T5-DHA-379

Power GUI Programming
with VisualAge™ for C++

Hiroshi Tsuji

Bob Love

William Law

Bruce Olson

WILEY COMPUTER PUBLISHING

John Wiley & Sons, Inc.

New York • Chichester • Weinheim • Toronto • Singapore • Brisbane

Publisher: Katherine Schowalter
Editor: Theresa Hudson
Managing Editor: Frank Grazioli
Assistant Managing Editor: Brian Snapp
Electronic Products, Associate Editor: Mike Green
Text Design & Composition: Bob Love and Hiroshi Tsuji

Designations used by companies to distinguish their products are often claimed as trademarks. In all instances where John Wiley & Sons, Inc. is aware of a claim, the product names appear in initial capital or all capital letters. Readers, however, should contact the appropriate companies for more complete information regarding trademarks and registration.

This text is printed on acid-free paper.

Copyright © 1997 by John Wiley & Sons, Inc.

All rights reserved. Published simultaneously in Canada.

This publication is designed to provide accurate and authoritative information in regard to the subject matter covered. It is sold with the understanding that the publisher is not engaged in rendering legal, accounting, or other professional service. If legal advice or other expert assistance is required, the services of a competent professional person should be sought.

This book is not sponsored in any part or in any manner by IBM. IBM does not endorse or represent the accuracy or appropriateness of any information contained herein. In addition, this book is not intended to replace IBM product documentation or personnel in determining the specifications and capabilities of any included products. You are responsible for the choice of all configurations and applications of computer hardware and software. You should discuss these choices with the proper IBM representative.

This book contains programs that are furnished as simple examples to provide illustration. These examples have not been thoroughly tested under all conditions. Therefore, the reliability, serviceability, or function of these programs is not guaranteed. All programs contained herein are provided to you "AS IS." THE IMPLIED WARRANTIES OF MERCHANTABILITY AND FITNESS FOR A PARTICULAR PURPOSE ARE EXPRESSLY DISCLAIMED.

Reproduction or translation of any part of this work beyond that permitted by section 107 or 108 of the 1976 United States Copyright Act without the permission of the copyright owner is unlawful. Requests for permission or further information should be addressed to the Permissions Department, John Wiley & Sons, Inc.

Library of Congress Cataloging-in-Publication Data:

ISBN: 0-471-16482-8
Printed in the United States of America
10 9 8 7 6 5 4 3 2 1

To the women in my life: Allison, Whitney, and especially Malinda.
— *W. L.*

To my wife and good friend, Sue, my daughter, Libbi, and my mother, Helen.
— *B. L.*

To my wife, Diane, my sons, John and Cory, and my parents, Gene and Myra.
— *B. R. O.*

To Teresa, Katie, and Jackson, with love.
— *H. T.*

Acknowledgments

We would like to extend thanks to those folks that helped us get this book written:

Kevin Leong, who was the driving force behind not only the first book, which he helped write, but also the set of C++ classes that became Open Class Library.

Our managers—Don Ingerslew, Al Groelle, Peter Spung, and Robert Leblanc—for supporting us.

All the readers and reviewers of our first book who gave us enough positive comments (and lists of corrections, in some cases) to encourage us to work on this revision.

All the developers that contributed to the success of VisualAge for C++. If you ever take a look at the module definition file for Open Class Library, or examine the link map for an application after statically linking with Open Class Library, you will find an assortment of rather strange segment names. The choice of these segment names attest to the hard work, camaraderie, and fun that the developers had while building Open Class Library. Many of these folks also helped review the book and its examples. Over the years, the segment names and the people who inspired them have included the following (there are still others waiting for the addition of more segments to Open Class Library):

I2001AMarksOdyssey	Mark Anderson	ICLAboveTheLaw	Bill Law
IJennsPen	Jennifer Becker-Fernald	ICLLeongGone	Kevin Leong
IOnAnotherBenge	Mark Benge	IAnotherLoveTune	Bob Love
IABernieWeekend	David Bernath	IMillerTime	Mike Miller
IBoezePhoneHome	John Boezeman	IJudyJudyJudy	Judy Oakley
IBonnanoRepublic	Jim Bonanno	IBruceKnee	Bruce Olson
IBrightBeak	Pete Brightbill	TheRightPrice	Brian Price
IMountainsOfBusch	Ed Busch	IShakAttack	Keith Shakib
IIsHaggarHorrible	Peter Haggar	IStangerHook	Robert Stanger
IHamiltonianQuill	Delores Hamilton	IGRedPepperStich	Marty Stich
ICLHarpersBizarre	Steve Harper	IProudMary	Mary Streble
ICLWannaHolliday	Jon Holliday	ITsujiNightLive	Hiroshi Tsuji
IHolmesBuilder	Paul Holmes	IWesWantsMore	Wes Wilson
IAbstractArt	Art Jolin	IYoungBloods	Michelle Young
ICLHello6Dave	Dave Lavin		

Finally, we would like to thank all of the users of Open Class Library. You gave us a reason to write our first book, and through your questions and problems, you continue to point out topics for us to discuss.

Contents

Preface

Welcome

Computer programming is rapidly changing. Each year seems to bring a new technology that must be mastered. Although your applications are more complex, and you want to deliver them on multiple platforms that are also getting more complex, your users are demanding easy-to-use applications. To help battle this strain, class libraries of reusable code and tools to generate code have now emerged.

You can use IBM VisualAge for C++ to make your programming life easier and to deliver the easy-to-use applications that your users demand. VisualAge for C++ is IBM's C++ development environment for the Windows and OS/2 operating systems. It includes a compiler, debugger, visual application builder, and a suite of other tools. When you use VisualAge for C++, you are likely also using or contemplating using IBM Open Class Library.

Open Class Library is particularly useful for creating a graphical user interface (GUI) with the look and feel of the native operating environment. Using these classes, you can produce better applications more quickly and more easily and use fewer lines of code than you could if you programmed directly to the operating system or presentation system. For example, you can write a simple "Hello World" program that runs on the OS/2, Windows NT, and Windows 95 platforms using the following lines of code:

```
#include <iframe.hpp>
void main ( )
{
  IFrameWindow frame( "Hello World" );
  frame.showModally();
}
```

This book is a guide to using this C++ class library. The primary audience for this book is current and future users of Open Class Library. For current users, we offer information and advice that you can immediately apply to get more out of Open Class Library and to improve the code you write. For new and future users, including those needing a cross-platform development tool or users of the Visual Builder who need to extend its generated code, we explain basics and give you the encouragement and confidence you need to leap into productive programming with Open Class Library. Whatever your background, if you are interested in Open Class Library, we welcome you as a reader.

We do not assume that you previously developed an application with a graphical user interface. Nor do we require that you are familiar with either the Windows or OS/2 operating systems. However, we do assume that you have reading knowledge of the C++ programming language.

About This Book

This book describes a significant part of Open Class Library. Because we have been part of the Open Class Library development team since its inception, we are in a unique position to write about it. This perspective allows us to provide practical and detailed usage information (including "under the covers" information), to warn against potential pitfalls we have seen others encounter, and to give insight into the design of Open Class Library, including ways you can extend it and improve the portability of your code. We provide the kind of information that you might only discover after extensive use of Open Class Library.

We primarily focus on the user-interface classes. In addition to the user-interface classes, we also describe classes not directly related to user interfaces, but ones that you need in order to use the user-interface classes. We cover the level of these classes included in IBM VisualAge for C++ for OS/2, Version 3.0 and IBM VisualAge for C++ for Windows, Version 3.5. We show how you can use these C++ classes to simplify the development of applications that are portable between the OS/2 and 32-bit Windows environments.

However, this book does not describe all of the Open Class Library. Specifically, we do not cover the complex mathematics, I/O stream, collection, database, 2-D graphics, multimedia, or Compound Document Framework classes. We also did not write this book as a reference manual to describe every function of the classes or as a guide for other tools of VisualAge for C++, such as the Visual Builder. The documentation included with VisualAge for C++ provides this type of information. In addition, if you intend to use the Visual Builder to construct Open Class Library applications, we recommend that you also read *VisualAge for C++ Visual Programming Handbook*, by Dale Nilsson and Peter Jakab.

Although VisualAge for C++ for Windows supports building Win32s applications, we do not discuss Win32s issues in this book and have not tested the example programs we provide with Win32s. Likewise, we do not address the AIX platform, although a subset of the functions available in VisualAge for C++ are available in the related product, IBM C Set ++ for AIX.

This book is a major revision of *OS/2 C++ Class Library: Power GUI Programming with C Set ++*. We wrote that book with Kevin Leong; Van Nostrand Reinhold originally published it. We have updated and broadened the scope of this book to include both VisualAge for C++ for OS/2 and VisualAge for C++ for Windows.

Conventions

Terms we define or emphasize appear in *italics*. Code, names of C++ classes and members, file names, programming key words and C++ reserved words appears in a `fixed-space font`. Command names and names of choices on a user interface appear in **bold**.

We use "you" to refer to you, the reader. We refer to a general user of a computer, or the person you are writing code for, as a "user."

Some class libraries use "container" to denote classes that hold things, such as lists, sets, stacks, and queues. Following the convention for VisualAge for C++, we use "collection" for this purpose and "container" to denote a specialized type of user-interface control. Finally, we use "operating system" or "presentation system" generically to refer to either the Windows or OS/2 operating system.

Throughout the book, we also sprinkle in secondary topics that you do not need in order to use the classes but which complement an understanding of Open Class Library. The discussions of secondary topics appear in side bars. An example of a side bar follows.

Side Bar Topics

Side bars such as this one contain discussions off the beaten path. For example, a side bar might focus on one of the following topics:

- Useful tips for GUI programming
- Design rationales behind Open Class Library
- C++ features utilized in Open Class Library
- Information about Windows or OS/2 programming to better use Open Class Library
- Tips for designing an object-oriented C++ class library

The Accompanying Disk

This book includes a CD-ROM that contains an extra chapter, example programs, and a trial copy of VisualAge for C++ for Windows, Version 3.5.

We include a PostScript file named extlib.ps for the chapter, "Custom Controls and Handlers." It is in the powergui directory of the CD-ROM. We published this chapter in the preceding version of this book; due to space and time constraints we include it on the disk, basically unaltered from how it originally appeared. We also provide the unaltered example code for this chapter on the CD-ROM. This chapter describes how you can create your own window, event, and event handler classes to extend Open Class Library. Although the discussion is in the context of using C Set ++ for OS/2 (the processor product to VisualAge for C++), the concepts that it presents are still relevant.

We provide 150 example programs, which appear in or are referenced by the text of this book. These coding examples range from simple to complex. We include them to help you under-stand the capabilities of the Open Class Library and to provide working code that you can use to speed development of your applications. You cannot sell the examples as your own and cannot add any of the classes we provide to a class library that you sell (see the file powergui\copyrght for licensing information). Other than those restrictions, we encourage you to reuse the code in the examples. The file powergui\read.me contains instructions for running and rebuilding the example programs, as well as a table for locating specific examples.

All but a few of the examples run on all of the following platforms: OS/2 Warp 3.0, Windows 95, Windows NT 4.0, and Windows NT 3.51. We tested these samples as best we could on these operating systems.

To run the example programs on the OS/2 operating system, we require you to install IBM VisualAge for C++ for OS/2, Version 3.0. Similarly, to run the examples on the Windows operating system, you must install IBM VisualAge for C++ for Windows, Version 3.5.

For those without the Windows version of the product, we include a trial, or "Try and Buy," copy. The trial copy and its associated files are located in the `trialva` directory. See `readme.txt` for installation instructions and `license.agr` for licensing information. Run `setup.exe` in either the Windows 95 or Windows NT operating system to install the trial copy. You can use the trial copy for 60 days after you install it.

Parts of this book assume you have applied a FixPak with corrective fixes for VisualAge for C++. For example, for some of the example programs to run properly, you must apply the latest FixPak for Open Class Library. Additionally, we discuss some features that were added to VisualAge for C++ for OS/2 in a FixPak, such as `IViewPort::expandableViewWindow` and `IWindow::disableMinimumSizeCaching`. The IBM Corporation makes available fixes for VisualAge for C++ in a variety of ways.

You can find information for obtaining FixPaks on the VisualAge for C++ home page on the World Wide Web: www.software.ibm.com/adv/visualage_c++.

At the time of this writing, some features added to VisualAge for C++ for Windows do not yet exist in VisualAge for C++ for OS/2. These features include the `ICommandConnectionTo` template class, `IWindow::setHelpId` function, and `IAcceleratorTable` class. Examples that use these features will not build on the OS/2 operating system until that support is added to VisualAge for C++ for OS/2. Examples that use other features new to VisualAge for C++, such as the `pmCompatible` styles, `IC_ID_CLOSE` macro, and `IBaseErrorInfo` class can be simplified once those features are added to VisualAge for C++ for OS/2. IBM may add these features in a FixPak for VisualAge for C++ for OS/2, which would make writing portable code easier.

One final note: we wrote most of these examples to get a point across as simply as possible. One simplification is that many of the examples construct windows using temporary, or "stack," storage in the `main` routine. Although there is nothing wrong with this technique from a coding correctness point of view, the code itself is not reusable. We encourage you to design your own applications with reuse in mind.

About the Authors

Hiroshi Tsuji

Hiroshi works for IBM as part of the Open Class Library development team in Research Triangle Park. He tries to frequent Yellowstone and Grand Teton National Parks but finds this is difficult to do from North Carolina. He enjoys playing volleyball (and probably would enjoy it even more if he were taller). He hopes to start dabbling with watercolors whenever work slows down.

Bob Love

Bob works for IBM as part of the Open Class Library development team in Research Triangle Park, North Carolina. He particularly enjoys his yearly trip to the high country to ski (it's actually closer to tumbling) black diamond runs with reckless abandon. That is Bob's daughter Libbi with him in the picture. As the stepfather of Open Class Library, he relies on his diverse background in parasitology, auto repair, and large-system computer repair for designing C++ classes and molding the future of Open Class Library.

William Law

Bill used to work at IBM developing C++ classes, including some that are now part of the Open Class Library. He is now the owner and operator of Solution Frameworks, a software consulting company in Silicon Valley. Bill continues to search for the right set of C++ and Java objects to make his job (and yours) easier.

Bruce Olson

Bruce works for IBM as part of the Open Class Library development team in Research Triangle Park, North Carolina. He is a native of Chicago where he began his career with IBM. His special interests include Artificial Intelligence and object-oriented software design. Bruce enjoys playing softball, reading, and coaching his two sons in various sports.

Although only the preceding names appear on the cover of this book, other members of the Open Class Library team also helped write this book. We are especially grateful to all the time and energy they gave. In particular, Jennifer, David, and Michael helped us write, revise, and review multiple chapters. Without the help of all the following authors, this book would have taken months longer to finish, assuming that we would have been able to finish it at all.

Jennifer Becker-Fernald

Jennifer works for IBM as part of the Open Class Library development team in Research Triangle Park. She enjoys fine wines, hiking with her dogs (Duke and Dutchess), travel, and skiing. Most of all, she likes to ride and show her horses. Jennifer is currently in search of a cheaper hobby.

David Bernath

David works for IBM as part of the Open Class Library development team in Research Triangle Park. After serving a stint as the manager of the class library team for the initial C Set ++ release, he regained his senses (with the help of his wife and two kids) and returned to programming. David enjoys skiing, golf, and soccer.

Michael Miller

Mike works for IBM as part of the Open Class Library development team in Research Triangle Park. He is the proud father of two, and he enjoys golf, ACC basketball, and good novels. When time permits, he likes to get away to the North Carolina beaches or the Virginia mountains.

Mark Benge

Mark works for Tivoli, an IBM Company, in Research Triangle Park. He used to be a member of the Open Class Library development team before his defection. Mark is a regular contributor to various OS/2 publications. He also gives presentations at conferences and customer sites, as long as an interpreter is present to translate his Southern colloquialisms.

Judy Oakley

Judy works for IBM as part of the Open Class Library development team in Research Triangle Park. She spends most of her free time pursuing a very mobile two-year old named Benjamin. When he's asleep, she manages to read, write, work out, play the church organ, and maintain a 60-acre farm populated by five dogs, one cat, and uncounted numbers of wild creatures.

We would also like to thank our copy editor (and rewrite artist), who often tried in vain to teach us the finer (or in some cases, the fundamental) points of the English language.

Delores Hamilton

Delores works for IBM in Research Triangle Park. Until recently she was the editor for the Open Class Library and Visual Builder development teams. She temporarily gave up her quilting hobby to spend her free time reining in our "cowboy" style of writing. Delores can be bribed with chocolate.

Road Map

We do not intend for you to read each chapter of this book in sequence like a novel. In many respects, this book is a hybrid of a reference manual and a user's guide with additional information such as design motivations. Because most of the classes that we describe in this book encapsulate the underlying presentation system, we provide introductory material that new users need to know about GUI programming to facilitate their understanding and use of Open Class Library. Conversely, experienced Windows or OS/2 programmers might want to relate a part of Open Class Library back to their understanding of the presentation system. We provide this information in the book where appropriate.

This mix of information can make it difficult to decide how to use this book. We provide this road-map information so that you can find information quickly when you are using the book as a reference. You can also use it to guide you through a more casual reading of the book.

The Structure of This Book

Some of the beginning chapters provide a foundation for the material in the remainder of the book. Other chapters you can read independently because they are mostly self-contained. This is especially true for the chapters that describe the various control classes of Open Class Library.

The following sections categorize the chapters of the book at a high level.

Introductory Chapters

The first three chapters contain introductory material. These chapters describe the flavor of programming using Open Class Library, graphical user interfaces, and presentation system concepts used by Open Class Library. You can skip some or all of this material depending on your background and interests.

General-Interest Chapters

Some chapters are of general interest to most readers of the book.

- Chapter 4 is highly recommended reading for everyone because it describes the event-handling architecture of Open Class Library. It also describes the common characteristics and behavior of all window classes in Open Class Library.

- Chapter 7, which describes the common characteristics and behavior of all control classes, builds on Chapter 4 because controls are specialized windows.

- Chapter 17 describes the event handler classes that you can use with most windows. This chapter is logically related to Chapter 4, which describes the concept of event handlers and their key role in Open Class Library.

- Chapter 26 describes the fundamental data types that Open Class Library provides, most notably the IString class. Open Class Library uses these data-type classes in the interfaces of many of its other classes, so you should become familiar with them.

Window Class Chapters

Chapters 5, 6, and 8-16 describe window classes or categories of classes such as edit controls. These chapters are mostly self-contained and can be read independently. You might want to read some or all of Chapters 1-4 and Chapter 7 before jumping into any of these chapters depending on your background and current needs. Chapters 13-16 are notable because they describe the classes that provide much of the value-add to using Open Class Library.

Non-Window Chapters

Chapters 18, 20-25, and 27 describe classes and components that are not windows. These classes are also self-contained and can be read independently. However, as is the case with the window class chapters, you might want to read portions of Chapters 1-4 before reading these chapters.

Advanced Topic Chapters

Chapters 19, 28, and 29 describe advanced topics that generally are independent of other chapters. The exception is Chapter 19 which covers advanced topics on frame windows not covered in Chapter 5. The other chapters cover topics such as performance and, therefore, only cover Open Class Library classes as they relate to these topics.

Chapter Details

Each chapter begins with road-map information for that chapter. This information describes how the chapter relates to the other chapters in the book. This section contains the following information:

- A summary of its contents
- The Open Class Library classes that it describes
- Reasons that you might want to skip the chapter
- Chapters you should read before reading the chapter
- Chapters that contain related information

Use this information to help you navigate through the book to best suit your needs and interests.

Chapter 1

Getting Started

- Introduces Open Class Library using two example programs
- Introduces basic window concepts used by Open Class Library
- Compares programming with Open Class Library to using Windows and OS/2 APIs
- You may want to skip this chapter if you are already familiar with Open Class Library.

Adding a graphical user interface (GUI) to a program is not a trivial undertaking. For even the simplest Windows application, you must deal with message queues, message dispatch loops, and window procedures. For an OS/2 application, you similarly face anchor blocks, message queues, message dispatch loops, and window procedures when programming to the Presentation Manager presentation system. To develop an application for both platforms, you must learn where overlap between their APIs exist and how to simulate overlap (if possible) where they do not. The APIs consist of functions, messages, and window classes.

An alternative to programming directly to system APIs is to use the User Interface Class Library, which is a part of Open Class Library. *Open Class Library* is a set of C++ class libraries shipped with IBM VisualAge for C++. Its user interface classes simplify the construction of a GUI by organizing presentation system concepts and by hiding complexity and programming pitfalls. This book tells you how to use this set of C++ classes.

What to Expect from This Chapter

This chapter is for readers new to Open Class Library, and introduces it using a couple of simple example programs. If you are already familiar with it, proceed to Chapter 3, 4, or to a later chapter describing a specific topic of interest to you.

For those of you continuing with this chapter, we spend some time relating use of the user interface classes to programming directly to Windows and OS/2 APIs. For readers with little or no experience with Windows or OS/2 programming, we weave in some basic presentation system concepts that Open Class Library uses. For those already well-versed in GUI programming, we compare programming with Open Class Library to programming directly with these APIs at the end of this chapter. Now, let's look at our first example program.

Displaying a Simple Window

Virtually everything you see on the screen is a *window*, a rectangular area with well-defined behavior. The IWindow class of Open Class Library represents windows in general.

Open Class Library provides several classes derived from IWindow to represent the predefined window types provided by the Windows and OS/2 operating systems, such as buttons, entry fields, and list boxes. These window types are commonly known as *controls*. Open Class Library directly supports these and many other built-in window types. Additionally, you can extend the IWindow class hierarchy to support controls of your own.

The Program

The following example illustrates a basic text editor using the IFrameWindow and IMultiLineEdit classes. This example consists of a handful of code, which is displayed in the window. Figure 1-1 shows the example running with VisualAge for C++ for Windows. The complete code also appears below.

Simple Example Program - getstart\start1\start1.cpp

```cpp
#include <iapp.hpp>
#include <iframe.hpp>
#include <imle.hpp>
#include <icconst.h>

void main ( )
{
  // Create a primary window that contains a read-only MLE.
  IFrameWindow
    primary( "Getting Started - Version 1" );
  IMultiLineEdit
    mle( IC_FRAME_CLIENT_ID, &primary, &primary,
         IRectangle(),
         ( IMultiLineEdit::classDefaultStyle
           | IMultiLineEdit::horizontalScroll )
         & ~IMultiLineEdit::wordWrap );
  primary.setClient( &mle );

  // Read this source file into the MLE, and position the
  // cursor at the top of the file.
  mle.importFromFile( __FILE__ );
  mle.setCursorLinePosition( 0 );

  // Set the input focus, and show the window.
  primary.setFocus();
  primary.show();

  // Start event processing.
  IApplication::current().run();
}
```

Because this is a simple example (the editor does not save any changes you make), we place all of the code in a single routine, main. main is the entry point of the program; it is the function called by the start-up code that the compiler adds. Although simple, this example still shows the basic structure needed in an application built with Open Class Library. The example constructs a primary (or main) window, gives it the input focus, shows it, and processes events until the user ends the application by closing the primary window.

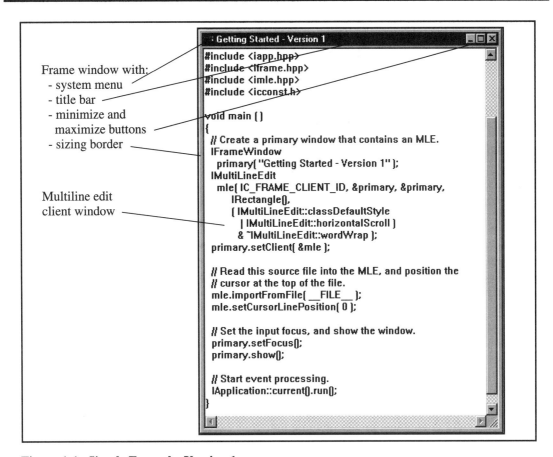

Frame window with:
- system menu
- title bar
- minimize and maximize buttons
- sizing border

Multiline edit client window

```
#include <iapp.hpp>
#include <iframe.hpp>
#include <imle.hpp>
#include <icconst.h>

void main ()
{
  // Create a primary window that contains an MLE.
  IFrameWindow
    primary( "Getting Started - Version 1" );
  IMultiLineEdit
    mle( IC_FRAME_CLIENT_ID, &primary, &primary,
      IRectangle(),
      ( IMultiLineEdit::classDefaultStyle
       | IMultiLineEdit::horizontalScroll )
      & ~IMultiLineEdit::wordWrap );
  primary.setClient( &mle );

  // Read this source file into the MLE, and position the
  // cursor at the top of the file.
  mle.importFromFile( __FILE__ );
  mle.setCursorLinePosition( 0 );

  // Set the input focus, and show the window.
  primary.setFocus();
  primary.show();

  // Start event processing.
  IApplication::current().run();
}
```

Figure 1-1. Simple Example, Version 1.

The primary window for the application actually consists of several windows, including a *frame window* and a multiline edit (MLE) control. We use the IFrameWindow class to create and represent the frame window. You can think of a frame window as the frame of a picture, since a frame window visually surrounds and provides some ornamentation for its client window. The client window in our example is the MLE. You can also think of a frame window as the frame of a building, in that it provides the basic structure and support for the rest of the elements of the window, such as the client window, and the following optional standard components:

- System menu
- Title bar
- Buttons to minimize and maximize the size of the window
- Sizing border

The simple way we construct our IFrameWindow object, named primary, causes it to use all of the above default components. These frame components are labeled in Figure 1-1. For the text of its title bar, the frame uses the **Getting Started - Version 1** string that we pass to the IFrameWindow constructor.

The MLE control with its scroll bars occupies the remainder of the frame's interior. It does this by being used as the frame's client window. The call to the setClient function of IFrameWindow establishes this relationship. Because a frame window routes many messages to its client window, you can locate most of the application-specific behavior for the entire window either with the frame window or its client window. Calling the importFromFile member function of the IMultiLineEdit object, mle, assigns it the source file of the program for its text. The compiler provides the name of the source file by expanding the __FILE__ macro. When you run this example, ensure the source file can be found in the current directory.

This is all you have to do to assemble the primary window. However, you still have to make it visible. To put it on the screen, call the show member function of the primary object. However, just before you do that, call its setFocus function so that your window has the input focus when the user sees it. All keystrokes go to the window with the input focus.

Finally, call IApplication::current().run() to cause events to be processed by your application. This call does not return until the display of the primary window ends, which, for example, occurs after the user closes the window by selecting **Close** from the system menu. At this point, the program has run to completion. We discuss event processing in more detail shortly.

The Make File

The next example shows the make file. You can build the example program by issuing the command **nmake** to build a Windows application or **nmake IC_PM=1** to build an OS/2 application.

Simple Example Make File - getstart\start1\makefile

```
CFLAGS = /Ft- /Gd+ /Ge+ /Gm+ /Wall+gnr-ppc-ppt-uni-vft-
LFLAGS = /PM:PM

!ifdef IC_PM
ODIR=.\os2
!else
ODIR=.\win
endif


ALL : CREATEDIR $(ODIR)\start1.exe

$(ODIR)\start1.exe : $(ODIR)\start1.obj
    icc $(CFLAGS) /B"$(LFLAGS)" /Fe$(ODIR)\start1.exe \
        $(ODIR)\start1.obj
```

```
$(ODIR)\start1.obj: start1.cpp
   icc $(CFLAGS) /C+ /Fo$(ODIR)\start1.obj start1.cpp
   copy start1.cpp $(ODIR)

CREATEDIR:
  @if not exist $(ODIR)* md $(ODIR)
```

In the OS/2 operating system, you can add the following line to your CONFIG.SYS file so you do not need to define IC_PM when you run nmake:

```
SET IC_PM=1
```

The prior make file, and all make files on the example disk, create a different directory for output when you run them in the OS/2 operating system than they do in the Windows operating system. You must run an example program in its output directory. For example, to run the "Getting Started" program on the Windows operating system, type **start1** in the GETSTART\START1\WIN directory; to run it on the OS/2 operating system, type **start1** in the GETSTART\START1\OS2 directory. See the topic "Example Program Make Files" in Chapter 3, "Tour of Open Class Library," for details on the make file options.

Adding Event Handling

While a user may only see a window in terms of its visual appearance, the implementation of a window consists of message-processing code. A window paints itself and acts on keystrokes and mouse input in response to the messages it receives. For example, when a frame window receives a message that the mouse pointer is over its sizing border, it changes the mouse pointer to a double arrow. Because a window is defined by the messages it receives and how it processes them, you can customize a window by changing how it handles specific messages.

The key role of messages stems from the fact that the presentation systems for both the Windows and OS/2 operating systems are message-driven. All windows communicate through messages with specific meanings and protocols, including a large set defined by the system. Some messages are requests for action, and some are notifications that a significant action has occurred. In both Windows and OS/2 programming, you place the message processing code for a window in a window procedure. You assign window procedures when registering a window class or subclassing individual windows.

Open Class Library represents messages as event objects. You process events routed to a window using event handler objects rather than window procedures. Thus, you can provide specialized behavior for a window by attaching a specialized event handler to it. Using event handlers, you can provide specialized processing for the selection of a push button, the selection of a menu item, or the character data typed by the user. A handler can be attached to—and thus service—a single window or many windows. You can attach any number of handlers to a window. Open Class Library provides a variety of handler classes for processing common events. Chapter 4, "Windows, Handlers, and Events," provides more details on events and handlers.

The previous example does not provide any special processing in response to user actions. It calls IApplication::current().run(), but this gives neither the frame window nor the MLE any customized behavior. As we hinted earlier, this function routes messages, which you can think of as event objects, to the message processing code of the appropriate window.

If you do not supply specialized event processing, keystrokes and mouse manipulations are handled in some default manner by the window. In our example, this means the user is limited to the default actions supported by the underlying operating system frame window (such as moving, sizing, and closing the window) and edit control (such as scrolling and selecting text). Next you can see how you can allow the user to do more by adding an event handler.

Creating a New Window Class

Before we describe the event handler we use, we will first isolate our existing windows into a C++ class. A class allows us to encapsulate our assemblage of windows into a single object. One benefit from this is that you create a reusable object. Then, if you need to display the same set of windows again, you only need to create a new object of this window class; you do not have to duplicate the code to construct and set up the individual windows. Another benefit is that you have the ability to control how a programmer using the class can manipulate the windows by controlling what functions appear in the public interface of the class. You can also build application-specific behavior into a window class by adding application-specific event handlers as part of the class.

Following is the class declaration and code for our window class, CodeWindow. The main differences from the previous example are the addition of a menu bar; the addition of functions to allow cutting, copying, and pasting of the MLE's text to and from the system clipboard; and the addition of a command handler of the class CutCopyPasteHandler.

We add a menu bar to the frame window via the style IFrameWindow::menuBar in the CodeWindow constructor. This style causes the frame window to create the menu bar by loading its definition from a resource file. The next topic in this chapter contains the definition of the menu. Next, we demonstrate how to use a command handler to tie together the menu bar and the functions we added to CodeWindow for cutting, copying, and pasting text.

Simple Code Window Interface - getstart\start2\start2w.hpp

```
#include <iframe.hpp>
#include <imle.hpp>
#include "start2ch.hpp"         // For CutCopyPasteHandler.

class CodeWindow : public IFrameWindow {
public:
  CodeWindow ( const char* title );
virtual Boolean
  cut    ( ),
  copy   ( ),
  paste  ( );

private:
// Disallow copy and assignment.
  CodeWindow ( const CodeWindow& );
CodeWindow
 &operator=  ( const CodeWindow& );
```

```
IMultiLineEdit
  mle;
CutCopyPasteHandler
  cmdHandler;
}; // CodeWindow
```

Simple Code Window Implementation - getstart\start2\start2w.cpp

```cpp
#include <icconst.h>
#include "start2w.hpp"
#include "start2.h"

CodeWindow::CodeWindow ( const char* title )
  : IFrameWindow ( title,
                   ID_CODEWINDOW,
                   IFrameWindow::classDefaultStyle
                   | IFrameWindow::menuBar ),
    mle( IC_FRAME_CLIENT_ID, this, this,
         IRectangle(),
         ( IMultiLineEdit::classDefaultStyle
            | IMultiLineEdit::horizontalScroll )
          & ~IMultiLineEdit::wordWrap ),
    cmdHandler ( )
{
  // Make the MLE the client window.
  this->setClient( &mle );

  // Read this source file into the MLE, and position the
  // cursor at the top of the file.
  mle.importFromFile( __FILE__ );
  mle.setCursorLinePosition( 0 );

  // Attach the command handler that will process
  // selections from the menu bar,
  cmdHandler.handleEventsFor( this );
}

IBase::Boolean CodeWindow::cut ( )
{
  Boolean didCut = false;
  if ( mle.hasSelectedText() )
  {      // Cut selected text from the MLE to the
         // system clipboard.
    mle.cut();
    didCut = true;
  }
  return didCut;
}

IBase::Boolean CodeWindow::copy ( )
{
  Boolean didCopy = false;
  if ( mle.hasSelectedText() )
  {      // Copy selected text from the MLE to the
         // system clipboard.
    mle.copy();
    didCopy = true;
  }
  return didCopy;
}
```

```
IBase::Boolean CodeWindow::paste ( )
{
  Boolean didPaste = false;
  if ( mle.clipboardHasTextFormat() )
  {       // Paste text from the clipboard to the MLE.
    mle.paste();
    didPaste = true;
  }
  return didPaste;
}
```

Here is how main looks now:

Version 2 Main Routine - getstart\start2\start2.cpp

```
#include <iapp.hpp>
#include "start2w.hpp"

void main ( )
{
  // Create a primary window that contains an MLE.
  CodeWindow
    primary( "Getting Started - Version 2" );

  // Set the input focus, and show the window.
  primary
    .setFocus()
    .show();

  // Start event processing.
  IApplication::current().run();
}
```

The Menu Bar

We define the menu bar in a resource file that is separate from our program code. Our menu bar consists of a **File** choice that displays a pull-down menu with a **Close** choice, and an **Edit** choice that displays a pull-down menu with choices for **Cut**, **Copy**, and **Paste**. Figure 1-2 shows the window running with VisualAge for C++ for OS/2. The user has selected part of the text and displayed the **Edit** pull-down menu.

If the user selects **Close** from the **File** menu, the menu choice runs a command to end the display of the window, just as if the user pressed Alt+F4 or selected **Close** from the system menu. We rely on the processing provided by Open Class Library and the operating system for handling this command. If the user selects **Cut**, **Copy**, or **Paste**, the selected menu item generates a command event our program must handle. We will have these menu items run the cut, copy, and paste member functions we added to our CodeWindow class. We cover the details of doing this in the next topic.

The resource file containing the menu bar definition follows, along with the include file that defines the constants shared between the resource file and our code. Note that the resource file defines the menu in the different formats required by the resource compilers used in the Windows and OS/2 environments.

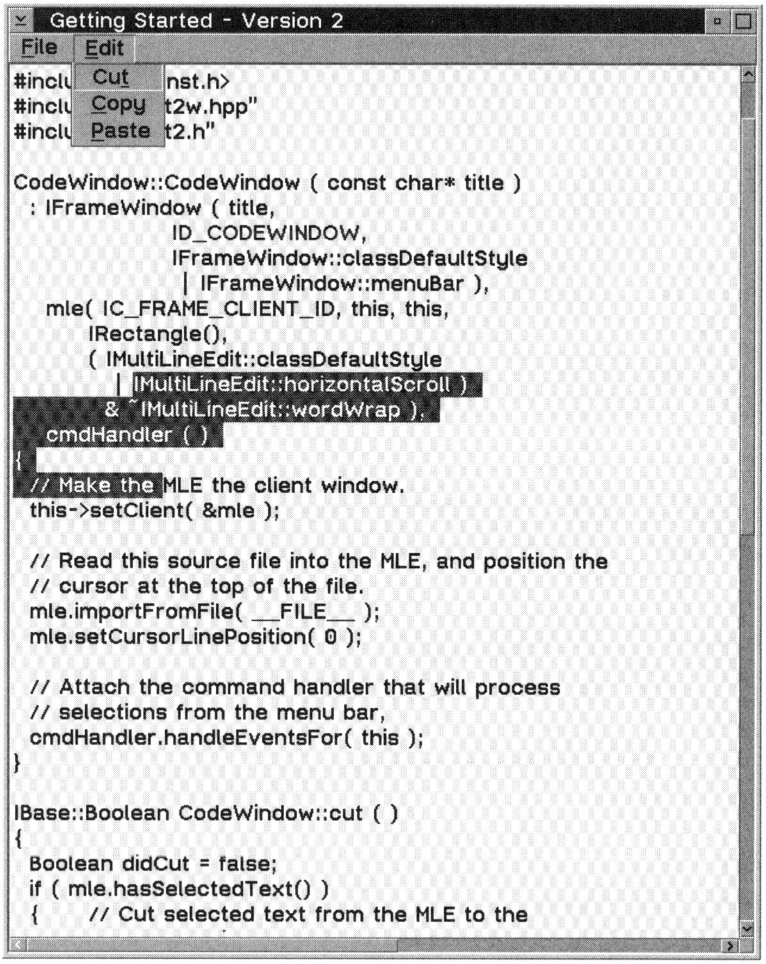

Figure 1-2. Simple Example, Version 2.

Resource Definitions - getstart\start2\start2.rc

```
#include "start2.h"

#ifdef IC_PM /* OS/2 resources */

#define INCL_WINFRAMEMGR        // For SC_CLOSE.
#define INCL_WINMENUS           // For MIS_SYSCOMMAND.
#include <os2.h>
```

```
MENU ID_CODEWINDOW
  BEGIN
    SUBMENU "~File",          ID_FILE
      BEGIN
        MENUITEM "Close",     SC_CLOSE, MIS_SYSCOMMAND
      END
    SUBMENU "~Edit",          ID_EDIT
      BEGIN
        MENUITEM "Cu~t",      CMD_CUT
        MENUITEM "~Copy",     CMD_COPY
        MENUITEM "~Paste",    CMD_PASTE
      END
  END

#else /* Windows resources */

ID_CODEWINDOW MENUEX
  BEGIN
    POPUP "&File",            ID_FILE
      BEGIN
        MENUITEM "Close",     SC_CLOSE
      END
    POPUP "&Edit",            ID_EDIT
      BEGIN
        MENUITEM "Cu&t",      CMD_CUT
        MENUITEM "&Copy",     CMD_COPY
        MENUITEM "&Paste",    CMD_PASTE
      END
  END

#endif
```

Resource Constants - getstart\start2\start2.h

```
// Window identifiers.
#define ID_CODEWINDOW 1000

// Command identifiers.
#define CMD_CUT        2001
#define CMD_COPY       2002
#define CMD_PASTE      2003

// Other menu-bar related identifiers.
#define ID_FILE        1001
#define ID_EDIT        1002
```

Creating a Command Handler

Command events are standard events that you need to process in your application. Typically, a user generates a command event by selecting a menu item or push button. When programming with Open Class Library, you place your processing of command events in command handlers, classes you derive from the ICommandHandler class.

In our example, we process command events that result from the user selecting the **Cut**, **Copy**, or **Paste** menu choices. We write our command handler in such a way that it calls the cut, copy, and paste functions we added to the CodeWindow class.

The CutCopyPasteHandler class is our command handler. To process application-specific commands (as opposed to system commands, such as the one the **Close** choice runs), the only virtual function we must override is ICommandHandler::command. This is shown in the class declaration that follows.

Command Handler Interface - getstart\start2\start2ch.hpp

```
#include <icmdhdr.hpp>

class CutCopyPasteHandler : public ICommandHandler {
protected:
virtual Boolean
  command ( ICommandEvent& event );
}; // CutCopyPasteHandler
```

Open Class Library calls our `command` virtual function to process all command events that reach the frame window that the command handler is attached to. The `IEvent::dispatchingWindow` member function returns this window. We use the `ICommandEvent::commandId` function to identify the command we are currently processing.

Command Handler Implementation - getstart\start2\start2ch.cpp

```
#include "start2ch.hpp"
#include "start2w.hpp"
#include "start2.h"

IBase::Boolean
  CutCopyPasteHandler::command ( ICommandEvent& event )
{
  Boolean stopProcessingEvent = false;
  CodeWindow* codeWindow =
                (CodeWindow*)event.dispatchingWindow();
  switch ( event.commandId() )
  {
    case CMD_CUT:
      codeWindow->cut();
      stopProcessingEvent = true;
      break;
    case CMD_COPY:
      codeWindow->copy();
      stopProcessingEvent = true;
      break;
    case CMD_PASTE:
      codeWindow->paste();
      stopProcessingEvent = true;
      break;
    default:
      break;
  }
  return stopProcessingEvent;
}
```

Open Class Library also provides event handler classes that let you process events other than command events. As a result, you can make the `CodeWindow` class sensitive to the size of the frame window, to specific keystrokes or mouse clicks, or to changes to the text of the MLE. We discuss these other event handler classes (`IResizeHandler`, `IKeyboardHandler`, `IMouseHandler`, `IEditHandler`, and others) in later chapters.

The Make File

The following is the make file we use to build this example. It is like the make file for the first example, but it compiles and links three source files instead of one and builds the resource file containing the menu bar into the program. Because the procedure for building Windows and

OS/2 resource files differs, the make file contains platform-specific rules. To build the program, you again issue the command **nmake** or **nmake IC_PM=1**.

Version 2 Make File - getstart\start2\makefile

```
CFLAGS = /Ft- /Gd+ /Ge+ /Gm+ /Wall+gnr-ppc-ppt-uni-vft-
LFLAGS = /PM:PM

!ifdef IC_PM
ODIR=.\os2
ORES=$(ODIR)\start2.res
RC=rc.exe -DIC_PM
!else
ODIR=.\win
ORES=
RC=irc.exe -Fo$(ODIR)\start2.res
!endif


ALL : CREATEDIR $(ODIR)\start2.exe

$(ODIR)\start2.exe : $(ODIR)\start2.obj $(ODIR)\start2w.obj \
                     $(ODIR)\start2ch.obj $(ODIR)\start2.res
!ifdef IC_PM
   icc $(CFLAGS) /B"$(LFLAGS)" /Fe$(ODIR)\start2.exe \
       $(ODIR)\start2.obj $(ODIR)\start2w.obj \
       $(ODIR)\start2ch.obj
   $(RC) $(ODIR)\start2.res $(ODIR)\start2.exe
!else
   icc $(CFLAGS) /B"$(LFLAGS)" /Fe$(ODIR)\start2.exe \
       $(ODIR)\start2.obj $(ODIR)\start2w.obj \
       $(ODIR)\start2ch.obj $(ODIR)\start2.res
!endif

$(ODIR)\start2.obj: start2.cpp start2w.hpp
   icc $(CFLAGS) /C+ /Fo$(ODIR)\start2.obj start2.cpp

$(ODIR)\start2ch.obj: start2ch.cpp start2w.hpp start2.h
   icc $(CFLAGS) /C+ /Fo$(ODIR)\start2ch.obj start2ch.cpp

$(ODIR)\start2w.obj: start2w.cpp start2w.hpp start2ch.hpp \
                     start2.h
   icc $(CFLAGS) /C+ /Fo$(ODIR)\start2w.obj start2w.cpp
   copy start2w.cpp $(ODIR)

$(ODIR)\start2.res: start2.rc start2.h
   $(RC) -r start2.rc $(ORES)

CREATEDIR:
  @if not exist $(ODIR)* md $(ODIR)
```

Programming without Open Class Library

Now, we need to take a step back and analyze our examples from the perspective of programming directly to Windows and OS/2 APIs. If you have programmed with either, you probably have noticed a large stylistic difference between the programs you have been writing and our example programs. For example, our code does not include WINDOWS.H, which is needed by traditional Windows programs. Likewise, our code (with the exception of the resource file) does not include OS2.H, OS2DEF.H, PMWIN.H, or any other files from the Developer's Toolkit for OS/2. We can avoid including these files because our examples do not call any Windows or OS/2 APIs.

So, where are the calls to the basic Windows APIs such as `GetMessage`, `TranslateAccelerator`, `TranslateMessage`, `DispatchMessage`, and `CreateWindowEx`? And, where are the calls to the corresponding set of OS/2 APIs (`WinInitialize`, `WinCreateMsgQueue`, `WinGetMsg`, `WinDispatchMsg`, `WinCreateWindow`, `WinDestroyMsgQueue`, and `WinTerminate`)? The answer is that Open Class Library calls these functions for you. Only the message dispatch loop (`GetMessage`/`DispatchMessage` and `WinGetMsg`/`WinDispatchMsg`) remotely surfaces in the form of a call to `IApplication::current().run()`. As for the `WinMain` function that Windows programmers are accustomed to, VisualAge for C++ uses `main` instead.

In case you have been wondering, essentially no difference exists between a standard control, such as an MLE created with `CreateWindowEx` or `WinCreateWindow`, and one created by an `IMultiLineEdit` object. Both are windows of the same operating system window class (`Edit` or `WC_MLE`, depending on the underlying platform) that supports the same basic set of messages.

While the windows on the screen are the same, Open Class Library simplifies the way you code to those windows by giving you a C++ interface. For example, you can call the `sizeTo` function of an `IMultiLineEdit` object to change the size of the MLE (rather than calling the Windows `SetWindowPos` API without the `SWP_NOMOVE` flag, or the OS/2 `WinSetWindowPos` API with the `SWP_SIZE` flag set in an `SWP` structure). Also, you can call the `isWritable` function of the `IMultiLineEdit` object to find whether the control allows user input (rather than checking if it has the Windows `MLS_READONLY` style or sending it the OS/2 `MLM_QUERYREADONLY` message). Best of all, you can modify the message processing of a window simply by using event handlers and their related event classes. You do this instead of providing an application-specific window procedure to the Windows APIs `SetWindowLong` and `RegisterClass` or to the OS/2 APIs `WinSubclassWindow` and `WinRegisterClass`. Often these window procedures degenerate into overly long `switch` statements.

Notice that the `ICommandEvent` object we process in our `command` function hides the actual operating system message we are processing, in this case, `WM_COMMAND`. The `ICommandEvent` class provides member functions that allow you to access information from the `WM_COMMAND` message without having to be aware of its underlying structure.

One last note: if you are a programmer who is used to the flexibility that the Windows or OS/2 APIs give, Open Class Library allows you full accessibility to the underlying system information that you are accustomed to working with. For example, you can access the `HWND` for a window from the `IWindow::handle` function and message identifiers and parameters through the `eventId`, `parameter1`, and `parameter2` member functions of `IEvent`. If you are an OS/2 programmer, you can even get a `HAB` from the `ICurrentThread` member function `anchorBlock`. As a result, you can mix code that uses system APIs with code that uses Open Class Library.

However, once you begin accessing the underlying system information, your code is no longer portable. To help you in this case, Open Class Library provides macros that allow you to conditionally compile platform-specific code. For example, it defines the macro `IC_WIN` or `IC_PM`, depending on whether you are compiling a Windows or OS/2 application. As a result, you can write code that looks like the following and still run it on both operating systems.

Using Platform-Specific Code - getstart\nonport\nonport.cpp

```cpp
#include <ibase.hpp>      // For IC_WIN or IC_PM.

#ifdef IC_PM
#define INCL_WINDIALOGS
#include <os2.h>
#else
#include <windows.h>
#endif

#include <imsgbox.hpp>
#include <istring.hpp>
#include <iwindow.hpp>

void main ( )
{
  // Call a platform-specific API and display a
  // platform-specific message.
#ifdef IC_PM
  WinAlarm( IWindow::desktopWindow()->handle(), WA_NOTE );
  IString
    msg( "This is an OS/2 application." );
#else
  Beep( 100, 100 );
  IString
    msg( "This is a Windows application." );
#endif

  IMessageBox
    msgBox( 0 );
  msgBox
    .setTitle( "Which Platform?" )
    .show( msg,
           IMessageBox::informationIcon
           | IMessageBox::okButton
           | IMessageBox::moveable );
}
```

Chapter 2

Object-Oriented User Interface
Fundamentals

- Explains the importance of graphical user interfaces to applications
- Presents the key user interface elements used by operating systems
- Introduces terminology used throughout the book
- Skip this chapter if you are familiar with graphical user interfaces.

An object-oriented, graphical user interface (GUI) is a visual metaphor of a real-world scenario, often a desktop. Within that scene are icons, representing actual objects, that you can access and manipulate with a pointing device. Both the Microsoft and IBM Corporations use this desktop analogy in their operating systems to provide ease-of-use and some consistency among applications. You expect to see consistency between applications and, thus, look for these common desktop elements. Both companies also publish guidelines to define and drive the standards for developing GUIs in today's applications. Whereas the Windows and OS/2 operating systems have different presentation layers and desktops, they share some common elements that applications also use. Because your users typically interact with the user interface first when they use your applications, you want to carefully design and implement it. A modern interface that offers tool bars, fly-over help, graphics, and advanced controls that appear on the desktop gains a competitive advantage over otherwise equivalent applications.

General Interface Guidelines

The *desktop* is the graphical user interface for both the Windows and OS/2 operating systems. As an object-oriented user interface, it displays objects—primarily data objects—on the screen. You perform actions on those objects, and the desktop can hide the fact that an action may result in the running of an application.

Both operating systems base their desktops on their guidelines for user interface design. The guidelines focus on the following key objectives:

- Focus on objects.
- Exploit knowledge transference.
- Leave the user in control.

These three objectives prevent your users from being impeded as they use your application's user interface.

Focusing on Objects

Objects are represented graphically (pictorially) as icons to assist you in associating a screen object with a corresponding real-world object. These icons let you manipulate objects on the screen, much as you would manipulate real-world objects. For instance, you can use a pointing device, usually a mouse, to touch and "feel" objects. This ability makes the objects more concrete.

Figure 2-1 shows the icon representation of several objects on the OS/2 desktop. The most fundamental object is the desktop window, which represents the entire screen and holds all other objects. At the most basic level, these other objects are *container objects*, *data objects*, and *device objects*.

Container objects hold other objects that typically are related to one another. Examples of containers are folders and the desktop window.

Data objects, such as files, documents, and charts, are the objects that users create and work with.

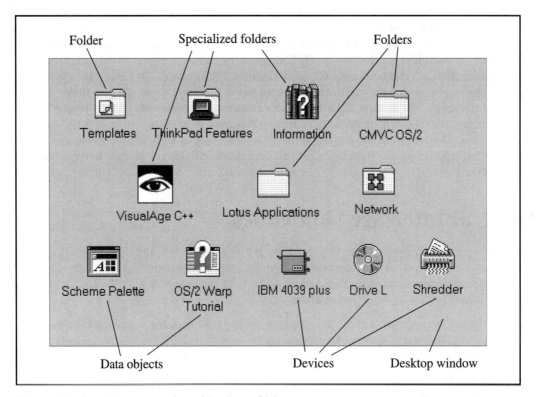

Figure 2-1. Icon Representation of Desktop Objects.

Device objects usually correspond to peripheral devices attached to your computer such as a printer or a disk drive. Logical devices, such as the OS/2 shredder, Windows recycling bin, sound mixer, or CD player, work without a corresponding physical object connected to your computer.

Using this model, you can concentrate on objects and the actions that apply to them. These actions include opening a document, selecting a choice for an object, or dragging and dropping an object. When interacting with objects, you end up running applications but your focus is on objects, not on applications and tools.

Figure 2-2 shows the objects on the Windows desktop. In addition, the open folders demonstrate different container views.

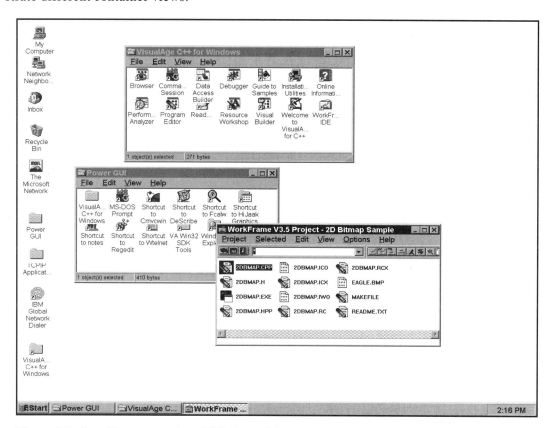

Figure 2-2. Icon Representation of Windows Objects.

Applying Learned Knowledge

A well-designed user interface minimizes the amount of information new users must learn to be productive. One way you can minimize users' learning and memory loads is to take advantage of information they already know. This is the principle of *knowledge transference*.

You and your users benefit if they can quickly become productive, simply by applying their learned knowledge to the way they use your application.

You can leverage knowledge transference by basing your user interface on mental models that the user is already familiar with. There are two ways to do this; apply real-world knowledge and be consistent.

First, let the user apply real-world knowledge to objects on the screen. You can encourage this by building your user interface around a familiar analogy, modeling application objects after tangible objects the user already knows. Users are less likely to be intimidated by or to forget familiar objects.

The analogy (or metaphor) for both the Windows and OS/2 desktops is a traditional business office. The screen represents a desktop where you can find folders, printers, a shredder or recycling bin, documents, and other data objects. You can act on these objects in much the same way you would work with the corresponding real-world objects. For example, you can print a document by dragging it to a printer icon.

Second, use knowledge transference by designing consistent interfaces in your applications. By using a recognized interface standard, such as the Common User Access (CUA) guidelines or the Windows Guidelines for Designing Interfaces, you reduce the amount of application-specific behavior your users encounter and have to remember. For your applications, you need to provide common navigation behavior for moving between windows or controls and common printing and deleting behaviors (drag and drop). These common behaviors, which are outlined by interface guidelines, are easier to learn and to remember because every conforming application reinforces the behavior. The desktop models a basic look and feel users expect in all applications. A single user interface also avoids the inevitable productivity loss when you have to stop to remember or recover from behaviors specific to a single application.

Leaving the User in Control

As a user, you want to be able to control the computer instead of being controlled by it. Specifically, you want to be free to complete tasks in the order you want, control the size and position of all windows, and change the font and color used by a window. You rightfully expect an application to show the status of lengthy operations, provide you the option of cancelling these operations, and allow you to correct errors.

This principle of leaving the user in control is important because few application developers can anticipate all of the ways that users might want to use an application or the restrictions that their customers may be working under.

Look and Feel of the Desktop

The following topics introduce the key user interface elements of the user interface. Included are the most important visual components (the container and notebook controls) and inter-action techniques (pop-up menus and direct manipulation). In Chapter 3, "Tour of Open Class Library," you learn how to use the library to write an application with this look and feel.

Windows and Views

To allow users to interact with an object, your application must display a window. For example, you might use a window to describe an object more fully than you can with an icon. An application can build complex windows by populating them with visible building blocks, called *controls.* These may be entry fields, simple text, or buttons.

For objects with default actions, the user double-clicks the object to execute that action. If the default action is to open the object, for example, the resulting window displays details of the object, which are called a *view* of the object.

A view is an object's user interface. It allows the user to see and change information or properties of the object. If an object has several ways to depict information about itself, then that object can support more than one kind of view.

Windows and OS/2 desktop folders support icon, tree, and details views. See the "Containers" topic in this chapter for more information. Most objects on the desktop window also allow you to open a properties, or settings, view. See the "Notebooks" topic in this chapter for more information.

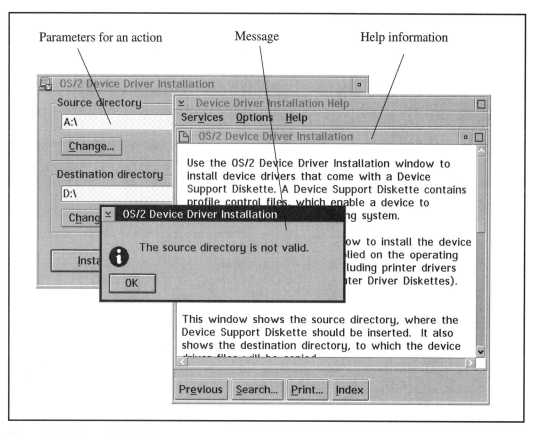

Figure 2-3. Example Windows.

A window can also display information other than an object view. For example, use windows to display messages and help information and to collect parameters for starting an action, as shown in Figure 2-3.

Not to be confused with the use of a window is the concept of *window relationships*. You can define a window independent of another window, such as a *primary window*, or in relationship to another window, such as a *secondary window*. Which windows you choose to make primary and which to make secondary depends on the context of the window—whether it is related to an existing window. Designers must be concerned about this concept more than users of those interfaces.

Use a primary window to display information that is independent of the information contained in other windows. For example, if your user opens an icon on the desktop, show a primary window. What a user does with those other windows does not affect the primary window.

Use a secondary window to further expand on information contained in a primary window. For example, you can show a secondary window when users open objects contained by a primary window, or you can prompt them for information about the objects. A secondary window cannot exist without its primary window, and it always appears on top of the primary window.

Some windows, like those displaying an object view, can be either a primary or secondary window. Others, like windows showing action choices, are always secondary windows.

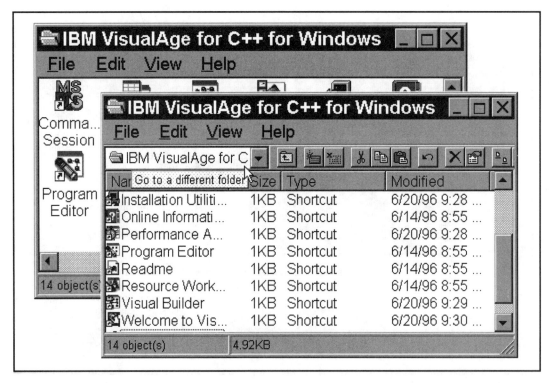

Figure 2-4. Opened Folders.

Containers

Figure 2-4 shows the windows that result from opening the VisualAge for C++ product folder. Both windows show different views of the same folder: icon and details.

A container holds objects and can display its objects in different views. An OS/2 container supports the following views: tree, icon, text, name, and details. The Windows container is composed of the list view and tree view control, which are native to the Windows environment.

Use the container control to implement a folder. Because the desktop prominently displays folders and other container objects, applications that want the same look and feel as the operating system use the container control frequently. Figure 2-5 shows the OS/2 System folder in a details, icon, and tree view.

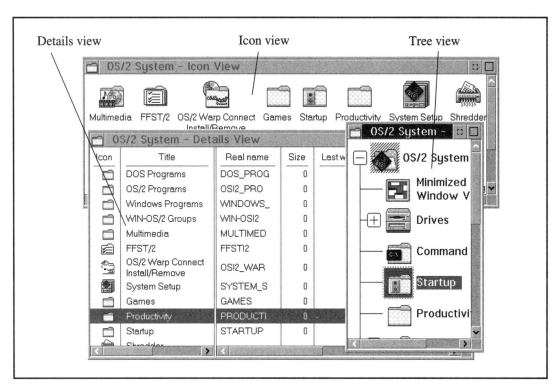

Figure 2-5. Container Views.

Notebooks

Figure 2-6 shows a primary window, containing the settings or properties view for a VisualAge for C++ WorkFrame Project object. Use a settings view to display the properties of a data or device object for users to modify. The Windows and OS/2 desktops use settings views to display configuration information for all of their objects.

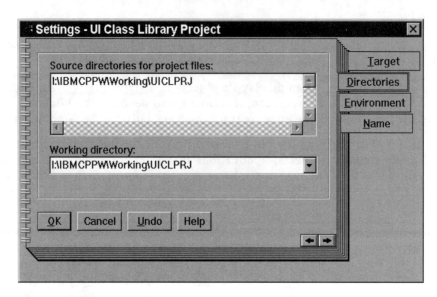

Figure 2-6. Settings View.

Typically, a notebook is used to display a settings view. The *notebook control* organizes a large amount of information by displaying windows as pages of information, which users can page through much like a real-world notebook. The settings view (and consequently the notebook control) is another key element of an application that copies the look and feel of the desktop.

Other Components of a Window

Windows can be composed of controls other than containers and notebooks. Figure 2-7 shows both a primary and secondary window provided by the VisualAge for C++ Debugger. Both windows include some of the standard components of a frame window, such as a system menu, window title (title bar), and sizing border. The primary window of this application uses a container control. The secondary window is composed of several controls, including an entry field, push buttons, and field prompts.

This application also adds *fly-over* (or *hover*) help, an information area, and multiple tool bars. These additional features are common in current GUIs and are beyond what is normally found on the desktop. Fly-over help displays short help windows that identify the object that the mouse pointer is positioned over. As users move their mouse pointers over various objects, different help windows are displayed. You can also display descriptive text for the object in a text control, such as the information area at the bottom of the window. A tool bar is a window with buttons that represent tools or menu items and actions. You can position the tool bar along the top, bottom, or sides of a frame window, or you can float it, positioning it anywhere on your desktop. You can also have multiple tool bars with a variety of tool bar buttons using text, bitmaps, or both. Look back at Figure 2-4 and notice that the details view container utilizes a tool bar with fly-over help for the tool bar. The tool bar is located beneath the menu.

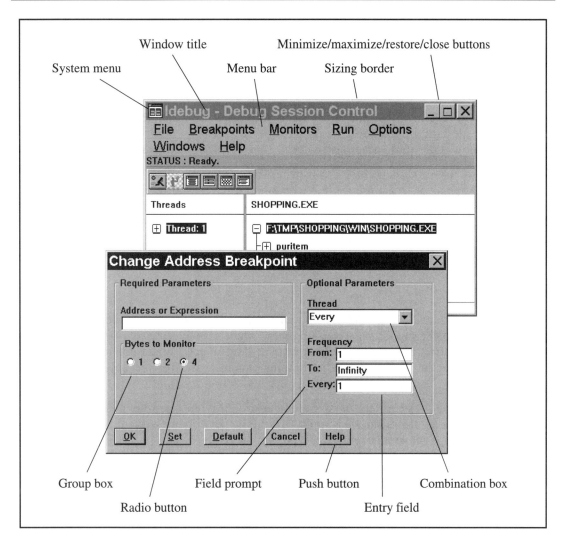

Figure 2-7. Components of a Window.

The fly-over help text, "Go to a different folder," is displayed when the mouse pointer is positioned over the drop-down combination box on the tool bar.

Interacting with the Desktop

Just as you can build a window in a variety of ways, you can also use several interaction techniques to control how users perform various actions. For the Windows and OS/2 desktops, users apply direct actions on objects by using drag and drop and pop-up menus.

Drag and drop is an example of a direct manipulation technique in which users use a mouse to directly alter an object. A pop-up menu offers a lesser degree of direct manipulation, but still more than a menu bar or push button that is physically separated from the object.

Drag and Drop

As with other direct manipulation techniques, drag and drop enables you to interact with objects on the desktop as touchable, real-world objects. It also lets you bypass intermediate steps and windows that would otherwise be necessary to perform an action.

A common use for drag and drop is to transfer data from an object (the source object) by selecting it, dragging it to another object (the target object), and releasing it there. You can also use drag and drop to move an object from one folder to another. Devices also respond to drag and drop; so, you can print a document by dropping it on a printer object or delete it by dropping it on a shredder object. To achieve the look and feel of the desktop, support drag and drop within your application.

Pop-Up Menus

Each object maintained by the Windows and OS/2 desktop provides a pop-up menu with actions that the object supports. A pop-up menu is not displayed until a user requests it by pressing mouse button 2 while the pointer is over that object. When displayed, the pop-up menu appears near the object and only contains choices valid for the object in its current context.

To achieve the same look and feel in your applications, provide a pop-up menu for each object in your user interface. Users can then apply an action to any object without having to access a menu bar. Figure 2-8 shows an example of a pop-up menu.

Figure 2-8. Pop-up Menu.

Chapter 3

Tour of Open Class Library

- Uses an example to show you how to build a graphical user interface using many of the components of Open Class Library
- Introduces other components of Open Class Library not used in the example
- Read Chapter 1 first if you are new to Open Class Library.
- Read Chapter 2 first if you are unfamiliar with graphical user interfaces.
- Skip this chapter if you have previously written code utilizing a wide range of the classes that Open Class Library provides.

This chapter's example application introduces the major components of Open Class Library. It uses many of the user-interface elements described in Chapter 2, "Object-Oriented User Interface Fundamentals," to show how different pieces of Open Class Library factor into different stages of application development.

First, we describe the application data objects that we need in our example. We then define views for those objects and build the code to display those views. In the process of doing this, we translate the major user window elements that the Windows and OS/2 desktops use into their corresponding components in Open Class Library. Next, we include the event handling code needed to process user actions. Then, we describe the user-interface classes not used in the example. Finally, we describe the classes in Open Class Library that address application issues beyond the user interface.

After you read this chapter, you will have a feel for the functionality that Open Class Library provides and for its programming style. You will also have learned that Open Class Library is comprised of a set of *frameworks*, which can save you significant time and effort in developing applications with robust, object-oriented, graphical user interfaces. A framework is a group of interrelated classes that are designed to solve a set of related problems. Frameworks reduce the amount of design and code you need to create and they allow you to focus on the unique aspects of your applications.

About the Example

The example in this chapter helps to describe Open Class Library and it provides a context for its use. But first, a disclaimer: our intent is not to use the example to teach either application design or class design.

For the example, we use a shopping list program which lets you create a list of things to buy. By keeping this example simple, we can focus on the basic concepts behind using the library. In some cases, we omit nonuser-interface code that would be essential for a real application. The code for the example, written as C++ classes, builds around the classes in Open Class Library. Portions of the code are shown throughout this chapter. You can find the complete example on the example program disk. Table 3-1 shows where you can find this example after you install the disk.

Table 3-1. Example Program Components

Component	Example Location
Main routine	latour\shopping\shopping.cpp
PurchaseItem class declaration	latour\shopping\puritem.hpp
PurchaseItem class implementation	latour\shopping\puritem.cpp
PurchaseItemView and nested class declarations	latour\shopping\puritemv.hpp
PurchaseItemView and nested class implementations	latour\shopping\puritemv.cpp
Resource file	latour\shopping\shopping.rc
Window and resource identifiers	latour\shopping\shopping.h
Make file	latour\shopping\makefile

Initial Tasks

Before you can start developing a user interface, you need to define the task. This means understanding the requirements of your customers so that you can design a user interface to help them perform their jobs.

This chapter presents developing code as a process of continual refinement. This process includes the design of user-interface objects and classes. A critical piece in developing the right solution is validating it with your customers, which we omitted because we have only hypothetical customers here.

Understanding the Problem

Suppose, in a series of lengthy conversations, you learn that your customers are experiencing many shopping-related woes as follows:

- Required items are not being purchased.
- Expenses are excessive because of unnecessary purchases.
- Items that need to be purchased are not documented, causing a loss of time, both in not buying them at the stores while there and in having to make extra trips back to those stores.

The customers are looking for an easy way to generate a shopping list. While they like the concept of a traditional hand-generated list, they insist that it does not do the job. It is difficult to maintain, does not encourage the proper amount of detail, and relies on an archaic technology. When pressed, the customers admit that others find their handwriting illegible. As a result, they are not satisfied with hand-generated shopping lists. They want a computer-age solution, one they can use on their personal computers at home. They also want the application to include typical items that they want to purchase. And, most importantly, the application must be easy enough for their young children to use it.

Defining the Objects

Once you understand the customers' problems and requirements, restate them in terms of objects. The first task is to identify the real-world objects with which the users work. If you cannot find reasonable objects, find real-world analogies for the tasks the users perform. The second task is to create corresponding objects in your user interface for these real-world objects.

The objects you choose are critical to the effectiveness of your user interface. To ensure that the objects work, your users must be able to easily correlate their mental models (of the problem domain) to your objects. For multiple users, you must select objects that all users can relate to, not always an easy task. Additionally, your choice of objects influences the actions you make available to your users, and it ultimately dictates how your users go about performing tasks. Thus, your ability to identify and depict readily identifiable objects is critical to your user interface.

Because, in this case, your customers are comfortable with a traditional shopping list, you can base your user-interface objects on that real-world object. So, design a shopping list object containing items your users want to purchase. Treat the items contained in the shopping list as objects, too. Each item to be purchased must have two attributes, a name and a quantity. Additionally, each one could have a preferred manufacturer, estimated price, and other relevant information. Each detail is an attribute, or data member, of an item to be bought. These attributes need not be treated as user-interface objects.

Defining the Actions

Next, you define the actions that each object supports. To do that, decide how the users interact with the objects and how the objects work together. This task focuses on answering questions such as the following ones:

- What happens when users open the object?
- How do users change the object?
- What other actions can users perform on the object?

In our example, opening a shopping list reveals a collection of items that need to be purchased. Users must be able to sort, save, print, and delete the shopping list. In turn, opening an item displays a window showing details about the item. In this window users can view and change attributes of the item. Users also must be able to create and delete items.

Consider various types of shopping lists, too. For example, one characteristic of grocery shopping is that people often need to buy the same things weekly. To make such a list easy to create, users need the application to keep a set of items that they can easily add to their grocery shopping lists when needed. In our example, we add a second list to hold these items. Because this list is not needed for every shopping list, we call it a "not-needed" list. Users will then be able to add these items to their shopping lists by moving them from the not-needed list to the shopping list, and they will be able to delete them again by moving the second list back into the not-needed list. Users can transfer items by using the tool bar, or by dragging and dropping the icons that represent the items between the two lists. When you select representational icons, your user interface also enables the customers' young children to use the application.

Although the shopping list and not-needed list are two separate objects in your user interface, they do not differ in terms of their fundamental data or behavior.

Modeling the Objects

Now, you begin transforming the user interface into code. At this point you can begin using the classes that Open Class Library provides.

A good place to start is by representing the nonvisual aspects of the application in terms of C++ classes. We define two data classes for our example, PurchaseList and PurchaseItem. The PurchaseList class represents a list containing items to buy. The shopping list and not-needed list are objects of this class. A PurchaseItem object represents an item to buy and is an entry held by a PurchaseList object.

You build data classes by assembling other data types. Represent data members, or attributes, with built-in C/C++ data types and with data type and collection classes that the library provides. The PurchaseList class is essentially a collection of PurchaseItem objects. The PurchaseItem class requires character string data for names and manufacturers, and it requires numeric data for prices. The example also stores the quantity and other miscellaneous information as character strings. By using character strings instead of numeric data, the application can store the unit of measure as part of the quantity, thus keeping the application simple.

Using the Data Classes of Open Class Library

Open Class Library provides a set of data type classes for you to use as well as for it to use when it implements its own classes. IString, IDate, ITime, IPoint, and ISize are some of the more commonly used data type classes.

Open Class Library provides a robust string class, IString, to handle character data. Thus, we use the IString class to represent all of the character-string data members of the PurchaseItem class. Figure 3-1 shows the data type classes that Open Class Library provides. All these classes derive from IBase, the base class of Open Class Library. Chapter 26, "Data Types," describes these data type classes in detail.

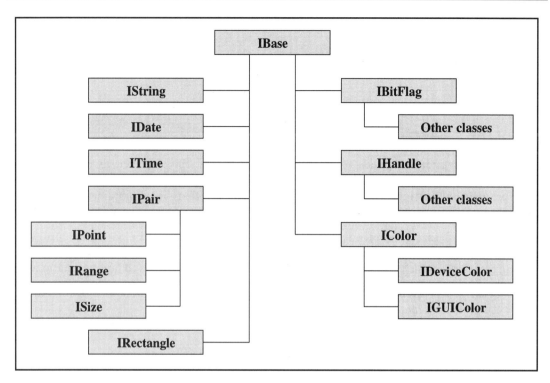

Figure 3-1. Hierachy of Data Type Classes.

Here is the first pass at declaring the PurchaseItem class. We later update this class declaration as we proceed through the chapter. In the class declaration, you find a constructor, functions to change each of the properties of a PurchaseItem object after you or the users create it, functions to query each of these values, and the object's private data members or attributes.

```
// An item you can add to a shopping list.
class PurchaseItem {
public:
  PurchaseItem       ( const IString& name,
                       const IString& quantity = "1",
                       const IString& manufacturer = IString(),
                       double price = 0,
                       const IString& notes = IString() );
PurchaseItem
  &setName           ( const IString& name ),
  &setQuantity       ( const IString& quantity ),
  &setManufacturer   ( const IString& manufacturer ),
  &setPrice          ( double price ),
  &setNotes          ( const IString& notes ),
  &addNotes          ( const IString& moreNotes );
IString
  name               ( ) const,
  quantity           ( ) const,
  manufacturer       ( ) const,
  notes              ( ) const;
double
  price              ( ) const;
```

```
private:
IString
  fName,
  fQuantity,
  fManufacturer,
  fNotes;
double
  fPrice;
};
```

Using the Collection Classes

Typically, an application needs to maintain collections of objects, such as a collection of invoices. Your first inclination may be to create a linked list for the list of items and then write an assortment of functions to add or remove items and to otherwise maintain the list. If you take advantage of the collection classes, however, this work becomes unnecessary.

The collection classes offer efficient implementations for a variety of classic data structures. These structures include sequences, queues, stacks, maps, and trees. By using these classes, you can create a complex list structure without having to write the code to build or maintain it.

You can easily implement the PurchaseList class using the collection classes. But first, let's look at the visual aspects of these objects.

Choosing Object Views

Once you identify your user-interface objects, you need to create *views*, or user interfaces, for those objects. First concentrate on defining the look of your views. Implementation comes later.

In the example, both the shopping list and not-needed list are containers of objects. Both containers display their objects as icons. Because the use of these two lists is so interconnected—a purchase item can appear in only one list at any time—we combine them into a single primary window. The purchase items are data objects. The main view for a purchase item is a settings view. We design this view using the basic controls provided by the presentation system, such as prompt text and entry fields. We organize the information comprising this view into pages of a notebook control that Open Class Library provides.

Figure 3-2 shows a drawing of the example program with these views.

Building Windows

Next, we start writing code to display these views. Open Class Library makes this task easier because it provides C++ classes for many of the window elements you typically need.

A logical place to start when you assemble your user-interface components is the IFrameWindow class. Use this class to create and manage both primary and secondary windows.

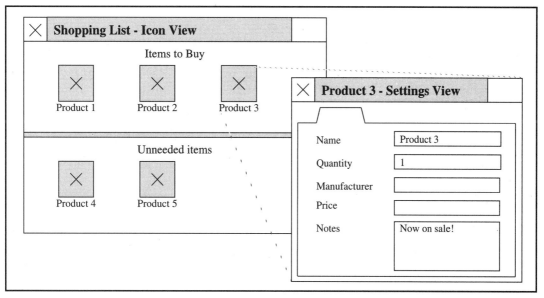

Figure 3-2. Views for the Example Application.

The `IFrameWindow` class supports two ways of building these desktop windows. The first is from a traditional Windows or OS/2 *dialog box*. A dialog box contains a definition of a frame window and the controls it contains. You can create dialog boxes using a dialog editor, such as the one that VisualAge for C++ provides.

The second way to build a window is to explicitly assemble the frame window and its components entirely within your program. This method enables you to build more complex and flexible windows than you can create by using a dialog editor.

Chapter 5, "Frame Window Basics," describes the role of the `IFrameWindow` class in building the basic parts of a window. Chapter 19, "Advanced Frame Window Topics," presents more detail and advanced topics related to frame windows.

Building the Primary Window

The primary window in the example displays the two `PurchaseList` objects. Displaying the primary window is quite simple. You need only the following code:

```
void main ( )
{
  // Create the primary window for the two container views.
  IFrameWindow primary( "Shopping List", ID_SHOPPINGLIST );

  // Give the frame the input focus, and show it.
  primary
    .setFocus()
    .show();

  // Start event processing.
  IApplication::current().run();
}
```

We create the frame window on the stack; that is, we do not use `operator new`. As a result, both the window and the `IFrameWindow` object are cleaned up by the time the `main` function returns. When the user closes the primary window, Open Class Library causes the call to `IApplication::current().run()` to return, causing `main` to end. The `IFrameWindow` object is deleted when it goes out of scope as defined by C++. We discuss the role of the `IApplication::current().run()` call later in this chapter and in Chapter 5, "Frame Window Basics."

We do not use a dialog box for the primary window, although the code at this point gives little indication of our intent. This code gives us an empty window with a title bar, system menu, and some standard behavior. We fill the window by assembling and adding its object view.

Building a View

You can assemble a view out of the controls that the presentation system provides. These controls include buttons, prompts, entry fields, containers, and notebooks. Open Class Library supplies classes for the controls available in the presentation system. The classes in the `IControl` class hierarchy represent these controls plus others that Open Class Library provides.

Figure 3-3 shows `IWindow` at the base of the window class hierarchy and the major division of the `IFrameWindow` and `IControl` classes below it. Figure 3-4 shows the `IControl` class hierarchy. See Table 7-1 for a mapping between Open Class Library classes and presentation system controls.

You can add a view into a frame window in two ways. The first is to place the controls comprising the view directly on the frame window, as is typical of a dialog box. The second is to build a separate window, which you can drop into the frame window to fill its *client area*.

The client area is the open area of a frame window. It is the area, or space, not occupied by the following frame-related components:

- Border
- Title bar
- System menu
- Minimize, maximize, hide, and restore buttons
- Menu bar
- Application-defined frame extensions

Chapter 19, "Advanced Frame Window Topics," describes frame extensions.

Open Class Library calls the window that occupies the client area the *client window* of the frame. Frame windows have built-in support for client windows so you can localize the visual characteristics of a window or

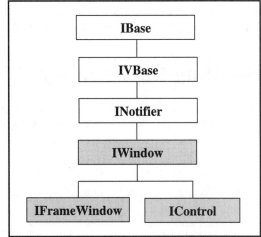

Figure 3-3. Base Window Class Hierarchy.

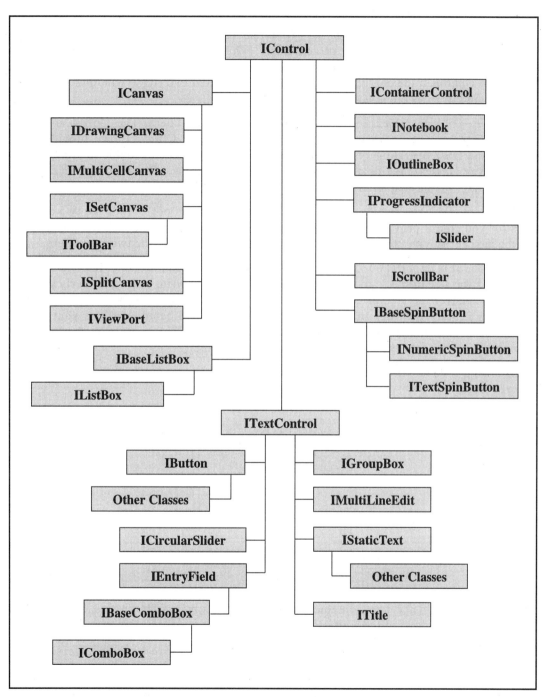

Figure 3-4. Hierarchy of the Control Classes.

specialized event processing for the entire window in the client window.

The primary window of the example uses its client window to display its object view. The view consists of the two PurchaseList containers. This combination of containers in the same primary window presents a problem because a frame window can have only one client window. Had we not combined the containers, we would have created two frame windows, each with a container window as its client window.

Using an ISplitCanvas object for the client window works well here. The ISplitCanvas class is a type of *canvas*, or advanced layout control, that Open Class Library provides. The Windows and OS/2 operating systems do not have any controls that provide the functionality of the canvas classes. We discuss canvases more in the topic, "Simplifying the Layout of Controls," later in this chapter and in detail in Chapter 15, "Canvases."

ISplitCanvas gives you two benefits. It manages the size and position of the two container views for you, and it provides a split bar between the two containers which the user can drag with the mouse. Moving the split bar causes ISplitCanvas to resize the two containers.

The first benefit is important because the user can readily change the size of the client window by changing the size of the frame window. You do not need to write code to properly size child windows whenever the size of the frame changes. Instead, you can rely on the support that Open Class Library provides to do this for you. The second benefit enables your users to directly manipulate the divider between the container views. This gives them the freedom to tailor how the client area is divided between the two containers.

The following code identifies the client window:

```
void main ( )
{
   // Create the primary window and its client window
   // for the two container views.
   IFrameWindow primary( "Shopping List", ID_SHOPPINGLIST );
   ISplitCanvas splitWindow( ID_LISTCLIENT, &primary, &primary );
   splitWindow.setOrientation( ISplitCanvas::horizontalSplit );

   // Use the split canvas as the client window.
   primary.setClient( &splitWindow );

   // Give the frame the input focus, and show it.
   primary
     .setFocus()
     .show();

   // Start event processing.
   IApplication::current().run();
}
```

We now need to add the two containers to the ISplitCanvas. We do this by making the containers child windows of the split canvas. No other calls are necessary.

Containers

Open Class Library provides the IContainerControl class for implementing container views and folders like the ones used by the desktop. The IContainerControl class displays a list of items in a details view, tree view, icon view, name view, or text view.

The examples implement the views for the two `PurchaseList` objects using the `IContainerControl` class. We use the icon view to show `PurchaseItem` objects as icons that users can manipulate.

In the example, we also use the `IContainerControl` class to implement the nonvisual aspects of the `PurchaseList` objects instead of using one of the collection classes. Had our example been more complex, we may have considered otherwise. (To simplify the example, we omit reading or storing the shopping list from or to a database or a file, and we assume the shopping list holds only a limited amount of data.)

Because `IContainerControl` can only contain objects derived from `IContainerObject`, we change `PurchaseItem` to derive from `IContainerObject`, as follows:

```
// An item you can add to a shopping list.
class PurchaseItem : public IContainerObject {
public:
...
};
```

One benefit of using `IContainerObject` is that it manages the name that the object displays in the container's icon view. We can use this functionality by removing the `fName` data member from the `PurchaseItem` class and implementing the `name` and `setName` functions to call the `IContainerControl::iconName` and `IContainerControl::setIconName` functions, respectively.

Here is how `main` looks now. It includes the code to create and set up the containers.

```
void main ( )
{
  // Create the primary window and its client window
  // for the two container views.
  IFrameWindow primary( "Shopping List", ID_SHOPPINGLIST );
  ISplitCanvas splitWindow( ID_LISTCLIENT, &primary, &primary );
  splitWindow.setOrientation( ISplitCanvas::horizontalSplit );

  // Use the split canvas as the client window.
  primary.setClient( &splitWindow );

  // Create the buy list and not-needed list containers.
  IContainerControl
    buyList( ID_BUYLIST, &splitWindow, &splitWindow ),
    dontBuyList( ID_DONTBUYLIST, &splitWindow, &splitWindow );

  // Set up the two containers.
  buyList
    .setTitle( "Items to buy" )
    .showTitle()
    .showTitleSeparator()
    .showIconView()
    .arrangeIconView()
    .setDeleteObjectsOnClose()
    .enableTabStop();

  dontBuyList
    .setTitle("Unneeded items")
    .showTitle()
    .showTitleSeparator()
    .showIconView()
    .arrangeIconView()
    .setDeleteObjectsOnClose()
    .enableTabStop;
```

```
    // Give the buy list the input focus and show the window.
    buyList.setFocus();
    primary.show();

    // Start event processing.
    IApplication::current().run();
}
```

Next, we create and add objects to the containers. The code, which initializes the PurchaseItem objects, substitutes for code in a real application that would read the initial values from a database or other file. The PurchaseItem class supplies all these initialization functions except setIcon, which IContainerObject provides. setIcon changes the icon that the container displays for an item.

```
    // Create some purchase items.
    PurchaseItem* p1 = new PurchaseItem( "Apple juice" );
    p1->setNotes( "Kids won't drink anything else." );
    PurchaseItem* p2 = new PurchaseItem( "Diskettes" );
    (*p2)
     .setQuantity( "1 box of 10 diskettes" )
     .addNotes( "3.5 inch, double-sided, high-density." )
     .addNotes( "Prefer preformatted." );
```

Chaining Functions

Perhaps you are wondering about the syntax we used to set up the two containers. We chained functions together by using the object returned by the previous call. With Open Class Library, you can chain most functions that set an attribute of an object. Because it throws exceptions to report errors, Open Class Library does not need to return an error code as the return value of these assignment functions. Instead, it returns a reference to the object being called.

Alternatively, we could have initialized the buyList object using individual statements:

```
    buyList.setTitle( "Items to buy" );
    buyList.showTitle();
    buyList.showTitleSeparator();
    buyList.showIconView();
    buyList.arrangeIconView();
    buyList.setDeleteObjectsOnClose();
```

The difference is one of coding style. Use chaining functions to emphasize that multiple functions are being called on the same object. However, this technique does have some disadvantages. For example, in the debugger, you cannot currently step over individual calls because the chained functions are a single C++ statement. Also the order of the chained functions is important because member functions of a class cannot return a reference to an object of a derived class, and you cannot call derived class functions on a base class object. For example, you can use the following code:

```
    IEntryField state(1,&frame,&frame);
    state
     .setText("North Carolina")
     .enableTabStop();
```

But, you cannot use this code:

```
    IEntryField state(1,&frame,&frame);
    state
     .enableTabStop()
     .setText("North Carolina");
```

enableTabStop returns an IControl&, and setText requires an ITextControl object.

```
PurchaseItem* p3 =
    new PurchaseItem( "Milk", "2 gallons", "Any", 3.75,
                      "Skim" );
PurchaseItem* p4 = new PurchaseItem( "Fruit snacks" );
p4->setNotes( "These are for the kids." );
PurchaseItem* p5 =
    new PurchaseItem( "Eggs", "1 dozen", 0, 1.50,
                      "Extra large size." );
p5->addNotes( "Be sure none are cracked." );
PurchaseItem* p6 =
    new PurchaseItem( "Power GUI Programming with VisualAge for
                      C++", "10", "John Wiley and Sons, Inc.",
                      49.95, "Updated for Windows release." );
(*p6)
 .addNotes( "Love the book!" )
 .setIcon( ID_THEBOOKICON );

// Fill the split windows.
dontBuyList
 .addObject( p1 )
 .addObject( p2 )
 .addObject( p3 )
 .addObject( p4 )
 .addObject( p5 );
buyList.addObject( p6 );
```

We add the above code to the main routine to finish setting up the containers. Figure 3-5 shows the resulting primary window and its two containers.

Chapter 13, "Container Control," describes the container control classes of Open Class Library in greater detail.

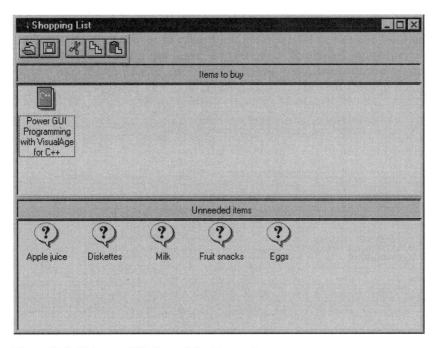

Figure 3-5. Primary Window of the Example.

Building the Secondary Window

We display a secondary window when users open a PurchaseItem object. To create a secondary window, we must provide it with an owner window (the owner is typically a primary window). By contrast, a primary window has no owner window. The following code shows what is required to display our secondary window:

```
// User has opened a PurchaseItem object.
// Create a secondary window with a settings view.
IFrameWindow* secondary =
  new IFrameWindow( ID_PURCHASEITEMVIEW, 0, &primary );
secondary->setAutoDeleteObject();
(*secondary)
 .setFocus()
 .show();
```

We create the secondary window using operator new, instead of creating the object on the stack. Because we display it as a modeless window, we cannot predict how long the window exists or how long we need the IFrameWindow object. This prevents us from creating the secondary window on the stack. We let Open Class Library automatically delete the IFrameWindow object when users close the window by calling IWindow::setAutoDeleteObject.

Building the View

We now build the view that the secondary window displays. To do this, we use a notebook to display a properties or settings view for the PurchaseItem object. Because this can be complicated, we first create another class to represent the frame window and the settings view.

We call this the PurchaseItemView class, and make it responsible for displaying the frame window containing the notebook and its two page windows. The constructor requires a PurchaseItem object, whose view we display. This class provides an updateDataObject function, which updates the PurchaseItem object with any changes users make to the settings values.

```
// Settings view for a PurchaseItem object.
class PurchaseItemView : public IFrameWindow {
public:
  PurchaseItemView ( PurchaseItem& purchaseItem,
                     unsigned long windowId,
                     IWindow* owner = 0 );

PurchaseItemView
 &updateDataObject ( );

protected:
PurchaseItemView
 &initializePage1  ( ),
 &initializePage2  ( );

private:
PurchaseItem
 &fPurchaseItem;
// The notebook and its windows are filled in later.
};
```

Next, we construct the `PurchaseItemView` object as a secondary window.

```
// User has opened a PurchaseItem object.
// Create a secondary window with a settings view.
PurchaseItemView* secondary =
  new PurchaseItemView( purchaseItem,
                        ID_PURCHASEITEMVIEW,
                        &primary );
secondary->setAutoDeleteObject();
```

Notebooks

Open Class Library provides the `INotebook` class for implementing notebooks, like those the desktop uses to display settings views. `INotebook` provides functions that you can use for these tasks:

- Manage the general look of the notebook
- Add and remove pages
- Access information about individual pages

We create two pages for the settings notebook in our example. Each page holds a *page window*, which is analogous to the client window of a frame. You can use any presentation system window as a page window. The first notebook page looks as depicted in Figure 3-2. The second page shows a bitmap of the first edition of this book. We add it to provide multiple pages for the notebook. (If the notebook had only one page then we wouldn't need the notebook!)

Following are the private data members we are adding to the `PurchaseItemView` class:

```
INotebook
  fNotebook;
IMultiCellCanvas
  fPage1,
  fPage2;
```

We discuss the class selected for the page windows shortly. But first, look at the `PurchaseItemView` constructor where we create the frame window and notebook. The code constructs the `INotebook`, configures it, and adds its pages. This is enough to give a functioning notebook control, although we still have to define its page windows.

```
PurchaseItemView :: PurchaseItemView
                         ( PurchaseItem& purchaseItem,
                           unsigned long windowId,
                           IWindow* owner )
  : IFrameWindow(windowId, 0, owner, IRectangle(),
                 IFrameWindow::defaultStyle()
                 | IFrameWindow::dialogBackground ),
    fPurchaseItem( purchaseItem ),
    fNotebook( ID_PURCHASEITEMBOOK, this, this ),
    fPage1( ID_PURCHASEITEMPAGE1, &fNotebook, &fNotebook ),
    fPage2( ID_PURCHASEITEMPAGE2, &fNotebook, &fNotebook )
{
  ITitle title( this, fPurchaseItem.name(),
                "Shopping List Settings View" );
  this->setClient( &fNotebook );
  fNotebook
   .setMinorTabSize( ISize( 0, 0 ) )
   .setBinding( INotebook::spiral );

  // Set up the first page of the notebook.
  this->initializePage1();
```

```
    // Set up the second page of the notebook.
    this->initializePage2();

    // Add the pages to the notebook.
    INotebook::PageSettings
      pageInfo( "1st", 0,
                INotebook::PageSettings::autoPageSize
                | INotebook::PageSettings::majorTab );
    fNotebook.addFirstPage( pageInfo, &fPage1 );
    pageInfo.setTabText( "2nd" );
    fNotebook.addLastPage( pageInfo, &fPage2 );

    // Size the frame window.
    IRectangle rectFrame =
      this->frameRectFor( IRectangle( IPoint( 0, 0 ),
                                      fNotebook.minimumSize() ));
    this->sizeTo( rectFrame.size() );
}
```

Chapter 14, "Notebook Control," further describes the notebook classes of the library.

Simplifying the Layout of Controls

The canvas classes supply a variety of functions. You saw some of them in the user-movable split bar supported by the ISplitCanvas class. Other canvas classes provide the ability to automatically size and position their child windows, based on their text and current font. Still another canvas class provides the ability to scroll any window.

The example has another place where it can exploit a canvas class. You can use the IMultiCellCanvas class to create the notebook page windows. This part of a settings view has the look of a traditional presentation system dialog box. It contains prompt text, entry fields, and a multiline entry field. The IMultiCellCanvas class allows these controls to automatically grow and shrink in size to fit the size of the notebook while remaining aligned. A dialog box does not give you this behavior.

First, we add the child controls of the first notebook page as private data members of the PurchaseItemView class:

```
    IMultiCellCanvas
      fPage1;
    IStaticText
      fNamePrompt,
      fQuantityPrompt,
      fManufacturerPrompt,
      fPricePrompt,
      fNotesPrompt;
    IEntryField
      fName,
      fQuantity,
      fManufacturer,
      fPrice;
    IMultiLineEdit
      fNotes;
```

To add child controls to the IMultiCellCanvas, we call its addToCell function. We provide relative positioning information for these child controls in terms of columns and rows. Figure 3-6 shows the look we want and the rows and columns we use for the IMultiCellCanvas.

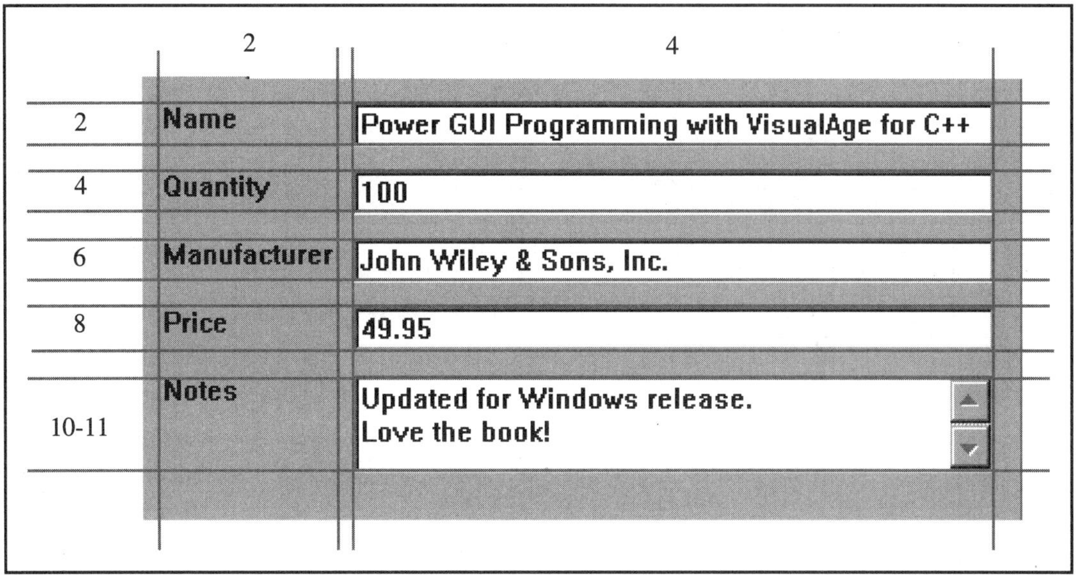

Figure 3-6. First Settings Page Composition.

The resulting changes to the `PurchaseItemView` constructor and the code to build the first notebook page follows:

```
PurchaseItemView :: PurchaseItemView
                         ( PurchaseItem& purchaseItem,
                           unsigned long windowId,
                           IWindow* owner )
  : IFrameWindow ( windowId, 0, owner, IRectangle(),
                   IFrameWindow::defaultStyle()
                     | IFrameWindow::dialogBackground ),
    fPurchaseItem( purchaseItem ),
    fNotebook( ID_PURCHASEITEMBOOK, this, this ),
    fPage1( ID_PURCHASEITEMPAGE1, &fNotebook, &fNotebook ),
    fNamePrompt( ID_NAMEPROMPT, &fPage1, &fPage1 ),
    fName( ID_NAME, &fPage1, &fPage1 ),
    fQuantityPrompt( ID_QUANTITYPROMPT, &fPage1, &fPage1 ),
    fQuantity( ID_QUANTITY, &fPage1, &fPage1 ),
    fManufacturerPrompt( ID_MANUFACTURERPROMPT,
                         &fPage1, &fPage1 ),
    fManufacturer( ID_MANUFACTURER, &fPage1, &fPage1 ),
    fPricePrompt( ID_PRICEPROMPT, &fPage1, &fPage1 ),
    fPrice( ID_PRICE, &fPage1, &fPage1 ),
    fNotesPrompt( ID_NOTESPROMPT, &fPage1, &fPage1 ),
    fNotes( ID_NOTES, &fPage1, &fPage1, IRectangle(),
            IMultiLineEdit::classDefaultStyle
              | IMultiLineEdit::ignoreTab )
{
  ...
  // Set up the first page of the notebook.
  this->initializePage1();
  ...
}
```

```
PurchaseItemView& PurchaseItemView :: initializePage1 ( )
{
  // Locate controls on the multicell canvas.
  fPage1
    .addToCell( &fNamePrompt,         2, 2 )
    .addToCell( &fName,               4, 2 )
    .addToCell( &tQuantityPrompt,     2, 4 )
    .addToCell( &fQuantity,           4, 4 )
    .addToCell( &fManufacturerPrompt, 2, 6 )
    .addToCell( &fManufacturer,       4, 6 )
    .addToCell( &fPricePrompt,        2, 8 )
    .addToCell( &fPrice,              4, 8 )
    .addToCell( &fNotesPrompt,        2, 10 )
    .addToCell( &fNotes,              4, 10, 1, 2 );

  // Allow MLE control to expand vertically with the window.
  fPage1.setRowHeight( 11, 0, true );

  // Allow MLE and entry fields to expand horizontally.
  fPage1.setColumnWidth( 4, 0, true );

  // Create bottom and right margins.
  ISize defaultCell = IMultiCellCanvas::defaultCell();
  fPage1
    .setRowHeight( 12, defaultCell.height() )
    .setColumnWidth( 5, defaultCell.width() );

  // Set up the child controls.
  ...

  return *this;
}
```

Although we omitted detailed description of the code, notice the following points. First, we did not specify any size and positioning information beyond columns and rows. These coarse units free us from over-exacting details such as the size of the current font or sizes of the currently displayed characters. Second, little code is required to create a window whose controls resize with the parent window. Figure 3-7 shows how the preceding code behaves in two differently sized notebooks.

Basic Controls

Open Class Library supplies classes for the basic controls provided by the Windows and OS/2 presentation systems. These include static controls, buttons, and controls that present the user with a list of items.

Examples of static controls include static text such as field prompts and instruction text, icons, bitmaps, and a boxed line with or without heading text. The library represents these static controls with the IStaticText, IIconControl, IBitmapControl, IGroupBox, and IOutlineBox classes. Chapter 8, "Static Controls," describes this group of control classes in greater detail.

Edit controls, such as an entry field for single line input, receive character input from the user. Open Class Library represents these controls with the IEntryField and IMultiLineEdit classes. Chapter 9, "Edit Controls," describes these classes.

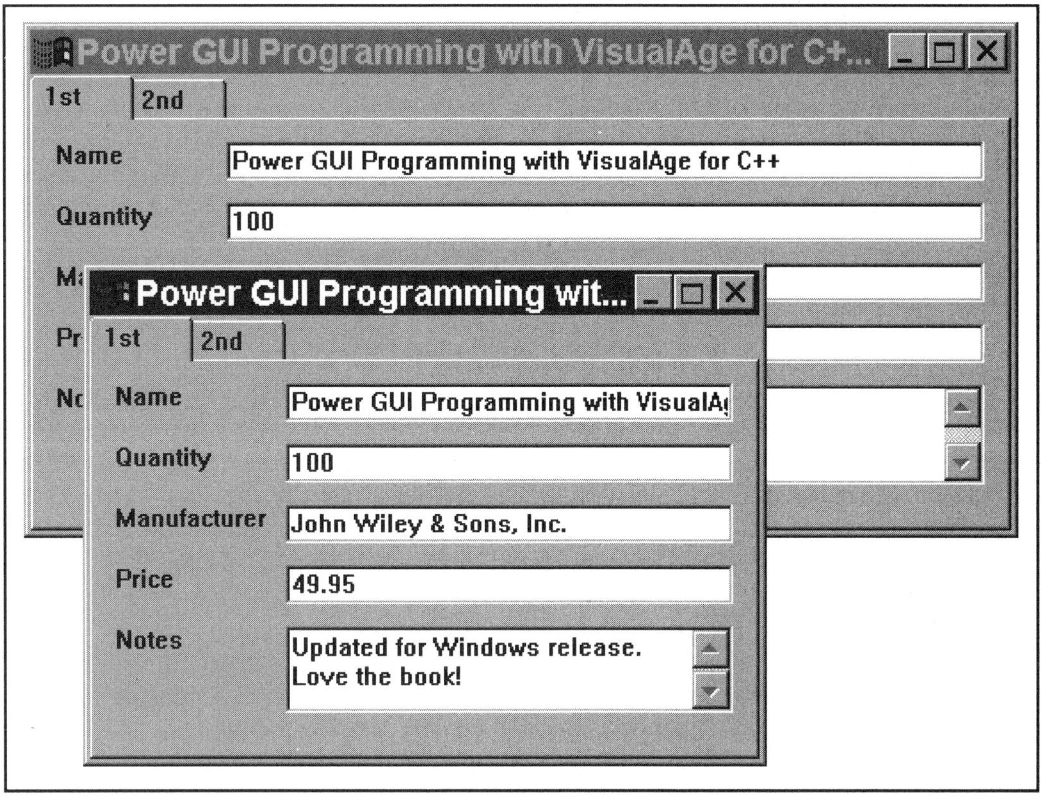

Figure 3-7. Sizing and Positioning Done by an IMultiCellCanvas.

The first notebook page of the example uses both `IEntryField` and `IMultiLineEdit` objects to collect information from the user. The following example shows how you can create and initialize these edit controls:

```
// Create a single-line entry field.
IEntryField fName( ID_NAME, &fPage1, &fPage1);
fName
 .setLimit(60)
 .setText( fPurchaseItem.name() )
 .enableTabStop()
 .enableGroup();

// Create a multiline edit field.
IMultiLineEdit fNotes( ID_NOTES, &fPage1, &fPage1,
                       IRectangle(),
                       IMultiLineEdit::classDefaultStyle
                         | IMultiLineEdit::ignoreTab);
fNotes
 .setText( fPurchaseItem.notes() )
 .enableTabStop()
 .enableGroup();
```

Buttons allow a user to select a choice, whether it is a single choice from a group of radio buttons, 0 or more choices from a group of check boxes, or an action to run from a group of push buttons or tool bar buttons. Open Class Library represents these controls with a set of button classes. The `IRadioButton` class represents a radio button; the `ICheckBox` and `I3StateCheckBox` classes represent check boxes; the `IPushButton` and `IGraphicPushButton` classes represent push buttons. With the `ICustomButton` and `ICustomButtonDrawHandler` classes, you can customize button drawing. `IToolBarButton` is a custom button specialized for use in a tool bar. It can display text, a bitmap, or both. `IAnimatedButton` is another custom button, which manages a set of bitmaps for animation. The example uses a push button on the second notebook page. Chapter 10, "Button Controls," describes this group of control classes.

You can display a list of items in a window other than a container. These list controls include the list box, combination box (which combines an entry field and list box), and spin button (which acts like a list box with only a single visible item). Open Class Library provides control classes for these types of list controls including `IListBox`, `IComboBox`, and `ITextSpinButton`.

The file dialog displayed when the push button is pressed shows some of these controls, including a list box and a combination box. However, the example does not create C++ objects to manage these controls. Chapter 11, "List Controls," describes this group of control classes in greater detail.

Slider Controls

Open Class Library supports three similar controls, the progress indicator, linear slider, and circular slider. Use the progress indicator, a read-only control, to show a value within a range such as the temperature on a mercury thermometer. It is a key component in building a progress indicator window that shows the status of a time-consuming task. The `IProgressIndicator` class represents a progress indicator control.

Use a slider or circular slider control to allow users to specify a value within a range such as a thermostat that they can control the temperature with. Use a circular slider to emulate dials such as stereo or video dials. The `ISlider` class represents a slider control and the `ICircularSlider` class represents a circular slider control. Chapter 12, "Slider Controls," describes these control classes in greater detail.

Menus

Menus list actions a user can run. These actions can apply to the application as a whole, such as an `Exit` choice, to a window or view, or even to a single control, such as `Cut`, `Copy`, or `Paste`. Menus are particularly useful for offering multiple action choices because you can group common menu choices together. You can organize menu items hierarchically, or you can simply separate them by dividers.

Open Class Library provides classes to represent different kinds of menus with a wide range of uses. For example, you can build menu bars and pop-up menus from resource files. You can dynamically create a menu bar or pop-up menu and dynamically change a menu bar, pop-up menu, or system menu. You can also use the `ISubMenu` class to temporarily change a menu until the user dismisses it. Once the user dismisses the menu, `ISubMenu` restores the menu to its original state. Chapter 6, "Menus and Keyboard Accelerators," describes these classes in greater detail.

Tool Bars

Use tool bars as an alternative to menus. Tool bars offer flexibility, a modern look, and a number of actions that are simultaneously visible to the user. You can easily add fly-over help or drag-and-drop support to a tool bar using classes that Open Class Library provides. Using direct manipulation, users can rearrange the tool bar buttons or add new buttons by dragging them from a menu. You can attach a tool bar to the top, bottom, or either side of a frame window, or you can allow it to float so users can place it anywhere on the desktop. Users can move a floating tool bar independently of the frame window, or they can "pin" it to the frame window so that it moves with the frame window.

The example program creates a tool bar that contains several buttons and is enabled for fly-over help. When you press one of these buttons, you see an informational message box that informs you that these buttons are not implemented in the example. Following is the code from the example that creates the tool bar:

Tool Bar Usage - latour\shopping\shopping.cpp

```
// Add a tool bar to the primary window.
IToolBar toolBar( ID_TOOLBAR, &primary );
IToolBarButton
  openButton( IC_ID_OPEN, &toolBar, &toolBar ),
  saveButton( IC_ID_SAVE, &toolBar, &toolBar ),
  cutButton( IC_ID_CUT, &toolBar, &toolBar ),
  copyButton( IC_ID_COPY, &toolBar, &toolBar ),
  pasteButton( IC_ID_PASTE, &toolBar, &toolBar );
toolBar
  .addAsLast( &openButton, true )
  .addAsLast( &saveButton )
  .addAsLast( &cutButton, true )
  .addAsLast( &copyButton )
  .addAsLast( &pasteButton )
  .disableDragDrop( );
```

Open Class Library provides the text and bitmaps for actions frequently found on a tool bar. These help you provide a common look and feel across applications and products. Tool bars typically contain buttons, although they can contain other controls provided by Open Class Library. Chapter 16, "Tool Bars, Fly-Over Help, and Custom Buttons," describes tool bars in greater detail.

Standard Dialogs

Open Class Library supports two special types of windows that most applications tend to need. These windows allow users to view and select a font or to select the name of one or more files. The presentation system terms for these windows are *font dialog* and *file dialog*. Open Class Library represents these dialogs with the IFontDialog and IFileDialog classes.

The example displays an `IFileDialog` object when the user presses the push button at the bottom of the second notebook page. This dialog allows users to pick a bitmap file from the list to replace the bitmap on the notebook page. Following is the handler that processes the push button event and creates the file dialog:

File Dialog Usage - latour\shopping\puritemv.cpp

```
IBase::Boolean PurchaseItemView::CmdHandler :: command
                                        ( ICommandEvent& event )
{
  Boolean stopProcessing = false;
  if (event.commandId() == ID_ICONBUTTON)
    {
    // set up the file dialog as a child of the desktop.
    IFileDialog::Settings settings;
    settings.setFileName( "*.bmp" );

    IFileDialog fileDlg( 0, fPurchaseItemView, settings );
    if ( fileDlg.pressedOK() )
    {
       fPurchaseItemView->updateBitmap(fileDlg.fileName());
    }
    stopProcessing = true;
  }

  return stopProcessing;
}
```

The Windows and OS/2 operating systems provide a default definition for the font and file dialogs. Figure 3-8 shows the file dialog. Chapter 18, "Fonts and Views," describes `IFontDialog` and `IFileDialog`.

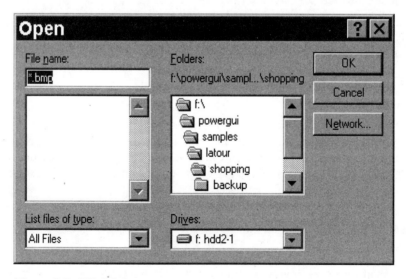

Figure 3-8. File Dialog.

Help and Messages

Open Class Library provides the `IHelpWindow` class for displaying help windows. Typically, these help windows are displayed as a result of the user pressing a help button or selecting help from a menu or tool bar.

Open Class Library also supports fly-over help for displaying short help messages for the window that the mouse pointer is positioned over. Typically, you use fly-over help for the buttons in a tool bar. Use the `IFlyText` and `IFlyHelpHandler` classes to add fly-over help to your application. Following is the code from the example for implementing fly-over help:

Fly-Over Help Usage - latour\shopping\shopping.cpp

```
// Add fly-over help to the tool bar.
IFlyText flyText( ID_FLYTEXT, &primary );
IFlyOverHelpHandler flyHandler( &flyText );
flyHandler
  .setDefaultText( "\0" )
  .setResourceLibrary( 0 )
  .handleEventsFor( &toolBar );
```

Open Class Library provides the `IMessageBox` class for displaying message windows. If the user fails to specify a name for a `PurchaseItem` object in its settings view, the example displays a message window containing an error message. Here is the code for displaying the message:

Message Box Usage - latour\shopping\puritemv.cpp

```
IMessageBox msg( this );
msg.show( "You must specify a name.",
        IMessageBox::okButton
        | IMessageBox::errorIcon
        | IMessageBox::moveable );
```

Figure 3-9 shows the resulting message window. Open Class Library error messages are normally loaded from a file to facilitate national language translation. Chapter 27, "Error Handling and Reporting," describes `IMessageBox`. Chapter 16, "Tool Bars, Fly-Over Help, and Custom Buttons," describes fly-over help. Chapter 23, "Using Help," describes how you can add other kinds of help to your application.

Direct Manipulation

The desktop uses an assortment of direct manipulation techniques. These techniques present different degrees of difficulty for you to implement support in your applications.

Some types of direct manipulation are built into the Windows and OS/2 operating systems, and they require no code to support them. For example, a user can move any frame window by dragging its title bar. With the OS/2 operating system, a user can also change the color of a window by dragging a color onto it from a color palette window.

Other types of direct manipulation are only partially built into the operating systems and require application code for you to fully support them. For example, you can create a frame window that users can size by dragging the borders. In the OS/2 operating system, users can change the size of the window's text by dragging a font from a font palette window. However,

Figure 3-9. Message Window.

in both cases, you are responsible for redistributing the contents of the window. The canvas classes, such as `IMultiCellCanvas` and `IViewPort`, provide support for these situations.

You also have drag and drop. While support for drag and drop is built into both operating systems, few applications support this direct manipulation technique because of its complexity. The Windows and OS/2 desktops, however, exploit this interaction technique—so much so that drag and drop is an important feature of both desktops. For your application to have the look and feel of the desktop, support the dragging and dropping of objects.

To illustrate the complexity involved, consider the code you must ordinarily provide for users to drag objects from a container. First, you must define what users can drag. Then, you must define what kinds of items the target window accepts from a drop. Finally, the source and target windows must send, receive and process a number of messages to exchange the dragged data.

Although it's tempting, omitting support for drag and drop in your application is not the right answer. Drag and drop can make some tasks easier and more intuitive for your users. In the example, by using drag and drop to move `PurchaseItem` objects between lists, users avoid the indirect step of accessing a menu or displaying a dialog to move an item.

With Open Class Library, you no longer have to get involved in complex drag-and-drop code. It provides a set of classes that you can use to easily support drag and drop in your application. These classes can even make a drag-and-drop interface easier to support than a menu-based one.

To support drag and drop in the example, we need to include the following code:

Main Partial Implementation - latour\shopping\shopping.cpp

```
// Support drag and drop of purchase items.
IDMHandler::enableDragDropFor( &buyList );
IDMHandler::enableDragDropFor( &dontBuyList );
```

We also need to implement a copy constructor and the `objectCopy` function (which calls the copy constructor) for the `PurchaseItem` class. After we implement `objectCopy`, users can copy container objects using direct manipulation.

Chapter 21, "Direct Manipulation," describes the drag-and-drop classes in greater detail.

Graphics Framework

Open Class Library provides classes for displaying two-dimensional (2D) graphics in your applications. These classes include a rich set of graphic primitives for 2D drawing, including lines, text, curves, boxes, and bitmaps. You can associate attributes with each primitive class to define its appearance, for example, its color and width. With these classes, you can draw an entire window or customize a window in your application. The graphics framework also provides a class that contains a list of graphics primitives for building complex graphics.

Multimedia Framework

Open Class Library provides classes to represent a wide spectrum of multimedia devices and capabilities. Examples of these devices include audio amplifier-mixers, CD audio players, digital video players, MIDI sequencers, and waveform audio players. Use this framework to implement an interface that looks and works like the controls of real electronic devices, such as stereos and video cassette recorders. Also, use this framework to enhance the interface of your application by adding audio, video, images, and animation.

Processing User Actions and System Events

Now that we have views and windows in place, our next step is to enable users to interact with these windows. In your applications, you do not have to provide all of the behavior for all of your windows, but you do have to provide application-specific behavior. Much of the standard behavior that an application needs is already built into the controls. What you need to provide are the interactions between windows and responses to user actions.

Event-Handling Framework

Open Class Library provides event and event-handler classes so that you can connect your window classes into the operating system's messaging model. Both are described in Chapter 4, "Windows, Handlers, and Events." With handlers, you can extend Open Class Library to provide application-specific logic to supplement or replace the default behavior that the

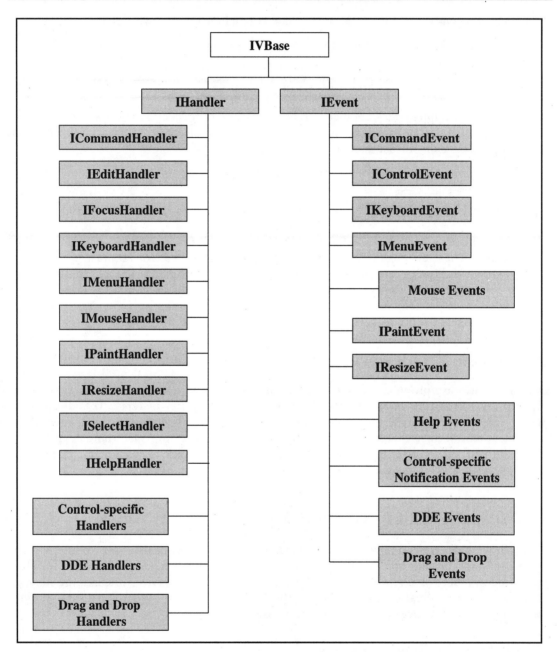

Figure 3-10. Hierarchy of Handler and Event Classes.

operating system or Open Class Library provides. Figure 3-10 shows the class hierarchy of the event-handling framework that Open Class Library provides.

For our example, let's take a look at the two kinds of event processing we need to provide. The first is to respond to a user's opening of a settings view for a PurchaseItem object by pressing the Enter key or double-clicking the mouse. The second is to update a PurchaseItem object with any changes that a user makes to the settings view window.

We showed the processing needed to open a PurchaseItemView a few pages ago. We only have to place it into a handler that detects an open event for a container object. The ICnrHandler class does just this. In this case, we can use the default processing of the handler class, which is to call the handleOpen function of the IContainerObject being opened. As a result, we can provide our application-specific code in a PurchaseItem::handleOpen function.

In the following code, we attach an ICnrHandler object to both container controls using the handleEventsFor function. As a result, this handler checks all events directed to the containers and processes the appropriate events.

Adding a Container Handler - latour\shopping\shopping.cpp

```
// Get default processing for an "open" event.
ICnrHandler cnrHandler;
cnrHandler
  .handleEventsFor(&buyList)
  .handleEventsFor(&dontBuyList);
```

Below, we show the handleOpen function that is called when a PurchaseItem is opened:

PurchaseItem::handleOpen - latour\shopping\puritem.cpp

```
void
  PurchaseItem :: handleOpen ( IContainerControl* container )
{
  // User has opened a PurchaseItem object.
  // Create a secondary window with a settings view.
  PurchaseItemView* secondary =
    new PurchaseItemView( *this,
                          ID_PURCHASEITEMVIEW,
                          container->parent() );
  secondary->setAutoDeleteObject();
  (*secondary)
    .setFocus()
    .show();
  this->IContainerObject::handleOpen( container );
}
```

Here, again, is what we did to enable drag and drop for our container controls:

Enabling Direct Manipulation - latour\shopping\shopping.cpp

```
// Support drag and drop of purchase items.
IDMHandler::enableDragDropFor( &buyList );
IDMHandler::enableDragDropFor( &dontBuyList );
```

Although we did not say so earlier, this is another case of "smart" default behavior provided by an event-handler class. This default processing does not require *any* other application-specific code.

The `CmdHandler` class updates the `PurchaseItem` with any updates that users make to the settings view, but only after they dismiss the view. The `CmdHandler` class also handles the events generated by clicking on the tool bar buttons. Following is the declaration of the `CmdHandler` class:

PurchaseItemView::CmdHandler Declaration - latour\shopping\puritemv.hpp

```
// Process command actions for a PurchaseItem.
class CmdHandler : public ICommandHandler {
public:
  CmdHandler     ( PurchaseItemView*  frame,
                   PurchaseItem&      purchaseItem );
protected:
virtual Boolean
  command        ( ICommandEvent& event ),
  systemCommand  ( ICommandEvent& event );

private:
  PurchaseItem
  &fPurchaseItem;
PurchaseItemView
  *fPurchaseItemView;
};   // class PurchaseItemView::CmdHandler
```

CmdHandler::systemCommand - latour\shopping\puritemv.cpp

```
IBase::Boolean PurchaseItemView::CmdHandler :: systemCommand
                                      ( ICommandEvent& event )
{
  Boolean stopProcessing = false;
  if (event.commandId() == ISystemMenu::idClose)
  {                  // View is being closed.
    if (fPurchaseItemView->validated())
    {                  // Save any changes.
      fPurchaseItemView->updateDataObject();
    }
    else
    {                  // Error, don't close the window.
      stopProcessing = true;
    }
  }

  return stopProcessing;
}
```

We describe specific event-handler classes in different chapters. For example, Chapter 17, "Reusable Handlers," describes the event-handler classes that you can use to extend the behavior of any window. The chapters that describe specific control classes also describe event handlers that are designed specifically for those controls.

Application Framework Objects

Application development involves more than creating objects to model the user's problem domain. You must also work with and be sensitive to the effects of operating system features in your applications because your application is still running in an operating system. A complex application needs to exploit the system's features.

For example, to take advantage of the multitasking power of the Windows and OS/2 operating systems, you must divide your application into multiple threads of execution and coordinate the processing done in those threads. Open Class Library provides classes to hide the complexity of doing this, as well as providing access to a system's information.

Applications

With the `IApplication` class, you can model attributes of your application. Use this class to store program arguments and to identify the location of your resource library. We provide an overview of resource libraries and their support in Open Class Library later in this chapter. You can also use `IApplication` to access information that the operating system maintains about your running application, or process.

The related `IProfile` class provides you with the functions to read and write application-specific data to the registry in the Windows operating system and to an initialization file in the OS/2 operating system. In that way you can save and restore information between invocations of your application.

You can accomplish much using Open Class Library without getting into the details of the application framework. All applications that use the window classes must include one critical line of code to enable this framework. This line starts the processing of operating system messages:

```
IApplication::current().run();
```

The example calls this function at the end of the `main` function. Chapter 20, "Applications and Threads," and Chapter 25, "Storing Data in a Profile," describe the classes mentioned here.

Threads

Maintaining a responsive user interface requires you to process events in a timely fashion. Otherwise, the machine can "hang." Users do not get any response to keyboard or mouse input. Thus, perform any event processing that takes appreciable time in a thread other than the message-processing thread of the application.

The Windows and OS/2 operating systems define two units of program execution, *threads* and *processes*. A process is essentially an application; it can be composed of many threads. Threads can run independently of one another, or they can be coordinated with semaphores. Open Class Library supports semaphores through the classes derived from `IResource` and `IResourceLock`.

By adding threads to your application, you allow users to continue interacting with the user interface, even while a time-consuming task runs on another thread. Open Class Library is designed with explicit support for multithreaded programs. Use the flexible `IThread` class to create threads. Unlike the C library function, `_beginthread`, the `IThread` class enables you to run C++ member functions in a separate thread. Chapter 20, "Applications and Threads," describes the thread and semaphore classes that Open Class Library provides.

Resources

You can build several types of resources, such as dialog boxes, bitmaps, and translatable text, into your application. You define these resources in a resource script file, process the file with a resource compiler, and bind the resulting resource file to a resource library. The resource library can be your executable (.EXE) file or a dynamic link library (.DLL) file.

Open Class Library provides classes to read resources out of either type of resource library. It also provides overloaded versions of functions in the IWindow class hierarchy that accept either the address of a character string or an entry in a string table resource. You can set the default resource file that your application uses by calling the setUserResourceLibrary function in the ICurrentApplication class.

The example uses some resources but binds them to its executable file. The executable file is the default user resource library that the IApplication class uses. Chapter 24, "Using Resources," describes the classes supporting application resources.

Dynamic Data Exchange Framework

Dynamic Data Exchange (DDE) is a protocol that enables your applications to communicate and exchange data with other applications in a client-server model. These other applications, such as Excel or Lotus 1-2-3, can be running in the OS/2 or Windows operating system.

Open Class Library provides event and event-handler classes to make it easy for your applications to use DDE in the role of either a client or server application. With these classes, you can create "hot" links to mirror data maintained by one application in another application. Changes to the data can be seen immediately in the second application.

Programming Objects

Open Class Library also provides classes to help you develop an application. Your users will likely never see evidence of these classes. However, without the help they can provide you, your users would likely have to wait longer to see your finished application.

Exceptions

The VisualAge for C++ compiler supports the ANSI C++ exception model. This error-handling model enables error-detecting code to throw an exception object, while a calling routine can catch the exception object to process the error.

Open Class Library throws exception objects to report error conditions. Open Class Library constructs these exception objects from exception classes that share a common hierarchy. The exception objects contain error data that identifies the function that throws the exception and the error's characteristics. Applications can catch these exceptions and also throw their own exception objects. You can use the exception classes that Open Class Library provides, or you can build your own based on these classes. Chapter 27, "Error Handling and Reporting," describes the C++ exception-handling support that Open Class Library provides.

Tracing

Open Class Library provides tracing support to help you gather run-time information about your program. Do not confuse this support with the Performance Analyzer tool that VisualAge for C++ provides. The analyzer enables you to view a log of all calls made by your running application. You can use it to identify performance bottlenecks and to observe the interactions between multiple threads.

Open Class Library provides the ITrace class and related macros so you can log application-specific string data from your program. You can find details in Chapter 28, "Problem Determination."

Notification Framework

Open Class Library provides a set of classes for implementing event- and attribute-change notification in your application. These notification classes include notifiers, observers, and notification events. The notification framework is different from the event-handling framework in one important way: whereas a handler can stop the dispatching of an event to the remaining handlers in the list, an observer cannot stop a notification from being sent to all observers registered for the notification. The notification framework is also designed to work with objects other than windows.

Streaming Framework

Open Class Library provides classes and global functions for streaming to and from memory or files. The global-streaming functions support the native C++ data types, the IString class, and the collection classes. Open Class Library also supplies functions for flattening and resurrecting these classes so that type information is not lost. Use the streaming framework to provide persistence for your model's data and objects.

Open Class Library's Obsolete Strategy

As Open Class Library has evolved, it has obsoleted classes and functions to improve consistency and design. Open Class Library provides a set of macros in IBASE.HPP that you can use to identify obsolete code and remove it from your application. The following macros are from IBASE.HPP:

```
#define IC_OBSOLETE_1    310
#define IC_OBSOLETE_2    400

#ifndef IC_OBSOLETE
 #ifdef IC_WIN
   #define IC_OBSOLETE  320
 #endif
```

```
#ifdef IC_PM
   #define IC_OBSOLETE   320
#endif
#ifdef IC_MOTIF
   #define IC_OBSOLETE   310
#endif
#ifdef IC_400
   #define IC_OBSOLETE   310
#endif
#ifdef IC_MVS
   #define IC_OBSOLETE   310
 #endif
#endif
```

Open Class Library defines a macro in the form IC_OBSOLETE_X for every version in which it obsoletes something. IC_OBSOLETE represents the obsolete level defined for each of the platforms. Open Class Library wrappers obsolete classes and functions in macros so you can remove them when you compile. The compiler then flags any usage of obsolete code in your application. For example, the first release in which Open Class Library obsoleted functions was represented by IC_OBSOLETE_1, and these functions appear in the class declarations as follows:

```
#if (IC_OBSOLETE <= IC_OBSOLETE_1)
    // Obsolete function here
#endif // IC_OBSOLETE
```

In the next major release, Open Class Library removed IC_OBSOLETE_1 functions (wrapped with IC_OBSOLETE_1 as in our example) from the headers, and did not ship their implementations with the product. Open Class Library only removes obsolete levels in major versions so that you have sufficient time to migrate your applications to replacement classes and functions. Notice that IC_OBSOLETE is conditionally defined so that you can define it to identify any obsolete functions in your code. For example, you could compile your application as follows:

```
icc -DIC_OBSOLETE 500 yourapp.cpp
```

In this example, you would receive error messages for any use of obsolete functions or classes. Because Open Class Library increments the release values with each release, you can easily identify functions obsoleted at a specific release level. For example, to identify only functions obsoleted with IC_OBSOLETE_1, compile your application with IC_OBSOLETE defined to 400. Note that you cannot run an application compiled with IC_OBSOLETE defined, even if you have no compile errors, because the class declarations do not match those that the product was built with.

To discourage their use, Open Class Library does not document its obsolete classes or functions in its product documentation. Likewise, we do not include obsolete classes or functions in this book or the accompanying example code.

Example Program Make Files

The make files for our example programs contain six items worthy of note:

- The compiler warning flags **/Wall+gnr-ppc-ppt-uni-vft-** maximize the number of warnings the compiler gives you for your own code; they minimize the warnings generated by using Open Class Library's header files.

- The compiler option **/Gm+** causes the examples to be built as multithreaded programs, a requirement for applications built with Open Class Library. If you do not include this flag, an error occurs during the compile. If you do not use the **/Ft-** option, use **/Gm+** when linking because template files processed at link time also need to be processed with **/Gm+**.

- The compiler option **/Gd+** causes the example to load VisualAge for C++ code at run time. This causes the example to require dynamic-link libraries (DLLs) for Open Class Library and the C/C++ run time. To eliminate the need for the DLLs, use **/Gd-** to statically link the VisualAge for C++ code into the executable files of the examples.

- We use the compiler—ICC.EXE—not only to compile the examples, but also to link them.

- We use the **/Ft-** option to correctly resolve C++ template functions. Although using this option results in larger object files, it does not affect the size of the executable file, and it eliminates linker errors that are typically difficult to resolve.

- We do not specify any static or import libraries when linking; instead, we rely on the library names to be resolved at link time from the names stored by the compiler in the object (.OBJ) files. The compiler stores library names based on the settings of the **/Gd** and **/Gm** options used at compile time, as well as any #pragma library statements it finds in header and include files that it reads at compile time. Note that the compiler does not generate references to import libraries for resolving calls to Windows APIs. Because the DLLs of Open Class Library load many of these system DLLs, usually you do not have to specify these import libraries when building with **/Gd+**. However, this is not the case when building without using **/Gd+**. In that case, you must include these import libraries to link without error in the Windows version of Open Class Library.

Chapter 4

Windows, Handlers, and Events

- Describes important window concepts and terminology, including differences between the Windows and OS/2 operating systems
- Describes the IWindow class, which is the base class for all window classes
- Describes the IEvent class, which is the base class for all event classes
- Describes the IHandler class, which is the base class for all event handler classes
- Discusses how IWindow, IHandler, and IEvent objects interact to implement the event-handling framework
- This chapter is highly recommended reading for all Open Class Library users.
- Read Chapter 3 before reading this chapter if you have not previously written code using the wide range of classes that Open Class Library provides.

Chapter 2, "Object-Oriented User Interface Fundamentals," describes how you compose the user interface of an application using a series of object views, action windows, and message windows. Chapter 3, "Tour of Open Class Library," shows how you build these views and windows using the classes derived from IWindow. In this chapter, we discuss the features that these window classes have in common.

As you build your application windows, you need to process data that your users update in these views and respond to user actions and system events. You accomplish these tasks using a series of event-handler classes derived from IHandler and event-data classes derived from IEvent. You learn to build these handlers and use them to process events.

You initiate and receive all communications from the underlying presentation system using these IWindow, IHandler, and IEvent derived objects. As you see in Figure 4-1, Open Class Library separates the processing of your requests *to* the presentation system from those you receive *from* it. You make requests to the presentation system by calling member functions of IWindow and its derived classes. You use these classes to create and destroy windows. You also use these classes to modify windows, including moving, sizing, hiding, and updating their contents.

Your application receives all messages from the presentation system via IHandler and its derived classes. For example, you can be notified when your user changes the contents of an entry field or selects a push button. These window and handler objects work together to provide you with a framework to control the behavior of your views.

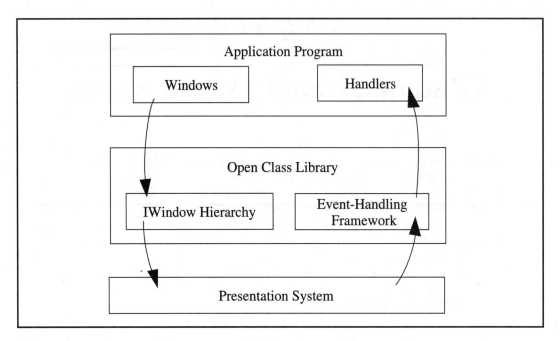

Figure 4-1. Separation of Messages to and from the Presentation System.

Open Class Library provides a wide range of handler classes. Some handlers are generic, in that you can use them with many different window classes. For example, IMouseHandler works with all window classes. Other handlers are specific to one window class. For example, you can only use IFrameWindowHandler for IFrameWindow and its derived classes. Handlers have corresponding event classes that identify the data specific to the events that the handlers process. Typically, the names of the handler and their event classes reflect their close association. For example, you use the IMouseEvent, IMouseClickEvent, and IMousePointerEvent classes with the IMouseHandler class. To help you choose the handlers and events you need to build your views, you find an overview of the event and event-handler classes' hierarchies later in this chapter. For more details on the generic handlers, see Chapter 17, "Reusable Handlers." For more details on specific handlers, see the chapters that describe the window classes that use each handler.

The event-handling framework connects your application to the presentation system's message-driven window model. If you need to work directly with the presentation system to accomplish tasks not supported by Open Class Library, read our discussion about the presentation system's message-driven model and the connection between it and the event-handling framework.

Window Basics

Visually, a presentation system window is a rectangular area on the display. In both the Windows and OS/2 operating systems, one or more pieces of code called *window procedures* control this visual element. These window procedures, or windows, handle events in the system such as mouse and keyboard input and painting the contents of the displayed window. When the presentation system captures keyboard and mouse input, it converts the input into specific messages with additional data unique to the message and then calls the window procedure. Each window in the presentation system has its own particular behavior, which is dictated by the way it handles messages. Whereas the presentation system requires all windows to exhibit a uniform behavior when responding to certain messages, other messages trigger a different window response. Each window can also send its own unique messages independent of the presentation system.

Parent-Child Relationships and Window Positioning

The *parent-child relationship* of windows refers to the visual relationship between windows in the presentation system. Child windows are always drawn on top of their parent window but cannot extend beyond it. If a child window does extend beyond its parent, the presentation system clips it to the boundary of the parent window. Figure 4-2 shows a parent window with a single child window that is not contained within its parent window. As this figure shows, you can only view the portion of the child window within the boundaries of the parent window.

The Windows and OS/2 operating systems use different coordinate systems to identify the position of windows on the display. In the Windows operating system, you specify all positioning information for a window relative to the *upper-left* corner of its parent window. Therefore, the position of a window in Windows is the offset of its upper-left corner from the upper-left corner of its parent. In the OS/2 operating system, you specify all positioning information for a window relative to the *lower-left* corner of its parent window. Therefore, the position of a window in the OS/2 operating system is the offset of its lower-left corner from the lower-left corner of its parent.

You specify the position and size of windows in terms of *picture elements* (*pels*). Figure 4-2 shows the relationship between a child window and its parent window. The child window is at horizontal offset "x" and vertical offset "y" from its parent's origin. In the Windows operating system, the child's "y" value is negative because it starts before or above its parent. In the OS/2 operating system, the child's "y" value is positive because it starts after or above its parent.

You can readily see that this difference in coordinate systems makes building portable applications difficult because you must calculate the position of all windows differently in each operating system. Fortunately, with Open Class Library you can pick a coordinate system and specify the location of all windows in that coordinate system. Open Class Library handles any difference to the native coordinate system for you. You learn more about this topic later in this chapter.

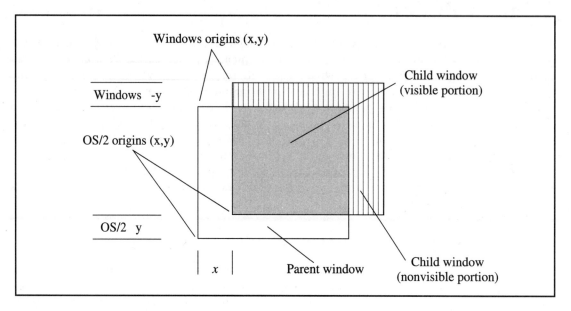

Windows origins (x,y)

Windows -y

OS/2 origins (x,y)

OS/2 y

x

Child window
(visible portion)

Parent window

Child window
(nonvisible portion)

Figure 4-2. Parent-Child Clipping and Window Positioning.

Because you can only view a child window within the bounds of its parent, you shouldn't be surprised to learn that the parent also controls whether the child window is visible. If the parent window is not visible, neither is the child. When you destroy a parent window, you automatically destroy all of its child windows, also.

Sibling Windows

Sibling windows have the same parent. *Sibling order* refers to the sequence in which sibling windows appear when they are painted on the display or when the user moves the cursor with the Tab key. Because sibling windows can overlap each other, the presentation system paints them in order from the bottom sibling to the top sibling. When sibling windows overlap, sibling order also determines which window receives mouse events that occur in the area where the siblings overlap. Be aware that the `IWindow::clipSiblings` style can cause the window that is actually underneath to appear to be on top. It is not, however, the one that receives mouse events.

In those parent windows that support tabbing, using the Tab key moves the cursor to the next sibling—proceeding from the top sibling to the bottom sibling. Using Shift+Tab moves the cursor from the bottom sibling to the top sibling.

By default, Open Class Library creates new windows at the bottom of the sibling order. Therefore, unless you specifically take steps to change it, sibling order is directly related to the order in which you create the windows. If two sibling windows overlap on the display, the window you create first covers a portion of the second window.

Frame windows are unique because when a user activates them, they dynamically change their sibling order to make themselves the topmost window. All topmost frame windows are siblings of each other; their parent is the desktop window.

The sibling order is not related to the location of windows on the display unless you take steps to position the windows in their sibling order. If you want the Tab key to move from the top of a list of entry fields to the bottom, explicitly create them in this order. You can adjust the order later, if needed.

Window Ownership

Whereas the choice of parent window establishes a visual relationship between windows, the *owner window* defines a path for message processing within the presentation system. Most windows on the Windows and OS/2 operating systems send a message to their respective owner windows to notify them of significant events in the windows. For example, they notify their owners when their contents change. The presentation system also routes some messages not processed by a window to its owner for processing.

A window always appears on top of its owner window and is hidden when its owner is minimized. This behavior is one thing that distinguishes a primary frame window from a secondary frame window. A *secondary frame window* has another frame window as its owner, and is always displayed on top of this window. A *primary frame window* does not have an owner and is independent of other frame windows in the same application.

With the OS/2 operating system, you can specify the owner when you create the window; the Windows operating system assigns the owner for you. If the parent window you specify when you create the window is not a top-level window, the Windows operating system identifies the top-level window of the parent and makes it the owner. If the parent window is a top-level window when you create it, Windows assigns this window as the owner. Further, with the OS/2 operating system, you can dynamically change the owner of a window; with the Windows operating system, you cannot.

Generally, you can use the parent window as the owner window for controls. See Chapter 7, "Controls," for considerations specific to controls.

The ownership of frame windows defines whether a window is a primary, secondary, or child window. Ownership of frame windows also becomes a factor during activation (when a frame window is closed, its owner gets activated) and clean up (when a frame window is destroyed, the frame windows that it owns are also destroyed). See Chapter 5, "Frame Window Basics," for further information.

Finally, here are two warnings relating to owner windows:

1. Always create a window on the same thread as its owner window. This is a restriction imposed by the OS/2 operating system, and we highly recommend it for the Windows operating system.

2. Ensure that you do not create a circular owner chain because an event can create an endless loop as it gets passed around the chain.

Window Input Focus

All presentation system windows share the same keyboard and mouse. Because these windows share those common resources, the presentation system requires a way to identify which window the keyboard or mouse input is sent to.

Windows receive keyboard input based on a window property called *input focus*. The window with input focus receives all keyboard input. Only one window at a time can have input focus, and only one window receives each keystroke. In the Windows operating system, if the focus window does not process the keystroke, the window dispatcher passes it up the window's owner chain until it is processed, effectively simulating how the OS/2 operating system routes these messages up the owner chain.

Each window that can receive input focus must provide a visual cue to the user. For example, a frame window's cue is to change the background color of the title bar; an entry field's cue is to display a text cursor.

Window Mouse Input

The presentation system does not use input focus to identify where to send mouse input. Instead, it checks the topmost window underneath the mouse to determine if it can accept the mouse message. If the window is registered to accept "hit test" messages, the presentation system sends it a hit test message (WM_NCHITTEST in the Windows operating system and WM_HITTEST in the OS/2 operating system) to determine whether the window processes mouse messages. Most windows pass this message on to the default window procedure. It returns a value based on whether the window is enabled (accepts the mouse input) or disabled (rejects the mouse input).

Some windows, like the static controls, appear transparent by responding to a hit test message with a return code that indicates that the window is transparent (HTTRANSPARENT in the Windows operating system and HT_TRANSPARENT in the OS/2 operating system). When this happens, the presentation system sends the same hit test message to the underlying window (usually the parent) to check whether it can receive the mouse message.

In the Windows operating system, the hit test message is always sent. In the OS/2 operating system, the message is not sent unless the window has the style CS_HITTEST. If a window does not have this style, the OS/2 operating system operates as if the window accepts mouse messages when it is enabled and rejects them when it is disabled.

The Desktop Window

The topmost window in the Windows and OS/2 operating systems is the desktop window. The primary function of the desktop window is to display a view of the objects located on the desktop. All of your application's visible top-level windows are child windows of the desktop window.

The Event-Handling Framework

To recap, a presentation system window contains a piece of code called a window procedure. All presentation-system-provided windows have their own window procedure. Through a process called *window subclassing*, the presentation systems in the Windows and OS/2 operating systems allow you to extend the behavior of their windows. When you subclass a window, you provide the presentation system with a window procedure for it to call instead of the current window procedure. A typical subclass procedure only processes some events and routes the remainder to the previous window procedure. If window subclassing occurs more than once for a window, a window can have a chain of window procedures. Each window procedure in the chain must either fully process a message or route the message to the next window procedure in the chain.

You use the derived classes of `IHandler` to process events associated with a window just as you would use a presentation system subclass procedure. Think of a handler as a way to add a particular behavior or protocol to a window. When you build handlers that are targeted to a specific behavior, you can easily reuse this behavior in a different window. You can also easily combine handlers to add more than one protocol to a window.

Window and Handler Separation

The use of event handler objects to mimic the presentation system's subclass procedures separates Open Class Library from other C++ libraries. Typically, other libraries capture events in the system and call virtual functions in the window hierarchy. If you want to process a particular event, you are forced to create a class, specify that it is derived from the window, and override a specific virtual function. This design can be easy to use but is not very flexible. In the next brief example, you see the difficulty in extending the behavior of a window designed in this manner.

You want to create an entry field that converts all lowercase characters to uppercase before displaying them in the entry field. To do this, you need to create a specific class of entry field. You specify that this class, `UpperCaseEntryField`, is derived from the library's existing entry field class and that it overrides a function of the class used to process keystrokes. You now use this function to convert characters to uppercase as the user enters lowercase characters.

Although you can build the `UpperCaseEntryField` easily, you now have two problems: how do you extend the behavior of this new class and how do you create an entry field that not only converts characters to uppercase, but also limits the characters that the users type to alphabetic characters? The answer is to create a new class, `UpperCaseAlphabeticEntryField`, which is derived from `UpperCaseEntryField`. In this new class, you again override the function used to process keystrokes to add the behavior to support alphabetic-only input. As a further refinement, you want an entry field that supports the alphabetic-only behavior without converting characters to uppercase. For this, you need to add yet another class to the hierarchy. As you can see, this approach leads you to many classes with obscure combinations of properties.

Even more important, consider how you would add behavior that converts characters to uppercase or how you would limit the users' input to alphabetic-only characters in a combination box or multiline edit control? Clearly, you cannot do this by deriving from either of the entry field classes that you already created. As a result, you must derive new classes from the library's combination box and multiline edit classes and add to them the same behaviors you already added to your entry field classes. Now, you cannot readily reuse your existing code.

Open Class Library fixes these problems by separating the processing of events into event-handler classes instead of including it with the window classes. Thus, you can build event-processing objects that are highly flexible. For example, you can create one handler to convert characters to uppercase and another handler to accept only alphabetic characters. You can then attach these handlers to any window that accepts keyboard input to add either or both behaviors. You write the code only one time. Open Class Library even provides templates so you can route handler callback functions to functions on your derived control classes. For more information, see Chapter 17, "Reusable Handlers."

From a Presentation System Message to Your Handler

You have seen in a general way how the presentation system creates events and how Open Class Library captures them and calls your handler objects for processing. You also have seen how the processing in a handler object is similar to the processing in a presentation system window subclass procedure. However, we left a gap between the presentation system sending the message and it arriving in your handler. Now we shall provide the missing pieces by describing how your handler receives a presentation system message. Figure 4-3 portrays this sequence of events.

The User Interface Subclass Procedure

An Open Class Library application is a presentation system application. Open Class Library itself provides a single window procedure that operates for most windows represented by IWindow objects (we ignore the exceptions for now). Every time you create an object derived from IWindow, the object registers this window procedure as a subclass window procedure. As a result, Open Class Library's window procedure gets the first chance to process all messages that the presentation system sends to the window (see Figure 4-3, step 1).

Messages Missing from the Subclass Procedure

In a few situations, Open Class Library's subclass procedure does not receive a message sent to one of the presentation system's window procedures. This occurs because the presentation system sends some notification messages as you create a window. Because Open Class Library does not subclass the window until after the window is created, its window procedure does not receive these messages. As a result, a handler attached to the window is not called to process these messages.

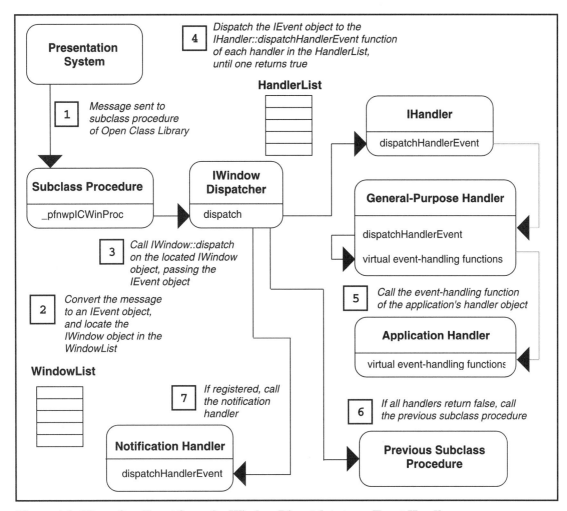

Figure 4-3. Flow of an Event from the Window Dispatcher to an Event Handler.

The primary job of the window procedure is to convert the presentation system message into a data package called an IEvent object (see Figure 4-3, step 2) and route the event to the correct IWindow object. It locates the window object in the current thread's collection of windows and calls the function IWindow::dispatch (see Figure 4-3, step 3). The dispatch function calls the handler and passes it the event.

The Collection of Windows

When the presentation system creates a window, it assigns the window a token called a *window handle*. The window handle is a unique value that the presentation system uses to identify the window. An application must pass this window handle to the presentation system after any request for services for a window. The presentation system also passes the window handle to a window procedure when it sends the window a message.

To fulfill its primary function, the window procedure uses the window handle that the presentation system provides to find the `IWindow` pointer of the C++ object for the window. It can do this because Open Class Library maintains keyed lists of all `IWindow` objects. It maintains a separate list for each thread. The window handle itself is the key used to retrieve the window object from the collection. The window procedure calls `IWindow::windowWithHandle` to retrieve the `IWindow` pointer with the handle from the current thread's collection of windows.

Once the window procedure finds the right window object, it calls the window object's dispatcher function, `IWindow::dispatch`, and passes it the event.

The Collection of Handlers

The window dispatcher's primary job is to call any handlers that have requested the window for a chance to process events. A handler registers this request by calling `IWindow::addHandler`. When a handler calls `addHandler`, the window adds the new handler to the top of its handler list. When the dispatcher calls the handlers in the list, it starts at the top of the list. This means the dispatcher always calls the last handler added before calling previously added handlers. Because of this ordering, you can add a handler that can replace some or all of the behavior of a handler already in the list.

To add a handler, call `IHandler::handleEventsFor` and pass it the `IWindow` object. This function calls `IWindow::addHandler`, which puts the handler in the window list.

Open Class Library adds this extra step in registering handlers to add a measure of type safety. Whereas `IWindow::addHandler` accepts any handler, some handlers only work with specific windows. When a handler limits the windows it can support, it then needs to override `IHandler::handleEventsFor` with its own versions to identify the `IWindow` derived classes it supports. It also needs to hide the `handleEventsFor` function which accepts an `IWindow` object by declaring the access for this function private.

Calling All Handlers

Starting with the handler at the top of its list, the window dispatcher calls the virtual function `IHandler::dispatchHandlerEvent` (see Figure 4-3, step 4). Every handler that inherits directly from `IHandler` must implement this function. The dotted lines in Figure 4-3 show that while the window dispatcher calls the `dispatchHandlerEvent` function in `IHandler`, the C++ virtual function mechanism routes the call to a derived class.

The function `dispatchHandlerEvent` in the class derived from `IHandler` has several responsibilities. It must return `true` to the dispatcher if the handler processed the event and does not want any other handlers or the default window procedure to process the event. If the function does return `true`, it also may be required to set an event result in the `IEvent` object received from the dispatcher. This result is specific to the event and requires the handler to distinguish details of specific Windows and OS/2 messages. The event result is not used in most events.

If a handler does not need to prevent dispatching of the event to other handlers and the default window procedure, its `dispatchHandlerEvent` function must return `false` to the window dispatcher.

Another responsibility of the handler is to package the information in the presentation system message into a form usable by the handler and to call a specific virtual function of the handler (see Figure 4-3, step 5).

When the window dispatcher receives `false` from a handler, it finds the next handler in the list and calls its `dispatchHandlerEvent` function. This process continues until a handler returns `true` or the dispatcher has exhausted all the handlers in the list. If any handler returns `true` (indicating that it processed the event), Open Class Library's subclass window procedure returns the event result in the message to the presentation system. The message is not processed by the presentation system's window procedure. If no handler returns `true`, then the subclass procedure calls the next window procedure in the subclass chain by calling `IWindow::defaultProcedure` (see Figure 4-3, step 6).

Modifying the Default Behavior of a Window

Every type of presentation system window belongs to a particular *window class*. Each class has a *class name* to identify the type of window, *class styles* to define characteristics of its windows, and a window procedure to process messages and draw the window. It is this window procedure that Open Class Library's window procedure calls if a handler did not process the event.

At times you need to extend the behavior of a class' window procedure for an event instead of replacing it completely. For example, you might want to add custom drawing on top of a window after any other handlers and after the window classes' window procedure has drawn the window. You need the other handlers to process the event, and you need the presentation system to provide its default processing before you perform your handler's action. You can do this in your handler by calling `IWindow::dispatchRemainingHandlers`, adding the additional processing, and returning `true` to the window dispatcher. The default behavior of this function calls `defaultProcedure` after calling the remaining handlers' `dispatchHandlerEvent` function.

At other times you might want the other handlers to process an event, but you want to do some processing before `defaultProcedure` is called. You can do this in your handler by calling `IWindow::dispatchRemainingHandlers` and specifying `false` for the optional argument `callDefProc`. You can then add the additional processing, call `defaultProcedure`, and return `true` to the window dispatcher.

Notifying Window Observers

After `IWindow::dispatch` calls all handlers in its list and calls the presentation system for the default processing of the message through a call to `IWindow::defaultProcedure`, it checks to see if any `IObserver` objects have been registered for notification messages. `IObserver` objects are registered by calling the function `addObserver` in `IWindow`'s base class, `INotifier`. If `IObserver` objects are registered, the dispatcher calls `dispatchHandlerEvent` on the `IWindowNotifyHandler` derived class attached to the window to allow it to pass the notification to its observers.

Window Handlers

Open Class Library ships a set of general-purpose handler classes that help to streamline window-event processing. These classes interpret the event identifier and call more specific event-handling functions. These event-handling functions are virtual functions that an application overrides to process an event. In addition, the handler classes convert the event to a specific event object that provides a detailed interpretation of the event parameters. Figure 4-4 displays the handler classes of Open Class Library.

To help you understand the work of these handlers better, we have broken them down into categories, which describe how you use them.

General Handlers

These handlers process common events applicable to many window classes. Thus, you can attach these handlers to different types of windows to add the same protocol or behavior to all of them. For example, you can add an IPaintHandler to both IEntryField and IMultiLineEdit objects.

Frame Window Handlers

These handlers process events for frame windows, and typically the frame constructor adds them automatically. This group includes handler objects for IFrameWindow, IFileDialog, and IFontDialog.

Control Handlers

These handlers work with specific controls in Open Class Library effectively extending the behavior of specific controls. You can attach most of these handlers to the control they extend or to the owner of the control. You can attach others only to the control itself.

Help Handlers

These handlers include IHelpHandler and IFlyOverHelpHandler. Use IHelpHandler objects to process events relating to help information. You can use this class only with frame windows. Use IFlyOverHelpHandler to implement *fly-over* (or *hover*) help for a window. You can use this class with any window.

Menu Handlers

These handlers dispatch menu events, such as requests for a pop-up menu. Do not use this class to process command events that occur because a user selects a menu item; use the ICommandHandler class to do that.

Draw-Item Handlers

These handlers replace or extend the default drawing behavior provided by some windows in Open Class Library.

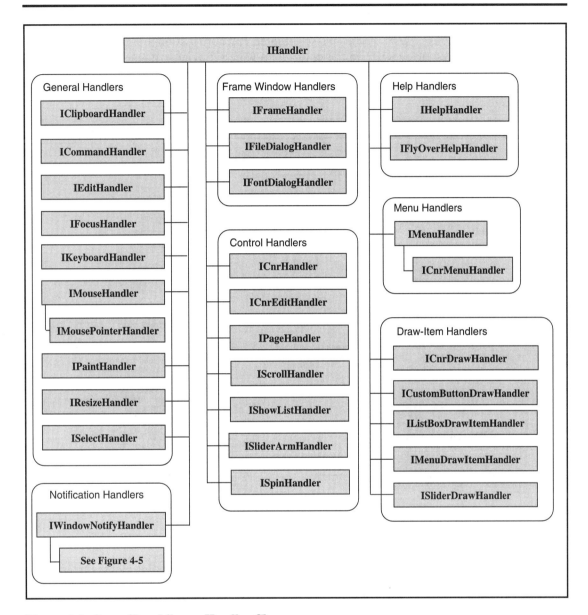

Figure 4-4. Open Class Library Handler Classes.

Notification Handlers

These handlers implement the INotifier protocol for IWindow and its derived classes. IWindowNotifyHandler provides notification for the INotificationIds identified in IWindow. Similarly, to implement additional notifications in the classes derived from

IWindow, the Open Class Library provides handler classes derived from IWindowNotifyHandler. These classes implement notification for messages from the presentation system specific to the controls to which they are attached. Then, they call the dispatchNotificationEvent function of their base class to ensure that all notifications occur for the window. Figure 4-5 shows the hierarchy of window notification classes.

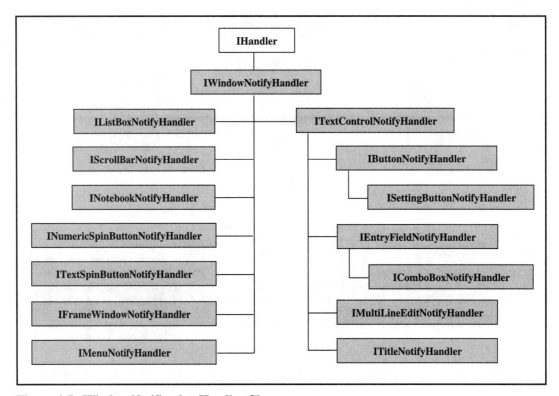

Figure 4-5. Window Notification Handler Classes.

Besides these handler classes, Open Class Library also provides handler classes to interpret direct manipulation (drag and drop) and dynamic data exchange (DDE) messages. See Chapter 21, "Direct Manipulation," for further discussion.

Handler Virtual Functions

When the window dispatcher calls a handler's dispatchHandlerEvent function, it passes an IEvent object. Based on information in the event object, the handler's dispatcher routes the event to one of the handler's own virtual functions. To process these events, create a class derived from the handler that overrides one or more of these *handle* (or *callback*) functions. Each function represents a related but independent event that you can choose to process in your derived class.

┌───┐

Naming Handler Callback Functions

In general, callback functions in the Open Class Library are named beginning with the word "handle." To shorten the names of the virtual callback functions in the IHandler hierarchy, the word "handle" is dropped from the function name because most of these functions are "handler" functions. It might help you, however, to read these virtual callback functions as if they started with the word "handle." For example, the command handler dispatcher calls ICommandHandler's virtual member function, command, to tell the handler to "[handle the] command."

└───┘

Event Objects

The IEvent object sent to a handler's dispatcher function contains the same untyped data received in the presentation system message. In this form it is not very useful or portable. It is the job of the handler, in combination with classes that inherit from IEvent, to provide this information in a form you can use. These inherited classes of IEvent contain functions you use to extract the data from the event object. A handler's dispatcher function passes these event objects to its callback functions and provides the additional data needed to process the event correctly. For example, the command handler's dispatcher passes an ICommandEvent when it calls the virtual command function. If the processing needs the identifier of the specific command, call ICommandEvent::commandId.

IEvent includes functions that extract the IWindow pointer of various windows related to the event. IEvent::window returns the IWindow pointer of the window contained in the event. Because the IWindow dispatcher routes owner-notification messages to the original source of the message, IEvent::window may not be the IWindow object you need. For this reason, IEvent provides two other functions. IEvent::dispatchingWindow returns the IWindow pointer of the window whose dispatch function called the handler with the event. IEvent::controlWindow returns the IWindow pointer of the window that originated the owner-notification event.

For example, a control sends a WM_DRAWITEM message to its owner to allow it the opportunity to take over drawing in the window. The window subclass procedure captures this message and sends it to the dispatcher of the control that originated the message before sending it to the dispatcher of the owner. (See "Rerouting Window Messages" for more information.) When a handler attached to the control receives the draw-item event, IEvent::dispatchingWindow is the IWindow of the control itself. When a handler attached to the owner of the control receives the event (because it was not processed by a handler attached to the control), IEvent::dispatchingWindow is now the owner of the window.

IEvent also includes functions to extract the message identifier and two event parameters. Open Class Library provides many event classes for you to use with the handler classes.

Event Parameters

To assist the classes that inherit from IEvent in translating message data so that it makes sense in a handler, Open Class Library also provides the class IEventData. With this class, you can create and render event parameters and event results from a variety of data formats. For example, this class contains constructors to create IEventData objects from combinations of numbers and characters. It also contains functions to extract these numbers and characters from the event data. Whereas these functions do provide a measure of type safety, the caller must read the real layout of the data. Usually, this work is done by Open Class Library's own handler and event classes. They provide a layer of abstraction for IEventData. Notice that the functions to retrieve the message parameters return IEventParameter1 and IEventParameter2 objects and the functions to query the message result return an IEventResult object. IEventParameter1, IEventParameter2, and IEventResult are synonyms (typedefs) for IEventData.

Event Results

Many events received from the presentation system do not require a return value. To provide a return value for those messages requiring a return value, a handler must call the function IEvent::setResult and pass it an IEventResult (IEventData) value. Throughout this book, we identify the events where setting the result is appropriate. When a handler dispatcher indicates it processed a message by returning true, the window dispatcher uses the IEvent::result function to retrieve the value and return it to the presentation system.

Rerouting Window Messages

In the discussion of window ownership, you saw how a presentation system window sends notification messages to its owner window for processing. Each presentation system window must determine what events need to be sent to its owner. Thus, the owner of a window can extend the behavior of the owned window by processing these messages.

To enable you to create windows that extend the functions of the presentation-system-provided windows, the window subclass procedure captures many owner notification messages and routes them to the window dispatcher of the window sending the notification. If the window's handlers do not process the message, the window subclass procedure sends the message on to the window dispatcher of the owner window.

Because of this rerouting of owner notification events, you and the classes in Open Class Library can create and add handlers directly to a control to extend the behavior of the control.

In the OS/2 operating system, the rerouted owner notification messages include all control notification messages (WM_CONTROL), messages to allow application drawing in a window (WM_DRAWITEM), messages to decide the size of an item in a window (WM_MEASUREITEM), and messages to dictate the type of pointer to be used over the window (WM_CONTROLPOINTER).

There are two additional owner notification messages, WM_COMMAND and WM_SYSCOMMAND, that the window subclass procedure does not route back to the push buttons or menus that send them. Whereas menus and push buttons do send these messages to their owners, they are not useful for extending the behavior of these controls. For this reason Open Class Library does not reroute these messages.

On the Windows platforms, most control notification messages are in the form of the WM_COMMAND message. To determine which of these messages require rerouting, the window subclass procedure inspects the second message parameter, or lParam, to see if it contains a control handle. The window subclass procedure reroutes only the subset of WM_COMMAND messages containing a control handle to the window dispatcher of the control that sent them. In addition, the 32-bit Windows common controls send WM_NOTIFY messages to each parent to notify it of events. The window subclass procedure also reroutes these messages to the window dispatcher of the common controls that sent them.

Finally, the 32-bit Windows platforms also send a number of messages that allow the parent of a control to change the text and background color of the control. The window subclass procedure also reroutes these messages to the window dispatcher of the controls that sent them. This includes WM_CTLCOLOREDIT, WM_CTLCOLORSTATIC, WM_CTLCOLORLISTBOX, WM_CTLCOLORSCROLLBAR, and WM_CTLCOLORBTN.

IWindow

The following topics describe the behavior that is common to all windows. This includes many public functions that you can use to change the characteristics of objects of classes derived from IWindow. For example, it includes functions to move and size a window, disable and enable user interaction with a window, and show or hide a window.

IWindow also has functions that affect the behavior of windows as they relate to other components and frameworks in Open Class Library. This behavior includes support for event dispatching, direct manipulation, the canvas classes, exception handling, and auto-deletion.

Finally, the IWindow interface includes protected functions, which derived classes use to implement their functions.

Window Constructors

You rarely need to create an IWindow object; usually, you create an object of a class that inherits from IWindow. However, you do have two constructors you can use to create a C++ "wrapper" object for an existing presentation system window. Use these constructors to attach the functions of Open Class Library to a window created outside Open Class Library. Use these constructors only when you do not know the type of the presentation system window. Most classes that inherit from IWindow have similar constructors that you need to use instead.

You might use these constructors if a portion of your application is a presentation system window procedure not written in C++. Or you might provide your development users a set of service routines in a dynamic link library (DLL). Then, you would associate Open Class windows to windows provided by the users of your service routines.

The IWindow constructors are:

```
IWindow     ( const IWindowHandle& handle);
IWindow     ( unsigned long        identifier,
              IWindow*             parent);
```

You can create one of these objects by providing the presentation system window handle or by providing the numeric identifier of the window and the IWindow pointer of its parent window. Use the first constructor when you know the window's handle. Use the second constructor when you do not know the window's handle but know its parent window (typically a dialog) and its window identifier.

You must follow one rule: never create more then one C++ object for any one presentation system window. If you do, IWindow rejects the second request by throwing an IInvalidRequest exception. You can easily determine if a C++ object exists for the window by calling IWindow::windowWithHandle if you know the handle of the window or IWindow::windowWithParent if you know the identifier and the parent IWindow. If these functions return a nonzero value for the IWindow pointer, the C++ object already exists for the window.

Window Styles

Almost all nonabstract classes that inherit from IWindow have a constructor that accepts a series of style values. The only way to set some window characteristics is to pass the style when you create the window. You can set other characteristics by using the style values or the specific functions provided in IWindow or its derived classes.

IWindow supports the following styles when you create a window of a derived class:

IWindow::noStyle

Use this style when you want to build a window without setting any style flags.

IWindow::visible

Use this style to create a visible window. By default, all window classes that inherit from IWindow, except frame and object windows, create their presentation system windows with this style. It allows you to create a frame with child windows and make them all visible by calling the function show on the frame window. Once you create a window, you can make the window visible using the function IWindow::show and invisible using the function IWindow::hide.

IWindow::disabled

Use this style to create a window that ignores keyboard and mouse input. Once you create a window, you can disable it using the function `IWindow::disable` and enable it using the function `IWindow::enable`. Disabling a window also disables the children of the window.

IWindow::clipChildren

Use this style to create a window that does not draw in the area occupied by its children. This is usually unnecessary. If you do use it, performance may decrease.

IWindow::clipSiblings

Use this style to create a window that does not draw over its sibling windows. This is only necessary for overlapping sibling windows when you cannot change their sibling order to have them draw correctly.

IWindow::clipToParent

Use this style to create a window that can paint outside its own boundary up to the boundary of its parent. Without this style, a window can only paint within its own boundary. This style is ignored on the Windows operating system.

IWindow::saveBits

Use this style to create a window that saves the screen area under the window as a bitmap. The window then uses the bitmap to restore the underlying screen area when it is closed. Do not use this style if the underlying screen area is likely to change. This style is ignored on the Windows operating system.

IWindow::synchPaint

Use this style to create a window that synchronously repaints itself instead of waiting for other events to be processed first. This style is ignored on the Windows operating system.

Whereas you cannot create an `IWindow` using one of these styles (because it has no constructor that accepts a style), you can use these styles to define the behavior of its derived classes. You can combine these style values using the C++ bitwise OR operator (`operator |`) with the styles defined for the particular class that inherits from `IWindow`. Except for `IWindow::visible`, you do not often need to use the `IWindow` styles.

Because all presentation system windows belong to a class and that class provides a set of predefined styles for the window, you cannot change these *class styles*. Some have corresponding window styles. Consequently, controls may exhibit behavior corresponding to these window styles although you never explicitly set the style for the control.

Window Positioning, Painting, and Visibility

IWindow provides functions that control the location, size, visibility, and usability of all Open Class Library windows. With these functions, you can move, size, hide, show, and disable windows. You can determine their position, size, visibility, and whether they respond to keyboard and mouse input. Besides determining a window's visibility, you can also determine if a visible window is the top window on the display. A visible window is not visible when another window covers it. You accomplish these tasks with these functions: moveTo, sizeTo, moveSizeTo, position, size, rect, show, hide, isVisible, isShowing, disable, enable, and isDisabled. The functions that set or return a window's position do so relative to the parent of the window.

You can also suspend the painting of a window, make changes to it, resume the painting, and refresh the window. Use this technique to make several changes without reflecting them in the window until they are all made. To do this, use the disableUpdate, enableUpdate, and refresh functions.

Window Identifier

The presentation system uses the window identifier and its parent window to uniquely identify one window from the other windows. IWindow provides functions to change the window identifier and to query the identifier of an existing window. You change the identifier of a window using setId, and you retrieve the window identifier for a window by calling id.

Window Recoordination

Because the Windows and OS/2 coordinate systems have a different origin, Open Class Library allows you to select one of these coordinate systems. It also provides a mapping layer to translate the coordinates you specify to those required by the native operating system. By default, functions in Open Class Library interpret the coordinates you specify in the coordinates of the native operating system. For the Windows operating system, these functions base the origin on the upper-left corner of the display. For the OS/2 operating system, they base the origin on the lower-left corner of the display.

If you want to use the OS/2 coordinate system, perhaps because you have already written code that uses Open Class Library on the OS/2 operating system, set the default coordinate system by calling ICoordinateSystem::setApplicationOrientation with a value of ICoordinateSystem::originLowerLeft.

To directly handle any messages from these operating systems that have point or rectangle information (it arrives in native coordinates), use functions in ICoordinateSytem to map these values so they can be ported. Use convertToApplication to convert points and rectangles from the operating system's coordinates system to the coordinate system you are currently using in your application. The reverse process works, too. Use convertToNative to convert points and rectangles from your application's coordinate system to the operating system's coordinate system. Also, use IRectangle::minX and IRectangle::minY to refer to the origin of a window regardless of the coordinate system.

Window Input Focus

The presentation system sends all keyboard input to the window with input focus. IWindow provides functions to change the window with input focus and to determine if a window currently has input focus. To change the input focus to another window, use setFocus; to determine if a window has input focus, call hasFocus.

C++ Object Lifetime Management

As you create and destroy your application's views, you must manage the lifetime of the C++ objects you use to compose those views. You must also ensure you do not write code that depends on the existence of either the C++ object or the presentation system window before they are created or after they cease to exist.

The task of managing the lifetime of a window object can be difficult because the C++ object and the presentation system window have independent lifetimes. You can create either of them first and destroy either of them last. This independence has ramifications you must consider as you write your code. For example, never write code in the destructor of a class derived from IWindow that depends on the existence of the presentation system window. Any function in Open Class Library that requires a presentation system window throws an IInvalidRequest exception if that window does not exist. Call IWindow::isValid to determine if the presentation system window still exists.

While you may want to take some action in a destructor while the presentation system window is still around, you must instead create a handler that captures the notification the presentation system sends before it destroys the window. The handler code to do this must process the presentation system message, WM_DESTROY, as in the following example:

```
//DestroyHandler interface
class DestroyHandler : public IHandler {
protected:
virtual Boolean
  dispatchHandlerEvent ( IEvent& event ),
  destroy              ( IEvent& event );
};

//DestroyHandler implementation
IBase::Boolean DestroyHandler::dispatchHandlerEvent ( IEvent& event )
{
  Boolean stopDispatching = false;
  switch (event.eventId())
  {
    case WM_DESTROY:
    {
      stopDispatching = this->destroy(event);
      break;
    }
  }
  return stopDispatching;
}

IBase::Boolean DestroyHandler::destroy ( IEvent& event )
{
  // Do your required processing here.

  // Return false so we don't stop WM_DESTROY processing.
  return false;
}
```

Even this code has restrictions. If the WM_DESTROY message is received because the application deleted the C++ object, all but the IWindow portion of the object (and its base classes) are destructed when the dispatcher calls the destroy handler.

To help you manage the C++ objects that accompany your windows, IWindow contains the following object and window management functions:

IWindow::setAutoDeleteObject

This function causes the window dispatcher to delete the C++ object for a presentation system window when the presentation system destroys the window. By default, the dispatcher does not delete the object because you might have created the object on the stack or as instance data of another object. Do not use this function unless you create the object using operator new and do not delete the object yourself.

If you use this function, the window dispatcher deletes the C++ object after ensuring there are no events still being dispatched to handlers attached to the window. The presentation system has already destroyed the window when the window dispatcher calls the C++ object destructor. Therefore, do not write code in the destructor that depends on a presentation system window being valid.

IWindow::setAutoDestroyWindow

The windows that inherit from IWindow use this function to cause the IWindow destructor to destroy the presentation system window. By default, the IWindow destructor destroys the presentation system window if the window constructor created it.

If the window constructor is a wrapper for an existing window, the IWindow destructor does not destroy the window unless you call this function. If you extend the windows in Open Class Library or create new ones of your own, you are responsible for correctly setting this up. The constructor of any class that inherits from IWindow and functions as a C++ wrapper for an existing presentation system window, must call this function with a value of false.

Sending and Posting Events

Earlier in this chapter, we described how a message leaves the presentation system and arrives in your handler. To simplify that description, we omitted a significant detail: the difference between sending and posting events.

The presentation system requires every program to provide a *message queue*. A message queue is a list the presentation system uses to store messages until the program is ready to process the message. To process messages in the message queue, a program contains a small piece of code called a *message loop*. The message loop takes the next message from the queue and routes it to the correct window procedure to process the message. Figure 4-6 shows the interaction between the presentation system, the message queue, and the message loop.

The Open Class Library's application framework shields you from the details of both the creation of the message queue and the routing of messages in the queue. When code in Open Class Library requires the existence of the presentation system and a message queue, the

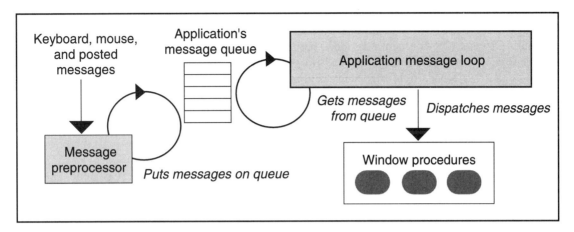

Figure 4-6. The Presentation System Message Queue.

framework initializes the presentation system and creates the message queue. You call typically `IApplication::current().run` to start processing messages in the queue. This function calls `IThread::current().processMsgs` which contains the actual message loop.

The presentation system only adds posted messages into the message queue. Therefore, posting a message is a way to add work to the end of the queue. The window procedure receives the message after it processes the messages ahead of it in the message queue.

When you post a message, control returns to you after the system places the message in the message queue. You do not know when the window procedure processes the message or if it processed the message without errors. The presentation system supplies a return value when you post a message. This return value only indicates whether the message made it to the queue; it does not tell you if the window procedure processed the message successfully.

Posting a message fails if the message cannot be placed in the message queue. Usually this occurs because a window procedure servicing the message queue is not processing messages in a timely manner, thus allowing the queue to become filled. On the OS/2 operating system, you may be able to remedy the problem by expanding the size of the message queue. You cannot change the size of the message queue on the Windows operating system. For details, see Chapter 20, "Applications and Threads."

If you send a message, the message is not put into the message queue. Instead, if the sender and receiver window are in the same thread, the presentation system calls the window procedure directly with the message. If the receiver is not in the same thread or the same process as the sender, the presentation system switches to the thread of the receiver and calls the appropriate window procedure directly. The sender is put on hold until the receiver processes the message.

When you send a message, the receiver processes the message completely before control returns to you. The return value, provided by the receiver of the message by calling `IEvent::setResult`, is usually an indication of its success or failure to process the message.

When you start building multi-threaded programs, the difference between sending and posting messages becomes very important. You do little to improve performance by placing code into a separate thread if it does nothing more then send messages to the primary thread. You only add the complexity of a multi-threaded program with none of its advantages. The program behaves as if it were a single-threaded program. The performance of the application may even suffer due to excessive thread switching.

`IWindow`, `IWindowHandle`, and `IMessageQueueHandle` all provide functions you can use to send and post messages to other windows and message queues. Each of these classes provides you with a different capability for sending and posting messages.

`IWindowHandle` provides the `sendEvent` and `postEvent` functions so you can send and post messages to windows that do not have a C++ object supporting them. For example, you might use these functions to send and post messages to windows created in another application. This class also provides the `sendEvents` and `postEvents` functions that allow you to broadcast messages to the children of a window. You can limit the broadcasting to frame windows or you can include all descendants of a window.

`IWindow` provides the `sendEvent` and `postEvent` functions so you can send and post specific types of events to windows with a C++ object. You can use the enumeration `IWindow::EventType` to send and post command, system command, help, and character events.

`IMessageQueueHandle` provides the `postEvent` and `postEvents` functions, so you can post (but not send) messages to one or more message queues. While you may find this capability useful for sending messages to the message queues of other applications, it has limited use in Open Class Library. This is because Open Class Library does not yet let you attach a handler to a message queue. If you posted a message to the message queue of Open Class Library, the message would never appear in a window's subclass procedure because the presentation system has no way to identify the correct window procedure. This means it also would not appear in one of your handlers.

A final warning before we leave the discussion of the message queue. The OS/2 operating system allows you to destroy the message queue. You should not use this brute force mechanism to terminate an Open Class Library application because once the message queue is destroyed, no further messages get distributed. This includes the `WM_DESTROY` messages that Open Class Library uses to auto-delete objects.

Sibling Order

The *sibling order* or *z-order* refers to the sequence that sibling windows should be visited when painting the windows on the display or moving the cursor between them with the `Tab` key. By default, Open Class Library creates all windows at the bottom of the sibling order. This causes windows to appear on top of siblings created before them and to receive the input focus resulting from the Tab key after them. You can change the sibling order after creation using the following functions:

positionBehindSibling

> Places the window behind the specified window in the sibling order.

positionBehindSiblings

Places the window behind all of its siblings in the sibling order.

positionOnSiblings

Places the window on top of all its siblings in the sibling order.

You can use the nested class `IWindow::ChildCursor` to iterate all of a window's children. This cursor class functions just like all the cursors in Open Class Library. It visits the child windows in the sibling order, from the top sibling to the bottom sibling. You can use `IWindow::childAt` to retrieve the window handle at any `ChildCursor` cursor location. This function returns a window handle instead of an `IWindow` pointer because not all child windows need to have a C++ object associated with them. For example, if you create a frame window from a dialog template, you would typically only create C++ objects for the controls on the dialog that require interaction.

The following code demonstrates how to hide all of a window's children:

```
// Find the parent window from its handle.
IWindow* parent = IWindow::windowWithHandle(handle);

// Build a child cursor.
IWindow::ChildCursor cursor(*parent);

// Visit all the child windows.
for (cursor.setToFirst(); cursor.isValid(); cursor.setToNext()){
  IWindowHandle childHandle = parent->childAt(cursor);
  IWindow* child = IWindow::windowWithHandle(childHandle);
  // The following code is only necessary if using some
  // non-C++ windows.
  // If the window has a C++ object, hide it.
  if (child)
     child->hide();
  // Else create a temporary C++ window object and hide it.
  else {
     IWindow(childHandle).hide();
  }
}
```

Exception Support

Chapter 27, "Error Handling and Reporting," describes the strategy and implementation of exceptions in Open Class Library. The basic strategy in Open Class Library is that *exception handling is error handling*. You should not see exceptions thrown by Open Class Library once you have removed your program errors and completed your application. If you wish to ignore things Open Class Library considers an error, you can add a `catch` block to your code to do so.

The interface between Open Class Library and the presentation system adds a unique problem to the C++ exception model. The presentation system sends messages to Open Class Library's subclass procedure. The subclass procedure routes these events to the window dispatcher and then on to a list of handlers.

If a library handler or one of your callbacks throws an exception, the C++ run time's exception handler unwinds the call stack until it finds a `catch` block for the exception. Figure 4-7 displays most of the call stack for an application that has implemented the `command` function in a class derived from `ICommandHandler`. In the call stack, you see that the `main` function is the

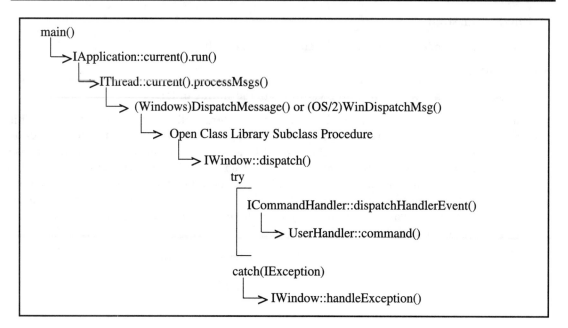

Figure 4-7. Call Stack from main() to Your Handler.

only application function above the command callback function in the handler. If your application throws an exception in the command callback function, it would not normally catch the exception until the exception reaches the main routine.

To catch exceptions that occur during the processing of events, IWindow::dispatch calls all handlers from within a try block. If a function below the dispatcher throws an exception of a class inherited from IException, the dispatcher catches the exception and calls the IWindow virtual function handleException. IWindow::handleException passes the exception on to an object of the class IWindow::ExceptionFn if your application registered an exception function. To register an exception function object, do the following:

1. Define a class derived from IWindow::ExceptionFn that implements the function handleException. If this function can correct the problem, it returns true. This causes the dispatcher to ignore the error and continue.

2. Create an object of your exception class.

3. Register this object with IWindow by calling the setExceptionFunction static function. If you previously called setExceptionFunction, subsequent calls return a pointer to the previous exception function object. Use this technique to chain exception functions.

If you do not register an exception function, or the one you did register returns false to indicate it could not correct the error, the IWindow function handleException rethrows the exception. Unless you execute the code in main within a try block, this rethrown exception causes the application to end.

Chapter 5

Frame Window Basics

- Discusses primary and secondary windows and the composition of applications using Open Class Library
- Describes the IFrameWindow, IFrameHandler, IFrameExtension, ITitle, and IInfoArea classes
- Introduces the IMenuBar, ISystemMenu, IAccelerator, and IAcceleratorTable classes
- Read Chapter 4 before reading this chapter.
- Chapters 6, 19, 20, and 24 cover related material.

This chapter describes the classes you use to manage the primary and secondary windows of your applications. Open Class Library provides the frame window class, IFrameWindow, and related classes for this purpose. Chapter 19, "Advanced Frame Window Topics," contains additional information on these classes.

Overview

The discussion of graphical user interfaces in Chapter 2, "Object-Oriented User Interface Fundamentals," introduces the basic definition of a *window* as a view of an object or a dialog with the user. In more concrete terms, a *frame window* is a presentation system window that manages the collection of controls that comprise such views.

In certain respects, a frame window is no different from any other control window in the following ways:

- All windows have a size and position.

- All have a parent window and can have an owner window.

- All support a basic set of functions, which is evident in the class hierarchy of Open Class Library; IFrameWindow derives from IWindow, as do all control window classes.

Various smaller-scale components—the title bar, menu bar, system menu, scroll bars, and client window—help comprise frame windows. Some controls are also composites such as a combination box control, which is comprised of an entry field and list box component.

What distinguishes frame windows from other kinds of windows is what distinguishes almost any class of object from another: behavior.

The frame window and the standard set of components that comprise it provide the following application-level function:

- The frame window manages these component windows to help ensure a common look and feel for all object views and action windows.

- The title bar manages the application's entry in the task bar on the Windows desktop and the window list on the OS/2 desktop, and allows you to move the frame window using direct manipulation.

- The system menu provides functions common to most applications: minimizing, maximizing, and restoring the view, closing the view and the application, accessing the window list, and moving and sizing the view on the desktop.

- The frame window allows you to size it through direct manipulation of the sizing border.

- The frame window processes certain events and routes others to the client window, allowing either the frame or client window to be the centralized location for application-specific processing.

- The frame window manages the relationships among related (owned) frame windows by enabling, disabling, moving, and closing these related frames in concert.

Thus, the frame window is the anchor for the visual representation of your application. IFrameWindow and its related classes provide a full set of functions for creating, tailoring, and managing frame windows and dialogs.

One important distinction between Open Class Library and regular Windows or OS/2 programming is that Open Class Library unifies frame windows and dialogs. To the IFrameWindow class, a dialog is just another attribute of a frame window.

Constructing Frame Windows

This topic explains how to construct your application's frame windows. You learn the three most common uses of frame windows and how to easily construct an IFrameWindow object for each. You also learn how to use dialog template resources to construct IFrameWindow objects.

In this section, you learn the IFrameWindow constructors that you use most often. Chapter 19, "Advanced Frame Window Topics," describes the full set of construction attributes and IFrameWindow constructors. Read that chapter if you need to do something more advanced than what we present here. You can accomplish most tasks, however, by using a small subset of the IFrameWindow constructor options.

Constructing Primary Windows

In most cases, the primary window of your application shows a view of the main object in your application. For example, the primary window of the shopping-list application presented in Chapter 3, "Tour of Open Class Library," is a view of the two lists that the application manages.

You create a primary window by constructing an `IFrameWindow` object that has the desktop window as its parent and no owner. Its lack of an owner is what distinguishes a primary window from a secondary window. We discuss secondary windows in more detail in the next topic.

Primary windows are independent views that do not close until the user explicitly closes them. The lifetime of primary windows is usually the same as the lifetime of your program. The code that reflects this use is almost always of the same form you saw in the example program presented in Chapter 3:

```
void main ( )
{
  IFrameWindow
    primary( ... );
  //...
}
```

You see this same basic application structure in most of the examples in this book. The primary frame window object is constructed when the program starts. The program processes user-initiated window events until the primary window closes and the frame window object is deleted. Then the program ends.

You read about the event-processing aspects of your application a little later. For now, we concentrate on techniques to construct the primary frame window itself.

Primary windows showing views of objects usually are not constructed from dialog template resources (see "Using Dialog Template Resources" in this chapter following the section on secondary windows). Because a primary window has the desktop window as its parent and has no owner, constructing this kind of frame window object is relatively straightforward.

The simplest constructor requires no arguments. The resulting frame window has the following characteristics:

- The default window identifier: `IC_DEFAULT_FRAME_ID`, defined in the file, `ICCONST.H`.

- The default parent window: the desktop window.

- The default owner window: none.

- The default initial size and position, as returned by the function `IFrameWindow::nextShellRect`.

- The default frame window style, as returned by the function `IFrameWindow::defaultStyle`.

- The default frame window title defined by a string table entry. This is obtained from the default application resource library using the frame window identifier, or, if no string resource is found, the name of the application's `.EXE` file.

These defaults are acceptable in many cases. The two attributes whose values you most likely need to supply in place of the defaults are the frame window identifier and the style. The window identifier for a frame also identifies its associated resources as specified by styles (such as a string for the title bar text, a menu bar, an accelerator table, and a minimized icon), and identifies its help subtable (see Chapter 23, "Using Help," for more information). Other constructors allow you to specify either or both a window identifier and style. If you need both, you can specify them in either order.

Constructing Secondary Windows

A secondary window is an `IFrameWindow` whose parent is the desktop window, but which is owned by another window—typically a primary window.

Ownership establishes the following behavior between frame windows:

- A frame window always stays on top of its owner window.

- A frame window minimizes and closes when the user minimizes or closes its owner window.

- When a frame window is closed, its owner window becomes the active window.

Use secondary windows in the following situations:

- To display views of subcomponents of the objects displayed in your primary view. For example, the properties (or settings) views of the shopping list entries shown in Chapter 3 are secondary windows.

- To display action windows to prompt the user for input to carry out an action selected by a menu choice. For example, the file dialog typically shown as a result of selecting the **Save as...** menu choice is a secondary window.

The lifetime of secondary windows is different from the lifetime of primary windows. Secondary windows are created whenever the user requests them, for example, when the user selects a menu item or double-clicks on a container object. Secondary windows can also be closed whenever the user chooses. As a result, most secondary windows are created using `operator new`. You may want to call `IWindow::setAutoDeleteObject` so that Open Class Library calls `operator delete` when the window closes.

Using Dialog Template Resources

You can create `IFrameWindow` objects from dialog template resources. You are most likely to use these kinds of frame windows as secondary action windows. Whereas the `IMultiCellCanvas` class provides another way to put a set of controls on a frame window and is superior to dialogs in many respects (see Chapter 15, "Canvases," for more details), you may have existing dialog templates you still want to use. In this topic you learn how to construct `IFrameWindow` objects from dialog template resources.

The following `IFrameWindow` constructors allow you to construct a frame window from a dialog template:

```
IFrameWindow ( unsigned long id = IC_DEFAULT_FRAME_ID,
               FrameSource source = tryDialogResource );
IFrameWindow ( const IResourceId &resId,
               IWindow* owner = 0,
               FrameSource source = tryDialogResource );
IFrameWindow ( const IResourceId &resId,
               IWindow* parent,
               IWindow* owner,
               FrameSource source= tryDialogResource );
```

The first constructor creates primary windows and the third creates child frame windows. So the second constructor is the one you use most often to construct frame windows from dialog templates. This is the same constructor you use to construct most standard secondary windows. The first parameter of each constructor identifies the dialog template to load, and it also provides the window identifier for the resulting frame window. See Chapter 24, "Using Resources," for more information on resource libraries and the `IResourceId` class.

The last parameter of each of these constructors is the enumerated type, `FrameSource`. This parameter allows you to control whether the constructor creates a frame window using a dialog template and to control the behavior of the constructor if a dialog template cannot be loaded. The following describes the behavior controlled by the `IFrameWindow::FrameSource` values:

IFrameWindow::dialogResource

> The constructor attempts to create a frame window from a dialog template in your resource library. If it cannot load the dialog template, it throws an exception. This is generally the desired behavior if you want to display a dialog.

IFrameWindow::noDialogResource

> The constructor creates a standard frame window. It does not attempt to load a dialog template. If you are not trying to display a dialog, this behavior is more efficient than the default.

IFrameWindow::tryDialogResource

> The constructor first attempts to create a frame window from a dialog template in your resource library. If it cannot load the dialog template, the constructor creates a standard frame window instead of throwing an exception. This is the default behavior.

The following example loads a secondary window from a dialog template:

Resource Definitions - frame1\dialog\dialog.rc

```
#include "dialog.h"

#ifdef IC_PM /* Define OS/2 resources. */
#include <os2.h>
```

```
DLGTEMPLATE ID_DIALOG
  BEGIN
    DIALOG "Dialog Title", ID_DIALOG, 10, 10, 100, 100, ,
            FCF_SYSMENU | FCF_TITLEBAR
      BEGIN
        CTEXT "Hello, World!", 0, 5, 30, 90, 48
        DEFPUSHBUTTON "OK", ID_OK, 5, 5, 40, 20
        PUSHBUTTON "Cancel", ID_CLOSE, 55, 5, 40, 20,
                    BS_SYSCOMMAND | NOT WS_TABSTOP
      END
  END
#else /* Define Windows resources. */
ID_DIALOG DIALOG LOADONCALL MOVEABLE DISCARDABLE
                         10, 10, 100, 100
CAPTION "Dialog Title" STYLE WS_BORDER | WS_CAPTION |
                        WS_DLGFRAME | WS_POPUP | WS_SYSMENU
  BEGIN
    CONTROL "Hello, World!", 0, "static", SS_CENTER | WS_CHILD,
                        5, 22, 90, 48
    CONTROL "OK", ID_OK, "button", BS_DEFPUSHBUTTON |
                        WS_TABSTOP | WS_CHILD,
                        5, 75, 40, 20
    CONTROL "Cancel", ID_CLOSE, "button", WS_CHILD,
                        55, 75, 40, 20
  END
#endif
```

Loading a Dialog Template - frame1\dialog\dialog.cpp

```cpp
#include <iapp.hpp>
#include <icmdhdr.hpp>
#include <iframe.hpp>
#include <imenubar.hpp>
#include "dialog.h"

class PrimaryCmdHandler : public ICommandHandler {
protected:
virtual Boolean
  command ( ICommandEvent& event );
}; // PrimaryCmdHandler

class DialogCmdHandler : public ICommandHandler {
protected:
virtual Boolean
  command ( ICommandEvent& event );
}; // DialogCmdHandler

class DialogFrameWindow : public IFrameWindow {
public:
  DialogFrameWindow ( unsigned long identifier,
                      IWindow*       owner );
 ~DialogFrameWindow ( );

private:
  DialogFrameWindow ( const DialogFrameWindow& );
DialogFrameWindow
 &operator=        ( const DialogFrameWindow& );
DialogCmdHandler
  cmdHandler;
}; // DialogFrameWindow

void main ( )
{
  // Create a primary frame window.
  IFrameWindow
    primary( "Primary Frame That Loads a Dialog Template" );
```

```
   // Create a menu bar and add a choice to open a dialog.
   IMenuBar
     menuBar( &primary );
   menuBar
#ifdef IC_PM
     .addText( ID_FILE, "~File" )
#else
     .addText( ID_FILE, "&File" )
#endif
     .addSubmenu( ID_FILE )
     .addText( ID_DIALOG_CMD, "Hello...", ID_FILE );

   // Create the command handler for the primary window.
   PrimaryCmdHandler
     cmdHandler;
   cmdHandler
    .handleEventsFor( &primary );

   // Set the focus and show the frame window.
   primary
    .setFocus()
    .show();

   IApplication::current().run();
}

IBase::Boolean
  PrimaryCmdHandler::command ( ICommandEvent& event )
{
   Boolean
     stopProcessingEvent = false;
   // Check for the "Hello..." menu choice.
   if ( event.commandId() == ID_DIALOG_CMD )
   {
     DialogFrameWindow *dialog =
       new DialogFrameWindow( ID_DIALOG,
                              event.dispatchingWindow() );
     (*dialog)
      .setAutoDeleteObject()
      .setFocus()
      .show();
     stopProcessingEvent = true;
   }
   return stopProcessingEvent;
}

IBase::Boolean
  DialogCmdHandler::command ( ICommandEvent& event )
{
   Boolean
     stopProcessingEvent = false;
   if ( event.commandId() == ID_OK )
   {
     DialogFrameWindow *dialog =
       (DialogFrameWindow*)( event.dispatchingWindow() );
     (*dialog)
      .setResult( event.commandId() )
      .close();
     stopProcessingEvent = true;
   }
   return stopProcessingEvent;
}
```

In this example, we use the command handler, `DialogCmdHandler`, to close the secondary window when the user selects the **OK** push button. Without this code, selecting the push button would do nothing. This behavior differs from that of a dialog displayed using Windows or OS/2 APIs, such as `DialogBox` and `WinDlgBox`. With these APIs, the dialog is dismissed when the user selects any push button not explicitly handled by the dialog procedure. Open Class Library suppresses this behavior, so that "undefined" push buttons are instead ignored.

Showing Frame Windows and Dialogs

In the preceding sections you learned what frame windows are and how to construct IFrameWindow objects. The next step is to show a frame window on the screen and initiate user interaction with your application.

Giving Your Frame the Input Focus

You frequently create frame windows upon initiation of your application. These are probably primary windows. If you create them in response to some action by the user during execution of your application, they are probably secondary windows. In both cases, the user expects the input focus to be transferred to the newly opened window.

An IFrameWindow object does not automatically set the focus to itself. You are responsible for explicitly calling the IWindow::setFocus member function. You can either set the input focus to the frame window itself or to a specific child control. If you set the focus to a frame window that has a client window, the frame gives the input focus to its client window.

Displaying Frame Windows

Frame windows, unlike controls, are not visible by default because frames typically require configuration after construction. If this were to happen while the frame is visible on the screen, the user would see the frame window flash when you add the menu bar, attach an information area, add a client window, and so on. So, by default, Open Class Library creates frame windows in the hidden state. You construct the frame, configure it—including giving it the focus as discussed above—and finally show it.

The conventional means of showing the frame is simply to call IFrameWindow::show. In the following typical application, you see the main function's implementation:

```
#include <iframe.hpp>

// Include other header files here.

void main ( )
{
  IFrameWindow
    mainWindow( MY_FRAME_ID );

  // Configure the frame here.

  // Give the frame the input focus and show it.
  mainWindow.setFocus();
  mainWindow.show();

  // Start event processing here (to be discussed).
}
```

Event Processing

Making your frame window visible on the screen does not enable the user to interact with it. Up to this point all communication with your window has been via calls to your frame window object. User input, entered using the keyboard or mouse, causes events to be posted to your application. You must set up your application to process these posted events before the user can interact with your window.

To help you understand what processing these events entails, consider the previous code example. The last line of the code presented above is a comment:

```
// Start event processing here (to be discussed).
```

What would this program do if we just left this line as a comment? Obviously, execution would simply flow off the end of `main` and the program would end. The user would see your frame window flash for just an instant before it disappears.

This reveals a bit about the code that must replace this comment. The code executed there must continue to execute while the frame window appears on the screen. The code required at that point in the program is a loop that obtains and processes window events. This loop is called a *message-processing loop* in presentation system terminology. In the terminology of Open Class Library, you would more accurately describe it as an *event-processing loop*.

Open Class Library encapsulates this event-processing loop within the function `ICurrentThread::processMsgs`. Invoke this function using the following expression:

```
IThread::current().processMsgs();
```

This expression needs to be added to the above example program where the comment indicates that event processing must occur.

We have not yet discussed in any detail the subject of threads of execution. Event processing occurs on a per-thread basis. Thus, the function that does this processing is a member function of a thread object. You can find details on threads and the relationship between threads and event processing in Chapter 20, "Applications and Threads."

In a single-threaded application these details are superfluous. Consequently, Open Class Library provides a simpler means of initiating the event-processing loop. You can use the following function instead:

```
IApplication::current().run();
```

This function's implementation consists solely of a call to the underlying `ICurrentThread` function described previously. The only difference is that you can access this function by including `IAPP.HPP` instead of `ITHREAD.HPP`. In a single-threaded application where the idea of threads is not applicable anyway, this approach might be preferred. The VisualAge for C++ sample programs use the `IApplication` version.

Once you have called `ICurrentThread::processMsgs` through either means, control does not return to the point of the call until all event processing on the thread stops. Chapter 20 discusses how you can force the processing of events to stop. However, generally you let Open Class Library manage ending the event-processing loop based on whether a primary or object window still exists. When a user or the application closes a primary or object window and no other primary or object windows are left on that thread, Open Class Library causes the call to `ICurrentThread::processMsgs` to end.

Displaying Application-Modal Frame Windows

`IFrameWindow` provides another way to display a frame window and process its events. This way is to display an application-modal frame window. When you display an application-modal frame window, its owner window becomes disabled. Any frame windows that are not in the owner chain of the application-modal frame window remain enabled.

The term *application-modal* derives from the more general term, *modal*. In the context of user interfaces, modal describes a window where the application limits the user's actions to a set of choices, or even a single choice. Application-modal means that the limitation extends only to the application's boundaries. Users can switch to another application; they just cannot use part or all of the rest of the application that displays the application-modal dialog. Hereafter, the term "modal" means "application-modal."

Use the member function `showModally` to show an `IFrameWindow` as a modal window. This function in effect contains an embedded event-processing loop. This is less surprising when you consider how you might use this function. Typically, you are processing an event at your primary window that signals your application to display a modal frame window. You could construct an `IFrameWindow` object from a dialog template and show it modally as follows:

```
{
  IFrameWindow
    dialog( DIALOG_ID, &mainWindow );

  dialog.setFocus();
  dialog.showModally();
}
```

The `showModally` call must not return until the user dismisses the dialog because, upon return, the `IFrameWindow` object goes out of scope and thus gets deleted. Your code eventually returns to process the next window event. Obviously, you do not want the `IFrameWindow` object deleted or the dialog destroyed until the user has dismissed it. You do not need to process events for your primary window until the user's dismissal of the dialog reenables it.

In effect, calling `showModally` is equivalent to calling `ICurrentThread::processMsgs` except that `showModally` has the following additional behavior:

- It disables the owner of the modal frame window.

- It makes the modal frame window visible.

- It returns when the user dismisses the modal window, which may be sooner than `ICurrentThread::processMsgs` would return (such as when a primary window still exists).

If the frame window you are showing does not have an owner window, you can use `showModally` instead of the `show` and `processMsgs` combination you saw previously. You can rewrite the previous simple code example as follows:

OS/2 Considerations for Modal Frame Windows and Dialogs

In the OS/2 operating system, the parent and owner windows of an application-modal frame window must not be the same. The reason becomes clear when you look again at what happens during the modal display of a frame window. To be modal means that the frame's owner window becomes disabled. When the OS/2 operating system disables a window, it disables all of its child windows as well. So, what happens if one of the owner's children is the modal frame window? You guessed it; the modal frame window also becomes disabled. A classic deadlock occurs because the user cannot dismiss the disabled modal window (being disabled, it accepts no user input) and the owner window remains disabled until the user dismisses the modal frame window.

Fortunately, in the OS/2 operating system, showModally detects when the frame's owner and parent are the same window. It throws an IInvalidParameter exception in such cases. You still must be careful, however, because this function does not detect the equally problematic situation where the parent of your modal frame is a child window of its owner. The safest course is to ensure that all your modal frame windows have the desktop window as their parent.

Another aspect is that the OS/2 operating system also attempts to circumvent this problem. When you load a dialog template resource, it checks to see that the dialog's parent and owner do not form an invalid combination. If they do, then it removes the owner window so that the dialog becomes a primary window. As a result, a program such as the following one does not initially disable the owner window, primary, as it does on the Windows operating system. You are left wondering why showModally is not working.

```
void main ( )
{
  IFrameWindow
    primary( "Main Window" ),
    // Next create a child frame from a dialog template.
    child( IResourceId( DIALOG_ID ), &primary, &primary );

  primary.show();
  child.setFocus();
  child.showModally();
  IThread::current().processMsgs();
}
```

Even if you do not use showModally and instead enter a conventional event-processing loop, you still lose the fact that the child frame is owned by the primary one. The OS/2 operating system discards this fact when it loads the child frame from the dialog template.

Modal Frame Window - frame1\modal\modal.cpp

```
#include <iframe.hpp>

void main ( )
{
  IFrameWindow
    mainWindow( "Modal Frame Window" );
```

```
    // Give the frame window the input focus.
    mainWindow.setFocus();

    // Process events.
    mainWindow.showModally();
}
```

Using this technique, you do not need to include the IAPP.HPP or ITHREAD.HPP header files.

You can test an IFrameWindow to see if showModally is displaying it in application-modal fashion by using the isModal function.

When you call showModally, control does not return to your code until the user closes the modal dialog. You can subsequently call IFrameWindow::result to query the "result" of the dialog, which can indicate the push button the user selected to dismiss the dialog. You set this result by calling IFrameWindow::dismiss. See "Closing Frame Windows" for details. True modal dialogs—that is, secondary frame windows displayed in application-modal fashion —have their disadvantages. The greatest disadvantage is that you prevent your users from interacting with your application views in the order that they prefer. They are instead limited to the order that your interface dictates.

Minimizing, Maximizing, and Restoring

Besides making your frame window appear on the screen, you can use various functions to modify its appearance. A frame window normally supports three different states: minimized, maximized, and normal. You can modify a frame's style so that it cannot be minimized or maximized by turning off the IFrameWindow styles minimizeButton and maximizeButton, respectively. The operating system disables these two choices on the system menu when you turn off (remove) these styles. It enables the **Restore** system menu choice only when the user has minimized or maximized the window. The Restore system menu choice returns a maximized window to its normal state.

The user can minimize, maximize, or restore a frame window using a variety of means, depending on how you configure the frame window. You can perform these actions from within your application code by calling the IFrameWindow member functions, minimize, maximize, and restore. However, use of these functions is rare. Normally, you let the user request these actions and let the system carry out the requests. Notice that minimize and maximize only work if you set the appropriate style; otherwise, these functions have no effect. Open Class Library does not call these functions when the user requests these actions using the minimize or maximize buttons or system menu choices. To detect when the user minimizes, maximizes, or restores your frame window, you must add an event handler that looks for the appropriate events that signal when the frame's state has changed. To process these events, you can derive from the MinMaxHandler class in the **frame1\minmax** example program included with this book.

You can query the size and position that your frame window has in each of these states. The frame window returns the corresponding IRectangle if you call the minimizeRect, maximizeRect, and restoreRect member functions of IFrameWindow.

OS/2 Considerations for Minimizing Dialogs

When you minimize a frame window with a minimized icon, the frame hides its client window, frame extensions, and other standard components (such as the title bar and system menu). This prevents these windows and their child windows from drawing on top of the minimized icon. Unfortunately, a frame window hides only those windows whose size and position it manages. If your frame window has other child windows that occupy the lower-left corner of the frame window, then those child windows draw on top of the minimized icon. This often happens when you load your frame from a dialog template because those frames do not have a client window. The only way to overcome this problem is to hide all of the frame's children when the user minimizes it. Of course, you would have to show these child windows again when the user later maximizes or restores the frame. See the **frame1\minmax** program included with this book for an example of how to do this.

Another issue related to minimized frames is how a frame window draws itself when it is minimized. When the user minimizes your frame, it draws its minimized icon. You can set that icon in one of two ways:

1. By using the `IFrameWindow::minimizedIcon` style when you construct the frame. The icon resource with the resource identifier you pass to the constructor is loaded automatically. This is the simplest and most common technique for setting your frame's minimized icon.

2. By calling `IFrameWindow::setIcon`. You can specify the icon as either a pointer handle or resource identifier.

In the Windows operating system, if your frame window does not have a minimized icon, then it draws a default icon when it is minimized. In the OS/2 operating system, however, the frame window paints itself normally after reducing its size to the size of a minimized icon. If the frame has a client window, the frame sizes the client window to fill the frame. The client window is not hidden in this case. If there is no client window, then only the lower-left corner of the frame window is visible in the minimized icon area. Because you probably did not design your frame to look right when drawn either way—with or without a resized client window—you should always provide a minimized icon if your frame can be minimized. The icon also looks nicer on the frame's system menu.

Closing Frame Windows

You have now learned about creating frame windows, making them visible on the screen, enabling the processing of user interaction, and working with the various states in which you can display the frame window. You will now learn what happens when the user closes a frame window.

Close Events

The following are ways for a user to close, or dismiss, a frame window:

- Double-click on the system menu
- Select **Close** from the system menu
- Press Alt+F4

Each of these methods is equivalent in terms of the event they generate: a system command event for the frame window.

The default frame window handler, which IFrameWindow attaches to all frame window objects, intercepts the system command event that signals that the frame is closing. This handler notifies the client window that the frame window is closing by sending it a modified close event. This pseudo-close event is an ICommandEvent with a command identifier of IC_ID_CLOSE (ISystemMenu::idClose), which triggers a call to the systemCommand virtual function of any command handlers attached to your client window. To perform some processing when your frame window closes, you can derive a specialized ICommandHandler that overrides the systemCommand function. Attach one of these handlers to your client window.

Open Class Library provides this processing on the OS/2 platform to avoid having a frame window send a WM_CLOSE message to its client window. A client window would, by default, process this message by posting a WM_QUIT message to the message queue of its thread. This message ends the event-processing loop described in the "Event Processing" topic. Because most threads end after their event-processing loops end, this can cause the application to end if it occurs on the main or only thread of the application.

The notification that the frame window handler sends to the client window is just that, a notification. You cannot prevent the frame window from closing by attaching a command handler to the client window that intercepts the close notification. To interrupt the frame closing—for example, to display a message box and prompt the user for confirmation—attach a command handler to your frame window instead. The following example program shows how you might implement such a handler:

Confirm Frame Closing - frame1\ok2close\ok2close.cpp

```
#include <icmdhdr.hpp>
#include <iframe.hpp>
#include <imsgbox.hpp>
#include <istattxt.hpp>
#include <isysmenu.hpp>
#include <ithread.hpp>

class CloseHandler : public ICommandHandler {
public:
// Use this function to attach this handler to your frame.
virtual CloseHandler
 &handleClosingOf( IFrameWindow& frame )
  {
    this->ICommandHandler::handleEventsFor( &frame );
    return *this;
  }
```

```
    // Override this function to insert your own "close" logic.
    virtual IBase::Boolean
      systemCommand ( ICommandEvent& event )
      {
        Boolean
          stopProcessingEvent = false;
        if ( event.commandId() == ISystemMenu::idClose )
        {
          IFrameWindow
            *frame = (IFrameWindow*)( event.dispatchingWindow() );
          IMessageBox
            prompt( frame );
          const char
            *text = "Press Cancel to keep the window open."
                    "  Press OK to let it close.";
          IMessageBox::Response
            rc = prompt.show( text,
                              IMessageBox::okCancelButton
                            | IMessageBox::informationIcon
                            | IMessageBox::moveable );
          if ( rc == IMessageBox::cancel )
          {
            stopProcessingEvent = true;
          }
        }
        return stopProcessingEvent;
      }
    private:
    virtual IHandler
     &handleEventsFor( IWindow* window )
      {
        return this->ICommandHandler::handleEventsFor( window );
      }
    }; // CloseHandler

    void main ( )
    {
      IFrameWindow
        frame( "Confirm on Close" );
      IStaticText
        client( IC_FRAME_CLIENT_ID, &frame, &frame );
      client
        .setAlignment( IStaticText::centerCenter )
        .setText( "Press Alt+F4 to close this window." );
      frame
        .setClient( &client );

      CloseHandler
        closeHandler;
      closeHandler
        .handleClosingOf( frame );
      frame
        .setFocus()
        .show();

      IThread::current().processMsgs();
    }
```

In the OS/2 operating system, the user has another way to close the frame window: selecting the **Close** choice on the frame window's pop-up menu in the window list. That presents even more complications. Selecting **Close** on the window list causes a WM_QUIT message to be posted directly to the frame window's message queue. Fortunately, this quit event can be detected. ICurrentThread::processMsgs, the Open Class Library function that processes these quit events, translates them to equivalent system command events. These events are just like those that are generated when the user double-clicks on the system menu. Therefore, you can process these events with a command handler, as described above, just as you would any other close event.

You can close an `IFrameWindow` under program control by calling its `close` member function. Call this function from a command handler, for example, to close a window when the user selects an application-specific push button. A conventional `WM_CLOSE` message is posted to the frame window, which `IFrameWindow` treats in the same manner as the system-close event generated when the user closes the window.

Throughout this book, we use the terms "close" and "dismiss" synonymously, usually to denote the user ending the display of a window. However, the functions `IFrameWindow::close` and `IFrameWindow::dismiss` are not equivalent, just similar. Calling `dismiss` hides a frame window whether you display it modally or modelessly. In this case, a close event is not generated so command handlers are not called. Because this function never causes the frame window to be destroyed, you can later show the window again without first having to create it. Calling `close` generates a close event and generally destroys the frame window (see the next topic for details).

Calling either `close` or `dismiss` on a modal frame window ends the `showModally` call that is displaying it. The same is true when the user closes a modal frame window. The value returned by `showModally` is the value you pass to `IFrameWindow::setValue` prior to calling `close` or the user closing the window (the value defaults to `IC_ID_CANCEL`, or 2, if you do not call `setValue`), or the `unsigned long` value you pass to `dismiss`. You can use this value, which can indicate the push button or command used to end the modal window, to determine the course of action for your application to take after returning from `showModally`. Note that by default, Open Class Library maps the user's closing of a modal frame window to the selection of a **Cancel** push button.

The following example uses `dismiss` and `showModally` to redisplay the same frame window each time the user selects the **Show the window again** push button. The underlying operating system window is not destroyed until the user selects the **Close** system menu choice. You can use this technique to show modal frame window dialogs over and over in your application (a confirmation dialog, for example). The following example examines the value returned by `IFrameWindow::result` to determine if the user closed the frame window by selecting the **Show the window again** push button, which causes the command handler to pass `AGAIN_CMD` to `IFrameWindow::dismiss`.

Dismissing a Window - frame1\dismiss\dismiss.cpp

```
#include <icmdhdr.hpp>
#include <iframe.hpp>
#include <ipushbut.hpp>
#include <istattxt.hpp>
#include <istring.hpp>
#include <icconst.h>

#if (IC_MAJOR_VERSION < 320)
   #define IC_ID_CLOSE  0x8004
#endif

#define AGAIN_CMD  100
```

```
class CmdHandler : public ICommandHandler {
public:
  CmdHandler ( IFrameWindow& frame )
    : frame( frame )
  {
    this->handleEventsFor( &frame );
  }
protected:
virtual Boolean
  command ( ICommandEvent& event )
  {
    Boolean
      stopProcessingEvent = false;
    if ( event.commandId() == AGAIN_CMD )
    {
       frame.dismiss( event.commandId() );
       stopProcessingEvent = true;
    }
    return stopProcessingEvent;
  }
private:
CmdHandler
 &operator= ( CmdHandler& );
IFrameWindow
 &frame;
}; // CmdHandler

void main ( )
{
  IFrameWindow
    frameWindow( "Using IFrameWindow::dismiss" );
  IStaticText
    text( IC_FRAME_CLIENT_ID, &frameWindow, &frameWindow );
  frameWindow
   .setClient( &text );

  IPushButton
    againButton( AGAIN_CMD, &frameWindow, &frameWindow );
  againButton
   .setText( "Show the window again" );
  frameWindow
   .addExtension( &againButton,
                  IFrameWindow::belowClient );

  CmdHandler
    handler( frameWindow );

  // Keep displaying the frame window until the user has
  // closed it via some means other than the "Again"
  // push button (for example, pressing Alt+F4).
  frameWindow
   .setResult( AGAIN_CMD);
  for ( int i = 1; frameWindow.result() == AGAIN_CMD; i++ )
  {
     text.setText( "Display Number " + IString( i ) );
     frameWindow.setResult( IC_ID_CLOSE );
     frameWindow.setFocus();

     frameWindow.showModally();
  }
}
```

Destroying the Window

The previous chapter discusses the relationship between the lifetime of operating system windows and the lifetime of IWindow objects. With frame windows, there is another twist to the window story. The closing of a frame window is distinct from the destruction of the underlying operating system window. The IFrameWindow class provides facilities you can use to connect these two events, thereby forcing the frame window to be destroyed when the user closes it. Given the facilities to connect the lifetimes of a window and its C++ object, this capability lets you force the IFrameWindow object to be deleted when the user closes the frame window.

Open Class Library calls this attribute of frame windows *destroy-on-close*. You can call IFrameWindow:setDestroyOnClose to enable or disable this attribute, and you can call IFrameWindow::willDestroyOnClose to query this attribute. By default, IFrameWindow enables this attribute by setting it to true.

If you disable the destroy-on-close attribute for a frame window, it still generates a close event that handlers can process when the user closes the window. However, Open Class Library neither hides nor destroys the window, so it remains on the screen.

Filling Your Frame Window

So far, you have learned the basic characteristics of all frame windows, the frame window infrastructure. Now, you learn ways to customize a frame window for your particular application.

The Client Area

The user can distinguish your application's frame windows by the contents of their client areas. The *client area* is that portion of your frame window not occupied by the standard frame components and frame extensions. The window that occupies the client area is the *client window*. Most of the time, your client window is one of the following:

container

> Use an IContainerControl object as the client window when your frame window shows a collection of objects for its view.

canvas

> Use a canvas class, usually IMultiCellCanvas, when your frame window shows action options.

notebook

> Use the INotebook class to show an object's properties or settings view, or another similar view.

multiple-line edit

Use the `IMultiLineEdit` class to display an object consisting solely of text.

view port

Use the `IViewPort` class to manage scrollable client windows.

If you load your frame window from a dialog template, it does not have a client window. The dialog's controls populate the client area of these dialog frames. These controls are direct descendants of the frame window, and the frame window paints the space between them.

Deriving Views from IFrameWindow

Many of the examples in this book show view classes derived from the `IFrameWindow` class. As with many matters of programming, there are trade-offs for using this technique.

Certainly, a view class can gain `IFrameWindow` functionality through composition. That is, the view class can include an `IFrameWindow` object as part of its member data rather than deriving from `IFrameWindow`. For some cases, this may give you a cleaner design.

However, the most compelling reason to derive views from `IFrameWindow` is to be able to use `IWindow::setAutoDeleteObject` to manage the lifetime of view objects created with `operator new`. As discussed previously in "Constructing Secondary Windows," you must create a view object that is displayed as a modeless secondary frame window using `operator new`. This requires a corresponding call to `operator delete` to avoid a memory leak. Open Class Library calls `operator delete` for you when it manages the lifetime of auto-delete windows.

Setting the Client Window

You identify your client window to the frame by calling `IFrameWindow::setClient`. The only argument is a pointer to the client window object.

The frame window automatically makes itself both the parent and owner of the client window. It also sets the client window's identifier to `IC_FRAME_CLIENT_ID`, whose value is defined in `ICCONST.H`. (For the OS/2 platform, this constant has the value of `FID_CLIENT`, which the OS/2 operating system uses to identify client area windows.) Because `IFrameWindow` modifies the identifier of a window when it is made the client window, you need to be careful to either give the window the identifier `IC_FRAME_CLIENT_ID`, or to not rely on your client window's identifier when writing your applications. You can access the client window via the frame window's `clientHandle` or `client` member functions.

Switching Client Windows

You can switch client windows whenever you like by calling `setClient` with a pointer to another client window. For example, you might do this when switching a frame window between settings and icons views. If your frame window already has a client window when you call `setClient`, then it changes the parent window of the previous client window to the object window. This causes the previous client window to be removed from the screen. The window reappears if you call `setClient` again, passing its address.

The following example of a `View` object uses a command handler to switch between the standard container views and a properties (or settings) view notebook:

```
class ViewHandler : public ICommandHandler {
//...
protected:
virtual Boolean
  command( ICommandEvent &event )
    {
    Boolean stopProcessingEvent = false;
    View *view = (View*)(event.window());
    switch( event.commandId() )
      {
      case VIEW_ICON:
        view->container()->showIconView();
        view->setClient( view->container() );
        stopProcessingEvent = true;
        break;
      case VIEW_TREE:
        view->container()->showTreeIconView();
        view->setClient( view->container() );
        stopProcessingEvent = true;
        break;
      case VIEW_DETAILS:
        view->container()->showDetailsView();
        view->setClient( view->container() );
        stopProcessingEvent = true;
        break;
      case VIEW_SETTINGS:
        view->setClient( view->settings() );
        stopProcessingEvent = true;
        break;
      default:
        break;
      }
    return stopProcessingEvent;
    }
//...
};

class View : public IFrameWindow {
public:
//...
// Get the view's container.
IContainerControl
 *container ( ) const
    {
    return &cnr;
    }
// Get View's settings notebook.
INotebook
 *settings ( ) const
    {
    return &nbk;
    }
```

```
//...
private:
IContainerControl
  cnr;
INotebook
  nbk;
//...
};
```

Sizing and Positioning via the Client Window

Because a frame window manages the size and position of its client window, you can only indirectly control the size and position of a client window through the size of its frame window and by adding or removing other standard component windows. But the client window is really the heart of your application's interface; so you want to be able to control its size and to wrap the frame window around a specific client rectangle.

To facilitate this, the `IFrameWindow` class provides a set of functions, shown in Table 5-1, which let you size and position the frame by specifying the client area dimensions. You use `IFrameWindow::clientRectFor` and `IFrameWindow::frameRectFor` to determine the size and position of either the frame or client window, given the size and position of the other. Once you know the size and position for the client window, call `IFrameWindow::moveSizeToClient` to size and position the frame window accordingly. These functions account for the space needed by the standard frame components and frame extensions, both of which you learn about in later topics in this chapter.

Table 5-1. Size and Position Functions of the IFrameWindow Class

Function	Description
moveSizeToClient	Sizes and positions the frame window so that the client window ends up with the specified size and position.
clientRectFor	Returns the size and position that the client window would have if the frame were to have the specified size and position.
frameRectFor	Returns the size and position that the frame window requires for the client window to have the specified size and position.

The Standard Frame Components

Whereas the client window provides the true character of your application, you can tailor the standard frame components as well. These include the title bar, menu bar, and system menu. `IFrameWindow` provides styles that control the presence of these components. For some, your only option is whether to have them present on your frame window. Others you can customize using classes that Open Class Library provides.

Title Bar

Open Class Library provides the `ITitle` class for accessing a frame window's title bar. `ITitle` has functions to help you compose your frame window titles using the following information:

- The object name
- The view name
- The view number (if multiple views of an object are open)

In the following example, the object name is "yourapp.ini," the view name is "Icon View," and the view number is 1. The `ITitle` object puts these components together so that your title text looks like this:

```
yourapp.ini - Icon View:1
```

Construct the title bar object by passing in a pointer to your frame window. You can optionally specify the title. If you do not provide a title, the title remains as it was and the `ITitle` object reflects those contents.

The following code example shows how to set a frame's title:

Accessing the Title Bar - frame1\titlebar\titlebar.cpp

```
IFrameWindow
  frame( "Original Title Bar Text" );

// Now replace the existing title bar text.
ITitle
  title( &frame, "yourapp.ini", "Icon View", 1 );
```

Note that the only way you can query and change a frame window's title is by creating an `ITitle` object for the frame. You can set the title text in its entirety or just change one component of a composite title.

If you have a simple title, you can deal simply with the text by calling `ITitle::text` and `ITitle::setText`.

Menu Bar

You can access the frame window's menu bar by creating an object of class `IMenuBar`. You construct it in a manner similar to the title by passing a pointer to the frame window whose menu bar you want to access. If the frame window already has a menu bar, the `IMenuBar` object becomes a wrapper for it. Otherwise, the `IMenuBar` object creates a new menu bar and attaches it to the frame. Read about menu bars in Chapter 6, "Menus and Keyboard Accelerators."

System Menu

Another frame-related menu that you sometimes need to access and manipulate is the system menu. To do this, you use an object of class `ISystemMenu`. You construct a system menu object by passing a pointer to the frame window.

The operating system enables and disables system menu choices according to the presence of their corresponding frame components. For example, if your frame does not have a sizing border, the **Size** menu choice is disabled. You can use an ISystemMenu object to add and remove items, and to enable some items such as the **Minimize** and **Maximize** choices. For more information about ISystemMenu, see Chapter 6, "Menus and Keyboard Accelerators."

Accelerator Table

An *accelerator table* contains entries that define short-cut key combinations and the commands that the user automatically triggers when pressing those keys. For example, when the user presses Alt+F4, an entry in the standard accelerator table causes a system command of type ISystemMenu::idClose (IC_ID_CLOSE) to be generated. An accelerator table differs slightly from the other frame components covered under this section in that an accelerator table is not visible on the screen.

Open Class Library provides several ways for you to work with accelerator tables. You can load an accelerator table resource and attach it to a frame by using the IFrameWindow::accelerator style when you construct an IFrameWindow object. You can use an IAccelerator object to load an accelerator table after the frame is constructed or to replace the accelerator keys used by the frame with a different set. You can also use an IAcceleratorTable object to query the accelerator keys used by a window, and to add, remove, or modify individual accelerator keys. See Chapter 6, "Menus and Keyboard Accelerators," for more information on accelerator tables.

Frame Extensions

Frame windows manage the layout of the standard frame components and the client window. To do this, frame windows use a set of events designed specifically for this purpose. Open Class Library intercepts these events and uses them to support application-defined frame components, called *frame extensions*. You can use frame extensions to reserve areas of a frame window's screen real estate to show controls of your choosing.

Open Class Library represents these frame extensions as objects of the class IFrameExtension. You rarely use this class directly. Instead, you simply provide the attributes of your frame extensions to the frame window, and the frame creates the underlying IFrameExtension objects for you.

Location

The following code displays a frame extension in several different regions of the frame window. Open Class Library identifies these regions by the values of the enumeration IFrameWindow::Location. You can see the resulting frame window, with its extensions, in Figure 5-1.

Frame Extension Sampler - frame1\frmextns\frmextns.cpp

```
#include <iframe.hpp>
#include <imenubar.hpp>
#include <istattxt.hpp>

void main ( )
{
  // Create a frame window and add a menu bar.
  IFrameWindow
    frame( "Title Bar" );
  IMenuBar
    menuBar( &frame );

  menuBar
#ifdef IC_PM
    .addText( 10, "~File" )
    .addText( 11, "~Edit" )
    .addText( 12, "~View" );
#else
    .addText( 10, "&File" )
    .addText( 11, "&Edit" )
    .addText( 12, "&View" );
#endif

  // Create some static text controls.
  IStaticText
    text1( 0, &frame, &frame ),
    text2( 0, &frame, &frame ),
    text3( 0, &frame, &frame ),
    text4( 0, &frame, &frame );
```

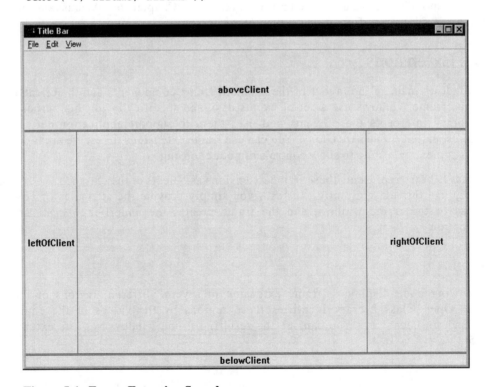

Figure 5-1. Frame Extension Sampler.

```
#ifdef IC_PM
  IStaticText
    text5( 0, &frame, &frame ),
    text6( 0, &frame, &frame ),
    text7( 0, &frame, &frame ),
    text8( 0, &frame, &frame );
#endif

  IStaticText::Alignment
    alignment = IStaticText::centerCenter;
  text1.setAlignment( alignment ).setText( "aboveClient" );
  text2.setAlignment( alignment ).setText( "belowClient" );
  text3.setAlignment( alignment ).setText( " leftOfClient " );
  text4.setAlignment( alignment ).setText( "rightOfClient" );
#ifdef IC_PM
  text5.setAlignment( alignment ).setText( "leftOfTitleBar" );
  text6.setAlignment( alignment )
       .setText( " rightOfTitleBar " );
  text7.setAlignment( alignment ).setText( " leftOfMenuBar " );
  text8.setAlignment( alignment ).setText( " rightOfMenuBar " );
#endif

  const unsigned long fixed = 150;
  const IFrameWindow::SeparatorType
    none = IFrameWindow::none,
    thin = IFrameWindow::thinLine,
    thick = IFrameWindow::thickLine;

  // Add the static text controls as frame extensions.
  frame
    .addExtension( &text1, IFrameWindow::aboveClient,
                   0.25, thick )
    .addExtension( &text2, IFrameWindow::belowClient,
                   thick )
    .addExtension( &text3, IFrameWindow::leftOfClient,
                   thin )
    .addExtension( &text4, IFrameWindow::rightOfClient,
                   fixed, thin );

#ifdef IC_PM
  frame
    .addExtension( &text5, IFrameWindow::leftOfTitleBar,
                   fixed, thick )
    .addExtension( &text6, IFrameWindow::rightOfTitleBar,
                   thin )
    .addExtension( &text7, IFrameWindow::leftOfMenuBar,
                   thick )
    .addExtension( &text8, IFrameWindow::rightOfMenuBar,
                   none );
#endif

  frame.setFocus ( );
  frame.showModally();
}
```

Size

You can specify the size of the frame extension in one of three ways:

- As an integral value. When you specify an integral value, the extension has a fixed width if it is leftOfClient or rightOfClient, or a fixed height if it is aboveClient or belowClient. The size of the extension is specified in pels and remains constant as the user resizes the frame window.

- As a floating point value. When you provide a floating point value, it is used to calculate the relative dimensions of the frame extension. For example, 0.33 would allocate one-third of the client area for the extension. The extension's size is recalculated to one-third the new width or height of the frame, as the user resizes it.

  The frame extension layout logic is simplistic. If you attach two frame extensions to the same portion of the frame using relative sizing, the size of the second one is calculated using the remaining space after the frame window allocates space for the first one. For example, placing one control aboveClient with size 0.33 and another belowClient with size 0.33 does not divide the client area up into three equal-sized pieces. The second extension only occupies two-ninths of the overall client area: one-third of the two-thirds that remain after the frame allocates space for the first extension.

- As a control's minimum size. If you add the extension without specifying an integral or floating point value, the size of the frame extension is determined by its minimum size. This allows the frame window to resize the extension when attributes that affect its size change, such as its font. See Chapter 15, "Canvases," for information on minimum sizes.

Separator Type

Another frame extension attribute is the *separator type*. This is the type of visual separator that the extension draws between itself and the frame component to which you attached it. Open Class Library supports three types of separators: none (IFrameWindow::none), a one-pel-wide line (IFrameWindow::thinLine), or a three-pel-wide line (IFrameWindow::thickLine). You identify these with the values of the enumeration IFrameWindow::SeparatorType. The previous example program uses all three.

Adding Frame Extensions

To add an extension to your frame, call IFrameWindow:addExtension. This function accepts the extension attributes described above—location, an optional size, and optional separator type—and requires a pointer to the window object that occupies the space for the extension. IFrameWindow overloads this function to distinguish the different kinds of sizing (relative, fixed, and minimum size). The separator type defaults to a thin line.

The previous example code shows how to use this function.

Removing and Resizing Extensions

You can remove frame extensions by calling IFrameWindow::removeExtension. As an argument, provide a pointer to the window object that occupies that extension.

You can call IFrameWindow::setExtensionSize to change the size of an existing frame extension. The arguments for this function are a pointer to the window occupying the extension and the new size. If there is no extension occupied by the window, then the function throws an IInvalidParameter exception.

Information Area

Open Class Library provides one control designed explicitly to use as a frame extension: IInfoArea. You use an object of this class to implement an information area for your frame window that displays descriptive text about the currently selected menu choice, that is, the menu choice that has the input focus. You can also display the long text associated with fly-over, or hover, help in the information area. See Chapter 16, "Tool Bars, Fly-Over Help, and Custom Buttons," for more information on fly-over help.

IInfoArea objects automatically attach themselves as frame extensions beneath the client area. They also attach themselves as a menu handler to the frame. When the user moves the cursor to a menu choice, the information area object detects the corresponding events and displays text corresponding to the current menu bar choice. The IInfoArea object displays the following kinds of text:

Inactive

The information area uses this text when the user has not selected any menu choice. The information area maintains the inactive text as a data member. You can query and set this text using inactiveText and setInactiveText. The default inactive text is blank.

Call IInfoArea::setInactiveText to specify that the information area can display other kinds of informational text. For example, you might use it to display similar text when the various controls on your window have the input focus, or as the user selects objects in your container. For example, on initial display of your frame window you might use:

```
infoArea
  .setInactiveText( "Press F10 to access the menu bar." );
```

Missing

The information area uses this text when it cannot find the informational text for a menu choice. To access the information area's missing text, call IInfoArea::missingText and IInfoArea::setMissingText. The default missing text is blank.

Disabled

The information area displays this text when a disabled menu choice has the input focus. It permits you to override the normal text for that choice. All menu choices use the same disabled text string. To access the information area's disabled text, call IInfoArea::disabledText and IInfoArea::setDisabledText.

If there is no disabled text, the information area displays the normal text for the menu choice.

Normal text

The information area displays this text when the user places the selection cursor on a menu choice. It obtains the text from its resource library using the menu item's identifier as the identifier for a string resource.

You can specify which resource library the information area searches. By default, it searches the default application resource library, which is obtained by calling `ICurrentApplication::userResourceLibrary`. You can set the application resource library by calling `ICurrentApplication::setUserResourceLibrary`.

To adjust the identifier used to search for the string resource, specify an offset value. The information area adds the offset value to the menu identifier to come up with the string resource identifier. You need to specify an offset value if the menu identifiers conflict with other string resource identifiers.

The information area extension occupies a fixed size at the bottom of the client area based on the size of its font. If your information text requires more or less space, you can call `IInfoArea::setLineCount` to set the height of the window.

The information area also tries to display information about the system menu choices, so you must supply string resources for the corresponding menu identifiers. The following is a sample resource script file, which shows how to define string resources for the system menu choices.

Information Area for the System Menu - frame1\infoarea\infoarea.rc

```
#include <icconst.h>

#ifdef IC_PM
  #define INCL_WIN
  #define INCL_WINFRAMEMGR   /* For SC_* */
  #include <os2.h>
  #include <ibase.hpp>

#ifndef IC_ID_CLOSE
  /* Define these constants which do not exist on */
  /* VisualAge C++ for OS/2, Version 3.0.         */
  #define IC_ID_CLOSE        SC_CLOSE
  #define IC_ID_MOVE         SC_MOVE
  #define IC_ID_SIZE         SC_SIZE
  #define IC_ID_MINIMIZE     SC_MINIMIZE
  #define IC_ID_MAXIMIZE     SC_MAXIMIZE
  #define IC_ID_SYSHIDE      SC_HIDE
  #define IC_ID_RESTORE      SC_RESTORE
  #define IC_ID_WINDOWLIST   SC_TASKMANAGER
#endif

#endif

STRINGTABLE
  BEGIN
    IC_ID_RESTORE   "Restore the frame window size and position."
    IC_ID_MOVE         "Move the frame window."
    IC_ID_SIZE         "Size the frame window."
    IC_ID_MINIMIZE     "Minimize the frame window."
    IC_ID_MAXIMIZE     "Maximize the frame window."
#ifdef IC_PM
    IC_ID_SYSHIDE      "Hide the frame window."
#endif
    IC_ID_CLOSE        "Close the frame window."
    IC_ID_WINDOWLIST   "Show the system window list."
  END
```

To use this information text for the system menu choices, compile this resource script file into a binary resource file and bind it to your application's default resource library. See Chapter 24, "Using Resources," for details on how to bind these resources to your application.

Chapter 6

Menus and Keyboard Accelerators

- Describes the classes provided by Open Class Library to work with keyboard accelerators and all of the various types of menus
- Describes the IMenu, IMenuItem, IMenuBar, IPopUpMenu, ISystemMenu, ISubmenu, IMenuHandler, IMenuEvent, IMenuDrawItemHandler, IMenuDrawItemEvent, IMenu::Cursor, ICommandHandler, ICommandEvent, and IAccelerator classes
- Chapters 5, 10, 13, and 17 cover related material.

This chapter describes the classes in Open Class Library that you use to build menus and add keyboard accelerators. A *menu* presents a list of choices to a user. The behavior of a menu is similar to the behavior that the button classes provide (see Chapter 10, "Button Controls"). A menu, however, extends the capability that buttons provide because it enables you to construct a complex list of choices, including nested choices. You can predefine it in a resource script file or a program can dynamically create it. A *keyboard accelerator*, an application-defined key or combination of keys, is closely related to a menu because you can include a keyboard accelerator to give your users a fast-path method for selecting each item on a menu.

Just as buttons do, the menu sends a command event to the window owning the menu when a user selects an item. Open Class Library provides a set of handler classes to handle command events and specific menu-related events. For example, when a user presses mouse button 2, the system sends an event to the application to display a pop-up menu. (In the OS/2 operating system, a user can also press the pop-up menu request key, Shift+F10.) The application receives another event when a user selects a choice from the menu. In addition, Open Class Library provides ways to alter the contents of the pop-up menu before it is displayed and to refresh the menu to its original state when the menu is dismissed.

This chapter describes the different kinds of menus that Open Class Library supports and shows you how to use the menu classes to create and manipulate the menus. It also includes examples to demonstrate how to code the following tasks:

- Construct menu bars and pop-up menus from a resource script file, and, dynamically, as your program is executing

- Define and use accelerator keys

- Add and remove items from a menu, including the system menu

- Change a menu item's text or bitmap

- Change whether a menu item is checked or disabled

- Draw your own menu items

About Menus

A menu is a window with a list of choices, and a *menu item* represents each choice in the list. A menu item includes the text or bitmap for the choice and describes how it is displayed. For example, menu items can be checked, disabled, framed by a box, or highlighted. When users select a menu item, it can generate a command event or help request, or it can display a *submenu*. A submenu is a menu window that the operating system displays when users select the menu item that contains a reference to the submenu. For our purposes, a submenu is any menu window displayed on request. This includes pull-down, cascade, and pop-up menus. Figure 6-1 shows a variety of the menus you can use in your applications.

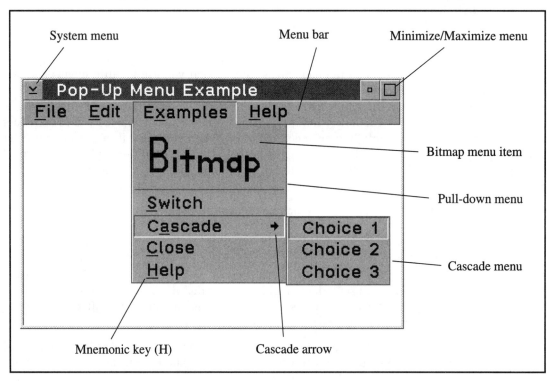

Figure 6-1. Different Kinds of Menus.

Menu Bar

A *menu bar* is a horizontal list of choices that appears below the title of many primary and secondary windows. Usually, all of the choices or menu items on the menu bar refer to submenus displayed when a user selects the item. These menu bar submenus are called *pull-down*, or *drop-down*, *menus*. For most applications, you define the menu bar contents using a resource script file, but you can create them dynamically as well.

Pull-Down Menu

Pull-down, or drop-down, menus are submenus associated with the menu bar. The name is a bit misleading because these menus only drop *down* if there is sufficient room below the menu bar to do so. If the menu bar is close to the bottom of the display, the presentation system displays the menu *above* the menu bar. A pull-down menu is hidden when a user selects a choice in the menu or moves the input focus off of the menu.

Cascade Menu

A *cascade menu* is a submenu associated with a menu item on a pull-down or pop-up menu. You use it to layer menu choices. The presentation system places an arrow sign next to each menu item with an associated cascade menu. When a user selects the item, the cascade menu is displayed beside the pull-down or pop-up menu. A cascade menu also can contain menu items with other cascade menus, thus enabling you to have multiple layers.

Conditional Cascade Menu

The difference between a *conditional cascade menu* and a cascade menu is that a conditional cascade menu is only displayed when a user selects the boxed arrow button next to the text. If a user selects anywhere else on the item, the default choice (the checked item in the submenu) in the cascade menu is automatically selected. The Windows operating system does not support conditional cascade menus.

Title Bar Menu

A *title bar menu* is a menu to the left or right of the title bar. For example, the system menu in the upper-left corner of a primary or secondary window is a title bar menu. Although Open Class Library does not support creating additional title bar menus, it does support adding and removing items from the system menu. The example disk contains code in the directory MENUS\TITLEBMP that demonstrates how to create a class as a wrapper for the minimize/maximize menu in the OS/2 operating system so that you can add menu items to it. Only the OS/2 operating system supports this technique.

Pop-Up Menu

A type of submenu, the pop-up menu, or *context menu*, is a vertical list of choices or menu items displayed when users click the pop-up menu mouse button. A pop-up menu contains action choices applicable to an object or a group of objects in a window. Although menu bars and title bar menus are associated with frame windows, you can use a pop-up menu with any window. You typically use them on the objects in a container control window. A pop-up menu can appear anywhere on the screen, but normally you display it next to the object at the position of the mouse pointer (if users use a mouse) or cursor (if users use the keyboard).

Keyboard Mnemonics and Accelerators

You can associate a mnemonic and a shortcut accelerator key with a textual menu item. Create a mnemonic by placing a mnemonic indicator (the tilde character in the OS/2 operating system, the ampersand character in the Windows operating system) before one character of the menu item's text. Make the mnemonic unique within the choices on a menu or submenu. The menu displays that menu item with the mnemonic character underlined. Open Class Library does not translate mnemonic characters across platforms, so for portable applications, place mnemonic text into a resource script file.

An accelerator is a key or combination of keys that you define in an accelerator table of a resource script file. When users press the accelerator keys, the presentation system dispatches a command event just as it does for a menu item selection. Identify the accelerators for menu choices by providing text on the right side of a menu item. For example, the **Cut** choice on an **Edit** menu usually includes **Shift+Delete** to the right. Then, instead of users selecting the menu and then **Cut**, they can invoke the cut action by holding down the Shift key, and pressing the Delete key. Although you identify a mnemonic in the text of a menu item, you do not define the accelerator key when you add a description of an accelerator to the text of a menu item. You must actually define an accelerator in an accelerator table of a resource script file, or you can define it dynamically by using the class IAcceleratorKey.

Users can invoke a mnemonic only from a menu with input focus; they can invoke an accelerator from anywhere in the window.

The Menu Classes

Figure 6-2 displays the classes in Open Class Library you use to work with menus. Use the IMenuBar, IPopUpMenu, and ISystemMenu classes to create menus and to add and remove items from the menus. These classes derive most of their behavior from their common base class IMenu.

Use IMenuItem to define the data, styles, and attributes of a menu item. You can create IMenuItem objects and add them to objects of any class that derives from IMenu. IMenu also has several functions that you can use to add items without creating an IMenuItem object.

IMenu and IWindow

The OS/2 operating system implements menus the same way it does other windows. Menus have a specific window class (WC_MENU), a size, a position, and window attributes such as modifiable fonts and colors. Applications can use the window handle to set and query attributes, and they can control the destruction of the window.

The Windows operating system implements menus differently based on the type of menu. For example, a menu bar is not a window; it is a specific nonclient area of the frame window. The operating system controls sizing, positioning, and painting. It implements submenus, such as pull-down menus and pop-up menus, as windows, but the similarity to the OS/2 operating system ends there. The Windows operating system creates a single window from a private window class and uses it for all submenus. Applications cannot access this window.

Because of these differences, be aware of the following details when writing portable code:

- Although IMenu derives from IWindow, do not manipulate menus as if they are windows. For example, color and font changes have no effect on Windows platforms.

- Use IMenuHandle to uniquely identify menus instead of IWindowHandle. Use IMenu::menuHandle instead of IWindow::handle to query for the handle. IMenuHandle wrappers the HMENU type on the Windows operating systems and the HWND type on the OS/2 operating system.

- Do not use IFrameWindow::handleFor(IFrameWindow::menuBar) to obtain the menu bar handle. Because this member function returns an IWindowHandle, it returns a window handle of 0 on the Windows operating system because a menu bar is not a window.

ISubmenu is a menu class that enables you to dynamically modify the contents of a pull-down or cascade menu. It keeps track of the dynamic changes made to the menu and automatically restores them when a user closes it. You do not create ISubmenu objects directly. Instead, IMenuHandler creates an ISubmenu object and passes it to its menuShowing function before the menu is displayed.

Open Class Library provides three general handlers to handle events that a menu window generates. IMenuHandler enables you to process the IMenuEvents related to creating and displaying a menu. This includes the following actions:

- Requesting a pop-up menu
- Selecting a menu item
- Displaying a submenu
- Closing a submenu

When you request a pop-up menu for a container window, use ICnrMenuHandler, a derived class of IMenuHandler. For more information on this special case, see "Container Pop-Up Menus" in Chapter 13, "Container Control."

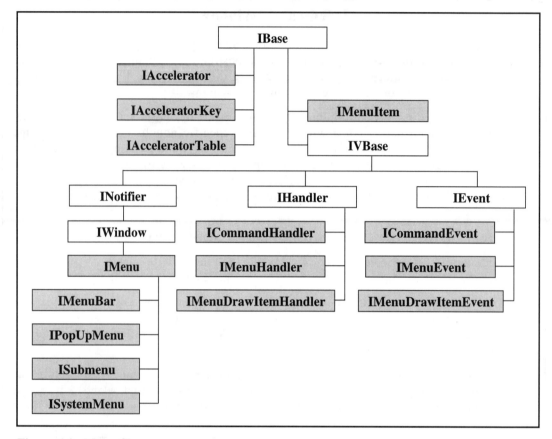

Figure 6-2. Menu Classes.

Use ICommandHandler to process the ICommandEvent that the window dispatcher sends when a user selects a menu item in a menu or presses an accelerator key.

To draw your own menu items, use IMenuDrawItemHandler. You must create these items with the IMenuItem::drawItem style.

Use IAccelerator or IAcceleratorTable to load a keyboard accelerator table from a resource file. Use IAcceleratorKey with IAcceleratorTable to manipulate individual accelerator keys.

Loading Menus from a Resource File

Usually, you use a resource script file to define a menu bar or pop-up menu and its layered submenus because they are simple to define. A second advantage is that you can translate the text in the file into foreign languages without modifying the source code. A third advantage is that you can change the menu structure without modifying the code.

Defining a Menu Resource

Both the Windows and OS/2 operating systems use a resource script language to define menu resources. Though similar, there are some differences. The following examples show a resource script file that defines a menu-bar resource. The two examples show the same resource but use the native script format for the respective operating system.

Typical Menu Resource Definition (Windows) - menus\menures\menures.rc

```
#include <windows.h>
#include "menures.h"
MI_BITMAP BITMAP  menures.bmp

MAIN_MENU MENUEX
  BEGIN
    POPUP "&File",  MI_FILE
      BEGIN
        MENUITEM "&New...",  MI_NEW
        MENUITEM "&Open...", MI_OPEN
        MENUITEM "&Save",    MI_SAVE
        MENUITEM "Save &as...", MI_SAVEAS
      END
    POPUP "&Edit",  MI_EDIT
      BEGIN
        MENUITEM "&Undo  \t Ctrl+U",     MI_UNDO
        MENUITEM SEPARATOR
        MENUITEM "&Cut   \t Shift+Delete", MI_CUT
        MENUITEM "Copy   \t Ctrl+Insert",  MI_COPY
        MENUITEM "&Paste \t Shift+Insert", MI_PASTE
      END
    POPUP "E&xamples",  MI_EXAMPLE
      BEGIN
        MENUITEM "",  MI_BITMAP  ,  BITMAP
        MENUITEM SEPARATOR
        MENUITEM "&Switch",  MI_SWITCH
        POPUP "C&ascade",  MI_CASCADE
          BEGIN
            MENUITEM "Choice 1",  MI_CASCADE1
            MENUITEM "Choice 2",  MI_CASCADE2
            MENUITEM "Choice 3",  MI_CASCADE3
          END
        MENUITEM "&Close",  SC_CLOSE
        MENUITEM "&Help",   MI_HELP
      END
    POPUP "&Help",  MI_HELP
      BEGIN
        MENUITEM "&General help...",  MI_GENERAL_HELP
        MENUITEM "&Extended help...", SC_HELPEXTENDED
        MENUITEM "&Keys help...",     SC_HELPKEYS
        MENUITEM "Help &index...",    SC_HELPINDEX
      END
  END
```

Typical Menu Resource Definition (OS/2) - menus\menures\menures.rc

```
#include <os2.h>
#include "menures.h"

BITMAP MI_BITMAP "menures.bmp"
```

```
MENU MAIN_MENU
  BEGIN
    PRESPARAMS PP_FONTNAMESIZE , "14.Helv"
    SUBMENU  "~File", MI_FILE
      BEGIN
        MENUITEM "~New...",   MI_NEW
        MENUITEM " Open...", MI_OPEN
        MENUITEM "~Save",     MI_SAVE
        MENUITEM "Save ~as...", MI_SAVEAS
      END
    SUBMENU "~Edit", MI_EDIT
      BEGIN
        MENUITEM "~Undo  \t Ctrl+U",    MI_UNDO
        MENUITEM SEPARATOR
        MENUITEM "~Cut    \t Shift+Delete", MI_CUT
        MENUITEM "Copy   \t Ctrl+Insert", MI_COPY
        MENUITEM "~Paste \t Shift+Insert",MI_PASTE
      END
    SUBMENU  "E~xamples", MI_EXAMPLE
      BEGIN
        MENUITEM "#1061",      MI_BITMAP, MIS_BITMAP
        MENUITEM SEPARATOR
        MENUITEM "~Switch"   MI_SWITCH
        SUBMENU  "C~ascade",          MI_CASCADE
          BEGIN
            MENUITEM "Choice 1",   MI_CASCADE1
            MENUITEM "Choice 2",   MI_CASCADE2
            MENUITEM "Choice 3",   MI_CASCADE3
          END
        MENUITEM "~Close",    SC_CLOSE,  MIS_SYSCOMMAND
        MENUITEM "~Help",     MI_HELP,   MIS_HELP
      END
    SUBMENU "~Help", MI_HELP
      BEGIN
        MENUITEM "~General help...",   MI_GENERAL_HELP
        MENUITEM "~Extended help...", SC_HELPEXTENDED,
            MIS_SYSCOMMAND
        MENUITEM "~Keys help...",       SC_HELPKEYS,
            MIS_SYSCOMMAND
        MENUITEM "Help ~index...",     SC_HELPINDEX,
            MIS_SYSCOMMAND
      END
  END
```

You can add the menu defined in this resource script file to the menu bar using the following code:

Loading a Frame Menu Resource - menus\menures\menures.cpp

```cpp
#include <iframe.hpp>
#include <iapp.hpp>
#include "menures.h"

void main()
{
// Create a frame window with a menu bar from a resource file.
IFrameWindow
   frame ("Menu Resource Example", MAIN_MENU,
          IFrameWindow::defaultStyle() | IFrameWindow::menuBar);

// Set the focus and show the application.
frame
  .setFocus()
  .show();
IApplication::current().run();
}
```

The menu resource definition consists mainly of MENUEX, POPUP and MENUITEM statements for Windows operating systems and MENU, SUBMENU and MENUITEM statements for the OS/2 operating system. All menu definitions begin with a MENUEX/MENU statement that contains a unique identifier for the menu. If you are creating an IFrameWindow with the IFrameWindow::menuBar style, make this identifier the same as the window identifier of the IFrameWindow object. In the Windows operating systems, the MENUEX keyword comes after the identifier, not before it as in the OS/2 operating system.

Within the BEGIN and END blocks of the MENUEX/MENU statement, you can put any number of POPUP/SUBMENU and MENUITEM statements. The POPUP/SUBMENU statement defines a pull-down menu for a menu bar, pop-up, or cascade menu. The MENUITEM statement specifies the item's text or bitmap, a unique identifier, plus any styles or attributes. If you don't specify a style or attribute, the system defaults the item style to MFT_STRING/MIS_TEXT (textual menu item) and the attribute to MFS_ENABLE/MIS_ENABLED. See Table 6-2 for a description of the MENUITEM styles and Table 6-3 for a description of the MENUITEM attributes.

To define a bitmap item, use an MFT_BITMAP/MIS_BITMAP style and associate the bitmap resource with the item. In the Windows operating system, you can only make this association after you load the menu resource. In the OS/2 operating system, you can make this association after loading the menu resource, or you can specify the identifier of the bitmap in the MENUITEM

MENU versus MENUEX

With the introduction of Windows 95, the Microsoft Corporation introduced a new API, *Extended Menus*, to interface to menus. With this API, all menu items can have a unique identifier, just as in the OS/2 operating system. Previous Windows platforms, including Windows 3.1 and Windows NT 3.51, only supported identifiers on command items but not on submenus and separators. Along with this new API, a new menu resource keyword, MENUEX, was created to support this functionality. By specifying this keyword instead of the MENU keyword, you can code your menu resource file with identifiers next to all menu items.

Because of the design of IMenu, Open Class Library requires applications to use the MENUEX keyword and to specify unique identifiers for all menu items in any Windows menu resources that applications define. This restriction applies to all applications that use IMenu and related classes to access menus. Open Class Library supports this keyword for all Windows platforms.

If no IMenu or related classes are required, you can develop an application that can use the original menu resource specification (MENU keyword) as long as you follow these restrictions:

- You must use the IFrameWindow::menuBar style on the IFrameWindow constructor to load the menu. This restricts the menu to text menu items because bitmap and draw-item styles require the use of the IMenu classes.

- You can use ICommandHandler objects to receive menu-generated command events, but you cannot use IMenuHandler and IMenuDrawItemHandler and their related events.

text. If you specify the bitmap identifier in the MENUITEM text, you must include the definition of the bitmap in a BITMAP statement in the resource script file. In the preceding example, we indicated the identifier of the bitmap for the MI_BITMAP MENUITEM by coding "#1061" for the text string.

Notice in the preceding example the following points:

- The MENUITEM SEPARATOR style defines an unselectable line to separate the menu items.

- To specify a mnemonic character on a text menu item, use a mnemonic indicator character in front of the character. In the Windows operating system, use the ampersand character (&) as the mnemonic indicator; in the OS/2 operating system, use the tilde character (˜) as the mnemonic indicator.

- On the OS/2 operating system, you can change the font or color of a menu by adding PRESPARAM statements.

- You can change the menu items to be system commands or requests for help by using the MIS_SYSCOMMAND or MIS_HELP styles. Also, use any of the predefined system command identifiers as the identifier of the menu item to get the operating system's default processing for these commands.

- There is no MENUITEM style to create a conditional cascade submenu. To use a conditional cascade menu, call IMenu::setConditionalCascade after you load the menu. Only the OS/2 operating system supports this.

Loading and Constructing a Menu Bar

After you have defined a menu resource, you have two ways to display the menu as a menu bar. You can include the IFrameWindow::menuBar style when you create your frame window. The frame window constructor then automatically loads the menu if it has the same numeric identifier as the frame window (see the preceding example). Or, you can create an IMenuBar object to load the menu resource. Using the IMenuBar object does not require you to use the same numeric identifier for the frame window and the menu. After you create the IMenuBar object, you can use it to modify the contents of the menu.

In the following example we load the same menu as the preceding example using an IMenuBar object. After loading the menu, we use the menu bar object to associate a bitmap for the bitmap menu item, and we change the **Cascade** menu item to a conditional cascade menu item. Only the Windows operating system requires the first step because the OS/2 operating system supports bitmap loading through a resource file. The second step has no effect in the Windows operating system because it doesn't support conditional cascades.

Using an IMenuBar - menus\menubar\menubar.cpp

```
#include <iapp.hpp>
#include <iframe.hpp>
#include <imenubar.hpp>
#include "menubar.h"
```

```
void main()
{
// Create a frame window.
IFrameWindow
  frame ("Menu Bar Example");

// Add the menu bar from a resource file.
IMenuBar
  menuBar(MAIN_MENU, &frame);

#ifdef IC_WIN
// For Windows, the bitmap is not automatically loaded into
// the menu, so load it now.
menuBar.setBitmap(MI_BITMAP, MI_BITMAP);
#endif

// Change the cascade to a conditional cascade.
menuBar.setConditionalCascade(MI_CASCADE, MI_CASCADE1);

// Set the focus and show the application.
frame
  .setFocus()
  .show();
IApplication::current().run();
}
```

Loading and Showing a Pop-Up Menu

You can add a pop-up menu to any window in Open Class Library. In the same way that you define a menu bar, you define a pop-up menu in your resource script file. You can load it during program initialization or wait until a user requests the menu. Whenever you load the pop-up menu, you must create a class derived from IMenuHandler and override IMenuHandler::makePopUpMenu to show the pop-up menu. Open Class Library calls this function when a user requests a pop-up menu for the control using either the keyboard or mouse. To display a pop-up menu, call IPopUpMenu::show and provide the location of the menu. This location is relative to the window that owns the pop-up menu. When a user requests a pop-up menu using the mouse, display the pop-up menu at the mouse pointer location. IMenuEvent::mousePosition returns the pointer location.

In the OS/2 operating system, the pop-up can also be requested via the keyboard. To determine which device requested the pop-up, use IEvent::parameter2().number2(). To load the menu on demand, create the IPopUpMenu object in your menu handler's makePopUpMenu function. When a user selects a menu item, the window that owns the menu receives the resulting command event.

The following code adds a pop-up menu to a static text control that is the client window of a frame window. We add a menu handler to the static text control to create and show the pop-up menu and a command handler to process the selection of menu items. Several operating system controls, such as the static text control, do not pass WM_COMMAND messages on to their owners. To ensure these messages are passed to your command handler, you have two choices. You can ensure that the owner of the pop-up menu is a window that passes these messages on to its owner (such as any of the canvas classes), or attach the command handler directly to the window that owns the pop-up menu. We used the latter in our example by making the static text control the owner of the pop-up menu and attaching the command handler to it.

Using Pop-up Menus - menus\txtpopup\txtpopup.cpp

```cpp
#include <iframe.hpp>
#include <istattxt.hpp>
#include <iapp.hpp>
#include <ipopmenu.hpp>
#include <imenuhdr.hpp>
#include <icmdhdr.hpp>
#include "txtpopup.h"

// Menu handler to capture pop-up menu requests.
class MenuHandler : public IMenuHandler
{
protected:
virtual Boolean
  makePopUpMenu(IMenuEvent& menuEvent);
};

// Command handler to capture menu commands.
class CommandHandler : public ICommandHandler
{
public:
  CommandHandler ( IStaticText& status)
          : aStatus(status) {}

protected:
virtual Boolean
  command             ( ICommandEvent& event );

private:
IStaticText
 &aStatus;
};

void main()
{
// Create a frame window with a menu bar and an
// accelerator table from a resource file.
IFrameWindow
  frame ("Pop-Up Menu Example", MAIN_MENU,
         IFrameWindow::defaultStyle() |
         IFrameWindow::menuBar |
         IFrameWindow::accelerator);

// Create a status area in the client
// and a command handler to write text in it.
IStaticText
  statusArea(ID_STATUS, &frame, &frame);
CommandHandler
  commandHandler(statusArea);

// Add the command handler to the frame to receive the
// menu commands and to the status area to receive any
// pop-up menu commands sent.
commandHandler
  .handleEventsFor(&frame)
  .handleEventsFor(&statusArea);

// Add a pop-up menu handler to the client status area.
MenuHandler
  textPopUpHandler;
textPopUpHandler.handleEventsFor(&statusArea);
```

```
// Set the focus and show the application.
frame
  .setClient(&statusArea)
  .setFocus()
  .show();
IApplication::current().run();
}

// Create and show the pop-up menu.
IBase::Boolean MenuHandler::makePopUpMenu(IMenuEvent& event)
{
  IPopUpMenu* popUp = new IPopUpMenu(POPUP_MENU,
                                event.dispatchingWindow());
  (*popUp)
    .show(event.mousePosition())
    .setAutoDeleteObject();
  return true;
}

IBase::Boolean CommandHandler::command( ICommandEvent& event )
{
  switch(event.commandId())
  {
    case MI_FILE         :
    case MI_NEW          :
    case MI_OPEN         :
    case MI_SAVE         :
    case MI_SAVEAS       :
    case MI_EDIT         :
    case MI_UNDO         :
    case MI_CUT          :
    case MI_COPY         :
    case MI_PASTE        :
    case MI_EXAMPLE      :
    case MI_BITMAP       :
    case MI_HELP         :
    case MI_GENERAL_HELP :
    case MI_CASCADE1     :
    case MI_CASCADE2     :
    case MI_CASCADE3     :
    {
        aStatus.setText(event.commandId());
        return true;
    }
  }
  return false;
}
```

You define a pop-up menu in a resource script file the same as you do a menu bar menu. We added the following menu resource statements to our resource script file to define a pop-up menu with the items on our **Edit** menu.

Pop-Up Menu Resource Definition (Windows) - menus\txtpopup\txtpopup.rc

```
POPUP_MENU MENUEX
  BEGIN
    MENUITEM "&Undo  \t Ctrl+U",        MI_UNDO
    MENUITEM SEPARATOR
    MENUITEM "&Cut   \t Shift+Delete", MI_CUT
    MENUITEM "Copy   \t Ctrl+Insert",  MI_COPY
    MENUITEM "&Paste \t Shift+Insert", MI_PASTE
  END
```

Pop-Up Menu Resource Definition (OS/2) - menus\txtpopup\txtpopup.rc

```
MENU POPUP_MENU
  BEGIN
    MENUITEM "~Undo  \t Ctrl+U",         MI_UNDO
    MENUITEM SEPARATOR
    MENUITEM "~Cut   \t Shift+Delete",  MI_CUT
    MENUITEM "Copy   \t Ctrl+Insert",   MI_COPY
    MENUITEM "~Paste \t Shift+Insert",  MI_PASTE
  END
```

Creating Menus Programmatically

Although most applications use the menu resource script file to define menus, you can create the menu bar and pop-up menus dynamically at run time. This is useful if the menu items vary depending on the state of the selected object or objects. For example, in a container view when multiple objects are selected, build a pop-up menu with items valid for all currently selected objects. There are several ways to accomplish this. First, you can define a menu resource that contains all possible menu items and submenus. After you load the menu, you can remove any menu items that do not apply to the currently selected objects. The other way, which we show in the next example, is to dynamically create the menu and then add the necessary menu items and submenus. You can use the same techniques in the example to dynamically create a menu bar. The only code that changes from the previous example is the definition of the makePopUpMenu function.

Dynamically Created Pop-Up Menus - menus\dynpopup\dynpopup.cpp

```
IBase::Boolean MenuHandler :: makePopUpMenu(IMenuEvent& event)
{
  // Create the pop-up menu.
  IPopUpMenu* popUp = new IPopUpMenu( event.dispatchingWindow(),
                                      POPUP_MENU );
  // Create menu items for "Close" and "Help."
  IMenuItem close(SC_CLOSE, IMenuItem::postSystemCommand);
  close.setText(SC_CLOSE);
  IMenuItem help(MI_HELP, IMenuItem::postHelp);
  help.setText(MI_HELP);

  // Add the menu items to the pop-up menu.
  (*popUp)
    .addText(MI_EDIT,    MI_EDIT)
    .addSubmenu(MI_EDIT)
      .addText(MI_UNDO,   MI_UNDO, MI_EDIT)
      .addSeparator(MI_EDIT)
      .addText(MI_CUT,    MI_CUT,   MI_EDIT)
      .addText(MI_COPY,   MI_COPY,  MI_EDIT)
      .addText(MI_PASTE,  MI_PASTE, MI_EDIT);
  (*popUp)
    .addText(MI_EXAMPLE, MI_EXAMPLE)
    .addSubmenu(MI_EXAMPLE)
      .addBitmap(MI_BITMAP, MI_BITMAP, MI_EXAMPLE)
      .addSeparator(MI_EXAMPLE)
      .addItem(close, MI_EXAMPLE)
      .addItem(help, MI_EXAMPLE)
    .setAutoDeleteObject();

  // Show the pop-up menu.
  (*popUp)
    .show(event.mousePosition());
  return true;
}
```

Note the following points:

- Although you can create the menu dynamically, you can still store the text for the menu items separately from the application code by defining a STRINGTABLE resource (not shown in our example) in your resource script file.

- To create submenus dynamically, first call IMenu::addText to create the menu item. Then, call IMenu::addSubmenu with the same numeric identifier to create the submenu.

- To mirror dynamic changes to a menu, use the IAcceleratorTable and IAcceleratorKey classes to make corresponding changes to accelerator keys.

- To cause the menu item selection to send a system command or help notification, construct a menu item with the appropriate styles and use IMenu::addItem to add them to the menu. (Reminder: Only the OS/2 operating system supports this capability.)

Defining Keyboard Accelerators

In the previous example, we added text to the right of our **Edit** menu items on the pop-up menu. This text describes how to invoke these items using accelerator keys. The \t in the text, which represents a tab character, aligns the following text in a separate column. To enable these accelerator keys, define an accelerator table with these keys and associate the table with the frame window or the window that owns the menu. To define an accelerator table, you can create an ACCELERATORS/ACCELTABLE resource in a resource script file or use the IAcceleratorTable and IAcceleratorKey classes to create the table dynamically. An accelerator table contains accelerator keys. Each accelerator key generates a command, system command, or help request when a user presses the key.

The accelerator table resource for our pop-up menu follows:

Accelerator Table Resource Definition (Windows) - menus\txtpopup\txtpopup.rc

```
MAIN_MENU ACCELERATORS
BEGIN
    "^U",          MI_UNDO,   ASCII
    VK_DELETE, MI_CUT,    SHIFT,    VIRTKEY
    VK_INSERT, MI_COPY,   CONTROL,  VIRTKEY
    VK_INSERT, MI_PASTE,  SHIFT,    VIRTKEY
END
```

Accelerator Table Resource Definition (OS/2) - menus\txtpopup\txtpopup.rc

```
ACCELTABLE MAIN_MENU
BEGIN
    "u",          MI_UNDO,   CHAR,        CONTROL
    "U",          MI_UNDO,   CHAR,        CONTROL
    VK_DELETE, MI_CUT,    VIRTUALKEY,  SHIFT
    VK_INSERT, MI_COPY,   VIRTUALKEY,  CONTROL
    VK_INSERT, MI_PASTE,  VIRTUALKEY,  SHIFT
END
```

After defining the accelerator table in a resource script file, you must add code to load the table. Similar to loading menus, you have two ways to load an accelerator table from a resource file. You can define the accelerator table with the same numeric identifier as your frame window and add the frame window style `IFrameWindow::accelerator` when creating the window.   Or, you can load the resource by creating an `IAccelerator` or `IAcceleratorTable` object.   `IAccelerator` enables you to load and associate an accelerator table with one window of your application or with all frame windows created on the current thread. The following example uses an `IAccelerator` object to load the accelerator table for our **Edit** menu items and to associate it with the frame window.

Loading an Accelerator Table - menus\accel\accel.cpp

```
#include <iaccel.hpp>
#include <iapp.hpp>
#include <icmdhdr.hpp>
#include <iframe.hpp>
#include <istattxt.hpp>
#include "accel.h"

// Command handler to capture menu commands.
class CommandHandler : public ICommandHandler
{
public:
  CommandHandler ( IStaticText& status )
          : aStatus(status) {}

protected:
virtual Boolean
  command               ( ICommandEvent& event );

private:
IStaticText
 &aStatus;
};

void main()
{
// Create a frame window with a menu bar.
IFrameWindow
  frame ("Pop-Up Menu Example", MAIN_MENU,
         IFrameWindow::defaultStyle()
           | IFrameWindow::menuBar);

// Load an accelerator table from the resource
// file and associate it with the frame window.
IAccelerator accelTable(MAIN_MENU, &frame);

// Create a status area as the client window
// and a command handler to write text in it.
IStaticText
  statusArea(ID_STATUS, &frame, &frame);
CommandHandler
  commandHandler(statusArea);

// Add the command handler to the frame to receive the
// menu commands and to the status area to receive any
// accelerator commands sent.
commandHandler
  .handleEventsFor(&frame)
  .handleEventsFor(&statusArea);

// Set the focus and show the application.
frame
  .setClient(&statusArea)
  .setFocus()
  .show();

IApplication::current().run();
}
```

You can also associate an accelerator table to a window using the IAcceleratorTable class. IAcceleratorTable duplicates much of the functionality of IAccelerator, although it lacks some of its lesser-used capabilities. The biggest difference between the two classes, however, is that you can use IAcceleratorTable with the IAcceleratorKey class to build an accelerator table dynamically, or query or modify individual accelerator keys.

You define an accelerator key with IAcceleratorKey using either an ASCII character code or an IKey::VirtualKey value defined in IKEY.HPP (for keys that have no obvious character code). Actually, IKey::VirtualKey is a typedef for unsigned long, thus allowing you to use virtual key values defined by the operating system that Open Class Library does not define in IKEY.HPP (perhaps because it is not a portable virtual key). You can also use the IAcceleratorTable::Cursor class to return the keys in an accelerator table as IAcceleratorKey objects.

IAcceleratorTable provides functions for adding an IAcceleratorKey object and removing an accelerator key with the same key combination as a specified IAcceleratorKey object. IAcceleratorTable also provides a nested Cursor class for iterating the accelerator keys in the table. You can use this class to return a key as an IAcceleratorKey object, to replace a specific accelerator key, or to remove a specific accelerator key.

Once you build an IAcceleratorTable object, call IWindow::setAcceleratorTable to associate the accelerator table with a window. An IAcceleratorTable object is also associated with a window if you specify the window when constructing the IAcceleratorTable object, or create the IAcceleratorTable object by calling IWindow::acceleratorTable. If associated at creation time, you can optionally cause any changes you make to the IAcceleratorTable object to be immediately reflected in the window.

We provide an example, in the directory MENUS\DYNACCEL on the example disk, that shows a selection handler using IAcceleratorTable and IAcceleratorKey to add and remove accelerator keys based on the selection or deselection of a check box:

Accessing Title Bar Menus

By default, a system menu is added to all primary and secondary windows in Open Class Library because the IFrameWindow::systemMenu style is a frame window default style. Access the system menu and its menu items by creating an ISystemMenu object. This lets you change the styles and attributes of the system menu items and add or remove items. The following example uses an ISystemMenu object to add a **Window** submenu to the system menu and to move most of the existing system menu items to this submenu. Use the function IFrameWindow::setIcon to replace the graphic displayed by the system menu. Figure 6-3 displays these changes in the system menu.

Accessing the System Menu - menus\sysmenu\sysmenu.cpp

```
#include <iapp.hpp>
#include <iframe.hpp>
#include <isysmenu.hpp>

#define MI_WINDOW 0x100

void main()
{
IFrameWindow
  frame ("System Menu Example");

// Provide a wrapper for the system menu.
ISystemMenu
  systemMenu(&frame);

// We want the "Window" submenu to be first in the list.
// This is accomplished by creating a menu item and
// setting its index to 0.  We later call addSubmenu
// to change it from a normal menu item to a submenu.
IMenuItem windowSubmenu(MI_WINDOW);
windowSubmenu
  .setIndex(0)

// Because we are not using a resource file, we need to handle
// the different mnemonic indicators.
#ifdef IC_PM
  .setText("~Window");
#else
  .setText("&Window");
#endif

systemMenu
  .addItem(windowSubmenu, ISystemMenu::idPulldown)
  .addSubmenu(MI_WINDOW);
```

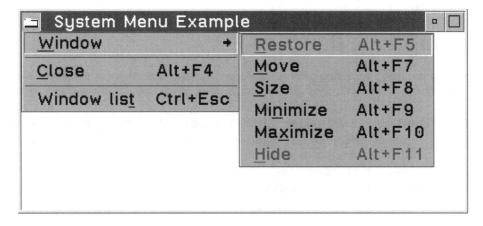

Figure 6-3. Altering a System Menu.

```
// Move some of the system menu items under
// the submenu we just added.
unsigned long itemsToMove[] =
    {ISystemMenu::idRestore, ISystemMenu::idMove,
     ISystemMenu::idSize, ISystemMenu::idMinimize,
     ISystemMenu::idMaximize, ISystemMenu::idHide};
for (int i=0; i<sizeof(itemsToMove)/sizeof(unsigned long); i++)
{
  // 1) Save the menu item data.
  // 2) Change the item's index to add it last.
  // 3) Delete the old menu item.
  // 4) Add the menu item under "Window".
  IMenuItem systemItem = systemMenu.menuItem(itemsToMove[i]);
  systemItem.setIndex(-1);
  systemMenu
    .deleteItem(itemsToMove[i])
    .addItem(systemItem, MI_WINDOW);
}

// Add an icon, set the focus, show the frame,
// and run the application.
frame
  .setIcon(ISystemPointerHandle(ISystemPointerHandle::folder))
  .setFocus()
  .show();

IApplication::current().run();
}
```

This example demonstrates how to do the following tasks:

- Access menu items in the system menu. The system menu provides a list of default items and the operating system enables and disables them automatically, depending on the state of the frame window. Each of these menu items has a unique identifier you can reference using constants defined in ISystemMenu or ICCONST.H. Table 6-1 lists the system menu items and their identifiers, values, and default behavior.

- Add an item as the first item in a menu by creating an IMenuItem object and then calling its setIndex function to set the index to 0.

Manipulating Menu Items

Most applications manipulate menu items at run time. The most commonly performed tasks include enabling and disabling menu items, adding and removing menu items, and checking and unchecking menu items.

IMenu provides functions you can use to change many common menu item characteristics. To use these functions, provide the menu item's numeric identifier. These functions include changing the text or bitmap using setText or setBitmap, adding or removing a check using checkItem or uncheckItem, enabling or disabling an item using enableItem or disableItem, and selecting an item using selectItem.

Use an IMenuItem object to query the state of a menu item (other than whether it is checked or enabled) or to alter other styles or attributes of the menu item.

Table 6-1. System Menu Items

Choice	OS/2 Constant	Windows Constant	Default Frame Processing
Restore	SC_RESTORE	SC_RESTORE	Restore is enabled when the window is maximized.
Move	SC_MOVE	SC_MOVE	Move is enabled if the window has a title-bar.
Size	SC_SIZE	SC_SIZE	Size is enabled if the window has size borders.
Minimize	SC_MINIMIZE	SC_MINIMIZE	Minimize is enabled unless the window is minimized.
Maximize	SC_MAXIMIZE	SC_MAXIMIZE	Maximize is enabled unless the window is maximized.
Hide	SC_HIDE	Not available	Hide is enabled if the window has a hideButton style.
Close	SC_CLOSE	SC_CLOSE	Close is always enabled.
Window List	SC_WINDOW	SC_TASKLIST	Window list is always enabled.

Using the Menu Item Class

IMenuItem is a "settings" type object that encapsulates information found in either the Windows MENUITEMINFO data structure or the OS/2 MENUITEM data structure. To change any menu item characteristic not directly supported by IMenu, build one of these objects. IMenu also returns an IMenuItem object when you query the characteristics of a menu item using IMenu::menuItem. You can then use the functions in IMenuItem to determine all characteristics of the menu item including the text or bitmap that it displays.

You can construct an IMenuItem object two ways. The first way is to provide the appropriate styles and attributes when you construct the IMenuItem object using the bitwise OR operator. When you construct IMenuItem objects in this way, do not combine any mutually exclusive choices. The second way is to let the styles and attributes default when constructing the IMenuItem object; then, use functions in IMenuItem to alter the menu item's characteristics. In fact, you must add several menu item characteristics, such as the text or bitmap and the index in its submenu, by using the IMenuItem functions.

You can use an IMenuItem object to add a new menu item or to change the characteristics of an existing menu item. To add an item, call IMenu::addItem with the IMenuItem object. To alter an existing menu item, call IMenu::setItem with the IMenuItem object.

Menu Item Styles

Menu item styles determine the type of menu item (how it looks and acts) and what kind of message it generates when a user selects it. Open Class Library represents these styles by IMenuItem::Style values. Table 6-2 lists the styles and functions you can use to alter or query

Table 6-2. IMenuItem Styles

Style Object	Related Functions	Definition and Description OS/2 / Windows Value
buttonSeparator	setLayout layOutType	Menu items with this style are buttons. They can only be selected with a mouse pointer. They are placed at the end of the menu, separated by a line. MIS_BUTTONSEPARATOR/not available
drawItem	setDrawItem isDrawItem	Menu items with this style must be drawn by the application with an IMenuDrawItemHandler. MIS_OWNERDRAW/MFT_OWNERDRAW
postHelp	setCommand commandType	Menu item with this style generate an IHelpEvent when selected. MIS_HELP/not available
postSystemCommand	setCommand commandType	Menu items with this style generate an ICommandEvent when selected. MIS_SYSCOMMAND/not available
separator	setSeperator isSeperator	Menu items with this style display a horizontal dividing line. MIS_SEPARATOR/MFT_SEPARATOR
split	setLayout layoutType	This style causes the menu items to display in a new row or column. MIS_BREAK/MFT_MENUBREAK
splitWithSeparator	setLayout layoutType	This style causes the menu items to display in a new row or column with a separator dividing it from the previous item. MIS_BREAKSEPARATOR/MFT_MENUBARBREAK
unavailable	setSelectable isSelectable	Users cannot move the cursor or select a menu item with this style. MIS_STATIC/MF_GRAYED

the style. It also includes a brief description of the style and its operating-system-equivalent value.

IMenuItem also provides a set of enumeration values you can use to alter the "layout" and "command type" styles using functions in IMenuItem. The setLayout and layoutType functions accept and return the normalLayout, splitLayout, splitWithSeparatorLayout, or buttonSeparatorLayout enumeration values. These constants are mutually exclusive and, with one exception, correspond to the styles you specify on construction. The value normalLayout corresponds to not specifying a layout style on construction. Similarly, the setCommand and commandType functions accept and return command, systemCommand, and `helpCommand`. The value `command` corresponds to not specifying a command type style on construction.

Menu Item Attributes

Menu item attributes determine how an item is displayed and whether a user can choose it. The default attribute is `IMenuItem::noAttribute`.

More so than with styles, it is the menu item's attribute values you need to change dynamically. For example, when you display an **Edit** menu, disable the **Paste** option if there is no valid data in the clipboard. Consequently, the `IMenu` functions directly support changing the commonly used attribute values. You can check, uncheck, disable, and enable a menu item by invoking the `checkItem`, `uncheckItem`, `disableItem`, and `enableItem` functions in `IMenu`. Because you typically want to change these menu item attributes dynamically, you see an example of this in the "Dynamic Submenus" topic later in this chapter. Table 6-3 lists the menu attributes and the functions you can use to set and query their values.

Table 6-3. IMenuItem Attributes

Attribute Object	Related Functions	Definition and Description OS/2 / Windows Value
checked	setChecked isChecked	Draws a check mark next to the item. MIA_CHECKED/MFS_CHECKED
disabled	setDisabled isDisabled	Disables the menu item, making it not selectable. MIA_DISABLED/MFS_DISABLED
framed	setFramed isFramed	Draws a frame around the menu item. MIA_FRAMED/not available
highlighted	setHighlighted isHighlighted	Displays the menu item with selected-state emphasis. MIA_HILITED/MFS_HILITED
noDismiss	setNoDismiss isNoDismiss	Menu items with this attribute, when selected, do not terminate the submenu. MIA_NODISMISS/not available

Adding and Removing Submenus

You have already seen how to load a menu from a resource file and how to dynamically construct a menu and add items to it. You can also combine these two strategies. For example, you can dynamically construct the menu and then load its submenus from a resource file. You load submenus using the function `IMenu::addSubmenu` by passing the resource identifier of a menu resource. The following example demonstrates this approach by modifying our `makePopupMenu` function to add the **Edit** and **Example** submenus from a resource, rather than creating them dynamically as we did previously. To do this requires that we add two new menu resources to our resource script file for the **Edit** and **Example** submenus.

Although we do not demonstrate it here, you can also remove a submenu by calling removeSubmenu with the identifier of the submenu item.

Submenu Resource Definition (Windows) - menus\addsubmn\addsubmn.rc

```
EDIT_MENU MENUEX
  BEGIN
    MENUITEM "&Undo  \t Ctrl+U",     MI_UNDO
    MENUITEM SEPARATOR
    MENUITEM "&Cut   \t Shift+Del", MI_CUT
    MENUITEM "Copy   \t Ctrl+Ins",  MI_COPY
    MENUITEM "&Paste \t Shift+Ins", MI_PASTE
  END

EXAMPLE_MENU MENUEX
  BEGIN
    MENUITEM "&Close",    SC_CLOSE
    MENUITEM "&Help",     MI_HELP
  END
```

Submenu Resource Definition (OS/2) - menus\addsubmn\addsubmn.rc

```
MENU EDIT_MENU
  BEGIN
    MENUITEM "~Undo  \t Ctrl+U",     MI_UNDO
    MENUITEM SEPARATOR
    MENUITEM "~Cut   \t Shift+Del", MI_CUT
    MENUITEM "Copy   \t Ctrl+Ins",  MI_COPY
    MENUITEM "~Paste \t Shift+Ins", MI_PASTE
  END

MENU EXAMPLE_MENU
  BEGIN
    MENUITEM "~Close",    SC_CLOSE,  MIS_SYSCOMMAND
    MENUITEM "~Help",     MI_HELP,   MIS_HELP
  END
```

Loading a Resource Submenu - menus\addsubmn\addsubmn.cpp

```
IBase::Boolean MenuHandler :: makePopUpMenu(IMenuEvent& event)
{
  // Create the pop-up menu.
  IPopUpMenu* popUp = new IPopUpMenu( event.dispatchingWindow(),
                                      POPUP_MENU );
  // Load the Edit and Example submenus from a resource file.
  (*popUp)
    .addText(MI_EDIT, MI_EDIT)
    .addSubmenu(MI_EDIT,    EDIT_MENU)
    .addText(MI_EXAMPLE, MI_EXAMPLE)
    .addSubmenu(MI_EXAMPLE, EXAMPLE_MENU)
    .setAutoDeleteObject();

  // Show the pop-up menu.
  (*popUp)
    .show(event.mousePosition());
  return true;
}
```

Using a Menu Cursor

Like other classes in Open Class Library, IMenu provides a nested Cursor class. You can use this class to iterate through the items in a menu or the submenu of a menu. There are also functions in IMenu to remove an item at a cursor location or add an IMenuItem object at the cursor location.

The following example iterates through the contents of the menu bar and displays the text associated with each menu item in a tree text container. Figure 6-4 displays the result of the program. We made one change to our resource script file for this example. Because the operating systems do not return a menu item definition when you create a separator using the MENUITEM SEPARATOR definition, we instead create a normal menu item with the style MFT_SEPARATOR/MIS_SEPARATOR. This approach also gives you the ability to change or remove this menu item because now it has its own identifier. We do not show the entire resource script file, but the separator definition in the Windows operating system is as follows:

```
MENUITEM "", MI_SEPARATOR, MFT_SEPARATOR
```

In the OS/2 operating system, it is as follows:

```
MENUITEM "", MI_SEPARATOR, MIS_SEPARATOR
```

Menu Cursor Example - menus\cursor\cursor.cpp

```cpp
#include <iapp.hpp>
#include <icnr.hpp>
#include <icnrobj.hpp>
#include <iframe.hpp>
#include <imenubar.hpp>
#include <imnitem.hpp>
#include "cursor.h"

void main()
{
IFrameWindow frame ("Menu Cursor Example");

// Add the menu bar from a resource file.
IMenuBar menuBar(MAIN_MENU, &frame);

// Create a container status area in the client.
IContainerControl
  statusArea(ID_STATUS, &frame, &frame);
statusArea
  .showTreeTextView()
  .setDeleteObjectsOnClose();

// Create menu cursors to display the menu bar contents
// in the client area.
IMenu::Cursor level1Cursor(menuBar);
for (level1Cursor.setToFirst();
     level1Cursor.isValid();
     level1Cursor.setToNext())
{
  IContainerObject* level1Object;
  IMenuItem level1Item =
            menuBar.elementAt(level1Cursor);
```

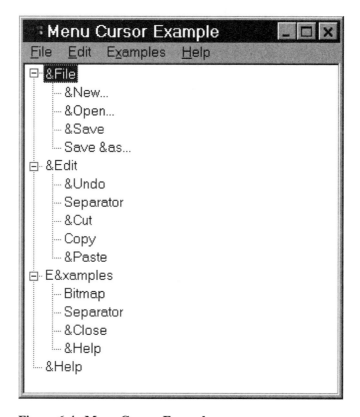

Figure 6-4. Menu Cursor Example.

```
if (level1Item.text().length()>0)
  level1Object = new IContainerObject(level1Item.text());
else if (level1Item.bitmap())
  level1Object = new IContainerObject("Bitmap");
else if (level1Item.isSeparator())
  level1Object = new IContainerObject("Separator");
else
  level1Object = new IContainerObject("Unknown");
statusArea.addObject(level1Object);

if(level1Item.submenuHandle())
{
  IMenu::Cursor level2Cursor(menuBar, level1Item.id());
  for (level2Cursor.setToFirst();
       level2Cursor.isValid();
       level2Cursor.setToNext())
  {
    IContainerObject* level2Object;
    IMenuItem level2Item =
                menuBar.elementAt(level2Cursor);
```

```
      if (level2Item.text().length()>0)
        level2Object = new IContainerObject(level2Item.text());
      else if (level2Item.bitmap())
        level2Object = new IContainerObject("Bitmap");
      else if (level2Item.isSeparator())
        level2Object = new IContainerObject("Separator");
      else
        level2Object = new IContainerObject("Unknown");
      statusArea.addObject(level2Object, level1Object);
    }
  }
}

// Set the focus and show the application.
frame
  .setClient(&statusArea)
  .setFocus()
  .show();

IApplication::current().run();
}
```

Responding to Menu Events

Menu windows send messages to their owners when significant events occur in the menu. For example, when a user selects an item, a command event is dispatched to the owner window. Open Class Library provides three general-purpose handler classes to deal with menu events: ICommandHandler, IMenuHandler, and IMenuDrawItemHandler. Usually, you must attach these handlers to the owner of the menu for them to function correctly. Table 6-4 lists and describes the event-handling functions of these handlers.

Processing Commands

To respond to a user choosing a menu item, create a class derived from ICommandHandler and override either the command or systemCommand function. Override systemCommand if the menu item is in the system menu or for the OS/2 operating system, if it has the IMenuItem::postSystemCommand (MIS_SYSCOMMAND) style. Identify the menu item selected by calling the function ICommandEvent::commandId. The text pop-up menu example earlier in this chapter demonstrates the typical use of a command handler. See Chapter 17, "Reusable Handlers," for more information on command handlers.

System Commands

Typically you do not need to process system commands. The value of using system commands is to achieve the default system behavior for actions such as close, move, or hide. You process system command events similar to the way you process regular application command events. However, to process the event you override ICommandHander::systemCommand instead of ICommandHander::command. If a user selects a menu item from the system menu and the numeric identifier of the item matches one of the system commands, the operating system intercepts the menu selection and invokes its default behavior. The constants listed in Table 6-1 are the menu item identifiers assigned to the predefined system menu items.

Table 6-4. Menu Event Handler Support

Handler Event Handler Function	Purpose
ICommandHandler::command ICommandHandler::systemCommand	Override either of these functions to respond to a user selecting a menu item. The event is sent to the systemCommand function if the item is in the system menu. In the OS/2 operating system, the event is also sent if the item has a postSystemCommand (MIS_SYSCOMMAND) style.
IMenuHandler::makePopUpMenu	Override this function to create and show a pop-up menu when a user presses mouse button 2, or the appropriate keys to request a pop-up menu.
IMenuHandler::menuSelected	Override this function to process the movement of the cursor to an item.
IMenuHandler::menuShowing IMenuHandler::menuEnded	Override these functions to process the showing or hiding of a submenu such as a pull-down or cascade menu.
IMenuDrawItemHandler::setSize IMenuDrawItemHandler::draw IMenuDrawItemHandler::highlight IMenuDrawItemHandler::unhighlight	Override these functions to draw an item in a submenu. The setSize function sets the size of the coordinates of the item. The draw function is called when the item must be redrawn completely. The highlight function is called when a user moves the cursor to an item. The unhighlight function is called when a user moves the cursor off the item.

Mimicking a Menu Command

You can code your application so that it emulates a user selecting a menu item. You do this with the IMenu::selectItem function. This function causes the menu window to post a command event to its owner, which dispatches either a command or systemCommand event to an ICommandHandler attached to the owner.

Dynamic Submenus

With Open Class Library, you can modify items in a submenu before it is shown and restore the changes after it is removed. Thus, you can alter your submenus before showing them without having to query the state of the items on the submenus to determine the changes you need to make. Prior to showing the submenus, assume that they are in a known state. You can achieve similar behavior by creating the submenus when you need them and deleting them after they are shown. However, having your program create the submenus once optimizes your use of submenus by minimizing their creation and destruction.

The ISubmenu class works with the menuShowing and menuEnded functions of IMenuHandler to handle dynamically created submenus. IMenuHandler calls its menuShowing function just before a submenu is displayed. It provides an ISubmenu object that you can use to alter the items. If your menuShowing function returns true, any changes you made with the ISubmenu object will be undone when the menu is dismissed and IMenuHandler calls its menuEnded function. The following code shows how to use submenus to disable the items dynamically on the **Edit** submenu when they are not valid:

Using ISubmenu Objects - menus\dynsubmn\dynsubmn.cpp

```
#include <iapp.hpp>
#include <icmdhdr.hpp>
#include <iframe.hpp>
#include <imenuhdr.hpp>
#include <imle.hpp>
#include <isubmenu.hpp>
#include "dynsubmn.h"

// Menu handler dynamically modifies a drop-down menu.
class MenuHandler : public IMenuHandler
{
public:
  MenuHandler (IMultiLineEdit& editWnd)
    : editWindow(editWnd) {}

protected:
virtual Boolean
  menuShowing    ( IMenuEvent& menuEvent,
                   ISubmenu&   submenuAboutToShow );

private:
IMultiLineEdit
 &editWindow;
};

// Command handler captures menu commands.
class CommandHandler : public ICommandHandler
{
public:
  CommandHandler ( IMultiLineEdit& status)
            : aStatus(status) {}

protected:
virtual Boolean
  command            ( ICommandEvent& event );

private:
IMultiLineEdit
 &aStatus;
};

void main()
{
// Create a frame window with a menu bar
// loaded from a resource file.
IFrameWindow
  frame( "Pop-Up Menu Example", MAIN_MENU,
         IFrameWindow::defaultStyle() | IFrameWindow::menuBar );

// Create an edit area in the client and a
// command handler to write in it.
IMultiLineEdit
  editArea(ID_EDIT, &frame, &frame);
CommandHandler
  commandHandler(editArea);

// Add the command handler to the frame so
// that it handles the menu messages sent.
commandHandler
  .handleEventsFor(&frame);
```

```
// Add a menu handler to dynamically alter the menu.
MenuHandler
   editMenuHandler(editArea);
editMenuHandler.handleEventsFor(&frame);

// Set the focus and show the application.
editArea.setFocus();
frame
   .setClient(&editArea)
   .show();
IApplication::current().run();
}

IBase::Boolean MenuHandler::menuShowing( IMenuEvent& event,
                                         ISubmenu&   submenu )
{
   // Enable and disable the appropriate "Edit" flags.
   Boolean modified = false;
   if(submenu.id() == MI_EDIT)
   {
      if(!editWindow.hasSelectedText())
      {
         submenu.disableItem(MI_COPY);
         submenu.disableItem(MI_CUT);
         modified = true;
      }
      if (!editWindow.isWriteable())
      {
         submenu.disableItem(MI_CUT);
         submenu.disableItem(MI_PASTE);
         submenu.disableItem(MI_READONLY);
         modified = true;
      }
      else
      {
         submenu.disableItem(MI_READWRITE);
         modified = true;
      }
      if(!editWindow.clipboardHasTextFormat())
      {
         submenu.disableItem(MI_PASTE);
         modified = true;
      }
   }
   return modified;
}
```

Drawing a Custom Menu Item

You can customize the appearance of a menu item by setting the IMenuItem::drawItem (MFT_OWNERDRAW/MIS_OWNERDRAW) style for the item. If you set this style, the menu sends messages to its owner to determine the size of the item and to paint, highlight, and unhighlight the item. IMenuDrawItemHandler provides event-handling functions to handle these events. The IMenuDrawItemHandler object calls its setSize function to determine the size of the menu item, its draw function to paint the item, its highlight function to draw highlight emphasis, and its unhighlight function to remove highlight emphasis. Attach the handler to the owner of the menu with the menu item that needs custom drawing.

The following example demonstrates how to draw a customized menu item, **Draw Item**, which has a larger font than normal. The item also turns red when a user selects it.

Drawing a Custom Menu - menus\drawmenu\drawmenu.cpp

```cpp
#include <iapp.hpp>
#include <icmdhdr.hpp>
#include <iframe.hpp>
#include <istattxt.hpp>
#include <ifont.hpp>
#include <imenubar.hpp>
#include <imndihdr.hpp>
#include <irect.hpp>
#include <istring.hpp>
#include <igrafctx.hpp>
#include <igstring.hpp>
#include "drawmenu.h"

// Menu handler captures draw item requests.
class MenuDrawHandler : public IMenuDrawItemHandler
{
public:
  MenuDrawHandler ()
      : font("Tms Rmn", 24) {}

protected:
virtual Boolean
  setSize       ( IMenuDrawItemEvent& event,
                  ISize&              newSize),
  draw          ( IMenuDrawItemEvent& event,
                  DrawFlag&           flag),
  highlight     ( IMenuDrawItemEvent& event),
  unhighlight   ( IMenuDrawItemEvent& event),
  drawText      ( IMenuDrawItemEvent& event,
                  Boolean             highlight);

private:
IFont
  font;
};

// Command handler captures menu commands.
class CommandHandler : public ICommandHandler
{
public:
  CommandHandler ( IStaticText& status)
          : aStatus(status)   {}

protected:
virtual Boolean
  command     ( ICommandEvent& event );

private:
IStaticText
 &aStatus;
};

void main()
{
IFrameWindow
  frame ("Draw Item Example");

// Add the menu bar from a resource file.
IMenuBar
  menuBar(MAIN_MENU, &frame);
// Associate a bitmap resource with the menu item.
menuBar.setBitmap(MI_BITMAP, MI_BITMAP);

// Change a menu item to the drawItem style.
IMenuItem drawItem = menuBar.menuItem(MI_DRAWITEM);
drawItem.setDrawItem();
menuBar.setItem(drawItem);
```

```
// Create a status area in the client and a
// command handler to write in it.  Add the
// command handler to the frame to handle
// menu commands.
IStaticText
  statusArea(ID_STATUS, &frame, &frame);
CommandHandler
  commandHandler(statusArea);
commandHandler
  .handleEventsFor(&frame);

// Add a MenuDrawHandler to the frame.
MenuDrawHandler
  drawHandler;
drawHandler
  .handleEventsFor(&frame);

// Set the focus and show the application.
frame
  .setClient(&statusArea)
  .setFocus()
  .show();
IApplication::current().run();
}

IBase::Boolean MenuDrawHandler :: setSize(IMenuDrawItemEvent& event,
                                          ISize& newSize)
{
  // Because text is unknown, set menu item width large
  // enough for 5 Ws and height to character height plus a pad.
  newSize.setWidth(font.textWidth("WWWWW"))
         .setHeight(font.maxCharHeight()+5);
  return true;
}

IBase::Boolean MenuDrawHandler :: highlight(IMenuDrawItemEvent& event)
{
   return drawText(event, true);
}

IBase::Boolean MenuDrawHandler :: unhighlight(IMenuDrawItemEvent& event)
{
   return drawText(event, false);
}

IBase::Boolean MenuDrawHandler :: draw(IMenuDrawItemEvent& event,
DrawFlag& flag)
{
   return drawText(event, false);
}
IBase::Boolean MenuDrawHandler :: drawText(IMenuDrawItemEvent& event,
                                           Boolean highlight)
{
  // This routine is based on the drawing being for text items
  // whose text is contained in a STRINGTABLE resource with an
  // ID that is the same as the item ID.
  IString str = IApplication::current().userResourceLibrary()
               .loadString(event.itemId());
  // Add pad to the left of the item text.
  str = " "+str;

  // Get the point to draw at, vertically center it, and provide
  // a wrapper for the graphic context for drawing use.
  IPoint point( event.itemRect().minXMinY() );
  point.setY(point.y() + 2);
  IGraphicContext gc(event.itemPresSpaceHandle());
```

```
  // If we highlight this, change the color to red.
  if (highlight)
    gc.setPenColor( IColor::red );

  // Otherwise, use the default menu text color.
  else
    gc.setPenColor(IGUIColor(IGUIColor::menuText));

  // Create a graphic string starting at the point with the
  // text and font requested.
  IGString text( str, point, font );
  text->drawOn( gc );

  return true;
}
IBase::Boolean CommandHandler::command( ICommandEvent& event )
{
  switch(event.commandId())
  {
    {
      try {
       aStatus.setText(event.commandId());
      } catch (...) {}
      return true;
    }
  }
  return false;
}
```

Figure 6-5 displays the results of this program.

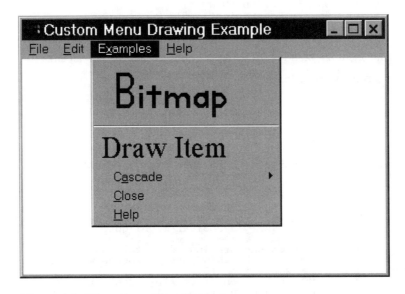

Figure 6-5. Menu Draw Item Example.

Chapter 7

Controls

- Describes the characteristics of all control classes in Open Class Library
- Describes the IControl class
- Read Chapter 4 before reading this chapter.
- Chapters 5, 8-18, and 26 cover related material.

Generally, a *control* is a specialized window—one that provides a well-defined and general-purpose interface, which makes it a highly reusable visual component. Both the OS/2 and Windows operating systems provide a robust set of controls, ranging from simple text prompts to complex controls for implementing notebooks and containers. These controls are the building blocks for constructing graphical user interfaces.

Open Class Library has control classes that you can use to exploit the controls that the operating system provides. With these classes, you can use these controls in an object-oriented manner in your applications. Figure 3-4 shows the hierarchy of control classes that Open Class Library provides. IControl is the base control class, and derives from IWindow.

These control classes represent all but a few of the public controls that the Windows and OS/2 operating systems supply. Table 7-1 shows the control that corresponds to each class derived from IControl. Controls that are not represented by an IControl class appear at the end of the table. The table lists the operating system controls in terms of their *window class names*, which is a precise way of identifying a type of control and its window procedure, class styles, and other associated attributes. Because Open Class Library represents some operating system controls with more than one class, a particular window style used by the control becomes the determining factor. These styles appear in parentheses in the table.

Open Class Library also goes beyond what the operating system provides by supplying additional control classes. These classes provide functionality you would not otherwise have without a substantial amount of work. Table 7-1 also identifies these classes by listing them with unmatched controls on one or both operating systems. For example, ICircularSlider has no corresponding control in the Windows operating system; IToolBar has no match in the OS/2 operating system; and IMultiCellCanvas is unique to both.

In the Windows operating system, IContainerControl, INotebook, IProgressIndicator, ISlider, INumericSpinButton, and ITextSpinButton also give you a choice. You can use these classes to create controls with a Windows look and feel, or controls that preserve the functionality, as well as the look and feel, of controls that the OS/2 operating system provides.

Table 7-1 (Part 1 of 3). Mapping of Open Class Library to Operating System Controls

Open Class Library Class	Operating System Window Class Name	
	Windows Platform	**OS/2 Platform**
I3StateCheckBox	Button (BS_3STATE, BS_AUTO3STATE)	WC_BUTTON (BS_3STATE, BS_AUTO3STATE)
IAnimatedButton	None	Like WC_GRAPHICBUTTON
IBitmapControl	Static (SS_BITMAP)	WC_STATIC (SS_BITMAP)
ICanvas	None	None
ICheckBox	Button (BS_CHECKBOX, BS_AUTOCHECKBOX)	WC_BUTTON (BS_CHECKBOX, BS_AUTOCHECKBOX)
ICircularSlider	None	WC_CIRCULARSLIDER
ICollectionViewComboBox	Like ComboBox	Like WC_COMBOBOX
ICollectionViewListBox	Like ListBox	Like WC_LISTBOX
IComboBox	ComboBox	WC_COMBOBOX
IContainerControl	SysListView32, SysTreeView32	WC_CONTAINER
ICustomButton	Button (BS_OWNERDRAW)	WC_BUTTON (BS_USERBUTTON)
IDrawingCanvas	None	None
IEntryField	Edit (without ES_MULTILINE)	WC_ENTRYFIELD
IFlyText	tooltips_class32	None
IGraphicPushButton	Like Button (BS_OWNERDRAW)	Like WC_BUTTON (BS_BITMAP, BS_ICON)
IGroupBox	Button (BS_GROUPBOX)	WC_STATIC (SS_GROUPBOX)
IIconControl	Static (SS_ICON)	WC_STATIC (SS_ICON, SS_SYSICON)
IInfoArea	Like msctls_statusbar32	None
IListBox	ListBox	WC_LISTBOX
IMMPlayerPanel	None	None
IMultiCellCanvas	None	None
IMultiLineEdit	Edit (ES_MULTILINE)	WC_MLE

Table 7-1 (Part 2 of 3). Mapping of Open Class Library to Operating System Controls

Open Class Library Class	Operating System Window Class Name	
	Windows Platform	**OS/2 Platform**
INotebook	Like a property sheet (but implemented with SysTabControl32)	WC_NOTEBOOK
INumericSpinButton	Combination of Edit and msctls_updown32	WC_SPINBUTTON
IOutlineBox	Static (SS_BLACKFRAME, SS_GRAYFRAME, SS_WHITEFRAME)	WC_STATIC (SS_FGNDFRAME, SS_HALFTONEFRAME, SS_BKGNDFRAME)
IProgressIndicator	Like msctls_progress32 (but implemented with msctls_trackbar32)	WC_SLIDER (SLS_READONLY)
IPushButton	Button (BS_PUSHBUTTON, BS_DEFPUSHBUTTON)	WC_BUTTON (BS_PUSHBUTTON, BS_DEFAULT)
IRadioButton	Button (BS_RADIOBUTTON, BS_AUTORADIOBUTTON)	WC_BUTTON (BS_RADIOBUTTON, BS_AUTORADIOBUTTON)
IScrollBar	ScrollBar	WC_SCROLLBAR
ISetCanvas	None	None
ISlider	msctls_trackbar32	WC_SLIDER (not SLS_READONLY)
ISplitCanvas	None	None
IStaticText	Static	WC_STATIC (SS_TEXT, SS_BKGNDRECT)
ITextSpinButton	Combination of Edit and msctls_updown32	WC_SPINBUTTON
ITitle	None	WC_TITLEBAR
IToolBar	Like ToolbarWindow32	None
IToolBarButton	Like the TBBUTTON structure passed to a ToolbarWindow32 control	None
IToolBarContainer	None	None
IView	None	None
IViewPort	None	None

Table 7-1 (Part 3 of 3). Mapping of Open Class Library to Operating System Controls

Open Class Library Class	Operating System Window Class Name	
	Windows Platform	**OS/2 Platform**
None	SysAnimate32	N/A
None	msctls_hotkey32	N/A
None	RichEdit	N/A
None	SysHeader32	N/A
None	N/A	WC_PENxxx
None	N/A	WC_VALUESET

For the former, the classes use controls that the operating system provides; for the latter, they use controls that Open Class Library provides. The chapters describing these classes list the trade-offs involved.

Although the control classes of Open Class Library are diverse, as a group they share fundamental design points. This chapter describes characteristics that apply to many or all of these control classes. Subsequent chapters describe usage considerations that are specific to a particular control class. We refer to those chapters as appropriate.

In this and following chapters, the term "window" includes controls.

Constructors

Almost all control classes provide two types of constructors: one that creates an operating system window and one that does not. Both types create a C++ object that represents an operating system window. Whether the constructor then creates the window itself or not (because the window already exists), differentiates the two types of constructors.

To understand the difference between the control constructors, you must distinguish between the lifetime of an operating system window and its corresponding C++ object. Whereas the lifetime of the two may be the same (you can make them the same using techniques described in Chapter 4, "Windows, Handlers, and Events"), they may also have independent lifetimes.

This discussion of constructors does not include the base control classes: `IControl`, `ITextControl`, `IButton`, and `ISettingButton`, `IBaseComboBox`, and `IBaseSpinButton`. You cannot construct objects of these classes because they have protected constructors or a pure virtual function. As a result, their constructors need little discussion. The purpose of these classes is to provide a common interface for their derived classes, common implementation for derived classes, or both.

Note that you do not need to construct C++ objects for all controls on a dialog box or a frame window displayed using APIs of the operating system. You only need an IWindow object to call C++ functions for the control (for example, to set or query its text) or to modify the behavior of the control by attaching an event handler to its C++ object.

Constructor That Creates an Operating System Window

The first type of constructor creates an operating system window. By default, the window is destroyed when the C++ object is destructed. This type of constructor is perhaps the type you use most often. Because of the number of arguments it supports, this type of constructor is also the most complex. Some arguments are optional, however, because they have default values. Generally, the samples in this book take advantage of these default values.

Following is the IEntryField constructor that creates an operating system window:

```
IEntryField ( unsigned long     windowIdentifier,
              IWindow*          parent,
              IWindow*          owner,
              const IRectangle& initial = IRectangle(),
              const Style&      style = defaultStyle() );
```

This IEntryField constructor uses the same arguments that all constructors of this type typically use. Although Chapter 4, "Windows, Handlers, and Events," covers the basics for these standard arguments, you find more information in the following topics.

Window Identifier

The window identifier argument is the identifier for the operating system window you create with this constructor. Although this argument is of type unsigned long, for portability purposes only use values in the range from 0 through 65535 (0xFFFF). For example, various Win32s and OS/2 APIs honor only the low-order word (two bytes) of this double-word (four-byte) value.

Despite its name, however, a window identifier does not uniquely identify a window; a window handle does this. Neither Open Class Library nor the operating system prevents you from assigning the same window identifier to multiple windows.

The following scenarios require that a window be uniquely identified by the combination of its window identifier and parent window or its window identifier and owner window:

- You call IWindow::windowWithParent, IWindow::handleWithParent, IWindow::windowWithOwner, the Windows API GetDlgItem, or the OS/2 API WinWindowFromID to locate the window.

- The window has an event handler attached to it or its owner window, and the handler processes an IControlEvent object or an object of a class derived from IControlEvent. Examples of such handlers are ISelectHandler, IPageHandler, and ICnrDrawHandler.

- The window is a scroll bar with an IScrollHandler attached to its owner window.

- You call the second type of control constructor that requires a parent window and window identifier.

Additionally, the following scenarios require that a window be uniquely identified by its window identifier:

- You want to display unique contextual help information for a control using help tables. Because a help table maps window identifiers to help panel identifiers, the identifiers of all windows that accept input focus, such as entry fields and buttons, must be unique across a frame window. If windows that accept input focus were to have the same window identifier, they would display identical contextual help information.

  As an alternative, however, you can assign a contextual help panel to a window using the `IWindow::setHelpId` function. Help support through this function has no dependencies on window identifiers, so a window does not require a unique identifier to display unique contextual help. See Chapter 23, "Using Help," for details on providing help for your application.

- You are displaying fly-over help for individual elements of a window. Fly-over help uses the identifier of the window underneath the mouse pointer to determine the appropriate help string to display.

Nevertheless, the safest way to program window identifiers is to use a unique one for each window that you create in a given frame window. Assign the value `IC_FRAME_CLIENT_ID`, which is defined in `ICCONST.H`, to all client windows and avoid using it for anything other than a client window. Call `IFrameWindow::setClient` to make a window the client window of the frame. If the window identifier is not already `IC_FRAME_CLIENT_ID`, setClient changes it to `IC_FRAME_CLIENT_ID`. As a result, any code that identifies the client window based on its window identifier must use the `IC_FRAME_CLIENT_ID` value to work correctly. Thus, the reason for assigning `IC_FRAME_CLIENT_ID` to all client windows is programming clarity. See Chapter 5, "Frame Window Basics," for more details.

To assign unique window identifiers, avoid using values reserved by the operating system and Open Class Library.

In the OS/2 operating system, for example, avoid using window identifiers reserved by the operating system for special child windows of a frame window. These reserved identifiers range from 0x8002 through 0x8013, and they are the `FID_*` values defined in the `PMWIN.H` file of the Developer's Toolkit for OS/2. The OS/2 operating system uses these values as the window identifiers for standard frame components, which it creates based on the frame window styles you specify. One example is the title bar, which gets a window identifier value of `FID_TITLEBAR`. `FID_CLIENT` is an exception to this rule, however, which is equivalent to the `IC_FRAME_CLIENT_ID` value discussed previously.

The OS/2 operating system has other reserved window identifiers that it uses with certain controls. For example, `PMWIN.H` also contains `CBID_*` values for the windows comprising a combination box control. These values are 0x029A and 0x029B. Additionally, `PMSTDDLG.H` of the Developer's Toolkit for OS/2 contains `CID_*` values for the windows comprising a container control. These values range from 0x7FF0 through 0x7FFA.

Open Class Library also reserves specific window identifiers. These are defined in ICCONST.H, and all have values greater than IC_ID_BASE (0x7000). For example, an IViewPort object creates child windows with window identifiers of IC_VIEWPORT_HORZSCROLLBAR, IC_VIEWPORT_VERTSCROLLBAR, and IC_VIEWPORT_VIEWRECTANGLE.

Other window identifiers double as command identifiers. For example, the command that a push button, graphic push button, custom button, or tool bar button generates has the same identifier as the button's window identifier. Therefore, avoid using these command identifiers as window identifiers for any of these buttons unless you intend them to generate that command.

Parent Window

The parent window argument identifies the parent window of the control you are constructing. This argument is of type IWindow*. The new control becomes a child window of this parent window. Chapter 4, "Windows, Handlers, and Events," describes the most important roles of a parent window.

All control windows must have a parent window. If you specify no parent window (by using an IWindow* value of 0), the control constructor you call typically throws an IInvalidParameter exception. Although you can use the desktop window as the parent of a control by using the value returned by IWindow::desktopWindow, this is not a typical usage.

You must construct the parent window before constructing its child windows. Otherwise, your application might fail with a protection exception. If you have a class that includes window objects as data members of a class, ensure that you list a parent window before any of its child windows in the class declaration. The order in which data members appear in a class declaration determines the order in which they are constructed, not their order in the initialization list of a constructor. Incorrectly ordering window objects in a class declaration can cause your application to fail.

Open Class Library also uses the parent window chain for processing help requests and accelerator keys. It passes unprocessed help requests to the parent window. As a result, a parent window can handle help requests for its child windows. For example, if users press the F1 key from a child window with no contextual help, a canvas displays the contextual help set using IWindow::setHelpId. Similarly, a keystroke in an entry field can get translated into a command or help request by an accelerator table assigned to a canvas or frame window in the entry field's parent window chain. See Chapter 6, "Menus and Keyboard Accelerators," for more information on accelerator tables.

It is sometimes useful to use an object window as a parent window. An object window hides its child windows, and thus prevents users from clicking on them with the mouse or tabbing to them with the keyboard. Calling the function IWindow::objectWindow returns a standard object window. Chapter 4, "Windows, Handlers, and Events," provides more details on object windows.

Owner Window

The owner window argument identifies the owner window of the control you are constructing. This argument is of type IWindow*. Generally, you use a control's parent window for its owner window, but you can create a control without an owner window. To do this, use a value of 0 to specify no owner. Using the value returned by IWindow::desktopWindow or IWindow::objectWindow is basically equivalent to using no owner, but not as efficient. As is the case with a parent window, you must construct an owner window before constructing any of the windows it owns.

The owner window for a control has three main uses. First, a window receives notification events from controls it owns. These notification events include WM_CONTROL, WM_COMMAND, WM_SYSCOMMAND, WM_MEASUREITEM, WM_DRAWITEM, WM_HSCROLL, and WM_VSCROLL. Second, a window receives keyboard and mouse events not processed by the controls it owns. Third, controls inherit colors and fonts from their owner windows. The "Colors and Fonts" topic later in this chapter discusses this.

The Windows operating system does not truly allow you to specify an owner window; instead, it assigns an owner window based on the parent window you choose. See Chapter 4, "Windows, Handlers, and Events," for more details. Open Class Library tries to simulate this behavior for the owner window you specify. However, it does not call event handlers to process owner notifications if the parent window does not have an IWindow representing it. This does not happen because the event-handling framework of Open Class Library does not otherwise see the message received by the true owner window (the parent window of the control). As a result, it cannot reroute the message back to the control or the owner window you specify.

Some control classes have additional considerations for either their owner windows or for their child windows. These are discussed in the chapters describing those classes. Also, some features, such as changing the mouse pointer using IFrameWindow::setMousePointer and fly-over help, may not work properly for controls whose owner chains do not lead to frame windows.

Size and Position

The size and position argument allows you to provide an explicit size and position for the window you are creating. This optional argument is of type const IRectangle&. Chapter 26, "Data Types," further describes the IRectangle class. Both the position and size values are treated as *pels* or *pixels*, which is the smallest unit addressable on a display screen. Restrict the dimensions of the size to values from 0 through 65535.

Typically, a control has an optimal size for painting. If the control is too big, it does not effectively use its entire rectangle. If too small, the contents of the control get clipped. For example, a static text control may not be able to display all of its text in a small rectangle.

This argument defaults to a zero-sized rectangle. This default value is only useful if you place the window into a context where it is sized by its parent window. In this case, any size and position value you specify here is ignored as well.

A child window is sized by its parent window in the following situations:

- When it is the client window

- When it is a frame extension of a frame window

- When it is a child window of most canvases

- In some cases, when you add it as a page window of a notebook.

Note that if you use the default rectangle and your window is not automatically sized, your window has no size and therefore is not visible. You can find further details in Chapter 5, "Frame Window Basics," Chapter 14, "Notebook Control," and Chapter 15, "Canvases."

Style

The style argument represents configuration options for the behavior or appearance of the control you are constructing. This optional argument is of type const Style&, where Style is a class nested within the declaration of the control class you are constructing. Chapter 26, "Data Types," further describes these Style classes that derive from the IBitFlag class.

If you are already familiar with Windows or OS/2 programming, you can use the Style classes to retain the programming style of creating controls with specific window styles. Each control class provides a set of style values that you can combine using the bitwise OR operator. This is similar to how you bitwise OR together Windows or OS/2 styles when calling the CreateWindowEx or WinCreateWindow APIs. You can also combine control-specific styles with IWindow::Style values, which are described in Chapter 4, "Windows, Handlers, and Events." Generally, you can also combine Style values with the IControl::tabStop and IControl::group styles, which we describe later in this chapter.

The Style classes also identify syntactic errors at compile time. Because they provide type safety, you cannot, for example, specify an IEntryField::Style value when constructing an IRadioButton object. You also receive a compiler error if you mistake the logical OR operator for the bitwise OR operator. For example, the following expression does not compile:

```
IControl::tabStop || IControl::group  // Error--Logical OR.
```

This correct expression does:

```
IControl::tabStop | IControl::group  // OK--Bitwise OR.
```

Semantic errors, however, are only identified at run time. This means a control constructor throws an exception when it detects a combination of incompatible styles. For example, the IEntryField class throws an exception if you specify the following style:

```
IEntryField::centerAlign | IEntryField::rightAlign
```

You cannot align the text contents of an entry field in two different directions like this. The semantics do not make sense.

Each control class also provides the static functions, defaultStyle and setDefaultStyle. These functions query and set the default style that the class uses. By calling setDefaultStyle, you can replace the default style value that Open Class Library provides. If you never call setDefaultStyle, defaultStyle returns the static classDefaultStyle object supplied by the control class. Even after calling `setDefaultStyle`, you can still retrieve the original default value by using `classDefaultStyle`.

Looking at the `IEntryField` constructor declaration again, you see that the default value for the constructor's style argument is the value returned by `IEntryField::defaultStyle`. This is the only way that the control classes use the `defaultStyle` function. As a result, the value it returns is only used when a window is created. Changing the default style by calling the `setDefaultStyle` function does not affect existing windows. Because any code in your application can call `setDefaultStyle` (which changes the default style used by subsequent calls to the constructor), you need to notify others who are developing your application about any call you make to this function. In this way, everyone can evaluate the impact on any code that uses the default style.

Instead of using `Style` classes when you construct a window object, you can construct your window objects using default styles and then call member functions to change the settings of individual styles. The control classes provide public member functions to query and change the settings of most styles.

Although you cannot consider the use of the `Style` classes to be totally safe from errors (remember that some style combinations cause errors that you see only at run time), you can rely on the member functions to disallow the same semantic errors at compile time. Examples of these style functions are `alignment` and `setAlignment` of `IEntryField`. `setAlignment` only accepts an enumeration that represents a valid alignment. You cannot specify a semantically incorrect value.

Even if you prefer the error-safe member functions to styles, you still cannot abandon the use of styles entirely. You can only set the behavior of some controls through styles when you create them. As an example, you cannot change the type of a combination box control after you have created the window. Thus, if you do not want the default type of combination box (specified by the style `IBaseComboBox::simpleType`), you must specify the `IBaseComboBox` style `dropDownType` or `readOnlyDropDownType` when you create the window.

Constructors That Represent an Existing Window

This type of constructor associates a C++ object with an existing window. It does not create a new operating system window. As a result, you can consider this type of constructor as a *wrapper* for a control because it adds a C++ interface around the window without altering it. Unlike the other type of constructor, the window is not destroyed by default when you delete its C++ object. Because the C++ object did not create the window, it does not destroy it either.

If you mistakenly use the other type of constructor to represent an existing window, you create a second window and interact with that new window, not the original window. If you create the new window so that it is not visible (perhaps it has no size because you used the default `IRectangle` value), you have no visual indication of what is wrong.

You have two ways to identify an existing window: by the combination of its window identifier and parent window or by its window handle. Thus, most control classes supply two constructors for providing a wrapper for an existing window.

Note that this type of constructor has restrictions on its use. First, you cannot create more than one C++ object for any window. We discuss this further in the "Copying Controls" topic in this chapter.

Second, ensure you match the type of the operating system window to the appropriate window class of Open Class Library. For example, avoid constructing an INotebook object for a list box control; instead, construct an IListBox object. Otherwise, unpredictable results can occur.

Third, for any window that you want to provide a wrapper, your process, or application, must have created it. If this is not the case, the startHandlingEventsFor function of IWindow throws an exception.

Window Identifier and Parent Window

You can usually identify a control by its window identifier and parent window. To use this constructor successfully, ensure that only one child window of the specified parent has that window identifier. Otherwise, unpredictable results can occur. The following is the corresponding constructor for IEntryField:

```
IEntryField ( unsigned long windowIdentifier,
              IWindow*       parent );
```

Use this type of constructor to provide a wrapper for controls on a dialog box because the window identifiers of controls on a dialog are usually readily available. However, you don't have to provide a wrapper for all child controls of a dialog box. You can use IFrameWindow to display a dialog box without constructing an object for any of its controls.

The parent window you pass to this constructor does not have to be a frame window; so, you can also use this constructor in other situations. For example, consider the spin button control, which is a *composite control* with a child entry field component. A composite control is one composed of more than one operating system window. You can construct an IEntryField object as a wrapper for the child entry field by specifying the INumericSpinButton or ITextSpinButton as the parent window and the window identifier of the entry field. The entry field has the same window identifier as the spin button.

The following is an example of using this type of constructor. It includes a test to check if the window is already represented by a C++ window object. In this case, spin is an ITextSpinButton object. If you try to provide a wrapper for a window that already has an IWindow object constructed for it, the constructor you call throws an IInvalidParameter exception.

Entry Field of a Spin Button - controls\ctors\ctors.cpp

```
// Construct an IEntryField for the existing window, the
// child window of the spin button.  Find it based on its
// window identifier after first checking for an existing
// IWindow object.
IEntryField
 *spinEF = (IEntryField*)
           IWindow::windowWithParent( spin.id(), &spin );
```

```
if ( ! spinEF )
{  // Because the window object does not exist,
   // construct a new one.
   spinEF = new IEntryField( spin.id(), &spin );
   spinEF->setAutoDeleteObject( true );
}

if ( spinEF )
{  // Now change its background color.
   // Note: For a window to retain a color change on the
   // Windows operating system, Open Class Library requires
   // that an IWindow object exist for the window for as long
   // as the color change is needed.  As a result, we keep
   // the IEntryField wrapper until the edit control is
   // destroyed.  We let Open Class Library manage the
   // deletion of the IEntryField* for us.
   // For the OS/2 operating system, we could simply delete
   // the IEntryField* immediately after changing the edit
   // control's color.
   spinEF->setBackgroundColor( IColor::cyan );
}
```

Window Handle

A window is uniquely identified by its window handle. Following is the constructor for
`IEntryField` that takes a window handle:

```
IEntryField ( const IWindowHandle& handle );
```

You might use this constructor when using Open Class Library to manipulate an operating
system window created outside of Open Class Library. You can also use this constructor to
create an `IWindow` object from a window handle returned by the class `IWindow::ChildCursor`.

Test for an existing C++ window object before you call this type of constructor by calling the
static `IWindow::windowWithHandle` function. This test is shown in the following code. It
provides a wrapper for the child entry field portion of a combination box control. We get the
window handle of the entry field by using its window identifier, 0x03E9 for the Windows
operating system (except for a `CBS_DROPDOWNLIST` type combination box, which has no child
entry field) and 0x029B for the OS/2 operating system (this is the value of `CBID_EDIT`, as
defined in `PMWIN.H`). If you try to provide a wrapper for a window that already has an `IWindow`
object constructed for it, the constructor you call throws an `IInvalidParameter` exception.

Entry Field of a Combination Box - controls\ctors\ctors.cpp

```
// Construct an IEntryField for the existing window, the
// child entry field of the combo box.  Find it based on its
// window handle after first checking for an existing
// IWindow object.
IEntryField
 *comboEF = 0;
IWindowHandle comboEFHwnd =
  IWindow::handleWithParent( ID_COMBOBOX_EF, combo.handle() );
if ( comboEFHwnd )
{
   // Note: In the Windows operating system, CBS_DROPDOWNLIST
   //type of combo boxes do not have a child entry field.
   comboEF = (IEntryField*)
            IWindow::windowWithHandle( comboEFHwnd );
   if ( ! comboEF )
```

```
    {  // Because the window object does not exist,
       // Construct a new one.
       comboEF = new IEntryField( comboEFHwnd );
       comboEF->setAutoDeleteObject( true );
    }
}                   // Else use the existing window object.

if ( comboEF )
{  // Now change its background color.
   // Note: For a window to retain a color change on the
   // Windows operating system, Open Class Library requires
   // that an IWindow object exist for the window for as long
   // as the color change is needed.  As a result, we keep
   // the IEntryField wrapper until the edit control is
   // destroyed.  We let Open Class Library manage the
   // deletion of the IEntryField* for us.
   // For the OS/2 operating system, we could simply delete
   // the IEntryField* immediately after changing the edit
   // control's color.
   comboEF->setBackgroundColor( IColor( 255, 127, 0 ) );
}
```

Copying Controls

You cannot create more than one object from the IWindow hierarchy for the same operating system window.   The IWindow::startHandlingEvents function, called from all window constructors, checks to ensure that a window is not already represented by another IWindow object.

Related to this, all classes derived from IWindow have a private copy constructor and assignment operator. Because these functions are inaccessible, you can neither duplicate an IWindow object by constructing it from another IWindow object nor by using operator=. One consequence is that you cannot create a collection of window objects using the collection classes of Open Class Library. You can, however, create a collection of pointers to window objects because you can freely copy pointers that reference the same window object.

Colors and Fonts

Both the Windows and OS/2 desktops enable users to configure the system colors and fonts used by all windows. In addition, the OS/2 operating system enables users to change the colors and fonts of individual windows. Similarly, your application can use Open Class Library to set and query the colors and fonts of individual windows. This topic describes colors and fonts together because they work similarly.

Although assigning specialized colors and fonts to controls can have a large amount of visual impact, you might want to avoid doing this. First, any windows that you tailor this way can discourage or prevent users from choosing their preferences in colors and fonts. Whereas OS/2 users can take the extra steps to open a Color Palette, Font Palette, or Scheme Palette window and replace your colors or fonts with ones they like, Windows users do not have this option. Setting the colors and fonts from an application does not leave the users in control. In the worst case, you may choose colors that some users cannot distinguish between because of display hardware or visual limitations such as color-blindness. Users may not be aware there is text they cannot see. Presumably, users have configured their system colors to avoid these colors, but that is of no consequence if you bypass those system colors. If it is important for your application to set colors or fonts, let users configure these colors in a properties, or settings, view.

Second, although you can set colors and fonts from your application, it is difficult to do so with portable code. For example, in the Windows operating system, you can only use a limited amount of customized colors in an application. Only the basic controls support this kind of customizing and only for background and foreground colors. But, in the OS/2 operating system, you can change the color of many of the individual parts of almost all controls (for example, the color of the borders of a push button), so these color choices would not be portable. Both operating systems provide a different set of system fonts and use different default fonts and font sizes for their windows. Thus, you run the risk that the same font is not available on both systems. Also, a font that is the proper size on one system can be the wrong size on the other.

If you still need to control colors and fonts, the following discussion explains how.

Open Class Library modeled its color and font support for the Windows platform based on the model that the OS/2 operating system uses. As a result, it behaves as follows on both the Windows and OS/2 operating systems:

- By default, a window uses the colors that users define for their systems.

- The application (or an OS/2 user) can assign the colors that a window uses.

- If a window is assigned a color, it uses its assigned colors.

- If a window is not assigned a color, it uses the default colors. The default color is determined in one of the following ways:

  - If a window somewhere in the owner chain has assigned colors, they become the default colors for the owned window.

  - If a window in the owner chain does not have assigned colors, it uses the system colors as its default.

So, when you change the colors of an owner window, that color propagates to the owned windows and then to the windows they own and on down the chain. For example, you may call `IWindow::setForegroundColor` on a notebook to change the color of its status text. However, this can also change the foreground color that all of the page windows of the notebook use because they also get the new default color. Fonts work the same way as colors.

Some windows do not draw text or paint with all colors. For example, an outline box control has no text, so it does not show its font when painting. Similarly, a frame window does not use a foreground color during painting. Nonetheless, when you assign a color or font to a window, it saves them. Even if that window does not use the color or font, the windows it owns can.

This leads to one last consideration about colors and fonts. Some controls do not require an owner window, such as `IStaticText`. This control does not issue any owner notification messages, and there is little need to catch its unprocessed keyboard and mouse events (except to be able to change the mouse pointer when it is over the static text control). However, you might give it an owner window just to support color changes. For example, if an IStaticText object has no owner window, and you or the users change the background color of its parent window, the background color of the text does not change to match the new background color of the parent window. If the parent window of the IStaticText object were also its owner window, the background color of the IStaticText object would change to match that of its parent window.

Setting and Querying Colors

To change the color a window uses, call the window's setBackgroundColor or setForegroundColor function. (More functions for setting different colors are available on the OS/2 platform, such as IWindow::setDisabledForegroundColor and IWindow::setBorderColor.) IWindow also contains functions to query the colors of a window, such as foregroundColor, backgroundColor, and borderColor. The query and set functions for colors all use IColor objects. Chapter 26, "Data Types," describes IColor and its derived classes. For Windows 95 compliance, only set colors so that users can alter them through the system settings. To do this, assign colors using IColor objects that you construct from an IColor::SystemColor enumeration.

You can also remove a previously assigned color from a window by calling a function such as IWindow::resetBackgroundColor. Calling this function causes the window to use a default background that is either inherited from its owner window chain or from the system.

Whenever the application or the users assign a window a new color, Open Class Library calls the window object's setLayoutDistorted function. See Chapter 15, "Canvases," for further details on this function.

In the Windows operating system, you need an IWindow object for the window before it can paint with a color. Thus, you cannot use a temporary IWindow object just to set a color because after the C++ object is deleted, the window cannot paint with any color you set through Open Class Library. In the OS/2 operating system, Open Class Library stores colors as presentation parameters within the operating system window, which the window can use during painting with or without a C++ object.

Setting and Querying Fonts

To set the font a window uses, call the window's setFont function or IFont::setWindowFont. See Chapter 18, "Fonts and Views," for details on the IFont class. You query a window's font by constructing an IFont object for the window, which contains complete information about the current font as in this example:

```
IEntryField myEntryField(ID_MYENTRYFIELD, &parent, &owner);
IFont controlFont(&myEntryField);
```

You can also remove a previously assigned font from a window by calling IWindow::resetFont. Calling this function causes the window to use a default font that is either inherited from its owner window chain or from the system.

The IWindow and the ITextControl classes also provide additional font-related functions. Use IWindow::characterSize to determine the average width and maximum height of a character in the current font of a window. ITextControl::displaySize returns the size required to show a specific text string on the screen given the control's current font. Both of these functions are useful for determining the optimal size for a window with its current font. Also, a window's setLayoutDistorted function is called whenever its font changes. See Chapter 15, "Canvases," for further details on this function.

One problem in hardcoding the font for a window in your application is that not all fonts are available on all machines. If a font is not available, a window may use a font that is very different from what you intended. Another problem becomes apparent if you run your application on the Japanese, Korean, or Chinese version of the OS/2 operating system. If you have translated your application so it displays double-byte text but your hardcoded font does not contain double-byte characters (as is the case with the Courier and Helvetica fonts), then the window may not display any text at all.

Tabbing and Cursor Movement

With Open Class Library, you can define *tab stops* and *groups* to specify how users move the cursor, or caret cursor, to change the control with input focus. Tab stops and groups determine rules for tabbing and moving the cursor, using the arrow keys for child windows of a frame or canvas window. No other window automatically provides keyboard navigation for its child windows. See Chapter 15, "Canvases," for more details. The child windows of a frame window can be a client window, frame extensions, or dialog-like controls for a frame window without a client window.

The order in which both tabbing and moving the cursor with the arrow keys proceeds through sibling windows is dictated by their sibling order, or *z-order* (as Windows and OS/2 APIs refer to it). See Chapter 4, "Windows, Handlers, and Events," for more information on sibling order.

The IControl class provides support for defining tab stops and groups. IControl is the base class for all control classes in Open Class Library. Although you often define tab stops and groups for the same window, they operate independently.

Tabbing between Windows

Tabbing between windows is automatically supported for child windows of a frame window or a canvas. In these cases, users presses the Tab key and the cursor moves to the next sibling window marked with a tab stop. When they press Shift+Tab, a *backtab*, the cursor moves to the previous sibling marked with a tab stop. The search wraps from the last sibling to the first when searching for the next sibling window and, similarly, from the first to the last when searching for the previous one.

The window with input focus may pass input focus to another window. For example, a static text control searches for another window to accept the cursor, a canvas moves the cursor to a child window marked with a tab stop, a radio button moves the cursor to the selected button in its group, and a combination box passes the input focus to its child entry field.

Some controls can process a Tab key to provide navigation within that control. In this case, its owner window does not receive the keystroke, and a canvas or frame window does not subsequently move input focus to another control. For example, a multiline edit control can conditionally treat the Tab key as character data. The `IMultiLineEdit::ignoreTab` style controls this behavior. Your users cannot use the Tab key to leave such a control.

When you use the first type of control constructor to create a window, mark a window with a tab stop by specifying the `IControl::tabStop` style. This style is equivalent to the `WS_TABSTOP` style that the Windows and OS/2 operating systems provide. You can query whether a window is marked with a tab stop by calling the `isTabStop` function of `IControl`, and you can add or remove a tab stop after the window has been created by calling `IControl::enableTabStop` or `IControl::disableTabStop`.

Cursoring between Windows

Like tabbing, moving the cursor between windows using the arrow keys is automatically supported for children of a frame window or a canvas. For these cases, users press the right or down arrow key to move the cursor to the next sibling window in the current group that can accept input focus. Users press the left or up arrow key to move the cursor to the previous sibling in the current group that can accept input focus. The search wraps from the last sibling to the first when searching for the next sibling. The opposite occurs when searching for the previous one.

A *group* is defined by its first window and includes all sibling windows up to where the next group starts. Therefore, all windows in a group must have the same parent window. Specify where a group starts by using the first type of control constructor and the `IControl::group` style when you create its first window. This style is equivalent to the `WS_GROUP` system style. You can query whether a control starts a group by calling `IControl::isGroup`, and you can split a group and combine groups by calling each control's `enableGroup` and `disableGroup` functions. All sibling windows that precede the first group are part of the last group.

The definition of a group is also critical to some basic operations of buttons, such as single-selection of a button within a group. See Chapter 10, "Button Controls," for more information.

Some controls process an arrow key to provide navigation within that control. In this case, an owner canvas or frame window does not receive the keystroke and does not subsequently move input focus to the next or previous control in the group. One example of this case is a list box. The arrow keys move the cursor to the next or previous list box item.

Preventing Keyboard Access to a Control

You can use the above information on tabbing and cursor movement to prevent users from using the keyboard to move to a control. To do this, do not mark the control with a tab stop. When you do not give a control the `IControl::tabStop` style, users cannot tab or backtab to it. Also, place the control in its own group. When you give a control and the one following it the `IControl::group` style, users cannot use the arrow keys to move the cursor to it because the arrow keys cannot cross groups.

Chapter 8

Static Controls

- Describes the read-only controls in the Open Class library, including the static text, bitmap, icon, group box, and outline box control classes
- Describes the IStaticText, IBitmapControl, IIconControl, IGroupBox, and IOutlineBox classes
- Read Chapter 7 before reading this chapter.
- Chapters 15 and 24 cover related material.

The static control classes allow you to display text strings, group related information in boxes, and show graphic images. This chapter describes the use of the static control classes, which include IStaticText, IBitmapControl, IIconControl, IGroupBox, and IOutlineBox. Figure 8-1 shows their class hierarchy. The IInfoArea class, which is also derived from IStaticText, is described in Chapter 5, "Frame Window Basics."

These controls are termed *static* in the sense that the user typically does not interact with them using the keyboard or mouse. Generally, an application also does not need to change their appearance on the screen, so visually they tend to be static or unchanging. Open Class Library

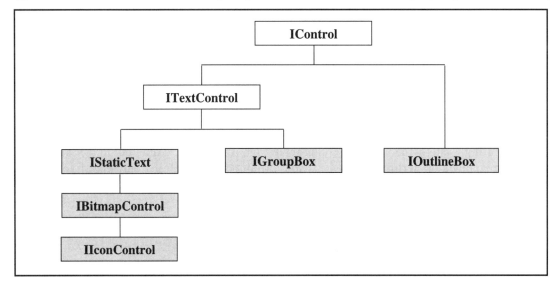

Figure 8-1. Static Controls Class Hierarchy.

also does not provide any event handlers specifically for use with these control classes. However, you can attach a general event handler, such as `IPaintHandler`, described in Chapter 17, "Reusable Handlers," to a static control.

Static Text

You can use the `IStaticText` class to display a string of text or even a block of color with no text. The text can be instructions for the window as a whole, a prompt for an entry field, a heading for a list box, or a status area whose contents you change dynamically.

Displaying Text

Once you construct an `IStaticText` object, you can assign a text string to it by calling the `setText` function. Unless the parent window of the `IStaticText` is an `ISetCanvas` or `IMultiCellCanvas`, you must manage the size of the control yourself. If the control is not sized large enough to contain all of its text, it clips the text at its window boundaries. If its size is larger than what is needed to display the text, it adds space around the text. `IStaticText` provides alignment styles so you can control what part of the text is clipped and where space is added. You can also use the member functions, `alignment` and `setAlignment`, to query and change the alignment.

You can enable *word wrapping* to cause the `IStaticText` object to write its text on multiple lines when the text does not fit on a single line. Use this style only if you are aligning the text to the top-left of the control. To see multiple lines of text, size the control tall enough so that it can contain more than one line of text.

`IStaticText` also provides text-drawing styles and corresponding member functions to add effects like underscore, strike out, and halftone text.

You can define a *mnemonic* for an `IStaticText` object the same as you can for buttons or menus. This is useful when you use a static text field as a label for an entry field because it allows you to define a fast path key to put the input focus in the entry field. This works because the operating system moves the input focus to the first control that can be tabbed to following the text field because the text field itself does not accept the input focus. If you specify the style `IStaticText::mnemonic` when constructing the `IStaticText` object, the ampersand character (&) on the Windows operating system and the tilde character (~) on the OS/2 operating system identifies the character that follows as a mnemonic. Visually, the mnemonic appears underlined and the tilde or ampersand is not shown, as you see in Figure 8-2. Without this style, the ampersand or tilde character appears as part of the text string. `IStaticText` has no corresponding member functions to set and query the mnemonic style.

Figure 8-2 shows the visual effect of using most of the styles provided by `IStaticText`. The code for this appears in the **menus\textstyl** example.

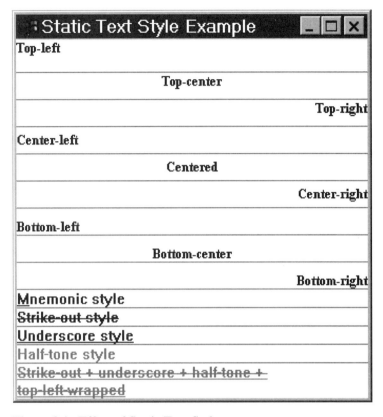

Figure 8-2. Effect of Static Text Styles.

Mnemonics Are Not Portable

The Windows and OS/2 operating systems use a different control character to specify a mnemonic. Open Class Library does not attempt to automatically translate Windows mnemonics to OS/2 mnemonics or vice versa. There are good reasons for this. Since the mnemonic character is part of the control's data, the library would have to change the data that you, the developer, told it to display. More than likely, the data would also have to be translated when you query for the contents of the control's data so that it matches the text you put into the control. The result of this is that both the ampersand and tilde characters would be unavailable for normal use in the control. The need for these characters is not all that uncommon.

Rather than imposing this restriction, Open Class Library requires you to specify the correct mnemonic character for the platform. The recommended way to do this is to use string resources that are different for the different platforms.

Displaying Color

You can create a block of color by simply not assigning the IStaticText object a text string to display. In this case, IStaticText uses its *fill* color to paint its entire rectangle. In the absence of a fill color, IStaticText uses the background color you assign. You can create a separator or divider by using an IStaticText window as a thin block of color with either a fill color or background color.

Of course, you can give an IStaticText object both color and text. By assigning either a fill or background color, you can show text on a block of color. If you use both the fill and background colors, IStaticText draws only the background of the text with the background color. It uses the fill color to paint any remaining space. Note that if you do not use the IStaticText::fillBackground style, the space which would have been painted with the fill color is not painted at all. The code example below illustrates most of these techniques. Figure 8-3 shows the resulting window.

Static Text Color Example - static\textclr\textclr.cpp

```
#include <icolor.hpp>
#include <iframe.hpp>
#include <iapp.hpp>
#include <istattxt.hpp>
#include <icconst.h>
#include <icoordsy.hpp>

void main ( )
{
  // Set the coordinate system to upper-left on all platforms.
  ICoordinateSystem::setApplicationOrientation(
      ICoordinateSystem::originUpperLeft);

  // Create the frame with a static text client.
  IFrameWindow frame( "Static Text Color Example" );
  IStaticText client( IC_FRAME_CLIENT_ID, &frame, &frame );
  frame.setClient( &client );
  client.setFillColor( IColor::green );

  // Display cyan block on the left.
  IStaticText left( 1, &frame, &frame );
  frame.addExtension( &left,
                    IFrameWindow::leftOfClient, 100 );
  left.setBackgroundColor( IColor::cyan );

  // Display text at the top of the client.
  IStaticText top( 2, &frame, &frame );
  frame.addExtension( &top,
                    IFrameWindow::aboveClient, 30 );
  top.setFillColor( IColor::yellow )
     .setForegroundColor( IColor::blue )
     .setBackgroundColor( IColor::white );
  top.setText( "This is blue on white text." )
     .setAlignment( IStaticText::centerCenter );

  // Add red horizontal separators.
  ISize screen( IWindow::desktopWindow()->size() ),
      separatorSize( screen.width(), 4 );
  IStaticText thinSeparator( 3, &client, &client );
  thinSeparator.setFillColor( IColor::red )
            .moveSizeTo( IRectangle( IPoint( 0, 10 ),
                                      separatorSize ));
```

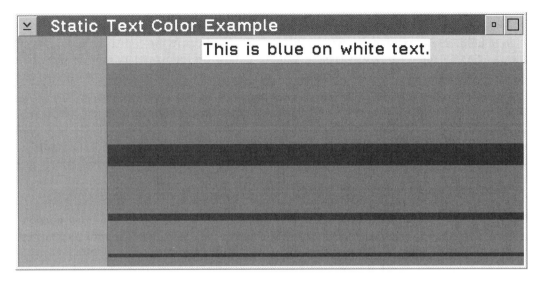

Figure 8-3. Static Text Color Usage.

```
IStaticText medSeparator( 4, &client, &client );
separatorSize.scaleBy( 1, 2 );   // Double the thickness.
medSeparator.setFillColor( IColor::red )
            .moveSizeTo( IRectangle( IPoint( 0, 50 ),
                                     separatorSize ));

IStaticText thickSeparator( 5, &client, &client );
separatorSize.scaleBy( 1, 3 );   // Now triple the thickness.
thickSeparator.setFillColor( IColor::red )
            .moveSizeTo( IRectangle( IPoint( 0, 110 ),
                                     separatorSize ));

// Size and show the window now.
frame.setFocus()
     .show();
IApplication::current().run();
}
```

Canvas Usage Considerations

The examples thus far in this chapter make heavy use of frame extensions because a frame window provides basic sizing and positioning of its extension windows. More likely, you will use the ISetCanvas and IMultiCellCanvas to automatically size and position static text windows. These classes are described in Chapter 15, "Canvases." However, be aware of the following three considerations when you use the IStaticText class with either a set canvas or multicell canvas.

First, if you are implementing a status or message area using the IStaticText class, call its setLimit function to indicate the minimum number of characters the field contains. If you do not call this function, the minimum size returned by the calcMinimumSize function of IStaticText determines the size needed by the control, based on its current text and font. If you change the text string displayed by an IStaticText window, this calculation is inadequate. Any change you make to the displayed text causes the canvas to flash as it updates all of its child windows based on the changed minimum size. By calling `setLimit`, you instruct `calcMinimumSize` to return a value based on how many characters the control must be big enough to hold. New text that fits within this size does not cause the canvas to update its child windows. See Chapter 15, "Canvases," for more details on the use of minimum sizes by the `ISetCanvas` and `IMultiCellCanvas` classes.

Second, `IStaticText::calcMinimumSize` does not allow static text to be displayed on more than one line. The value it returns is the size needed to display all of the control's text on a single line. As a result, static text on an `ISetCanvas` or `IMultiCellCanvas` is only displayed as a single line of text, even if the `IStaticText` object uses word wrapping. To support word wrapping, provide your own minimum size for a static text control. For example, you can create a class derived from `IStaticText` that overrides the `calcMinimumSize` function. You could implement this function using the `minTextWidth` and `textLines` functions of `IFont`.

Third, if you are using an `IStaticText` object as a fill box or separator, you must manage its minimum size. This is necessary because `IStaticText::calcMinimumSize` returns a minimum size of (0, 0) if the control has no text to display. If the minimum size of the `IStaticText` needs to be calculated dynamically, create a class derived from `IStaticText` that provides its own implementation for `calcMinimumSize`. Otherwise, assign the static text control a minimum size by calling its `setMinimumSize` function. The following example shows how you can incorporate these canvas considerations into your code. Figure 8-4 shows the resulting window.

Canvas Considerations for Static Text - static\textcv\textcv.cpp

```
#include <ifont.hpp>
#include <iframe.hpp>
#include <iapp.hpp>
#include <imcelcv.hpp>
#include <iradiobt.hpp>
#include <iselhdr.hpp>
#include <istattxt.hpp>
#include <istring.hpp>
#include <icconst.h>

// Objects of this class support writing their text across
// multiple lines when they are made a child window of a
// multicell or set canvas.  The text is wrapped to fit in a
// percentage of the parent window's width.  Because this class
// relies on the function IFont::textLines, it does not support
// double-byte characters.
class MultiLineStaticText : public IStaticText {
public:
  MultiLineStaticText ( unsigned long id,
                        IWindow* parent,
                        IWindow* owner,
                        IStaticText::Style style =
                          IStaticText::defaultStyle() )
    : IStaticText( id, parent, owner, IRectangle(), style ),
      parentFraction( 0.5 )
  {
    this->disableMinimumSizeCaching();
    this->setAlignment( IStaticText::topLeftWrapped );
  }
virtual MultiLineStaticText
 &setFraction        ( double fraction )
  {
    parentFraction = (fraction > 1) ? 1 : fraction;
    return *this;
  }
```

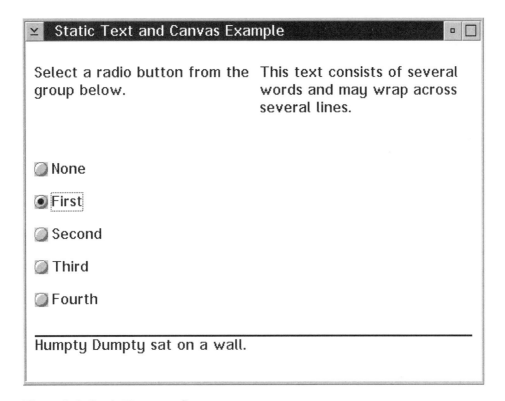

Figure 8-4. Static Text on a Canvas.

```
virtual double
  fraction             ( ) const
  { return parentFraction; }
protected:
virtual ISize
  calcMinimumSize      ( ) const
  {
    unsigned long recommendedWidth =
      (unsigned long)(this->parent()->size().width() *
          this->fraction());

    // Get the current font information to see what size the
    // text needs to be.
    IFont font( this );
    unsigned long minWidth = font.minTextWidth( this->text() );

    // At least show the longest word.
    if (recommendedWidth < minWidth)
      recommendedWidth = minWidth;

    unsigned long lines =
      font.textLines( this->text(), recommendedWidth );

    return ISize( recommendedWidth,
                  lines * font.maxCharHeight() );
  }
```

```
private:
double
  parentFraction;
MultiLineStaticText ( const MultiLineStaticText&);
MultiLineStaticText& operator= ( const MultiLineStaticText&);
};

// This class is used to dynamically change the text of a
// static text control to help illustrate the benefits of
// using the IStaticText::setLimit function.
class HumptyDumptySelectHandler : public ISelectHandler {
public:
  HumptyDumptySelectHandler ( IStaticText* outputArea )
  { output = outputArea; }
protected:
virtual Boolean
  selected       ( IControlEvent& event )
  {
    char* text = " ";
    switch ( event.controlWindow()->id() )
    {
      case 1:
        text = "Humpty Dumpty sat on a wall.";
        break;
      case 2:
        text = "Humpty Dumpty had a great fall.";
        break;
      case 3:
        text = "All the King's horses and all the King's men,";
        break;
      case 4:
        text = "Couldn't put Humpty together again.";
        break;
      default:
        break;
    }
    if (output)
    {
      output->setText( text );
    }
    return false;
  }
private:
IStaticText
 *output;
};

void main ( )
{
  IFrameWindow frame( "Static Text and Canvas Example" );
  IMultiCellCanvas client( IC_FRAME_CLIENT_ID, &frame, &frame );
  frame.setClient( &client );

  // Create child windows.
  IStaticText
    output   ( 10, &client, &client ),
    separator( 11, &client, &client );
  output.setLimit( 45 );
  separator
   .setFillColor( IColor::black )
   .setMinimumSize( ISize( 10, 2 ) );

  IMultiCellCanvas
    headings( 14, &client, &client );
  MultiLineStaticText
    heading1( 12, &headings, &headings ),
    heading2( 13, &headings, &headings );
```

```
heading1
  .setFraction( 0.4 )
  .setText( "Select a radio button from the group below." );
heading2
  .setFraction( 0.4 )
  .setText( "This text consists of several words and may"
               + IString( " wrap across several lines." ));

headings
  .addToCell( &heading1,  1, 1 )
  .addToCell( &heading2,  3, 1 );
headings
  .setColumnWidth( 1, 10, true )
  .setColumnWidth( 2, 10, true )
  .setColumnWidth( 3, 10, true );

IRadioButton
  none  ( 0, &client, &client ),
  first ( 1, &client, &client ),
  second( 2, &client, &client ),
  third ( 3, &client, &client ),
  fourth( 4, &client, &client );
none
  .setText( "None" )
  .enableTabStop()
  .enableGroup();
first.setText( "First" );
second.setText( "Second" );
third.setText( "Third" );
fourth.setText( "Fourth" );

client
  .addToCell( &headings,  2, 2, 2 )
  .addToCell( &none,      2, 4 )
  .addToCell( &first,     2, 6 )
  .addToCell( &second,    2, 8 )
  .addToCell( &third,     2, 10 )
  .addToCell( &fourth,    2, 12 )
  .addToCell( &separator, 2, 14, 2 )
  .addToCell( &output,    2, 15, 2 );
client
  .setColumnWidth( 3, 0, true )
  .setColumnWidth( 4,
                   IMultiCellCanvas::defaultCell().width() );

unsigned long defaultHeight =
                 IMultiCellCanvas::defaultCell().height();
client
  .setRowHeight( 1,  defaultHeight, true )
  .setRowHeight( 3,  defaultHeight, true )
  .setRowHeight( 13, defaultHeight, true )
  .setRowHeight( 16, defaultHeight, true );

HumptyDumptySelectHandler selHdr( &output );
selHdr.handleEventsFor( &client );

// Size and show the window now.
frame
  .moveSizeToClient( IRectangle( IPoint( 50, 50 ),
                                 client.minimumSize() ))
  .setFocus()
  .show();

IApplication::current().run();
}
```

Bitmap and Icon Controls

With the `IBitmapControl` and `IIconControl` classes, you can display a graphical image. The image can be either a bitmap or icon. You can store the bitmap in a resource library or bind it to the executable program. The bitmap can also be a system-provided bitmap or one your application has already loaded. Your sources for an icon are similar. You can store the icon in a resource library or bind it to the executable program. It can also be a system-provided icon or one that your application has already loaded.

You can display a bitmap using the `IBitmapControl` class. Because `IIconControl` derives from `IBitmapControl`, you can use `IIconControl` to display either an icon or a bitmap.

Showing a Graphical Image

When you create a bitmap control, you can provide it a bitmap to display. Once you have constructed an `IBitmapControl` window, you can dynamically replace the original bitmap with another by calling `IBitmapControl::setBitmap`.

Likewise, when you create an icon control, you can provide it an icon to display. Once you have constructed an `IIconControl` window, you can replace the original icon by calling either the `setBitmap` or `setIcon` function. `setBitmap` assigns the `IIconControl` a bitmap to display. `setIcon` assigns it an icon.

If you use an `IIconControl` to display an icon created with screen or inverse colors, do not use the `IWindow::clipChildren` style on the parent window of the `IIconControl`. Otherwise, the icon's appearance is unpredictable because the display of screen or inverse colors is dependent on what is on the screen when the icon is drawn. `IWindow::clipChildren` keeps the parent window from painting the area where the icon appears.

Sizing the Graphical Image

As you change the size of an `IBitmapControl` or `IIconControl` window, it sizes its bitmap or icon to fill its window boundaries. This means both `IBitmapControl` and `IIconControl` automatically stretch and compress an image, as necessary, to fit it into its window rectangle.

In many cases, it is necessary to show a bitmap or icon in its actual size, that is, not distorted or scaled through stretching or compression. You do this by sizing the `IBitmapControl` or `IIconControl` to the actual size of the bitmap or icon, thus preventing the `IBitmapControl` or `IIconControl` itself from growing or shrinking. You can get the actual size of the bitmap or icon displayed by either of these classes by calling their `calcMinimumSize` function indirectly through `minimumSize`. For example, you can size an `IIconControl` by using the following code:

```
// Construct the IIconControl.
IIconControl icon( ... );

// Size the icon to its true size.
icon.sizeTo( icon.minimumSize() );
```

You can also construct an `IBitmapControl` with the `IBitmapControl::sizeToBitmap` style, or an `IIconControl` with the `IIconControl::sizeToIcon` style. These styles direct the `IBitmapControl` or `IIconControl` to size itself to the actual size of the respective bitmap or icon each time you assign it a new bitmap or icon. However, these styles do not guarantee that the size of the `IBitmapControl` or `IIconControl` cannot be changed. So, be sure to place the `IBitmapControl` or `IIconControl` in a context where its size cannot be changed if you always want to show the exact image of a bitmap or icon.

For example, perhaps you want to show a fixed-size bitmap or icon on an `IMultiCellCanvas`. If you cannot ensure that the row and column of the multicell canvas will not grow, add an intermediate `ISetCanvas` object between the multicell canvas and the bitmap or icon control. The `ISetCanvas` keeps any size changes that the multicell canvas tries to make on its child windows from affecting the graphic image.

Showing Text

Because both `IBitmapControl` and `IIconControl` derive from `IStaticText`, you can show text on top of the graphic image by calling `setText`. Be sure you do not use the `IStaticText::fillBackground` style. This erases the bitmap or icon when the text is drawn. Assigning text also changes the minimum size of the object.

Processing User Interaction

Appropriately for a static control, `IBitmapControl` and `IIconControl` display bitmaps and icons that the user is not intended to interact with. There are other means of creating a bitmap or an icon that the user can interact with. Among these alternatives are the `IGraphicPushButton` class (see Chapter 10, "Button Controls"), the `IContainerControl` and `IContainerObject` classes (see Chapter 13, "Container Control"), the `IMouseHandler` class to detect mouse button clicks (see Chapter 17, "Reusable Handlers"), and drag and drop (see Chapter 21, "Direct Manipulation").

Example

The following example code shows an icon and bitmap on an `IMultiCellCanvas`. The `IIconControl` displays the icon at its actual size. The `IBitmapControl` allows the canvas to enlarge the bitmap along with the frame window. Figure 8-5 shows the resulting window.

Icon and Bitmap Example - static\iconbmp\iconbmp.cpp

```
#include <ibmpctl.hpp>
#include <iframe.hpp>
#include <iapp.hpp>
#include <iiconctl.hpp>
#include <imcelcv.hpp>
#include <istattxt.hpp>
#include <icconst.h>
#include "iconbmp.h"

void main ( )
{
  IFrameWindow frame( "Icon and Bitmap Example" );
```

```
// Put the icons and bitmaps on an expandable canvas.
IMultiCellCanvas client( IC_FRAME_CLIENT_ID, &frame, &frame );
frame.setClient( &client );

// Create the background bitmap.
IBitmapControl bmp1( 1, &client, &client, ID_CPPBITMAP );

// Create labels for the graphic images.
IStaticText
  bmpHeading   ( 0, &client, &client ),
  iconHeading  ( 0, &client, &client );
bmpHeading
 .setText( "Bitmap - Sized by canvas" )
 .setAlignment( IStaticText::centerCenter )
 .disableFillBackground();
iconHeading
 .setText( "Icon - Actual size" )
 .setAlignment( IStaticText::centerCenter )
 .disableFillBackground();

// Create an icon.
IIconControl icon1( 1, &client, &client,
                    ID_CPPICON, IRectangle(),
                    IIconControl::classDefaultStyle
                      | IIconControl::sizeToIcon );

// Put the child windows in the multicell canvas.
client
 .addToCell( &bmp1,        1, 1, 5, 7 )
 .addToCell( &bmpHeading,  1, 2, 5 )
 .addToCell( &iconHeading, 2, 5, 3 )
 .addToCell( &icon1,       3, 4 );
```

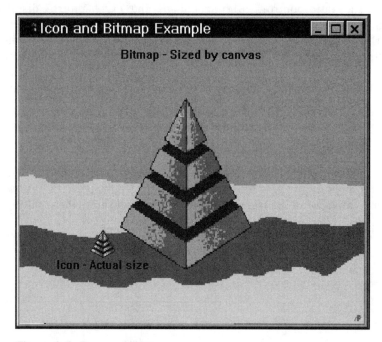

Figure 8-5. Icon and Bitmap.

```
    // Assign expandable columns and rows.
    client
      .setColumnWidth( 2, 1, true )
      .setColumnWidth( 4, 1, true )
      .setColumnWidth( 5, 3, true )
      .setRowHeight( 3, 4, true )
      .setRowHeight( 6, 1, true );

    // Show the window now.
    frame.setFocus()
         .show();
    IApplication::current().run();
}
```

Icon and Bitmap Resources - static\iconbmp\iconbmp.h

```
#define ID_CPPICON        1
#define ID_CPPBITMAP      1
```

Icon and Bitmap Constants - static\iconbmp\iconbmp.rc

```
#include "iconbmp.h"

#ifdef IC_PM /* OS/2 resources */
ICON    ID_CPPICON      .\os2\cpp.ico
BITMAP  ID_CPPBITMAP    cpp.bmp

#else  /* Windows resources */
ID_CPPICON     ICON   .\win\cpp.ico
ID_CPPBITMAP   BITMAP cpp.bmp
#endif
```

Group Box and Outline Box

You may, at times, want to provide a stronger way to relate information logically than simply by locating it together. The group box control offers a commonly used way to create a stronger association than that. Visually, a group box draws a rectangular border just inside its window boundaries; a text label forms part of its top border. You can use the group box to organize information by placing related elements inside the borders of the group box. The IGroupBox class represents a group box control.

An outline box gives you an easy way to draw a common graphic—a rectangular border. You can use this control in the same manner as a group box, to group together logically related information. An outline box draws its border just inside its window boundaries and has the look of a group box without text. Figure 8-6 shows a group box and an outline box.

Usage Considerations

Neither a group nor outline box paints its entire screen area. Instead, each box only draws its borders, and a group box draws its text. They do not paint over their interiors. As a result, you can create a group or outline box that visually contains sibling windows by positioning and sizing the group or outline box around them.

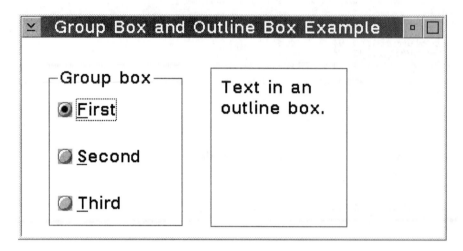

Figure 8-6. Group Box and Outline Box.

You can get the same visual effect by making the windows contained by a group box or outline box the child windows of those controls.   However, if you do this, you lose automatic processing of the Tab and cursor arrow keys to move the input focus among these child windows. Dialog-box behavior, like cursor movement, is provided only to child windows of a frame window or a canvas. In the OS/2 operating system, another drawback of using a group or outline box as a parent window is its effect on the mouse. Child windows stop receiving mouse clicks and do not change the appearance of the mouse pointer.

When you size an IGroupBox window, make it large enough to contain its text, its surrounding border, and the windows it encloses. A group box only displays a single line of text, which can be clipped if the window is too narrow to display it all. So, try to limit the amount of text you assign to a group box. You assign text using the setText function.

Do not confuse a group box with the effect of using the IControl::group style. A group box only gives visual effects. Also, due to the problems in using an IGroupBox as the child window of an ISetCanvas, ISetCanvas provides an alternate way to get the visual effect of a group box. See Chapter 15, "Canvases," for details.

Example

The following code displays the window shown in Figure 8-6. Three radio buttons are sized and positioned to appear within the border of the group box. Static text is sized and positioned to appear within the border of the outline box. All the controls are sibling windows.

Group Box and Outline Box Example - static\boxes\boxes.cpp

```cpp
#include <icanvas.hpp>
#include <iframe.hpp>
#include <iapp.hpp>
#include <igroupbx.hpp>
#include <ioutlbox.hpp>
#include <iradiobt.hpp>
#include <istattxt.hpp>
#include <icconst.h>
#include <icoordsy.hpp>

void main ( )
{
  // Set the coordinate system to upper-left on all platforms.
  ICoordinateSystem::setApplicationOrientation(
      ICoordinateSystem::originUpperLeft);

  IFrameWindow frame( "Group Box and Outline Box Example" );
  ICanvas client( IC_FRAME_CLIENT_ID, &frame, &frame,
                  IRectangle( IPoint(), ISize( 390, 200 )));
  frame.setClient( &client );

  // Create a group box with radio buttons.
  IGroupBox group( 1, &client, &client,
                   IRectangle( IPoint( 30, 10),
                               ISize( 150, 170 )));
  group.setText( "Group box" );

  ISize buttonSize( 130, 30 );
  IRadioButton
    first ( 2, &client, &client,
            IRectangle( IPoint( 40, 40 ), buttonSize )),
    second( 3, &client, &client,
            IRectangle( IPoint( 40, 90 ), buttonSize )),
    third ( 4, &client, &client,
            IRectangle( IPoint( 40, 140 ), buttonSize ));
  first
   .setText( "First" )
   .enableTabStop()
   .enableGroup();
  second.setText( "Second" );
  third.setText( "Third" );

  // Create an outline box with text.
  IOutlineBox outline( 5, &client, &client,
                       IRectangle( IPoint( 210, 10 ),
                                   ISize( 150, 170 )));
  IStaticText text( 6, &client, &client,
                    IRectangle( IPoint( 220, 20 ),
                                ISize( 130, 150 )));
  text
   .setAlignment( IStaticText::topLeftWrapped )
   .setText( "Text in an outline box." );

  // Size and show the window now.
  frame
   .moveSizeToClient( IRectangle( IPoint( 50, 30 ),
                                  client.size() ))
   .setFocus()
   .show();
  IApplication::current().run();
}
```

Chapter 9

Edit Controls

- Describes the edit control classes in Open Class Library
- Describes the ITextControl, IEntryField, IMultiLineEdit and IEditHandler classes
- Read Chapters 4 and 7 before reading this chapter.
- Chapters 11, 15 and 17 cover related material.

This chapter describes the entry field and multiline edit control classes supported by Open Class Library. You use these controls to collect character input from the user and to present text for users to edit or view. It also describes the abstract text control class from which the edit controls and other text-based controls derive their basic behavior. These controls work with character text and are enabled to support double-byte character data.

The Edit Classes

Figure 9-1 shows the classes in Open Class Library that you use with edit controls. IEntryField and IMultiLineEdit create edit controls and set and select text from the controls. These classes derive their base functional behavior from ITextControl, their common base class.

ITextControl provides a small base set of functions that are common to all text-based controls in Open Class Library. These functions enable you to set and query the text within the control, as well as to query for other specific information about the text and related items. You can set the text of the control using two different forms of ITextControl::setText. The first form enables you to specify the string directly; the second form enables you to set the text indirectly by specifying the resource identifier of an item in a string table. Use ITextControl::text to query for the current string set in the text control and ITextControl::textLength to get the length of that current string in bytes.

IEntryField represents an edit control that enables only a single line of text and is used to prompt and collect information from the user. IMultiLineEdit also represents an edit control but one that enables more than one line of text and contains enough editing capabilities to enable you to use it as a simple text editor.

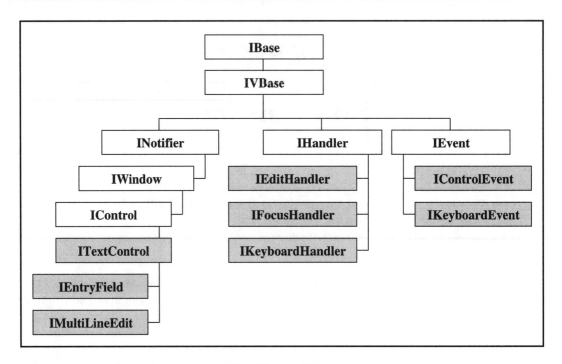

Figure 9-1. Edit Controls and Related Handlers and Events.

The following code fragment shows the derived text functions applied to `IEntryField` and `IMultiLineEdit` objects:

Basic Text Functions - editctls\simple\simple.cpp

```
// Set the text of the entry field.
myEntryField.setText( "Common Text Operations" );

// Query the text of the entry field.
IString text = myEntryField.text();

// Find the length of the text in the entry field.
int length = myEntryField.textLength();

// Now apply the same functions to an MLE.
myMLE.setText( "Common Text Operations" );
text = myMLE.text();
length = myMLE.textLength();
```

In addition to the basic functions listed above, `ITextControl` also provides a couple of helper functions that are useful in edit operations and control layout. Call `clipboardHasTextFormat` to determine whether a paste operation is valid for the text control. This function checks the clipboard for the existence of a text string from a prior cut or copy operation. You can retrieve the size of the rectangle needed to display the current string with the current font for the window using `ITextControl::displaySize`.

Common Text Operations

You can create an `IEntryField` or `IMultiLineEdit` object using the standard constructors described in Chapter 7, "Controls." Both classes share many common interfaces beyond the common set of functions they derive from `ITextControl`.

Selected Text Operations

Selected text operations are another common set of functions. Both classes support the capability to select text and query selected text. Additional functions also act on selected text. Generally, you let the users select the text by swiping it with the mouse with the selection button pressed or by holding down the Shift key and moving the cursor using the keyboard. However, you can select text with `selectRange` by specifying the start and end points. If you do not specify parameters, `selectRange` selects all of the text in the edit control. Use `selectedRange` to retrieve the range selected and `selectedTextLength` and `selectedText` to get the size of the selected text and the actual text selected, respectively.

Additional selected text functions include `clear` and `discard`. The differences between the clear and discard operations are that `clear` replaces the selected text with blanks and `discard` deletes the selected text. Both functions throw an exception if the control does not have any selected text. You can test for this condition by calling `hasSelectedText`.

Don't Forget to Prompt Your User

Because many operations are only valid for selected text, your applications need to provide visual clues to your users about these operations. Menu items representing selected text actions need to be disabled when no text is selected and enabled when text is selected. See an example of this in Chapter 6, "Menus and Keyboard Accelerators." It uses `IMenuHandler` to dynamically modify a submenu.

Clipboard Operations

Open Class Library supports clipboard operations for edit controls. Both `IEntryField` and `IMultiLineEdit` classes provide `cut`, `copy`, and `paste` functions to transfer data to and from the clipboard. Users must select the text to use `cut` and `copy`, and the clipboard must contain text to use `paste`. Otherwise, the function you call throws an exception. Use `hasSelectedText` as a check prior to using `cut` or `copy` and `clipboardHasTextFormat` as a check prior to `paste`. The `cut` function removes the selected text and puts the data in the clipboard. The `copy` function only copies the data to the clipboard. The class `IClipboard` also has functions for storing data and testing the type of data in the clipboard.

Additional Common Interfaces

Common interfaces declared by `IEntryField` and `IMultiLineEdit` classes include the following ones:

- `setLimit` and `limit`, which you use to set and query the text limit

- `hasTextChanged`, `setTextChanged`, and `resetTextChanged`, which you use to set, reset, and query to determine if the text in the control was modified since you last checked it

- `setCursorPosition` and `cursorPosition`, which you use to set and query the position of the cursor

- `enableDataUpdate`, `disableDataUpdate`, and `isWriteable`, which you use to set, reset, and query to determine if the user can modify the text in the control

- `removeAll`, which you use to delete the entire contents of the edit control

The Entry Field Control

An entry field's window styles determine its behavior. These styles are set when you create the control. `IEntryField` provides functions to enable and disable some of these styles after the edit window is created, but most of these are supported only in the OS/2 operating system. The Windows operating system does not support dynamic modification of styles for their native controls, including entry fields. Therefore, functions such as `enableAutoTab`, `disableMargin`, and `setAlignment` only work in the OS/2 operating system, so avoid them in portable code. We discuss a few of the entry field styles here.

You can prevent users from entering text into an entry field by making it read-only. Specify this using the `IEntryField::readOnly` style. This is the only edit control style that you can modify dynamically on the Windows operating system; you can change it by using `enableDataUpdate` and `disableDataUpdate`.

Entry Field Styles

To justify text within an entry field control, use the styles `IEntryField::leftAlign`, `IEntryField::centerAlign`, and `IEntryField::rightAlign`. These styles do not automatically remove leading or trailing blanks from the text. Use the `IString` member functions `strip`, `stripLeading`, and `stripTrailing` to do that.

Use the `IEntryField::autoScroll` style to determine whether the text in an entry field scrolls to show the current typing point.

If you remove the `IEntryField::margin` style, the entry field does not draw the border. Note that drawing a border does not change the size of the text or edit region of the entry field. The text or edit region containing the text determines the size and position of an entry field. The border, if present, is drawn around the text region. You can use another style, `IEntryField::border3D`, to specify a three-dimensional border instead of a solid line. This style affects only 32-bit Windows programs; it has no effect in the OS/2 or Windows 3.1 operating systems.

Use the `IEntryField::unreadable` style to create an entry field that accepts a password. Instead of displaying the user's actual input, the entry field displays asterisks to protect the password. In the Windows operating system, this style always provides left alignment of the text, ignoring any alignment styles set.

The `IEntryField::autoTab` entry field style causes the cursor to move to the next control when a user enters the last character of the text limit. The text limit is the maximum number of characters that a user can enter into the control. The default text limit is 32 bytes. You can change the text limit with the `setTextLimit` member function. The text limit also determines the minimum size of the entry field in an `ISetCanvas` or `IMultiCellCanvas` window. Note that the auto tab behavior is only supported in the OS/2 operating system. Specifying this style in the Windows operating systems has no effect.

You set a style to enable double-byte character input. Two defined styles accept a mixture of single and double-byte characters: `mixedData` and `dbcsData`. Use `mixedData` when you want the text limit to include shift-out and shift-in characters, which are needed to convert the value to an EBCDIC code page. Open Class Library supports double-byte, immediate conversion, and input mode. Note that these styles are not necessary on the Windows operating system and have no effect.

If you size an entry field too short vertically for its font, the Windows operating system may not show the text in the entry field, and the user cannot change focus to the control. To correct this problem, either size the entry field taller or change its font.

The Multiline Edit Control

Like entry fields, the multiline edit control's window styles define its behavior. Also like entry fields, you must set these styles when you create the control if you want portable code. The Windows operating system restricts these styles. We discuss a few of the multiline edit styles here.

Use `IMultiLineEdit::wordWrap` to cause the edit control to start a new line when text exceeds the horizontal size of the control instead of scrolling the text. Specify `IMultiLineEdit::horizontalScroll` or `IMultiLineEdit::verticalScroll` to add the respective scroll bars to the control.

Both edit control classes have several common styles. You can make the multiline edit control read-only by specifying the `IMultiLineEdit::readOnly` style. To add a border around the text region, use the `IMultiLineEdit::border` style. Note that the default style for `IMultiLineEdit` enables word-wrapping and provides a vertical scroll bar and a border. In the 32-bit Windows operating systems, you can also create a multiline edit control with 3D borders by specifying `IMultiLineEdit::border3D` style.

In the OS/2 operating system, you can also change the behavior of the Tab key. When you use the `IMultiLineEdit::ignoreTab` style, the cursor does not skip to the next control when the user presses the Tab or backtab key. This enables users to tab inside the multiline edit window. It is also the default behavior in the Windows operating system, and you cannot change it. When the edit control processes tab keys, you can specify the locations of the tab stops using the `setTab` function.

The multiline edit control performs best for text under 4KB and fastest for text up to 32KB. Anything greater than that may cause the performance to degrade unacceptably. Although you can use the multiline edit control for large files, a maximum size limit exists on some platforms. For both the Windows 95 and Windows 3.1 operating systems, the maximum amount of text that you can place in the control is less than 64K.

When using an `IMultiLineEdit` in an `ISetCanvas` or `IMultiCellCanvas` window, define its minimum size. The default for Open Class Library is 100 by 100 pixels.

Simple Text Editor

The multiline edit control is often referred to as a simple text editor. The typing and editing functions are part of the multiline edit control; your program does not have to provide them.

`IMultiLineEdit` provides functions to insert text from a data buffer or file into the window, and to save the contents in the window to a file. You can insert text at the current position (add), at the end of the contents of the window (addAsLast) or at a specific position (addAtOffset). By default, these functions insert up to the first null character in the specified text. If you want to insert a string that contains more than one null character, you must specify its buffer size.

The `importFromFile` function inserts the contents of a data file into the window at the current position of the cursor. You can export all of the contents using `exportToFile` or just the selected text using `exportSelectedTextToFile`.

When inserting and saving text, you specify an end-of-line character format. Table 9-1 lists the formats you can use.

Line operations are a feature of multiline edit controls not found in entry fields. You can insert a specific line of text or remove a specific line of text. The `addLineAsLast` function appends a new line of text to the end. You insert a line of text at a specific line number with the `addLine` function. The line number is the number of lines from the beginning of the edit control as the lines would be displayed, which is based on the control size and word-wrapping. The carriage-return and line-feed, line-break sequence is ignored and the number is zero-based. You remove a line of text using the `removeLine` function. In addition to the common cursor operations listed previously, `IMultiLineEdit` also provides `setCursorLinePosition` to set the cursor to the beginning of a specific line number and `cursorLinePosition` to query the specific line number location of the cursor. Use `numberOfLines` to retrieve the total number of lines in the control and `visibleLines` to retrieve the number of visible lines. Both of these functions return an incorrect value unless the multiline edit window is visible. You can scroll

Table 9-1. End-of-Line Character Formats

EOLFormat Enumerator	Description
cfText	Uses carriage-return (CR) and line-feed (LF) characters to end a line. The tab characters separate words within a line. A null character signals the end of the data. This is the default format.
noTran	Uses a LF character to end a line. noTran guarantees that any text imported into the multiline edit control in this format can be recovered in exactly the same form when it is exported. This format is supported only in the OS/2 operating system.
MLEFormat	Uses CR-LF characters to end a line. During importing, MLEFormat ignores the character sequence of CR-CR-LF, but it denotes word-wrapping during exporting.

the text vertically to place a line at the top of the window using setTop, and you can retrieve the line number of the topmost line using top.

IMultiLineEdit also provides the ability to restore the contents in the control to the state they were in before the last change. Not all actions can be undone. Call isUndoable to check whether you can undo any actions performed before you invoke the undo function.

The multiline edit control has some restrictions. They are as follows:

- Currently, the OS/2 operating system limits the multiline edit control to accept only bitmap fonts.

- In certain situations, overrunning the text limit causes an alarm, but the character is added, anyway. This happens if you create the multiline edit control with undo disabled. Open Class Library does not support this style, but you may encounter controls created with it. For example, a container in the details view displays a multiline edit window that exhibits this behavior to support direct editing.

Event Handlers

Open Class Library provides three handler classes for you to use with these edit control objects:

- IEditHandler, which you use to validate nonkeyboard input, such as text copied from the clipboard. IEditHandler calls its edit virtual function whenever the contents of an edit control change. This handler is called after the control has been visibly updated with the change. You can attach this handler to either the edit control or its owner window.

- IKeyboardHandler, which you use to capture keystrokes, typically to validate input. Attach this handler to the edit control. See Chapter 17, "Reusable Handlers," for more details on IKeyboardHandler.

- IFocusHandler, which you use for handling focus change events. These occur when a control gains or loses the input focus, such as when the user tabs to and from the control. You can attach this handler to either the edit control or its owner window. Note that you cannot change the window with the input focus by using the gotFocus or lostFocus virtual functions. One way around this restriction is to post a user message from the focus handler. You can then implement a handler for the user message to change the window with the input focus. This strategy, however, may not work. The control itself may be implementing the same behavior (for example, a combination box control in the OS/2 operating system), and its posted message may get processed after yours.

The following code is an example of IEditHandler being used to ensure only alphabetic characters are typed into an entry field:

IEditHandler implementation - editctls\logon\logon.cpp

```
// Edit handler that checks password for alphabetic characters.
class PasswordHandler : public IEditHandler
{
public:
  PasswordHandler( IEntryField* ef, IPushButton* pb )
     : entryPW(ef), OkButton(pb) {}
protected:
virtual Boolean
  edit          ( IControlEvent& evt )
  {
    // Get the password contents on each update.
    password = entryPW->text();

    // If the user enters a nonalphabetic key, disable the OK
    // push button so that the dialog cannot be dismissed.
    if (!(password.isAlphabetic()))
      OkButton->disable();
    else
      OkButton->enable();
    return true;
  }
private:
IEntryField
 *entryPW;
IPushButton
 *OkButton;
};
```

Chapter 10

Button Controls

- Describes the various button control classes in Open Class Library
- Describes the IPushButton, IGraphicPushButton, ISettingButton, ICheckBox, I3StateCheckBox, IRadioButton, and ISelectHandler classes
- Read Chapter 7 before reading this chapter.
- Chapter 16 covers the specialized button classes ICustomButton, IToolBarButton, and IAnimatedPushButton. Chapter 17 covers related material.

This chapter describes most of the classes in Open Class Library that you use to add buttons to your applications. Buttons are controls that users press to select a choice or to initiate an immediate action. The classes in Open Class Library that allow users to initiate an action inherit from the class `IPushbutton`; `IPushButton` itself is the primary class that provides this behavior. However, the classes in Open Class Library that allow users to select a choice inherit from the abstract class `ISettingButton`. Open Class Library also provides button classes that replace the default drawing for push buttons. We describe these `ICustomButton` derived classes, including `IToolbarButton` and `IAnimatedPushButton`, in Chapter 16, "Tool Bars, Fly-Over Help, and Custom Buttons." Figure 10-1 displays the button control class hierarchy.

Common Button Behavior

It is hard to discuss the behavior of the button classes as a whole because the button controls do not always behave alike even though they look alike. The button classes have more similarities because of their common `IWindow`, `IControl`, and `ITextControl` inheritance than because they inherit from `IButton`. Buttons also function as members of a group, and in several button classes, it is this group characteristic that dominates the behavior of the button. For these reasons, it is more informative to discuss the buttons in terms of their individual characteristics. However, all buttons exhibit the following behavior:

- You can simulate a press of the button by calling the function `IButton::click`. Note that if you have an `ISelectHandler` object attached to the button object and call `IButton::click`, the `ISelectHandler::selected` virtual function is called. This is not the case, however, when you call the similar `ISettingButton::select` function.

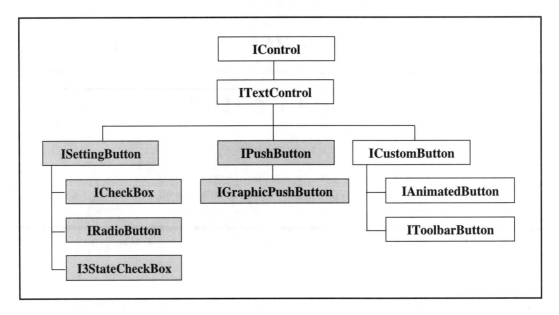

Figure 10-1. Button Classes.

- You can set or query the highlighted state of a button by calling the functions `IButton::unhighlight`, `IButton::highlight`, and `IButton::isHighlighted`. The presentation system normally only displays the highlighted state of a button when users select the button either by pressing mouse button 1 or by pressing the space bar when focus is on the button. It removes the highlighted state when users release the mouse button or space bar. If you call `highlight`, the button remains in the highlighted state until you call `unhighlight` or users select the button manually.

- You can create the button with the style `IButton::noPointerFocus`. The presentation system does not transfer focus to a button that you created with this style when users press the button. However, this style does not disable the use of the keyboard to transfer focus to the button. You can use this style for any button class, but it is not very useful on buttons other than push buttons. See the topic "Help Push Buttons" later in this chapter for its primary use in push buttons.

Push Buttons

When users select them, push buttons cause an immediate action. Use them, then, to start or cancel an action, request help, or display an action view or a settings view. In response to a button press, Open Class Library dispatches an `ICommandEvent` to the owner of the button with the command-event identifier set to the identifier of the button. This behavior is similar to the behavior of menus, and this similarity means you can process an action choice that occurs from a menu or push button in the same way.

On the OS/2 operating system, you can create push buttons with or without a border. Create a push button without a border by using the `IPushbutton::noBorder` style or remove the border later by calling `IPushbutton::removeBorder` after creating the button. The Windows operating system ignores both of these requests.

System Command Push Buttons

Also, as with menus, you can change the `ICommandHandler` callback from `command` to `systemCommand`. You can do this because Open Class Library calls `ICommandHandler` in response to a button press. To change a push button to send a system command notification in this manner, create it with the style `IPushButton::systemCommand`, or call `IPushButton::enableSystemCommand` after you create the push button.

The value of changing a push button to generate a system command is that the presentation system works for you. It executes the default behavior for system commands without your writing any additional code. The window identifier of the push button is the command identifier in the command event. To generate a system command that the presentation system recognizes, you must assign the button one of the system command identifiers defined in `ISystemMenu`. See the topic "Push Button Example" in this chapter for an example that uses system command push buttons.

Help Push Buttons

Again, as with menus, you can change the notification that the push button sends when a user presses it to a help request. Changing a push button to a help button initiates an attempt to find and display the help information for the control with input focus. To change a push button to a help button, either create the button with the `IPushButton::help` style or call `IPushButton::enableHelp` after you create the push button.

By default, the presentation system changes input focus to the push button when a user presses it. If you create the button with the `IPushButton::help` style, the presentation system displays help for the push button itself. To add a push button to display *context-sensitive help* (help for the control with input focus), add the `IButton::noPointerFocus` style. With this style, the operating system leaves input focus on the control that had it before the user selected the push button with the mouse. Thus, a user can request help for any control in the view with input focus by using the mouse to select a help push button.

In the OS/2 operating system only, if you create buttons as part of a dialog template, you can add the `systemCommand`, `help`, and `noPointerFocus` styles using the Presentation Manager styles, `BS_SYSCOMMAND`, `BS_HELP`, and `BS_NOPOINTERFOCUS`.

The Default Push Button

A *default push button* is a button that is automatically selected when a user presses the Enter key—even when input focus is *not* on a push button. The default push button is useful because it allows your users to type in fields on the view and press Enter to process the data without having to move the cursor to a specific button. To make a push button a default button, either create it with the `IPushButton::defaultButton` style, or call `IPushButton::enableDefault` after you create the push button.

When you add the `defaultButton` style to a push button, the push button displays a thick border and temporarily becomes the default push button. A user can change the default push button by using the Tab key to put input focus into a group of push buttons and then use the left and right arrow keys to move input focus, along with the default style, to another push button. When the user moves to a control that is not a push button, the push button that you specified to be the default becomes the default push button again.

Create only one push button with the `defaultButton` style for each frame window. This button must be a child of the frame or a child of a canvas window.

If you create your buttons as part of a dialog template, you can create a default button by using the control type `DEFPUSHBUTTON` instead of `PUSHBUTTON`.

The Group Behavior of Push Buttons

Ensure that the first (usually the left-most or top-most) push button in a set has a style of `IControl::group` and `IControl::tabStop`. A push button with the `group` style becomes the first button in a group of buttons. A push button with the `tabStop` style receives input focus when the user tabs to the control. Add the group style to only one button in a set of push buttons. If you add the group style to more than one push button, you create more than one logical group; the left and right cursor keys no longer allow your users to move among all of the push buttons. To add the group style to a push button, create it with the `IControl::group` style or call `IControl::enableGroup`. If the group style is already added to a button, call `IControl::disableGroup` to remove it.

Although only one push button in a set should have the group style, you can add tabbing behavior to more than one push button by creating it with the `IControl::tabStop` style or by calling `IControl::enableTabStop`. The Tab key moves focus to every push button with the `tabStop` style.

If you create your buttons as part of a dialog template, the `tabStop` style is the default. You remove it using the `NOT WS_TABSTOP` style. Add the `group` style using the presentation system's `WS_GROUP` style.

Graphic Push Buttons

Use the `IGraphicPushButton` class to add a bitmap or icon image to a push button. You can also add text to the graphic push buttons because this class inherits from `IPushButton`. The graphic push button displays the text on top of the graphic image. And, it behaves identically to a normal push button.

You can use the `IGraphicPushbutton::sizeToGraphic` style to cause the graphic push button to size itself to the size of the graphic image. Use this style especially if you are putting the graphic push button into one of the canvas classes. If you do not use this style, you are responsible for creating the graphic push button in the correct size to contain the graphic image.

If you do not use an icon that uses screen or inverse colors, add the `IWindow::clipChildren` style to the graphic push button to optimize the drawing of the push button.

Push Button Handlers

Open Class Library does not provide specialized handlers for the push button classes but it does use its own specialized handers internally on the Windows platforms to simulate the `IPushButton` styles `systemCommand`, `help`, and `noPointerFocus`.

You cannot use an `ISelectHandler` to capture the selection of a push button because Open Class Library does not call `ISelectHandler::select` when a user presses a button. Instead you use an `ICommandHandler` to capture button presses as command events.

Push Button Example

The following example demonstrates our recommended approach for adding push buttons to an action view. The client area of the action view contains a multicell canvas. Inside the multicell canvas is a set canvas with both normal and graphic push buttons. The set canvas is the best approach for displaying buttons because it relieves you of calculating the size and position of the buttons, regardless of the font you use to display text on the buttons or the size you use for the graphic images.

The first push button, with the text **OK**, contains the `tabStop` and `group` styles. Thus, users can tab to the push buttons as a group and then move the cursor among them with the left and right arrow keys. The **OK** push button also contains the `defaultButton` style, so it is activated when users press the Enter key. The last push button, with the text **Help**, contains the `help` and `noPointerFocus` styles. When users press it, they can see context-sensitive help for the other controls in the frame window, such as other push buttons. The **Cancel** push button is a system command push button with the identifier `ISystemMenu::idClose`. Therefore, it acts the same as **Close** on the system menu.

Push Button Example - buttons\pushbut\pushbut.cpp

```
#include <iframe.hpp>
#include <ipushbut.hpp>
#include <igraphbt.hpp>
#include <imcelcv.hpp>
#include <isetcv.hpp>
#include <iapp.hpp>
#include <ihandle.hpp>
#include <icconst.h>
#include <isysmenu.hpp>
#include "pushbut.h"
```

```cpp
void main()
{
// Create a frame window with a multicell canvas
// as the client window.
IFrameWindow
  frame ("Push Button Example");
IMultiCellCanvas
  client(IC_FRAME_CLIENT_ID, &frame, &frame);

// Create a set canvas to hold the push buttons.
ISetCanvas
  buttons(ID_BUTTONS, &client, &client);

// Create the push buttons in the set canvas.
IPushButton
  ok(ID_OK, &buttons, &buttons),
  cancel(ISystemMenu::idClose, &buttons, &buttons);

IGraphicPushButton
  bitmap(ID_BITMAPBUTTON, &buttons, &buttons,
         ISystemBitmapHandle(ISystemBitmapHandle::program)),
  icon(ID_ICONBUTTON, &buttons, &buttons,
         ISystemPointerHandle(ISystemPointerHandle::folder));

IPushButton
  help(ID_HELP, &buttons, &buttons, IRectangle(),
       IPushButton::defaultStyle() |
       IPushButton::noPointerFocus);

// Indicate that the bitmap button should base its size on
// the size of the bitmap.
bitmap.enableSizeToGraphic();

// Set default button to "OK" and make this
// button the first of the group.
ok
  .enableDefault()
  .setText("OK")
  .enableTabStop()
  .enableGroup();

// Make the Cancel button a "Close" system command so
// the application closes when it is pressed.  Note
// that we created the button with the id
// ISystemMenu::idClose.
cancel
  .enableSystemCommand()
  .setText("Cancel");

// Make the Help button show help when pressed (in
// this application, we have not defined any help
// to display).
help
  .enableHelp()
  .setText("Help");

// Add the controls to the multicell canvas.
client
  .addToCell(&buttons, 2, 6, 3, 1);

// Allow for some growth in the canvas.
client
  .setRowHeight   (1, 20, true);
```

```
// Put the canvas in the client and show the window.
frame
  .setClient(&client)
  .setFocus()
  .show();

IApplication::current().run();
}
```

Figure 10-2 displays shows the output of this program.

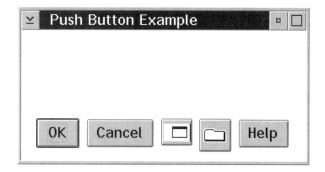

Figure 10-2. Push Button Example.

Setting Buttons

As Figure 10-1 shows, Open Class Library provides three classes of settings buttons: IRadioButton, ICheckBox, and I3StateBox. Whereas you use push buttons to initiate an immediate action, you use settings buttons to display settings or state information. ISettingButton adds the interface to enable you to select, deselect, and query the selection state with the functions select, deselect, and isSelected. ISettingButton also adds the interface to allow you to enable and disable auto-selection and to query the state of auto-selection with the functions enableAutoSelect, disableAutoSelect, and isAutoSelect.

Radio Buttons

You use radio buttons to allow your users to choose from a small list of mutually exclusive items. Radio buttons function like the radio buttons on a car—only one button can be selected at a time. When users select a radio button, the selection emphasis is removed from the previously selected radio button. If you have a large list of mutually exclusive choices, use a single selection list box instead of radio buttons to display the choices.

The Group Behavior of Radio Buttons

Ensure that you put each set of radio buttons into a single group by adding the group style to the first radio button. To add the group style, either create the radio button with the `IControl::group` style or call `IControl::enableGroup` after you create the radio button.

As you learned in Chapter 4, "Windows, Handlers, and Events," the sibling order determines the order in which windows are visited when users press the cursor arrow keys. The radio button's position in the sibling order also determines the value returned from `IRadioButton::selectedIndex`. If you create your radio buttons from top (with the group style) to bottom, the top radio button is assigned an index of 0, the second is 1, and so on. If a user does not select a radio button, the function returns -1. You can call this function on any radio button in the group to find the index of the currently selected radio button. Be aware that any nonbutton siblings of your buttons can cause the indexes to be nonsequential because the nonbutton siblings also have indexes. Therefore, create all radio buttons in a single group with no intervening controls.

Selection of Radio Buttons

`IRadioButton` has two styles that affect a user's ability to select radio buttons: `IRadioButton::autoSelect` and `IRadioButton::noCursorSelect`. By default, you create radio buttons with the `IRadioButton::autoSelect` style. This style causes the radio button to be selected when a user clicks on the button with the mouse. If you remove this style, you must select the radio button because the user is no longer able to select it. Also, without the `IRadioButton::autoSelect` style, an `ISelectHandler` attached to the radio button does not call `ISelectHandler::selected`.

By default, users just move the cursor to the radio button to select it. However, cursor selection only works if the radio button is a child window of a frame window or a canvas window. To turn off this behavior, create the radio buttons with the `IRadioButton::noCursorSelect` style or call `IRadioButton::disableCursorSelect` after you create each button. When you create a radio button with this style, the button is not selected when input focus is moved to the button using the cursor. The user selects the radio button by using the mouse or by pressing the space bar when the button has input focus.

Radio Button Handlers

If you need to perform an action when a user selects a radio button, you can add an `ISelectHandler` to the radio button. You might add such a handler to enable or disable other choices in the view when the user selects a particular radio button.

Do not use the function `ISelectHandler::enter` unless you want to treat a double-click as something other than another single-click. By default, `ISelectHandler::enter` calls `ISelectHandler::selected` when a user presses a button. Normally, you override `ISelectHandler::selected` to process radio button selections.

Radio Button Example

We have modeled the following example after the OS/2 Desktop Settings dialog for changing the background of the desktop. The example demonstrates the use of an `ISelectHandler` to capture a select event of a radio button and perform an action. When you select the **Color** radio button, we disable `ISetCanvas` for **Image** and its child windows that display the image data. When you select the **Image** radio button, we enable these windows. Figure 10-3 displays the results of this example.

Radio Button Select Handler - buttons\radio\radio.cpp

```cpp
#include <iframe.hpp>
#include <iradiobt.hpp>
#include <imcelcv.hpp>
#include <istattxt.hpp>
#include <icombobx.hpp>
#include <ipushbut.hpp>
#include <isetcv.hpp>
#include <iapp.hpp>
#include <iselhdr.hpp>
#include <icconst.h>
#include "radio.h"

// Declare the radio button select handler
class SelectHandler : public ISelectHandler
{
public:
  SelectHandler ( ISetCanvas& canvas)
      : _canvas(canvas)   {}

protected:
virtual Boolean
  selected    ( IControlEvent& event );

private:
ISetCanvas
 &_canvas;
SelectHandler& operator=(const SelectHandler&);
};

void main()
{
IFrameWindow
  frame ("Radio Button Select Handler Example");
IMultiCellCanvas
  client(IC_FRAME_CLIENT_ID, &frame, &frame);

// Set 1 for radio buttons; set 2 for bitmap name.
ISetCanvas
  set1(ID_SET1, &client, &client),
  set2(ID_SET2, &client, &client);

// Add the set 1 buttons.
IRadioButton
  image(ID_IMAGE, &set1, &set1),
  color(ID_COLOR, &set1, &set1);
IPushButton
  changeColor(ID_CHANGECOLOR, &set1, &set2);

set1.setText("Background type");
set2.setText("Image");
```

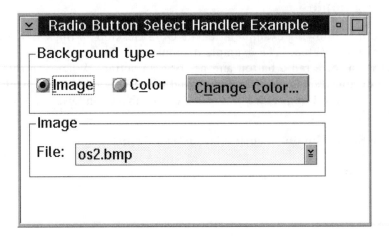

Figure 10-3. Radio Button Select Handler.

```
// Add text to the buttons.  Note that
// mnemonics are platform-sensitive.
#ifdef IC_PM
  image.setText("~Image");
  color.setText("C~olor");
  changeColor.setText("C~hange Color...");
#else
  image.setText("&Image");
  color.setText("C&olor");
  changeColor.setText("C&hange Color...");
#endif

// Add the set 2 text and combination box.
IStaticText
  fileLeader (ID_FILESTATIC, &set2, &set2);
IComboBox
  fileName   (ID_FILENAME, &set2, &set2, IRectangle(0,0,0,0),
             IComboBox::dropDownType | IWindow::visible);

fileLeader.setText("File:");
fileName.setText("os2.bmp");

// Enable tab stops.
image.enableTabStop();
fileName.enableTabStop();

// Select the color choice.
image.select();

image.disableAutoSelect();
color.disableCursorSelect();

// Add the sets to the client canvas.
client
 .addToCell(&set1, 2, 2)
 .addToCell(&set2, 2, 3);

// Allow for some growth in the canvas.
client
 .setRowHeight   (4, 10, true);
```

```
// Create and add select handler.
SelectHandler selectHandler(set2);
selectHandler.handleEventsFor(&set1);

// Put the canvas in the client and show the application.
frame
  .setClient(&client)
  .setFocus()
  .show();

IApplication::current().run();
}

IBase::Boolean SelectHandler::selected ( IControlEvent& event )
{

  switch(event.controlId())
  {
    case ID_IMAGE :
    case ID_COLOR :
    {
      // Test to see if we should enable or disable
      Boolean enable =  (event.controlId() == ID_IMAGE);

      // If image button is selected, Enable the canvas and
      // its children; otherwise, disable the canvas and its
      // children.  Although disabling the canvas disables
      // the children, they don't look disabled unless
      // we explicitly disable them.
      IRadioButton* button =
                  (IRadioButton*)event.controlWindow();
      if (button && button->isSelected())
      {
        _canvas.enable(enable);
        IWindow::ChildCursor cursor(_canvas);
        for(cursor.setToFirst();
            cursor.isValid();
            cursor.setToNext())
        {
          IWindow* child = IWindow::windowWithHandle(
                      _canvas.childAt(cursor));
          child->enable(enable);
        }
      }
      break;
    }
  }
  return false;
}
```

Check Boxes

A *check box* is a button control that contains a small box with a text string to the right of it. In objects of the class ICheckBox, this square can be in one of two states: checked or unchecked. Each time users select the check box, it toggles from one state to the other.

You can use check boxes in two ways: To allow users to choose from a small list of items that are not mutually exclusive or to represent the on and off state of a single item. Using them as a small list of items is similar to using a multiple-selection list box. In fact, if you have a large list of items, consider using a multiple-selection list box instead.

Also, use check boxes to represent the on or off state of a single item. For example, the **Sort** page of the OS/2 Desktop Settings has a check box labeled, "Always maintain sort order." If you check this box, the OS/2 Desktop maintains the sort order; otherwise, it does not.

The `I3StateCheckBox` and `ICheckBox` classes are similar except that the three-state check box has three possible states. Besides the checked and nonchecked states of the check box, the three-state check box has a halftone state. Each time users select the three-state check box, it toggles to one of these states.

The desktop publishing system we used to prepare most of this manuscript uses three-state check boxes effectively in its style sheets. We create these style sheets in a hierarchy. For certain attributes of these style sheets, we indicate that we explicitly want the behavior by checking a box, explicitly do not want the behavior by unchecking the box, or want the behavior of an inherited style sheet by leaving the box in its halftone state.

The Group Behavior of Check Boxes

To put check boxes that are used together into a single group, create the first check box in the group with the `IControl::group` style or call `IControl::enableGroup` on the first check box after you create it. Also, add the `IControl::tabStop` style to the first check box so that users can tab to the check boxes as a group.

Selection of Check Boxes

Like the `IRadioButton` class, the `ICheckBox` and `I3StateCheckBox` classes support an auto-select style called `ICheckBox::autoSelect` or `I3StateCheckBox::autoSelect`. By default, you create check boxes with the auto-select style. This style causes a check box to be selected or deselected, depending upon its state at the time, when a user clicks on it. If you remove this style, your must explicitly select the check boxes because the user is no longer able to do so.

Check Box Handlers

You can add an `ISelectHandler` to a check box to determine when the check box is checked, not checked, or halftone.

Only use a select handler if you need immediate processing when the check box is checked or unchecked (for example, to enable or disable other choices). Otherwise, simply query its selection state when you need it. When you use a select handler, be aware that `ISelectHandler` calls its `selected` function when your users select and deselect the button (and make it halftone). Query the check box directly if you need to distinguish these states.

Chapter 11

List Controls

- Describes the control classes you can use to display lists of items in Open Class Library
- Describes the IBaseListBox, IListBox, ICollectionViewListBox, IBaseComboBox, IComboBox, ICollectionViewComboBox, IBaseSpinButton, INumericSpinButton, ITextSpinButton, ISelectHandler, IEditHandler, IFocusHandler, IShowListHandler, IListBoxDrawItemHandler, IListBoxDrawItemEvent, and ISpinHandler classes
- Read Chapter 7 before reading this chapter.
- Chapters 9, 13, and 17 cover related material.

This chapter describes three controls that display items in a list: list box, combination box, and spin button. Figure 11-1 displays the Open Class Library classes that support these controls and their associated handler and event classes.

The container, described in Chapter 13, "Container Control," is another control that displays its items in a list. If you need to display many items or require more than a simple layout of the data, the container may be a better choice.

You create list controls using the same types of constructors that almost all classes derived from `IControl` support. See Chapter 7, "Controls," for details of these constructors.

The List Box

A *list box* is a rectangular window that displays a scrollable list of read-only items. Associated with each item in the list box is a text string and a handle. Without any action on your part, the list box displays the text string for each item. However, you can use the item handle to display a bitmap or other information for the item. Doing this requires you to draw the items in the list box. See the "Custom List Box Example" topic later in this chapter for more information.

Open Class Library provides two classes for creating list boxes. `IListBox` is the original Open Class Library list box class. `ICollectionViewListBox` is a template class that displays items from an Open Class Library collection class object in a list box. Because you can modify the contents of the list box only by changing the collection, `ICollectionViewListBox` provides a level of model-view separation. The *Visual Builder* that ships with VisualAge for C++ typically generates objects of this class instead of `IListBox`. `IListBox` and

199

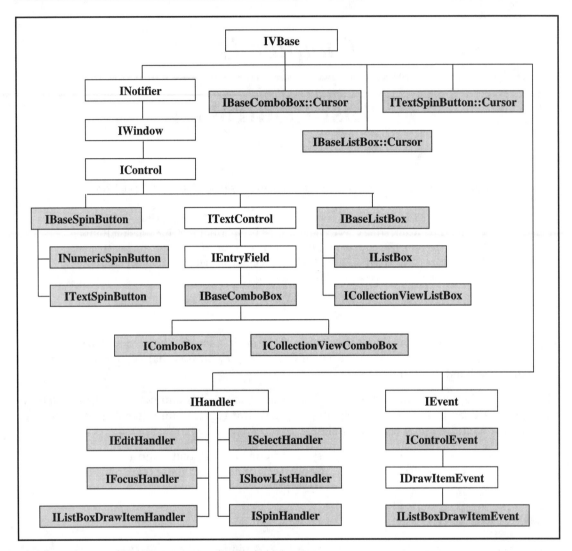

Figure 11-1. The Window, Handler, and Event Classes for Lists.

`ICollectionViewListBox` derive from `IBaseListBox`, which is an abstract class that contains the functions common to its derived classes.

A list box always contains a vertical scroll bar that it enables when it contains more items than it can display in its visible region. If it can display all the items, it disables the scroll bar. To display items wider than the visible area of the list box you add a horizontal scroll bar using the style `IBaseListbox::horizontalScroll`. Like the vertical scroll bar, the list box enables the horizontal scroll bar to scroll items that do not fit in its visible region.

By default the list box automatically shrinks its height so it does not display a partial bottom row. Add the style `IBaseListBox::noAdjustPosition` to stop the list box from adjusting its height. Do not use this style if the list box is the child of an `IMultiCellCanvas`, `ISetCanvas`, or `ISplitCanvas` because it can cause the screen at the bottom of the list box to remain unpainted.

In 32-bit Windows operating systems, you can get a 3-D border around the list box by specifying the style `IBaseListBox::border3D`. This style has no effect in other platforms.

Selecting List Box Items

The list box supports three forms of selection: single, multiple, and extended. Create multiple and extended selection list boxes by constructing them with the `IBaseListBox` `multipleSelect` or `extendedSelect` styles. You create a single-selection list box if you do not specify one of these styles.

In a *single-selection list box* a user can select only one item at a time. Selecting an item always deselects any previously selected item. Although you can display a single-selection list box without a selected item, one always becomes selected once a user interacts with the list box. A user selects an item by clicking it with the mouse or by moving the selection cursor onto an item and pressing the space bar. The only way to deselect an item is to select another item.

With a *multiple-selection list box*, you can select 0, one, or many items at a time. A user selects items by clicking them with the mouse or by moving the selection cursor onto an item and pressing the space bar. If you select an already selected item, the list box deselects the item. You can also select noncontiguous ranges of items in a multiple-selection list box.

An *extended-selection list box* is an enhanced form of a single-selection list box. Extended selection is appropriate for situations in which a user usually wants to select only one item, but occasionally wants to select more than one. Users can select multiple items by dragging the mouse across them. They can also select multiple items using the mouse or up and down arrow keys with the Shift key or Ctrl key pressed. They use the Shift key to select ranges of items. And, if they press the Ctrl key they can select noncontiguous items. If they select an unselected item without the Shift key or Ctrl key pressed, the list box first deselects all previously selected items.

All list boxes move the selection cursor to an item if a user types the first character of an item. In a single-selection list box, this produces the effect of first character selection.

Handling List Box Events

As Figure 11-1 shows, you can use several handler and event classes to process events for a list control. Of these you can use `IListBoxDrawItemHandler`, `ISelectHander`, and `IFocusHandler` (and their associated event classes) with a list box.

`ISelectHandler` calls its `selected` function when a user selects an item in the list box, and it calls its `enter` function when a user presses the Enter key or double-clicks the mouse on an item. Each of these functions receives an `IControlEvent` object with information about the event. (The Enter key can also select a default push button, which causes a command handler to be called.)

`IFocusHandler` calls its `gotFocus` function when the list box receives the keyboard focus and it calls its `lostFocus` function when it loses the keyboard focus. Do not change the window with the input focus in either of these functions. This rule applies regardless of the kind of control `IFocusHandler` is processing events for.

`IListBoxDrawItemHandler` provides the event-handling functions that you can override to replace the default drawing of list box items. The `IListBoxDrawItemEvent` class provides the information you need to draw the list box items and to draw selection emphasis. You only use these classes if you want to draw the items with special effects, such as icons or bitmaps. The list box automatically draws text items for you. An example described later in this chapter shows how to use these two classes.

The Combination Box

A *combination box* combines the behavior of an entry field with that of a list box. The value of a combination box is the value displayed in the entry field. Selecting a value from the list box places that value in the entry field. A user can type text in the entry field or select an item in the list box to fill the entry field unless the combination box is a read-only drop-down type. A read-only drop-down combination box forces its value to be one of the items in its list box. There are three different types of combination boxes:

simple

> This type of combination box always displays its list box. Create this type of combination box with the `simpleType` style. This is the default.

drop-down

> The visibility of the list box is under the control of the user for this type of combination box. Create this type of combination box with the `dropDownType` style.

read-only drop-down

> This type of combination box is a read-only version of the drop-down combination box. Create this type of combination box with the `readOnlyDropDownType` style.

Open Class Library provides two classes for creating combination boxes. `IComboBox` is the original Open Class Library combination box class. `ICollectionViewComboBox` is a template class that displays items from an Open Class Library collection class object in a combination box. Because you can modify the contents of the combination box only by changing the collection, `ICollectionViewComboBox` provides model-view separation. The Visual Builder that ships with VisualAge for C++ typically generates objects of this class instead of

IComboBox. IComboBox and ICollectionViewComboBox derive from IBaseComboBox, which is an abstract class that contains the functions common to its derived classes.

A simple combination box always displays its list box below the entry field. A drop-down combination box normally does not display its list box. The combination box provides a button, called a *drop-down button*, next to its entry field. When a user selects the drop-down button, the combination box displays its list box if it is hidden and removes it if it is visible. The read-only drop-down combination box is nothing more than a read-only version of the drop-down combination box, meaning you cannot type in the entry field. You cannot change the type of the combination box after creating the control.

In 32-bit Windows operating systems, you can get a 3-D border by specifying IBaseComboBox::border3D. This style has no affect in other platforms.

A combination box is a composite control made up of an entry field and a list box. To process keystrokes in the combination box, attach a keyboard handler to the entry field portion of the combination box. To do this, first create an IEntryField wrapper for the entry field using the constructor that takes a window identifier and parent window. CBID_EDIT, which is defined in PMWIN.H, is the identifier for the entry field in the OS/2 operating system. In the Windows operating system, the window identifier is 0x03E9. The parent window of the entry field is the combination box for both operating systems. In the Windows operating system, a read-only drop-down combination box does not have a child entry field to wrap, but there is normally no reason to attach a keyboard handler to a read-only control.

There are additional considerations when you use an IComboBox object in an IMultiCellCanvas object. See Chapter 15, "Canvases," for information on how to correctly use IComboBox with IMultiCellCanvas.

Selecting Combination Box Items

The list box portion of the combination box only supports single selection because its sole purpose is to aid the entering of data in the entry field of the combination box. When a user types the first letter in the entry field, the list box scrolls the list of items so it displays the items that begin with the character. The simple and drop-down combination boxes do not restrict what a user can type into the entry field to those items in its list box because this is the role of the read-only drop-down combination box.

Handling Combination Box Events

Of the handler classes displayed in Figure 11-1, you can use IShowListHandler, IEditHandler, ISelectHandler, and IFocusHandler with a combination box.

IShowListHandler calls its listShown function when the combination box is about to display its list box. This occurs when a user presses the drop-down button on a drop-down combination box. However, because a user can use the up and down arrow keys to scroll the list inside the entry field without ever displaying the list box, you cannot use this handler to initialize the contents of the list box.

IEditHandler calls its edit function when a user or your program changes the contents of the combination box entry field. ISelectHandler calls its selected function when a user selects an item in the list box. See Chapter 9, "Edit Controls," for more information on IEditHandler and ISelectHandler.

You can use IFocusHandler to detect when a combination box gains or loses focus. In the Windows operating system, attach the handler to either the IComboBox object or to its owner window. IControlEvent::controlWindow identifies the IComboBox object. In the OS/2 operating system, a focus handler attached to a read-only drop-down combination box or the owner of an IComboBox object is never called. You must attach the focus handler to a simple or drop-down combination box because the handler actually detects focus-change events for the child entry field of the combination box. As a result, IControlEvent::controlWindow identifies the entry field (it returns 0 if an IEntryField wrapper object does not exist), rather than the IComboBox.

List Box and Combination Box Items

Once you have constructed a list control you need to add items to it. The IListBox and IComboBox classes provide similar functions for operations, such as adding and removing items. ICollectionViewListBox and ICollectionViewComboBox require you to make all additions, removals, and changes to the list box items through their associated collection object. IBaseListBox and IBaseComboBox provide similar functions for selecting items. Because of these similarities, we describe the behavior of the list box and combination classes together.

Adding and Removing Items

IListBox and IComboBox provide functions to add items by passing a character string or resource identifier. You can use them as follows:

- By specifying the position to add an item in the list as a 0-based index using the add function

- By adding an item at the top or bottom of the list using the addAsFirst and addAsLast functions

- By adding an item in ascending or descending alphabetical order in the list using the addDescending and addAscending functions

- By adding an item relative to a cursor

The code to add list box items from the list box example described in a later topic follows:

Adding List Box Items - listctls\drawlist\drawlist.cpp

```
// Add the items to the list box by creating an
// IString from the item data address.
for(int i=0; i< sizeof(items)/sizeof(ListItem); i++)
{
   list.add(i, IString((unsigned long)&items[i]));
}
```

You can remove all items in a list or an item at a 0-based index position.

Selecting Items

When a user selects an item in a list box, the list box highlights the item. When a user selects an item in a combination box, it highlights the item and moves the value of the item to its entry field. You can also select an item in a list box or combination box programmatically. To select a single item in the list, use the `select` function, which requires a 0-based index of the item as an argument. If you do not know the index of an item, use the `locateText` function to retrieve the index based on the text of the item.

For the combination box and single-selection list box, selecting an item deselects any previously selected item. Because a multiple-selection list box enables users to select more than a single item, they must explicitly deselect items to remove the selection emphasis. No matter what type the list box or combination box is, you can deselect all items by calling `deselectAll`.

Obtain the index of the selected item in the list by calling the `selection` function or test if an item at an index position is selected by calling the `isSelected` function. With a multiple-selection list box, you can query the number of selected items by calling the `numberOfSelections` function. Use a cursor to get the selected items.

Finding Items Using Cursors

A *collection cursor* is a standard mechanism in Open Class Library for moving through the elements of a collection. Because the list box and the combination box are collections of items, both of these classes provide a nested class to iterate their items. These cursor classes, `IBaseListBox::Cursor` and `IBaseComboBox::Cursor`, have the standard functions of all cursors: `setToFirst`, `setToNext`, `setToPrevious`, `setToLast`, `isValid`, and `invalidate`. Because a multiple-selection list box can have multiple items selected, you can also create a cursor to iterate just the selected items in the list box.

Custom List Box Example

The custom list box example simulates the behavior of a class-hierarchy browser to show you how to replace the default drawing of items in a list box. This includes drawing both bitmaps and text for the list box items, and drawing the highlight state of each item. Figure 11-2 shows the running example.

Besides demonstrating how to draw list box items, we also demonstrate an alternative to storing handles for the list box items. First, you must store the data necessary to draw an item in an object. Then, you can convert the address of this object to a text string and use it as the item's text. When it is time to draw an item, you can use the functions of `IString` to convert the text string back into an address to the object, retrieve the actual text string of the item, and display it in the list box. This is the technique we use in the list box custom-drawing example.

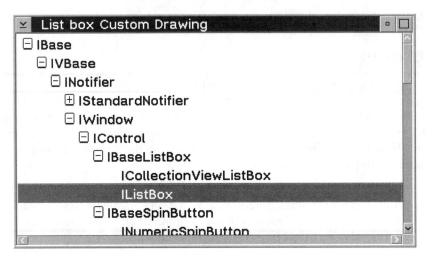

Figure 11-2. Custom List Box Drawing.

One note about this technique: Because the item text in the list box is not the actual text, first-character selection does not work correctly.

The Spin Button

The *spin button* is a visual control that displays a collection of items, one at a time, in the entry field, also called the *spin field*, portion of the spin button. The collection itself is an ordered collection, the ends of which connect to form a complete ring of items. The spin button displays up and down arrow buttons, called *spin arrows*, that allow users to use the mouse to scroll, or spin, the contents of the spin button within its entry field. They can also scroll the contents using the keyboard up and down arrow keys.

Open Class Library provides two classes for creating spin buttons, INumericSpinButton and ITextSpinButton. Both derive from IBaseSpinButton, which is an abstract class that contains the functions common to its derived classes. A numeric spin button contains a contiguous range of integers. A text spin button contains an array of text strings and, therefore, you can use one to display a noncontiguous collection of numbers as text strings.

Using Spin Button Styles

The spin button supports multiple entry fields controlled by a single set of spin arrows. You accomplish this by building one spin button with the style IBaseSpinButton::master and one or more spin buttons with the style IBaseSpinButton::servant. The master spin button contains the spin arrows that control the scrolling of both the master and servant spin fields. The spin arrows control the spin field with the focus. After constructing a servant spin button, call the function IBaseSpinButton::setMaster to identify the master spin button. A typical example for a set of master and servant spin buttons is an editable date display containing individual month, day, and year fields. We use this as an example in this chapter.

`IBaseSpinButton::pmCompatible` is only available in the Windows platform. Specifying this style gives you a spin button with the same look and feel as the OS/2 operating system spin button. Set the same `pmCompatible` style for all associated master and servant spin buttons. In 32-bit Windows operating systems, you can get a 3-D border around a spin button created without the `IBaseSpinButton::pmCompatible` style by specifying the style `IBaseSpinButtonx::border3D`. This style has no effect in other platforms.

There are several other styles that you can specify when you create a spin button. You can change any of the following styles dynamically using functions provided in `IBaseSpinButton`:

- Build a read-only spin button by adding the `IBaseSpinButton::readOnly` style. A read-only spin button limits the choices that your users can make to those in the spin button's collection. Without this style, you must validate the data that a user types.

- Increase the rate that the spin button spins the data in the spin field by adding `IBaseSpinButton::fastSpin`. With this style, the spin button skips some entries. If you use the `ISpinHandler` class (described in the next topic) to synchronize the movement of master and servant spin buttons, do not use this style. The spin button omits scrolling to some items in the spin button's collection to speed up scrolling. If your spin handler depends on being notified when a user scrolls past these skipped items, it will not work correctly with this style.

- Justify the data in the entry field using one of the `IBaseSpinButton` styles: `leftAlign`, `centerAlign`, or `rightAlign`.

All of the spin button styles have accessors for determining the style's current setting.

Handling Spin Button Events

Of the handler classes displayed in Figure 11-1, you can use `IEditHandler`, `ISpinHandler`, `IFocusHandler`, and `IKeyboardHandler` with a spin button. `IEditHandler` calls the `edit` function when a user or your program changes the contents of the spin button's entry field.

`ISpinHandler` enables you to process the events relating to the use of the spin arrow or the keyboard arrow keys. `ISpinHandler` calls the `arrowUp` function when a user clicks on the up arrow button or presses the up arrow key. Similarly, it calls the `arrowDown` function when a user clicks on the down arrow button or presses the down arrow key. Finally, it calls the `spinEnded` function when a user releases a spin arrow or arrow key.

`IFocusHandler` calls the `gotFocus` function when the spin button receives the input focus, and it calls the `lostFocus` function when it loses the input focus. Do not change the window with the input focus in either of these functions.

You can also use an `IKeyboardHandler` with an `ITextSpinButton` or `INumericSpinButton` object, but you must attach it to the entry field portion of the spin button. Create an `IEntryField` wrapper for the entry field portion of the spin button using the constructor requiring a window identifier and parent window. The parent window of the entry field is the spin button and the ID is the same as that of the spin button.

Spin Button Items

You can restrict the number of characters or numbers displayed in the spin button using the `IBaseSpinButton::setLimit` function.   To check the current limit use the `IBaseSpinButton::limit` function.

Adding and Removing Items

The only way to add items to a numeric spin button is with the function `INumericSpinButton::setRange`. This does not stop your users from entering a number outside this range, but they are unable to scroll to a number outside this range using the spin arrows or arrow keys. If you call `setRange` while a numeric value outside the specified range is in the spin field, the spin button spins to the nearest valid value in the range. If you want to keep this out-of-bounds value in the spin field when you change the range, you can do so by passing `true` as the second parameter to the `setRange` function. There is no function to remove values in the middle of the range that you specify on the `setRange` function. You can only specify a new range of values. The `range` function returns the current range.

There are many functions provided for adding, removing, and replacing items in a text spin button. The `ITextSpinButton::Cursor` class is one mechanism that you can use to work with the collection of items. This cursor class has the standard function of all cursors in Open Class Library: `setToFirst`, `setToNext`, `setToPrevious`, `setToLast`, `isValid`, and `invalidate`.

`ITextSpinButton` provides the following ways to add items:

- Specify the text or string resource identifier and position for each new item. The position is specified as a 0-based index or using a cursor.

- Specify an array of text strings, a 0-based index for the position to add the array at, and the number of strings in the array.

- Specify the text or string resource identifier of the new item that you want to insert at the top or bottom of the list using `addAsFirst` and `addAsLast`.

The following code is from the date control example provided with this chapter, and it demonstrates how to add the months of the year to a month spin button:

Adding Spin Button Items - listctls\spinbut\datectrl.cpp

```
...
// Load the Month spin button
for (int i=1;
     i < 13;
     i++)
{
   month().addAsLast(IDate::monthName((IDate::Month)i));
}
...
```

You can remove all items from the spin button or only the item at a cursor position. You can also replace an item at a cursor position by specifying the text or string resource identifier.

Finding Items

You might want to determine if a particular string is contained in a text spin button. Although no function does this directly, you can accomplish this by iterating through the spin button collection. `ITextSpinButton` provides two overloaded versions of `elementAt` to retrieve items from the spin button collection. The first takes a 0-based index, and the second takes an `ITextSpinButton::Cursor` object.

Spinning to an Item

You can use the `IBaseSpinButton::spinUp` and `IBaseSpinButton::spinDown` functions to spin a text or numeric spin button the specified number of times. The default is to spin the button one time.

Use the `INumericSpinButton::spinTo` function when you are not sure if the number that you want to spin to is in the current range. This function takes a value to spin to and a `Boolean` for specifying the behavior you prefer when the specified number is outside the range. If you specify `true`, the button spins to the closest limit of the range. The default is `false`, which causes the function to throw an `IInvalidParameter` exception if the number is not in the range.

`ITextSpinbutton` provides three overloaded versions of `spinTo` for complete flexibility in spinning to an item. The simplest version takes a 0-based index. The second version takes a character string and an optional `Boolean`, which indicates whether case-sensitivity matters when searching for a match. The default is `false`, which means to ignore the case. The last version takes an `ITextSpinButton::Cursor` object.

Setting and Validating the Current Value

`INumericSpinButton::setValue` is the only function that sets the current value of a numeric spin button to a number outside of the current range. You can also use this function to set the value to a number in the range. Be aware that `setValue` does not extend the range to include the specified number. The `INumericSpinButton::value` function returns the current value displayed in the spin field. To determine if the currently displayed number is in the range, use the `INumericSpinButton::isSpinFieldValid` function. The `Boolean` argument is not used for numeric spin buttons.

`ITextSpinButton::setText` sets a text spin button's current value to a string not contained in its collection. You can also use it to set the value to one of the items in the collection. This string is not added to the collection of spin button items. Use `ITextSpinButton::text` to retrieve the current value in the spin field. You can use the `ITextSpinButton::isSpinFieldValid` function to determine if the current text displayed in the spin field is contained in the spin button collection. This function takes a `Boolean` argument, which indicates if case-sensitivity matters. If you specify `true`, the text must match a value in the collection exactly. This argument defaults to `false`. There is no function to clear a spin button's current value. Use the `setText` function to set the current value to a space or a 0-length string.

Master and Servant Date Control Example

The spin button example demonstrates how to use master and servant spin buttons to create a control that enables a user to edit the month, day, and year fields of a date. The class `DateControl` inherits from `IMultiCellCanvas` and on construction creates the spin buttons to show and edit the individual fields of a date. `DateControl` also creates the `ISpinHandler`-derived class `DateSpinHandler` to capture the spin events of its spin buttons. This handler updates the month and year fields when the day and month fields exceed their range.

The following code sets the spin buttons to the current date. It also associates the servant spin buttons with the master spin button so that the spin arrows control all of the spin buttons.

Setting up the Spin Buttons - listctls\spinbut\datectrl.cpp

```
year()
   .setRange(aYearRange)
   .setLimit(4);
year()
   .spinTo(aDate.year());

month()
   .setMaster(year())
   .setLimit(12);
month()
   .setText(aDate.monthName());

day()
   .setRange(IRange(1,32))
   .setMaster(year())
   .setLimit(2);
day()
   .spinTo(aDate.dayOfMonth());
```

Figure 11-3 shows the running example.

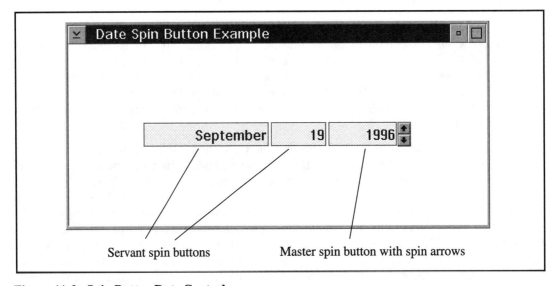

Servant spin buttons   Master spin button with spin arrows

Figure 11-3. Spin Button Date Control.

Chapter 12

Slider Controls

- Describes the classes provided by Open Class Library for using a progress indicator or slider
- Describes the IProgressIndicator, ISlider, ICircularSlider, ISliderArmHandler, and ISliderDrawHandler classes
- Read Chapter 7 before reading this chapter.
- Chapters 9, 11, and 17 cover related material.

Open Class Library provides three control classes for displaying and selecting a value from a range in addition to those described in Chapter 11, "List Controls." These classes are IProgressIndicator, ISlider, and ICircularSlider. This chapter describes these classes, which you can use to create and manipulate progress indicator and slider controls. It also describes the specialized event handler classes for these controls: ISliderArmHandler and ISliderDrawHandler. Figure 12-1 shows the hierarchy for these classes.

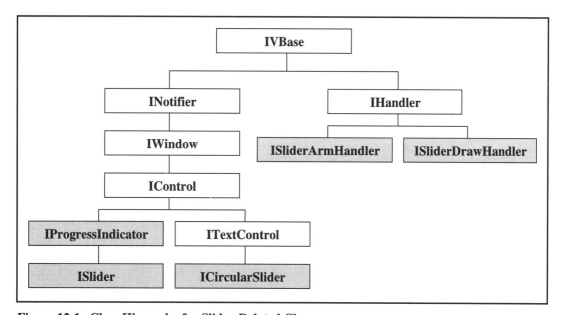

Figure 12-1. Class Hierarchy for Slider-Related Classes.

A *linear slider* displays a value through the position of its arm. A user can modify that value by sliding the arm back and forth along the slider shaft. Typically, you use a slider in cases where the value is a numeric quantity in a continuous range of possible values. The values could be in units of feet, meters, decibels, or percentages, for example. You can provide a scale next to the slider shaft to allow a user to easily match the position of the arm to a value.

Whereas a *circular slider* has similar use to a linear slider, it has a different appearance. The model for a circular slider is a twistable knob (or dial), such as you use to control the volume on a radio or stereo receiver. Multimedia applications often use circular sliders.

Figure 12-2 shows an example of each of these three types of controls.

By using the ISliderArmHandler class, you can detect when the value of any of these three controls changes; whereas by using the ISliderDrawHandler class, you can provide custom painting for a progress indicator or linear slider. However, ISliderDrawHandler is not available for all types of an IProgressIndicator or ISlider object in the Windows operating system (see the "Custom Painting" topic). Note that although you can also use the IEditHandler and IFocusHandler classes with these controls (as well as with other control classes such as IEntryField), we do not describe these event handler classes in this chapter. ISliderArmHandler is better suited for the slider classes than IEditHandler because IEditHandler does not provide a virtual function equivalent to ISliderArmHandler::moving.

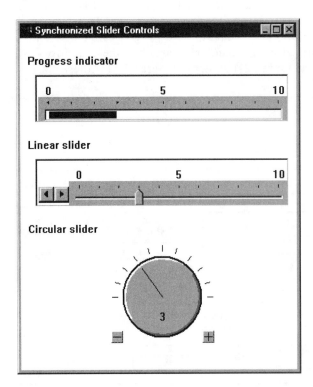

Figure 12-2. Progress Indicator, Linear Slider, and Circular Slider.

Progress Indicator

Applications must stay responsive to user interaction, even while performing time-consuming operations. To be user-friendly, they also must provide feedback to the user on the status of long-running tasks. Chapter 20, "Applications and Threads," discusses the use of the IThread class for creating multithreaded applications to address the first requirement; this section describes the IProgressIndicator class for addressing the second.

Use the IProgressIndicator class to create and manipulate progress indicator controls. You can use progress indicators to display status graphically. Figure 12-3 shows a progress indicator. Note that IProgressIndicator does not give you a complete window, only a progress indicator control. To use this class, you must still place the control within a frame window and, optionally, add static text and push buttons to the window as shown in the figure.

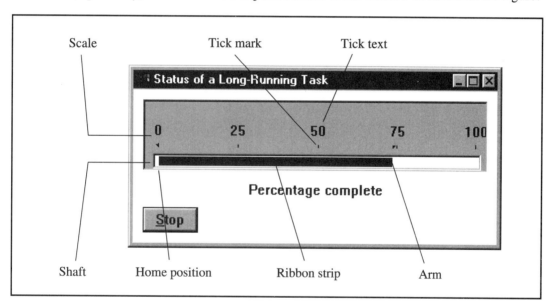

Figure 12-3. Progress Indicator Example.

The following definitions apply to progress indicators, as well as linear sliders. These areas of a progress indicator are labeled in Figure 12-3 and in Figure 12-4 for a linear slider.

Arm

> The arm represents the current value of the control. To provide a visual indicator of its value, a progress indicator uses its arm to size its *ribbon strip* (see definition in this list). Users cannot move the arm of a progress indicator using the keyboard or mouse, as they can with a slider. Only the application can change the arm position such as by calling IProgressIndicator::moveArmToTick. See the topic, "Progress Indicator Arm Operations," for more details.

Shaft

The horizontal or vertical track that the arm moves along. The shaft represents the control's entire range of possible values.

Home position

The end of the shaft that serves as the starting or base location for the arm.

Ribbon strip

The area of the shaft between the home position and the arm. When you specify the `IProgressIndicator::ribbonStrip` style, the control paints this area a different color than the rest of the shaft.

Tick

An incremental value along the shaft. Progress indicators and sliders position their ticks evenly along their shafts. A tick is not visible, but it can have a tick mark and tick text that are.

Tick mark

An optional mark identifying the position of a tick.

Tick text

An optional label indicating the value that a tick represents. The tick text is centered on the tick.

Scale

The area along the shaft occupied by tick marks and tick text. The scale shows the range of values represented by the control.

Creating a Progress Indicator

`IProgressIndicator` has the same standard constructors that almost all control classes provide. Chapter 7, "Controls," describes these constructors and their common parameters. However, in its constructors for creating an operating system window, `IProgressIndicator` provides arguments for defining the number of ticks in a scale and the space between ticks.

The `tickSpacing` parameter sets the number of pixels, or pels, between each tick on the scale. Be careful when you use this parameter because if you specify a value other than 0, you fix the length of the shaft and scale at that value multiplied by one less than the number of ticks. This can cause strange painting problems if you or the user makes the progress indicator window shorter than this fixed length. If you use the default value of 0 for tick spacing, the progress indicator calculates the length of the shaft to best fit within the size of the progress indicator. The progress indicator continues to calculate the length for the shaft and scale whenever you change the number of ticks or whenever you or the user changes the size of the progress indicator. We recommend that you specify 0 for tick spacing unless you must have complete control over the length of the shaft. Sizing a progress indicator can be problematic, however, even when using the default value for tick spacing. See the topic "Sizing a Progress Indicator" for more information.

`IProgressIndicator` provides styles for customizing the appearance and behavior of a progress indicator. You use these styles with the constructors that create an operating system window. The only styles you cannot change after constructing a progress indicator are those that control the following:

- The horizontal or vertical orientation of the control

  The styles `IProgressIndicator::horizontal` and `IProgressIndicator::vertical` control the orientation.

- The location of the shaft within the progress indicator

  Use the `IProgressIndicator` alignment styles (`IProgressIndicator::alignCentered`, `IProgressIndicator::alignTop`, `IProgressIndicator::alignBottom`, `IProgressIndicator::alignLeft`, and `IProgressIndicator::alignRight`) to control how white space is added above and below a horizontal shaft and left and right of a vertical shaft. This white space creates space for the scale. See the topic "Sizing a Progress Indicator" for related information.

  You can override the alignment style by manually positioning the shaft using `IProgressIndicator::setShaftPosition`. This function, however, is not available in the Windows platform if you do not use the style `IProgressIndicator::pmCompatible`.

- The portability between objects of the Windows and OS/2 versions of the class

  The controlling style, `IProgressIndicator::pmCompatible`, is only available on the Windows platform. We refer to an object created with this style as a *PM-compatible* control. The code you write for this object is highly portable between the OS/2 and Windows operating systems both functionally and visually. However, the resulting window is a control that Open Class Library provides rather than a control that the Windows operating system provides.

  If you do not use this style in the Windows operating system, the object uses the track bar control, a control the operating system provides. If the Windows operating system updates the look of this control, the look of an `IProgressIndicator` window automatically gets the same look. We refer to this version of a progress indicator, or slider, as the *native-Windows* version of the class. Such an object does not support all functions of the class, however. For example, you cannot customize tick marks and color or provide specialized painting, because the Windows track bar control does not offer such support. See the topics "Setting Up a Progress Indicator" and "Custom Painting" for more details.

  For most people, the use of native visuals is a higher priority than the availability of all functions. As a result, most applications will not likely build a progress indicator using the `IProgressIndicator::pmCompatible` style.

- A border around the control

  The controlling style, `IProgressIndicator::border3D`, has an affect only in 32-bit Windows operating systems.

With `IProgressIndicator`, you can also modify other elements of a progress indicator, including characteristics associated with other `IProgressIndicator::Style` values (see the next topic).

Following is an example of constructing an `IProgressIndicator` object as a data member of a class. The constructor creates an operating system window with five ticks and specifies a tick-spacing value of 0.

Constructing a Progress Indicator - slider\progind\progind.cpp

```
progressIndicator( 100, &canvasClient, &canvasClient,
                   IRectangle(), 5, 0,
                   ( IProgressIndicator::defaultStyle()
                       & ~IProgressIndicator::alignCentered )
                     | IProgressIndicator::alignBottom ),
```

Setting Up a Progress Indicator

By default, a progress indicator has a horizontal shaft centered in the window, a scale above the shaft, the home position at the left end of the shaft, and a ribbon strip. The home position is the starting point for numbering ticks and calculating offsets used by functions such as `armTickOffset`. Give the progress indicator a ribbon strip; otherwise, the user cannot see the value of the control (depending on the operating system and your use of the `IProgressIndicator::pmCompatible` style).

Although you can specify ticks and tick spacing for two scales, you can only use one scale, the *primary scale*, at any time. A progress indicator paints the tick marks and tick text for the primary scale only. And, any calls to tick-related functions, such as `setTickLength`, `setTickText`, and `moveArmToTick`, also apply to the primary scale only. Because you can dynamically change which scale is the primary scale using `IProgressIndicator::setPrimaryScale`, this function causes ticks and tick marks to move from one side of the shaft to the other. Construct the `IProgressIndicator` object with the `alignCentered` style to prevent one of its scales from being clipped. Or, change the ticks and tick marks in the scale by replacing the definition of the primary scale. Do this by calling `setTicks`, `setTickLength`, and `setTickText`. Either technique, however, can cause the length of the shaft to change if you change the number of ticks or the tick spacing.

By default, the tick marks of a progress indicator have a length of 0 (except for the native-Windows version, which always draws tick marks for the first and last ticks). Because a progress indicator does not paint tick marks unless they have a nonzero length, call `setTickLength` with a nonzero length to make them visible. The `setTickLength` function is overloaded. Thus, you can assign all tick marks the same zero or nonzero length with one call, or you can set the length of each tick mark individually. For the native-Windows version of the control, any nonzero value you pass to `setTickLength` causes the tick mark to be drawn with a predetermined length. The exact value you specify is not used. In the OS/2 platform and in the Windows platform when you use the style `IProgressIndicator::pmCompatible`, the value you pass sets the length of the tick mark in pixels.

To add text to the scale, use `setTickText`. Both `setTickLength` and `setTickText` identify a tick using a 0-based index from the home position. Both throw an exception if you specify an invalid index.

The following code sets the tick marks and tick text for the progress indicator shown in Figure 12-3. This example uses few ticks in the scale because a large number of ticks can lead to painting and sizing problems. See the next two topics for more details.

Setting Tick Marks and Tick Text - slider\progind\progind.cpp

```
// Set the length of the tick marks and define the tick text for
// the progress indicator.  We minimize the number of ticks to
// avoid sizing problems and to avoid clipping or overlapping
// the tick text.
progressIndicator
  .setTickLength( 10 );
for ( int i = 0; i <= 4; i++ )
{
  progressIndicator
    .setTickText( i, IString( i * 25 ) );
          // Label ticks with "0," "25," "50," "75," "100".
}
```

Finally, you can customize a progress indicator by changing its colors. Use setBackgroundColor to set the background and setForegroundColor to set the color of the tick marks and tick text. The native-Windows version has limited color support because the Windows track bar control does not support customizing colors. For this version, you can change the color of only the tick marks and the area surrounding the track bar control.

Additionally, only the OS/2 and PM-compatible versions allow you to customize the color of the ribbon strip or shaft, but they require you to use the ISliderDrawHandler class to do this. See the topic "Custom Painting" for details.

Sizing a Progress Indicator

Sizing a progress indicator is difficult because you have to consider the following factors:

- Orientation
- Number of ticks and tick spacing
- Shaft position and breadth
- Lengths of tick marks
- Tick text size based on the current font

As an indication of how difficult this is, IProgressIndicator currently uses only one of these factors in its calcMinimumSize routine. This function returns a fixed value of approximately ISize(100,30) or ISize(30,100) based on the orientation of the control.

Sizing the length of a progress indicator is difficult because you can only indirectly size the length of its shaft and scale. The number of ticks determines how the shaft and scale spread out. Any pixels that cannot be evenly divided between all ticks become white space at the ends of the shaft and scale. As a result, using a large number of ticks, N, can potentially result in a large amount of white space at each end of the shaft: $(N/2)-1$ pixels in the worst case. Reducing the number of ticks reduces the amount of potential white space. See the next topic, "Progress Indicator Arm Operations," for information on this technique. In the OS/2 platform and in the Windows platform when you use the IProgressIndicator::pmCompatible style, the control may not paint the shaft if you size the control so small that the shaft does not have at least one pixel for each tick.

One reason to indirectly size the length of the shaft is to control the amount of white space around the ends of the shaft. Only the boundary of the control clips tick text, so tick text for the first and last ticks could be clipped if the first and last ticks are too close to the edge of the control (because tick text is centered on a tick). To prevent this tick text from being clipped, you must prevent the shaft from extending to the edges of the control. By creating white space at the ends of the shaft, you are creating room for the tick text at the ends of the shaft. For tick text not at the ends of the shaft, if the scale is not wide or tall enough, depending on the orientation of the control, the tick text can overlap adjacent tick text. Minimizing the number of ticks with tick text and limiting the length of tick text for a horizontal progress indicator helps to prevent this overlap.

Sizing the other dimension of a progress indicator (the height when using a horizontal shaft or width when using a vertical shaft) is only slightly less difficult. To avoid extra white space around the breadth of the shaft, do not use the `IProgressIndicator::alignCentered` style. (The two exceptions are: you are changing the primary scale at run time, or you need the white space for better esthetics for the optional border on 32-bit Windows platforms). Because the control centers only the shaft when you use this style, rather than the combination of the shaft and scale, you must size the control larger than you think you would need to fit the scale. Otherwise, what you see is a large amount of white space on the side of the shaft not occupied by the primary scale.

Progress Indicator Arm Operations

`IProgressIndicator` provides two functions for moving the arm along the shaft. The first is `moveArmToTick`, which does not require you to know the number of pixels between ticks. When calling this function, you identify the tick with its 0-based index from the home position. The second function is `moveArmToPixel`.

Use `moveArmToPixel` when you need greater precision in positioning the arm than ticks allow, such as minimizing the number of ticks to avoid some of the sizing problems described in the previous topic. Do not create a progress indicator with the `snapToTickMark` style if you are using this function because this style prevents you from placing its arm between ticks. If necessary, you can convert ticks to pixels or pixels to ticks by using the member functions `tickSpacing`, `armRange`, and `numberOfTicks`. `tickSpacing` returns the number of pixels between ticks; `armRange` returns the number of pixels in the scale (the length of the scale in pixels is one less than this value); `numberOfTicks` returns the number of ticks in the scale. The following example calls `armRange` and `moveArmToPixel` to move the arm to a percentage of the total shaft length, as specified by the `percentToUse` variable. This code works regardless of the number of ticks in the scale and the size of the progress indicator.

Setting the Arm Position - slider\progind\progind.cpp

```
unsigned long
  totalPixels = progressIndicator.armRange() - 1,
  newArmOffset = totalPixels * percentToUse / 100;
progressIndicator
 .moveArmToPixel( newArmOffset );
```

The Underlying Operating System Window

Open Class Library implements the native-Windows version of both IProgressIndicator and ISlider as *composite controls*, controls that are composed of several windows. Both use a surrounding window that contains a TRACKBAR_CLASS control. This implementation is used to add tick text, which the TRACKBAR_CLASS does not support, as well as scroll buttons in the case of ISlider. This implementation does not prevent you from sending TBM_* Windows messages to the window handle returned by the handle function of an IProgressIndicator or ISlider object, however. The surrounding window, whose window handle is actually returned, routes TBM_* messages that it receives to the TRACKBAR_CLASS control. Such code is not portable to the OS/2 operating system.

The OS/2 operating system does not provide separate progress indicator and linear slider controls. Both are implemented with the WC_SLIDER control class, and a style differentiates the two. Open Class Library provides both an IProgressIndicator class and an ISlider class. It does this for two reasons: the visual appearance of a progress indicator and typical linear slider differ significantly, and the WC_SLIDER control class supports functions that do not apply to a progress indicator.

In the OS/2 operating system and in the Windows operating system when you use the style IProgressIndicator::pmCompatible, calling moveArmToTick or moveArmToPixel to initially position the arm to its initial position. Either specify a value for tick spacing or ensure that the progress indicator has a size before you move the arm. Otherwise, Open Class Library throws an exception because the shaft has no length. If you do not set tick spacing, you must either ensure that the layout routine for the parent canvas gets run or that you set the size of the progress indicator window before you move the arm.

We discuss the query functions armTickOffset and armPixelOffset in the next section on linear sliders, because they are most useful for finding the position of the arm after the user has moved it.

Linear Slider

The ISlider class creates and manipulates a linear slider control. ISlider is derived from IProgressIndicator and, therefore, inherits all of the capability that IProgressIndicator provides. As a result, the previous topics that describe IProgressIndicator apply to ISlider objects as well. Also, because sliders are not read-only, ISlider has additional styles and functions to support user interaction. Figure 12-4 shows a typical linear slider.

Visually, the biggest difference between a progress indicator and linear slider is in their arms. For a slider, the arm is clearly visible and the user can drag it with the mouse to change the value of the control. Although a linear slider supports a ribbon strip, its arm is the primary visual indicator for its value. Linear sliders also support the following optional user interface elements:

Slider buttons

Buttons at one end of the shaft. When you select a slider button with the mouse, the slider arm moves one increment (tick spacing) in the indicated direction. One consequence of minimizing the number of ticks to improve the sizing of a slider (as recommended in the topic "Sizing a Progress Indicator") is that users have a coarser level of control over the movement of the arm when they use the slider buttons.

Detent

A user-selectable mark on the scale supported on the OS/2 platform and on the Windows platform when you use the IProgressIndicator::pmCompatible style. You can place a detent anywhere along the scale; it does not have to be placed at a tick position. Selecting a detent with the mouse moves the arm to the detent (or the closest tick if you are using the IProgressIndicator::snapToTickMark style). See the topic "Adding Detents" for more information.

A linear slider thus gives a user several ways of moving the arm. For example, you can use the mouse to drag the slider arm, select the shaft on either side of the arm, select a slider button, or select a detent. When the slider has the input focus you can also use the keyboard to move the slider arm by pressing the arrow keys, Home key, or End key.

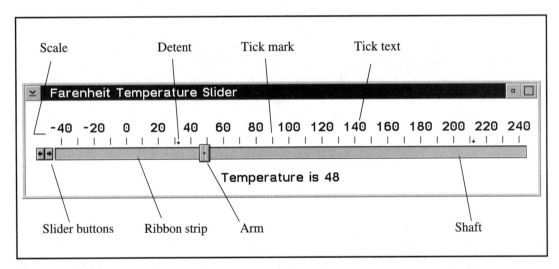

Figure 12-4. Linear Slider Example.

Creating a Slider

ISlider provides constructors identical to those that IProgressIndicator provides. As a result, the information and recommendations given earlier in this chapter for constructing IProgressIndicator objects also applies to ISlider objects. Especially note the recommendations for the tickSpacing parameter.

To add slider buttons, specify one of the four button styles (for example, `ISlider::buttonsLeft`) on the constructor. `ISlider` provides no functions for later adding or moving the buttons. For horizontal sliders, add the buttons to the left or right of the slider shaft. For vertical sliders, add the buttons above or below the slider shaft. You can also create a slider without buttons by not using any of the button styles.

Finding the Position of the Arm

The `armTickOffset` and `armPixelOffset` functions of `IProgressIndicator` are essential for sliders because the user can move the arm. These functions return the location of the arm. `armTickOffset` returns the number of ticks from the home position of the scale to the tick closest to the arm. `armPixelOffset` returns the number of pixels from the home position to the arm position. If your slider does not use the style `IProgressIndicator::snapToTickMark`, which allows the user to drag the arm between ticks, query the arm position using `armPixelOffset`. Then, map it to an application value using the total pixels in the scale, which is available from the `IProgressIndicator::armRange` function.

The following code uses `armPixelOffset` to update a static text control with the new value of the slider, as done for Figure 12-4. It demonstrates the use of `armPixelOffset` and `armRange` to determine where the user has moved the arm.

Querying the Arm Position - slider\slider\tempview.cpp

```
ISlider *slider = (ISlider*)event.controlWindow();

// We need to deal with pixel offsets instead of ticks because
// we have only 29 ticks but need to appear to support 281.
unsigned long
  totalPixels = slider->armRange() - 1,
  armOffset = slider->armPixelOffset();
long temperature =
  armOffset * ( 281 - 1 ) / totalPixels - 40;
temperatureText->setText( IString( "Temperature is " )
                          + IString( temperature ) );
```

Adding Detents

You can use detents to mark special values on the slider scale. Detents are similar to tick marks, except you can place them anywhere along the slider scale, and users can select a detent with the mouse. Selecting a detent moves the arm directly to the detent position. Users can also move the arm to the previous or next detent by holding down the Shift key and pressing the left or right arrow key. The native-Windows version of the linear slider, however, does not support detents. Also, do not add detents to a slider whose size can change because `ISlider` does not attempt to adjust the position of a detent.

The following code adds detents at 32 degrees and 212 degrees on the Fahrenheit slider in Figure 12-4. The detents mark the freezing and boiling points on this temperature scale. Use the `addDetent` function to add a detent at a pixel offset, which is measured from the home position on the slider. `addDetent` returns a unique detent identifier, which the `detentPosition` and `removeDetent` functions require to identify a detent. Note that the `tickPosition` function returns the offset of a tick from the left edge of the linear slider window, not from its home position. As a result, before you can pass this value to addDetent, you must convert it to the number of pixels from the home position. Do this by subtracting the position of tick 0, which is located at the home position, from your value. Because the slider in the example does not have ticks where we want the detents, we instead convert degrees to pixels and avoid ticks altogether.

Adding Detents - slider\slider\tempview.cpp

```
// Force the canvas to size the slider, and size the frame
// window around the client so the slider does not resize.
ISize
  clientMinimumSize( canvasClient.minimumSize() );
(*this)
  .moveSizeToClient( IRectangle( IPoint( 50, 50 ),
                                 clientMinimumSize ) );

// Translate degrees to pixel offsets from tick 0.
// The total number of pixels spans 280 degrees (-40 to 240).
unsigned long
  totalPixels = farenheitSlider.armRange() - 1;
unsigned long
  pixelsToFreezing = (32 + 40) * totalPixels / 280 + 1,
  pixelsToBoiling = (212 + 40) * totalPixels / 280 + 1;

// Add detents for freezing and boiling temperatures using
// the above pixel offsets.
farenheitSlider
  .addDetent( pixelsToFreezing );
farenheitSlider
  .addDetent( pixelsToBoiling );
```

Circular Slider

A circular slider is similar functionally to a linear slider, although it looks quite different. A circular slider uses many of the same elements used by a linear slider, such as an arm, ticks, tick marks, and buttons. However, its most important feature is its dial. Users change the value of a circular slider by turning the dial, which moves the arm. They can do this by direct manipulation with the mouse, by selecting the new arm position with the mouse, by selecting the increment or decrement slider button with the mouse, or by pressing the left or right arrow keys. These elements are labeled in Figure 12-5. Unlike a linear slider, a circular slider does not have tick text, detents, multiple scales, or a ribbon strip.

Although the Windows operating system does not provide a control equivalent to the WC_CIRCULARSLIDER control available in the OS/2 operating system, Open Class Library offers one through the class ICircularSlider.

Constructing a Circular Slider

ICircularSlider provides the standard constructors described in Chapter 7, "Controls." However, because the Windows operating system does not provide a circular slider control, you do not have a way to create a circular slider without using the ICircularSlider constructor that creates a window. As a result, in the Windows operating system you have little opportunity to use the constructors that wrapper an existing circular slider control.

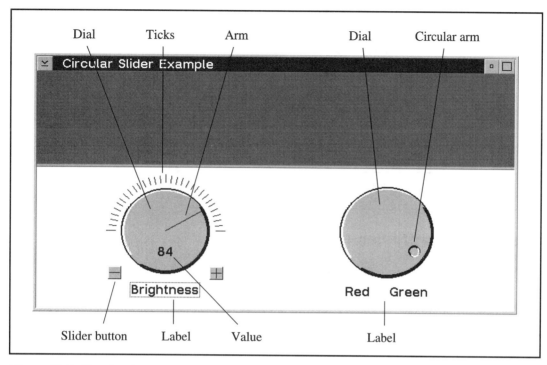

Figure 12-5. Circular Slider Example

ICircularSlider provides no functions for changing the setting of any of its style values following construction. So, you must decide the look that you want your circular slider to have and specify the appropriate ICircularSlider::Style values to get that look when you construct the object. A number of the styles affect the working of other styles or functions. These relationships are shown in Table 12-1.

The calls to construct the two circular slider objects in Figure 12-5 follow. The two circular sliders, brightnessSlider and redGreenSlider, are data members of another class.

Circular Slider Example - slider\cslider\cslider.cpp

```
brightnessSlider( ID_BRIGHTNESS_CSLIDER,
                  &sliderCanvas, &sliderCanvas, IRectangle(),
                  ICircularSlider::buttons
                    | ICircularSlider::displayValue
                    | ICircularSlider::jumpToPointer
                    | ICircularSlider::label
                    | ICircularSlider::midpoint
                    | ICircularSlider::proportionalTicks
                    | IControl::tabStop
                    | IWindow::visible ),
redGreenSlider( ID_REDGREEN_CSLIDER,
                &sliderCanvas, &sliderCanvas, IRectangle(),
                ICircularSlider::circularArm
                  | ICircularSlider::jumpToPointer
                  | ICircularSlider::label
                  | ICircularSlider::noTicks
                  | IControl::tabStop
                  | IWindow::visible ),
```

Table 12-1. ICircularSlider::Style Dependencies

Style	Effect
ICircularSlider::buttons	If not set, calls to ICircularSlider::setIncrementBitmaps and ICircularSlider::setDecrementBitmaps are ignored.
ICircularSlider::full360	If set, the styles ICircularSlider::displayValue and ICircularSlider::buttons are ignored.
ICircularSlider::label	If not specified, the control does not display text specified via ITextControl::setText.
ICircularSlider::noTicks	If specified, the styles ICircularSlider::midpoint and ICircularSlider::proportionalTicks are ignored.

Using a Circular Slider

Programming a circular slider differs from using a linear slider. ICircularSlider derives from ITextControl, so it is separate from ISlider in the class hierarchy. Calling ITextControl::text and ITextControl::setText queries and sets an optional label below the dial of the circular slider rather than the value indicated by the dial. To make this label visible, create the circular slider object with the style ICircularSlider::label.

To access the value of the control, use ICircularSlider::value. This function returns a numeric value that you can optionally display in the dial by using the style ICircularSlider::displayValue. The value is always within the range of values that you pass to ICircularSlider::setArmRange (similar to how you set up an IScrollBar). As a result, you can work directly with application values in contrast to mapping from application values to ticks and pixel offsets when you use the ISlider class. To set the value of a circular slider, call ICircularSlider::setValue. This function moves the arm by turning the dial, and it changes the text that the control optionally displays in the dial.

You indirectly set the number of ticks through the setArmRange and setTickSpacing functions. Unlike tick spacing in a linear slider, which is the number of pixels between ticks on the scale, tick spacing in a circular slider is the amount of the range between tick marks as well as the amount the arm is moved when the user selects a slider button or presses the left or right arrow keys. A circular slider gives you no way to label ticks.

The following code shows how we set up the circular sliders in Figure 12-5.

Circular Slider Example - slider\cslider\cslider.cpp

```
// Set up the circular sliders.
brightnessSlider
 .setBackgroundColor( sliderCanvas.backgroundColor() )
 .setMinimumSize( ISize( 50, 50 ) );
brightnessSlider
 .setArmRange( IRange( 0, 100 ) )
 .setTickSpacing( 1 )
 .setText( "Brightness" )
 .enableTabStop()
 .enableGroup();
```

```
redGreenSlider
  .setBackgroundColor( sliderCanvas.backgroundColor() )
  .setMinimumSize( ISize( 50, 50 ) );
redGreenSlider
  .setArmRange( IRange( 0, 255 ) )
  .setTickSpacing( 10 )
  .setText( "Red    Green" )
  .enableTabStop()
  .enableGroup();
```

Monitoring Value Changes

You can detect changes to the values of a progress indicator, linear slider, or circular slider using the ISliderArmHandler class. This handler lets you process changes to the arm position (made by a user or the application) as they are made. Open Class Library also supports the IEditHandler class for these controls. The IEditHandler::edit function is equivalent to ISliderArmHandler::positionChanged. However, IEditHandler has no function that corresponds to ISliderArmHandler::moving, which is called when the user drags the arm of a linear slider or the dial of a circular slider with the mouse. You can attach either handler to the control you are monitoring or to its owner window. Regardless of where the handler is attached, IControlEvent::controlWindow returns a pointer to the progress indicator or slider you are monitoring. IControlEvent::dispatchingWindow returns a pointer to the window to which the handler is attached.

You should have few occasions to need to monitor changes to an IProgressIndicator because it relies on your application to change its value (a user has no way to move its arm). For a linear slider or circular slider, you need an ISliderArmHandler or IEditHandler only if you need to process a value change before the user dismisses the window, such as to adjust the volume of a sound recording as it plays. To process changes to the value of a slider, create a class derived from ISliderArmHandler and override positionChanged, moving, or both virtual functions. Generally, you will want to process both virtual functions in the same manner. One way of doing this is to implement both to call a common function.

The following example shows the use of a class derived from ISliderArmHandler that monitors changes to a circular slider. The nested ArmHandler class overrides the positionChanged and moving functions of ISliderArmHandler. Both functions call a valueChange virtual function. As a result, this handler class processes all changes to the position of the arm through a single function (valueChange). An object of this class is attached to each of the circular sliders shown in Figure 12-5, and it updates the color displayed above the circular sliders as users turn their dials.

ICircularSlider Example - slider\cslider\cslider.hpp

```
...
class ArmHandler : public ISliderArmHandler{
  public:
    ArmHandler        ( ColorWindow* window );
  protected:
  virtual Boolean
    positionChanged ( IControlEvent& event )
    { return this->valueChange( event ); }
  virtual Boolean
    moving          ( IControlEvent& event )
    { return this->valueChange( event ); }
```

```
    virtual Boolean
      valueChange ( IControlEvent& event );
    private:
    ColorWindow
     *colorWindow;
    }; // ColorWindow::ArmHandler
...
```

ISliderArmHandler Example - slider\cslider\cslider.cpp

```
...
ColorWindow::ArmHandler::ArmHandler ( ColorWindow* window )
  : ISliderArmHandler( ),
     colorWindow( window )
{ }

IBase::Boolean
  ColorWindow::ArmHandler::valueChange ( IControlEvent& event )
{
  ICircularSlider
   *cslider = (ICircularSlider*)event.controlWindow();
  if ( cslider->id() == ID_BRIGHTNESS_CSLIDER )
  {
    colorWindow->updateBrightness( cslider->value() );
  }
  else if ( cslider->id() == ID_REDGREEN_CSLIDER )
  {
    unsigned char
      green = (unsigned char)( cslider->value() );
    colorWindow->updateColor( (unsigned char)( 255 - green ),
                              green,
                              0 );
  }
  return false;
}
```

Custom Painting

The OS/2 and PM-compatible versions of IProgressIndicator and ISlider support customized painting through the IProgressIndicator::handleDrawItem style and the ISliderDrawHandler class. With this style and handler you can replace the default painting otherwise provided for the background, shaft, ribbon strip, and arm. You can replace any or all of this default painting by creating a class derived from ISliderDrawHandler and overriding the appropriate virtual function or functions. You can attach your custom paint handler object to either the IProgressIndicator or ISlider you are modifying, or to its owner window. IDrawItemEvent::itemRect returns only the portion of the window that the handler is responsible for painting. Depending on your painting code, you may need to test for the control's shaft orientation and home position.

The **slider\sliddraw** program on the examples disk illustrates custom painting of a progress indicator using ISliderDrawHandler. The example provides implementations for the drawBackground, drawRibbonStrip, and drawShaft virtual functions in the derived class, DrawHandler.

Although you can change the background color of a progress indicator or linear slider simply by calling IProgressIndicator::setBackgroundColor, you must use ISliderDrawHandler to customize the color of a ribbon strip.

Chapter 13

Container Control

- Describes the primary classes you use to build container controls: IContainerControl, IContainerObject, and IContainerColumn
- Describes adding pop-up menus to containers using the class ICnrMenuHandler
- Describes iterating, sorting, and filtering containers using the IContainerControl::Iterator, IContainerControl::CompareFn, and IContainerControl::FilterFn classes
- Describes editing data in the container using the ICnrEditHandler, ICnrEditEvent, ICnrBeginEditEvent, and ICnrEndEditEvent classes
- Describes custom drawing in the container using the ICnrDrawHandler, ICnrDrawItemEvent, and ICnrDrawBackgroundEvent classes
- Describes the implementation of the container classes on the Windows and OS/2 operating system native controls
- Read Chapters 4 and 7 before reading this chapter.
- Chapters 6, 9, 16, 22, and 25 cover related material.

`IContainerControl` and its related classes provide a rich set of capabilities for storing, viewing, and manipulating objects in containers. These objects represent other containers of objects or items such as programs, data files, and devices. Because Open Class Library implements its containers using many classes and member functions, we provide a number of samples to get you started building basic containers and other samples that demonstrate the advanced features of the container. We also discuss the design of the container classes to help you extend these classes with features of your own.

`IContainerControl` uses the native container controls of each operating system to implement much of its interface. Because the native controls are different between the Windows and OS/2 operating systems, and because the native container on the OS/2 operating system has more function than the Windows operating system container, Open Class Library also provides a separate implementation of the OS/2 container on the Windows operating system. To help you choose the right implementation for your needs, we discuss the features that are not portable using the native containers. Refer to the *IBM Open Class Library Reference* for a detailed description of the container restrictions on the Windows operating system.

Because objects stored in a container are not windows, they cannot participate in the normal event-dispatching scheme in Open Class Library. However, Open Class Library does provide special handler functions to connect objects in containers to many container window events.

These handlers, described later in this chapter, capture those presentation system messages that occur over the objects in a container and call virtual functions on the objects.

The Container Model

For our purposes, a *container* is a control window that stores and displays non-window elements called *objects* in one of several views. A container displays the same set of objects in several different views, but only one view at a time. Each of these views displays the characteristics of its objects in a different way. Some views, such as the name and text view, are basic and using them is straightforward. Others, like the icon, tree, and details view, are rich in function and require more understanding to use them effectively. Before you learn the details of the container's views, you need to know the model that the container uses to store its objects. This model determines the appearance of the objects in the various views of the container.

The model of objects in the container is a combination of three different models—an ordered list, a hierarchical tree, and a *messy desk*. The container stores objects added at the root level of the hierarchy in an ordered sequence. These root-level objects are visible in all views of the container, and in several views the container displays objects in the same order that they exist in the ordered list.

Although the container displays root-level objects in all views, it only displays descendants of these objects in a tree view. In all other views, the container ignores these descendant objects. If you want to display descendant objects in a view other than the tree view, create another container and add these objects at the root level.

The messy desk, or icon view, allows you to specify an icon and its location within the container for each root-level object. The icon view displays these icons along with the object's text at the location you specify. Typically, you allow your users to control the location of these icons so they can choose the location for these icons in the container.

Figure 13-1 demonstrates the relationship between the ordered list and the hierarchical model of the container. In this figure, the root-level objects 1, 2, and 3 are visible in all container views. The objects 11, 12, 21, and 211 are only visible in the tree view of the container because they are descendent objects.

Constructing Containers

As you would expect of a class derived from IControl, you use IContainerControl like the other control classes in Open Class Library. Usually, you create a container as the client window of a frame window. You can also use a container as a child of any canvas class described in Chapter 15, "Canvases." Unlike other control classes, IContainerControl does not provide behavior to size itself in a canvas when its contents change.

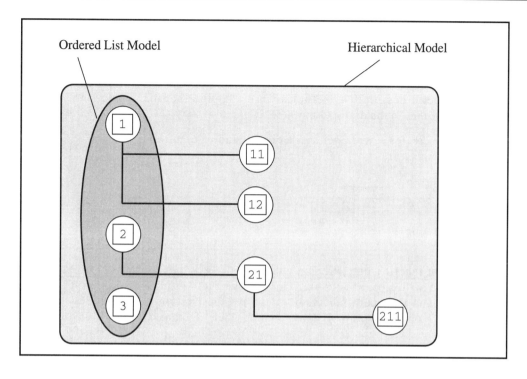

Figure 13-1. The Ordered List and Hierarchical Tree Models of Objects in a Container.

IContainerControl provides support for the control portion of a container, and it supports the same basic three constructors provided by all classes that derive from IControl: one that creates an operating system window and two that provide a wrapper for an existing operating system window.

```
IContainerControl (
        unsigned long      id,
        IWindow*           parent,
        IWindow*           owner,
        const IRectangle&  location = IRectangle(),
        const Style&       style = defaultStyle(),
        const Attribute&   attribute = defaultAttribute());
IContainerControl (
        unsigned long id,
        IWindow*        parentDialog);
IContainerControl (
        const IWindowHandle& handle);
```

The first constructor creates an operating system container. This constructor accepts a numeric identifier for the container and an IWindow* for its parent and owner windows. Optionally, the constructor also accepts the position and size (as an IRectangle) and the styles and attributes of the container. If you use the container as a client of a frame window, Open Class Library ignores the position and size you specify on this constructor.

Use the second and third constructors to create an `IContainerControl` wrapper for an existing container by specifying the container's handle or the container's numeric identifier and the `IWindow*` of its parent and owner. Use the window handle constructor to connect a container created independently of Open Class Library to the event-handling functions in Open Class Library. Use the numeric identifier constructor as a wrapper for a container dialog resource. The dialog constructor has limited usefulness in a container because you cannot specify the objects for the container in the dialog template.

The following code creates a container as the client window of a frame window:

```
main()
{
    IFrameWindow        frame (0x0100);
    IContainerControl cnr (0x0101,
                            &frame,
                            &frame);
    frame.setClient(&cnr);
    frame.show();
}
```

Like all classes that inherit from `IWindow`, you can call `IWindow::setAutoDeleteObject` on a container allocated with `operator new`. This causes the `IWindow` dispatcher to delete the container object when the operating system destroys the container window. By default, an `IContainerControl` object does not delete itself when the operating system destroys the container window.

Container Styles and Attributes

When you create a container using the constructor that creates the presentation window, you can optionally specify a series of values for the nested classes `IContainerControl::Style` and `IContainerControl::Attribute`. Styles and attributes map to the container styles and attributes defined by the OS/2 native container. The intended difference between them is that you cannot change styles after you construct the container, while you can change attributes. In reality, you can change some container styles and all attributes after construction using various `IContainerControl` functions.

Besides the styles added from its inherited classes, `IWindow` and `IControl`, you can construct `IContainerControl` with the following additional `Style` values:

IContainerControl::readOnly

Creates a container that prohibits the user from editing the text.

IContainerControl::autoPosition

Creates a container that automatically determines the location of icons in the icon view. This style prevents users from moving icons to a new location.

IContainerControl::singleSelection

Creates a container that limits selection to one container item at a time. Call `IContainerControl::setSingleSelection` to enable single selection after you create the container.

This is the default style.

Single selection is the only selection type currently supported in the tree view.

IContainerControl::multipleSelection

Creates a container that allows users to select multiple items. Call `IContainerControl::setMultipleSelection` to enable multiple selection after you create the container.

IContainerControl::extendedSelection

Creates a container with an enhanced version of single selection. Extended selection allows users to select discontiguous sets of container items. Call `IContainerControl::setExtendedSelection` to enable extended selection after you create the container. This style is only supported when you use it in conjunction with the `IContainerControl::pmCompatible` style.

IContainerControl::verifyPointers

Verifies that an object exists in the container before using it. Use this style during development, but because it imposes a performance penalty, remove the style when you have finished debugging your application. When you use this style, the container fails any request made using an invalid object by throwing a C++ exception (usually an `IAccessError`). This style is only supported when you use it in conjunction with the `IContainerControl::pmCompatible` style.

IContainerControl::pmCompatible

Creates an OS/2 style container on the Windows operating system. This style is ignored on the OS/2 operating system. See the topic "The IContainerControl::pmCompatible Style" later in this chapter for more details.

IContainerControl::classDefaultStyle

Creates a container with default styles. The `IContainerControl` default styles are `IContainerControl::singleSelection` and `IWindow::visible`.

The function `IContainerControl::defaultStyle` returns the value of the data member `IContainerControl::currentDefaultStyle`. This member is initialized during static object construction to the value `IContainerControl::classDefaultStyle`. Call the static member `IContainerControl::setDefaultStyle` to change the value of `IContainerControl::currentDefaultStyle`.

IContainerControl::noSharedObjects

Improves container performance when you don't add the same objects to more than one container. The performance benefit is highest during the deletion of a container or the deletion of a large number of objects.

Use the following mutually exclusive attributes to set the initial view of the container:

IContainerControl::textView

> Displays objects in the text view. Call `IContainerControl::showTextView` to show the text view after you construct the container.

IContainerControl::iconView

> Displays objects in the icon view. Call `IContainerControl::showIconView` to show the icon view after you construct the container.

IContainerControl::nameView

> Displays objects in the name view. Call `IContainerControl::showNameView` to show the name view after you construct the container.

IContainerControl::detailsView

> Displays objects in the details view. Call the `IContainerControl::showDetailsView` to show the details view after you construct the container.

Add the following attribute to the text, icon, and name views:

IContainerControl::treeView

> Displays objects in one of the tree views. Call the `IContainerControl` functions, `showTreeIconView`, `showTreeNameView`, or `showTreeTextView` to show the tree view after you construct the container. If you specify an attribute of `IContainerControl::treeView` without also including one of the attributes `IContainerControl::nameView`, `IContainerControl::textView`, or `IContainerControl::iconView`, the container displays the tree icon view.

Add the following attribute to the text or name views:

IContainerControl::flowedView

> Causes the container to display its items in a series of vertical lists instead of a single vertical scrollable list. Call the `IContainerControl` functions `showFlowedTextView` or `showFlowedNameView` to show a flowed text or flowed name view after you construct the container. If you create a container without the `IContainerControl::pmCompatible` style on the Windows operating system, the container always flows container objects.

The container title is a text string that the container displays above the objects in the container. The following attributes affect the title in the container:

IContainerControl::readOnlyTitle

> Prohibits users and your program from editing the title. Call `IContainerControl::enableTitleUpdate` to allow users to edit of a container title after you construct the container, or call `IContainerControl::disableTitleUpdate` to disable editing once you've enabled it.

IContainerControl::titleSeparator

Adds a horizontal separator line under the container title. Call `IContainerControl::showTitleSeparator` to show the title separator after you construct the container.

IContainerControl::detailsViewTitles

Adds a heading above each column in the details view. Call `IContainerControl::showDetailsViewTitles` to show the details view titles after you construct the container.

IContainerControl::visibleTitle

Adds a title above the objects in the container if the title field contains text. Call `IContainerControl::showTitle` to show the container title after you construct the container.

Use the following mutually exclusive attributes to align the title:

IContainerControl::alignTitleCentered

IContainerControl::alignTitleLeft

IContainerControl::alignTitleRight

Aligns the title. Call `IContainerControl::setTitleAlignment` with one of the `IContainerControl::TitleAlignment` values `left`, `right`, `centered` to change the alignment of the container title after you construct the container.

The following attributes enable you to custom draw either items in the container or the background of the container. We describe custom drawing in more detail later in this chapter.

IContainerControl::handleDrawItem

Allows you to draw each item in the container. This style causes the container to dispatch an `ICnrDrawItemEvent` to an `ICnrDrawHandler` to draw each item in the container. Call `IContainerControl::enableDrawItem` to cause this event to be dispatched after you construct the container. This attribute is ignored on the Windows operating system unless you create the container using the `IContainerControl::pmCompatible` style.

IContainerControl::handleDrawBackground

Allows you to draw the background of the container. This attribute causes the container to dispatch an `ICnrDrawBackgroundEvent` to an `ICnrDrawHandler` to draw the background of the container. Call `IContainerControl::enableDrawBackground` to cause this event to be dispatched after you construct the container. This attribute is ignored on the Windows operating system unless you create the container using the `IContainerControl::pmCompatible` style.

The following attributes affect the type of emphasis used during direct manipulation. These attributes do not affect the emphasis used in the icon view or the tree view.

IContainerControl::orderedTargetEmphasis

Requests that the container draw a black line between container objects to show that the target of a direct manipulation operation occurs between items. Call `IContainerControl::setOrderedTargetEmphasis` to set ordered target emphasis after you construct the container.

IContainerControl::mixedTargetEmphasis

Requests that the container draw a black line between container items or a solid border around a container item. This shows that the target of a direct manipulation is between container items or on top of a container item, depending upon the location of the drag pointer. Call `IContainerControl::setMixedTargetEmphasis` to set mixed target emphasis in the container after you construct the container.

The following attribute causes the container to draw lines to connect items in the tree view:

IContainerControl::visibleTreeLine

Draws lines to connect items in the tree view. Call `IContainerControl::showTreeLine` to show the tree line after you construct the container. When you create a container on the Windows operating system without the style `IContainerControl::pmCompatible`, the tree lines are always visible.

The following attribute causes the container to draw small icons instead of normal size icons on its nontext views:

IContainerControl::miniIcons

Draws small icons on its nontext views. Call `IContainerControl::showMiniIcons` to show small icons after you construct the container.

The IContainerControl::pmCompatible Style

In the OS/2 operating system, `IContainerControl` implements its behavior using the native container control with the class name `WC_CONTAINER`. This same control, with all the functions it supports, is available to you using VisualAge for C++ for Windows. When you create containers on the Windows operating system using the `IContainerControl::pmCompatible` style, the `IContainerControl` class implements its behavior using a ported version of the `WC_CONTAINER` control. Consider using this style if you build your application for both the Windows and OS/2 operating systems and you require the additional function provided by the `WC_CONTAINER` control.

In many cases, it is more important to build an application with the look and feel of the native presentation system than it is to achieve easy portability. If you do not specify the `IContainerControl::pmCompatible` style on the Windows operating system, `IContainerControl` builds its containers using the Windows native container controls. If you choose to create a container without this style, be aware that there are `IContainerControl` functions that Open Class Library does not support due to limitations in the Windows native container controls. These include the functions for filtering container objects and handling draw-item events for container objects.

In the OS/2 operating system, the `WC_CONTAINER` control provides all of the views supported by `IContainerControl`. In the Windows operating system when you create a container without the `IContainerControl::pmCompatible` style, the Windows list view control (`SysListView32`) provides most of the views, including the text view, icon view, name view, and details view. The Windows tree view control (`SysTreeView32`) provides the tree views. You can still switch between all views on the Windows operating system just as you can on the OS/2 operating system. You can do this because the `IContainerControl` class creates the `SysListView32` or `SysTreeView32` controls when necessary to support the current view. To avoid unnecessary overhead, create your containers with the style that represents the view you intend to display. This ensures that you do not get the overhead associated with the opposite view until your user chooses to display this view. For example, if you create a container where the initial view is a text view, icon view, name view, or details view, `IContainerControl` does not create a `SysTreeView32` control. Conversely, if you create a container where the initial view is a tree view, `IContainerControl` does not create a `SysListView32` control.

Creating Container Objects

The class `IContainerObject` is a required base class for all objects added to a container. You are also required to allocate these objects using `IContainerObject::operator new`. It is an error to allocate an `IContainerObject` or a class derived from `IContainerObject` on the stack or as instance data of another object. Open Class Library throws an `IInvalidRequest` exception when it detects this condition. This is described in more detail when we discuss the design of the container classes later in this chapter.

While there are no required parameters for constructing an `IContainerObject`, you usually construct one using text and an icon. You can specify the text and icon pair directly as a string and an icon handle or as resource identifiers. If you use resource identifiers, the container loads the text and icons from the applications's resource library. Additionally, you can construct container objects by making a copy of an existing object. The following examples demonstrate several ways to construct container objects:

```
// Declare a pointer to an IContainerObject.
IContainerObject* object;

// Create an object using the default constructor with
// no icon or text.
object = new IContainerObject();

// Create a text-only object.
object = new IContainerObject("Just Text");

// Create an object by loading the text and icon from
// a resource file.
object = new IContainerObject(ID_OBJECTTEXT, ID_OBJECTICON);

// Create an object by making a copy of an existing object.
IContainerObject* object2 = new IContainerObject(*object);
```

Adding Objects to Containers

Once you create an object, you add it to a container as a root-level object in the ordered model or as a descendant of another object in the hierarchical model. You use the functions IContainerControl::addObject and IContainerControl::addObjectAfter to add an object to both models. As we describe in the topic "Icon View," you can also position the icons for an object in the messy desk model that the icon view uses.

By default, you add objects at the end of the container's ordered list. If you specify a parent object, it is added as the last child of that parent object by default. Use IContainerControl::addObjectAfter to add an object after a specified object at the root level or at any descendant level. You can add an object first by specifying 0 for the afterObject parameter.

Assume that we have already created the container cnr, and the objects root1, root2, root3, root1Child1, root1Child2, and root1Child3. The following code adds these objects to a container so that they appear in the tree view shown in Figure 13-2:

```
// Add the root objects.
cnr.addObject(root1);
cnr.addObject(root2);
cnr.addObject(root3);

// Add root1Child2 and root1Child3 under root1.
cnr.addObject(root1Child2, root1);
cnr.addObject(root1Child3, root1);

// Add root1Child1 as the first child of root1.
cnr.addObjectAfter(root1Child1, 0, root1);
```

Notice that we used IContainerControl::addObjectAfter with a 0 afterObject parameter to add root1Child1 as the first child of root1.

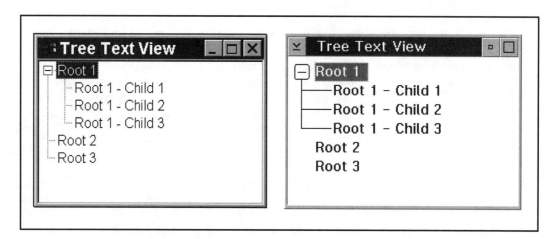

Figure 13-2. Windows (left) and OS/2 (right) Container Tree Text View.

The container control also supports adding the same object to more than one container. When you update an object that exists in multiple containers, you update the object in all containers. See "Container Object Attributes" later in this chapter for the details on using objects in multiple containers.

For most of the container's views, you can use IContainerObject directly without deriving from it. However, as you learn later, you must derive from IContainerObject to display data in a details view or to process events routed to the object by the container's handlers.

If you add a large number of objects to the container, the amount of time needed to add the objects to the container can become unacceptably long. See "Building Large Numbers of Container Objects" for techniques to improve the time it takes to create and add objects to the container.

Text View

The text view, the simplest of all views, displays a text string representation of all root-level objects in a vertical list. Scroll bars move the text into view when necessary.

The flowed-text view is the same as the text view except it displays the text strings in multiple columns instead of a single vertical list. Figure 13-3 displays the text view in the Windows and OS/2 operating systems. As in all container text strings on the OS/2 operating system, you can use a newline character ('\n') to cause the text to be displayed across multiple lines. The native container in Windows does not support displaying text across multiple lines in this manner.

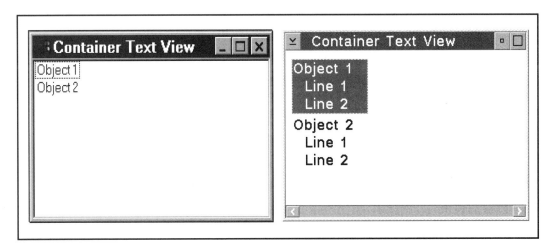

Figure 13-3. Windows (left) and OS/2 (right) Text View Containers.

Name View

The name view, an extension of the text view, displays an icon representation of root-level objects to the left of the text string. Similarly, the flowed-name view is a variation of the flowed-text view that displays the icon and text string pairs in multiple columns instead of a single vertical list. Figure 13-4 displays the name view in the Windows and OS/2 operating systems.

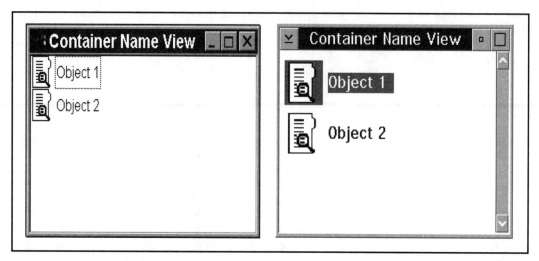

Figure 13-4. Windows (left) and OS/2 (right) Name View Containers.

Icon View

The icon view displays both an icon and text string representation of root-level objects in the container. The container centers the text string below the icon. Unlike the other views, the container displays the icon and text string pairs based on specific coordinates that it stores with each object.

The Icon View Coordinate System

The easiest way to position icons in the icon view is to create the container with the style IContainerControl::autoPosition. This causes the container to calculate the location of icons when the container is first displayed, anytime an object is added or removed, and whenever the container window is sized. This result is often unsatisfactory because it doesn't allow the user to reposition icons in the container. It is important to allow the user to decide on the position of icons in the container by dragging them to a new location.

Positioning icons in a container icon-view window requires you to understand the relationship between the container's *workspace* and the visible display area or *view port* into this workspace. The container workspace is an independent coordinate system that the container uses to position icons when you add objects to a container.

The visible area of the container is a view port into this workspace that a user can move with the scroll bars, and that you can move under program control. The smallest rectangle that encompasses all objects in the container defines the bounds of the workspace. These bounds limit the movement of the view port on the workspace. When you first create the container, the view port is located at the origin of the workspace (0,0).

Figure 13-5 displays the location of the container's bounded workspace in an actual view of the objects in the icon view (the view port). We created this container by specifying a frame window size just large enough to display all of the objects. We then called `IContainerControl::arrangeIconView` to position the icons. Finally, we sized the frame window to include the top two icons. Because the origin of the container and the origin of the workspace are at position (0,0), the nondisplayed objects are at a negative workspace coordinate. The user can adjust the position of the view port on the workspace with the scroll bars, or you can adjust it by calling a container scroll function. In neither case can you or the user move the view port outside the bounded workspace of the container. This means the container

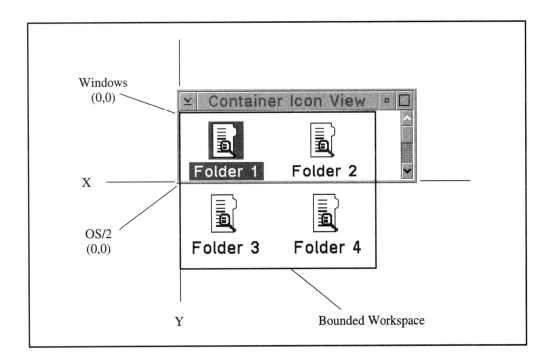

Figure 13-5. The Bounded Workspace of the Container.

in Figure 13-5 cannot be scrolled horizontally. This is obvious to the user because no horizontal scroll bars are present; it is not so obvious when you try it in code.

When you add objects to a container created without the style `IContainerControl::autoPosition`, their location in the container is not consistently defined on all operating systems. Containers on the OS/2 operating system and containers with the style `IContainerControl::pmCompatible` on the Windows operating system place them at workspace location (0,0). This means that without further action on your part, the icons appear one on top of the other in the bottom left corner of the container window. To correct this situation, call `IContainerControl::arrangeIconView`. This has the same one-time effect as using the `IContainerControl::autoPosition` style, while still allowing you or the user to reposition specific objects in the icon view. Containers on the Windows operating system without the style `IContainerControl::pmCompatible` automatically arrange the icons when you first put them in the container.

You can manually arrange the icons by calling `IContainerControl::moveIconTo` on each object. Following this, scroll the container to position the view port on the workspace. Be aware that `IContainerControl::moveIconTo` sets the position of the icon, regardless of any text. Because the amount of text is variable, it can become quite difficult to position the icon and text pairs so that they don't overlap.

To give your users maximum flexibility and yet keep your code simple, we recommend the following actions:

- Call `IContainerControl::arrangeIconView` after you have added objects for the first time.

- Save the location of the icons in a profile when the user closes the application.

- When the user opens the application, check the profile for this data and use it to position the icons.

- Provide an **Arrange** choice on the menu to allow the user to request automatic arrangement of the icons.

Even when you include these, you still have the job of deciding where to add a new object when the user hasn't told you where to place it. Depending on your strategy for solving this problem, it can be quite difficult. You can call `IContainerControl::objectUnderPoint` to locate a place in the current view port that does not already contain an object. However, it is easier to code, and probably more understandable for your users, if you position new objects in a fixed location and let the users move them to their preferred location.

Position an object's icon in the workspace using workspace coordinates by calling `IContainerControl::moveIconTo`. However, when you query the location of an object's icon, the container returns the result in container window coordinates. When necessary, call `IContainerControl::convertToWorkspace` to convert a rectangle in window coordinates to a rectangle in workspace coordinates.

Tree View

As you learned earlier, the tree view displays the hierarchical model of the container. The tree-text view displays this hierarchy using only the text string of the object. The tree-icon view and the tree-name view display an icon with the text string to the right of the icon. In addition to the icon and text pair, the tree-icon view also displays separate icons for expanding and collapsing the branches of the tree. Figure 13-6 displays the three tree views of the container in the native container of the Windows operating system.

The default expand icon in the tree-text view and the tree-name view is a plus sign (+) and the collapse icon is a minus sign (-). Collapse and expand the branches of the tree-name view by clicking the mouse on the parent object's icon. Single-click the icon on the OS/2 operating system and double-click the icon on the Windows operating system. You also can collapse and expand the branches of the tree using the keyboard + and - keys when input focus is on a parent icon.

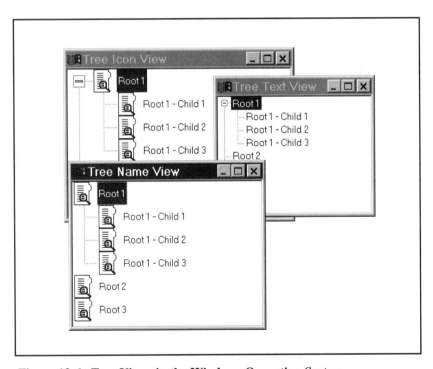

Figure 13-6. Tree Views in the Windows Operating System.

You can alter several features of a tree view as follows:

- To remove the line used to connect a child icon to its parent, call `IContainerControl::hideTreeLine`, or construct the container without the attribute `IContainerControl::visibleTreeLine`. To replace the line later, call `IContainerControl::showTreeLine`.

- To change the thickness of the tree line, call `IContainerControl::showTreeLine` and specify a thickness, in pels, for the `treeLinePixelWidth` parameter.

- To change the amount of space child icons are offset from their parent icon, call `IContainerControl::setTreeViewIndent`.

- To replace the expand and collapse icons with your own custom icons, call `IContainerControl::setTreeItemIcons`.

- To alter the size of the expand and collapse icons, call `IContainerControl::setExpandIconSize`.

Details View

The details view of the container displays data for root-level objects in columns with optional headings at the top of each column. Although the container displays many types of data, it only supports user editing of text data. User editing of text is covered later in the topic "Editing Container Text."

To use the details view, derive a class from `IContainerObject` and add whatever data you need displayed as member data of the new class. Also, create an object of `IContainerColumn` for each column of data and add these columns to the container. Because `IContainerColumn` is tightly coupled to the data in your object, specify the type of the data and the offset of the data in your object.

Building a Details View Object

The following class defines the minimum information that a `Developer` class needs for the details view to display a developer's name, CompuServe identifiers as text strings, and an icon to represent the developer's role.

```
class Developer : public IContainerObject
{
  public:
  Developer    ( const IString&  name,
                 unsigned long   iconId,
                 const IString&  compuServeId);
      : IContainerObject(name, iconId),
        fCompuServeId(compuServeId)
    {}
```

```
enum Column {kNameColumn, kIconColumn, kCompuServeIdColumn };
static IContainerColumn
  *createAndOrphanColumnFor ( IContainerControl& container,
                              Column           column);
static void
  createAllColumnsFor      ( IContainerColumn&  container);

private:
IString
  fCompuServeId;
};
```

Notice that the `Developer` object only requires one new data member, an `IString`, to store a developer's CompuServe identifier. We can store the developer's name and an icon in the `iconViewText` and `icon` fields of `IContainerObject`.

We have also added two static functions to create column objects for displaying the object in the details view. The first function, `createAndOrphanColumnFor`, creates and adds a specific `IContainerColumn` object to the argument container. You indicate which column you want added to the container by specifying a value for the `Column` enumeration argument. When you use this function, you must keep track of and delete any column objects that you request the `Developer` object to build.

The second static function, `Developer::createAllColumnsFor`, automatically builds a default set of `IContainerColumn` objects and adds each to the argument container. It calls `Developer::createAndOrphanColumnFor` for each column to create and add it to the container and then it calls `IContainerControl::setAutoDeleteColumns` to cause the container to delete the column objects when it is closed.

As the implementation of these functions shows in the following example, the creation of the `IContainerColumn` objects requires the offset of the data in the container object. Here, the macro `offsetof`, defined in `STDDEF.H`, returns the offset of the `strCompuServeId` field in the `Developer` object.

```
IContainerColumn*
 Developer::createAndOrphanColumnFor( IContainerControl& container,
                                      Column            columnType)
{
  IContainerColumn* newColumn = 0;
  if (columnType == Developer::fNameColumn)
    newColumn = new IContainerColumn(
                          IContainerColumn::isIConViewText );
  else if (columnType == Developer::fIconColumn)
    newColumn = new IContainerColumn(
                          IContainerColumn::isIcon  );
  else if columnType == Developer::fCompuServeIdColumn)
  {
    unsigned long offset = offsetof(Developer, fCompuServeId);
    newColumn = new IContainerColumn( offset );
  }
  // Ensure that a new column is created.
  IASSERTSTATE(newColumn != 0);

  return newColumn;
}
```

Defining Column Objects

An object of the class `IContainerColumn` defines the characteristics of a single column of data in the details view. Each column of data relates to one piece of data in the container object. The column object includes the following characteristics:

- The type of data in the column. The container can display character strings, numbers, dates, times, and an icon.

- The offset of the data within the container object. The container uses this information to draw the data in the column.

- The data to be displayed in the column heading and its type. Column headings can contain text or an icon.

- Any additional column formatting information, such as justification, or the use of column separator lines.

You usually construct an `IContainerColumn` using the offset of the data displayed in the column and, optionally, the style of the column heading and column data. By default, both the column heading and the column data contain vertically centered, left-aligned, and read-only text. In our `Developer` object, we added the static functions `createAndOrphanColumnsFor` and `createColumnFor` to return `IContainerColumn` objects for the data in our object. This approach has an advantage because it keeps the existence of data offsets out of your object's interface.

> ## IString Implementation Note
>
> You may have noticed we are using `IString` instead of character pointers for our text data. We can do this because the class `IString` was designed to be used in read-only situations as a replacement for a character array. It can do this because an instance of `IString` is four bytes long and contains only a pointer to the character data stored in the `IString`. Thus, an `IString` is, by definition, binary-compatible with a character pointer. It is read-only, because you must change the data of the `IString` using `IString` functions.

`IContainerColumn` has another constructor you can use to create a column that displays the `icon` or `iconViewText` stored in the base portion of an `IContainerObject`. We use this constructor in our `Developer` object to create a column object for the developer's name and icon. This constructor does not require the offset of the data in the column because the container calculates this information.

The columns for displaying our `Developer` object appear as follows:

```
IContainerColumn
    name(IContainerColumn::isIconViewText);
IContainerColumn
    iconId(IContainerColumn::isIcon);
IContainerColumn
    compuServeId(Developer::compuServeIdOffset());
```

Pay attention to the following points when you build your objects and columns:

- The data type must match the actual type of data. If you indicate that the data is text, the container uses the data as a pointer to a text string. You will likely get an access violation if the types do not match.

- You can put heterogeneous objects into a container, but you can create problems if you are not careful. If you create a column object for data of a specific type at a specific offset in an object, every object in the details view must have data of that type present at that offset. This is not checked. It is your job to ensure that it is done. If you use heterogeneous objects in a container, create column objects only for data members that exist in a common base class.

Adding Column Objects to the Container

After you create an `IContainerColumn` object, add it to a container using either `IContainerControl::addColumn` or `IContainerControl::addColumnAt`. Use `addColumn` to add the column after an existing column; if you don't provide a reference column, the container adds the column as the last column. Use `addColumnAt` to add the column using an `IContainerControl::ColumnCursor`; the container adds the column after the column pointed to by the cursor. Unlike container objects, you can only add column objects to a single container.

In the OS/2 operating system and in the Windows operating system for containers with the style `IContainerControl::pmCompatible`, you can display icons, text, numbers, dates, and times in the data of the columns. You can also display icons and text in the column's heading. However, there are a number of restrictions to consider if you use native containers in the Windows operating system. Because these restrictions are well documented in the *Open Class Library Reference* under the `IContainerColumn` class description, you can read them there. To build details-view containers that work well as native containers on both operating systems, follow these guidelines:

- Create an `IContainerColumn` object using the constructor that takes a `DataSource` enumeration with the value `IContainerColumn::isIcon` and add it as the first column in the container using default values for both the `HeadingStyle` and `DataStyle` parameters. Call `IContainerColumn::setHeadingText` if you want a heading above the icon in the OS/2 operating system; this text is not used for the Windows native container.

- Create a second `IContainerColumn` object using the same constructor with the value `IContainerColumn::isIconViewText` and add it as the second column in the container. Call `IContainerColumn::setHeadingText` to add the heading text used for the icon-view text in the OS/2 operating system and for the combined icon and icon-text column for the Windows native container.

- Do not build `IContainerColumn` objects using the style `IContainerColumn::icon` because the Windows native container only supports icons in the first column.

- If possible, use the defaults for both `DataStyle` and `HeadingStyle` when you create column objects. If you do specify these styles, they must be text and are read-only.

Using Dates and Times in the Details View

As you read earlier, the container can format and display both dates and times in the fields of a details view. You can also use Open Class Library classes `IDate` and `ITime` to format and store dates and times as string data. If you want to give your users the ability to directly edit the dates and times, store this information as a character pointer or an `IString`. The container's built-in support for dates and times does not support user editing.

To use the container's built-in date and time support, store the date and time data in your container object in a form identical to the Developer's Toolkit for OS/2 structures `CDATE` and `CTIME`. Also, construct an `IContainerColumn` with `IContainerControl::DataStyle` enumeration values of `IContainerColumn::date` or `IContainerColumn::time`. The **cnr\cdata** program shows our `Developer` object with `CDATE` and `CTIME` support added and container columns to display this information. Note that this example shows the layout of both `CDATE` and `CTIME`. The **cnr\uidate** program shows our `Developer` object with support for the classes `IDate` and `ITime` instead of `CDATE` and `CTIME`.

Adding a Split Bar

A *split bar* is a movable vertical border that you use to separate a range of columns in the details view. Call `IContainerControl::setDetailsViewSplit` to add a split bar to a details view. The parameters for this function identify the last column to appear on the left side of the split bar and the initial location of the split bar, in pixels, from the left side of the details view. Call `IContainerControl::showSplitBar` to show the split bar and call `IContainerControl::hideSplitBar` to hide it.

The native container in the Windows operating system does not support separately scrollable windows in the details view. If you do not use the `IContainerControl::pmCompatible` style when you build your container, `IContainerControl` ignores calls to add or reposition the split bar. The Windows native container does allow users to reposition the border of all columns in the details view whereas the OS/2 container does not.

To add a split bar to a container displaying the details of our `Developer` object after the name column and to specify an initial location 125 pixels from the left side of the container, you would include this code:

```
cnr.setDetailsViewSplit( &name, 125 );
cnr.showSplitBar();
```

Although adding a split bar to a container is easy, you can run into complications with the details-view container. In containers, the columns on the right side of the split bar are in a separate presentation system window than those on the left side. To clarify this, recall the relationship of the container window or view port to the container workspace. Because of this relationship, the two split windows move independently in a horizontal direction. But, they move together in a vertical direction. To determine if a column is in the left or the right window, call `IContainerControl::isColumnRight`.

Another complication occurs because `IContainerControl::detailsObjectRectangle` (which returns the window rectangle bounding an object in the details view) returns only the area on one side of the split bar. The `Boolean` that you specify for the `rightWindow` parameter determines on which side it returns. Call `IContainerControl::splitBarOffset` to find the location of the split bar.

Moving and Copying Objects in the Container

`IContainerControl` provides two powerful functions to move or copy objects in a container. `IContainerControl::moveObjectTo` supports moving objects in both the ordered and hierarchical model, and it supports changing the icon position in the icon view. It also supports moving objects from one container to another if both containers are in the same process. Because not all moves in a container are valid, `moveObjectTo` returns `false` rather than throwing an exception when it cannot move the object. Trying to move an object to one of its descendants is an example of an invalid move. You can also call `IContainerControl::isMoveValid` prior to attempting a move to determine if you can make the move.

`IContainerControl::copyObjectTo` supports copying objects in both the ordered and hierarchical models. It also supports copying objects from one container to another if both containers are in the same process. If you create a class that inherits from `IContainerObject` and you ever plan to call `IContainerControl::copyObjectTo`, you must override and implement `copyObjectTo` in the derived class. Because the container's built-in direct manipulation support calls `copyObjectTo` to copy objects as the result of a direct manipulation copy operation, you must implement `copyObjectTo` if you enable direct manipulation. If you do not implement `copyObjectTo` in your derived class, `IContainerObject::copyObjectTo` throws an `IInvalidRequest` exception when it is called instead of your version.

`IContainerControl` does not provide support to move or copy objects between two containers in different processes. To do this, you need to use an inter-process communications vehicle to transfer the data of an object from one process to another. The Dynamic Data Exchange (DDE) classes in Open Class Library, provide this vehicle. See Chapter 22, "Dynamic Data Exchange Framework," for a description of these classes.

Managing the Lifetime of Container Objects

Managing the lifetime of objects in containers can become quite complex because your objects can exist in one container, multiple containers, or no containers at all. Many helper functions in the container help you handle this complexity.

Removing and Deleting Objects

Just as constructing an object is an independent event from adding that object to a container, removing an object from a container is an independent event from deleting it. You can remove an object from a single container or all containers simultaneously. You can remove a single object by its address or by using an `IContainerControl::ObjectCursor` or an `IContainerControl::TextCursor`. You can also remove all selected objects or all objects in the container simultaneously. The following examples show how you remove objects from a container:

```
// Remove the object with the cursor.
IContainerObject* pobject = cnr.cursoredObject();
cnr.removeObject(pobject);

// Remove all objects in a container.
cnr.removeAllObjects();

// Remove all selected objects in a container.
cnr.removeSelectedObjects();

// Remove the first object with an ObjectCursor.
IContainerControl::ObjectCursor objectCursor(cnr);
objectCursor.setToFirst();
if (objectCursor.isValid())
  cnr.removeObjectAt(objectCursor);

// Remove the last object with the text "Delores."
IContainerControl::TextCursor textCursor(cnr, "Delores");
textCursor.setToLast();
if (textCursor.isValid())
  cnr.removeObjectAt(textCursor);
```

When you remove an object that contains descendants in the hierarchical model, `IContainerControl` removes all of its descendants.

When you delete an object, `IContainerControl` removes the object from all containers with the object prior to deleting it. When you delete an object with descendants in the hierarchical model, `IContainerControl` removes and deletes all descendants in all containers. The container builds a list of the objects requiring deletion, removes them from their respective containers, and calls each object's destructor. Similar to the process you use to remove objects, you can request the container to delete all objects, delete all selected objects, or to delete an object at a particular cursor location.

Automatic Deletion of Objects

In many cases, you only add objects to a single container and want the objects deleted when the user closes the container. If you do not need an object beyond its use in a particular container, call `IContainerControl::setDeleteObjectsOnClose` on that container. Calling this function causes the `IContainerControl` destructor to remove all its objects and then to call the destructor of those objects that do not exist in other containers. Those objects that exist in other containers remain there.

Managing objects in multiple containers imposes a performance penalty on your application, especially during the deletion of container objects, because `IContainerControl` must handle the use of the object in other containers. If you do not share objects among multiple containers, create your containers with the `IContainerControl::noSharedObjects` style. This style cause the container to ignore the code that handles objects that exist in multiple containers.

Locating Container Objects and Columns

Using three nested cursor classes of `IContainerControl`, you can iterate the objects and columns in a container. Cursors are "smart" placeholders to a current object in a container. By using a cursor to maintain a current position in the container, you can have multiple place-holders in the same container. These cursors also limit the amount of data stored with the container because you create them only for as long as you need them.

As you learn in the following topics, several arguments to the cursors' constructors change the behavior of the cursors. In effect, you create a different kind of cursor depending on the values of these arguments.

Object Cursor

Use `IContainerControl::ObjectCursor` to find container objects that match a particular emphasis attribute that you specify when you create the cursor. The cursor supports all the emphasis types of `IContainerObject` including these:

> `IContainerObject::none`
>
> `IContainerObject::inuse`
>
> `IContainerObject::selected`
>
> `IContainerObject::cursored`

You also can change the order in which this cursor finds objects in the container. Objects can be found in *item order* or in *Z-order*. Item order is the order of the objects in the hierarchical and ordered models. Z-order is the painting order of the icons in the icon view because icons can be on top of each other.

Finally, several options control how the objects are found in the hierarchic model. You can choose to iterate only the root-level objects of the ordered model, all objects including those in the hierarchical model, the direct descendants of a single object, or all descendants of an object.

In a container with the `IContainerControl::singleSelection` style and in all tree view containers, a single object is selected at a time. In addition, this object is always the container object with input focus. Therefore, instead of using an object cursor to find the selected object, call `IContainerControl::cursoredObject`.

You can construct an object cursor in the following ways:

```
// Create an object cursor for all container objects,
// including subtree objects.
IContainerControl::ObjectCursor allObjects(cnr);

// Create an object cursor for the direct children of root1.
IContainerControl::ObjectCursor root1Direct(cnr,root1);

// Create an object cursor for all children of root1.
IContainerControl::ObjectCursor root1All(cnr, root1, true);
```

```
// Create an object cursor for all selected objects in item order.
IContainerControl::ObjectCursor allSelected(cnr,
                  IContainerObject::selected);

// Create an object cursor for all selected objects in Z-order.
IContainerControl::ObjectCursor allSelected(cnr,
                  IContainerObject::selected,
                  IContainerControl::zOrder);
```

Although you create object cursor in different ways, you use them with the same cursor loop to iterate the container, as follows:

```
for(allObjects.setToFirst();
    allObjects.isValid();
    allObjects.setToNext()) {
  IContainerObject* pcnrobj = cnr.objectAt(cursor);
}
```

Text Cursor

Use an IContainerControl::TextCursor to return objects that match a particular text string. Create a text cursor by providing the text string and the following optional Boolean arguments:

isCaseSensitive

Determines if the text match is case sensitive. If true, make the case of the text identified on the TextCursor constructor the same case as the object's text for the object to be found. If false, the default, text searches are not case sensitive.

isFirstInRecord

If true, the text identified on the TextCursor constructor must match the text in the object, starting from the beginning of the string. If false, the text can be anywhere in the string. By default, text searches examine the entire string for a match.

isExactMatch

If true, the text identified on the TextCursor constructor must exactly match the entire text string for an object to be found. If false, the default, an exact match is not required.

Construct and use text cursors just as you do other cursors, as follows:

```
// Create a text cursor to find all objects with "the" in their text.
IContainerControl::TextCursor theCursor(cnr, "the");

// Create a text cursor to find all objects starting with "An."
// Match the case as well.
IContainerControl::TextCursor anCursor(cnr, "An", true, true);

// Use the theCursor to hide all objects with "the."
for(theCursor.setToFirst();
    theCursor.isValid();
    theCursor.setToNext()) {
  IContainerObject* pcnrobj = cnr.objectAt(theCursor)->hide();
}
```

Column Cursor

Use `IContainerControl::ColumnCursor` to return the columns added to the container. Add an additional `Boolean` argument if you want to limit the search to visible columns in the container, as follows:

```
// Hide all visible columns.
IContainerControl::ColumnCursor visibleColumns(cnr, true);
for(visibleColumns.setToFirst();
    visibleColumns.isValid();
    visibleColumns.setToNext()) {
    IContainerColumn* pcnrcol = columnAt(visibleColumn)->hide();
}
```

One restriction for all cursors in the container (and the rest of Open Class Library) is that these cursors become invalid if additions or removals occur to the cursor's collection. Consequently, do not add or remove objects or columns without setting the cursor to a valid value during the cursor `for` loop. You can make a minor variation in the cursor `for` loop to overcome this restriction. The following example uses a cursor loop to remove all objects that match our previously created `theCursor`. Instead of advancing the text cursor to the next item in the collection, the code continually resets the cursor to the first item. The action of resetting the cursor to a known value validates the cursor after it has been invalidated by the call to `IContainerControl::removeObject`.

```
for(theCursor.setToFirst();
    theCursor.isValid();
    theCursor.setToFirst()) {

    IContainerObject* pcnrobj = cnr.objectAt(theCursor);
    cnr.removeObject(pcnrobj);
}
```

Applying Behavior to Objects

As you already learned, you use cursors to loop through a container and retrieve objects or columns that match various characteristics. A slight variation of this technique is to loop through a container and call a function for each object in the container. The `IContainerControl::Iterator` class provides this capability. The steps involved in using an iterator are as follows:

1. Define a class derived from `IContainerControl::Iterator` and implement the function `applyTo`. The container calls this function for each object and passes it a pointer to the object. When called, this function must return a `Boolean` value to indicate if the iteration should continue; it returns `true` to continue the iteration and `false` to stop it.

2. Declare an object of the new derived class.

3. Call `IContainerControl::allObjectsDo` and provide the iterator object as an argument.

Suppose, for example, you want to translate any icon text containing the string "alarm" to upper case. You can do this using the following code:

```
// Create the derived class and implement applyTo.
class FoldIconText : public IContainerControl::Iterator{
virtual Boolean
  applyTo( IContainerObject* object)  {
      //  Update the state of the object.
      IString iconText = object->iconText();
      if(iconText.includes("alarm")) {
          iconText.upperCase();
          object->setIconText(iconText);
      }
      return true;
  }
};

// Declare an object of the iterator.
FoldIconText toUpper;

// Apply the function to the container.
cnr.allObjectsDo(toUpper);
```

Sorting Objects in the Container

You can sort objects in the container using their icon text by calling IContainerControl::sortByIconText or by using an application-provided comparison function. Using an application comparison function, you can sort the objects in the container in any number of ways. When you call sortByIconText, the container provides its own comparison function to do the sorting.

The steps involved in providing your own sort behavior are as follows:

1. Define a class derived from IContainerConrol::CompareFn and implement the function isEqual. Code isEqual to return an integer value that is:

    - Less than zero, if the first object is less than the second object.
    - Zero if the first object is equal to the second object.
    - Greater than zero if the first object is greater than the second object.

2. Create an object of the newly defined comparison class.

3. Call IContainerControl::sort and pass the comparison function object.

The following example sorts our previously defined Developer objects by the value of their compuServeId fields. To accomplish this, we compare the identifiers using the national language-support-enabled function, IContainerControl::nlsCompare.

```
// Define the comparison function and implement isEqual.
Class CompareCServeIds : public IContainerControl::CompareFn{
virtual int
  isEqual(IContainerObject* developer1,
          IContainerObject* developer2,
          IContainerControl* container){
    return nlsCompare(((Developer*)developer1)->compuServeId(),
                      ((Developer*)developer2)->compuServeId());
  }
};
```

```
// Create an object of the comparison function.
CompareCServeIds compareIds;

// Invoke the sort funtion.
cnr.sort(compareIds);
```

Hiding or Filtering Container Objects

Containers created with the style `IContainerControl::pmCompatible` support the notion of invisible, or filtered objects. Use filtering as a way to display a subset of the objects in a container without removing the objects from the container's collection. The container does not display invisible objects but because they remain in its collection of objects you can iterate them using an object cursor. Hide a visible object by calling `IContainerControl::hideObject` and show a hidden object by calling `IContainerControl::showObject`. You can also hide and show objects by building your own filter function. Like the sort function, `hideObject` and `showObject` use filter functions internally to hide and show objects.

The steps for providing your own filter behavior are as follows:

1. Define a class derived from `IContainerConrol::FilterFn` and implement the function `isMemberOf`. Code `isMemberOf` to return `true` if the container should display the object and `false` if it should not.

2. Create an object of the newly defined filter class.

3. Call `IContainerControl::filter` and pass the filter-function object.

The following example hides any of our previously defined `Developer` objects if they don't have a value for their `compuServeId` fields.

```
// Define the filter function and implement isMemberOf.
Class ValidCServeIds : public IContainerControl::FilterFn
{
virtual int
  isMemberOf(IContainerObject* developer,
             IContainerControl* container)
  {
    if(((Developer*)developer)->compuServeId().length()>0)
      return true;
    return false;
  }
};

// Create an object of the comparison function.
ValidCServeIds cServeIds;

// Invoke the filter function.
cnr.filter(cServeIds);
```

Editing Container Text

The container supports user editing of the text in the container title, the text associated with an icon, the column headings of the details view, and the object data of the details view. In addition, you can initiate the editing of text in your program using functions in

IContainerControl. Before the text can be edited, you must enable editing in the field and ensure the field contains character data. You can meet the requirement for character data by using a character array or the class IString.

Enabling User Editing

By default, the user cannot edit text in the container. To enable user editing, complete these tasks:

- Ensure the field to be edited is text data using either an IString or a character pointer.

- Enable editing for an object by calling IContainerControl::enableDataUpdate and passing the object.

- Create an object of the class ICnrEditHandler or a class that inherits from ICnrEditHandler and invoke the function handleEventsFor.

The fields in the container that support text editing may have construction styles, functions that can be invoked after construction, or both to enable editing in the field. To edit any data in an object you must call IContainerControl::enableDataUpdate. In addition, if the object data to be edited is in a column of the details view, construct the column without the IContainerColumn::readOnly data style (this style is set by default). Alternatively, call IContainerColumn::enableDataUpdate after you construct the IContainerColumn.

To enable editing of the container title, call IContainerControl::enableTitleUpdate. To enable editing of the column headings in the details view, construct the columns without the IContainerColumn::readOnly heading style or call the IContainerColumn function enableHeadingUpdate.

Initiating and Terminating Editing

Use IContainerControl functions to initiate and terminate editing in the container. The following IContainerControl functions support editing:

editContainerTitle

Opens an edit field on an edit-enabled container title.

editColumnTitle

Opens an edit field on an edit-enabled column heading in the details view. The field must contain character data.

editObject

Opens an edit field on an edit-enabled container object in any of the container's available views. Use an optional parameter of this function to specify a column in the details view so that you can open an edit field on the data of a column. A field in the details view must contain character data.

Handling an Edit Change Request

Use the classes `ICnrEditHandler` and `ICnrEditEvent` to add specific behavior during the process of editing data in the container. `ICnrEditHandler` supports the following notifications:

beginEdit

> Called by the edit handler and passed an `ICnrBeginEditEvent` following a request to open a container edit field. `ICnrEditHandler::beginEdit` creates and attaches an `IMultiLineEdit` object to the edit control opened by the container. If you override this function, call the base class function before adding your custom behavior.

reallocString

> Called by the edit handler when it needs to reallocate the storage to contain new data in a field. `ICnrEditHandler::beginEdit` provides complete support for data reallocation. In particular, the edit handler can identify the type of data used for fields managed by the container (title, details headings, and icon text) and handles reallocation automatically.

> Consider overriding `reallocString` in an edit handler only if your object data is a mixture of `IString` objects and character pointers.

endEdit

> Called by the edit handler and passed an `ICnrEndEditEvent` after the container has been updated with the new data of the edit field. `ICnrEditHandler::endEdit` deletes the `IMultiLineEdit` object added by `ICnrEditHandler::beginEdit`. If you override the behavior of this function, call the base class implementation after you complete your processing.

The `IMultiLineEdit` object provides a wrapper class for the edit field that the presentation system container uses for editing text. You can replace this object with a different object that inherits from `IMultiLineEdit`, but you cannot replace the actual container's edit field. Your class must still provide a wrapper for the container's multiline edit field. You do not need to replace the `IMultiLineEdit` object because you can adjust the behavior of the edit field by attaching your own edit handler to the existing edit control.

Container Object Attributes

Objects stored in a container have several different attributes. Because an object can exist in more than one container, many of these attributes reflect the state of an object in a particular container. For example, an object can be visible in one container but hidden in another. The container classes provide functions to help you answer the following two questions about an attribute:

1. What is the state of an object's attribute in a particular container? For example, is the object customer1 visible in container1? Answer this question by calling the object and providing the container or by calling the container and providing the object. For example:

    ```
    object1->isVisible(container1);
    container1->isVisible(object1);
    ```

2. What is the state of an attribute in all places where the object resides? If you have not added an object to a container, the object answers the question based on its state data. If you have added the object to one or more containers, the object answers the question by determining its state in all containers holding the object. For example, an object returns false to IContainerObject::isVisible unless it is visible in all its containers. Always answer this question by calling the attribute functions of the object without supplying a container, as follows:

    ```
    object1->isVisible();
    ```

For example, consider two containers, container1 and container2, and an object, object1. Initially, object1 is not in either container. The following code demonstrates the use of the container functions to query the attributes of an object:

```
object1->hide();
object1->isVisible();                // NO
object1->show();
object1->isVisible();                // YES (even though it is not
                                     // in a container).

container1->addObject(object1);
container2->addObject(object1);

object1->hide(container1);
object1->isVisible();                // NO

object1->isVisible(container1);  // NO
container1->isVisible(object1)   // NO (same question)

object1->isVisible(container2);  // YES
container2->isVisible(object1);  // YES (same question)
```

Setting and Querying Object Attributes

You can modify the following container object attributes:

Visibility

The ability to see an object in the container on the display. An object is visible unless you explicitly hide it. Hide an object either by calling IContainerControl::hide or by using a filter function (as we showed earlier). Determine an object's visibility by calling IContainerControl::isVisible or IContainerObject::isVisible.

Cursored emphasis

An object with input focus. Change the object with cursored emphasis by calling `IContainerControl::setCursor`. Only a single object at a time can have cursored emphasis in a container. Therefore, setting the cursored emphasis to one object removes cursored emphasis from another. Removing an object with cursored emphasis causes the container to apply cursored emphasis to a different object.

You cannot explicitly turn cursored emphasis off. Don't try to use an `ObjectCursor` to remove an object with cursored emphasis. If you use the normal cursor loop, it can remove many or all of the objects in the container. This happens because the container automatically shifts the cursored emphasis to the next object.

You can determine if an object has cursored emphasis by calling `IContainerControl::isCursored`. You can determine which object has cursored emphasis by calling `IContainerControl::cursoredObject`.

Selection emphasis

A highlighted object or group of objects that the user wants to perform an action on, such as copy or move. Selection emphasis shows the highlighted target of the user's action. Typically a user selects an object or a group of objects, and applies a specific behavior to these objects. In a single-selection container, setting the selection emphasis to a new object removes selection emphasis from the prior object with selection emphasis. Call `IContainerControl::setSelected` to set selection emphasis on an object and call `IContainerControl::removeSelected` to remove it. Determine if an object has selected emphasis by calling `IContainerControl::isSelected`.

In-use emphasis

A highlighted object that is currently in-use. This emphasis might occur when the user opens a view on the object. Call `IContainerControl::setInUse` to set in-use emphasis on an object and call `IContainerControl::removeInUse` to remove it. Determine if an object has in-use emphasis by calling `IContainerControl::isInUse`.

Refresh state

A state of an object that determines whether the container updates the view of the object on the display. To make a series of changes to an object without updating the display, set an object's refresh state to off. To do this, call `setRefreshOff`, make the changes, call `setRefreshOn`, and then call `refresh`.

The container also has a refresh state which enables you to make changes to a group of objects without updating the container. If you turn off the container's refresh state, your changes to an object are not seen even if the refresh state of the object is on. Turn off the container's refresh state by calling `IContainerControl::setRefreshOff`. After you make your changes, turn refresh on by calling `IContainerControl::setRefreshOn` and then `IContainerControl::refresh`.

Open status

An opened object. By default, the container sets in-use emphasis on when an object is opened and removes it when an object is closed. Set an object to the open state by calling `IContainerObject::setOpen` and to the closed state by calling `IContainerObject::setClosed`. Determine if an object is open by calling `IContainerObject::isOpen`.

Direct edit status

An object enabled for editing. As described earlier, the text data associated with an object cannot be edited by the user or under program control unless you enable the object for editing. Enable an object for text editing by calling `IContainerControl::enableDataUpdate` or `IContainerObject::enableDataUpdate`. Disable an object for update by calling `IContainerControl::disableDataUpdate` or `IContainerObject::disableDataUpdate`. Determine if an object can be edited by calling `IContainerControl::isReadOnly` or `IContainerObject::isReadOnly`.

Expanded or collapsed state in tree view

An object's state when its descendants are viewable or hidden. Hide the descendants of an object by collapsing a branch of the tree and restore them by expanding the branch of the tree. Collapse a branch of the tree by calling `IContainerControl::collapse` and expand a collapsed branch by calling `IContainerControl::expand`. Determine if the descendants of an object are collapsed by calling `IContainerControl::isCollapsed` or `IContainerControl::isExpanded`.

Target Emphasis

A highlighted object that is the target of a user's direct-manipulation action. Determine if an object is the target of a direct manipulation by calling `IContainerControl::isTarget`.

Source Emphasis

A highlighted object that is the source of a user's action. The container shows an object with source emphasis when the user is dragging it with the mouse and when a user requests a pop-up menu for the object. Determine if an object has source emphasis by calling `IContainerControl::isSource`. The container classes call the functions `showSourceEmphasis` and `hideSourceEmphasis` in `IContainerControl` to add and remove source emphasis during direct manipulation and while showing a pop-up menu.

Handling Object Change Notification

The container classes provide a series of event notifications when the values of object attributes in the container change. The base container handler, `ICnrHandler`, captures these notifications and routes them to virtual functions within the handler. By default, when the attributes of an object change, the handler calls virtual functions on the changed object. The container classes do *not* create an `ICnrHandler` by default. If you need to process the virtual functions in your `IContainerObject` derived class, create an `ICnrHandler` object and call its function handleEventsFor to attach it to the container. Unlike many other handlers, you do not need to derive from ICnrHandler to use it.

The base container handler captures the following changes and passes them to an object for processing.

The user presses Enter or double-clicks mouse button 1.

The handler calls ICnrHandler::enter and passes it an ICnrEnterEvent object to describe the details of the event. If the enter occurs over an object, ICnrHandler::enter calls IContainerObject::handleOpen to process the action; otherwise, the function does nothing.

The selection status of an object changes.

The handler calls ICnrHandler::selectedChanged and passes it an ICnrEmphasisEvent object to describe the details of the event. Then, selectedChanged calls the IContainerObject::handleSelectedChange and indicates whether the selection emphasis was acquired or released. Note that the container usually sends two events for each user's changing of the emphasis—one event for the object losing the emphasis and one event for the object acquiring the emphasis.

The cursored status of an object changes.

The handler calls ICnrHandler::cursoredChanged and passes it an ICnrEmphasisEvent object to describe the details of the event. Then, cursoredChanged calls IContainerObject::handleCursoredChange and indicates whether the cursored emphasis was acquired or released. Similar to selection notification, the container dispatches an event both for the object acquiring the cursor and for the one losing it.

The in-use status of an object changes.

The handler calls ICnrHandler::inuseChanged and passes it an ICnrEmphasisEvent object to describe the details of the event. Then, inuseChanged calls IContainerObject::handleInuseChanged and indicates whether the in-use emphasis was acquired or released.

Advanced Features

Using Help in the Container

The native help facilities of the Windows and OS/2 operating systems provide a powerful facility for displaying help information for an application. Chapter 23, "Using Help," discusses adding help to Open Class Library applications. In addition to the contextual window help available to all windows, the container classes allow you to display help for objects in any of the available views and for the individual columns in the details view during direct editing.

To use help in objects of the container, create the container's default handler, `ICnrHandler`, and call its function `handleEventsFor`. In addition, if you provide column help during a direct edit in the details view, create an `ICnrEditHandler` and call its function `handleEventsFor`.

When the container's default handler detects a request for help, it calls `ICnrHandler::help` to process the request. If the help request occurs over an object, `ICnrHandler::help` checks to determine whether an edit field is currently open on a column of the details view. If so, it calls `IContainerColumn::helpId` to determine the identifier of the help panel to display for the column. If a column is not currently being edited, it calls `IContainerObject::helpId` to determine the help panel to display for the object. If a help panel is not returned in either of these cases, it calls `IWindow::helpId` to determine if a help panel is set for the container. If the handler finds a help panel in any of these situations, it calls the static function `IHelpWindow::helpWindow` to determine the help window for the container and then calls `IHelpWindow::show` to display the help panel.

Because the objects and columns of the container are not presentation system windows, you do not need to add information to the help table or subtable in your resource file. Identify the help panel to be displayed at run time by providing the actual panel identifier (the `RES=` tag in the `IPF` file) of the help panel.

Help for Container Objects

To provide help for an object in the container, override the function `helpId` in your `IContainerObject`-derived class and return the help panel that you want displayed. Then you can provide help at the class level for objects in the container. Also, with a little additional code, you can provide help for each individual object in the container. For example, to add help for each of our `Developer` objects, add the following functions to the class:

Container Help - cnr\help\devmodel.cpp

```
Developer& Developer::setHelpId ( unsigned long helpId )
{
  this->fHelpId = helpId;
  return *this;
}

unsigned long Developer::helpId ( ) const
{
  if(this->fHelpId!=0)
    return this->fHelpId;
  else
    return PANEL_DEVELOPER_UNKNOWN;
}
```

To specify help for a `Developer` object, call `setHelpId` to store the help panel identifier in the `Developer` instance data. If you do not call this function for an object, the container displays the help panel for "unknown developers."

Help for Container Columns

Because IContainerColumn is a class designed to be used without derivation, its help strategy is different from that of IContainerObject. IContainerColumn contains a data member to store the help panel identifier similarly to the way we extended the Developer object in the last example. To show column help, call IContainerColumn::setHelpId with a valid panel identifier. Because a user cannot directly select the columns in the container (selection occurs on the entire row of data), the container can only display column help if a user opens a column for editing. Thus, you cannot provide column help in a read-only container.

Customized Container Edit Controls

The container classes provide the capability to enhance the edit behavior of the container in several ways. The simplest way is to create a keyboard handler as a derived class of IKeyboardHandler and to override the behavior of the virtual function key. To use this handler, create an ICnrEditHandler object and call the function setMLEHandler with the newly-created keyboard handler object. For example, the following code prevents a user from typing the character "A" in the container's edit field.

KeyboardHandler Interface - cnr\edithdr\keyhdr.hpp

```
#include <ikeyhdr.hpp>
#include <istring.hpp>

class KeyboardHandler : public IKeyboardHandler {
protected:
virtual Boolean
  characterKeyPress ( IKeyboardEvent& event )
  {
    // Reject any 'A' characters.
    IString strChar = event.mixedCharacter();
    if (strChar.isSBCS()  &&  strChar -- 'A')
    {
       event.setResult(true);
       return true;
    }
    return false;
  }
};
```

KeyboardHandler Usage - cnr\edithdr\edithdr.cpp

```
#include <iframe.hpp>
#include <iapp.hpp>
#include <icnrctl.hpp>
#include <icnrobj.hpp>
#include <icnrhdr.hpp>
#include <icnrehdr.hpp>
#include <icconst.h>
#include "keyhdr.hpp"

void main()
{
// Create the frame and a container.
IFrameWindow frame("Container Keyboard Edit Handler");
IContainerControl cnr(IC_FRAME_CLIENT_ID, &frame, &frame);
```

```
// Create and attach the container handlers.
ICnrEditHandler editHandler;
ICnrHandler cnrHandler;
editHandler.handleEventsFor(&cnr);
cnrHandler.handleEventsFor(&cnr);

// Create the keyboard handler and pass it to
// the container's edit handler to use whenever
// an MLE is created.
KeyboardHandler keyHandler;
editHandler.setMLEHandler(&keyHandler);

// Add an object for editing.
IContainerObject* object;
object = new IContainerObject("Object 1");
cnr
  .addObject(object)
  .enableDataUpdate(object);

// Put the container into the text view and
// give it the focus.
cnr
  .showTextView()
  .setFocus();

// Put the container in the client and
// show the frame.
frame
 .setClient(&cnr)
 .show();

// Start processing messages.
IApplication::current().run();
}
```

Another way to alter the processing of the container's edit control is to acquire a pointer to the IMultiLineEdit control during the processing of the edit handler's function beginEdit. Then use it to call functions on the multiline edit control that alter its behavior. Remember to call the base class implementation of beginEdit before trying to use the multiline edit control because this function creates the wrapper for the container's multiline edit control.

Container Pop-Up Menus

IContainerControl can display pop-up menus using a pop-up menu handler and the IPopUpMenu class. Because you need to be able to show pop-up menus on the objects in the container (and one for the container itself), Open Class Library provides the class ICnrMenuHandler to determine the object under the mouse. Consequently, derive a class from ICnrMenuHandler, instead of IMenuHandler, and override its popUpMenu function. This example shows you how to do that:

```
// Declare a derived class of the container's menu handler.
class DeveloperMenuHandler : public ICnrMenuHandler
{
protected:
Boolean
 makePopUpMenu(IMenuEvent& menuEvent);
};
```

```
// Provide the implementation of makePopUpMenu.
Boolean DeveloperMenuHandler::makePopUpMenu(IMenuEvent& menuEvent)
{
  // If the mouse is on an object, create a menu for the object.
  // Add support for a container window menu if
  // the mouse isn't over an object.

  IContainerControl* container =
                (IContainerControl*)(menuEvent.window());

  if(popupMenuObject()) {
    IPopUpMenu* popUpMenu = new IPopUpMenu(POPUP_MENU, container);
    popUpMenu->setAutoDeleteObject();
    popUpMenu->show(menuEvent.mousePosition());
    return true;
  }
  return false;
}
```

To use the preceding handler, create an object of the handler and call its `handleEventsFor` function. This is not shown in the preceding example, but it is included in the **cnr\popup** program on the examples disk. A restriction of the container's pop-up menu handler is that you must attach it to the container itself; the handler does not work correctly attached to the container's owner.

Also, within the pop-up menu handler's `makePopUpMenu` function, you must create the pop-up menu using the container as the `owner` parameter. We show this line of code in bold type in the preceding example.

Building Large Numbers of Container Objects

It might be necessary to display more items in a container than the performance characteristics of the container can reasonably support. To overcome this problem, Open Class Library provides two techniques to minimize the time it takes to build and display objects in the container. The first technique, called *record caching*, allows you to show the container with a subset of the total records. The container dispatches notification events as a user scrolls the container to allow you to dynamically adjust the actual records in the container. This technique is limited because the scroll bars in the container reflect the actual items in the container, not the full set of items you intend your users to view.

To enable caching in the container, call `IContainerControl::enableCaching` and pass the *delta value*. The delta value is a count of objects from the top and bottom ends of the container. The container uses this count to form boundaries at the top and bottom of the container. When the user scrolls past either boundary, the container dispatches an `ICnrQueryDeltaEvent` to `ICnrHandler::deltaReached`. The `ICnrQueryDeltaEvent` object provides information describing the current location of the scroll bar in the container. Use this event to adjust the objects in the container by removing objects from one end and adding new objects to the other end, depending on which way the user moves the scroll bar.

The second technique optimizes how you create and add container objects by allowing you to allocate and add objects as a group instead of one at a time. Open Class Library provides this capability with the class `ICnrAllocator` in combination with functions in `IContainerControl` and `IContainerObject`.

Follow these steps to use `ICnrAllocator`:

1. Allocate the storage for your objects by creating an `ICnrAllocator` object. Because `ICnrAllocator` allocates the storage for a group of objects, provide it with the number of objects and the size of each object. Use the C macro `sizeof` on your `IContainerObject`-derived class to determine the size to pass to the `ICnrAllocator` constructor. The following example creates an allocator for 5,000 `IContainerObjects`.

```
ICnrAllocator allocator( 5000, sizeof(IContainerObject));
```

2. Create your objects using the version of `IContainerObject::operator new` that accepts an `ICnrAllocator` object. This function uses the storage already acquired by the `ICnrAllocator` object rather than allocating a separate block of storage for each object.

```
IContainerObject* object = new(allocator) IContainerObject("object");
```

3. Add your new objects to a container using one of the functions in `IContainerControl` that accepts an `ICnrAllocator` as an argument.

```
container.addObjects(allocator);
```

The **cnr\cnralloc** program on the examples disk demonstrates how to add objects to a container both with and without an `ICnrAllocator` and it shows the time you can save if you use `ICnrAllocator`.

Custom Drawing

The container normally handles the painting of icons, text, and its own background, and does so sufficiently well to meet the needs of most applications. When needed, an application on the OS/2 operating system or on the Windows operating system that uses the style `IContainerControl::pmCompatible`, can handle some of this drawing. The container classes do not currently support custom drawing on the native Windows container. Even for the containers Open Class Library supports, custom drawing can be difficult unless you limit the support your container provides. Some of the difficulties in providing custom drawing in these two containers are as follows:

- The container supports multiple lines of text in all fields that support text. This includes titles, icon text, column headings, and the data stored in the details view.

- The container does not send a separate notification for drawing selection emphasis. If you decide to draw the text or icon of an item, you must also draw cursored, selection, in-use, source, and target emphases.

- The container is composed of several different windows. The title in all views and the data to the left and right of a split bar in the details view are child windows of the container.

- Drawing the background in anything other than a solid color or pattern is difficult because of the relationship between the container workspace and the view port on that workspace and because the container adds scroll bars when it determines they are needed.

If you choose to change the default drawing performed by the container, we recommend that you finish the rest of your application first. The following steps describe how to use the support that the container classes provide for drawing.

To handle drawing the background of the container, follow these steps:

1. Derive a class from `ICnrDrawHandler`, override `drawBackground`, and implement your drawing of the background.

2. Create an object of your draw handler and call its function `handleEventsFor` to attach the handler to the container.

3. Call `IContainerControl::enableDrawBackground` to cause the container to dispatch an `ICnrDrawBackgroundEvent` object to your handler.

To handle drawing items in the foreground of the container, follow these steps:

1. Derive a class from `ICnrDrawHandler` and override one or more of the following functions. If you do not provide one of these functions, the container does the drawing. If you override a function, you must draw the emphasis states of the items and the items themselves.

   ```
   ICnrDrawHandler::drawIcon
   ICnrDrawHandler::drawText
   ICnrDrawHandler::drawTreeIcon
   ICnrDrawHandler::drawDetailsItem
   ICnrDrawHandler::drawTitle
   ```

2. Create an object of your draw handler and call its function `handleEventsFor` to enable it.

3. Call `IContainerControl::enableDrawItem` to cause the container to dispatch an `ICnrDrawItemEvent` object to your handler.

Under the Covers

Open Class Library implements `IContainerControl` differently depending upon the operating system and the styles you use to create an `IContainerControl`. Particular differences are as follows:

OS/2 operating system

- `IContainerControl` uses the native `WC_CONTAINER` control.

Windows operating system

- When you create an IContainerControl *without* the style IContainerControl::pmCompatible, IContainerControl creates the native SysListView32 and SysTreeView32 controls on top of a window it creates with the class name "ICL Native Container." See Figure 13-7.

- When you create an IContainerControl *with* the style IContainerControl::pmCompatible, IContainerControl creates a version of the container control that Open Class Library provides. It looks and behaves like the native OS/2 container control and has the class name WC_CONTAINER.

Because you may need to modify or extend the behavior in IContainerControl or its related classes, we spend some time discussing how to accomplish this.

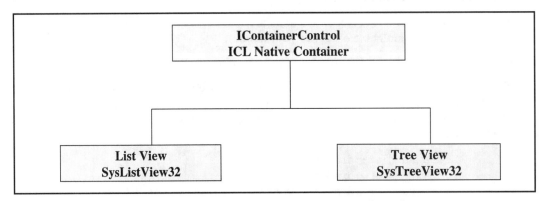

Figure 13-7. Windows IContainerControl without the pmCompatible Style.

IContainerControl

IContainerControl encapsulates the window and collection portion of the behavior found in the operating system containers it uses. In the OS/2 operating system, an application performs operations on the WC_CONTAINER control by sending it messages starting with the characters "CM_" (for Container Message). IContainerControl functions that need to perform operations on the WC_CONTAINER control build the appropriate CM_ messages and call IWindow::sendEvent to send them to the WC_CONTAINER control.

In the Windows operating system, an application performs operations on the SysListView32 and SysTreeView32 controls by composing messages starting with "LVM_" (for List View Message) for SysListView32 and "TVM_" (for Tree View Message) for SysTreeView32. The Windows operating system also provides a set of macros to help in composing these messages. For example, the macro ListViewGetItem expands to a call to SendMessage with an LVL_GETITEM message identifier. Open Class Library typically uses the macros to invoke functions in the Windows native containers.

Rather than providing separate implementations of its functions for the native Windows containers, IContainerControl uses the same functions to send these messages to its top-level window, the ICL Native Container control. A handler attached to this window captures these messages and routes the appropriate calls to either the native SysListView32 or SysTreeView32 container. This approach isolates the differences between the two implementations to a few files, leaving the majority of the container code common across all platforms.

IContainerObject on the OS/2 Native Container

The primary structure that the WC_CONTAINER window class uses exists in two different versions in the OS/2 operating system: RECORDCORE and MINIRECORDCORE. MINIRECORDCORE, as its name implies, is a slimmed-down version of the RECORDCORE data structure that the OS/2 developers added to reduce storage demands. The following points describe their differences:

- You can only display a single icon using a MINIRECORDCORE structure, whereas you can display both bitmaps and icons in minimized and regular versions using a RECORDCORE structure.

- You can only store a single text string in MINIRECORDCORE structure, whereas you can store a different text string for each of the four major views in RECORDCORE structure.

- You can store collapsed and expanded icons and bitmaps in the RECORDCORE structure for the tree name view.

IContainerObject is built on the MINIRECORDCORE structure, and therefore does not use the additional features of the RECORDCORE structure. As Figure 13-8 shows, the storage of an IContainerObject is contiguous with a MINIRECORDCORE structure.

When you create an IContainerObject using operator new, the base MINIRECORDCORE is initialized. The base portion of this object is not accessible to a client program. The container object stores the address of the base record during construction.

Although it is okay to derive a C++ object from a C structure (there is no difference between the two except the default access; a struct is public and a class is private), IContainerObject is not derived from the MINIRECORDCORE structure. A private header file, provided with the source code only, re-declares the contents of MINIRECORDCORE as a separate class, IMiniCnrRecord. IContainerObject::operator new allocates an IMiniCnrRecord object whenever an IContainerObject is constructed. The operator new in IContainerObject calls the WC_CONTAINER via CM_ALLOCRECORD to allocate enough memory for the user portion of IContainerObject, IContainerObject itself, and IMiniCnrRecord. It stores the pointer to the IMiniCnrRecord in the IContainerObject field called pbase. All that operator new in the private class IMiniRecordCore does is return a pointer to the MINIRECORDCORE portion of the object.

Because the WC_CONTAINER works with RECORDCORE and MINIRECORDCORE addresses, and IContainerObject works with object addresses, you may need to convert these addresses in the interface between IContainerObject and the Presentation Manager container.

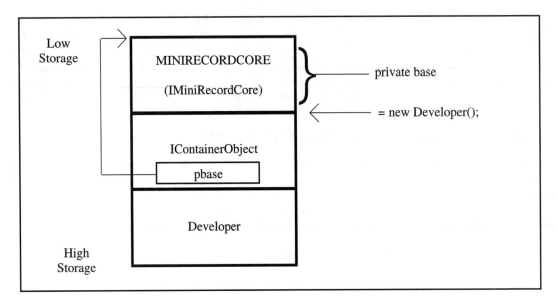

Figure 13-8. Layout of IContainerObject Storage.

Use the following code to convert from `IMiniCnrRecord` (MINIRECORDCORE) to `IContainerObject`:

```
IContainerObject* IObjFromRec(const IMiniCnrRecord* pcnrrec){
  if (pcnrrec)
    return  (IContainerObject*)(((char*)pcnrrec) + pcnrrec->cb);
  return 0;
}
```

Use the following code to convert from `IContainerObject` to `IMiniCnrRecord`:

```
IMiniCnrRecord* IRecFromObj(const IContainerObject* pcnrobj) {
if(pcnrobj)
  return ((IContainerObject*)pcnrobj)->baseRecord();
return 0;
}
```

As indicated earlier, one requirement of `IContainerObject`, or any of the classes that inherit from it, is that you must allocate its storage using `operator new` because the Presentation Manager container requires storage to be allocated by sending it a `CM_ALLOCRECORD` message. You cannot allocate this storage yourself.

You may have noticed that you can create an `IContainerObject` before you create an `IContainerControl`. Also, you cannot specify a container when you create a container object. So where is the container that allocates container objects? `IContainerControl` maintains an allocation container for each thread for the specific purpose of acquiring storage for `IContainerObjects`. This allocation container allows you to create an `IContainerObject` or a class derived from `IContainerObject` independently of any containers in the application.

IContainerObject on the Windows Native Container

Although in the previous topic you learned how Open Class Library implemented IContainerObject in the OS/2 operating system and the PM-compatible container in the Windows operating system, the details apply to the implementation of IContainerObject on the Windows native container. This is because IContainerObject uses the same IMiniCnrRecord base to store information it needs for objects in the Windows native containers.

Catching Container Exceptions

Open Class Library uses a strategy to only throw exceptions when an error occurs; it does not use exceptions for conveying the results of a request. If one of the container functions throws an exception, you usually have a mistake in your code. In most situations, you do not need to add try-and-catch code before calling container functions in a shipped application.

The primary exception returned from a call to a container function occurs when the presentation system container indicates that a request sent via an internal message failed to work. When this happens, the container function throws an IAccessError exception to identify the appropriate presentation system message along with any error text that the presentation system returns concerning the failure.

Unfortunately, in many cases the presentation system returns an error indicating only that the parameters to the function were invalid, not the details of what is invalid.

Tips and Techniques

The following topics discuss coding examples that we provide on the examples disk to extend the capability of the container.

Dynamic Creation of Objects and Columns

A requirement of showing objects in the details view is that you must put all details-view data in a class derived from IContainerObject, and you must report the offset of that data when you create the IContainerColumn for displaying the data. This doesn't work very well if you don't know the layout of the object until run time. As it turns out, with a few added restrictions and some creative programming, you can overcome this limitation.

The **cnr\dynobj** program on the examples disk demonstrates how to dynamically create IContainerObjects to display details-view data. The primary requirement is that you must store all data in the object as an IString. The creative part is to provide a class derived from IContainerObject with a special version of operator new with an argument indicating the number of fields in the object. The operator new function uses this count to allocate storage for the correct number of IStrings. Further, we use C++ placement syntax to construct the IStrings during the object's constructor without allocating storage (because the operator new function already allocated the storage as part of the object's storage). All access to the data in the object occurs via an index into the array of IStrings in the object.

The following code demonstrates the implementation of the operator new function that allocates storage based on the number of fields and it demonstrates the object constructor that allocates the IStrings using placement syntax. The entire example is on the examples disk.

```
// Operator new for variable number of fields.
void* TableObject::operator new(size_t size)
{
  void* tableObject = IContainerObject::operator new( size +
                   (size_t)fgFieldCount*sizeof(IString));
  return(tableObject);
}

// Primary TableObject constructor.
TableObject::TableObject( )
            : IContainerObject(0)
{
  IASSERTSTATE(TableObject::fgFieldCount != 0)
    // Call global operator new using placement syntax.
    // This does not allocate any storage, but the
    // constructor gets called.
    for(unsigned long s=1; s<fgFieldCount; s++)
    {
        new(&fFieldArray[s]) IString();
    }
}
```

Spreadsheet Behavior in the Details View

Typically, users initiate editing in the details view by clicking on an item with mouse button 1 to open an edit field on a column and close the edit field by clicking the mouse outside the edit field (in the OS/2 operating system, users open an edit field by click mouse button 1 while holding down the Alt key). You may have an application where you want a default editing behavior that more closely resembles how you edit in a spreadsheet. By defining a few keyboard accelerators and creating a specialized handler, you can achieve a details view that provides the editing function you need. You might include the following behavior:

- An edit field is usually open in the details view.

- The tab keys move the edit field from column to column. The edit field wraps to the next row after it moves to the last column, and it moves the previous row after it moves to the first column.

- The up and down arrow keys move the edit field from row to row.

- The view port is scrolled automatically to keep the edit field in view.

To enable the use of this spreadsheet behavior with other containers, we build this behavior into a specialized handler that you can attach to any container. For the simplicity of this handler, we have coded the example to use an accelerator table that equates specific keyboard keys to the functions in the spreadsheet handler that move the edit field. You can also accomplish this using a keyboard handler and processing the keys directly or by using IAcceleratorTable with the IAcceleratorKey class to build an accelerator table dynamically. The complete example is in the **cnr\spreadsh** program on the examples disk.

Chapter 14

Notebook Control

- Describes the Open Class Library classes you can use to build settings (or property) views
- Describes the INotebook, INoteBook::PageSettings, INoteBook::Cursor, IPageHandle, IPageHandler, IPageHelpEvent, IPageEvent, IPageSelectEvent, IPageRemoveEvent and INoteBookDrawItemEvent classes
- Read Chapter 7 before reading this chapter.
- Chapters 5, 15, 17, and 23 cover related material.

The INotebook class creates a control that displays information in a manner similar to a real notebook. It includes several features of a real notebook such as pages, tabs, and an optional binding. Because it is a software notebook, you can also add unique features such as page buttons to rapidly turn the pages of the notebook, a status area, and tab scroll buttons to scroll the tabs when there are more tabs than the notebook can display at one time. You can also add text, bitmaps, or both to your notebook tabs. Use the notebook control to organize related information and to easily retrieve that information.

An INotebook object functions like other control objects in Open Class Library. You can use a notebook as the client window of a frame window, as a frame extension, or within any canvas object. Usually, you create a notebook as the client window of a frame window. While you can place any window onto a page of the notebook, it is best to limit your choice to frame windows and the canvas classes. You can also attach handlers to the notebook to provide special processing.

Using Notebooks and Tab Controls

Both the Windows and OS/2 operating systems use the notebook to provide settings or property views using pages with tabs. The notebook tabs define the different categories of an object's attributes; the contents of the pages provide the details. INotebook supports the controls that both operating systems provide for these views.

The OS/2 operating system provides settings notebooks for all workplace objects. Open Class Library bases the INotebook class on the OS/2 notebook control and supports major and minor tabs, bindings, and a status area. You can use this notebook on both the Windows and OS/2 operating systems.

Additionally, in the Windows operating system, the Open Class Library implements the INotebook class using the Windows tab control. You can use the native tab control to display the properties associated with an object and provide a user interface consistent with that of the operating system.

The Windows tab control differs from the OS/2 notebook in the following ways:

- The tab control supports only major tabs. As a result, all minor and non-tab pages in existing applications are converted to major tabs when executed on the Windows operating system. Tab orientation and shape settings are ignored as the Windows tab control only supports rounded major tabs with their orientation limited to the top of the control. The Windows tab control centers the tab text and tab text alignment settings are also ignored.

- The Windows tab control automatically sizes the tabs unless you specify a size using INotebook::setMajorTabSize.

- The Windows tab control supports the placement of text and bitmaps on the same tab.

- The Windows tab control supports multiple rows of tabs that keep all of the tabs visible to the user.

- The Windows tab control supports owner drawing of the tabs. However, you must specify INotebook::handleDrawTabs during INotebook construction to enable the owner draw support. The owner-drawn tabs must all be the same width.

- The Windows tab control contains no binding or back pages area. The INotebook's implementation of this control ignores the binding and back pages settings.

- The Windows tab control contains no status text line so this is ignored as well.

- The Windows tab control contains no page buttons. If you specify a page button setting, it is ignored.

The Windows tab control is the default selection on the Windows operating system. To use the OS/2-style notebook, use INotebook::pmCompatible when you construct your notebook. Figure 14-1 shows the default notebook control on the Windows operating system.

Constructing a Notebook

The INotebook class supports the same basic three constructors that all control classes provide in Open Class Library. One constructor creates a new presentation system notebook window and the other two create a wrapper object for an existing notebook window.

In the Windows operating system, the constructors that create an INotebook object for an existing control assume that the application interacts with the control only via the INotebook object, because it creates a clipping window and manipulates the pages when the user selects tabs. Use the constructor that creates a new window when you use the tab control.

When you delete an INotebook object, the notebook destructor by default destroys the window only if the notebook constructor created it. Therefore, if you use the first constructor to create the window, the destructor will destroy it. If you use a constructor that creates a wrapper for an existing window, the destructor does not destroy the window. Call IWindow::setAutoDestroyWindow to change the default behavior in both of these cases.

Typically, you create a notebook as the client window of a frame window using IFrameWindow::setClient as in the following simple example:

Simple Notebook Example - notebook\simple\simple.cpp

```
#include <inotebk.hpp>
#include <iframe.hpp>
#include <iapp.hpp>
#include <icconst.h>

main()
{
  IFrameWindow frame ("Simple Notebook");
  INotebook notebook (IC_FRAME_CLIENT_ID, &frame, &frame);

  frame
    .setClient(&notebook)
    .setFocus()
    .show();
  IApplication::current().run();
}
```

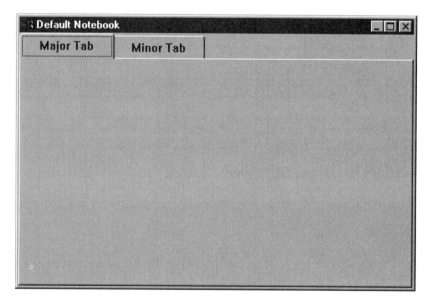

Figure 14-1. Default Windows Notebook Control.

Changing the Notebook's Style

There are many different ways to change the look and feel of a notebook. There are styles you can specify at construction, and there are functions to change these styles after you create the notebook. When you specify a style on the notebook constructor, you are making a series of choices. Some of these choices are independent and some are not. If you use the constructor styles, you must ensure that no conflicts occur. The style functions try to insulate you from making these types of mistakes. The majority of these styles apply to the PM-compatible notebook control only and are ignored when you use the Windows tab control. Figure 14-2 shows the major components of a notebook.

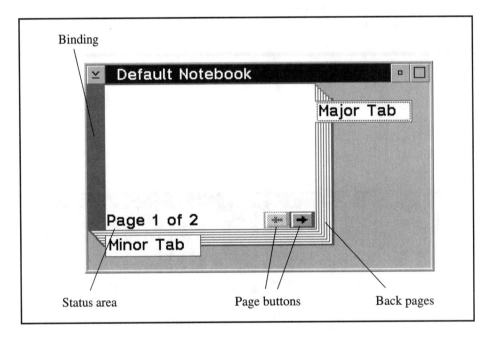

Figure 14-2. Components of a Notebook.

Creation Styles

You create a notebook with either a spiral binding or a solid binding using one of the following styles:

```
INotebook::solidBinding
INotebook::spiralBinding
```

The back pages of a notebook are the recessed edges, which give the notebook a three-dimensional effect. The notebook style, which specifies the location of the back pages, identifies the corner where the pages intersect.

You can put the back pages intersection in any corner using one of the following styles:

```
INotebook::backPagesBottomRight
INotebook::backPagesBottomLeft
INotebook::backPagesTopRight
INotebook::backPagesTopLeft
```

Page buttons move through the pages of the notebook one page at a time. The left page button brings the previous page into view in the notebook, and the right page button brings the next page of the notebook into view. The notebook places the page buttons on the corner where the back pages intersect.

The tabs of a notebook allow a user to move rapidly through the sections of the notebook. You can put the major tabs on any side of the notebook and their placement sets the location of the binding. The notebook puts the binding on the side opposite the tabs. If major tabs are on the right, the binding is on the left. Specify the location of the major tabs using one of the following styles:

```
INotebook::majorTabsRight
INotebook::majorTabsLeft
INotebook::majorTabsTop
INotebook::majorTabsBottom
```

The minor tabs of a notebook allow a user to move within a major tab section of a notebook. The notebook sets the location of the minor tabs based on the location of the back pages and the location of the major tabs. The notebook always puts the minor tabs on the back page edge that does not already contain the major tabs. If the back pages are on the bottom right and the major tabs are on the right, the notebook places the minor tabs on the bottom.

You can create the tabs with rounded corners, square corners, or as a polygon using one of the following styles:

```
INotebook::roundedTabs
INotebook::squareTabs
INotebook::polygonTabs
```

If a tab contains text (it can contain a bitmap instead), you can justify the text using one of the following styles:

```
INotebook::tabTextLeft
INotebook::tabTextRight
INotebook::tabTextCenter
```

The status area of the notebook displays information about the current page, such as "Page 1 of 3." The notebook always puts the status area on the same line as the page buttons. You can justify the text in the status area using one of the following styles:

```
INotebook::statusTextLeft
INotebook::statusTextRight
INotebook::statusTextCenter
```

Style Functions

If you do not code the style on the first constructor for your notebook, the static member INotebook::classDefaultStyle determines the style. This style specifies the original default style for the INotebook class and yields a notebook with the back pages on the bottom right, the major tabs on the right, a solid binding on the left, square-shaped tabs, centered tab text, and left-justified status text. The default style gives the look used by the settings or properties views of the operating system. Figure 14-1 displays the default view of the notebook.

You can change the notebook's default style to a style of your own choosing by calling the function `INotebook:setDefaultStyle`. For instance, to change the default style of new `INotebook` objects and to put a spiral binding of the notebook at the top with the minor tabs on the left, you would code the following:

```
INotebook::setDefaultStyle(INotebook::backPagesBottomLeft |
                           INotebook::spiralBinding       |
                           INotebook::majorTabsBottom      |
                           INotebook::roundedTabs          |
                           INotebook::tabTextCentered      |
                           INotebook::statusTextLeft);
```

Once you create the notebook, you can change its style using functions in `INotebook`. `INotebook` defines an additional set of enumerations to represent the notebook's binding, orientation, tab shape, and text alignment. You provide values of these enumerations to the `INotebook` functions, which cause a change in the notebook's style. These functions are `setBinding`, `setOrientation`, `setTabShape`, `setStatusTextAlignment`, and `setTabTextAlignment`.

For example, the values of `INotebook::Binding` are `INotebook::spiral` and `INotebook::solid`. To change a notebook binding from solid to spiral, you would code the following:

```
notebook.setBinding (INotebook::spiral);
```

One difference exists between the styles you use at construction and the enumerations you use to modify these styles after creating the notebook. The styles used to specify the location of the back pages and the location of the major tabs are merged into a single enumeration called `Orientation`. `Orientation` can have one of the following values:

```
INotebook::backpagesBottomTabsRight
INotebook::backpagesTopTabsRight
INotebook::backpagesBottomTabsLeft
INotebook::backpagesTopTabsLeft
INotebook::backpagesRightTabsTop
INotebook::backpagesLeftTabsTop
INotebook::backpagesRightTabsBottom
INotebook::backpagesLeftTabsBottom
```

You use these values after you create your notebook as we did previously with the notebook binding. For example, to change the binding and orientation, you would code the following:

```
notebook.setBinding( INotebook::spiral );
notebook.setOrientation( INotebook::backpagesBottomTabsRight );
```

Adding Pages in a Notebook

The last topic explained how you can create and modify the style or appearance of a notebook. You usually construct your notebooks in a style consistent with others in the system and, therefore, do not need to spend much time adjusting notebook styles. As in a real notebook, the value of a notebook is its content. This topic shows you how to add value to your notebook by filling it with useful pages.

On one level, a notebook is simply an ordered collection of pages. Each page has certain characteristics. The primary characteristic is the application window it shows on the page. To try to keep things straight, we refer to the portion of the notebook that contains the application window, tabs, and status information, as a *page* of the notebook. We call the application window that you display on a page a *page window*.

Logically, each page window is associated with a page of the notebook. However, the notebook creates a single window to control and handle keyboard and mouse input for all pages of the notebook. The main purpose of the window that holds the page window is to clip the page window so it does not paint over tabs or other notebook contents. When you add a page window to the notebook, the notebook makes this window the parent of your page window. As you select different pages in the notebook, it updates the information associated with a page, such as the text or bitmap on a tab and the status text. The notebook also hides the current page and makes the one you selected visible.

Page Settings

The nested class `INotebook::PageSettings` describes the characteristics of a notebook page. You use a `PageSettings` object to identify the characteristics of a page prior to adding it to the notebook. Once you add a page to the notebook, you use `INotebook` functions to update this information. If you call a function on a `PageSettings` object after putting the page in the notebook, it has no effect on the actual page in the notebook. The name `PageSettings`, instead of simply `Page`, reflects the use of the class in establishing the initial settings of a page. You can also use one object of this class to add multiple pages with the same characteristics or to query the current state of a page in a notebook.

A `PageSettings` object defines the attributes for a page of the notebook: the use of major or minor tabs, the page's autosizing behavior, the text or bitmap for tabs, and the text for status. You specify the attributes of a page using a nested class of `INotebook::PageSettings` called `INotebook::PageSettings::Attribute`. This class is similar to a style class and has constant values defined for its valid values. By default, pages are created with no attributes. You specify the type of tabs on a page using one of the following attributes:

```
INotebook::PageSettings::majorTabs
INotebook::PageSettings::minorTabs
```

A page cannot have both a major and a minor tab with different text. If you insert a page without a tab style, it does not have a tab on the page and it becomes a part of the section containing the closest prior tab page. The Windows tab control only supports major tabs and converts all minor and non-tab pages in your application to major tab pages.

To add status text or cause the notebook to autosize the page, use the following attributes:

```
INotebook::PageSettings::statusTextOn
INotebook::PageSettings::autoPageSize
```

The Windows tab control contains no status text line, and it ignores the status text and alignment settings.

If you use the `autoPageSize` attribute, a page window is automatically resized when a user resizes the notebook. Otherwise, you are responsible for sizing your page windows.

The notebook can also create a `PageSettings` object to indicate the current settings of a page in the notebook. You identify the page with an `IPageHandle` object. We discuss the functions that return a page handle later in this chapter. Again, modifying the `PageSettings` object returned from the notebook has no affect on the actual page in the notebook. In addition to its value of describing the characteristics of a page, it is useful as a template to create a new page in the notebook with the same or modified characteristics.

Besides the characteristics of the page, you can use the PageSettings nested class to store a single piece of application data with a page. You can then use this to store the identity of the object viewed on a page so it can be used later.

Page Handles

Once you add a page to the notebook, you identify it with an IPageHandle object. You use an IPageHandle on most of the operations affecting the characteristics of the page and to remove the page from the notebook.

INotebook has a number of functions to add pages to the notebook and each returns an IPageHandle object for the page. Besides identifying the position of the page in the notebook's collection, such as first or last, you add the page by providing a PageSettings object and an optional window to put on the page. You can also use some of these functions to add a page before or after another page. You can specify this "reference" page using either an IPageHandle or an INotebook::Cursor (which we discuss shortly).

In the next example, we imaginatively name it notebook, and add three pages to it. The first page needs a bitmap as the major tab and needs to contain a frame window created from a dialog template with the resource identifier, ID_DIALOG1. The second page needs a major tab with the text "no window," and does not have a page window. The third page needs a minor tab with the text "dialog3," and should contain a dialog window with the resource identifier, ID_DIALOG3. The status area contains information identifying the current page seen in the notebook. We do not show the definition of the actual dialogs, but the code to build the notebook is as follows:

Adding Notebook Pages - notebook\addpages\addpages.cpp

```
#include <inotebk.hpp>
#include <iframe.hpp>
#include <iapp.hpp>
#include <ihandle.hpp>
#include <ifont.hpp>
#include <ipoint.hpp>
#include <icconst.h>
#include "addpages.h"

void main()
{
  IFrameWindow frame ("Adding Notebook Pages");
  INotebook    notebook (IC_FRAME_CLIENT_ID, &frame, &frame);

  // Dialog1 & Dialog3
  IFrameWindow
    dialog1(ID_DIALOG1, &notebook, &notebook),
    dialog3(ID_DIALOG3, &notebook, &notebook);

  // Use one of the system bitmaps for the tab.
  ISystemBitmapHandle page1Bitmap(ISystemBitmapHandle::drive);
```

```
      // Add Page 1 to the notebook with a bitmap, major tab,
      // and dialog1.
      INotebook::PageSettings pageData1 (
              page1Bitmap,
              "Page 1",
              INotebook::PageSettings::statusTextOn |
              INotebook::PageSettings::majorTab);
      notebook.addLastPage( pageData1, &dialog1);

      // Add Page 2 to the notebook with text and major tab,
      // but no window.
      INotebook::PageSettings pageData2 (
              "no window",
              "Page 2",
              INotebook::PageSettings::statusTextOn |
              INotebook::PageSettings::majorTab);
      notebook.addLastPage( pageData2);

      // Add Page 3 to the notebook with text, minor tab,
      // and dialog3.
      INotebook::PageSettings pageData3 (
              "dialog3",
              "Page 3",
              INotebook::PageSettings::statusTextOn |
              INotebook::PageSettings::minorTab);
      notebook.addLastPage( pageData3, &dialog3);

      // Size the tabs to fit the text.
      IFont noteFont(&notebook);
      ISize tabSize(ISize(noteFont.minTextWidth("no_window Page_3"),
                  noteFont.maxCharHeight()) + ISize(6,6));
      notebook
        .setMajorTabSize(tabSize)
        .setMinorTabSize(tabSize);

      // Show the application and process messages.
      frame
        .setClient(&notebook)
        .show();
      IApplication::current().run();
   }
```

Sizing Tabs

The Windows tab control automatically sizes the tabs according to the size of its contents.

The PM-compatible version of INotebook does not currently provide the capability to automatically size its tabs to best fit their contents. As a result, you must explicitly set the size of both the major and minor tabs to something large enough to contain their largest piece of data. While you can separately size major and minor tabs, you cannot uniquely size individual tabs.

The previous example contains code that works well for finding the size needed to contain the text in the tabs. It passes a string containing all the words used on the tabs to the function IFont::minTextWidth. minTextWidth returns the size of the largest word. Note that we have replaced blanks with underscores (so that multiple-word tab text is treated as a single "token") and have added a little extra size for padding. An alternative approach would be to use the function IFont::textWidth on each individual string and loop for all the tabs.

Like all presentation system windows, the notebook changes its font when you drag a new font from the OS/2 Font Palette or modify your Windows Control Panel settings. However, the notebook does not change the size of the tabs to accommodate an increase or decrease in the space required to display the tab text. If you want to add this function to your notebooks, you can do so by providing a class that derives from INotebook, and implements the function setLayoutDistorted to dynamically resize the tabs. See Chapter 15, "Canvases," for more information on the setLayoutDistorted function.

If you want tab text to be in a specific font, do not call IWindow:setFont to make the notebook use the font. This propagates the font to all the page windows. A better strategy would be to use IPageHandler to draw the tab text using that font instead of using the default drawing with the font of the notebook.

In the OS/2 operating system, if you do not have any minor tabs, set the minor tab size to ISize(0,0). This removes space that the notebook would otherwise reserve for minor tabs, even if you do not have any. This is useful if you later choose to add a minor tab.

Adding Windows to a Page

A *page window* is the window associated with a page of the notebook. As you have already seen, this association is accomplished by specifying the window when the page is added to the notebook or after the page is in the notebook using INotebook::setWindow.

You can define page windows using a variety of different windows, but you usually choose one of the following:

- An IFrameWindow created from a dialog template and loaded from a resource file
- One of the ICanvas classes (primarily IMultiCellCanvas)

Chapter 15, "Canvases," describes the advantages that the canvas classes have over dialog templates. The advantages of using a canvas are even more important when building a notebook because you now have the task of trying to get a group of dialogs to look right given a fixed size for the notebook. This is hard enough that some developers resort to resizing the notebook to fit the contents of the current page. Visually, the notebook grows or shrinks as the user leafs through the pages of the notebook. We do not recommend this approach, primarily because it violates one of our user-interface design goals—*leave the user in control*. Allow the user to determine the position and size of the windows on the desktop and do not design your application so that it takes this ability away.

There are other reasons to use the canvas classes to compose the views in your page windows. For one, you can use the views displayed in the pages of a notebook in other places in your application, perhaps even other notebooks. You do not want to fix the size of these views just because they are going to be displayed in the same notebook. The problem is further complicated if you decide to delay building some of the pages until a user turns to that page. Because you have not created the page yet and its size is specified in a resource independent from your application, you do not know how big to make the notebook to contain it (unless, of course, you build all the page windows of your application at a fixed size). If you still are not convinced, read Chapter 15, "Canvases," and see what can happen when you drop a font on a dialog template using the OS/2 Font Palette window.

We hope we have convinced you that the canvas classes are the way to go in building the pages of a notebook. Nevertheless, Open Class Library supports dialog templates, and you might have situations where you need to use them (especially if you are supporting an existing application).

Dialog Pages

To create a page window from a dialog template, construct an `IFrameWindow` using the frame window constructor that takes an `IResourceId` and a parent and owner `IWindow*`. Unless you are putting the dialog template into a view port, both the parent and the owner of the frame window *must* be the notebook.

Use the class `IViewport` between the page and your dialog template window to automatically add scroll bars when the notebook page reaches a size that would cause the page window to be clipped. This technique gives you some measure of support for dynamically sized windows. If you use a view port, the parent and owner of the view port must be the notebook and the view port must be the parent and owner of your dialog template window. Add the view port as the page window. Specify `INotebook::PageSettings::autoPageSize` as the style for the page.

If you use `IFrameWindow` objects as the page windows for a notebook, and all the frame windows or dialogs have a nonzero initial size, the notebook returns the smallest size it needs to contain all of its page windows at their initial size as its minimum size. This is a useful feature for initially sizing a notebook to an optimal size.

Matching Dialog Colors on a Page

There is a problem with the example used in the topic "Page Handles." While the background of the dialog page window is gray, the typical dialog background color, the background of the page itself is white. Thus, a white border shows around the outside of the dialog page window and the background of the tabs are white. We can fix this by changing the colors of these areas of the notebook to the color of a dialog background. The `INotebook::pageBackground` is the area around the page and includes the background of the tabs and the status area. It also includes any area of the page not covered by the dialog page window. We need to add the following code to our dialog example:

```
// Set the color of the page parts to that of a dialog
// background.
notebook
  .setPageBackgroundColor(
          (IGUIColor::dialogBgnd)
  .setMajorTabBackgroundColor(
          (IGUIColor::dialogBgnd);
```

The following example demonstrates how to use a view port on a page of the notebook:

View Port on a Notebook Page - notebook\vportdlg\vportdlg.cpp

```cpp
#include <inotebk.hpp>
#include <iframe.hpp>
#include <iapp.hpp>
#include <ihandle.hpp>
#include <ifont.hpp>
#include <ipoint.hpp>
#include <ivport.hpp>
#include <icolor.hpp>
#include <icconst.h>
#include "deferacc.hpp"
#include "vportdlg.h"

void main()
{
   // Create the frame, notebook, and view port.
   IFrameWindow frame ("ViewPort Notebook");
   INotebook    notebook (IC_FRAME_CLIENT_ID, &frame, &frame);
   IViewPort    viewport (0x102, &notebook, &notebook);

   // Set the window and the page to the
   // color of a dialog background.
   frame.setBackgroundColor(
            (IGUIColor::dialogBgnd);
   notebook
     .setPageBackgroundColor(
            (IGUIColor::dialogBgnd)
     .setMajorTabBackgroundColor(
            (IGUIColor::dialogBgnd);

   // Create a dialog on the view port.
   IFrameWindow dialog1(ID_DIALOG1, &viewport, &viewport);
#ifdef IC_PM
   DeferAccelerators accelHdr;
   accelHdr.handleEventsFor(&dialog1);
#endif

   // Declare a page settings with text, major tab, and
   // a dialog.
   INotebook::PageSettings pageData =
                INotebook::PageSettings (
                        "dialog1",
                        "Page 1",
                        INotebook::PageSettings::autoPageSize |
                        INotebook::PageSettings::statusTextOn |
                        INotebook::PageSettings::majorTab);
   notebook.addLastPage( pageData, &viewport);

   // Make sure the tabs are big enough.
   IFont noteFont(&notebook);
   ISize tabSize(ISize(noteFont.minTextWidth("Page_1"),
            noteFont.maxCharHeight()) + ISize(6,6));
   notebook.setMajorTabSize(tabSize);

   // Set the client and show the window.
   frame
     .setClient(&notebook)
     .show();
   IApplication::current().run();
}
```

The `DeferAccelerators` class in the previous example prevents the dialog from processing accelerator keys in the OS/2 operating system. Omitting this handler causes default accelerator keys for a frame to be processed by the dialog instead of the frame window containing the notebook. The accelerator keys are Alt+F4 for Close, Alt+F7 for Move, Alt+F8 for Size, Alt+F9 for Minimize, and Alt+F10 for Maximize. So, pressing Alt+F4 would close the page window and leave the notebook with an empty page. This does not occur on the Windows operating system.

Canvas Pages

Two canvas classes provide the essential ingredients for building page windows. You already learned how to use the IViewport class to add scroll bars to your dialog page windows. The IMultiCellCanvas class provides the ability to easily create dialogs that are insensitive to changes in font, screen resolution, or window size. As you do for the dialog page windows, create the canvas classes used as page windows with the notebook as their parent and owner.

If you use IMultiCellCanvas objects as the page windows for a notebook and all the canvases have an initial size of ISize(0,0), the notebook returns the smallest size it needs to contain all of its page windows (sized to their minimum sizes) as the notebook's minimum size. This is a useful feature for initially sizing a notebook to an optimal size.

Chapter 15, "Canvases," provides examples and additional information on using the canvas classes.

Finding Pages Using the Notebook Cursor

A *collection cursor* is a standard mechanism in Open Class Library for moving through the elements of a collection. Because a notebook is a collection of pages, INotebook provides the nested class INotebook::Cursor to iterate notebook pages. The INotebook::Cursor class has the standard protocol of all cursor classes: setToFirst, setToNext, setToPrevious, setToLast, isValid, and inValidate. The cursor class relieves you of having to store page handles when the pages are first added to the notebook because they can be retrieved in a logical order. For example, to find the page of the notebook that contains the window dialog2, you code the following:

```
INotebook::Cursor cursor(notebook);
for (cursor.setToFirst(); cursor.isValid(); cursor.setToNext()) {
  if (notebook.window(cursor) == dialog2)
    // Do something.
}
```

Keep the lifetime of a cursor object as short as possible because changes to the notebook can cause the cursor to become invalid. The best approach is to declare cursors on the stack and to avoid calling functions that cause pages to be added or removed. The addition and removal of pages after the creation of a cursor causes the cursor function isValid to return false.

In addition to the standard protocol, INotebook::Cursor also has functions that set the cursor location and then return the page handle at the cursor location: first, next, previous, and last. There are also functions to return the page handle at the cursor location and to set the cursor directly to a known page: current and setCurrent.

The cursor movement functions return 0 for the page handle if the requested operation cannot be accomplished. A 0 handle is not a valid page handle and results in an exception if you use it as input to one of the notebook's functions. You must also ensure a page handle is valid prior to calling the setCurrent function because it is not checked. A handle is not valid if you remove the page from the notebook. The `current` and `setCurrent` functions can be useful if you are iterating a notebook and need to add or remove pages and still maintain the integrity of the cursor. Do this by storing the current handle with a call to `current`, adding or removing pages, and then restoring the cursor to the saved value with a call to `setCurrent`. Just be sure you do not remove the page with the restored page handle.

Requesting and Updating Page Information

The page handle is the primary identifier you use to query or change the data associated with the pages of a notebook. As we discussed in the previous section, you can store this handle when you add the page or determine it later using a cursor. There are also functions of the notebook that you can use to return page handles: `topPage`, `firstPage`, `nextPage`, `previousPage`, and `lastPage`. The top page is the page that you see when the notebook is visible, and it changes as you flip through the pages of the notebook.

The notebook itself has no means of keeping track of a current page, so the functions `nextPage` and `previousPage` require a reference page. If you use these functions, you assume the primary duty of the cursor—keeping track of the current page.

Once you know the page handle, you can determine a wealth of information about the page. You can query the current settings of the page describing the status line, the existence and type of the tab, the text or bitmap of the tab, and any application data you stored with the page. You also use the page handle to query the window associated with the page.

Removing Pages

Like you do with many of the functions in the notebook, remove pages by supplying the `IPageHandle`, which was returned when the page was created. The function `INotebook::removePage` accepts either a handle directly or determines the handle from an instance of an `INotebook::Cursor`. You can remove pages of a notebook by calling `INotebook::removeAllPages` to empty the notebook or `INotebook::removeTabSection` to remove pages associated with a major or minor tab section. An invalid handle in any of these functions or a request to remove a tab section for a page without a tab results in an `IAccessError` exception.

Handling Notebook Events

In addition to the handlers described in Chapter 17, "Reusable Handlers," which you can use in a notebook as you use them in other controls in Open Class Library, the notebook has handlers specific to the pages of the notebook. Use `IPageHandler` to receive notification of events affecting the pages of the notebook. Attach the page handler either directly to the notebook or to the owner of the notebook. The page handler is not called if it is attached to the page windows. When the page handler receives one of these events, it creates a corresponding event object and dispatches that object to the appropriate `IPageHandler` virtual function. Table 14-1

Table 14-1. IPageHandler Notification Functions

Virtual Function	Description
drawTab	Called when a tab is drawn on the notebook.
help	Called when a user requests help for the notebook when the selection cursor is on a tab.
remove	Called when a page is removed from the notebook.
resize	Called when the size of the application page window has changed.
select	Called when a user selects a new page in the notebook and it is brought to the top of the notebook.
selectPending	Called when a selection is pending on another page in the notebook. This member is supported on the Windows operating system only and is used to save the state of the outgoing page and to prevent the user from turning to another notebook page.

shows the `IPageHandler` virtual functions that you can use to process events in the notebook. You can override these virtual functions to supply customized processing of a page event. The return value from the virtual functions specifies whether Open Class Library passes the page event to another event for additional processing.

Delayed Addition of Pages

One of the best uses of an `IPageHandler` is to support the creation of page windows when a user selects the pages instead of building all of the page windows prior to showing the notebook. Adding a window to the page after it is in the notebook requires the page handle and a call to the function `INotebook::setWindow`.

In the following example, we create the page window for the first page when we create the notebook. We wait until a user selects the other pages of the notebook before we create their page windows. We store the dialog identifier of the page window as application data in the page when adding the page to the notebook. When the window dispatcher calls the page handler to process the select event, the handler loads the dialog and adds it to the notebook. It then sets the application data field to 0 to indicate that the page window has already been created.

Delayed Addition of Notebook Windows - notebook\select\select.cpp

```
#include <inotebk.hpp>
#include <ipagehdr.hpp>
#include <iframe.hpp>
#include <iapp.hpp>
#include <ihandle.hpp>
#include <ifont.hpp>
#include <ipoint.hpp>
#include <icolor.hpp>
#include "select.h"
```

```cpp
// The page handler for capturing page select
// events (used to delay dialog creation).
class PageSelectHandler : public IPageHandler {
protected:
virtual Boolean
  select ( IPageSelectEvent &event );
};

void main ( )
{
  // Create the frame and the notebook.
  IFrameWindow frame ("Delayed Addition of Pages");
  INotebook    notebook (ID_NOTEBOOK, &frame, &frame);

  // Make the page parts the same color as the dialog.
  notebook
    .setPageBackgroundColor(
             (IGUIColor::dialogBgnd)
    .setMajorTabBackgroundColor(
             (IGUIColor::dialogBgnd);

  // Declare a page settings object.
  INotebook::PageSettings pageData(
          INotebook::PageSettings::statusTextOn |
          INotebook::PageSettings::majorTab |
          INotebook::PageSettings::autoPageSize);

  // Set up page 1 with text, a major tab, and a dialog.
  // User data is 0 because we load the dialog here.
  pageData
    .setTabText("Page 1")
    .setStatusText("Page 1")
    .setUserData(0);

  // Create the dialog for the top page
  // and add the page to the notebook.
  IFrameWindow dialog1(ID_DIALOG1, &notebook, &notebook);
  notebook.addLastPage( pageData, &dialog1);

  // Set up page 2 with text, a major tab, and a dialog.
  // We store the dialog ID in user data and use it
  // later to load the dialog.
  pageData
    .setTabText("Page 2")
    .setStatusText("Page 2 - no window yet")
    .setUserData(ID_DIALOG2);

  // Add page 2 to the notebook without a dialog.
  notebook.addLastPage( pageData );

  // Repeat the above for page 3.
  pageData
    .setTabText("Page 3")
    .setStatusText("Page 3 - no window yet")
    .setUserData(ID_DIALOG3);
  notebook.addLastPage( pageData );

  // Size the tabs to fit the text.
  IFont noteFont(&notebook);
  ISize tabSize(ISize(noteFont.minTextWidth("no_window Page_3"),
                      noteFont.maxCharHeight()) + ISize(6,6));
  notebook
    .setMajorTabSize(tabSize)
    .setMinorTabSize(tabSize);

  // Create and energize a page handler to capture "select"
  // events so we can add the missing dialogs.
  PageSelectHandler pageHandler;
  pageHandler.handleEventsFor(&frame);
```

```
      // Put the notebook in the client and show the frame.
      frame
        .setClient(&notebook)
        .show();
      dialog1.setFocus();

      // Run the application.
      IApplication::current().run();
}


IBase::IBoolean PageSelectHandler::select  ( IPageSelectEvent &event )
{
   IPageHandle selectedPage = event.pageHandle();
   INotebook* notebook = event.notebook();
   INotebook::PageSettings pageData =
                 event.notebook()->pageSettings(selectedPage);
   unsigned long dialogId = pageData.userData();

   // If we have a dialog ID in user data, the frame needs to
   // be created.
   if (dialogId != 0) {
      IFrameWindow* dialog = new IFrameWindow(
                                    dialogId,
                                    notebook,
                                    notebook);

      // Size the dialog to the size of the page.
      (*dialog).sizeTo((*notebook).pageSize());

      // Put the page on the notebook, and set user data to
      // zero to indicate that we've added the page window.
      IString statusText
              = pageData.tabText() + " has been added";
      (*notebook)
         .setWindow( selectedPage, dialog)
         .setUserData(selectedPage, 0)
         .setStatusText(selectedPage, statusText);
   }

   else
   {    // Page window already loaded.
      (*notebook)
         .setStatusText(selectedPage, pageData.tabText());
   }
   return false;
}
```

Changing Notebook Colors

As you do with all Open Class controls, you change the colors in the PM-compatible notebook using member functions in INotebook that accept an IColor object. These functions define all the parts of a notebook that can have colors independently set. You can also query the color of different areas of the notebook. The color functions are not supported for the tab control due to a Windows limitation.

The color functions supported in INotebook are as follows:

```
INotebook::backgroundColor
INotebook::hiliteBackgroundColor
INotebook::majorTabBackgroundColor
INotebook::majorTabForegroundColor
INotebook::minorTabBackgroundColor
INotebook::minorTabForegroundColor
INotebook::pageBackgroundColor
INotebook::resetMajorTabBackgroundColor
INotebook::resetMajorTabForegroundColor
INotebook::resetMinorTabBackgroundColor
INotebook::resetMinorTabForegroundColor
INotebook::resetPageBackgroundColor
INotebook::setMajorTabBackgroundColor
INotebook::setMajorTabForegroundColor
INotebook::setMinorTabBackgroundColor
INotebook::setMinorTabForegroundColor
INotebook::setPageBackgroundColor

IWindow::foregroundColor
IWindow::resetBackgroundColor
IWindow::resetForegroundColor
IWindow::resetHiliteBackgroundColor
IWindow::setHiliteBackgroundColor
```

For example, to change the background color of your page, you would code the following:

```
notebook.setPageBackgroundColor( IColor::red )
```

Note the following items about these functions:

- Changing the notebook window background color can change the color of notebook children that do not have their own background color. The presentation system and Open Class Library passes this color change request to all windows that the control owns. If a child window has the same color area and you have not explicitly set it to its own color, it acquires the new color in this area. Therefore, changing colors in the notebook can cause changes to the page windows on the notebook.

- The Windows tab control does not provide color-support APIs. All tab control colors are based upon the default system colors. The INotebook's implementation of this control ignores the color settings.

- Calling setForegroundColor changes the color of the notebook's status line text and, potentially, the foreground color of page windows.

- Changing the selection cursor color can change the color of notebook child windows that use a highlight background color.

Displaying Notebook Help

Chapter 23, "Using Help," discuses how you add help text to your application using Windows native help or IBM's Information Presentation Facility (IPF). Some people have trouble adding help to the notebook control because the notebook allows you to put the focus onto the tabs of the notebook. The problem arises because the tabs are non-window elements of the window used to implement the page. They are not individual windows for which you can provide an entry in a help table. In fact, on the OS/2 operating system, the tab with the selection cursor does not have to be the tab on the page currently displayed.

If you want to show help when the focus is on a notebook tab, create an `IPageHandler` and add it to the notebook to process help requests. When you receive the help notification, you must decide to show help either for the tab with the selection cursor or for the top page in the notebook. You can determine the page with the selection cursor by calling `IPageHelpEvent::pageHandle`, and show the appropriate help panel. You can determine the top page of the notebook by calling `INotebook::topPage`. The operating system shows help for the top page when help is requested with the selection cursor on a tab.

Smart Guides

You can use the notebook control to create a *smart guide* or *wizard*, a notebook that guides a user through a set series of tasks and the pages are displayed based upon the choices that the user makes. This allows for a consistent interactive model for goal-oriented task support.

To illustrate a smart guide, we create a more complex notebook sample that incorporates many of the topics that we discuss in this chapter, including delayed addition of pages and help support. Figure 14-3 displays the first page of the finished smart guide. In the following topics, we code our interface for the various classes used in the smart guide.

Designing a Smart Guide

Our smart guide design is a framework that is composed of a number of classes, but you only create a few of them to build a smart guide application. The two primary class types are `SmartGuide` itself and a series of classes derived from `SmartPage`.

`SmartGuide` has several roles, as follows:

1. It is a collection of smart pages. This collection is a hierarchy implemented by the `IMutliwayTree` collection class. When you add smart pages to this collection, you provide a reference page that identifies where to attach a new page in the tree. Like any good collection, `SmartPage` has functions to iterate the pages in its collection. `SmartPage` provides the nested class `Cursor` like most collections do in Open Class Library.

2. It builds the view to display smart pages. To do this, it creates an `IFrameWindow` with an `INotebook` in the frame's client area. Prior to building the view the first time, it determines the size of the view by calling `SmartPage::minimumSize` on each smart page and then ensures that the notebook is big enough to contain the largest page.

3. It handles navigation through the pages of the notebook. The tree structure you create when you add smart pages establishes the paths that your users might take when they move through the smart guide. When you first show the smart guide after it builds the frame window and the notebook, `SmartGuide` calls `SmartPage::createAndOrphanPage` on the root smart page. Thereafter, when users press the **Next** button on the smart guide, it calls `SmartPage::currentChoice`. `SmartGuide` uses this value to determine which branch of the tree to follow next. It then calls `createAndOrphanPage` on the `SmartPage` stored at that branch to display the next page of the notebook.

`SmartPage` has the same three primary roles that `SmartGuide` has:

1. It must indicate its minimum size by implementing `SmartPage::minimumSize`.

2. It must implement `SmartPage::createAndOrphanPage` to create a view of its contents.

3. It must implement `SmartPage::selectedChoice` to indicate the current choice on its page. Because the class `SmartPage` itself does not support page selection, it always indicates that its first (and only) branch is selected.

`SmartPage` also stores text for the tab of the notebook and a help id that `SmartGuide` uses to display help when a user presses the **Help** button.

Although `SmartPage` defines the protocol that all smart pages must follow, you cannot create a `SmartPage` directly because it does not implement `SmartPage::createAndOrphanPage`. To show the usefulness of these smart pages, we provide two classes that derive from `SmartPage`. The first of these, `TextSmartPage`, serves as an information-only page with a label at the top and scrollable information below it. Call `TextSmartPage::setPageLabel` to specify the text to use for the label, and call either `TextSmartPage::setPageText` to specify the text directly or `TextSmartPage::setPageTextFile` to identify a file that contains the text.

`SingleChoiceSmartPage`, which we derive from `TextSmartPage`, finally provides the ability we have been looking for in our smart guide: it allows you to specify choices that `SmartGuide` can use to select different branches of the tree. Call `TextSmartPage::addChoice` with a text string to add choices and call `TextSmartPage::setSelectedChoice` to establish a default selection. You can also pass an optional help id when you call `addChoice`. This allows the `SmartGuide` to display choice sensitive help.

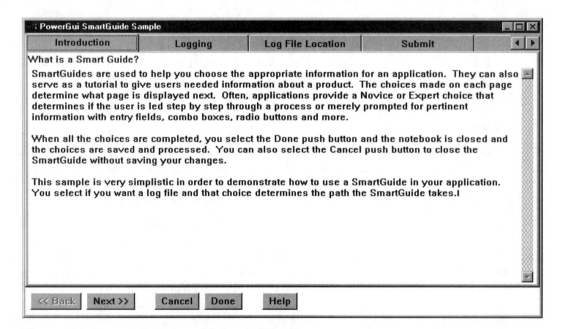

Figure 14-3. Example of a Smart Guide or Wizard.

Because `SmartGuide` walks down the selected branches of its tree and creates a page in the notebook with tab text for each page, it is a good idea to always provide default selections. Then your users can jump ahead if they are familiar with your smart guide. Each time your users change a choice in the smart guide, `SmartGuide` again walks down the selected branches and rebuilds the notebook pages if necessary. It does not rebuild the page views themselves; they are kept around and used again if the page comes back into the selected path and a user selects the page.

When `SingleChoiceSmartPage` builds its view in response to `SmartGuide` calling its `createAndOrphanView` function, it first builds an `ISplitCanvas` and then calls `createAndOrpanView` of its parent `TextSmartPage` class to build the label and scrollable information in the top of the view port. It then creates an `ISetCanvas` in the bottom of the view port. If you have only added a small number of choices, it adds an `IRadioButton` for each choice to the set canvas. If you have coded a larger number of choices, it instead creates an `IListBox` in the set canvas.

Behind the scenes of the primary smart guide classes are a number of implementation classes that tie the framework together. There is a command handler to capture the command events resulting from the **Back**, **Next**, **Cancel**, and **Help** buttons on the notebook. There is a page handler to capture page selection so that the smart page views are only created when users select the page. And there is a `SmartInfo` class that stores the information associated with each node of the tree. This includes the smart page view returned from `createOrOrphanPage` and the count of the number of children at the node. `SmartInfo` objects are stored in a `SmartTree` (which is a basic `IMultiwayTree`).

Another feature of the `SmartGuide` is that you can add the same page to multiple branches of the tree. For example, no matter which choice a user makes, you probably always want to display a "Mission complete" panel. Supporting this feature is the reason that `SmartGuide::addPage` accepts a handle instead of a `SmartPage`. The handle uniquely identifies the node containing the `SmartPage`. This is necessary because the same `SmartPage` can exist at multiple nodes. We demonstrate this capability in the example which follows. Figure 14-4 shows the flow of the example and demonstrates how the same page views exist at multiple nodes.

Caution: We have not provided you with a complete smart guide application that you can use out of the box. We did not implement all of the pieces we discussed in this topic.

Creating a Smart Guide

In this application, we first define the class `SmartPage` to determine the behavior of the pages in our notebook. Because of the special needs of the smart guide, the notebook needs to have additional functionality. We also define a `TextSmartPage` class derived from `SmartPage`, which adds a label and descriptive text to the notebook page. This class overrides the same functions for creating the page.

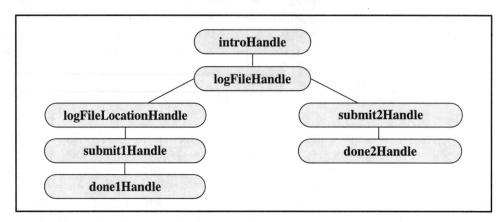

Figure 14-4. Flow of the Smart Guide Sample.

SingleChoiceSmartPage provides support for making a choice and then displays the next page based on that choice. This class demonstrates the logic needed for a smart guide, or wizard, but provides minimal support for removing or changing the choice. We provide the help ID for the choice so that a user can request information before making a selection.

The final class, SmartGuide provides our collection behavior with a tree of node records with a pointer to the page. On the Windows operating system, this is an IMultiwayTree; on the OS/2 operating system, this is an ITree collection. Here, we also define our navigation and panel creation functions needed to show the smart guide and refresh the pages to rebuild the notebook after a user makes a choice. We only display the push buttons when they are valid for a particular page.

Note that the behavior of the smart guide is predicated by the current choice, and a user cannot go to pages that would have otherwise been displayed. We also use canvases and sizing algorithms to determine the size of our pages and use MLEs for our text in order to provide text-wrapping and scrolling features.

Smart Guide Notebook - notebook\smrtguid\smrtguid.hpp

```
#include <istring.hpp>
#include <ibitflag.hpp>
#include <irect.hpp>

class IWindow;
class IFrameWindow;
class INotebook;
class IMultiCellCanvas;
class IPageSelectEvent;
class IPageHandle;
class IPushButton;
class IHelpWindow;
class SmartGuideList;
class SmartGuidePageHandler;
class SmartGuideCommandHandler;
class SmartChoiceSelectHandler;
class SmartChoiceList;
class SmartPageInfoList;
class SmartTree;
class SmartPageInfo;
```

```
//   SmartPage is an abstract base class that defines the protocol
//   for pages in a SmartGuide.  This includes help for the
//   page (not implemented), text for the notebook tab,
//   the protocol to specify the size of the view for the page,
//   and the protocol to create the view of the page.
//
class SmartPage    {

public:
/*---------------------------- Constructors ----------------------*/
SmartPage ( )
  : fTabText(""),
    fHelpId (0)
  { }
virtual
 ~SmartPage ( )
  { }

/*--------------------------- Panel Creation ----------------------*/
virtual ISize
  minimumSize     ( ) const;

virtual IWindow*
  createAndOrphanPage ( IWindow*         parent,
                        IWindow*         owner,
                        const IRectangle& initialRect) = 0;

/*---------------------- Navigation and Choice -------------------*/
// The following function is called by the SmartGuide when
// navigating to the next page in the notebook.  All choices are
// zero based.  The 0 returned here causes traversal to
// the first leg of the node.  Multi-choice smart pages overide this to
// pick other legs.
virtual unsigned long
  currentChoice  ( )  const { return 0; }

// The following function is called by SmartGuide to determine
// if it can enable the "Done" button.
virtual Boolean
  isOKToClose    ( IString& closeErrorIfFalse ) const;
/*--------------------------- Panel Text --------------------------*/
virtual SmartPage
 &setTabText     ( const IString& tabText);

virtual IString
  tabText        ( ) const;

/*--------------------------- Displaying Help --------------------*/
// The following functions store and retrieve a help identifier
// for the page.
virtual SmartPage
 &setHelpId      ( unsigned long helpId);

virtual unsigned long
  helpId         ( ) const;

private:
/*--------------------------- Hidden Members ---------------------*/
  SmartPage ( const SmartPage& );
SmartPage
 &operator=    ( const SmartPage& );

IString
 fTabText;
unsigned long
 fHelpId;

}; // SmartPage
```

```
// TextSmartPage is a SmartPage that adds a label
// and non-editable text to the page.
//
class TextSmartPage : public SmartPage
{
typedef SmartPage
  Inherited;
public:
/*--------------------------- Constructors ----------------------*/
  TextSmartPage ( )
    : fPageLabel ( "" ),
      fPageText ( "" )
    {}

/*--------------------------- Panel Creation --------------------*/
virtual ISize
  minimumSize      ( ) const;

virtual IWindow*
  createAndOrphanPage ( IWindow*          parent,
                        IWindow*          owner,
                        const IRectangle& initialRect);

/*--------------------------- Panel Text ------------------------*/
virtual TextSmartPage
 &setPageLabel    ( const IString& pageLabel),
 &setPageText     ( const IString& pageText),
 &setPageTextFile( const IString& pageTextFile);

virtual IString
  pageLabel      ( ) const,
  pageText       ( ) const,
  pageTextFile   ( ) const;

private:
/*--------------------------- Hidden Members --------------------*/
   TextSmartPage ( const TextSmartPage& );
TextSmartPage
 &operator=   ( const TextSmartPage& );
IString
 fPageLabel,
 fPageText,
 fPageTextFile;
IMultiCellCanvas
 *fMultiCellCanvas;
};

// SingleChoiceSmartPage is a SmartPage that adds
// the ability for the page to display multiple
// choices and overrides "currentChoice" to
// enable the SmartGuide to pick different paths.
//
class SingleChoiceSmartPage : public TextSmartPage
{
typedef TextSmartPage
  Inherited;
public:

/*--------------------------- Constructors ----------------------*/
   SingleChoiceSmartPage  ( )
    : fSmartChoiceList  ( 0 ),
      fNumberOfChoices  ( 0 ),
      fSelectedChoice   ( 0 ),
      fSelectHandler    ( 0 ),
      fSelectionWindow  ( 0 )
    {}
```

```
/*--------------------------- Panel Creation ----------------------*/
virtual ISize
  minimumSize      ( ) const;

virtual IWindow*
  createAndOrphanPage ( IWindow*           parent,
                        IWindow*           owner,
                        const IRectangle& initialRect);

/*----------------------- Navigation and Choice -------------------*/
virtual SingleChoiceSmartPage
 &addChoice ( const IString&  choiceText,
             unsigned long   helpId = 0 );

virtual SingleChoiceSmartPage
 &setSelectedChoice   ( unsigned long choiceIndex);

virtual unsigned long
  currentChoice        ( ) const;

virtual IString
  choiceTextAtIndex    ( unsigned long index);

unsigned long
  numberOfChoices      ( ) const;

virtual Boolean
  isOKToClose     ( IString& closeErrorIfFalse ) const;

/*--------------------------- Displaying Help -------------------*/
// Override the following function to return a choice sensitive
// help id. You specify the help id on the constructor.

virtual unsigned long
  helpId    ( ) const;

private:
/*--------------------------- Hidden Members --------------------*/
  SingleChoiceSmartPage ( const SingleChoiceSmartPage& );
SingleChoiceSmartPage
 &operator-   ( const SingleChoiceSmartPage& );
SmartChoiceList
 *fSmartChoiceList;
unsigned long
  fNumberOfChoices;
unsigned long
  fSelectedChoice;
SmartChoiceSelectHandler
 *fSelectHandler;
IWindow
 *fSelectionWindow;
};

// SmartGuide contains all smart pages and controls:
// 1) Telling a page to create its windows
// 2) Navigation through the pages of the guide
// 3) Cancel and Close requests
class SmartGuide
{
public:
class Cursor;

/*--------------------------- Constructors ----------------------*/
  SmartGuide    ( const IString&  guideName);
```

```
/*----------------------- Navigation and Choice -------------------*/
unsigned long
  addPage ( SmartPage*        smartPage,
                 unsigned long   referencePageHandle=0);
virtual Boolean
  isOKToClose     ( IString& closeErrorIfFalse ) const;

/*------------------------- Panel Creation --------------------*/
virtual SmartGuide
 &show          ( ),
 &refreshPages  ( );

virtual ISize
  newPageSize   ( ) const;

/*------------------------- Displaying Help -------------------*/
virtual SmartGuide
 &setHelpWindow     ( IHelpWindow& helpWindow );

/*------------------------- Cursor Functions ------------------*/
enum IterationOrder
{
   selectedOrder,
   topDown,
   bottomUp
};

SmartPage
 *pageAtLocation ( Cursor& cursor) const;

  class Cursor {
  public :
  /*----------------------- Constructors ---------------------*/
    Cursor   ( SmartGuide&              smartGuide,
             SmartGuide::IterationOrder  order =
                                      SmartGuide::selectedOrder);
   virtual
     ~Cursor ( );

  /*----------------------- Page Iteration -------------------*/
  virtual Boolean
    setToFirst    ( ),
    setToNext     ( ),
    setToPrevious ( ),
    setToLast     ( ),
    isValid       ( ) const;

  void
    setCurrent ( unsigned long smartPageHandle );

  private:
  /*----------------------- Hidden Members -------------------*/
  Cursor        ( const Cursor& cursor );
  Cursor
   &operator=   ( const Cursor& cursor );

  /*----------------------- Private --------------------------*/
  void
   *fTreeCursor;
  SmartGuide
   &fSmartGuide;
  SmartGuide::IterationOrder
    fOrder;
  friend class SmartGuide;
  };
/*------------------------- Debug Functions -------------------*/
virtual IString
  asString      ( ) const,
  asDebugInfo   ( ) const;
```

```
protected:
/*----------------------------- Callback Functions ------------------*/
virtual Boolean
  handlePageSelect  ( IPageSelectEvent& event ),
  handleBack        ( ),
  handleNext        ( ),
  handleCancel      ( ),
  handleDone        ( ),
  handleHelp        ( ),
  handleRefresh     ( );

SmartPageInfo
 *pageInfoAtLocation ( Cursor& cursor) const,
 *pageInfoWithHandle ( const IPageHandle& pageHandle) const;

private:
/*------------------------- Hidden Members -----------------------*/
SmartGuide        ( const SmartGuide& );
SmartGuide
 &operator=  ( const SmartGuide&);

/*----------------------------- Private --------------------------*/
// Consider moving the following to a private data class.
IString
  fGuideName;
SmartTree
 *fSmartTree;
SmartPageInfoList
 *fPageInfoList;
SmartPageInfo
 *fCurrentPageInfo;
IFrameWindow
 *fFrameWindow;
INotebook
 *fNotebook;
IPushButton
 *fBackButton,
 *fNextButton,
 *fCancelButton,
 *fDoneButton,
 *fHelpButton;
SmartGuidePageHandler
 *fPageHandler;
SmartGuideCommandHandler
 *fCommandHandler;
ISize
 fLastPageSize;
IHelpWindow
 *fHelpWindow;
friend class SmartGuidePageHandler;
friend class SmartGuideCommandHandler;
friend class Cursor;
};
...
```

In the implementation file, we create our notebook pages, add tab text, labels, choices, and determine the path of the pages. We also create objects of the SmartGuide, SingleChoiceSmartPage, and TextSmartPage classes as shown in the following code:

Smart Guide Notebook - notebook\smrtguid\training.cpp

```
#include <iapp.hpp>
#include <iostream.h>
#include "smrtguid.hpp"
```

```
void main ( )
{
   SmartGuide smartGuide("PowerGui SmartGuide Sample");
   TextSmartPage  introPage;
   introPage
    .setPageLabel("What is a Smart Guide?")
    .setPageTextFile("smrtpag1.txt")
    .setTabText("Introduction");

   SingleChoiceSmartPage  logFile;
   logFile
    .addChoice("Yes")
    .addChoice("No")
    .setSelectedChoice(0)
    .setPageLabel("Specify whether you want to keep a log file.")
    .setPageTextFile("smrtpag2.txt")
    .setTabText("Logging");

   SingleChoiceSmartPage  logFileLocation;
   logFileLocation
    .addChoice("Current Path")
    .addChoice("Root directory")
    .setSelectedChoice(0)
    .setPageLabel("Choose a log file location.")
    .setPageTextFile("smrtpag3.txt")
    .setTabText("Log File Location");

   TextSmartPage  submitPage;
   submitPage
    .setPageLabel("Press \"Done\" to Finish.")
    .setPageText("")
    .setTabText("Submit");

   TextSmartPage  donePage;
   donePage
    .setPageLabel("SmartGuide Complete.")
    .setPageText("Ok.  Thanks.")
    .setTabText("Done");

   unsigned long introHandle, logFileHandle, logFileLocationHandle,
          submit1Handle, submit2Handle, done1Handle, done2Handle;

   // Flow of the smart guide (See Figure 14-4).
   introHandle = smartGuide.addPage(&introPage);
   logFileHandle = smartGuide.addPage(&logFile, introHandle);
   logFileLocationHandle = smartGuide.addPage(&logFileLocation,
                                             logFileHandle);
   submit1Handle = smartGuide.addPage(&submitPage, logFileLocationHandle);
   done1Handle   = smartGuide.addPage(&donePage, submit1Handle);
   submit2Handle = smartGuide.addPage(&submitPage, logFileHandle);
   done2Handle   = smartGuide.addPage(&donePage, submit2Handle);

   cout << smartGuide.asDebugInfo();

   smartGuide.show();
   cout << smartGuide.asDebugInfo();
   IApplication::current().run();
}
```

For each page in the notebook, we include a file that contains the text displayed on that page. We then dynamically load this file using setPageTextFile. To run the sample, ensure that you have these text files in the current directory.

Chapter 15

Canvases

- Describes the canvas classes of Open Class Library, which represent advanced visual layout controls
- Describes the ICanvas, IMultiCellCanvas, ISetCanvas, ISplitCanvas, and IViewPort classes
- Read Chapter 7 before reading this chapter.
- Chapters 5, 8, 10, 16, and 18 cover related material.

The canvas classes are a set of window classes that you can use to implement dialog-like windows, that is, windows with several child controls. These windows are useful for showing views of objects as pages in a notebook and for prompting the user for information to run an action. What differentiates the canvas classes from traditional dialog boxes are the added features they provide to support more robust user interfaces.

This chapter describes these classes, which include ICanvas, IMultiCellCanvas, ISetCanvas, ISplitCanvas, and IViewPort. They are characterized as follows:

ICanvas	Provides base dialog-box-like behavior
IMultiCellCanvas	Arranges child windows according to relative sizing and positioning information
ISetCanvas	Lines up child windows into rows and/or columns
ISplitCanvas	Provides split bars between child windows
IViewPort	Scrolls a window of information

Figure 15-1 shows the class hierarchy. Although IDrawingCanvas also derives from ICanvas, we do not describe it here. Chapter 16, "Tool Bars, Fly-Over Help, and Custom Buttons," describes IToolBar and IToolBarContainer, which are derived from ISetCanvas.

Why Use Them?

The canvas classes offer help for solving problems that software developers who program to system APIs often struggle with, ignore, or don't even recognize as problems! Specifically, the canvas classes offer help as follows:

- They overcome limitations of dialog boxes (the mechanism that the operating system gives you for implementing dialog-like windows).

- They provide dialog-box behavior outside of dialog boxes.

- They offer advanced window layout features that the operating system does not provide.

The following sections describe each of these points.

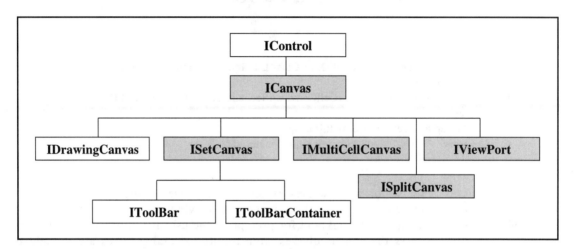

Figure 15-1. Canvas Class Hierarchy.

Overcoming Limitations of Dialog Boxes

The `IMultiCellCanvas` and `ISetCanvas` classes address a key weakness of dialog boxes: dialog boxes require that an application provide absolute positioning and sizing for all child controls. This design point can make dialog boxes cumbersome to use during development because the text in a dialog often changes as you modify the design of your application. A single change sometimes affects the size and position of several controls. You face the same problems if you want to change text dynamically at run time.

Canvases also support some routine direct-manipulation actions better than dialog boxes do. These actions include dragging the sizing border of a frame window and, in the OS/2 operating system, dropping a font onto a window. `IMultiCellCanvas` and `ISetCanvas` change the size and position of their child controls when a user performs either of these actions.

Dialog Box Basics

You define a dialog box with a dialog template, which you define at run time as a structure or statically to produce a dialog resource that you build into your program. You can use a dialog editor tool, such as the one included with VisualAge for C++, to build a dialog resource. Alternatively, you can hand-craft a text file equivalent to one that a dialog editor produces. We have done that for most of the dialog resources you see in this book. After defining a

dialog template, you call operating system APIs to display it. You can also use the
IFrameWindow class to display a dialog box from a dialog resource. See Chapter 5, "Frame
Window Basics," for more information.

An example of a dialog resource in a resource script file follows. The file contains statements
to define equivalent OS/2 and Windows dialogs, although we show only those for the Windows
dialog here. Figure 15-2 shows the dialog box in the OS/2 operating system.

Dialog Box Definition - canvas\lunchdlg\lunchdlg.rc

```
#include "lunchdlg.h"

ID_LUNCH_DIALOG DIALOG 8, 5, 217, 166
STYLE WS_POPUP | WS_VISIBLE | WS_CAPTION | WS_SYSMENU | WS_DLGFRAME
CAPTION "Lunch"
FONT 8, "System"
{
    LTEXT               "Select your lunch preferences:",
                        ID_LUNCH_TEXT, 4, 5, 186, 8, SS_LEFT
    GROUPBOX            "Food", ID_FOOD, 11, 19, 93, 74, BS_GROUPBOX | WS_GROUP
    AUTORADIOBUTTON     "&Hamburger", ID_HAMBURGER, 18, 31, 72, 10,
                        BS_AUTORADIOBUTTON | WS_GROUP | WS_TABSTOP
    AUTORADIOBUTTON     "&Cheeseburger", ID_CHEESEBURGER, 18, 47, 72, 10
    AUTORADIOBUTTON     "Hot &dog", ID_HOTDOG, 18, 63, 72, 10
    AUTORADIOBUTTON     "&Pizza", ID_PIZZA, 18, 79, 72, 10
    GROUPBOX            "Beverage", ID_BEVERAGE, 114, 19, 93, 74,
                        BS_GROUPBOX | WS_GROUP
    AUTORADIOBUTTON     "&Milk", ID_MILK, 121, 31, 79, 10,
                        BS_AUTORADIOBUTTON | WS_GROUP | WS_TABSTOP
    AUTORADIOBUTTON     "&Soft drink", ID_SOFTDRINK, 121, 47, 79, 10
    AUTORADIOBUTTON     "&Juice", ID_JUICE, 121, 63, 79, 10
    AUTORADIOBUTTON     "&Water", ID_WATER, 121, 79, 79, 10
    GROUPBOX            "Side orders", ID_SIDEORDERS, 11, 97, 196, 45,
                        BS_GROUPBOX | WS_GROUP
    AUTOCHECKBOX        "Sa&lad", ID_SALAD, 18, 109, 63, 10,
                        BS_AUTOCHECKBOX | WS_GROUP | WS_TABSTOP
    AUTOCHECKBOX        "&French fries", ID_FRIES, 90, 109, 63, 10,
                        BS_AUTOCHECKBOX | WS_GROUP | WS_TABSTOP
    LTEXT               "Other", ID_REQUESTPROMPT, 21, 125, 40, 8, SS_LEFT
    EDITTEXT            ID_REQUEST, 64, 124, 135, 10
    DEFPUSHBUTTON       "OK", ID_OK, 5, 149, 40, 14,
                        BS_DEFPUSHBUTTON | WS_GROUP | WS_TABSTOP
    PUSHBUTTON          "Cancel", ID_CANCEL, 49, 149, 40, 14, NOT WS_TABSTOP
    PUSHBUTTON          "Help", ID_HELP, 93, 149, 40, 14, NOT WS_TABSTOP
}
```

One of the biggest enticements for using dialog boxes is their automatic support for the
following basic keyboard and button behavior:

- Tabbing and cursor movement
- Default push buttons
- Mnemonics
- Cursor selection of radio buttons
- Mutually exclusive selection of radio buttons

However, dialog boxes are not dynamic in nature; this is their major shortcoming. The canvas
classes address this limitation, while also providing the same basic keyboard and button
support usually associated only with dialog boxes. We later show how to use ISetCanvas and
IMultiCellCanvas to create windows equivalent in appearance and basic behavior to the
dialog box in Figure 15-2.

Figure 15-2. OS/2 Dialog Box.

One area that the canvas classes do not handle is separating the definition of a dialog box from your executable code. You have to weigh the benefits of using canvases against the loss of using dialog template files and the tools written for them. Because the benefits that the canvas classes offer are enormous, do not discard them hastily.

Relative Positioning of Controls

You can use the `IMultiCellCanvas` and `ISetCanvas` classes to replace the drudgery of specifying exact positions and sizes for dialog controls. Both classes determine the positions and sizes for their child windows based on relative positioning information, such as which child window is located before which and the minimum size that each child window returns.

The amount of code you need to provide is minimal. In most cases you can use the minimum size values that Open Class Library provides. You can also create complex arrangements of controls by combining canvases, and you can fine-tune each canvas as to how it lays out its child windows.

Independence from Changing Text

Changing the text in a dialog template, such as the text in a push button or the prompt for an entry field, can adversely affect the layout of its controls. The main reasons for this brittleness are as follows:

1. You must specify the exact location and size of all controls in all your dialog templates.

2. It is not always obvious how to optimally size a control. For many controls, the optimal size is dependent on the text strings that they display. If you change the text, you may need to change the size.

3. The optimal position for a control is dependent on the positions and sizes of the controls around it. If you change one, you may need to change the position of the controls surrounding it and even the size of the dialog box itself.

Take, for example, the definition of the push buttons shown in Figure 15-2. The resource file uses the following rules to size and position them:

*   Each push button has a height of 14 dialog units (the units of measure you use to define dialog boxes).

*   Each push button has a width of 40 dialog units, regardless of its text string.

*   Each push button is positioned 5 dialog units above the bottom of the dialog box.

*   The first push button is 5 dialog units from the left edge of the dialog box, and each subsequent push button is horizontally separated from the previous by 4 dialog units.

If you need to change the **OK** push button to **Place order**, you know that you only have to change the resource script file. However, the new text no longer fits in the push button. How much wider should you make this button?

This specific case is not much of a problem because this change only affects the size of the first push button and the position of the ones following it. Additionally, most dialog editors provide a way to position and align a row of controls, and some even provide a recommended size for push buttons based on their text. However, IMultiCellCanvas and ISetCanvas can do all of this work automatically for you; you can even change the text at run time.

Next, let's say you need to add a fifth choice, **Chicken sandwich**, in the middle of the **Food** group box. For the screen changes, this change requires far more work than changing the **OK** push button. Adding this radio button requires you not only to enlarge the **Food** group box horizontally and vertically, but also to shift two of the food radio buttons vertically to make room for the new **Chicken sandwich** radio button. You also have to move the **Beverage** group box and its four radio buttons to the right, while keeping it aligned with the top of the **Food** group box. You need to enlarge the dialog box itself and move the controls further below or above the **Food** group box to make room for its larger size. Generally, dialog editors are cumbersome for making all these changes. However, the IMultiCellCanvas and ISetCanvas classes can do this work for you automatically.

Independence from Changing Fonts

In the OS/2 operating system, one of the more complicated issues to deal with is the effect of font changes on the appearance of your windows. Although controls repaint themselves when they get a new font, they do not alter their size. Likewise, if you change the font that a dialog box or any of its child controls uses, the dialog box does not adjust the size or position of its child controls. Therefore, changing a font on a dialog box can cause text to be clipped or cause a control to look inappropriately sized for its text.

Figure 15-3 shows the same dialog box that appears in Figure 15-2 after changing the font of six of its controls. Now the **Cheeseburger** radio button, the **French fries** check box, and the **Cancel** push button are no longer wide enough to contain their text, and the **Select your lunch preferences:** prompt and the **Other** entry field are no longer tall enough to hold their text.

How much of a problem is this? An OS/2 user can change fonts at any time by dragging one from a Font Palette window and dropping it onto any window or control. The Windows operating system, however, does not provide a way for a user to change the font that an individual window uses.

Open Class Library addresses the dynamics that font changes cause by using minimum sizes. Both IMultiCellCanvas and ISetCanvas use the minimum sizes that their child windows return in order to size and position those child windows. Most of the window classes in Open Class Library use font-size information to calculate their minimum size. These canvases rely on these font-sensitive routines not only to initially size and position each child window, but also to update the size and position of child windows when a font is changed. Figure 15-4 shows the dialog, now implemented with the ISetCanvas class, after dropping the same fonts as we did for Figure 15-3. For more information on how the control classes return minimum sizes, see the topic "Using Minimum Sizes in Open Class Library" near the end of this chapter.

Figure 15-3. OS/2 Dialog Box after Changing Fonts.

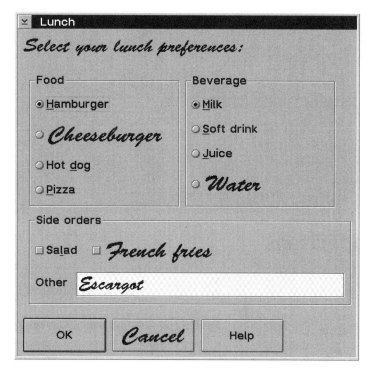

Figure 15-4. Dialog Box Built with ISetCanvas after Dropping a Font.

Sizable Dialog Boxes

Dialog-like windows tend to be fixed in size. Ideally, however, dialogs should have sizing borders and should size their child windows to best utilize the size of the dialog box. Creating sizable dialogs benefits your users because they can take better advantage of different display resolutions and fonts by sizing a window to best suit their customized systems.

The operating system does not prevent you from adding sizing borders to dialog boxes, yet most application developers don't do this. Why not? The probable reason is that the work you need to do to support a window that sizes intelligently is not trivial.

`IMultiCellCanvas` provides a solution. With this canvas class, you can identify the white space and child windows that the canvas grows or shrinks as it changes size. Although we have not discussed Figure 15-12 yet, it shows how `IMultiCellCanvas` can provide sizing support for the lunch dialog.

Dialog-Box Behavior outside a Dialog Box

The canvas classes provide the same kind of keyboard and button support that you might expect only from a dialog box. For example, they allow the Tab and arrow keys to move the input cursor between controls. If you create a window with child controls and use a window other than a canvas or frame as their parent, you may lose dialog-box behavior that you need.

The potential loss of this dialog-box behavior is a major reason for continuing to use a dialog box. You probably want to avoid emulating the operating system's dialog-box support because it's difficult to do and the canvas classes already provide this support. The topic "The ICanvas Class" explains what this support includes.

Difficult Implementations Made Easy

The canvas classes provide features beyond what you can get using dialog boxes. We already mentioned that you can use `IMultiCellCanvas` to support a sizable dialog. The canvas classes also provide other layout-related features, such as split bars that a user can move with the mouse and automatic scrolling support for any window. See the topics describing the `ISplitCanvas` and `IViewPort` classes for more information.

Class Comparisons

Table 15-1 provides a comparison of features among the five canvas classes. Several of the entries in the table include a number. The meanings of these numbers follow the table.

Table 15-1. Comparison of Canvas Classes

	ICanvas	ISetCanvas	IMultiCellCanvas	ISplitCanvas	IViewPort
Sizes and positions child windows	No	Yes	Yes	Yes	Yes (1)
Uses minimum size of child windows	No	Yes (2)	Yes (3)	No	Yes (1)
Imposes restrictions on child windows	No	No	Yes (4)	No	Yes (5)
Responds to resizing	No	No	Yes (6)	Yes (7)	Yes (8)

The following notes apply to Table 15-1. Later sections in this chapter that describe the specific canvas class provides more detail.

1. A view port makes a child window appear to scroll by repositioning it. If the window being scrolled initially has a size of (0,0), the view port sizes it to its minimum size. Otherwise, it does not size the child window.

2. A set canvas can grow a child window beyond its minimum size based on the pack option you choose. (See the topic "Pack Options" later in this chapter.)

3. A multicell canvas can grow a child window beyond its minimum size if the child window lies in an expandable row or column or if it lies in a row or column that is grown to hold a sibling window with a larger minimum size than the child window's.

4. You must call IMultiCellCanvas::addToCell for each child window of the canvas. This enables the canvas to manage the size and position of the child window.

5. A view port can have only one child window.

6. A multicell canvas resizes child windows that lie in an expandable row or column.

7. A split canvas resizes all of its child windows so that together they fill the canvas.

8. A view port updates its scroll bars to reflect what portion of the window being scrolled is now visible.

The ICanvas Class

ICanvas is the base canvas class. It provides dialog-box behavior that all other canvas classes inherit. Although you can construct an ICanvas object, it has the least functionality of all the canvas classes; its dialog-box behavior is the only processing that it provides to its child windows. You must size and position child windows because ICanvas does not.

Supplying Dialog-Box Behavior

All of the canvas classes automatically support the same type of keyboard and button behavior that a dialog box provides. For a canvas to provide this support to its child windows, make the canvas the owner of its child windows.

Cursor Movement

In a dialog box, a user can move the input cursor, or caret, from one control to another with the Tab and arrow keys. Canvases provide the same support for their child windows. The topic "Tabbing and Cursor Movement" in Chapter 7, "Controls," describes how to define cursor movement behavior for a control, whether it is a child window of a canvas or a dialog box.

The child window of a canvas can be another canvas. If the child canvas has child windows of its own to which your users can tab, the Tab key moves the input cursor between those child windows and the sibling windows of the canvas. Figure 15-5 illustrates this behavior. (Note,

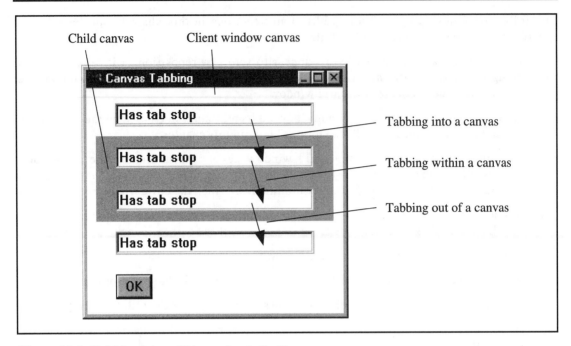

Figure 15-5. Tabbing into, within, and out of a Canvas.

however, that the arrow keys cannot be used to jump between child windows of different windows.) The **canvas\cvtab** program on the examples disk contains the code for this window.

Tab key support in ICanvas is one example of how dialog-box behavior is implemented to support the nesting, or embedding, of canvases. By using canvases within canvases (a canvas as the child window of another canvas), you can build complex layouts of controls.

Default Push Buttons

A *default push button* is the push button that becomes selected when a user presses the Enter key. The operating system draws the default push button with a thick border. See Chapter 10, "Button Controls," for more information on creating default push buttons.

Canvases support default push buttons in the same way that dialog boxes do. This support includes identifying the original default push button for a window, changing the default push button to the push button with the input focus, restoring the original default when a window other than a push button receives the input focus, and selecting the default push button when a user presses the Enter key.

Mnemonics on Buttons

A *mnemonic* is a character associated with a control. A user can type this character to move the input cursor to that control. The operating system underlines the mnemonic character. See Chapter 10, "Button Controls," for more information on defining mnemonics. After the user types a mnemonic character (sometimes together with the Ctrl or Alt key) on a dialog box, the button that uses that mnemonic is selected. Canvases provide this same support for their child button controls.

Radio Button Selection

Chapter 10, "Button Controls," describes two aspects of radio button selection usually associated only with dialog boxes. One is the automatic selection of a radio button when a user presses the Tab or arrow keys to give it the input focus. The other is *mutually exclusive selection* when only one radio button in a group can be selected at a time. The canvas classes provide this dialog-box behavior for their child radio buttons using the same information that a dialog box uses (the `IControl::group` style and absence of the `IRadioButton::noCursorSelect` style).

Creating a Window with ICanvas Objects

The following example creates four `ICanvas` objects: a client window and three color squares. The constructor calls appear in the following code. Figure 15-6 shows the resulting window. Because the color squares do not have any child windows, we could use `IStaticText` objects in their place. We use `ICanvas` objects instead to show the additional constructor examples.

We must explicitly size and position the child windows of an `ICanvas` object—in this case, the `ICanvas` and `IPushButton` child windows of the client window. Although you can control exactly where and how large you want these child windows to be, `ICanvas` provides no support

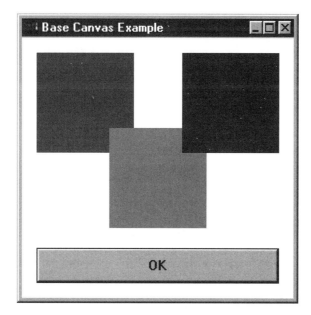

Figure 15-6. ICanvas Example.

for resizing child windows when a font or text changes or when the size of the frame window changes. These are features that `ISetCanvas` and `IMultiCellCanvas` offer.

Simple Canvas - canvas\cvsimple\cvsimple.cpp

```cpp
#include <iapp.hpp>
#include <icanvas.hpp>
#include <icolor.hpp>
#include <icoordsy.hpp>
#include <iframe.hpp>
#include <ipushbut.hpp>
#include <isysmenu.hpp>
#include <icconst.h>

#define MARGIN          15
#define COLOR_SIZE      100
#define COLOR_OVERLAP   25
#define BUTTON_PAD      20
#define BUTTON_HEIGHT   35

void main ( )
{
  // Position windows relative to the upper left as the
  // Windows operating system does.
  ICoordinateSystem::setApplicationOrientation
    ( ICoordinateSystem::originUpperLeft );

  IFrameWindow
    frame( "Base Canvas Example" );
  ICanvas
    client( IC_FRAME_CLIENT_ID, &frame, &frame );

  // Create three color squares using ICanvas objects,
  // specifying their position and size.
  ISize
    colorSize( COLOR_SIZE, COLOR_SIZE );
  ICanvas
    red  ( 1, &client, &client,
            IRectangle( IPoint( MARGIN, MARGIN ), colorSize ) ),
    green( 2, &client, &client,
            IRectangle( IPoint( MARGIN + COLOR_SIZE - COLOR_OVERLAP,
                                MARGIN + COLOR_SIZE - COLOR_OVERLAP ),
                        colorSize ) ),
    blue ( 3, &client, &client,
            IRectangle( IPoint( MARGIN + 2 * COLOR_SIZE
                                       - 2 * COLOR_OVERLAP,
                                MARGIN ),
                        colorSize ) );
  red
   .setBackgroundColor( IColor::red );
  green
   .setBackgroundColor( IColor::green );
  blue
   .setBackgroundColor( IColor::blue );

  IPushButton
    ok( ISystemMenu::idClose, &client, &client,
        IRectangle( IPoint( MARGIN,
                            MARGIN + 2 * COLOR_SIZE
                                   - COLOR_OVERLAP + BUTTON_PAD ),
                    ISize( 3 * COLOR_SIZE - 2 * COLOR_OVERLAP,
                           BUTTON_HEIGHT ) ) );
  ok
   .enableDefault()
   .enableSystemCommand()   // For ISystemMenu::idClose.
   .setText( "OK" )
   .enableTabStop()
   .enableGroup();
```

```
    // Size and show the window now.
    ISize
      clientSize( client.minimumSize() + ISize( MARGIN, MARGIN ) );
    frame
      .setClient( &client )
      .moveSizeToClient( IRectangle( IPoint( 100, 100 ), clientSize ) )
      .setFocus()
      .show();

    IApplication::current().run();
}
```

The ISetCanvas Class

The `ISetCanvas` class is the simplest canvas class that you can use to build dialog-like windows that dynamically update their layouts at run time. This class positions and sizes its child windows according to their sibling order, their minimum sizes, and a set of options that you specify. You can characterize a set canvas as a window that automatically sizes its child windows and lines them up, typically in the order that you create them.

Terms and Features of a Set Canvas

The lines into which a set canvas arranges its child windows are termed *decks*. A deck can be oriented horizontally with child windows laid out in rows from left to right or vertically with child windows laid out in columns from top to bottom. (This direction-independent term is convenient for discussing a set canvas because `ISetCanvas` has a number of formatting options available for both row-based and column-based layouts. "Deck" has no particular orientation, horizontal or vertical.)

Generally, a set canvas works best for child windows of similar size such as a row of push buttons, a group of check boxes or radio buttons, or a matrix of bitmaps or icons. `ISetCanvas` provides you with pack and alignment options for handling differently sized child windows. These options work best for similarly sized child windows.

A set canvas also supports a *pad* and *margin* size. Pad is the amount of space that the set canvas adds between adjacent child windows in a deck and between adjacent decks. Margin is the amount of space that it adds around its group of decks. The size of both the pad and margin defaults to the average character width and maximum character height of the initial font used by the canvas. Figure 15-7 illustrates these terms.

If the size of the set canvas is not large enough to display all of its child windows, the canvas clips them at its bottom and right edges. If the size of the canvas is larger than what is needed to contain all of its child windows, it adds white space below and to the right of its decks.

Sizing and Positioning Child Windows

You do not need to make any calls to add a control to a set canvas. You only need to make the canvas the parent window of the control.

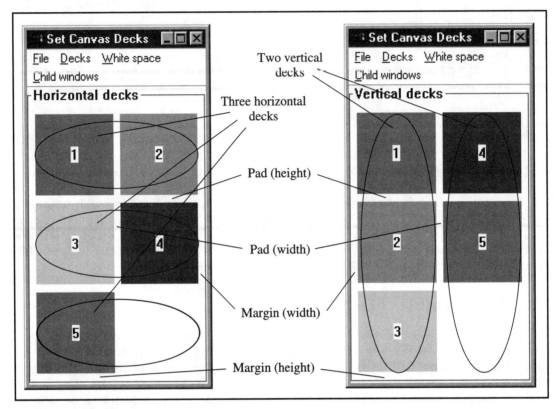

Figure 15-7. Set Canvas Terms.

The most important factors that ISetCanvas uses for sizing and positioning its child windows are their sibling order, deck information, and the minimum size that each of its child windows returns. The pack option that you choose is the next important factor. Other settings, such as alignment and pad, are the least important factors.

Sibling Order

A set canvas orders its child windows in decks according to their sibling order. A set canvas arranges its child windows in their sibling order from left to right in horizontal decks and from top to bottom in vertical decks. The Tab and arrow keys move the input cursor between the child windows in this same order.

Number and Direction of Decks

ISetCanvas gives you different ways to control the look of the decks you create. For example, Figure 15-7 shows two set canvases with more than one deck. The left one displays its child windows in three horizontal decks (rows); the right one, in two vertical decks (columns). ISetCanvas provides functions for setting and querying the orientation and number of its decks and styles to set the orientation. The **canvas\setdecks** program on the examples disk shows the use of many of these functions. This example displays the windows in Figure 15-7.

By default, a set canvas organizes its child windows into horizontal decks. You can set or change the direction of the decks by specifying a deck orientation style when constructing the set canvas or by calling setDeckOrientation.

Use the setDeckCount function to specify the maximum number of decks into which a set canvas distributes its child windows. By default, a set canvas places all of its child windows into a single deck. If you specify more than one deck, the set canvas splits its child windows into decks as evenly as possible by number. Because the size of the child windows plays no part in determining how many are placed in each deck, ISetCanvas works best with similarly sized child windows. As you saw in Figure 15-7, the set canvas distributed five child windows across three horizontal and two vertical decks. If you specify more decks than the number of child windows, a set canvas places each child window into a separate deck. The extra decks are empty and take up no space.

You can also use the ISetCanvas::decksByGroup style to create decks. If you use this style, the set canvas ignores any calls to setDeckCount and no longer tries to balance the number of child windows in each deck. It instead places each child window with the IControl::group style into a new deck.

Decks of a set canvas never overlap. The canvas arranges multiple horizontal decks vertically from top to bottom and multiple vertical decks from left to right. The decks are separated by a pad amount (see the topic, "Pad and Margin," for more information).

The size of a deck is determined by the child windows it holds. The height of a horizontal deck is the height of the tallest child window in the deck; its width is the sum of the widths of the child windows in the deck and the pads between them. The width of a vertical deck is the width of the widest child window in the deck; its height is the sum of the heights of the child windows in the deck and any pads between them.

Minimum Size

A set canvas sizes a child window based on the minimum size that the child window returns from its minimumSize function. Although ISetCanvas never sizes a child window smaller than its minimum size, the canvas can grow a child window beyond its minimum size according to the pack option you use. The topic "Pack Options" describes the effects of the different pack options. For more information on minimum sizes, see the topic "Using Minimum Sizes in Open Class Library" near the end of this chapter.

Pad and Margin

ISetCanvas supplies a default amount of space between child windows. This space is called *pad*. You can change the separation of adjacent windows in a deck or of adjacent decks in a set canvas by changing the pad with ISetCanvas::setPad.

Do not confuse pad with *margin*, which is the amount of space that a set canvas adds between the edge of the canvas and its child windows. The margin does not add space between child windows, and the pad does not add space around the entire collection of child windows. Call ISetCanvas::setMargin to modify the default margin.

The **canvas\setdecks** example calls ISetCanvas::setPad and ISetCanvas::setMargin.

Both pad and margin have a horizontal (width) and vertical (height) component. The deck orientation of the canvas determines how it uses the pad value. A set canvas with horizontal decks uses the pad width to separate child windows within a deck, and the pad height to separate decks. A set canvas with vertical decks uses the pad width to separate decks, and the pad height to separate child windows within a deck.

You can also add a group pad value by calling ISetCanvas::setGroupPad. This causes the set canvas to add additional space between a child window with the IWindow::group style and the child window preceding it in the deck. The group pad does not affect the first window in a deck, nor the space between decks.

Using the ISetCanvas::even pack option can cause child windows in a deck to be separated by more than the pad amount. See the next section, "Pack Options," for details.

Pack Options

The *pack options* control adjustments that a set canvas makes to its child windows to compensate for different minimum sizes. The adjustments may alter the size of the child windows and their placement in a deck. Changing the pack option does not affect spacing between decks, which is determined exclusively by the pad size. Table 15-2 compares the different pack options that ISetCanvas provides.

Table 15-2. ISetCanvas Pack Options

Pack Option	Changes child window sizes?	Changes child window positions?	Notes
tight	No. Child windows remain at their minimum sizes.	No. Child windows remain separated by the pad size.	The default pack option.
even	No. Child windows remain at their minimum sizes.	Yes. The set canvas adds space between child windows in a deck as needed to align windows across multiple decks. This creates the effect of both rows and columns of child windows.	Acts like the tight pack option if the canvas has only one deck. This pack option usually causes the length of a deck to grow, because the canvas adds white space between child windows in a deck to cross-align decks.
expanded	Yes. The set canvas makes its child windows the same size, that of the largest minimum height and width.	No. Child windows remain separated by the pad size.	Child windows across multiple decks are aligned, like the even pack option.

Alignment Options

If all child windows do not have the same minimum size, and you do not use the ISetCanvas::expanded pack option, you can use the alignment options to control how a child window is positioned within a deck (alignment otherwise has no affect). The alignment options do not move decks, however, which are always aligned to the top and left edges of a set canvas.

For a horizontal deck with the ISetCanvas::tight or ISetCanvas::even pack option, you can shift all child windows vertically to align them with the top or bottom of the deck, or center them vertically in the deck. For a vertical deck with the ISetCanvas::tight or ISetCanvas::even pack option, you can shift all child windows horizontally to align them against the left or right edge of the deck, or center them horizontally in the deck. If you use the ISetCanvas::even pack option and its child windows occupy more than one deck, you can also align the child windows both horizontally and vertically.

Figure 15-8 shows the difference between the different pack options, and the effect of using top-left alignment. The **canvas\setpack** program on the examples disk contains the code that displays this window.

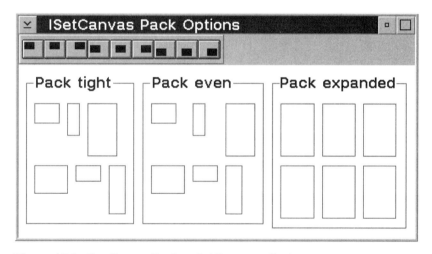

Figure 15-8. Set Canvas Pack and Alignment Options.

Creating a Row of Push Buttons

The ISetCanvas class is well-suited for managing a row of push buttons. Simply by placing push buttons in a set canvas, the canvas can evenly space them, automatically size them, and change their size and position when fonts and text change at run time.

An example of a set canvas with three push buttons follows. The lunch dialog, shown in Figure 15-4, uses this set canvas. The **canvas\setlunch** program on the examples disk contains the rest of the code for this lunch dialog.

Push Buttons in a Set Canvas - canvas\setlunch\pushbtns.hpp

```
#include <ipushbut.hpp>
#include <isetcv.hpp>
#include <icconst.h>

#ifdef IC_PM
  // Define special window identifiers not originally
  // included in VisualAge for C++ for OS/2, V3.0.
  #ifndef IC_ID_OK
    #define IC_ID_OK      1
  #endif
  #ifndef IC_ID_CLOSE
    #define IC_ID_CLOSE  0x8004
  #endif
#endif

class MyStandardPushButtons : public ISetCanvas {
public:
  MyStandardPushButtons ( unsigned long id,
                          IWindow*        parentAndOwner )
    : ISetCanvas( id, parentAndOwner, parentAndOwner ),
      ok( IC_ID_OK, this, this ),
      cancel( IC_ID_CLOSE, this, this ),
      help( IC_ID_HELP, this, this )
  {
    (*this)
     .setMargin( ISize() )
     .setPackType( ISetCanvas::expanded );
               // Make all the buttons the same size.
    ok
     .enableDefault()
     .setText( "OK" )
     .enableTabStop()
     .enableGroup();
    cancel
     .enableSystemCommand()  // For the Close system command.
     .setText( "Cancel" );
    help
     .enableHelp()
     .disableMouseClickFocus()
     .setText( "Help" );
  }
private:
  MyStandardPushButtons ( const MyStandardPushButtons& );
MyStandardPushButtons
 &operator=             ( const MyStandardPushButtons& );
IPushButton
  ok,
  cancel,
  help;
}; // MyStandardPushButtons
```

The set canvas displays the three push buttons in a single row, separated by the default pad amount. We use the `ISetCanvas::expanded` pack option to keep the size of the three buttons the same—the largest any of them needs based on their current text and font.

Adding a Group Box

It is not unusual for a dialog box to use group boxes to visually associate related information. For example, the dialog box shown in Figure 15-2 uses three group boxes. However, controls like a group box that surround or overlap other controls do not work well as a child window of an `ISetCanvas`, because a set canvas does not allow its child windows to overlap.

ISetCanvas gives you a way to achieve this look without a group box control. The group boxes you see in Figures 15-4, 15-7, and 15-8 are a result of using this capability. To cause a set canvas to draw a group box around itself, call ISetCanvas::setText. The set canvas uses the text string you pass to setText as the label of the group box. If you do not specify any text, the previously displayed group box is removed. Calling setText causes the minimum size of the set canvas to change to include or remove the space needed to show the group box.

The IMultiCellCanvas Class

As with ISetCanvas, you can use the IMultiCellCanvas class to build a window with the look of a dialog box. Also like ISetCanvas, it sizes and positions its child windows based on their minimum sizes.

However, IMultiCellCanvas is more complex than ISetCanvas, so you can arrange its child windows in ways not possible with a set canvas. Its child windows do not have to be aligned, can be separated by different amounts of space, and can overlap one another. Because sibling order does not determine the arrangement of child windows, you have greater control over how the Tab and cursor arrow keys work. But the most obvious difference between the two canvas classes is how IMultiCellCanvas can automatically adjust the size and position of its contents as it is sized: it has the ability to grow and shrink child windows as its size grows and shrinks.

Terms and Features of a Multicell Canvas

Picture a multicell canvas as divided into rows and columns. These are the units you use to position child windows relative to one another. Unlike window or dialog coordinates, rows and columns are not fixed-size units. For example, the width of one column may differ from the width of another in the same canvas. You identify columns and rows by their number. Both are 1-based and numbered sequentially, columns from left to right and rows from top to bottom.

The intersection of each column and row forms a *cell*. The cell is the fundamental unit of screen space for IMultiCellCanvas. The size of a cell is the width of its column and height of its row. You identify a cell by its column and row. Thus, the cell at the top-left corner of a multicell canvas is cell 1, 1.

You assign each child window a unique starting cell and a number of adjoining cells to occupy. A multicell canvas sizes its child windows to completely fill the cells you define for them. IMultiCellCanvas allows child windows to overlap, so more than one child window can occupy a cell. Additionally, because a cell does not have to contain a child window, you can create space around or between child windows by leaving some cells empty.

You can also mark rows and columns to be expandable. If the height of a multicell canvas is larger than the sum of the heights its rows require, the canvas divides the extra space among its expandable rows. Similarly, if the width of the canvas is larger than the sum of the widths its columns require, the canvas divides the extra space among its expandable columns.

If the size of a multicell canvas is not large enough to display all of its child windows, the canvas clips them at its bottom and right edges. If the size of the multicell canvas is larger than needed to contain all of its child windows, the canvas adds white space below and to the right of its child windows, unless it has expandable rows or columns. In this case, the canvas grows the size of its expandable rows and columns to absorb the extra space.

Adding and Positioning Child Windows

Unlike the other canvas classes, to add a child window to a multicell canvas, you must do more than just make the canvas its parent window. You must also call `IMultiCellCanvas::addToCell`. This function assigns the child window to one or more adjoining cells of the canvas. If you fail to call `addToCell` for a child window, the canvas does not manage its size or position.

By adding child windows to occupy the same cell or range of cells, you can overlap child windows. However, `IMultiCellCanvas` does not allow two child windows to start in the same cell (cannot have the same cell for their upper-left corners). The most common types of windows to overlap are a group box, for overlapping the sibling windows it contains within its border, and a combination box control with a drop-down list box, for sharing the portion of the screen where its list box displays with sibling windows. The topic "Adding Special-Case Child Windows" discusses special considerations for both.

Because `addToCell` conveys positioning information, `IMulticellCanvas` uses sibling order only to determine the order in which the input cursor cycles through its child windows when the user presses the Tab or cursor arrow keys.

Creating White Space

You can create space between child windows of a multicell canvas by leaving an empty cell between them, that is, a cell that no child windows occupy. You can create a margin around its child windows, similar to the margin explicitly supported by `ISetCanvas`, by leaving empty its first and last rows and first and last columns.

The width of an empty column and height of an empty row both default to ten pels, the default cell size. You can query and set this size using `IMultiCellCanvas::defaultCell` and `setDefaultCell`. You can also give a row or column, whether empty or not, a specific height or width by calling `setRowHeight` or `setColumnWidth`.

To create a right and bottom margin, use `setColumnWidth` and `setRowHeight`. A multicell canvas creates only as many rows and columns as you specify. It creates all rows up to the highest numbered one that you pass to `addToCell` or `setRowHeight`. It creates all columns up to the highest numbered one that you pass to `addToCell` or `setColumnWidth`. Therefore, if you need an empty column beyond the rightmost column that you specify to `addToCell`, specify it on a call to `setColumnWidth`. If you do not want to change the default width of the empty column, call `setColumnWidth`, as follows:

```
canvas
  .setColumnWidth( LAST_COLUMN,
                IMultiCellCanvas::defaultCell().width() );
```

Creating a Window with IMultiCellCanvas Objects

In Figure 15-6, you saw a window implemented with the ICanvas class. The code for a similar
window implemented with IMultiCellCanvas follows. Figure 15-9 shows the columns and
rows holding the color blocks and the push button child windows, and it shows the empty
columns and rows used for margins. Each of the child windows occupies multiple rows or
columns. This is necessary so that the color blocks overlap and the push button spans the
widths of the color blocks.

Simple IMultiCellCanvas - canvas\mcsimple\mcsimple.cpp

```cpp
#include <iapp.hpp>
#include <icolor.hpp>
#include <iframe.hpp>
#include <imcelcv.hpp>
#include <ipushbut.hpp>
#include <isysmenu.hpp>
#include <icconst.h>

void main ( )
{
  IFrameWindow
    frame( "Multicell Canvas Example" );
  IMultiCellCanvas
    client( IC_FRAME_CLIENT_ID, &frame, &frame );

  // Create three color squares using ICanvas objects.
  // Do not let the squares get smaller than 20x20 pels.
  ICanvas
    red  ( 1, &client, &client ),
    green( 2, &client, &client ),
    blue ( 3, &client, &client );
  red
   .setBackgroundColor( IColor::red )
   .setMinimumSize( ISize( 20, 20 ) );
  green
   .setBackgroundColor( IColor::green )
   .setMinimumSize( ISize( 20, 20 ) );
  blue
   .setBackgroundColor( IColor::blue )
   .setMinimumSize( ISize( 20, 20 ) );

  // Create a push button.
  IPushButton
    ok( ISystemMenu::idClose, &client, &client );
  ok
   .enableDefault()
   .enableSystemCommand()  // For ISystemMenu::idClose.
   .setText( "OK" )
   .enableTabStop()
   .enableGroup();

  // Position child windows in the canvas.
  client
   .addToCell( &red,    2, 2, 2, 2 )
   .addToCell( &green,  3, 3, 3, 2 )
   .addToCell( &blue,   5, 2, 2, 2 )
   .addToCell( &ok,     2, 6, 5 );
```

```
    // Use expandable rows and columns so that the squares always
    // fill the canvas.  Set the overlap amount to be 25% of the
    // child windows' width and height via the ratios we pass to
    // setColumnWidth and setRowHeight.
    ISize
      defaultCellSize = IMultiCellCanvas::defaultCell();
    client
      .setColumnWidth( 2, 3, true )
      .setColumnWidth( 3, 1, true )
      .setColumnWidth( 4, 2, true )
      .setColumnWidth( 5, 1, true )
      .setColumnWidth( 6, 3, true )
      .setColumnWidth( 7, defaultCellSize.width() )
      .setRowHeight( 2, 3, true )
      .setRowHeight( 3, 1, true )
      .setRowHeight( 4, 3, true )
      .setRowHeight( 7, defaultCellSize.height() );

    // Size and show the window now.
    frame
      .setClient( &client )
      .setFocus()
      .show();

    IApplication::current().run();
}
```

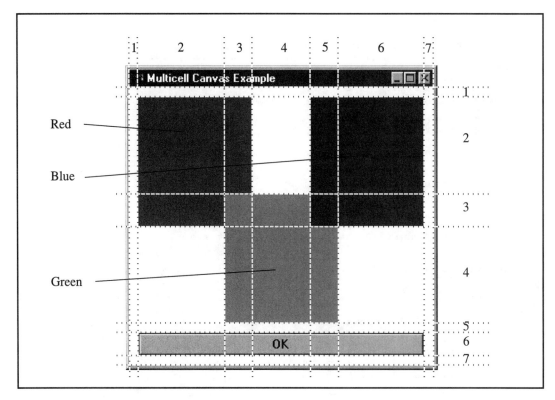

Figure 15-9. Cells in a Multicell Canvas.

The first addToCell call places the red color block at column 2, row 2 of the canvas. This child window spans two columns and two rows. We place the green child window at column 3, row 3, and the blue child window at column 5, row 2. The green block spans three columns and two rows, and the blue spans two columns and two rows. Thus, we align the top edge of the red and blue blocks in row 2 and overlap portions of the color blocks in columns 3 and 5 and in row 3. The **OK** push button appears below them in row 6. It spans the entire width of the three color blocks because it occupies columns 2 through 6. Columns 1 and 7 and rows 1 and 7 provide a margin around the child windows.

More on Positioning and Sizing Child Windows

A multicell canvas positions and sizes its child windows based on their minimum sizes. However, a number of other factors also affect the layout of its controls. These include the following factors:

- The initial sizes of its rows and columns. Specify these sizes by calling setRowHeight or setColumnWidth. Otherwise, each size defaults to the width or height that IMultiCellCanvas::defaultCell returns.

- The number of columns and rows that a child window occupies.

- The use of expandable rows or columns.

These factors determine the width of the columns and height of the rows of the canvas, which in turn set the sizes of its cells. IMulticellCanvas positions and sizes its child windows to fill the cells that they occupy.

Using Minimum Sizes

A multicell canvas never sizes a child window smaller than the minimum size that the child window returns from its minimumSize function. (For more information on minimum sizes, see the topic "Using Minimum Sizes in Open Class Library" near the end of this chapter.) Because a multicell canvas sizes a child window to fill the cells it occupies, the canvas can size the child window larger than its minimum size.

If a child window occupies a single column, its minimum size can cause the canvas to increase the width of the column. The same applies to rows. If the width of the child window's minimum size exceeds the column's width, the larger value becomes the column's new width.

If a child window spans several columns, its minimum size can also cause the canvas to increase the width of a column. However, a canvas only does this if the width of the child window's minimum size is greater than the combined widths of the columns it occupies. In this case the canvas increases the width of the expandable columns. If none of the columns that the child window occupies is expandable, the canvas increases the width of the child window's starting (first) column. Again, the same applies to rows.

Creating Expandable Rows and Columns

If you compare the code for the similar windows in Figure 15-6 and 15-9, you might not see much difference; the line count is comparable. The major difference is that the ICanvas version explicitly positions and sizes its child color-block windows; the IMultiCellCanvas version does not. Instead, the multicell canvas does the positioning and sizing based on calls to addToCell, setColumnWidth, and setRowHeight.

Actually, there is another difference. The code for the second example uses setColumnWidth and setRowHeight to make some of the columns and rows expandable. This feature gives the IMultiCellCanvas version sizing support; the ICanvas version and dialog boxes lack this support. As the user changes the size of the frame window, the multicell canvas automatically sizes the color blocks, keeping them equal in size. It sizes the color blocks and the **OK** push button to fit the size of the canvas, overlapping the color blocks by 25% of their widths and heights. Additionally, if we change the text or font of the push button, the canvas automatically updates the size of the button to accommodate the change. Figure 15-10 shows how the IMultiCellCanvas version responds to changes in frame sizes.

By default, columns and rows are not expandable, so their sizes are not dependent on the size of the multicell canvas. You can make a column or row expandable by passing a value of true as the third argument to setColumnWidth or setRowHeight. By creating expandable rows and columns, you cause a multicell canvas to size its child windows and white space based on the size of the canvas. If the canvas is wider or taller than what its columns and rows minimally

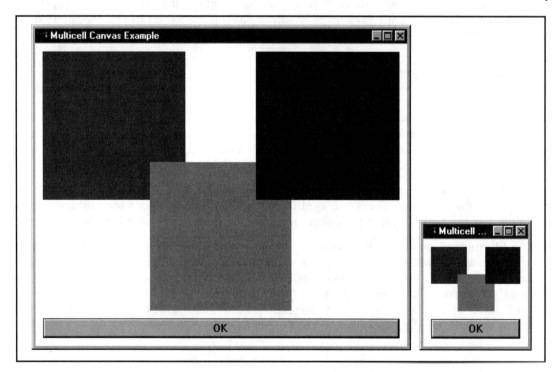

Figure 15-10. Differently Sized Multicell Canvases with Expandable Rows and Columns.

need, it divides this extra space among its expandable columns and rows. It does this by dividing this space proportionally, according to the widths and heights of the expandable columns and rows before expanding them.

As mentioned in the previous topic, if a child window occupies more than one row or column of which none is expandable, the multicell canvas can grow the child window's starting row and column. This behavior gives unexpected results in some cases. You can correct this potential problem by making one or more rows or columns expandable. The **canvas\mcbad** program on the examples disk is a variation of the **canvas\mcsimple** example that we used to create Figure 15-10, but without the expandable rows or columns. The resulting window shown in Figure 15-11, with the green block almost entirely covered by the blue block, looks far different from the ones in Figure 5-10. Therefore, because expandable rows and columns give you greater control over the size of shared rows and columns, they are useful even if you do not add sizing borders to frame windows.

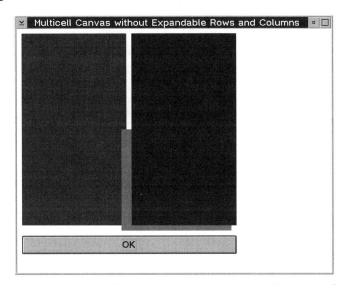

Figure 15-11. Multicell Canvas Needing Expandable Rows and Columns.

Look at the `IMultiCellCanvas` version of the lunch dialog shown in Figure 15-12. It looks much like the `ISetCanvas` version shown in Figure 15-4 and the dialog box shown in Figure 15-2. However, this `IMultiCellCanvas` version uses expandable rows and columns to provide sizing support for the dialog in addition to the support for text and font changes that it shares with the `ISetCanvas` version. Figure 15-13 shows the `IMultiCellCanvas` version after enlarging the frame window. The code follows.

Figure 15-12. Lunch Dialog Built with IMultiCellCanvas.

Lunch Dialog using IMultiCellCanvas - canvas\mclunch\mclunch.cpp

```cpp
#include <iapp.hpp>
#include <icheckbx.hpp>
#include <ientryfd.hpp>
#include <iframe.hpp>
#include <igroupbx.hpp>
#include <imcelcv.hpp>
#include <iradiobt.hpp>
#include <istattxt.hpp>
#include <icconst.h>

#include "pushbtns.hpp"        // For MyStandardPushButtons.
#include "mclunch.h"

void main ( )
{
  IFrameWindow
    frame( "Lunch",
           ID_LUNCH_DIALOG,
           IFrameWindow::classDefaultStyle
             & ~IFrameWindow::maximizeButton
             & ~IFrameWindow::minimizeButton
             | IFrameWindow::dialogBackground );

  // Create the client window.
  IMultiCellCanvas
    client( IC_FRAME_CLIENT_ID, &frame, &frame );
```

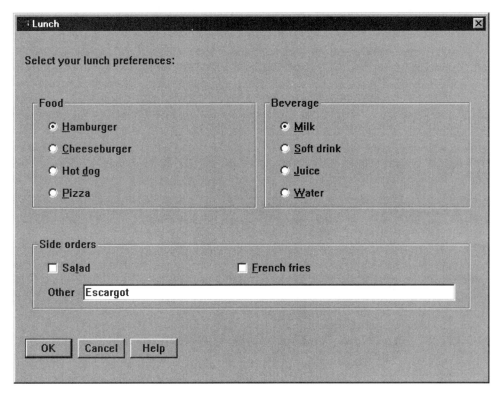

Figure 15-13. Expanded Multicell Canvas Lunch Dialog.

```
// Create the heading text.
IStaticText
  headingText( ID_LUNCH_TEXT, &client, &client );
headingText
 .setText( ID_LUNCH_TEXT );

// Create the "Food" group box and its choices.
IGroupBox
  food( ID_FOOD, &client, &client );
food
 .setText( ID_FOOD );
IRadioButton
  hamburger    ( ID_HAMBURGER,    &client, &client ),
  cheeseburger( ID_CHEESEBURGER, &client, &client ),
  hotdog       ( ID_HOTDOG,       &client, &client ),
  pizza        ( ID_PIZZA,        &client, &client );
hamburger
 .setText       ( ID_HAMBURGER )
 .enableTabStop()
 .enableGroup   ();
cheeseburger
 .setText( ID_CHEESEBURGER );
hotdog
 .setText( ID_HOTDOG );
pizza
 .setText( ID_PIZZA );
```

```
// Create the "Beverage" group box and its radio buttons.
IGroupBox
  beverage( ID_BEVERAGE, &client, &client );
beverage
  .setText( ID_BEVERAGE );
IRadioButton
  milk      ( ID_MILK,      &client, &client ),
  softDrink( ID_SOFTDRINK, &client, &client ),
  juice     ( ID_JUICE,     &client, &client ),
  water     ( ID_WATER,     &client, &client );
milk
  .setText     ( ID_MILK )
  .enableTabStop()
  .enableGroup  ();
softDrink
  .setText( ID_SOFTDRINK );
juice
  .setText( ID_JUICE );
water
  .setText( ID_WATER );

// Create the "Side orders" group box and its choices.
IGroupBox
  sideOrders( ID_SIDEORDERS, &client, &client );
sideOrders
  .setText( ID_SIDEORDERS );
IMultiCellCanvas
  checkBoxes ( 1, &client, &client ),
  requestPair( 2, &client, &client );
ICheckBox
  salad( ID_SALAD, &checkBoxes, &checkBoxes ),
  fries( ID_FRIES, &checkBoxes, &checkBoxes );
salad
  .setText     ( ID_SALAD )
  .enableTabStop()
  .enableGroup  ();
fries
  .setText     ( ID_FRIES )
  .enableTabStop()
  .enableGroup  ();
IStaticText
  requestPrompt( ID_REQUESTPROMPT, &requestPair, &requestPair );
requestPrompt
  .setAlignment( IStaticText::centerLeft )
  .setText     ( ID_REQUESTPROMPT );
IEntryField
  request(ID_REQUEST, &requestPair, &requestPair );
request
  .enableTabStop()
  .enableGroup();

// Create the push buttons.
MyStandardPushButtons
  pushButtons( 4, &client );

// Position and size child windows of the multicell canvases
// by assigning them to cells.
ISize
  defaultCellSize = IMultiCellCanvas::defaultCell();
client
  .addToCell( &headingText,   2,  2,  14 )
  .addToCell( &food,          3,  5,  5,  11 )
  .addToCell( &hamburger,     5,  8 )
  .addToCell( &cheeseburger,  5,  10 )
  .addToCell( &hotdog,        5,  12 )
  .addToCell( &pizza,         5,  14 )
```

```
        .addToCell( &beverage,      9,   5,   6,   11 )
        .addToCell( &milk,          11,  8 )
        .addToCell( &softDrink,     11, 10 )
        .addToCell( &juice,         11, 12 )
        .addToCell( &water,         11, 14 )
        .addToCell( &sideOrders,    3,  18, 12,  7 )
        .addToCell( &checkBoxes,    5,  21,  8 )
        .addToCell( &requestPair,   5,  23,  8 )
        .addToCell( &pushButtons,   2,  27, 14 );
     client
        .setColumnWidth( 6,  defaultCellSize.width(), true )
        .setColumnWidth( 12, defaultCellSize.width(), true )
        .setColumnWidth( 16, defaultCellSize.width() )
        .setRowHeight  ( 1,  defaultCellSize.height(), true )
        .setRowHeight  ( 3,  defaultCellSize.height(), true )
        .setRowHeight  ( 17, defaultCellSize.height(), true )
        .setRowHeight  ( 25, defaultCellSize.height(), true )
        .setRowHeight  ( 28, defaultCellSize.height(), true );

     checkBoxes
        .addToCell( &salad,         1,  1 )
        .addToCell( &fries,         3,  1 );
     checkBoxes
        .setColumnWidth( 2, defaultCellSize.width(), true )
        .setColumnWidth( 4, defaultCellSize.width(), true );

     requestPair
        .addToCell( &requestPrompt, 1,  1 )
        .addToCell( &request,       3,  1 );
     requestPair
        .setColumnWidth( 3, 0, true );

     // Select the default choices.
     hamburger
        .select();
     milk
        .select();

     // Size and position the frame window.
     IRectangle
        clientRect( IPoint( 50, 50 ), client.minimumSize() );
     frame
        .setClient( &client )
        .moveSizeToClient( clientRect );

     // Show the dialog now.
     frame
        .setFocus()
        .show();

     IApplication::current().run();
  }
```

Some controls do not return a context-sensitive minimum-size value, such as ILISTBox, IMultiLineEdit, IContainerControl, and ISplitCanvas. Consider placing these controls into cells with expandable rows and columns. If you effectively use expandable rows and columns, you do not need to supply these classes with a minimum size specific to their content.

Independently Sizing Child Windows

You can use multiple canvases for positioning child windows that coincidentally lie in the same column or row. Do not forcibly align windows that are not logically related. If the size of one of the child windows changes, a multicell canvas continues to align windows from independent parts of the overall window, which can give unexpected results.

Look again at the `IMultiCellCanvas` version of the lunch dialog in Figure 15-11 as an example. This window uses a multicell canvas as the client window. This canvas contains the majority of the controls on the lunch dialog. The client window aligns the choices within each group box by placing them in the same column. It also aligns choices in the **Food** and **Beverage** group boxes by placing them in the same rows. Finally, it aligns the borders of the **Food** and **Side orders** group boxes at the left edge of the window and the **Beverage** and **Side orders** group boxes at the right edge of the window.

The lunch dialog also uses three other canvases. The first is a set canvas for the push buttons. Although it appears we could align the **Cancel** push button and the entry field by placing them in the same column of the multicell canvas, these two controls are not related. By adding this alignment, changes to the prompt text of the entry field could cause the **OK** push button to grow or the **Cancel** button to shift to the right. This alignment would not look right, so we do not want a change to the prompt text affecting the size or position of any other control. For this reason, the example uses an additional multicell canvas just for managing the prompt text and the entry field. Because these two controls are related, we want any size changes to one to take only the other into account. Similarly, the dialog uses a multicell canvas to insulate the check boxes from formatting changes that affect the radio buttons. Although you could also create additional multicell canvases to insulate each group of radio buttons from the other, adding too many layers of canvases affects performance.

Another reason to isolate independent groups of controls into separate canvases is to minimize the factors contributing to the size of a given column or row. Once you exceed multiple factors, it becomes harder to control the outcome of a layout.

Removing Child Windows

Generally, you do not need to clean up a multicell canvas before you delete it. However, to delete or even temporarily remove a child window from a multicell canvas that you are currently displaying or are planning to display again, you need to use the `IMultiCellCanvas::removeFromCell` function.

`removeFromCell` is the counterpart to `addToCell`. Use `removeFromCell` so a multicell canvas no longer manages the position and size of a given window. Call `removeFromCell` prior to deleting a child window if the canvas might thereafter try to position and size it.

This function is not a replacement for destroying a child window or deleting a child window object. To completely remove a child window from a multicell canvas, you must also either delete the child window you no longer need or change its parent window. Otherwise, it remains on the canvas, keeping its last position and size. If you only want to temporarily remove a child window, change its parent to the object window that `IWindow::objectWindow` returns. This hides the child window and prevents a user from tabbing to it until you change its parent window back to the multicell canvas. Call `addToCell` at that time.

Adding Special-Case Child Windows

The topic "Canvas Usage Considerations" in Chapter 8, "Static Controls," provides information on adding an `IStaticText` object to a multicell canvas. Follow the techniques there for using an `IStaticText` object to display anything other than a single line of unchanging text.

With `IMultiCellCanvas` you also need to take special steps to ensure that a combination box or group box control properly overlaps sibling windows. Both controls share the characteristics of having a top portion that typically does not overlap other controls and a bottom portion that typically does. For a combination box, the top portion is the entry field component of the control; the bottom portion is where it displays its drop-down list box. For a group box, the text is its top portion; the area inside its borders is the other. In a multicell canvas, you want the top portion of these controls to fully occupy a row so that sibling windows in rows below cannot overlap them.

Combination Boxes

If you create the combination box control with the `IBaseComboBox::dropDownType` or `IBaseComboBox::readOnlyDropDownType` styles, its list box appears only on demand. The area over which the list box appears is an ideal place to locate other controls. This area must be part of the combination box control's window rectangle, and can extend below the bottom of the parent window. `IMultiCellCanvas` uses the `IWindow::layoutAdjustment` function to support the special needs of this control (`IBaseComboBox` overrides this function). To use this support, add a combination box object that occupies only a single row of a multicell canvas. The canvas places the entry field of the combination box entirely within this row. Then, call `IBaseComboBox::setMinimumRows` to specify the height of the list box in number of rows.

If you create a combination box control with the `IBaseComboBox::simpleType` style, it always displays its list box. No special considerations apply to adding this type of combination box control to a multicell canvas.

The following example adds a simple and drop-down type combination box to a multicell canvas. The list box of the drop-down type overlaps two radio buttons below it.

IMultiCellCanvas with Combination Boxes - canvas\mccombo\mccombo.cpp

```
#include <iapp.hpp>
#include <icombobx.hpp>
#include <iframe.hpp>
#include <imcelcv.hpp>
#include <iradiobt.hpp>
#include <istring.hpp>
#include <icconst.h>

void main ( )
{
  IFrameWindow
    frame( "Multicell Canvas with Combination Boxes" );
  IMultiCellCanvas
    client( IC_FRAME_CLIENT_ID, &frame, &frame );
```

```
// Create a combination box without a drop-down list box that
// does not overlap any sibling windows.  Also create one with
// a drop-down list box that overlaps some radio buttons.
IComboBox
   simpleCombo( 1, &client, &client ),
   dropDownCombo( 2, &client, &client, IRectangle(),
                  IComboBox::classDefaultStyle
                  & ~IBaseComboBox::simpleType
                  | IBaseComboBox::dropDownType );
simpleCombo
 .enableTabStop();
dropDownCombo
 .setMinimumRows( 8 )
 .enableTabStop();

// Fill the combination boxes with some items.
simpleCombo
 .addAsFirst( "Simple-type combination box" );
simpleCombo
 .addAsLast( "Second item" );
simpleCombo
 .addAsLast( "Third item" );
simpleCombo
 .setText( simpleCombo.itemText( 0 ) );
dropDownCombo
 .addAsFirst( "Drop-down type combination box" );
dropDownCombo
 .addAsLast( "Second item" );
dropDownCombo
 .addAsLast( "Third item" );
dropDownCombo
 .addAsLast( "Fourth item" );
dropDownCombo
 .addAsLast( "Fifth item" );
dropDownCombo
 .addAsLast( "Sixth item" );
dropDownCombo
 .addAsLast( "Seventh item" );
dropDownCombo
 .addAsLast( "Eighth item" );
dropDownCombo
 .setText( dropDownCombo.itemText( 0 ) );

// Create radio buttons below the drop-down combination box.
IRadioButton
   left1( 3, &client, &client ),
   left2( 4, &client, &client );
left1
 .setText( "Button 1" )
 .enableTabStop()
 .enableGroup();
left2
 .setText( "Button 2" );

// Create radio buttons to the right of the combination boxes.
IRadioButton
   right1( 5,  &client, &client ),
   right2( 6,  &client, &client ),
   right3( 7,  &client, &client ),
   right4( 8,  &client, &client ),
   right5( 9,  &client, &client ),
   right6( 10, &client, &client );
right1
 .setText( "Button A" )
 .enableTabStop()
 .enableGroup();
right2
 .setText( "Button B" );
```

```
right3
  .setText( "Button C" );
right4
  .setText( "Button D" );
right5
  .setText( "Button E" );
right6
  .setText( "Button F" );

// Position the child windows in the canvas.  Note that we place
// the drop-down combination box in a single row.  We control the
// height of its list box using its setMinimumRows function.
client
  .addToCell( &simpleCombo,    2, 2, 1, 5 )
  .addToCell( &dropDownCombo, 2, 8 )
  .addToCell( &left1,          2, 10 )
  .addToCell( &left2,          2, 12 )
  .addToCell( &right1,         4, 2 )
  .addToCell( &right2,         4, 4 )
  .addToCell( &right3,         4, 6 )
  .addToCell( &right4,         4, 8 )
  .addToCell( &right5,         4, 10 )
  .addToCell( &right6,         4, 12 );

// Grow the canvas vertically between the radio buttons;
// grow the combination boxes horizontally.
client
  .setRowHeight( 1,   10, true )
  .setRowHeight( 3,   10, true )
  .setRowHeight( 5,   10, true )
  .setRowHeight( 7,   10, true )
  .setRowHeight( 9,   10, true )
  .setRowHeight( 11, 10, true )
  .setRowHeight( 13, 10, true )
  .setColumnWidth( 2, 10, true );

// Size and show the window now.
frame
  .setClient( &client )
  .moveSizeToClient( IRectangle( IPoint( 100, 200 ),
                                 client.minimumSize() ) )
  .setFocus()
  .show();

IApplication::current().run();
}
```

Group Boxes

In the IMultiCellCanvas version of the lunch dialog, we used group boxes but did nothing special to add them to the canvas. As a result, these group boxes use the default row height to reserve space to hold their labels' text. Changing the font that these controls use or that the dialog uses can cause a control in a row below it to overlap that text. Use the following class, GroupBoxForMultiCell, to solve this problem. This class derives from IGroupBox and requires you to identify the starting row that it occupies in its parent multicell canvas. GroupBoxForMultiCell uses this information to set the height of the row to fit the height of its text whenever its font changes. It overrides IWindow::setLayoutDistorted to provide this support. See the topic, "Processing 'Layout Events' with the setLayoutDistorted Function," for more information.

IMultiCellCanvas with Smarter Group Boxes - canvas\mcgroup\mcgroup.hpp

```
#include <ifont.hpp>
#include <igroupbx.hpp>
#include <imcelcv.hpp>

class GroupBoxForMultiCell : public IGroupBox {
public:
  GroupBoxForMultiCell ( unsigned long       windowId,
                         IMultiCellCanvas* parentAndOwner,
                         unsigned long       row = 0 )
      : IGroupBox( windowId, parentAndOwner, parentAndOwner ),
        fRow( row )
  { }
GroupBoxForMultiCell
 &setMultiCellRow ( unsigned long row )
    {
      fRow = row;
      return this->setRowHeight();
    }

protected:
virtual GroupBoxForMultiCell
 &setLayoutDistorted ( unsigned long flagsOn,
                       unsigned long flagsOff )
    {
      if ( flagsOn & IWindow::fontChanged )
      {
        this->setRowHeight();
      }
      this->IGroupBox::setLayoutDistorted( flagsOn, flagsOff );
      return *this;
    }

private:
  GroupBoxForMultiCell ( const GroupBoxForMultiCell& );
GroupBoxForMultiCell
 &operator=            ( const GroupBoxForMultiCell& );
GroupBoxForMultiCell
 &setRowHeight ( )
    {
      if ( fRow )
      {
        IFont
          font( this );
        IMultiCellCanvas
          *canvas = (IMultiCellCanvas*)( this->parent() );
        ( *canvas)
          .setRowHeight( fRow, font.maxCharHeight() );
      }
      return *this;
    }
unsigned long
 fRow;
}; // GroupBoxForMultiCell
```

The ISplitCanvas Class

Use the ISplitCanvas class to separate windows with a split bar that a user can move by dragging it with button 1 of the mouse. The split bar looks and acts much like the one an OS/2 container control displays in the details view.

Features of a Split Canvas

A *split canvas* manages the position and size of its child windows, so that together with the split bars they occupy the entire area of the canvas. If the split canvas changes size, it resizes its child windows so they still fill it, maintaining the ratio of their sizes. In the simplest case of a single child window, the split canvas keeps the size of the child window identical to its size, and does not draw a split bar.

A split canvas arranges its child windows in their sibling order, either horizontally from left to right in a single row or vertically from top to bottom in a single column. Between its child windows it draws split bars. Therefore, if a split canvas has N child windows, it creates N-1 split bars. Vertical split bars separate horizontally-arranged child windows; horizontal split bars separate vertically-arranged ones. A split canvas does not limit the number of child windows it supports and requires no calls to add a child window.

When a user positions the mouse pointer over a split bar, the pointer changes to a double-headed arrow. A user can drag a vertical split bar left or right; a horizontal split bar, up or down. Moving a split bar causes the split canvas to change the sizes of the two windows that the split bar separates. A user cannot move the split bar using the keyboard.

Figure 15-14 shows a split canvas with five child windows. Vertical split bars separate the child windows. The mouse pointer is over the split bar separating the fourth and fifth child windows. The code that creates the window follows.

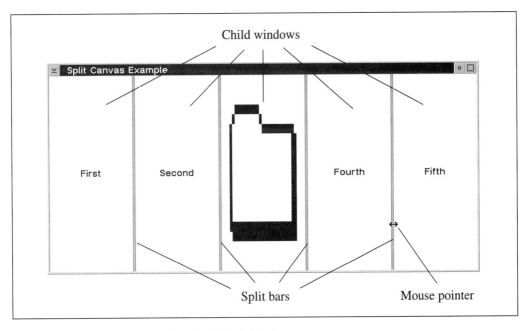

Figure 15-14. Split Canvas with Vertical Split Bars.

Simple Split Canvas Example - canvas\splittxt\splittxt.cpp

```cpp
#include <iapp.hpp>
#include <ibmpctl.hpp>
#include <iframe.hpp>
#include <isplitcv.hpp>
#include <istattxt.hpp>
#include <icconst.h>

void main ( )
{
  IFrameWindow
    frame( "Split Canvas Example" );
  ISplitCanvas
    client( IC_FRAME_CLIENT_ID, &frame, &frame );

  // Create five child windows.
  IStaticText
    st1( 1, &client, &client ),
    st2( 2, &client, &client );
  IBitmapControl
    bmp( 3, &client, &client, ISystemBitmapHandle::folder );
  IStaticText
    st4( 4, &client, &client ),
    st5( 5, &client, &client );
  st1
    .setText( "First" )
    .setAlignment( IStaticText::centerCenter );
  st2
    .setText( "Second" )
    .setAlignment( IStaticText::centerCenter );
  st4
    .setText( "Fourth" )
    .setAlignment( IStaticText::centerCenter );
  st5
    .setText( "Fifth" )
    .setAlignment( IStaticText::centerCenter );

  // Size and show the window now.
  frame
    .setClient( &client )
    .setFocus()
    .show();

  IApplication::current().run();
}
```

Manipulating Split Bars

The distinguishing feature of a split canvas is its split bars. ISplitCanvas gives you some control over their look, including placement, thickness, and color.

A split canvas draws either vertical or horizontal split bars. You can specify which type of split bars you want by using a style when constructing the canvas or by calling ISplitCanvas::setOrientation after creating the canvas. Setting the orientation of the split bars determines whether the split canvas arranges its child window horizontally or vertically. Although you cannot create a split canvas that uses both vertical and horizontal split bars, you can simulate this look by using a second split canvas as the child window of the first, where each uses a different orientation for its split bars. The **canvas\complex** program on the examples disk shows this combination. However, users are limited to being able to move only one split bar at a time. They cannot move a horizontal split bar from one split canvas and a vertical split bar from another by dragging them from the point where they meet.

You can position split bars but only by setting the relative sizes of the child windows that they separate. Use the ISplitCanvas member function, setSplitWindowPercentage, to set them. Similarly, never change the size of a child window except by calling setSplitWindowPercentage.

If the split canvas has vertical split bars, the percentage that you pass to setSplitWindowPercentage only affects the width of a child window. Its height remains the height of the canvas. Similarly, this value only affects the height of a child window separated by horizontal split bars. If you do not assign percentages, the split canvas sizes its child windows equally.

If you set the percentage of one child window, set the percentage of all of them. If you set the percentage of only one window, you can get unpredictable results because you cannot predict what percentages the other child windows will use. A user can change the original percentages by dragging a split bar. Additionally, while the sum of the percentages returned by splitWindowPercentage for each child window is always 100%, the sum of the percentages you pass to setSplitWindowPercentage may not be.

If the sum of the percentages you specify is not 100%, ISplitCanvas treats the percentages as ratios. For example, you can assign percentages of 5, 5, and 10 for the three child windows of a split canvas with vertical split bars. The canvas then sizes the first and second child windows to occupy 25% of the available width and the third child window to occupy 50%.

Because you can treat the percentages you pass to setSplitWindowPercentage as ratios, you can accomplish near-exact positioning of split bars by passing, in pels, the size that you want each child window sized to. You can account for the amount of screen space each split bar occupies by calling ISplitCanvas::splitBarThickness.

Adding Special-Case Child Windows

A split canvas does not paint between its split bars. Its child windows paint the entire area of the canvas except for its split bars. As a result, windows that adjust the size of their rectangles or do not paint their entire rectangles do not work well in a split canvas. Such windows include combination boxes, icons that use screen or inverse colors, group boxes, and outline boxes.

In the OS/2 operating system, frame windows also do not work well as child windows of a split canvas, but for a different reason. A split canvas relies on the sibling order of its child windows to not change, but users do precisely this when they activate a child frame window.

You can compensate for both situations by adding a multicell canvas between the split canvas and the problem child windows. Make the multicell canvas a child window of the split canvas, make the problem window the only child window of the multicell canvas, and place the problem window into an expandable row and column of the multicell canvas. Also, use setMinimumSize to give the problem window a small minimum size so that the user sees no difference between how the split canvas sizes this window and an actual child window. The **canvas\splitprb** program on the examples disk illustrates this technique.

The IViewPort Class

The `IViewPort` class supports the scrolling of any window, such as a bitmap, notebook, drawing canvas, or canvas with child windows. A user can scroll the window using the keyboard. If you specify styles to add scroll bars, a user can also scroll the window using the mouse. In this case, the view port creates a vertical scroll bar to the right of and a horizontal scroll bar below the window being scrolled. `IViewPort` manages the size of the scroll bars' scroll boxes, and updates their positions as it scrolls your window.

`IViewPort` thus gives you functional scroll bars. Open Class Library provides the base scroll classes: `IScrollBar`, `IScrollHandler`, and `IScrollEvent`. However, unless you implement a handler class derived from `IScrollHandler`, any scroll bar you create does not actually scroll data. `IViewPort` uses the `IScrollHandler` class to provide an easy-to-use implementation for scrolling a window.

`IViewPort` also gives another way to implement windows that a user can size freely. With a view port, a user can scroll the contents of a frame window or notebook when the window is no longer large enough to display it all.

Terms and Features of a View Port

You usually treat the view port as a single window, but it is actually four different windows. The first is the view port itself, which is the parent and owner window of the remaining windows. The next two windows are horizontal and vertical scroll bars. The last window is a *view rectangle*. The view rectangle is the area of the view port not occupied by the scroll bars and the little square where the scroll bars meet. The `IViewPort` class creates all four windows when you construct a view port.

The *view window* is the window that a view port scrolls. You supply the view window and identify it by making it a child window of the view port. Open Class Library uses the term *view window* rather than *child window* because the view window does not remain a child of the view port. Once you display the view port, `IViewPort` changes the parent window of the view window to the view rectangle. The view port scrolls the view window within the view rectangle. Only the portion of the view window that lies within the view rectangle is visible.

A view port supports only one view window. To replace the view window, remove it from the window hierarchy of the view port by destroying the window or changing its parent window. Then, you can add a new view window by making it a child window of the view port.

Figure 15-15 shows the parent-child relationship of the different windows combined in a view port. Note that the parent window of the view window is the view rectangle. The figure also shows the window identifiers that `IViewPort` assigns to its component windows. Open Class Library defines these window identifiers in `ICCONST.H`.

Figure 15-16 shows a view port scrolling a bitmap. The component windows of the view port are labeled. Although the portion of the view window (the bitmap) outside of the view port is not actually visible, the figure shows it superimposed behind the view port to illustrate the relative portion of the bitmap displayed in the view rectangle. As the view port scrolls the

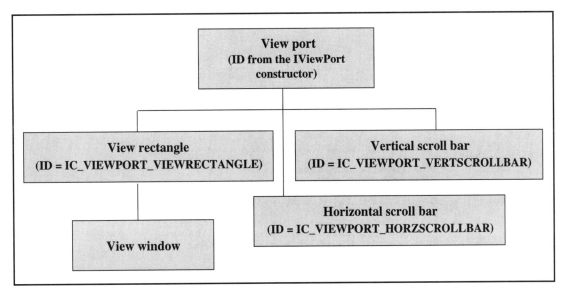

Figure 15-15. Hierarchy of Windows Managed by a View Port.

bitmap, IViewPort moves the bitmap around and users see only the portion positioned within the view rectangle.

Creating a View Port

The following example displays the view port shown in Figure 15-16. We create the view port to always show its horizontal and vertical scroll bars by using the IViewPort::alwaysHorizontalScrollBar and IViewPort::alwaysVerticalScrollBar styles (it never displays its scroll bars if you use the styles IViewPort::noHorizontalScrollBar and IViewPort::noVerticalScrollBar, and only displays them when the view window can be scrolled if you specify IViewPort::asNeededHorizontalScrollBar and IViewPort::asNeededVerticalScrollBar). We take care not to specify conflicting styles, such as the combination of IViewPort::asNeededHorizontalScrollBar and IViewPort::alwaysHorizontalScrollBar. If we do use conflicting systems, the IViewPort constructor throws an IInvalidParameter exception.

This example also uses the IViewPort::noViewWindowFill style to optimize the drawing of the view window. This style is generally equivalent to using IWindow::clipChildren. It prevents the view port from clearing the old image of the view window as it is being scrolled. The window being scrolled does this when it paints. Do not use this style with view windows that do not paint their entire rectangles, such as icons that use screen or inverse colors.

Bitmap in a View Port - canvas\vportbmp\vportbmp.cpp

```cpp
#include <iapp.hpp>
#include <icconst.h>
#include <ibmpctl.hpp>
#include <iframe.hpp>
#include <iscroll.hpp>
#include <ivport.hpp>
#include "vportcmd.hpp"
#include "vportbmp.h"

void main ( )
{
  // Create the frame window and its client view port.
  IFrameWindow
    frame( IFrameWindow::classDefaultStyle
           | IFrameWindow::menuBar );
  IViewPort
    vport( IC_FRAME_CLIENT_ID, &frame, &frame, IRectangle(),
           IViewPort::classDefaultStyle
             & ~IViewPort::asNeededHorizontalScrollBar
             & ~IViewPort::asNeededVerticalScrollBar
             | IViewPort::alwaysHorizontalScrollBar
             | IViewPort::alwaysVerticalScrollBar
             | IViewPort::noViewWindowFill );

  // Set up the bitmap for the view port to scroll.  We make it
  // the view window by making it the child window of the view
  // port.  By not sizing the view window, the view port sizes
  // it to its minimum size.
  IBitmapControl
    bmp( 1, &vport, &vport, ID_DEFAULTBMP );

  // Double the amount of a "line" scroll and increase by half
  // the width of the scroll bars.
  unsigned long
    scrollIncrement =
            vport.verticalScrollBar()->minScrollIncrement() * 2;
  ( *( vport.verticalScrollBar() ) )
    .setMinScrollIncrement( scrollIncrement )
    .sizeTo( ISize( IScrollBar::systemScrollBarWidth( true )
                                             * 3 / 2, 0 ) );
  ( *( vport.horizontalScrollBar() ) )
    .setMinScrollIncrement( scrollIncrement )
    .sizeTo( ISize( 0,
                    IScrollBar::systemScrollBarWidth( false )
                                             * 3 / 2 ) );
  // Add command handlers for the menu bar choices.
  NewBitmapCmdHandler
    cmdHdr1( &bmp );
  cmdHdr1
   .handleEventsFor( &vport );
  SizeBitmapCmdHandler
    cmdHdr2( &bmp, &vport );
  cmdHdr2
   .handleEventsFor( &vport );
  ScrollViewCmdHandler
    cmdHdr3( &vport );
  cmdHdr3
   .handleEventsFor( &vport );

  // Show it all now.
  frame
   .setFocus()
   .show();

  IApplication::current().run();
}
```

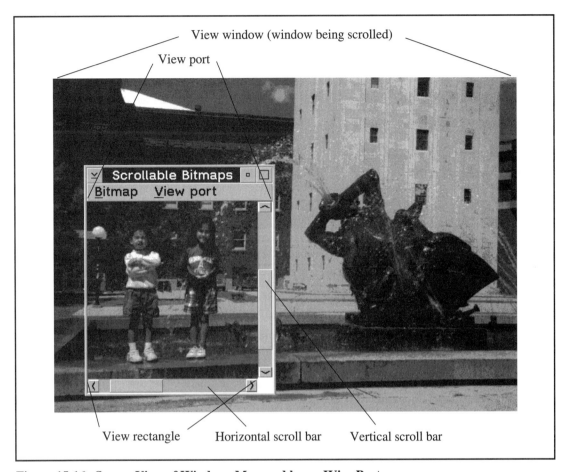

Figure 15-16. Screen View of Windows Managed by an IViewPort.

Scrolling the View Window

If the view window is larger than the view rectangle, you can scroll the view window. Otherwise, the view port disables scrolling because all of the view window is already visible, and it positions the view window in the upper-left corner of the view rectangle. Any white space in the view rectangle appears below and to the right of the window being scrolled. This is the only case where a view port displays any white space in the view rectangle. This is also the default position for the view window view when you display a view port, so any position you initially give the view window is discarded.

A view port allows scrolling with the keyboard or mouse. Table 15-3 shows which keys the view port translates into scrolling actions (assuming neither the view window nor any of its child windows processes the key first), and it shows how they compare to using the mouse. The table also shows the default scroll amounts that each scroll bar uses, which are based on the average character width and maximum character height of the initial font of the view port. Changing the font of a view port after it has been constructed does not change these scroll

Table 15-3. View Port Scrolling

Scroll Type	Key	Mouse Action	Default Scroll Amount
Vertical page scroll	Page Up, PgUp, Page Down, PgDn	Click the shaft of the vertical scroll bar above or below the scroll box.	The height of the view rectangle minus the vertical line scroll amount
Vertical line scroll	Up arrow, down arrow	Click the scroll arrows of the vertical scroll bar.	Half of the maximum character height of the initial font of the view port
Horizontal page scroll	Ctrl+Page Up, Ctrl+PgUp, Ctrl+Page Down, Ctrl+PgDn	Click the shaft of the horizontal scroll bar left or right of the scroll box.	The width of the view rectangle minus the horizontal line scroll amount
Horizontal line scroll	Left arrow, right arrow	Click the scroll arrows of the horizontal scroll bar.	The average character width of the initial font of the view port

amounts. See the next topic, "Accessing the Scroll Bars," for how to change these scroll amounts.

You can also scroll the view window from your application by calling the view port's `scrollViewVerticallyTo` and `scrollViewHorizontallyTo` functions. These functions cause a view port to both scroll the view window and update the position of the scroll box in the appropriate scroll bar. The value you pass to these functions is the offset in pels from the top-left corner of the view window to the point that you want to see in the upper-left corner of the view rectangle. For example, to show the upper-left corner of the view window, pass a value of 0 to both `scrollViewVerticallyTo` and `scrollViewHorizontallyTo`. Calling `moveTo` on the view window does not update the scroll boxes of the scroll bars.

The following code shows how you can scroll a view window horizontally so that the middle portion of the view window is displayed in the view rectangle. Figure 15-16 shows the view window scrolled this way. This code uses the `viewWindowSize` and `viewWindowDrawRectangle` functions of `IViewPort`. `viewWindowSize` returns the size of the view window; `viewWindowDrawRectangle` returns the portion of the view window currently visible in the view rectangle. The `clViewPort` variable is a pointer to an `IViewPort` object.

Bitmap in a View Port - canvas\vportbmp\vportcmd.cpp

```
...
IRectangle
  viewWindow( IPoint(), clViewPort->viewWindowSize() ),
  visibleView( clViewPort->viewWindowDrawRectangle() );
visibleView
 .centerAt( viewWindow.center() );
( *clViewPort )
 .scrollViewHorizontallyTo( visibleView.left() );
...
```

Accessing the Scroll Bars

Access the scroll bars of a view port using the `IViewPort` functions, `horizontalScrollBar` and `verticalScrollBar`. By using `IScrollBar` functions on the objects that these functions return, you can customize the scroll bars. For example, the **canvas\vportbmp\vportbmp.cpp** code you saw earlier increases the widths of the scroll bars and the amount they scroll the view window when a user selects their scroll arrows.

Setting the Size of the View Window

`IViewPort` provides three ways for you to set the size of the view window. The size of the view window determines if the view port enables scrolling and how it sizes the scroll boxes of the scroll bars.

To size most view windows, give them a non-zero size. Specify an `IRectangle` argument when you construct the view window or call the `sizeTo` or `moveSizeTo` functions before you first show the view port. You will probably do this for all view windows except multicell canvases and set canvases, and you will possibly do this for notebooks, drawing canvases, and bitmaps. Note that `IViewPort` cannot scroll a view window with an actual width or height greater than 32,767 pels.

If you change the size of the view window after you display the view port, notify the view port of the change by calling its `setLayoutDistorted` function. See the topic "Processing 'Layout Events' with the setLayoutDistorted Function" for details on using this function.

The second way to size a view window is to use its minimum size. If the size of the view window is `ISize(0, 0)` when you first show the view port, the view port sizes the view window to its minimum size. In the case of using `IMultiCellCanvas` and `ISetCanvas`, the minimum size is large enough to show all of their child windows. `IViewPort` automatically detects if the minimum size of its view window changes and updates its scroll bars accordingly. Note that `IViewPort` cannot scroll a view window with a size greater than 32,767 pels.

Some windows size especially well when grown larger than their minimum size, such as a multicell canvas with expandable rows or columns. When using a view port to scroll such a window, construct the view port with the `IViewPort::expandableViewWindow` style. When the size of the view rectangle is larger than the minimum size of the view window, the style causes `IViewPort` to grow the view window to fill the view rectangle. As a result, this style causes `IViewPort` to grow and shrink the view window as its size grows and shrinks. However, `IViewPort` stops shrinking the view window at its minimum size, enabling it for scrolling at that point. Note that for VisualAge for C++ for OS/2, 3.0, Open Class Library added the `IViewPort::expandableViewWindow` style in a FixPak. See the **canvas\complex** program on the examples disk for usage of this style.

The final way to size a view window is to call `IViewPort::setViewWindowSize`, specifying a logical size for the view window. The next topic describes this technique.

Giving a View Window a Logical Size

Calling `IViewPort::setViewWindowSize` gives the view window a logical size. The view port treats the view window as if it were sized to its logical size rather than its actual size. The two sizes can be quite different. `IViewPort` continues to create, size, and position the scroll bars for you, and it notifies you when a user scrolls the view window. `IViewPort` also continues to size and position the scroll boxes of its scroll bars but does this based on the logical size of the view window. However, you must manage all aspects of the view window's appearance, perhaps even giving it the look of being scrolled.

So, why use a logical size? You use it primarily to avoid creating a full-size view window while taking advantage of the scroll bar management code that `IViewPort` provides. One case where you might want to use a view window with a logical size is to scroll a large graphic object. Perhaps instead of creating and drawing the entire object, you want to draw only the part a user is currently viewing. Perhaps you want to scroll a large array of entry fields. However, you can neither afford the start-up time needed to create all of the controls nor the resulting depletion of system resources. You only want to create the controls that the user sees at one time and to give the appearance that you are scrolling many more. Perhaps you want to scroll a window whose width or height exceeds 32,767 pels, which is the physical size limit that `IViewPort` handles.

To implement a view window with a logical size, in addition to calling `IViewPort::setViewWindowSize`, create a class derived from `IViewPort` and override the `IViewPort::positionViewWindow` function. `IViewPort` calls this function whenever the application or a user scrolls the view window. You are responsible for the appearance of the view window based on the position information that the view port reports. Use `positionViewWindow`, which ordinarily scrolls the view window, to provide this specialized processing. The `IViewPort` class has already updated the position of the scroll boxes when it calls `positionViewWindow`.

The **canvas\vportlog** example creates a view window with a logical size. Figure 15-17 shows the resulting window, a view port scrolling a view window that appears to be 0x40000 (262,144) pels wide and 0x80000 (524,288) pels high. The physical size of the view window is only as large as the display, however. The example overrides the virtual function `IViewPort::positionViewWindow` to do the following:

1. Update the contents of the drawing canvas view window based on the logical portion of the view window that the view port reports is currently visible (the `buildGraphicList` function relies on `IViewPort::viewWindowDrawRectangle` to identify the logical portion of the view window now visible)

2. Force the paint handler for the drawing canvas to be called by calling `IWindow::refresh`

3. Prevent the `IViewPort` class from actually scrolling the view window by not calling `IViewPort::positionViewWindow`, which scrolls the view window

In this code, `clViewWindow` represents the view window with a logical size:

View Window with a Logical Size - canvas\vportlog\vportlog.cpp

```
LogicalSizeViewPort& LogicalSizeViewPort::positionViewWindow
                            ( const IWindowHandle& viewWindow,
                              const IRectangle& viewRectangle )
{
   // Do not call IViewPort::positionViewWindow, which scrolls
   // the window.

   // Prepare the view window so it appears to scroll when it
   // paints; then force it to paint.
   this->buildGraphicList();
   clViewWindow
     .refresh();

   return *this;
}
```

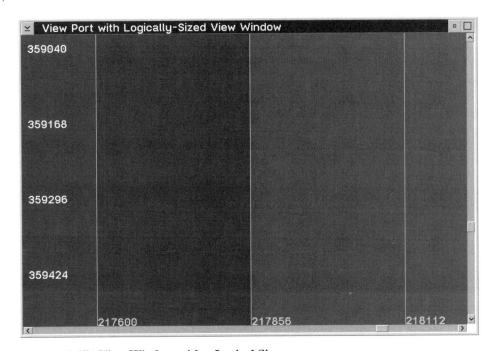

Figure 15-17. View Window with a Logical Size.

IViewPort supports logical sizes exceeding 32,767 pels by scaling the logical size units to a different set of units for the scroll bars to use. This approach imposes some restrictions on the application, however. First, recognize that the values passed to and returned by IViewPort are in logical size units. Second, IScrollBar functions that handle the scrollable range, scroll box range, scroll box position, and visible count use scaled values. The IScrollBar functions that handle scrolling amounts such as setPageScrollIncrement use logical size units. Third, to modify the page scroll amount, override IViewPort::setupScrollBars to set the new scroll amount. Do this after calling IViewPort::setupScrollBars, which resets the page scrolling increment to use the default value in logical size units. The **canvas\vportlog** example shows the use of these techniques.

Canvas Class Combinations

You can mix and match the canvas classes because Open Class Library imposes no restrictions on which windows you can make the child window of another. Many of these combinations work well, allowing you to create complex windows using the technique of composition. Others offer benefits but require some tips to make them work right. Several of these combinations are used in the **canvas\complex** program on the examples disk. Still, others provide little benefit. This section groups the possible combinations into these different categories.

These combinations work well:

- ISetCanvas in an ISetCanvas, IMultiCellCanvas, or IViewPort

- IMultiCellCanvas in an IMultiCellCanvas

- ISplitCanvas in an ISplitCanvas

- IViewPort in an ICanvas or an ISplitCanvas

- ICanvas in an ICanvas, ISetCanvas, IMultiCellCanvas, or IViewPort

These combinations can work effectively but need additional code:

- ISplitCanvas in an IMultiCellCanvas or IViewPort

  You must provide the split canvas with a reasonable minimum size. You could also explicitly size the split canvas before it is displayed when it is in a view port.

- IViewPort in an IMultiCellCanvas or ISetCanvas

  You must assign a reasonable minimum size to the view port.

- IMultiCellCanvas in an IViewPort

  To support expandable rows and columns in the multicell canvas, specify the IViewPort::expandableViewWindow style when creating the view port. See a previous topic, "Setting the Size of the View Window," where we discuss the IViewPort class for more information.

These combinations either do not work well or provide little or no value:

- ISetCanvas in an ICanvas or ISplitCanvas

  ICanvas neither sizes nor positions an ISetCanvas. If the minimum size of the set canvas changes (because of a font change for example), ICanvas does not change the size of the set canvas accordingly. An ISetCanvas only has one best size, so an ISplitCanvas will likely cause the set canvas to clip its child windows.

- `IMultiCellCanvas` in an `ICanvas`, `ISetCanvas`, or `ISplitCanvas`

  `ICanvas` neither sizes nor positions an `IMultiCellCanvas`. If the minimum size of the multicell canvas changes (because of a font change for example), `ICanvas` does not change the size of the multicell canvas accordingly. Neither `ICanvas` nor `ISetCanvas` support dynamically growing a multicell canvas with expandable rows or columns. An `ISplitCanvas` will likely cause the multicell canvas to clip its child windows.

- `ISplitCanvas` in an `ICanvas` or `ISetCanvas`

  `ISplitCanvas` tends to work best in situations where it can be dynamically sized, such as when it is used as the client window of a frame window. Neither `ICanvas` nor `ISetCanvas` provides support for growing a child window this way. You must also provide the split canvas with a minimum size for it to work decently on a set canvas.

- `IViewPort` in an `IViewPort`

  A double set of scroll bars offers little value.

- `ICanvas` in an `ISplitCanvas`

  An `ICanvas` only has one best size, so an `ISplitCanvas` will likely cause it to clip its child windows.

Behind the Scenes

This section describes two areas of support that are key to implementing the canvas classes. Both areas build canvas support into the entire window hierarchy; their interface appears in the `IWindow` class. With minimum size support, you can add any window to a multicell or set canvas. Canvases use the `IWindow::setLayoutDistorted` function to determine when to update their contents. Some examples in this chapter have already touched on these areas.

Using Minimum Sizes in Open Class Library

`IMultiCellCanvas` and `ISetCanvas` use minimum sizes as the basis for how they size their child windows.

For each child window, you can use the minimum size Open Class Library provides or supply your own. The minimum size that Open Class Library provides suffices in most cases because most control classes dynamically factor in the size needed by its fixed-size and variable-sized elements, such as text. The most notable exceptions are `IContainerControl`, `IListBox`, `IMultiLineEdit`, `IOutlineBox`, and `ISplitCanvas`. Your application needs to set their minimum sizes. Supply a minimum size for these to use them as child windows of a multicell or set canvas; otherwise, their minimum sizes default to `ISize(100, 100)`.

If you supply a minimum size, be aware that `IMultiCellCanvas` and `ISetCanvas` typically size a child window to its minimum size. Therefore, consider a minimum size to be the smallest size you want a control sized to but pick a size that gives a usable control. Do not use the smallest size that a control can be. For example, although you could size a list box so that it displays only a single character at a time, no user would tolerate using it to scroll through several hundred items.

You have two ways to supply a minimum size for a window. The easiest is to call the window's setMinimumSize function. Because this function fixes the value of the minimum size until you call it again, it is not well suited for a minimum size that can be changed outside of your code (unless you are calling it from a handler). Alternatively, you can create a derived control class that provides an implementation of the calcMinimumSize function. This solution can potentially return a different minimum size whenever it is called, based on the current environment.

IMultiCellCanvas and ISetCanvas get a child window's minimum size by calling its minimumSize function. IWindow::minimumSize returns the value set by calling IWindow::setMinimumSize. If there is no such value or the value has been reset by a call to IWindow::resetMinimumSize, IWindow::minimumSize calls the virtual calcMinimumSize function. However, a class' implementation of calcMinimumSize can potentially be a time-consuming operation that typically returns the same value for the same object.

To improve the performance of IMultiCellCanvas and ISetCanvas, Open Class Library caches calculated minimum sizes. For VisualAge for C++ for OS/2, 3.0, Open Class Library added this support in a FixPak. As a result, once a multicell or set canvas gets the minimum size of a child window, it uses that value instead of requiring another call to the child window's calcMinimumSize function. It uses this value until the child window indicates that its minimum size has changed. Specifically, IWindow::minimumSize calls IWindow::savedMinimumSize to retrieve a value it previously cached, and it calls IWindow::saveMinimumSize to cache a value obtained by calling calcMinimumSize. In this way, IWindow::minimumSize avoids calling calcMinimumSize until the minimum size changes. To notify a parent canvas that the minimum size value it calculates has changed, a window must call its own setLayoutDistorted function, passing the IWindow::minimumSizeChanged flag. See the next topic for details on this function. To disable the caching of minimum size values for a window, call its IWindow::disableMinimumSizeCaching function.

Processing "Layout Events" with the setLayoutDistorted Function

A key to implementing the canvas classes is using the IWindow member function setLayoutDistorted. This function provides a canvas with notifications that potentially require it to update the position and sizes of its child windows. The canvas classes provide implementations of this virtual function to process significant layout events reported as flags passed to the setLayoutDistorted function. Canvases use this mechanism to react to changes at run time, such as changes to the text or font used by a child window.

Any window can generate these "layout events" simply by calling its own setLayoutDistorted function or that of its parent window. Although a window calls setLayoutDistorted to report a change that can affect how it appears on a canvas, the function does not require the window to be a child window of a canvas. The window calls the function to report a change; the window being called determines if the change has any relevance. Open Class Library already contains many calls to setLayoutDistorted to report a variety of layout events.

Most windows do not process most, if not all, of the flags passed to their setLayoutDistorted function. Similarly, each canvas class checks for only those events that affect how it manages its child windows. For example, IMultiCellCanvas and ISetCanvas update the layouts of their child windows whenever any of their minimum sizes change. These canvas classes detect minimum size changes by testing for the IWindow::childMinimumSizeChanged flag in their setLayoutDistorted functions. ICanvas and ISplitCanvas ignore this flag, however, because they do not size or position child windows based on their minimum sizes. As a result, the way each canvas implements its setLayoutDistorted function determines how responsive it is to changes at run time, and reflects those characteristics that are important to its layout routine.

Some of the differences between how the various canvas classes process setLayoutDistorted account for the traits shown in Table 15-4. Table 15-4 describes the flags you can pass to setLayoutDistorted, the IWindow::Layout enumerations. You can pass a single flag or several bitwise flags ORed together. The first argument to setLayoutDistorted is the set of flags being enabled, and the second is the set of flags being disabled. Note that many entries in the table have a number next to the text. The meaning of these numbers is explained following the table.

If a window overrides setLayoutDistorted, it must pass any flags it does not process to the setLayoutDistorted function of the class it derives from. In many cases, this turns out to be IWindow::setLayoutDistorted; in other cases, ICanvas::setLayoutDistorted. Both have important implementations.

IWindow::setLayoutDistorted applies the flags being enabled to the flags it has stored, removes the flags being disabled, and then stores the new result. You can subsequently test for flags it stores using IWindow::isLayoutDistorted. It then routes some flags on to the setLayoutDistorted function of the parent window. For example, if a window calls its own setLayoutDistorted function, passing the IWindow::minimumSizeChanged flag, IWindow::setLayoutDistorted stores this flag and calls the parent window's setLayoutDistorted function, passing it the IWindow::childMinimumSizeChanged flag. If the parent window is an ISetCanvas or IMultiCellCanvas, the canvas runs its layout routine to update the appearance of its child windows. This, in turn, can cause the minimum size of the canvas to change, which can result in its parent canvas running its layout routine, as a result of more calls to setLayoutDistorted. To see how, let's examine how canvases implement setLayoutDistorted.

Unlike a minimum size change, most functions that change a canvas do not cause it to immediately update the layout of its child windows. For example, calling IMultiCellCanvas::addToCell does not cause a multicell canvas to immediately run its layout routine, which allows you to call addToCell numerous times with little performance cost. Instead the following occurs:

1. IMultiCellCanvas::addToCell calls IMultiCellCanvas::setLayoutDistorted to turn on the canvas' IWindow::layoutChanged flag.

2. IMultiCellCanvas::setLayoutDistorted calls the ICanvas::setLayoutDistorted function.

3. `ICanvas::setLayoutDistorted` calls `IWindow::setLayoutDistorted`, which stores the `IWindow::layoutChanged` flag to indicate that it has an update pending.

4. If the `IWindow::immediateUpdate` flag is not enabled, as is the case when calling `IMultiCellCanvas::addToCell`, the update remains pending until the next time the canvas paints. Thereafter, making the canvas visible or calling `IWindow::refresh` to force the canvas to paint causes it to run its `layout` routine.

Therefore, to force a canvas to update its layout when it has no update pending, you must also call its `setLayoutDistorted` function, passing the bitwise OR of `IWindow::layoutChanged` and `IWindow::immediateUpdate`. For example, if you change the size of the window that a view port is scrolling, you must explicitly report the change in this manner. Otherwise, even when you force the view port to paint, it will not call its `layout` routine.

Because a canvas runs its `layout` routine only when it receives the `IWindow::layoutChanged` or `IWindow::immediateUpdate` flags, you can also prevent a canvas from updating its child windows by intercepting these flags in the `setLayoutDistorted` function of a class derived from a canvas. One scenario for doing this would be to prevent a multicell canvas from running its `layout` routine multiple times when you update the text of several child button controls. By overriding `setLayoutDistorted`, you can block the canvas from temporarily detecting these changes reported as `IWindow::childMinimumSizeChanged` flags, so it can later run its `layout` routine only once to incorporate all changes.

The final consideration applies to control classes you create that provide a `calcMinimumSize` function. For a multicell or set canvas to detect when the minimum size of the control changes, the control must call its `setLayoutDistorted` function, passing `IWindow::minimumSizeChanged`. All window classes in Open Class Library do this. With the introduction of minimum size caching, discussed in the previous topic, not calling `setLayoutDistorted` this way can cause a multicell or set canvas to not detect changes to the minimum size.

Table 15-4 (Part 1 of 2). Flags to Pass to setLayoutDistorted

IWindow::Layout Enumeration	Usage	IWindow::setLayout-Distorted Behavior	Canvases That Process It
windowCreated	Automatically turned on when you construct a window object.	Calls the parent window, passing the IWindow::childWindow-Created flag.	None.
childWindowCreated	Turned on by IWindow::setLayoutDistorted.	None.	ICanvas (1), ISetCanvas (1), ISplitCanvas (1), IViewPort (1).
colorChanged	Automatically turned on when you construct a window object and by IWindow::dispatch when you or a user changes a color.	None.	N/A.

Table 15-4 (Part 2 of 2). Flags to Pass to setLayoutDistorted

IWindow::Layout Enumeration	Usage	IWindow::setLayout-Distorted Behavior	Canvases That Process It
sizeChanged	Turned on by IMultiCellCanvas, ISplitCanvas, and IViewPort when they are resized.	None.	ISplitCanvas (1), IViewPort (2).
minimumSizeChanged	Turned on by a window (including ICanvas, ISetCanvas, and IMultiCellCanvas) when its minimum size has changed.	Calls the parent window, passing the IWindow::childMinimum-SizeChanged flag.	N/A.
childMinimumSize-Changed	Turned on by IWindow::setLayoutDistorted.	None.	ISetCanvas (2), IMultiCellCanvas (2), IViewPort (3).
fontChanged	Automatically turned on when you construct a window object and by IWindow::dispatch when you or the user changes a font.	Calls the parent window, passing the IWindow::fontPropogated flag, if the new font is inherited from the owner window. Otherwise it turns off the IWindow::fontPropogated flag.	ISetCanvas (4).
fontPropogated	Automatically turned on by IWindow::setLayoutDistorted.	None.	All (5).
layoutChanged	Turned on by some functions of a canvas that affect its layout or by its setLayoutDistorted function (see the last column).	None.	All (6).
immediateUpdate	Turned on by some functions of a canvas that affect its layout.	None.	All (7).
windowDestroyed	Automatically turned on when you delete a window object.	Calls the parent window, passing the IWindow::childWindow-Destroyed flag.	None.
childWindowDestroyed	Turned on by IWindow::setLayoutDistorted.	None.	ICanvas (1), ISetCanvas (1), ISplitCanvas (1), IViewPort (1).

The following notes apply to Table 15-4:

1. The canvas enables the `IWindow::layoutChanged` flag.

2. The canvas enables the `IWindow::layoutChanged` and `IWindow::immediateUpdate` flags.

3. If the view window initially has a size of (0, 0), the `IViewPort` enables the `IWindow::layoutChanged` and `IWindow::immediateUpdate` flags.

4. If the `ISetCanvas` is displaying text for a group-box label, it enables the `IWindow::layoutChanged` flag.

5. Once its `IWindow::fontPropogated` flag is enabled, a canvas stops running its `layout` routine until `IWindow::setLayoutDistorted` resets the flag. In the OS/2 operating system, this minimizes the amount of reformatting when a user drops a font.

6. When the canvas receives a paint event, it runs its `layout` routine.

7. If the canvas is visible, it runs its `layout` routine.

Table 15-4 also identifies some other uses for the `setLayoutDistorted` function, such as overriding it in a derived class to detect when a user changes the font or color of the window. You can check for a notification of a font change by testing the first argument for the `IWindow::fontChanged` flag and a color change by testing the first argument for the `IWindow::colorChanged` flag. For example:

```
MyWindow& MyWindow::setLayoutDistorted
                ( unsigned long flagsOn, unsigned long flagsOff )
{
  if (flagsOn & IWindow::fontChanged)
  {
     // Process a change in font here.
  }
  if (flagsOn & IWindow::colorChanged)
  {
     // Process a change in color here.
  }

  IWindow::setLayoutDistorted( flagsOn, flagsOff );
  return *this;
}
```

Chapter 16

Tool Bars, Fly-Over Help, and Custom Buttons

- Describes how you build tool bars using the classes IToolBar, IToolBarButton, IToolBarFrameWindow, and IToolBarContainer
- Describes the fly-over help support that the classes IFlyOverHelpHandler and IFlyText provide
- Describes how you use the tool bar building blocks, ICustomButton, ICustomButtonDrawHandler, and ICustomButtonDrawEvent to build your own specialized button classes
- Describes how you build animated push buttons using the class IAnimatedPushButton
- Read Chapters 10 and 15 before reading this chapter.
- Chapters 5, 7, 17, 23, and 24 contain related information.

In just a few years, tool bars have become a ubiquitous feature in user-interface design. Don't even think about building an application without a tool bar to provide your users with a fast path to their most common tasks. In this chapter, you learn how Open Class Library makes building this portion of your application easy. You also learn the design points of the tool bar and how to use its building blocks in windows other than tool bars and how to extend them with your own unique features.

Tool Bar

Although we usually describe a tool bar as if it is a single entity, Open Class Library implements its tool bar using two different ISetCanvas-derived tool bar classes. The first of these, IToolBar, usually contains special buttons called tool bar buttons, but it can also contain any class derived from IWindow. When you see the words "tool bar" in this chapter, think IToolBar. IToolBar has the interface for adding and removing windows and for determining the location of a tool bar relative to its owning frame window.

The second ISetCanvas-derived tool bar class, IToolBarContainer, contains IToolBar objects. You learn about IToolBarContainer in this chapter, but you don't create these objects yourself. Open Class Library creates IToolBarContainer objects as it needs them to contain the tool bars you create.

A Tool Bar Is a Set Canvas

As you see in Figure 16-1, both `IToolBar` and `IToolBarContainer` derive from `ISetCanvas`. This derivation provides many of the important characteristics of `IToolBar` and `IToolBarContainer`.

For example, because `IToolBar` derives from `ISetCanvas`, it can contain any class derived from `IWindow`. Even though `IToolBar` has an explicit add and remove interface that `ISetCanvas` does not, it is `ISetCanvas` that makes this possible by handling the layout of the windows in a tool bar. In practice, besides the tool bar buttons that the class `IToolBarButton` provides, the only other control you use in a tool bar is a drop-down combination box. To simplify our discussion in the remainder of this chapter, we discuss the tool bar as if it contained only tool bar buttons. Because tool bar buttons are such an important component of the tool bar, we discuss their use and design prior to discussing the tool bar itself.

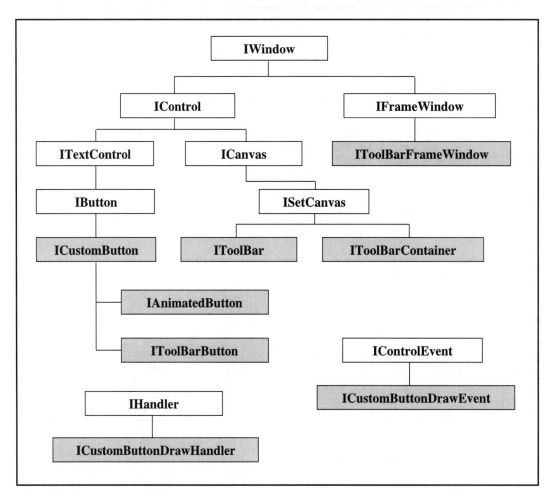

Figure 16-1. Tool Bar Classes.

Creating Tool Bar Buttons with Text and Bitmaps

IToolBarButton has a single constructor with the following declaration:

```
IToolBarButton   ( unsigned long     id,
                    IWindow*          parent,
                    IWindow*          owner,
                    const IRectangle& initial = IRectangle(),
                    const Style&      style = defaultStyle() );
```

This constructor is the same constructor that Open Class Library provides for all classes that derive from IWindow. Because IToolBarButton is a control that only Open Class Library provides and not a wrapper for an operating system control, you cannot create an IToolBarButton using either an IWindowHandle or a numeric identifier and the IWindow pointer of its parent window. Table 16-1 summarizes the IToolBarButton::Style values you use to construct tool bar buttons.

If you create an IToolBarButton with the IToolBarButton::useIdForBitmap style, the IToolBarButton constructor attempts to find a bitmap resource that matches the numeric identifier you provide it. If the identifier is not in the range of bitmaps that Open Class Library provides (Open Class Library reserves the range above IC_ID_BASE), the constructor attempts to load the bitmap using the application's resource library that is returned from IApplication::current().userResourceLibrary(). Conversely, if the identifier is in the range of bitmaps that Open Class Library provides, the constructor tries to load the bitmap using the resource library returned from IApplication::current().resourceLibrary().

Similarly, if you create IToolBarButtons with the IToolBarButton::useIdForText style, the IToolBarButton constructor attempts to find a text resource that matches the numeric identifier you provide it. If the identifier is not in the range of string table resources that Open Class Library provides, the constructor attempts to load the text using the application's resource library. Conversely, if the identifier is in the range of string table resources that Open

Table 16-1. IToolBarButton Style Values

IToolBarButton Styles	Description
bitmapAndTextVisible	Displays both the bitmap and text in the button
bitmapVisible	Displays only the bitmap in the button
classDefaultStyle	The combination of IToolBarButton::bitmapVisible, IToolBarButton::useIdForBitmap, IToolBarButton::useIdForText, IToolBarButton::standardFormat, IButton::noPointerFocus, and IWindow::visible
noDragDelete	Does not allow a user to drag the button to the desktop shredder
standardFormat	Displays the button using the rules for standard formatting (see the topic "Standard Tool Bar Buttons")
textVisible	Displays only the text in the button
usedIdForBitmap	Attempts to load a bitmap using the ID value
useIdForText	Attempts to load a text string using the ID value

Class Library provides, the constructor tries to load a string table resource using the library's resource library.

Alternatively, you can call `IToolBarButton::setBitmap` to specify either a numeric identifier to load a bitmap using the same rules that the `IToolBarButton` constructor uses, or you can provide the `IBitmapHandle` of an existing bitmap. You can specify the text for the tool bar button in the same way, but you call the `setText` functions of `ITextControl` to do so.

Three construction styles affect the appearance of the bitmap and text displayed in a tool bar button. You can create tool bar buttons with only the text visible using the `IToolBarButton::textVisible` style, only the bitmap visible using the `IToolBarButton::bitmapVisible` style, or both the text and bitmap visible using the `IToolBarButton::bitmapAndTextVisible` style. The constructor throws an `IInvalidParameter` exception if you specify more than one of these styles.

You can also call `IToolBarButton::setView` with one of the `IToolBarButton::View` enumeration values of `IToolBarButton::bitmapView`, `IToolBarButton::textView`, or `IToolBarButton::bitmapAndTextView` after you construct the tool bar button to change the contents of the button.

Although you can construct tool bar buttons to show only bitmaps, only text, or bitmaps and text together, and you can call `IToolBarButton::setView` to change what these buttons display after you construct them, you usually change the view of the entire tool bar rather than changing individual buttons. To change the view of all buttons on a tool bar, call `IToolBarButton::setButtonView` and supply one of the `IToolBarButton::View` enumeration values described in the previous paragraph. You can also create an `IToolBar` with one of the `IToolBar` styles `buttonBitmapVisible`, `buttonTextVisible`, or `buttonBitmapAndTextVisible`. `IToolBar::buttonBitmapVisible` is the default style.

Using Transparency with Tool Bar Buttons

Icons are a special type of bitmap that the operating system draws transparently on top of existing data on the display. In addition to the bitmap of the primary image, an icon also contains a *mask bitmap*. The operating system uses the mask bitmap to change some of the bits in the primary bitmap to the color already on the display. In effect, the mask bitmap identifies every bit in the primary bitmap that should remain the color of the bit already on the display. With this support, you can create images that appear to be nonrectangular on the display.

The operating system also uses the mask bitmap to draw the transparent bits of the primary bitmap using colors that are the inverse of those on the display. The primary use of this feature is to draw selection emphasis around the icon's primary image.

One restriction that you need to be aware of when you use icons is that the operating system predefines their size and changes them to this predefined size when you load them from a resource file. This makes it difficult for you to use icons for images in a wide variety of sizes.

Tool bar buttons support the transparency that icons provide without the restriction the operating system imposes on the size of icons. When you create a tool bar button that uses transparency, `IToolBarButton` creates an `IGBitmap` object that examines the bitmap you supply and builds a mask bitmap based on the location of the bits in the bitmap that are in the transparent color. It then uses this mask bitmap to draw the tool bar button transparently in a way that is similar to the way that the operating system draws icons.

To use this transparency support, choose an infrequently used color as the transparent color and use it as the background of your bitmap images. Then, call `IToolBarButton::setTransparentColor` to set the transparent color for a single button, or call the static function `IToolBarButton::setDefaultTransparentColor` to set the default transparent color for all subsequent tool bar buttons.

Open Class Library provides you with a set of built-in bitmaps that already has a transparent color. You use these bitmaps by constructing an `IToolBarButton` with one of the tool bar button constants defined in `ICCONST.H`. These constants are described in the "Constructors" topic of the `IToolBarButton` class in the *Open Class Library Reference*. If you don't call `IToolBarButton::setDefaultTransparentColor`, the value returned by the static member `IToolBarButton::defaultTransparentColor` is the color that these built-in bitmaps require for transparency. This color is `IColor::pink` and has the RGB values of Red=255, Green=0, and Blue=255. If you want to use some of the Open Class Library-provided bitmaps in your application, create your bitmaps with the same pink transparent color that Open Class Library uses. Alternatively, you can call `setTransparentColor` on each button you create with its own transparent color, or, if you change the default transparent color to match your bitmaps, call `setTransparentColor(IColor::pink)` on the buttons that use Open Class Library-provided bitmaps.

If you do not want to use transparent bitmaps, call the `IToolBarButton` static function `clearDefaultTransparentColor` to disable support for transparency. If you disable the support for transparency, do not use Open Class Library-provided bitmaps because the background color of the bitmaps remain pink. Also, if you disable support for transparency, use a separate latched bitmap for each latchable tool bar button so that your users can distinguish the difference between the latched and unlatched states. By default, `IToolBarButton` uses the mask bitmap to draw a different transparent color in the latched state; without support for transparency in the button, it is cannot to do this. See "Latchable Tool Bar Buttons" later in this chapter for further details.

Standard Tool Bar Buttons

To help you achieve a consistent look and feel in the tool bar buttons of an application and to optimize the drawing of tool bar buttons, Open Class Library provides the `IToolBarButton::standardFormat` style to construct tool bar buttons. *Standard formatting* refers to the size of tool bar bitmaps, the width of tool bar text, and the number of lines of tool bar text. Call the `IToolBar` static functions `setStandardBitmapSize`, `setStandardTextLines`, and `setStandardTextWidth` to set the standard parameters that `IToolBar` uses to create all tool bar buttons with the `IToolBar::standardFormat` style. `IToolBar` uses these static values to draw the bitmap and text of all standard tool bar buttons at the same size.

Because tool bar buttons with the `IToolBar::standardFormat` style have a consistent, unchanging size, the drawing routines in `IToolBar` use this information to optimize the drawing of these buttons. They do this by creating and caching a bitmap for each standard tool bar button. After the brief initial delay in creating these bitmaps, standard tool bar buttons paint faster than tool bar buttons without the style.

Latchable Tool Bar Buttons

Because IToolBarButton inherits from ICustomButton, you can create tool bar buttons with the ICustomButton::latchable style. Latchable buttons toggle between a latched and an unlatched state each time a user presses the button. By default, Open Class Library changes the background of a latched button and transparently draws the button's bitmap and text on top of the new background. You must create tool bar buttons using a transparent color for IToolBarButton to correctly draw the latch state of these buttons. See the topic "Transparent Tool Bar Buttons" earlier in this chapter for details on creating transparent tool bar buttons. Alternatively, you can call IToolBarButton::setLatchedBitmap to use a different bitmap in the latched state.

In the topic "Grouping Buttons on the Tool Bar," you learned how to use the IControl::group style to arrange tool bar buttons into groups on a tool bar. The IControl::group style not only groups buttons visually, it also affects the behavior of tool bar buttons with the ICustomButton::autoLatch style. Buttons in the same group with the auto-latch style behave like a set of radio buttons. When a user presses one button in a group of auto-latch buttons, the button enters into and then displays the latched state. At the same time, other auto-latch buttons in the same group return to the unlatched state.

Creating Tool Bars

With IToolBar, you can group buttons on the tool bar, specify the amount of space, or *pad*, between these groups of buttons, specify the amount of pad between buttons, and specify the amount of pad around the sides of the tool bar. Again, it is ISetCanvas that provides the interface for and implementation of all of these features. When you indicate that you want to create a new group of buttons on the tool bar, IToolBar adds the IControl::group style to the first window in the group by calling IControl::enableGroup. ISetCanvas uses this style, along with the group pad you've specified, to lay out the windows in the correct groups. For further details, see the topic "Grouping Buttons on a Tool Bar" later in this chapter.

You create tool bars using the following two constructors:

```
IToolBar ( unsigned long          identifier,
           IFrameWindow*          owner,
           Location               location = aboveClient,
           Boolean                groupWithPreceding = false,
           const Style&           style=defaultStyle());
IToolBar ( unsigned long          identifier,
           IToolBar*              precedingToolBar,
           Boolean                groupWithPreceding = false,
           const Style&           style=defaultStyle());
```

Use the first of these constructors to create a single tool bar in one of the IToolBar::Location areas. Use the second constructor to create a tool bar after an existing tool bar (the precedingToolBar argument in this constructor) in the IToolBar::Location of the preceding tool bar. Table 16-2 summarizes the IToolBarButton::Style values that you use to construct tool bars. The following topics discuss tool bar locations and tool bar grouping in more detail.

Table 16-2. IToolBar Style Values

IToolBar Styles	Description
buttonBitmapAndTextVisible	Displays both the bitmap and text in all tool bar buttons
buttonBitmapVisible	Displays only the bitmap in all tool bar buttons
buttonTextVisible	Displays only the text in all tool bar buttons
classDefaultStyle	The combination of IToolBar::filterMisfits, IToolBar::bitmapVisible, and IWindow::visible
filterMisfits	Automatically removes windows in a horizontal tool bar that exceed the misfit width
noDragDrop	Disables direct manipulation to and from the tool bar and its tool bar buttons

Tool Bar Locations

When you create a tool bar for a frame window, you specify the location where you want the tool bar placed relative to that frame window. You specify the location on the `IToolBar` constructor with one of the following values of the enumeration `IToolBar::Location`:

```
IToolBar::aboveClient
IToolBar::belowClient
IToolBar::leftOfClient
IToolBar::rightOfClient
IToolBar::floating
IToolBar::hidden
```

`IToolBar::hidden` creates an invisible tool bar. The remaining tool bar locations are displayed in Figure 16-2.

Frame Extension Tool Bars

When you use one of the first four `IToolBar::Location` values to create a tool bar or to change its location using `IToolBar::setLocation`, `IToolBar` positions itself inside the frame window relative to the client window. The first time you create an `IToolBar` object in one of the four client-related areas, `IToolBar` creates an `IToolBarContainer` and calls `IFrameWindow::addExtension` to put the `IToolBarContainer` into the appropriate frame extension area. `IToolBar` then makes itself a child window of the tool bar container. As we explain shortly, it is this use of `IToolBarContainer` that allows you to create more than one tool bar in each client-related area.

Because most applications position their tool bars above the client window, `IToolBar::aboveClient` is the default location used if you do not specify an `IToolBar::Location` value on the constructor.

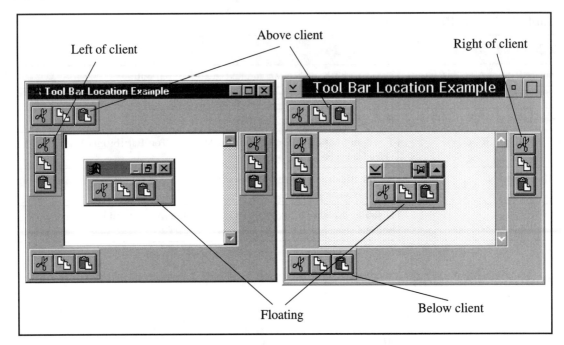

Figure 16-2. Tool Bar Locations in the Windows (Left) and OS/2 Operating Systems.

Floating Tool Bars

When you create a tool bar with the location IToolBar::floating, or when you change the location to floating using IToolBar::setLocation, IToolBar puts the tool bar into the client area of a separate frame window. It creates this frame window by calling IToolBar::floatingFrame the first time that the tool bar needs a floating frame window. This function creates and returns an IToolBarFrameWindow. IToolBar then calls IFrameWindow::setClient to make itself the client window of the floating frame window. Unlike tool bars created in one of the frame extension areas, an IToolBar in a floating frame window is not the child of an IToolBarCanvas. Because of this, you can only put a single tool bar inside the client area of a floating frame window.

If you want to create a different floating frame for your tool bars, you can derive a class from IToolBarFrameWindow and build a different frame window. Then, derive another class from IToolBar and override the function IToolBar::floatingFrame and create and return your floating frame window replacement.

Depending upon which operating system you use, IFloatingFrameWindow has several useful functions. In both the Windows and OS/2 operating systems, IToolBarFrameWindow has buttons that allow a user to show and hide the tool bar contained in the client window. With this feature, shown in Figure 16-3, your users can "roll up" the buttons in the tool bar to conserve screen real estate when they are not using them, and then they can roll them back down when they need to use them.

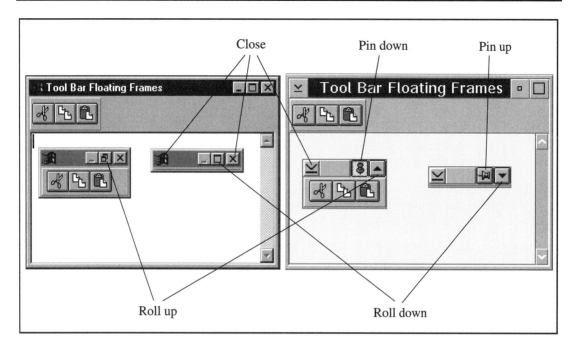

Figure 16-3. Buttons in Floating Tool Bar Frame Windows.

In the OS/2 operating system, `IToolBarFrameWindow` has a "pin" button that allows the floating tool bar to be attached to its owning frame window so that it moves with the frame window. This button is not currently supported in the Windows operating system.

Grouping Buttons on the Tool Bar

For many of your applications, you do not need to create more than a single tool bar. Just create a default tool bar as a frame extension above the client window and use the group behavior of `IToolBar` to separate the buttons on the tool bar into logical groups. You start a new group of buttons by setting the `startNewGroup` parameter to `true` when you add a new button or move an existing button to a new location.

By default, `IToolBar` leaves 8 pixels of space between groups of buttons. You can call `IToolBar::setGroupPad` to change the group pad for a single tool bar or call the static function `IToolBar::setDefaultGroupPad` to change it for all subsequently created tool bars. Figure 16-4 displays groups of buttons on a tool bar with the group pad set to 16 pixels.

Adding Decks to a Tool Bar

We started our discussion of tool bars by pointing out that `IToolBar` inherits its layout behavior from its `ISetCanvas` parent class. As you learned in Chapter 15, "Canvases," `ISetCanvas` supports laying out its child windows into decks. As you would expect, you can take advantage of this feature in the tool bar. In the code following, we create the same tool

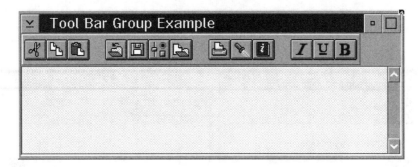

Figure 16-4. Using Group Pad with Tool Bar Buttons.

bar as the one shown in Figure 16-4 except that we create it to the left of the client window, and we call `ISetCanvas::setDecks` to change the layout to two decks. Figure 16-5 displays this tool bar.

Tool Bar with Decks - toolbar\tbardeck\tbardeck.cpp

```
#include <iframe.hpp>
#include <itbar.hpp>
#include <itbarbut.hpp>
#include <imle.hpp>
#include <iapp.hpp>
#include <icconst.h>

void main()
{
IFrameWindow
  frame ("Tool Bar With Decks Example");

// Create an MLE for the client area.
IMultiLineEdit
  mle(IC_FRAME_CLIENT_ID, &frame, &frame);
```

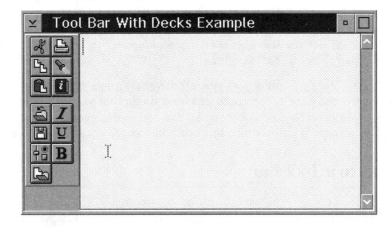

Figure 16-5. Tool Bar with Two Decks to the Left of the Client.

```
// Create a tool bar to the left of the client window.
IToolBar
  leftOfClient(0x01, &frame, IToolBar::leftOfClient);

// Create some library-supplied tool bar buttons.
IToolBarButton
  cutButton        (IC_ID_CUT,       &leftOfClient, &leftOfClient),
  copyButton       (IC_ID_COPY,      &leftOfClient, &leftOfClient),
  pasteButton      (IC_ID_PASTE,     &leftOfClient, &leftOfClient),
  openButton       (IC_ID_OPEN,      &leftOfClient, &leftOfClient),
  saveButton       (IC_ID_SAVE,      &leftOfClient, &leftOfClient),
  printButton      (IC_ID_PRINT,     &leftOfClient, &leftOfClient),
  locateButton     (IC_ID_LOCATE,    &leftOfClient, &leftOfClient),
  helpButton       (IC_ID_HELP,      &leftOfClient, &leftOfClient),
  boldButton       (IC_ID_BOLD,      &leftOfClient, &leftOfClient),
  italicButton     (IC_ID_ITALIC,    &leftOfClient, &leftOfClient),
  underscoreButton(IC_ID_UNDERSCORE,&leftOfClient,&leftOfClient),
  settingsButton (IC_ID_SETTINGS,&leftOfClient, &leftOfClient),
  copyToButton     (IC_ID_COPYTO,    &leftOfClient, &leftOfClient);

// Add the buttons to the tool bar.
leftOfClient
  .addAsLast ( &cutButton )
  .addAsLast ( &copyButton )
  .addAsLast ( &pasteButton )
  .addAsLast ( &openButton, true )
  .addAsLast ( &saveButton )
  .addAsLast ( &settingsButton )
  .addAsLast ( &copyToButton )
  .addAsLast ( &printButton, true )
  .addAsLast ( &locateButton )
  .addAsLast ( &helpButton )
  .addAsLast ( &italicButton, true )
  .addAsLast ( &underscoreButton )
  .addAsLast ( &boldButton );

leftOfClient.setDeckCount(2);

frame
  .setClient (&mle)
  .setFocus()
  .show();
IApplication::current().run();

}
```

Using Multiple Tool Bars

For those times when you need more flexibility, either because you have a lot of buttons on your tool bar or because you want to control the display of different sets of buttons on the tool bar, Open Class Library allows you to put any number of tool bars into one of the frame extension areas. You can do this because the top-level window in every frame extension area is an IToolBarContainer and, like its parent ISetCanvas, IToolBarContainer can lay out and display any number of child windows.

When you create the first IToolBar in one of the client-related locations, the IToolBar constructor automatically creates an IToolBarContainer, calls IFrameWindow::addExtension to put it into the correct frame extension area, and creates the new IToolBar as a child of the IToolBarContainer. If an IToolBarContainer already exists in the frame extension, the IToolBar constructor creates the new IToolBar as a child of the existing IToolBarContainer.

Figure 16-6 shows a tool bar that looks almost exactly like the tool bar in Figure 16-5. In Figure 16-5, we got two columns of buttons by setting the deck count of a single tool bar to 2. If you look carefully at Figure 16-6, you see that there are four tool bars inside a tool bar container. In most situations, your users would not notice the difference, but there is an important distinction between the two examples. Because we built the second example with a separate tool bar for each group of buttons, we can manipulate these groups as a whole. For example, we could add a settings notebook to our program that allowed our users to choose which tool bars they wanted to use and under what circumstances they needed them. It is also a simple matter to hide and show entire tool bars. And even more important, your users can directly manipulate these tool bars using the mouse. The code for this tool bar follows:

Multiple Tool Bars - toolbar\tbarmult\tbarmult.cpp

```
#include <iframe.hpp>
#include <itbar.hpp>
#include <itbarbut.hpp>
#include <imle.hpp>
#include <iapp.hpp>
#include <icconst.h>

void main()
{
IFrameWindow
  frame ("Tool Bar Container Example");

// Create an MLE for the client area.
IMultiLineEdit
  mle(IC_FRAME_CLIENT_ID, &frame, &frame);

// Create a number of tool bars to the left of the client.
IToolBar
  leftOfClient11(0x01, &frame, IToolBar::leftOfClient),
  leftOfClient12(0x01, &frame, IToolBar::leftOfClient, true),
  leftOfClient21(0x01, &frame, IToolBar::leftOfClient),
  leftOfClient22(0x01, &frame, IToolBar::leftOfClient, true);

// Create some library-supplied tool bar buttons.
IToolBarButton
 cutButton      (IC_ID_CUT,  &leftOfClient11, &leftOfClient11),
 copyButton     (IC_ID_COPY, &leftOfClient11, &leftOfClient11),
```

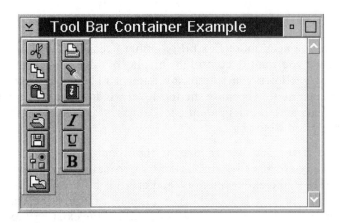

Figure 16-6. Multiple Tool Bars to the Left of the Client Window.

```
  pasteButton   (IC_ID_PASTE,&leftOfClient11, &leftOfClient11),
  openButton    (IC_ID_OPEN, &leftOfClient12,&leftOfClient12),
  saveButton    (IC_ID_SAVE, &leftOfClient12,&leftOfClient12),
  settingsButton(IC_ID_SETTINGS,&leftOfClient12,&leftOfClient12),
  copyToButton  (IC_ID_COPYTO, &leftOfClient12,&leftOfClient12),
  printButton   (IC_ID_PRINT, &leftOfClient21, &leftOfClient21),
  locateButton  (IC_ID_LOCATE,&leftOfClient21, &leftOfClient21),
  helpButton    (IC_ID_HELP,  &leftOfClient21, &leftOfClient21),
  boldButton    (IC_ID_BOLD,  &leftOfClient22, &leftOfClient22),
  italicButton  (IC_ID_ITALIC,&leftOfClient22, &leftOfClient22),
  underscoreButton(IC_ID_UNDERSCORE,&leftOfClient22,
                   &leftOfClient22);

// Add the buttons to the tool bar.
leftOfClient11
  .addAsLast ( &cutButton )
  .addAsLast ( &copyButton )
  .addAsLast ( &pasteButton );
leftOfClient12
  .addAsLast ( &openButton)
  .addAsLast ( &saveButton )
  .addAsLast ( &settingsButton )
  .addAsLast ( &copyToButton );
leftOfClient21
  .addAsLast ( &printButton)
  .addAsLast ( &locateButton )
  .addAsLast ( &helpButton );
leftOfClient22
  .addAsLast ( &italicButton)
  .addAsLast ( &underscoreButton )
  .addAsLast ( &boldButton );

frame
  .setClient (&mle)
  .setFocus()
  .show();
IApplication::current().run();

}
```

Direct Manipulation Support

Unlike many other controls in Open Class Library, the tool bar is enabled for direct manipulation by default. With direct manipulation enabled, your users can use the mouse to do the following tasks:

- Reorganize the buttons within a tool bar
- Move buttons to a different tool bar
- Reorganize the tool bars within a frame extension area
- Move a tool bar to a different frame extension area or make it a tool bar within a floating frame window
- Change the bitmap displayed within a tool bar by dropping a bitmap file onto it

Although Open Class Library enables all of these direct-manipulation features by default, before your users can take advantage of them, you must first do some work. For example, if you want to allow your users to be able to rearrange the buttons on the tool bar or move them to a different tool bar, add code to save their new locations in a profile and use them to create the tool bars on subsequent uses of your application. If for any reason you do not want to do this, turn off the direct-manipulation support in your tool bars. To disable that support, either create the `IToolbar` object with the style `IToolBar::noDragDrop` or call `IToolBar::disableDragDrop` after you create the tool bar.

Removing Misfits in Vertical Tool Bars

Until now, we have not discussed the fact that tool bars can contain any `IWindow`-derived class. In most cases, you put these windows into a tool bar in the same way that you do tool bar buttons. In practice, many `IWindow`-derived classes such as list boxes, notebooks, and containers serve no function in a tool bar. The drop-down combination box and the entry field are controls that you might find useful, but only on a horizontal tool bar. Their width makes them unsuitable for a vertical tool bar. For this reason, `IToolBar` includes *misfit filtering*. `IToolBar` filters, or temporarily removes, any control from a vertical tool bar that exceeds the value that you supply for a misfit width. By specifying an appropriate misfit width, you can add combination boxes and entry fields to a vertical tool bar that do not display if your user drags the tool bar to one of the vertical frame extension areas.

You control misfit filtering with the `IToolBar::filterMisfits` style. This style is on by default. You can call `IToolBar:enableMisfitFiltering` and `disableMisfitFiltering` to turn filtering on and off after constructing a tool bar, and you can call `IToolBar::isMisfitFilteringEnabled` to determine whether filtering is active.

You can also set the misfit width used to construct new tool bars, but you cannot control the misfit width of an individual tool bar. Call the static function `IToolBar::setDefaultMisfitWidth` to change the misfit width for tool bars and call `IToolBar::defaultMisfitWidth` to determine the misfit width for new tool bars.

Fly-Over Help

Open Class Library provides classes that you can use to add support for *fly-over* (or hover) help to your applications. Fly-over help displays brief informational or instructional text for the window that is underneath the mouse pointer. Using this form of help, users can quickly identify the function of or get instructions for using a graphical button or any other element in a user interface by moving the mouse to that window. Users neither request help by pressing the F1 key or a mouse button nor explicitly dismiss it. More important, users do not have to move the input focus to the control for which they want help, and the window with input focus does not lose that focus to a help window. As a result, users do not have to change the state of a window. The frame window, however, does have to be active (a control that has the frame in its parent window chain must have input focus) before fly-over help can be displayed.

The text displayed in fly-over help is not in the form of a traditional help panel (see Chapter 23, "Using Help".) Instead a user sees a short, single line of text displayed in an `IFlyText` window, a longer text string displayed in any control derived from `ITextControl`, or both. Figure 16-7 shows an example of both short and long text strings. The fly-over text window is positioned near the window that is beneath the mouse pointer. In practice, neither the short nor long text string can be very long. As a result, it is perhaps best to use fly-over help to inform or to suggest usage rather than to provide details.

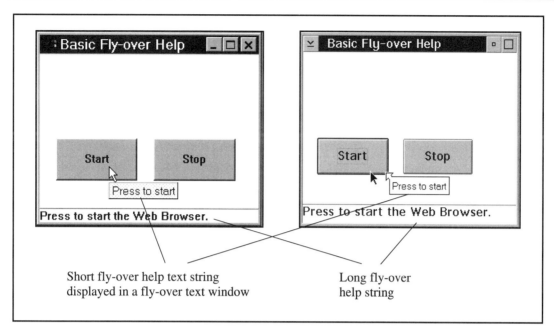

Figure 16-7. Fly-Over Help Features on the Windows (Left) and OS/2 operating systems.

Fly-over help is particularly well suited for tool bar buttons that typically do not accept input focus. (Without input focus, a user cannot request contextual help with the F1 key.) In addition, these buttons generally do not display text; they display bitmaps or icons whose meanings may not be obvious to a user. We include an example of fly-over help for a tool bar later in this chapter.

Adding fly-over help to your application requires minimal changes to your user interface (for example, an added control to display the long text or a menu choice for a user to be able to enable or disable this feature). You also need only add a minimum of code to support fly-over help because you can use the `IFlyOverHelpHandler` and `IFlyText` classes without having to derive your own classes. You do, however, need to plan how to assign window identifiers to ensure that the appropriate fly-over help is displayed for the appropriate controls. We describe the role of window identifiers in the section, "Specifying Fly-over Help Text."

You do not have to provide fly-over help text for every window and control in your application. In fact, you probably do not want to provide fly-over help for relatively unimportant elements in your user interface, such as static controls. A good first step is to supply fly-over help only on tool bar buttons.

Creating and Attaching the Fly-Over Help Handler

`IFlyOverHelpHandler` is the most important class for supporting fly-over help. Unlike using most event-handling classes, you do not have to create your own class derived from `IFlyOverHelpHandler` to add fly-over help support. You simply construct an

`IFlyOverHelpHandler` object and attach it to appropriate windows in your application. You create an `IFlyOverHelpHandler` using one of the following constructors:

```
IFlyOverHelpHandler ( IFlyText*      flyText,
                      unsigned long initialDelay = 100,
                      unsigned long delay        = 100 );

IFlyOverHelpHandler ( ITextControl* longText,
                      unsigned long initialDelay = 100,
                      unsigned long delay        = 100 );

IFlyOverHelpHandler ( IFlyText*      flyText,
                      ITextControl* longText,
                      unsigned long initialDelay = 100,
                      unsigned long delay        = 100 );
```

Displaying Long Fly-Over Text

Before you create the fly-over help handler, you need to create the controls that display the help text. You can create an `IFlyText` object for short text, an `ITextControl`-derived object for long text, or both controls to display short and long text simultaneously.

You typically use an `IStaticText` object or an `IInfoArea` object for displaying long text. If you do not specify a window to display long fly-over help, the text is never shown to the users. Therefore, to stop displaying long fly-over help, pass a 0, which indicates no window, to `IFlyOverHelpHandler::setLongTextControl`.

Displaying Short Fly-Over Text

`IFlyOverHelpHandler` only displays short fly-over text in an `IFlyText` window or an object of a class derived from `IFlyText`. `IFlyText` includes enough standard behavior that you typically do not need to derive from it.

The fly-over text window that `IFlyText` creates appears only when there is short fly-over text to be displayed. When the mouse pointer is over a window without short fly-over text, or if the mouse has not yet stopped over a window with short fly-over text, the fly-over text window is not visible. When it is visible, the fly-over help handler sizes it so that the short fly-over text appears on a single line. If the text contains carriage-return and line-feed characters (CR/LF), `IFlyText` strips them off prior to displaying the text.

In the Windows operating system, `IFlyText` displays its text using the Tool Tip control. This control positions itself relative to the mouse pointer.

Currently, in the OS/2 operating system, `IFlyOverHelpHandler` positions the fly-over text window on a corner of the window that is beneath the mouse pointer. The handler first tries to place the fly-over text window below and to the right of the window beneath the pointer. If the fly-over text window does not fit on the display, the handler then tries to position it below and to the left of the window. The final two positions that the handler tries are above and to the left and above and to the right. As you see in Figure 16-7, a corner of the fly-over text window contains an arrow that points to the window underneath the mouse pointer.

While this positioning in the OS/2 operating system ensures that the fly-over text window never covers the window that a user wants to learn about, it has some weaknesses. The first drawback is that the fly-over text window can be displayed far from the mouse pointer and, consequently, far from a user's attention. Second, the entire fly-over text window does not appear entirely within the boundaries of the display if the window beneath the mouse pointer is too large. Third, the fly-over help window may appear to be positioned far from the right boundary of a window because the edge of a window can extend beyond where you expect it to. For example, the right edge of a check box or radio button might extend considerably past the end of the text.

The fly-over text window is always a child window of the desktop window. This allows it to be placed anywhere on the screen, including outside your application's frame window. You can specify the owner of the fly-over text window, however. In practice, the owner needs to be either a frame window or 0. Using 0 allows you to use the same `IFlyText` object for multiple frame windows. Using a frame window as the owner allows you to limit the lifetime of the presentation system window of the `IFlyText` object to that of its owning frame window (a frame window destroys all windows that it owns when it is destroyed). If you call `IWindow::setAutoDeleteObject` on the `IFlyText` object, Open Class Library deletes the C++ object when the presentation system window is destroyed. The owner window has no other significance beyond this.

Most of the preceding fly-over text attributes, including window location and size, arrow shape, and window border, are not configurable. If this standard behavior is acceptable, using `IFlyText` is extremely easy because typically you only need to construct a fly-over text window and pass it to an `IFlyOverHelpHandler`. And, you only need to call a function of an `IFlyText` object to change the font or color of its text.

If you do not specify a window to display short fly-over help, the text is never shown to the user. Likewise, to stop displaying short fly-over help, pass a 0, which indicates no fly-text window, to `IFlyOverHelpHandler::setFlyTextControl`.

Specifying the Timer Delay

To control the display of help text, use the `IFlyOverHelpHandler` constructors to specify two time-delay intervals. The delays exist so that a user who is randomly moving the mouse (without intending to explore the user interface), does not see a series of fly-over help text windows. The `initialDelay` parameter controls the initial display of fly-over help. This is the delay between when users stop the mouse pointer over a window and when they first see the fly-over help displayed. The default `initialDelay` is 100 milliseconds. The `delay` argument controls subsequent displays of fly-over help. Its default is also 100 milliseconds.

Attaching the Fly-Over Help Handler

After you create the controls for displaying help text and the fly-over help handler, attach the handler to appropriate windows so that the handler can detect when a user positions the mouse pointer over a window or one of its child windows. If you plan to add fly-over help only to your tool bar buttons, simply attach an `IFlyOverHelpHandler` object to the tool bar.

If you plan to add fly-over help to other controls in your application, the process is more complicated. The design of fly-over help might require you to attach the handler to lower-level child windows. If you do not want to provide fly-over help for all controls on a given frame window, attach the handler to the windows that have fly-over help text further down the parent and owner chain. You might want to do this because you cannot ensure that all windows that need unique fly-over help text use unique window identifiers or because the combination of window identifiers and offsets might not identify the correct strings in all cases. See the topic "Providing Unique Window Identifiers" for further details.

Specifying Owner Windows

Before you can provide fly-over help for a window, ensure that its owner window chain leads to a window where you have attached a fly-over help handler. That window in the owner chain must also exist in the parent chain of the window for which you are providing fly-over help. Therefore, you can only provide fly-over help for child windows.

Do not expect a fly-over help handler attached to a window in the owner chain of a frame window to process fly-over help requests for the frame window. Because frame windows do not ordinarily pass the messages that the fly-over help handler uses (WM_MOUSEMOVE, WM_CONTROLPOINTER in OS/2 operating system or WM_SETCURSOR in the Windows operating system) to their parent or owner window, such a handler is not called when the mouse is over the frame window.

Using a Fly-Over Help Handler with a Mouse Handler

If you use an IFlyOverHelpHandler with an IMouseHandler, the fly-over help handler might stop working. This happens because both handlers process the same mouse messages. If you override IMouseHandler::mouseMoved or IMouseHandler::changeMousePointer, IMouseHandler can process the WM_MOUSEMOVE message and either the WM_CONTROLPOINTER message in the OS/2 operating system or the WM_SETCURSOR message in the Windows operating system. This prevents an IFlyOverHelpHandler from being called. Note that this can occur even if the mouse handler is not attached to the same window as the IFlyOverHelpHandler but is somewhere in the owner chain.

Disabling Fly-Over Help

Users may want a way to stop fly-over help after they are familiar with an application. With IFlyOverHelpHandler, you can independently disable the display of short text and long text. Call IFlyOverHelpHandler::setFlyTextControl(0) to disable short text or call IFlyOverHelpHandler::setLongTextControl(0) to disable long text. You can also call IHandler::disable to disable the handler itself, thus disabling both short and long text.

Composite Controls

A control implemented with multiple windows is a *composite control*. Typically, you program to such controls without knowing this. Composite controls appear and act as a single window. For example, the combination box is a composite control. To design a composite control, you usually expend considerable effort to make the windows behave as one window. Supporting fly-over help for such controls, such as for the composite controls that Open Class Library provides, requires additional work.

Specifying Fly-Over Help Text

The `IFlyOverHelpHandler` class gives you two ways to specify the help text it displays for a window. The first is to associate the identifier of the window with a text string in a string table resource. The second is to associate the handle of the window with a text string. Each method has its advantages and disadvantages. Note that you cannot use both techniques for the same window. For example, you cannot supply short text based on a window identifier and long text via a window handle.

Specify Fly-Over Help Based upon Window Identifiers

The fly-over help handler checks if you specified help text for the window handle before trying to load the text from a string table resource. To specify help text for a window handle, call `IFlyOverHelpHandler::setHelpText` and pass it the window handle and the short and long text strings. (You can specify the help text either as an `IString` or as an `IResourceId`.) Calling this function is the only way you can provide help text for a window without a corresponding C++ object. It is also the easiest way to display different fly-over help for windows with corresponding C++ objects that have the same window identifier. For example, in the OS/2 operating system, the child entry-field controls of combination-box controls always have a window identifier of `CBID_EDIT`.

Specify Fly-Over Help using Resource Identifiers

If you do not call `IFlyOverHelpHandler::setHelpText` for a window handle, the handler determines the fly-over help text for a window from its window identifier. This is similar to the design of `IInfoArea` that you use with menus (see Chapter 5, "Frame Window Basics," for details on the `IInfoArea` class). Like `IInfoArea`, `IFlyOverHelpHandler` reads the help text from a string table resource. `IFlyOverHelpHandler` determines the identifier of the help text string in the string table by adding a numeric offset to the identifier of the window beneath the mouse pointer. The offsets for retrieving the short and long help text strings both default to 0. Short text is displayed in a fly-over text window; long text is displayed in a text control. If you plan to show different short and long text strings, change at least one of these offsets. Call `IFlyOverHelpHandler::setFlyTextStringTableOffset` to set the offset of the short help text strings, and call `IFlyOverHelpHandler::setLongStringTableOffset` to set the offset of long help text strings.

Each `IFlyOverHelpHandler` reads text strings from a single string table resource that is loaded from a single resource library. Call `IFlyOverHelpHandler::setResourceLibrary` to specify a resource library for the handler to load these text strings. If you do not call this function, the handler loads text strings from the application resource library, which you set by calling `IApplication::current().setUserResourceLibrary()`.

Although each `IFlyOverHelpHandler` reads its strings from a single resource library, you can use more than one fly-over help handler for the same frame window. Each handler can then read its strings from a different resource library. However, this approach does not work well unless both handlers write their text to different short and long help text controls. You can do this easily for the short text because you simply construct another `IFlyText` control. The long text is more of a problem because you typically do not want to use two controls to display the long text.

Displaying Default Fly-Over Help Text

If the mouse pointer is over a window that has a fly-over help handler attached to it or a window in its parent chain, but it has no fly-over help defined for it, `IFlyOverHelpHandler` displays its default text. You can change the default text through the function `IFlyOverHelpHandler::setDefaultText`. If you do not call this function, no text is displayed as the default text.

Providing Unique Window Identifiers

Perhaps the most difficult part of setting up fly-over help strings in a string table is using window identifiers and offsets that result in a unique set of strings. This problem is further complicated by a possible conflict with the strings that `IToolBarButton` and `IInfoArea` use. If you use an `IInfoArea` window and display fly-over help by window identifiers, you must ensure that menu identifiers do not conflict with window identifiers to avoid using fly-over help strings as information text for menus.

The following sample, shown in Figure 16-7, demonstrates how to complete the following tasks:

- Specify a resource library for string resources

- Specify a short and long offset for resources

- Use text strings that are not automatically loaded from a resource library for short and long help text

Basic Fly-Over Help Implementation - toolbar\flybasic\flybasic.cpp

```
#include <iframe.hpp>
#include <ipushbut.hpp>
#include <iinfoa.hpp>
#include <iflytext.hpp>
#include <iflyhhdr.hpp>
#include <icoordsy.hpp>
#include <icanvas.hpp>
#include "flybasic.h"
```

```
void main( )
{
   ICoordinateSystem::setApplicationOrientation(
              ICoordinateSystem::originUpperLeft );
   IFrameWindow frame("Basic Fly-over Help");
   ICanvas client (IC_FRAME_CLIENT_ID, &frame, &frame);
   frame.setClient(&client);

   // Create the fly-over text for short text and an info area
   // for long text.
   IFlyText flyText(ID_FLYTEXT, &frame);
   IInfoArea infoArea(&frame);

   // Create the fly-over help handler and attach it to the
   // frame.
   IFlyOverHelpHandler flyHandler( &flyText, &infoArea);
   flyHandler.handleEventsFor(&frame);

   // Set the string table offsets into the handler.
   flyHandler.setFlyTextStringTableOffset(FLYTEXT_OFFSET);
   flyHandler.setLongStringTableOffset( LONGTEXT_OFFSET);

   // Create buttons that have fly-over and long text.  The
   // first button's text comes from the application resource
   // file and the second button's text is specified here.
   IPushButton resourceButton( ID_BUTTON1, &client, &client,
                          IRectangle(20, 100, 120, 150));
   resourceButton.setText(ID_BUTTON1);

   IPushButton textButton (ID_BUTTON2, &client, &client,
                          IRectangle(140, 100, 240, 150));
   textButton.setText( "Stop");
   flyHandler.setHelpText( textButton.handle(),
                          "Press to Stop",
                          "Press to stop the Web Browser.");

   // Show the window and start the application.
   frame
    .setFocus()
    .show();

   IApplication::current().run();

}
```

Basic Fly-Over Help Constants - toolbar\flybasic\flybasic.h

```
#define FLYTEXT_OFFSET     500
#define LONGTEXT_OFFSET    1000

#define ID_BUTTON1         1
#define ID_BUTTON2         2
#define ID_FLYTEXT         3
```

Basic Fly-Over Help Resources - toolbar\flybasic\flybasic.rc

```
#include "flybasic.h"

STRINGTABLE PRELOAD
BEGIN
   ID_BUTTON1,                 "Start"
   ID_BUTTON1+FLYTEXT_OFFSET,  "Press to start"
   ID_BUTTON1+LONGTEXT_OFFSET, "Press to start the Web Browser."
END
```

Providing Fly-Over Help for a Tool Bar

Providing additional help for tool bar buttons is perhaps one of the best uses of fly-over help for the following reasons:

- These buttons may not otherwise have text associated with them.

- By default, these buttons do not accept input focus. Therefore, a user cannot request contextual help with the F1 key.

In addition to providing fly-over help for the buttons on a tool bar, you might also consider grouping your buttons logically into different tool bars and adding help for the group of buttons by providing it for each tool bar.

If you support the ability to drag and drop menu items onto a tool bar, and if you provide fly-over help for tool bar buttons, then you also need to provide fly-over help for these tool bar buttons that a user can create.

The following example demonstrates the addition of fly-over help to a simple tool bar. It shows you how to add fly-over help for both the buttons of the tool bar and the tool bar itself.

Tool Bar Fly-Over Help - toolbar\flytbar\flytbar.cpp

```cpp
#include <iframe.hpp>
#include <ipushbut.hpp>
#include <iinfoa.hpp>
#include <iflytext.hpp>
#include <iflyhhdr.hpp>
#include <icanvas.hpp>
#include <itbar.hpp>
#include <itbarbut.hpp>
#include "flytbar.h"

void main( )
{
  // Create the frame, a canvas for the client, and
  // the tool bar.
  IFrameWindow frame("Tool Bar Fly-over Help");
  ICanvas client (IC_FRAME_CLIENT_ID, &frame, &frame);
  frame.setClient(&client);


  // Create the fly-over text for short text and an info area
  // for long text.
  IFlyText flyText(ID_FLYTEXT, &frame);
  IInfoArea infoArea(&frame);

  // Create the fly-over help handler for our own resources
  // and attach it to the frame.
  IFlyOverHelpHandler flyHandler( &flyText, &infoArea);
  flyHandler.handleEventsFor(&frame);

  // Set the string table offsets for our resources.
  flyHandler.setFlyTextStringTableOffset(FLYTEXT_OFFSET);
  flyHandler.setLongStringTableOffset( LONGTEXT_OFFSET);


  // Create a tool bar for edit controls.
  IToolBar editToolBar (ID_EDITTOOLBAR, &frame);
```

```
   // Create the edit buttons from IOC-supplied tool bar
   // buttons and add them to the tool bar.
   IToolBarButton cut(IC_ID_CUT, &editToolBar, &editToolBar);
   IToolBarButton copy(IC_ID_COPY, &editToolBar, &editToolBar);
   IToolBarButton paste(IC_ID_PASTE, &editToolBar, &editToolBar);
   editToolBar
     .addAsLast(&cut)
     .addAsLast(&copy)
     .addAsLast(&paste);

   // Create a special application tool bar.
   IToolBar launchToolBar (ID_LAUNCHTOOLBAR, &editToolBar, true);

   // Create a tool bar button of our own and add it
   // to the tool bar.
   IToolBarButton launchBrowser
         (ID_LAUNCHWEB, &launchToolBar, &launchToolBar);
   launchToolBar.addAsLast (&launchBrowser);

   // Show the window and start the application.
   frame
     .setFocus()
     .show();

   IApplication::current().run();

}
```

Tool Bar Fly-Over Help - toolbar\flytbar\flytbar.h

```
#define FLYTEXT_OFFSET      500
#define LONGTEXT_OFFSET    1000

#define ID_EDITTOOLBAR       1
#define ID_LAUNCHTOOLBAR     2
#define ID_FLYTEXT           3
#define ID_LAUNCHWEB         4
```

Tool Bar Fly-Over Help - toolbar\flytbar\flytbar.rc

```
#include <icconst.h>
#include "flytbar.h"

STRINGTABLE PRELOAD
BEGIN
   ID_EDITTOOLBAR,                    ""
   ID_EDITTOOLBAR+FLYTEXT_OFFSET,   "Editing Tools"
   ID_EDITTOOLBAR+LONGTEXT_OFFSET,  "Tools used to transfer data
                                     to and from the clipboard"
   IC_ID_CUT,                "Cut"
   IC_ID_COPY,               "Copy"
   IC_ID_PASTE,              "Paste"
   IC_ID_CUT+FLYTEXT_OFFSET,    "Cut selected text to clipboard"
   IC_ID_COPY+FLYTEXT_OFFSET,   "Copy selected test to clipboard"
   IC_ID_PASTE+FLYTEXT_OFFSET,  "Paste from clipboard to cursor"
   IC_ID_CUT+LONGTEXT_OFFSET,    "Removes text with selection
                                 emphasis from document and stores
                                 it in the system clipboard."
   IC_ID_COPY+LONGTEXT_OFFSET,   "Copies text with selection
                                 emphasis from document and stores
                                 it in the system clipboard."
   IC_ID_PASTE+LONGTEXT_OFFSET, "Pastes text from the system
                                 clipboard to the cursor location in
                                 the document."
   ID_LAUNCHTOOLBAR,                  ""
   ID_LAUNCHTOOLBAR+FLYTEXT_OFFSET,"Start external applications"
   ID_LAUNCHTOOLBAR+LONGTEXT_OFFSET, "Starts tools that run
                                 outside of the document."
```

```
    ID_LAUNCHWEB,                    "Web Browser"
    ID_LAUNCHWEB+FLYTEXT_OFFSET   "Press to Start Web Browser"
    ID_LAUNCHWEB+LONGTEXT_OFFSET  "Press to start web browser"
END

#ifdef IC_PM /* PM resources */
BITMAP   ID_LAUNCHWEB     web.bmp

#else    /* Windows resources */
ID_LAUNCHWEB  BITMAP      web.bmp
#endif
```

Custom Buttons

Custom buttons are buttons that you can use to replace or extend the drawing for a button while retaining the button behavior of a push button. Open Class Library provides this capability in the `ICustomButton` and `ICustomButtonDrawHandler` classes. In fact, `IToolBarButton` achieves most of its specialized drawing by deriving from `ICustomButton`.

`ICustomButton` adds several features not found in push buttons, and you do not need to derive from `ICustomButton` to use them. For example, `ICustomButton` supports latching a button like you do with `IToolBarButton`. In fact, `IToolBarButton` directly inherits its latch behavior from `ICustomButton`.

`ICustomButton` also examines its text for newline ("\n") characters and flows characters that follow to the next line. `ICustomButton::calcMinimumSize` uses this information to determine the size of the window needed to contain these multiple lines of text. If you include `ICustomButtons` in a canvas class that allows child windows to determine their size, it automatically sizes itself around its text.

`ICustomButton` also draws its borders in a 3D style.

The following example demonstrates how to create an `ICustomButton` with multiple lines of text and latching behavior. Figure 16-8 displays the results of this example.

Simple Custom Button Example - toolbar\cbutsimp\cbutsimp.cpp

```cpp
#include <iframe.hpp>
#include <ianimbut.hpp>
#include <isetcv.hpp>
#include <iapp.hpp>
#include <icconst.h>

void main()
{
IFrameWindow
  frame ("Simple Custom Button Example");

// Create a set canvas for the client area.
ISetCanvas
  client(IC_FRAME_CLIENT_ID, &frame, &frame);

// Create the custom button as a latchable button.
ICustomButton
  customButton(11, &client, &client);

customButton
  .enableLatching()
  .setText("This is a \n latchable \n custom button!");
```

```
// Put the canvas in the client area and show the application.
frame
  .setClient(&client)
  .setFocus()
  .show();
IApplication::current().run();

}
```

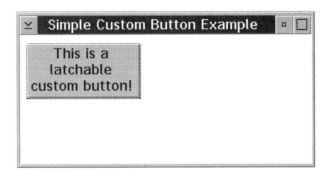

Figure 16-8. Simple Custom Button Example.

Building Enhanced Custom Buttons

Even though ICustomButton is a useful button as is, its real purpose is to allow you to code your own custom drawing for a button. You do so by deriving from ICustomButtonDrawHandler and overloading one or all of its virtual functions. You then attach your new class to ICustomButton. Depending upon how much of the drawing behavior of ICustomButtonDrawHandler you'd like to change, you might also need to derive from ICustomButton. For example, if you want to do anything that changes the size of the window for the button, you need to override ICustomButton::calcMinimumSize so that your button correctly determines its size for canvas windows.

When ICustomButtonDrawHandler detects that an ICustomButton needs to be drawn, it calls ICustomButtonDrawHandler::drawButton to handle the drawing. ICustomButtonDrawHandler::drawButton calls, in order, drawBorder, drawBackground, and drawForeground. Then, if the button is disabled, it calls drawDisabledEmphasis.

In addition to drawing the border, ICustomButtonDrawHandler::drawBorder shrinks the drawing area by the size of the border and the margin. It does this by calling ICustomButtonDrawEvent::setDrawingArea with the size of the new drawing area. Because of this change to the drawing area, you do not need to know the size of the border when you draw the background and foreground.

In the **toolbar\cbuthdr** program on the examples disk, we demonstrate how to extend a custom button to change its drawing behavior. The example adds a bitmap to the text for the button and changes the bitmap as it toggles between latched and unlatched. Because we have increased the size of the custom button by the size of our bitmap, we derive from ICustomButton to change its minimum size calculation and to store our latched and unlatched bitmaps. To draw the bitmap, we only need to override a single function,

`ICustomButtonDrawHandler::drawForeground`, to draw our bitmap onto the button. Because we want to utilize the ability of `drawForeground` to split the text over multiple lines, we first draw our bitmap, and then we reduce the size of the drawing area by the size of our bitmap and call the inherited member `drawForeground` to draw the text.

Animated Buttons

`IAnimatedButton` extends `ICustomButton` to provide a simple but limited method for drawing *animated push buttons*. Animated buttons show motion by continuously displaying a set of graphic images. You provide `IAnimatedButton` with a set of bitmaps to define these graphic images. When you activate animation, the button cycles through the set and draws each bitmap on a time interval.

Specify the bitmaps for `IAnimatedButton` by providing an `IResourceId` for the first button you want to display and the count of all bitmaps. The numeric identifiers of the additional bitmaps must be in exact numeric order following the first bitmap, and they must be in the same resource library.

Call `IAnimatedButton::setAnimationRate` to change the time interval. The default animation rate is one per second.

Open Class Library also provides a number of animated buttons that you can use. Call `AnimatedButton::setBitmaps` with one of the values of the enumeration `IAnimatedButton::AnimatedButtons`.

The **toolbar\animated** program on the examples disk demonstrates how to create animated buttons using bitmaps in a resource file and how to create animated buttons using the animation buttons that Open Class Library provides.

Location of Example Code for Figures

Many of the figures in this chapter are screen captures of example programs not included in this chapter. Table 16-3 describes where you can find this code on the examples disk provided with the book.

Table 16-3. Location of Example Programs for Figures

Sample Location	Figure	Figure Description
samples\toolbar\tbarlocs	16-2	Tool Bar Locations in the Windows and OS/2 Operating Systems
samples\toolbar\tbarfrms	16-3	Buttons in Floating Tool Bar Frame Windows
samples\toolbar\tbargrps	16-4	Using Group Pad with Tool Bar Buttons
samples\toolbar\tbardeck	16-5	Tool Bar to the Left of the Client with Two Decks
samples\toolbar\tbarmult	16-6	Multiple Tool Bars to the Left of the Client

Chapter 17

Reusable Handlers

- Describes the event handler classes in Open Class Library that can be used with almost any of the window classes
- Describes the ICommandHandler, ICommandConnectionTo<>, ICommandEvent, IKeyboardHandler, IKeyboardConnectionTo<>, IKeyboardEvent, IMouseHandler, IMouseConnectionTo<>, IMouseEvent, IMouseClickEvent, IMousePointerEvent, IPaintHandler, IPaintConnectionTo<>, IPaintEvent, IResizeHandler, and IResizeEvent classes
- Read Chapter 4 before reading this chapter.
- Chapters 5, 6, 9-16, 19, and 22-24 cover related material.

The windows and controls you can create with Open Class Library provide standard behavior that will suit most of your needs. Still, you will find occasions when you need to use event handler classes to modify or extend this default behavior. Chapter 4, "Windows, Handlers, and Events," describes the architecture for event processing in Open Class Library.

This chapter describes event handler classes that you can use with any class in the IWindow class hierarchy and their corresponding event classes. These handler classes are as follows:

- Command handler (ICommandHandler and ICommandConnectionTo<>)
- Keyboard handler (IKeyboardHandler and IKeyboardConnectionTo<>)
- Mouse handler (IMouseHandler and IMouseConnectionTo<>)
- Window-paint handler (IPaintHandler and IPaintConnectionTo<>)
- Window-size handler (IResizeHandler)

At the time of this writing, the handler template classes—ICommandConnectionTo, IKeyboardConnectionTo, IMouseConnectionTo, and IPaintConnectionTo—were not available in VisualAge for C++ for OS/2, 3.0.

We describe other event handler classes in the following chapters:

- Chapter 6, "Menus and Keyboard Accelerators," for IMenuHandler and IMenuDrawItemHandler

- Chapters 9-12 for control-related handlers, including IEditHandler, ISelectHandler, IListBoxDrawItemHandler, ISliderArmHandler, and others

- Chapter 13, "Container Control," for container-specific handlers

- Chapter 14, "Notebook Control," for IPageHandler

- Chapter 16, "Tool Bars, Fly-Over Help, and Custom Buttons," for `IFlyOverHelpHandler`

- Chapter 19, "Advanced Frame Window Topics," for `IFrameHandler`

- Chapter 21, "Direct Manipulation," for drag and drop handlers

- Chapter 22, "Dynamic Data Exchange Framework," for `IDDEClientConversation` and `IDDETopicServer`

- Chapter 23, "Using Help," for `IHelpHandler`

Command Handler

As described in Chapter 2, "Object-Oriented User Interface Fundamentals," an object-oriented user interface presents visual objects to the user. A user performs tasks by acting on those objects, such as selecting a menu choice. A number of these actions result in command events in Open Class Library.

The `ICommandHandler` class provides a structured means for processing command events. Command processing represents a higher level of abstraction than responding directly to the user-interface events that generate command events. A command event can result from a user selecting a choice from a menu bar or pop-up menu, from pressing an accelerator key, or from selecting a push button. We describe these three sources of command events in Chapter 6, "Menus and Keyboard Accelerators," and Chapter 10, "Button Controls." Typically, command processing takes place at a frame window or its client window.

Open Class Library represents command events with the `ICommandEvent` class. A command can be either a *system command* or an *application command*. The operating system defines and typically processes a system command. An example is the Close command that a user invokes by selecting the **Close** choice from the system menu or pressing the Alt+F4 accelerator key. This command closes a frame window. An application defines its own application commands and must provide their implementation as well. An example is an Open or Save command, which has a specific meaning to your application. When you create a menu item, accelerator key, or push button that runs a command, you also identify if the command is a system command.

To provide an implementation for an application or a system command, use the `ICommandHandler` class or the template class `ICommandConnectionTo`, which derives from it.

Querying Command Information

To process a command, a command handler (or the function called by an `ICommandConnectionTo` object) relies on the information available from the `ICommandEvent` object it receives. This object represents a command invoked by a user or the application.

The `ICommandEvent::commandId` function returns the identifier for the command. The *command identifier* matches the identifier of the user-interface element that generates the command. For example, if a user selects a menu choice, the identifier of the menu item is the identifier of the resulting command.

The `ICommandEvent::source` function returns an enumeration that identifies whether a user invoked the command using a menu item, accelerator key, or push button. This information, however, probably does not alter how you process a command.

Using ICommandHandler

To use the `ICommandHandler` class, create a class derived from it. In your derived class, provide an implementation for one or more of the virtual functions of `ICommandHandler`. Override the `command` virtual function to process application commands and override `systemCommand` to process system commands. Both functions are passed a reference to an `ICommandEvent` object that identifies the command and how it was invoked.

An example of a simple command handler follows.

Simple Command Handler Example - genhdrs\cmdhdrs\cmdhdr1.hpp

```
#include <ibase.hpp>          // For IC_PM/IC_WIN.
#ifdef IC_PM
  #define INCL_DOSPROCESS     // For DosBeep.
  #include <os2.h>
  #define BEEP(frequency,duration) (DosBeep(frequency,duration))
#else
  #include <windows.h>        // For Beep.
  #define BEEP(frequency,duration) (Beep(frequency,duration))
#endif

#include <icmdhdr.hpp>
#include "cmdhdrs.h"

class OneBeepCmdHandler : public ICommandHandler {
protected:
virtual Boolean
  command ( ICommandEvent& event )
  {
    Boolean dontPassOn = false;
    if ( event.commandId() == ID_ONE_BEEP_CMD )
    {
      BEEP( 100, 100 );
      dontPassOn = true;
    }
    return dontPassOn;
  }
}; // OneBeepCmdHandler
```

Using ICommandConnectionTo

An alternative to deriving from `ICommandHandler` and overriding the `command` and `systemCommand` functions is to use the template class `ICommandConnectionTo`. Use this class to locate the code that processes a command in any class, rather than one derived from `ICommandHandler`. For example, you can use this support to add command processing to a class derived from `IWindow` without having to multiply inherit from `ICommandHandler` and without having to create a protocol for a command handler to access data in the window class. You can simplify design issues by using this class, although your command processing code likely will not be reusable (command processing code generally is not very reusable because it tends to be closely tied to window data anyway).

To use the ICommandConnectionTo class, instantiate the ICommandConnectionTo template and create an object of the new template class. The constructor requires that you pass it an object of the class you used to instantiate the template class and a member function of the object. The member function must accept a reference to an ICommandEvent object as its only argument. When Open Class Library calls an ICommandConnectionTo object to process a command event, the template object calls the member function of the object you specified when you constructed it. It calls this member function to handle both application and system commands. Unfortunately, an ICommandEvent object does not identify whether it represents an application or system command. As with a conventional command handler, you attach an ICommandConnectionTo object to a window by calling its handleEventsFor function.

The **cmdhdrs\enablcmd** example, which appears in the "Disabling Commands" topic later in this chapter, uses the ICommandConnectionTo class.

Application Commands

Open Class Library reserves a number of application command identifiers, mostly for predefined tool bar buttons. These command identifiers are defined in both ICCONST.H (such as IC_ID_OPEN) and ICMD.HPP (such as ICommand::kOpenId). Because the values in ICCONST.H are known at compile time, you can use them in switch statements and resource files. These commands all have identifiers greater than IC_ID_BASE (0x7000). Open Class Library leaves the implementation of these commands to your application, because their meaning is specific to an application.

As you learned in the topic, "Using Dialog Template Resources," in Chapter 5, "Frame Window Basics," Open Class Library ignores application commands that are not processed by a command handler. Therefore, if you display a window using the IFrameWindow class and a user invokes a command that your application does not explicitly process, no action occurs.

System Commands

Table 17-1 shows the system commands supported by both the Windows and OS/2 operating systems. Chapter 6, "Menus and Keyboard Accelerators," lists the system commands that appear on a default system menu.

Because the operating system provides an implementation for its system commands, you do not need a command handler to get default processing for them. However, if you provide a command handler and override the systemCommand function, you can replace the default processing. By returning a value of true from systemCommand, you prevent the operating system from processing the command. The Close system command, which corresponds to ISystemMenu::idClose, ICommand::kCloseId, and IC_ID_CLOSE, is typically the only one you might need to process. Chapter 5, "Frame Window Basics," provides an example of doing that.

Avoid using system commands outside of the system menu. The Windows operating system does not support this, and Open Class Library on the Windows platform only supports the Close system command on menu bars or pop-up menus. For a Windows application, Open Class Library supports the OS/2 model of running system commands from push buttons and

Table 17-1. Portable System Commands

Command Identifier		Default Action
icconst.h Value	**ICommand Value**	
IC_ID_CLOSE	kCloseId	Closes the frame window
IC_ID_MOVE	kMoveId	Allows a user to move the frame window using the keyboard or mouse
IC_ID_SIZE	kSizeId	Allows a user to size the frame window using the keyboard or mouse
IC_ID_MINIMIZE	kMinimizeId	Minimizes the frame window if it has a minimize button next to its title bar
IC_ID_MAXIMIZE	kMaximizeId	Maximizes the frame window if it has a maximize button next to its title bar
IC_ID_RESTORE	kRestoreId	Restores the frame to its previous size and position if it is minimized or maximized
IC_ID_SYSHIDE	kHideId	Hides the frame window (minimizes the frame window in the Windows operating system)

accelerator keys, but only if you enable system command support through the `IPushButton` and `IAcceleratorKey` classes.

Also, avoid trying to define your own system commands. The Windows operating system does not support this. Even in the OS/2 operating system, your system command is essentially an application command because the system does not provide any default behavior for it.

Routing of Command Events

Push buttons, menu items, and accelerator keys generate command events differently. A push button routes a command event to its owner window. A menu item routes a command event to the owner of the menu, which is typically a frame window. An accelerator key causes a command event to be routed to the window owning the accelerator table, which also is typically a frame window.

`ICanvas`, its derived classes, and `IContainerControl` (if it has an `ICnrMenuHandler` attached to it) forward command events that they receive to their owner windows. A frame window forwards all unprocessed application commands to its client window. Although it processes all system commands itself, a frame window also sends a Close system command to its client window as a notification whenever it closes. No other type of window forwards command events to another window.

These rules are the basis for choosing where to attach a command handler.

Attaching a Command Handler

Generally, the best window to attach a command handler to is a frame window or its client window. Therefore, you can use these windows as focal points for processing command events, regardless of their source. Call a handler's `handleEventsFor` function to attach the handler to a window.

Most command handlers work equally well at either window. However, if your frame window has no client window, attach your command handler to the frame window. If your command handler processes system commands other than Close, attach it to the frame window. If the client window is not an `ICanvas`, one of its derived classes, or an `IContainerControl` with an `ICnrMenuHandler` attached to it, attach the command handler to the client window. If the last two criteria apply, you may need to attach your command handler to both windows or split it into two classes.

You can also define commands and command handlers that are specific to a particular control. For example, by creating a pop-up menu or accelerator table owned by a control you can cause command events to be routed directly to that control. Controls do not generally pass the command events that they receive to any other window. To process these commands, attach a command handler to the control itself.

Avoiding Potential Pitfalls

Some subtle problems can cause your command handling to go awry. The following topics describe these.

Conflicts with Other Classes

Both the `ICnrMenuHandler` and `IFrameHandler` classes conduct specialized processing of command events. `ICnrMenuHandler` causes a container to forward command events to its owner window. `IFrameHandler` causes a frame window to forward command events to its client window. As a result, these handlers can prevent command handlers that are attached to a frame or container window from receiving a command event.

Consider this processing if you attach a command handler and either an `ICnrMenuHandler` or `IFrameHandler` to the same window. Once the event dispatcher of Open Class Library calls `ICnrMenuHandler` or `IFrameHandler` to process a command event, it does not call any subsequent handlers, including command handlers, attached to the same window. Therefore, if you are using a container menu handler (and the container is not a client window) or your own frame handler, attach all command handlers *after* it so that the command handlers are called *before* it. The **genhdrs\cmdhdrs** program on the example disk shows this technique.

Generating Your Own Command Events

You can invoke command processing from your application by explicitly sending or posting a command event. Send and post events using the `sendEvent` and `postEvent` functions of `IWindow` or `IWindowHandle`. To create an application command event, specify an event identifier of WM_COMMAND or the IWindow::EventType enumeration, IWindow::command. To create a system command event, specify an event identifier of WM_SYSCOMMAND (or the IWindow::EventType enumeration, IWindow::systemCommand). Match the format of the event parameters to the message parameters documented by the operating system for the WM_COMMAND and WM_SYSCOMMAND messages.

The Windows and OS/2 operating systems require the message parameter data to be in different formats. For example, in the Windows operating system, the IEventParameter2 value must be 0 so that it can be distinguished from a control notification message, which also uses WM_COMMAND for its message identifier. The OS/2 operating system stores flags in IEventParameter2.

An example of how to send your own command event follows.

Simple Command Handler - genhdrs\cmdhdrs\cmdhdr2.hpp

```
#include <ibase.hpp>          // For IC_WIN/IC_PM.
#ifdef IC_PM
  #define INCL_DOSPROCESS     // For DosBeep.
  #define INCL_WINWINDOWMGR   // For CMDSRC_OTHER.
  #include <os2.h>
  #define BEEP(frequency,duration) (DosBeep(frequency,duration))
#else
  #include <windows.h>        // For Beep.
  #define BEEP(frequency,duration) (Beep(frequency,duration))
#endif

#include <icmdhdr.hpp>
#include "cmdhdrs.h"

class TwoBeepCmdHandler : public ICommandHandler {
protected:
virtual Boolean
  command ( ICommandEvent& event )
  {
    Boolean dontPassOn = false;
    if ( event.commandId() == ID_TWO_BEEP_CMD )
    {
      // Issue the first beep; then send a command event to
      // invoke another command handler to do the second beep.
      BEEP( 200, 100 );
      event.window()
        ->sendEvent( IWindow::command,
#ifdef IC_PM
                     IEventParameter1( ID_ONE_BEEP_CMD ),
                     IEventParameter2( CMDSRC_OTHER, false ) );
#else
                     IEventParameter1( ID_ONE_BEEP_CMD, 3 ),
                     IEventParameter2( 0 ) );
#endif
      dontPassOn = true;
    }
    return dontPassOn;
  }
}; // TwoBeepCmdHandler
```

Because command events are relatively easy to send and because command handlers are easy to create, you may be tempted to use a command event as a general notification event. Resist doing this. Instead, use either an application-defined event and event handler class or the notification framework.

There are several reasons for not using command events for this purpose. First, Open Class Library treats the field that identifies the source of the command (the high word of `IEventParameter1` in the Windows operating system or the low word of the `IEventParameter2` value in the OS/2 operating system) as if it contains only that value instead of data that you choose. Open Class Library reserves the high-order bit of that field when it processes application and system commands. If you must store an unconventional value in this field (not a source value documented for `WM_COMMAND` or `WM_SYSCOMMAND` messages), send or post the command event directly to the window that has the command handler attached to it so that it processes the command. If you allow the command event to be passed from a canvas or container client window to the frame or from a frame window to its client window, Open Class Library alters the value in this field before your command handler receives it. If the value you store has the high-order bit set, the frame window does not route the command event to its client window as it normally does.

Second, in the Windows operating system, if you store a non-zero value in `IEventParameter2`, Open Class Library does not call command handlers to process the event. The event instead represents a control notification event, which may cause Open Class Library to call an edit handler or select handler to process the event.

Third, in the OS/2 operating system, a frame window discards command events while a user is moving or sizing it. As a result, a command handler (especially if it is attached to the frame window) may never be called to process a command event posted to it from another thread, depending on the user's actions.

Disabling Commands

You must synchronize the availability of a command across all of its possible sources. Open Class Library does not handle this; the operating system handles some but not all cases.

To disable a command, disable all menu items and push buttons that run that command. By disabling a menu choice or push button, you not only give a user a visual indication that the command is not available, but you also prevent the menu choice or push button from generating a command event.

The other command source you need to handle is an accelerator key. Both the Windows and OS/2 operating systems enable and disable accelerator keys that run application commands whenever an item in the menu bar that runs the same command is enabled or disabled. This support does not help you if you are not using a menu bar or the accelerator key you want to disable does not have a corresponding item in the menu bar. In these cases, consider notifying the appropriate command handler not to process the command that you want to disable, or consider using the `IAcceleratorTable` and `IAcceleratorKey` classes to remove the accelerator key from the window.

Generally, the operating system manages the availability of system commands. For example, it disables the Maximize system command when a frame window is maximized. The Windows and OS/2 operating systems, however, do not handle accelerator keys that generate a system command as effectively as accelerators that generate application commands. Both discard a disabled system command that a user invokes with an accelerator key—but only after generating a WM_SYSCOMMAND message that Open Class Library processes by calling your command handlers. If you process system commands, add the appropriate checks to determine if the system command is enabled or disabled. If you have a push button that runs a system command, you similarly need to decide when to enable and disable the push button.

The following example enables and disables the Close system command. When a user selects a push button, the ICommandConnectionTo object calls the CloseTestWindow::processCommand function to process the resulting command. Note that this function can still be called to process a Close system command (IC_ID_CLOSE) invoked by pressing Alt+F4, even after the application disables the **Close** choice in the system menu.

Enabling and Disabling the Close Command - genhdrs\enablcls\enablcls.cpp

```cpp
#include <iapp.hpp>
#include <icmdhdr.hpp>
#include <iframe.hpp>
#include <imnitem.hpp>
#include <imsgbox.hpp>
#include <ipushbut.hpp>
#include <isetcv.hpp>
#include <istattxt.hpp>
#include <isysmenu.hpp>
#include <icconst.h>

#ifdef IC_PM
  // Define the system command identifier not originally
  // included in VisualAge for C++ for OS/2, V3.0.
  #ifndef IC_ID_CLOSE
    #define IC_ID_CLOSE  0x8004
  #endif
#endif

#define ID_TOGGLE_CLOSE  100

class CloseTestWindow : public IFrameWindow {
public:
  CloseTestWindow ( );
protected:
Boolean
  processCommand ( ICommandEvent& event );
private:
  CloseTestWindow ( const CloseTestWindow& );
CloseTestWindow
 &operator=          ( const CloseTestWindow& );
IStaticText
  instructions;
ISetCanvas
  buttons;
IPushButton
  closeButton,
  enableDisableButton;
ISystemMenu
  systemMenu;
ICommandConnectionTo< CloseTestWindow >
  cmdConnection;
static const IString
  closeInstructions,
  cannotCloseInstructions,
  enableCloseString,
  disableCloseString;
}; // CloseTestWindow
```

```
void main ( )
{
  CloseTestWindow
    frame;
  frame
    .setFocus()
    .show();
  IApplication::current().run();
}

const IString
  CloseTestWindow::closeInstructions( "You can close the window."
                        "  However, try disabling the Close command." ),
  CloseTestWindow::cannotCloseInstructions( "You cannot close the"
                        " window until you enable the Close command." ),
  CloseTestWindow::enableCloseString( "Enable the Close Command" ),
  CloseTestWindow::disableCloseString( "Disable the Close Command" );

CloseTestWindow::CloseTestWindow ( )
  : IFrameWindow( "Disabling the Close System Command" ),
    instructions( IC_FRAME_CLIENT_ID, this, this ),
    buttons( 1, this, this ),
    closeButton( IC_ID_CLOSE, &buttons, &buttons ),
    enableDisableButton( ID_TOGGLE_CLOSE, &buttons, &buttons ),
    systemMenu( this ),
    cmdConnection( *this, CloseTestWindow::processCommand )
{
  instructions
    .setText( closeInstructions );
  closeButton
    .enableSystemCommand()
    .enableDefault()
    .setText( "Close the Window" )
    .enableTabStop()
    .enableGroup();
  enableDisableButton
    .setText( disableCloseString );
  cmdConnection
    .handleEventsFor( this );

  (*this)
    .setClient( &instructions )
    .addExtension( &buttons, IFrameWindow::belowClient );
}

// This is the function that the ICommandConnectionTo<> object calls.
IBase::Boolean
  CloseTestWindow::processCommand ( ICommandEvent& event )
{
  Boolean
    stopProcessingEvent = false;
  switch ( event.commandId() )
  {
    case IC_ID_CLOSE:
    {    // Assume this is a system command.
      IMessageBox
        msgBox( this );
      const char
        *text;

      // When the Close system menu item is disabled, our command
      // handler usually is not called to process this system
      // command.  However, it is called when a user presses an
      // accelerator key for the Close command (Alt+F4)--even
      // though the system eventually ignores this request.  So
      // we must check if the system menu choice is disabled before
      // processing the Close command.
```

```
          if ( systemMenu.isItemEnabled( IC_ID_CLOSE ) )
          {      // Close is enabled.
             text = "The window is closing.  Select OK to continue.";
          }
          else
          {
             text = "The Close command is disabled.  You must enable"
                   " it to close the window.";
          }

          msgBox
            .show( text,
                   IMessageBox::okButton
                 | IMessageBox::informationIcon
                 | IMessageBox::moveable );
          break;
        }
        case ID_TOGGLE_CLOSE:
        {      // Assume that this is an application command.
          // Toggle the enabled state of Close on the system menu.
          Boolean
            enableClose = ! systemMenu.isItemEnabled( IC_ID_CLOSE );
                   // Negate the current state.
          systemMenu
            .enableItem( IC_ID_CLOSE, enableClose );

          // Toggle the enabled state of the Close button.
          closeButton
            .enable( enableClose );
          instructions
            .setText( enableClose ? closeInstructions :
                                    cannotCloseInstructions );
          enableDisableButton
            .setText( enableClose ? disableCloseString :
                                    enableCloseString );

          stopProcessingEvent = true;
          break;
        }
        default:
          break;
      }
    return stopProcessingEvent;
}
```

When a Command Handler Is Not Called

In the Windows and OS/2 operating systems, a user can get the effect of running a system command by using direct manipulation. In these cases, a user does not actually invoke a system command, so a command handler is not called to process these actions. For example, a user can size a frame window by dragging its sizing border with the mouse. This action bypasses the **Size** choice on the system menu. A user can also move a frame window by dragging its title bar with the mouse, bypassing the Move system command.

The Windows operating system also uses WM_COMMAND messages for control notifications (in place of the WM_CONTROL message used by the OS/2 operating system). However, command handlers do not process these notifications. Use control-specific event handlers, such as IEditHandler and ISelectHandler, to process these events.

Keyboard Handler

Use a keyboard handler to process the individual keystrokes that a window receives. With this capability, you can alter the way any window processes keyboard input. For example, you can restrict the characters that an entry field accepts or provide specialized cursor movement in or between controls. Open Class Library supplies this support through the classes IKeyboardHandler, IKeyboardConnectionTo, and IKeyboardEvent.

A keyboard handler, however, does not process some keys well. Generally, these keys relate to command processing, or users can configure them as part of their system so you cannot hardcode them in your application. Table 17-2 shows some of these keys and how you can process them.

For example, you may want a user to press F5 to run a Refresh command, or Ctrl+O to run an Open command. The use of a keyboard handler to process these keys may seem an obvious solution for implementing this support. However, it is better to implement such command keys as accelerator keys whose resulting command actions you can then process with a command handler. If you later decide to let a user run the same command from the menu bar or a pop-up menu, you already have the code to process the command in place.

A keyboard handler is not called when a user presses an accelerator key. These events are converted immediately into command events.

Table 17-2. Keys Best Handled with Other than a Keyboard Handler

Key	Recommended Handler	Notes
Enter (to run a command)	ICommandHandler	The handler is only called if you have a default push button.
Enter (to open a container object)	ICnrHandler	The handler is also called when the user double-clicks a container object.
Esc (to close a window)	ICommandHandler	The handler is only called if you have an entry for the key in an accelerator table.
Other keys to run actions (such as Ctrl+O to run an open command)	ICommandHandler	The handler is only called if you have an entry for the key in an accelerator table.
F1 (to request help)	None	Your application can satisfy these help requests using help resource tables or the IWindow::setHelpId function (see Chapter 23, "Using Help," for more information).
Shift+F10 (to display a pop-up menu in the OS/2 operating system)	IMenuHandler ICnrMenuHandler	These handlers are also called when a user uses a mouse to request a pop-up menu. The OS/2 operating system allows a user to configure this combination of keys.
Keys to select a button, menu item, or notebook tab	None	Specify a character in the text of the button, menu item, or notebook tab to be a mnemonic.

Using IKeyboardHandler

To use the IKeyboardHandler class, create your own class derived from it and implement one or more of its virtual functions. Using these virtual functions, you can process common types of keyboard events as well as any and all keyboard events. Each of these functions is passed a reference to an IKeyboardEvent object that identifies the key (or combination of keys) being pressed or released. These functions are scanCodeKeyPress, virtualKeyPress, characterKeyPress, and key.

A keyboard handler can call more than one of its virtual functions to process a keyboard event. However, it only calls those virtual functions that are appropriate for the event. For example, IKeyboardHandler only calls its key function to process a key release; it calls its other virtual functions only to process a key press. A keyboard handler calls its virtual functions in the following order.

1. scanCodeKeyPress
2. virtualKeyPress
3. characterKeyPress
4. key

If you return a value of true from any of these virtual functions, Open Class Library does not pass the event on to any other virtual functions of your keyboard handler or to any other handlers for additional processing.

Using IKeyboardConnectionTo

An alternative to deriving from IKeyboardHandler and overriding its virtual functions is to use the template class IKeyboardConnectionTo. The relationship between this class and IKeyboardHandler is the same as between ICommandHandler and ICommandConnectionTo.

Key Press vs. Key Release

A key can be in one of four states, as shown in the diagram below: (1) up, (2) moving from an up state to a down state, (3) held down, and (4) moving from a down state to an up state.

The diagram also shows the type of keyboard event (press or release) associated with each key state. A key press event occurs when a key is in the up-to-down transition or is held down to generate repeated key presses. A key release event occurs when a key is in the down-to-up transition. No keyboard event is generated as a result of a key being in an up state.

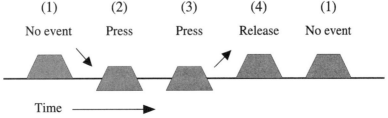

To use the IKeyboardConnectionTo class, instantiate the IKeyboardConnectionTo template and create an object of the new template class. The constructor requires you pass it an object of the class you used to instantiate the template class and up to two member functions of that object. One member function is for processing presses of character keys; the other is for presses of virtual keys. The member functions must accept a reference to an IKeyboardEvent object as their only argument. As with a conventional keyboard handler, you attach an IKeyboardConnectionTo object to a window by calling the object's handleEventsFor function. When Open Class Library calls an IKeyboardConnectionTo object to process the press of a character or virtual key, the object calls the appropriate member function of the object you specified when you constructed it.

Processing Keyboard Events

Keyboard handlers receive a reference to an IKeyboardEvent object. This object identifies the key and determines if it was pressed or released. You can process a keyboard event using either the IKeyboardHandler or IKeyboardConnectionTo class.

The value returned by the keyboard handler determines whether Open Class Library allows any additional processing for the event. If you return a value of true, Open Class Library does not pass the event on to another function of the keyboard handler or to any other handlers for additional processing.

Note that Open Class Library calls a keyboard handler to process a key before the window receives it and attempts to validate it. As a result, your keyboard handler is called to process key events that the window may later discard. For example, an entry field discards character keys that would cause the contents of the control to exceed its text limit. As a result, depending on the purpose of your keyboard handler, you may need to duplicate the control's validation logic.

Character Key Press

An IKeyboardHandler object calls its characterKeyPress virtual function to process the press of a *character key*, a key with an ASCII character code. Because you focus on character data when using the characterKeyPress function, this may be the virtual function of IKeyboardHandler you override the most. Character data typically is the most important information that your application's data objects, such as customer objects, collect from the users. You can also process a key press that has an associated character code using the IKeyboardConnectionTo class.

Although the Esc, Enter, Tab, Shift+Tab, and destructive backspace keys are keys with character codes, process these key presses with the virtualKeyPress function instead of the characterKeyPress function.

You can call the character or mixedCharacter function of IKeyboardEvent to retrieve the character code of the key that a user pressed. You can only call the IKeyboardEvent::character function to process single-byte data. If you call this function and the character is more than one byte, it throws an IInvalidRequest exception. Before your program can process multi-byte keyboard input, such as when a user is running your application on a Japanese, Chinese, or Korean version of the operating system, you must call the `IKeyboardEvent::mixedCharacter` function. `mixedCharacter` can return either a single-byte or multi-byte character. To determine the type of character, check the length of the character string or test the character using the `IString::isSBCS` or `IString::isDBCS` function.

Note that a keyboard handler handles some Ctrl key combinations differently in the Windows and OS/2 operating systems. For example, pressing Ctrl+h on the Windows operating system causes the `virtualKeyPress` function to be called (the virtual key is `IKeyboardEvent::backSpace` and `IKeyboardEvent::isCtrlDown` returns true). In the OS/2 operating system, pressing Ctrl+h causes the `characterKeyPress` function to be called (the character is **h** and `IKeyboardEvent::isCtrlDown` returns true). The difference reflects different keyboard models in the two operating systems.

The following code shows two examples of keyboard handlers that use `characterKeyPress` to provide specialized processing for character data. The first limits the character data that a user types to hexadecimal digits. The second converts lowercase characters to uppercase as a user types. Both keyboard handlers show how to replace a key (see the topic, "Replacing a Keyboard Event and Other Information," for details), and the first also shows how to discard a key press. The example uses the two handlers attached to the same windows and different windows. They are also attached to entry fields, a combination box, and a multiline edit control to show their versatility. In this example, we use the handlers to enhance a dialog created with the Dialog Editor. Figure 17-1 shows the effect of the handlers; a user has typed the same keys into all of the controls.

HexKeyboardHandler - genhdrs\keybd\hexkeybd.hpp

```
#include <ibase.hpp>          // For IC_PM/IC_WIN.
#ifdef IC_PM
  #define INCL_WINDIALOGS    // For WinAlarm.
  #define INCL_WININPUT      // For KC_CHAR, VK_DELETE.
  #include <os2.h>
#else
  #include <windows.h>
#endif

#include <ikeyhdr.hpp>
#include <istring.hpp>
#include <iwindow.hpp>

// This keyboard handler restricts character input to
// hexadecimal digits (0-9, a-f, A-F).
class HexKeyboardHandler : public IKeyboardHandler {
protected:
virtual Boolean
  characterKeyPress ( IKeyboardEvent& event )
  {
    Boolean badKey = true;
    Boolean dontPassOn = true;

    IString strChar = event.mixedCharacter();
    if ( strChar.isSBCS() )
    {                            // The character is single-byte.
      if ( strChar.isHexDigits() )
      {                          // '0'-'9', 'A'-'F', 'a'-'f'.
        badKey = false;    // Valid hexadecimal digit.
        dontPassOn = false;  // Pass the event to the window.
      }
    }
```

```
          else if ( strChar == " " )
          {                          // Space bar is pressed.
             badKey = false;         // Replace it with the Delete key.
#ifdef IC_PM
             IEventParameter1
               param1( event.parameter1().number1() & ~KC_CHAR,
                       event.parameter1().char3(), 0 );
             (*event.window())
              .sendEvent( IWindow::character,
                          param1,
                          IEventParameter2( 0, VK_DELETE ) );
                   // Discard scan code and character data.
#else
             (*event.window())
              .sendEvent( IWindow::character,
                          IEventParameter1( 0, 1 ),
                          IEventParameter2( VK_DELETE ) );
                   // Discard scan code and character data.
#endif
          }
          // Throw away any other character key.
       }                             // End single-byte input.

    if ( badKey )
    {
#ifdef IC_PM
       WinAlarm( IWindow::desktopWindow()->handle(),
                 WA_WARNING );
#else
       Beep( 100, 100 );
#endif
    }
    return dontPassOn;
  }
}; // HexKeyboardHandler
```

Uppercase Keyboard Handler - genhdrs\keybd\uckeybd.hpp

```
#include <ikeyhdr.hpp>
#include <istring.hpp>
#include <iwindow.hpp>

// This keyboard handler example converts lowercase characters
// to uppercase as a user types.
class UppercaseKeyboardHandler : public IKeyboardHandler {
protected:
virtual Boolean
  characterKeyPress ( IKeyboardEvent& event )
  {
    Boolean dontPassOn = false;
    IString strChar = event.mixedCharacter();
    if ( strChar.isSBCS()  &&  strChar.isLowerCase() )
    {                      // Single-byte 'a'-'z' is pressed.
       // Convert the character to uppercase by generating
       // another keyboard event with its uppercase character.
#ifdef IC_PM
       IEventParameter2 param2( strChar.upperCase()[0],
                                event.parameter2().number2() );
                   // Only change the character to uppercase.
       event.window()->sendEvent( IWindow::character,
                                  event.parameter1(),
                                  param2);
```

```
#else
        IEventParameter1 param1( strChar.upperCase()[0] );
                        // Only change the character to uppercase.
        event.window()->sendEvent( IWindow::character,
                                   param1,
                                   event.parameter2() );
#endif
        dontPassOn = true;      // Don't pass on the original event.
    }
    return dontPassOn;
  }
}; // UppercaseKeyboardHandler
```

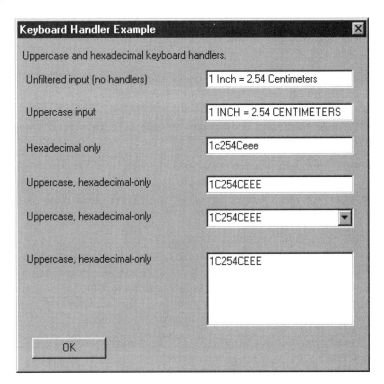

Figure 17-1. Window with Keyboard Handlers.

Because keyboard handlers only process keyboard data, you cannot use a keyboard handler to verify all changes to the contents of a control such as an entry field. A keyboard handler does not detect when a user cuts text from a control, pastes text from the clipboard into a control, or drags text to or from your control. It also does not detect changes made via calls to setText, SetWindowText, or WinSetWindowText. However, you can detect and verify all of these changes to an entry field using the IEditHandler class.

Perhaps you are wondering if you also can process keyboard changes to an entry field with IEditHandler. You can. However, whereas you can use IKeyboardHandler to verify a key before its effect is seen on the screen, an IEditHandler is not called until after the control has been updated with a key.

Virtual Key Press

A *virtual key* generally does not have an associated ASCII character code so it cannot be identified by a character code. Examples of virtual keys are Enter, Esc, Tab, Home, Caps Lock, and F5.

An `IKeyboardHandler` object calls its `virtualKeyPress` virtual function to process the pressing of a virtual key. You can also process these key presses using the `IKeyboardConnectionTo` class.

The `IKeyboardEvent::virtualKey` function identifies the virtual key that is pressed. The enumeration it returns corresponds to (but is not identical in value to) a `VK_*` virtual key value defined in `WINUSER.H` or `PMWIN.H`.

Note that you cannot detect an F1 or F10 key press using the `virtualKey` function because an application does not detect these events during normal processing. The operating system processes these keys as accelerator keys before a keyboard message is generated. Chapter 6, "Menus and Keyboard Accelerators," discusses accelerator keys, and Chapter 23, "Using Help," discusses help support in more detail.

Although the Windows operating system provides virtual key values for alphanumeric keys, `IKeyboardHandler` does not call its `virtualKeyPress` function to process these key presses. Override the `characterKeyPress` virtual function to process these keys, which include the space bar, a-z, A-Z, and 0-9 keys.

Many keyboards have redundant keys that you can process identically to or differently from each other. For example, most have two Enter keys that are represented by different virtual keys, `IKeyboardEvent::enter` and `IKeyboardEvent::newLine`. However, you cannot differentiate between other keys duplicated on the numeric keypad, such as Insert/Ins, Delete/Del, Home, End, Page Up/PgUp, and Page Down/PgDn using the `virtualKeyPress` function. Use the `scanCodeKeyPress` or `key` function to make these distinctions.

Scan Code Key Press

A *scan code* is a value generated by keyboard hardware to identify a key, where each key top on the keyboard has a unique value. Because the same key (and therefore, scan code) can result in a different character, depending on the current code page, using scan codes is not an ideal way to process most keys. Therefore, you might never find a need to use this function. Nevertheless, an `IKeyboardHandler` object calls its `scanCodeKeyPress` virtual function to process a key press based on its scan code value.

The `IKeyboardEvent::scanCode` function returns the scan code associated with the key press. Do not assume that the key identified by the `IKeyboardEvent` passed to this function is a character key or a virtual key. Test the event with the `IKeyboardEvent::isCharacter` function before attempting to query the character code of the event, and use `IKeyboardEvent::isVirtual` before querying the virtual key code.

Not all key presses have an associated scan code value. For example, an ASCII character generated when a user presses the Alt key and keys a three-digit ASCII code on the numeric keypad does not have a scan code value.

Key Releases and Other Miscellaneous Key Events

A keyboard handler calls its `key` virtual function to process all keyboard events that another virtual function has not processed. As a result, this is a catchall function that does not filter events. Do not assume that a keyboard event passed to this function is a key press (it might be a key release), that it has an ASCII character code, that it is a virtual key, or that it has a scan code. Test the event with functions such as `IKeyboardEvent::isCharacter` to determine what information it holds before calling functions to extract specific data. If you try to extract data that the keyboard event does not contain, the function you call typically throws an `IInvalidRequest` exception. You can test whether the event is a key release by calling `IKeyboardEvent::isUpTransition`.

Some of the keyboard events you receive might appear to be useless, but they aren't. So, return a value of `false` from your `key` function when it encounters a keyboard event it cannot handle. In this way, the keyboard event can be passed on to another keyboard handler or to the operating system, which can have dependencies on receiving seemingly useless keyboard events.

Attaching a Keyboard Handler

You can attach a keyboard handler to any window, although generally you only attach a keyboard handler to a window that accepts the input focus, such as an entry field. To understand the options for attaching keyboard handlers, we next discuss message passing as it relates to keyboard events. In the Windows operating system, Open Class Library does much of this processing to emulate the processing that the OS/2 operating system provides. (In describing this processing, we do not distinguish the behavior that the operating system provides from the behavior Open Class Library provides.)

When a user presses a key, the keyboard event is first checked against the accelerator keys of the window with the input focus, the accelerator keys of the windows in its parent chain, and those of the message queue. If the keyboard event is not an accelerator key, the window with the input focus receives the event. If this window does not process the keyboard event, it is passed to the window's owner. As long as a keyboard event goes unprocessed by handlers and window procedures, it continues up the owner window chain. With this message-passing logic, a window that never accepts the input focus can still receive keyboard events by being the owner window of a control that can take the input focus.

Now, let's discuss entry fields specifically. Although an entry field processes almost all character key presses itself, it typically does not process a Tab key. This key is passed to the owner window of the entry field for processing. If the entry field is on a frame window or canvas, that window receives the Tab key which enables it to supply tabbing support.

The previous code example uses a combination box control, which is a composite control made up of an entry field, list box, and a window that provides overall management of the various component windows. In the code example, we attach the keyboard handlers to the entry field window of the combination box rather than to the combination box itself. Because the entry field processes almost all character key presses, it does not pass them to its owner window. As a result, had we attached our keyboard handlers to the combination box, the handlers would have had no effect on the behavior of the control. Thus, when you attach a keyboard handler, be aware of composite controls and potentially the keyboard message processing behavior of windows in the owner chain.

How you want your keyboard handler to function determines which window you attach it to. If the handler provides support for a specific window or if it processes a key that a control typically processes, attach the keyboard handler to that window or control. If the handler processes keys that controls do not typically process such as Tab or Enter, consider attaching it to the window where the owner window chain of your controls converge.

Replacing a Keyboard Event

You cannot alter the keyboard event passed to a virtual function of IKeyboardHandler simply by changing the value of its IEventParameter1 or IEventParameter2 component. The event handler classes that Open Class Library provides only allow a virtual function to change the IEventResult component of an event; all other changes are discarded. As a result, to get the effect of changing the event parameters of an IKeyboardEvent, send a new keyboard event to the window to replace the original IKeyboardEvent. Then return a value of true to prevent further processing of the original keyboard event. We illustrate this in the GENHDRS\KEYBD\UCKEYBD.HPP file in the previous code example.

If you use this technique to send a new keyboard event to the window your handler is attached to, be sure not to introduce an endless loop. In the previous example, UppercaseKeyboardHandler avoids an endless loop by not creating a new keyboard event for a valid key, one that already represents an uppercase character. If you cannot avoid an endless loop when sending a new keyboard event to the same window, try passing the new keyboard event to the window's IWindow::dispatchRemainingHandlers function or the handler's IHandler::defaultProcedure function and then returning true from your virtual keyboard handler function.

Combining Keyboard Events

The operating system might combine several identical keyboard events into a single keyboard event. You can detect if the system has done this by calling IKeyboardEvent::repeatCount. Typically, a single IKeyboardEvent represents more than one keyboard event only when your application is no longer processing messages in a timely manner (within 0.1 seconds). For example, your application could be overloaded with user input, or it could be delayed in processing a message. You can ignore the repeatCount function to avoid overwhelming a user with a flood of keyboard data when your application finally catches up on its input processing.

Mouse Handler

With a pointing device, usually a mouse, a user can perform actions directly on objects, thus avoiding the need to access the menu bar. The Windows and OS/2 operating systems support three uses for a mouse: to select and open objects, to move and copy objects using drag and drop, and to display pop-up menus.

You can use the `IMouseHandler` class to detect when a user moves the mouse or presses and releases any of the mouse buttons. With this handler, you can create a specialized role for the mouse in your user interface beyond what the operating system provides. To use a mouse handler, create your own class derived from `IMouseClickHandler` and implement one or more of the virtual functions, `mouseClicked`, `mouseMoved`, and `mousePointerChange`. These functions are passed a reference to an associated event object, `IMouseClickEvent`, `IMouseEvent`, and `IMousePointerEvent`, respectively.

As an alternative to using the `IMouseHandler` class, you can create an `IMouseConnectionTo` object that calls similar functions in any object you specify. The relationship between this class and `IMouseHandler` is the same as between `ICommandHandler` and `ICommandConnectionTo`.

You do not need to use a mouse handler to get the mouse support already built into the operating system, such as how clicking an entry field gives it the input focus, dragging a title bar moves a frame window, or dragging the sizing border of a frame window changes its size. Table 17-3 shows some of the standard mouse actions that a handler other than `IMouseHandler` processes better.

Table 17-3. Mouse Actions Best Handled with Other than a Mouse Handler

Mouse Action	Recommended Handler	Notes
Click a button	ICommandHandler, ISelectHandler	This is equivalent to using the space bar or a mnemonic.
Click or double-click a list box row	ISelectHandler	This is equivalent to using the space bar or Enter key.
Click a scroll bar	IScrollHandler	This is equivalent to scrolling with arrow keys or the Page Up and Page Down keys.
Click a notebook tab	IPageHandler	This is equivalent to using the space bar or a mnemonic.
Click a menu item	ICommandHandler	This is equivalent to using the Enter key or a mnemonic.
Displaying a pop-up menu with button 2	IMenuHandler, ICnrMenuHandler	In the OS/2 operating system, users can display a pop-up menu using Shift+F10 (they can configure the mouse button and key combination).
Drag and drop	IDMSourceHandler, IDMTargetHandler	There are no equivalent keys. In the OS/2 operating system, users can configure the mouse button.

Processing Mouse Button Events

An `IMouseHandler` object calls its `mouseClicked` function whenever the state of a mouse button changes. The `IMouseClickEvent` object that is passed to this function identifies the button, its new state, and the position of the mouse pointer, and it identifies whether a user pressed an augmentation key (Shift, Alt, or Ctrl). You can also process a mouse button event using the `IMouseConnectionTo` class. It passes a reference to an `IMouseClickEvent` to the member function it calls.

The `IMouseClickEvent::mouseNumber` function identifies the mouse button that changed state. It returns a button number based on whether the user configured the mouse for left-handed or right-handed use through the desktop. *Mouse button 1* is the left mouse button on a right-handed mouse and the right mouse button on a left-handed mouse. *Mouse button 2* is the right mouse button on a right-handed mouse and the left mouse button on a left-handed mouse.

The `IMouseClickEvent::mouseAction` function identifies the button state change. The event can be a mouse button press, release, *single-click* (a press followed by an immediate release), *double-click* (two consecutive single-clicks), or *chord* (the simultaneous pressing of button 1 and button 2).

Two other functions return information about the location of the mouse pointer. The `IMouseEvent::windowUnderPointer` function returns the window that the mouse pointer is over. This "top" window is not necessarily the window that the mouse handler is attached to because the handler can be processing a mouse-click event that it received from an owned

---

Actions That Generate Multiple Mouse Events

The operating system generates single-click, double-click, and chord events based on button press-and-release events that have occurred, but only after the system has already dispatched some of the constituent events to the appropriate window. As a result, your mouse handler processes these composite mouse events only after seeing all of the component events. The following mouse actions generate the following mouse-click events.

Single-click

1. Down
2. Up
3. Single-click

Double-click

1. Down
2. Up
3. Single-click
4. Double-click
5. Up

Chord

1. Down (first button pressed)
2. Down (second button pressed)
3. Chord
4. Up (first button released)
5. Up (second button released)

window or a transparent window (the topic "Attaching a Mouse Handler" provides more information on transparent windows). The `IMouseEvent::mousePosition` function returns the location of the mouse pointer on the screen at the time of the event. The location is in device units (or pels) relative to the origin of the window that the handler is attached to. (The origin is dependent on the coordinate system currently in use, which you set via `ICoordinateSystem::setApplicationOrientation`.) When the event is passed up the owner chain, the top window remains the same, although the pointer location changes to become relative to the new window receiving the event.

Processing Mouse Movements

An `IMouseHandler` object calls its `mouseMoved` function whenever a user moves the mouse pointer in the window that the handler is attached to. You can override this function to track the position of the mouse pointer and to perform processing based on that position. You can also process the movement of the mouse pointer across a window using the `IMouseConnectionTo` class. Both `IMouseHandler::mouseMoved` and the member function that `IMouseConnectionTo` calls are passed a reference to an `IMouseEvent` object.

In the following example, an `IMouseConnectionTo` object calls the `ShapeWindow::processMouseMovement` member function to display a text string based on the position of the mouse pointer. The window contains an `IDrawingCanvas` window that displays a collection of geometric shapes. The `ShapeWindow::processMouseMovement` function determines which shape the mouse pointer is over. In the code, the `graphicList` data member is the collection of shapes, and `gc` is a pointer to the `IGraphicContext` that the drawing canvas uses. Figure 17-2 shows the window.

Mouse Movement Example - genhdrs\mousemov\mousemov.cpp

```cpp
// This is the function that the IMouseConnectionTo<> object calls.
IBase::Boolean ShapeWindow::processMouseMovement ( IMouseEvent& event )
{
  if ( event.windowUnderPointer() ==
        event.dispatchingWindow()->handle() )
  {    // The mouse pointer is over the drawing canvas.
    IGraphic
     *graphicUnderMousePointer =
        graphicList.topGraphicUnderPoint( event.mousePosition(), *gc );
    char
     *infoText = "Move the mouse pointer over a shape.";

    // Test if the mouse pointer is over a shape.
    if ( graphicUnderMousePointer )
    {        // Now figure out which shape.
      switch ( graphicUnderMousePointer->id() )
      {
        case ID_CIRCLE:
          infoText = "Circle";
          break;
        case ID_SQUARE:
          infoText = "Square";
          break;
        case ID_RECTANGLE:
          infoText = "Rectangle";
          break;
```

```
            case ID_TRIANGLE:
              infoText = "Triangle";
              break;
            case ID_ELLIPSE:
              infoText = "Ellipse";
              break;
            case ID_PENTAGON:
              infoText = "Pentagon";
              break;
            default:
              break;
          }
        }

      instructions
        .setText( infoText );
    }
    return false;
}
```

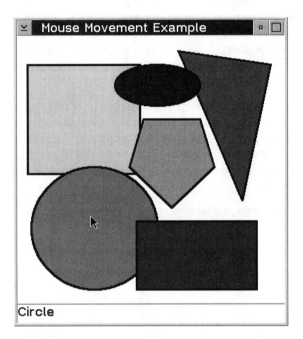

Figure 17-2. Mouse Movement Example.

Changing the Mouse Pointer

You can change the appearance of the mouse pointer for a single window by overriding the IMouseHandler::mousePointerChange function. This function receives a reference to an IMousePointerEvent object. This object does not identify the position of the mouse pointer within the window, however. You can also process the appearance of the mouse pointer in a particular window using the IMouseConnectionTo class.

To identify a new mouse pointer to use, call `IMousePointerEvent::setMousePointer` from your `mousePointerChange` function or from the member function called by an `IMouseConnectionTo` object; then, return `true`. Do not call `IEvent::setResult` because this overwrites the value that `IMousePointerEvent::setMousePointer` stores.

You can also change the mouse pointer for a frame window and its child windows by calling `IFrameWindow::setMousePointer`. You do not need to use a mouse handler in this case. The frame window must own its child windows for this function to work because the frame window must receive mouse-pointer change messages from the windows it owns.

If you build a custom control using multiple windows, attach the handler returned by `IMousePointerHandler::defaultHandler` to all of the component windows that are owned by another window. This handler passes unprocessed mouse-pointer change events to the window's owner.

Attaching a Mouse Handler

You can attach a mouse handler to any window. The handler is called to process not only those mouse events that occur while the mouse pointer is over the window it is attached to, but also the mouse events that get passed to the window from a window that it owns.

The operating system routes mouse events to the topmost window that the mouse pointer is over. The OS/2 operating system then routes unprocessed button-up, button-down, and double-click events up the owner window chain. Open Class Library emulates this behavior on the Windows operating system. So as long as these mouse-click events are not processed, they continue to be passed up the owner window chain. Several controls routinely process mouse-click events, such as buttons and scroll bars, so an owner window does not typically receive every mouse-click event that its owned windows receive.

However, single-click, chord, and mouse move events are not sent up the owner window chain in either operating system. Therefore, it is safest to attach a mouse handler directly to the window you need to capture mouse events for. For composite controls, it is not always obvious which window is receiving mouse events. For example, an OS/2 container control in the details view has child windows to the left and right of the split bar. These windows intercept most mouse events, keeping them from reaching the container control itself.

You have one other variable to consider. A window can appear to be transparent to mouse events, so that even though the mouse pointer is directly over the window, the operating system dispatches mouse events to the window behind it. For example, a disabled control in the Windows operating system typically functions as if it is transparent to mouse events. Also, how a window processes the `WM_NCHITTEST` message in the Windows operating system or the `WM_HITTEST` message in the OS/2 operating system can cause the operating system to treat it as transparent. For example, `IGroupBox` and `IOutlineBox` windows are transparent to mouse events. The operating system routes all mouse events that occur over these controls to the window that is behind them at the position of the mouse pointer.

The **genhdrs\mouseclk** example uses a mouse handler that logs all mouse button events it receives to a list box. Because it attaches this handler to all controls on the window, you can see how the rules for the passing of unprocessed mouse events influence which windows receive which events.

Capturing the Mouse

Sometimes, it is useful to receive mouse events even when the mouse is not over your window. Although this is not the default behavior of the operating system, your mouse handler can process such events if you call `IWindow::capturePointer`. This function call causes the window to capture all mouse events. The operating system routes them to the capturing window, regardless of what window the mouse pointer is over. This can prevent the users from being able to interact with the system and other applications, so capture the mouse only when you need all mouse events and only for a limited time.

Window Paint Handler

Provide painting logic for a window by attaching a paint handler to the window. Any painting you do with any other event handler will likely get overwritten when the window processes a paint event. To create a paint handler, derive from the `IPaintHandler` class and override the `paintWindow` virtual function. Alternatively, you can create an object of the class `IPaintConnectionTo`, identifying the member function of an object that you want called to process a paint event.

The operating system sends a `WM_PAINT` message (which maps to a paint event, the `IPaintEvent` class, in Open Class Library) to a window whenever the window must update an *invalidated* portion of its screen. The invalidated portion of a window is the part of it that is visible but does not accurately represent the window. A window is only called to be painted when it is both visible and has non-zero dimensions.

A window can be invalidated whenever a user or the application sizes it larger or causes it to be uncovered by another window, or when the application makes it visible or explicitly invalidates it. Calling drawing functions, such as `TextOut`, `WinDrawText`, or graphics APIs of the operating system, does not cause a window to become invalidated. To invalidate a window from your application, call `IWindow::refresh`, the `InvalidateRect` or `RedrawWindow` Windows APIs, or the `WinInvalidateWindow` or `WinUpdateWindow` OS/2 APIs. Never explicitly send a `WM_PAINT` message to a window.

Some window classes provide draw-item handlers, which enable you to do specialized painting of a specific part of a control window. Draw-item handlers provide finer granularity than a paint handler. Where these classes are available, use them instead of a paint handler for customizing the drawing of a specific kind of window.

Using a Paint Handler

Open Class Library calls a paint handler when the operating system determines that a window it is attached to needs to be updated. The `IPaintEvent` object passed to the handler provides information functions and functions that allow you to do rudimentary painting. The `clearBackground` and `drawText` functions provide implementations for simple painting operations such as drawing a rectangle of color or string of text. For more complex painting, use the 2-D graphics classes of Open Class Library or the graphics APIs of the operating system.

The `IPaintEvent::presSpaceHandle` function gives you a surface that you can apply painting operations against. This function returns the handle of a display device context on the Windows operating system and of a presentation space on the OS/2 operating system (by default, the handle of a cached-micro presentation space). If you use the graphics APIs of the operating system, pass this handle to those calls. You can also use this handle to construct an `IGraphicContext` object that the 2-D graphics classes need. We use "graphic context" in the rest of this chapter to represent an `IGraphicContext` object, a display device context, or a presentation space.

The `IPaintEvent::rect` function identifies the portion of the window that requires updating. Actually, this rectangle is the boundary of the invalidated portion of the window as well as the boundary of the clip region set into the graphic context that `IPaintEvent::presSpaceHandle` returns. (The invalidated region and clip region might have a more complicated shape than a rectangle, however.) Any drawing you do into this graphic context is consequently limited to this rectangle; therefore, any drawing you do outside this rectangle does not appear on the screen. You can modify the clip region by calling `IGraphicContext::setClipRegion` so that your painting is not limited to replacing only invalidated portions of the window.

You can also provide your own graphic context for painting by using one of the following options.

- Derive from the window class that the paint handler is attached to and override `IWindow::presSpace` to return the graphic context of your choice. `IPaintEvent::presSpaceHandle` calls this function before using the invalidated portion of the window to set the clip region of the graphic context. `IPaintEvent` calls `IWindow::releasePresSpace` in its destructor.

- In your paint handler's `paintWindow` function (or in the function called by an `IPaintConnectionTo` object), pass the graphic context of your choice to `IPaintEvent::setGraphicContext`. This function gives you the option of using the invalidated portion of the window to set the clip region of the graphic context. Thereafter, `IPaintEvent::presSpaceHandle` returns this graphic context. You must free this graphic context.

- If the window is an `IDrawingCanvas`, you can store the graphic context by calling `IDrawingCanvas::setGraphicContext`. The **genhdrs\mousemov** example uses this function. The drawing canvas uses this graphic context to paint its graphics list. You must free this graphic context.

The clipping styles that you assign your window affect the invalidated area and consequently the clip region that you get from a paint event. IWindow::clipSiblings causes the operating system to exclude the area occupied by sibling windows that overlap the window from the invalidated area. This style causes a window to remain visually behind its siblings. IWindow::clipChildren causes the area occupied by a window's child windows to be excluded from its invalidated area. Although the use of these styles adds performance overhead, they can improve the look of how a window paints in certain circumstances.

The Boolean value you return from your paint handler determines if Open Class Library allows any additional processing for the event.

The following paint handler uses the 2-D graphics classes to draw two diagonal lines over a window after the window first paints itself. Figure 17-3 shows a window using this paint handler along with another paint handler that inverts the colors of half of the window it is attached to.

Paint Handler Example - genhdrs\painthdr\painthdr.cpp

```cpp
class XWindowPaintHandler : public IPaintHandler {
public:
protected:
virtual Boolean
  paintWindow ( IPaintEvent& event );
};  // XWindowPaintHandler

IBase::Boolean
  XWindowPaintHandler::paintWindow ( IPaintEvent& event )
{
  IWindow
   *windowToPaint = event.dispatchingWindow();

  // Save the clip region in case the window clears it
  // as part of its painting.
  IGraphicContext
    gc( event.presSpaceHandle() );
  IRegionHandle
    origClipRegion( gc.clipRegion() );

  // Let the window paint its contents.
  (*windowToPaint)
    .dispatchRemainingHandlers( event, true );

  // Reset the clip region in case the window cleared it
  // as part of its painting.
  gc
    .setClipRegion( origClipRegion );

  // Now draw the two diagonal red lines.
  IRectangle
    windowRect( windowToPaint->rect().moveTo( IPoint() ) );
  IGLine
    diag1( windowRect.bottomLeft(), windowRect.topRight() ),
    diag2( windowRect.bottomRight(), windowRect.topLeft() );
  IGraphicBundle
    bundle( gc );
  bundle
    .setMixMode( IGraphicBundle::overPaint )
    .setPenType( IGraphicBundle::solid )
    .setPenEndingStyle( IGraphicBundle::rounded )
    .setPenWidth( 2 )
    .setPenColor( IColor::red );
```

```
diag1
  .setGraphicBundle( bundle )
  .drawOn( gc );
diag2
  .setGraphicBundle( bundle )
  .drawOn( gc );

return true;
}
```

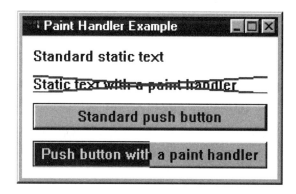

Figure 17-3. Paint Handler Example.

Attaching A Paint Handler

You can attach a paint handler to any window, but attach it only to the window or windows it paints. Unprocessed paint events are not routed to any other windows for processing.

Avoiding Potential Pitfalls

Custom painting of some controls can be a problem because not all of their painting is controlled by WM_PAINT messages. For example, the operating system updates the look of a button when it is selected and the look of an entry field as the user types characters into it—without generating a paint message. This action severely hampers your ability to alter the look of these controls with a paint handler because your paint handler will not be called to update the control in these cases. This, in turn, leads to out-of-sync conditions. The **genhdrs\painthdr** example shows this problem with a paint handler attached to a push button. Clicking the push button causes the operating system to directly update its screen contents. The operating systems use this shortcut to provide immediate feedback to a user. You can use this technique, too, but you must duplicate painting logic to be sure your window paints the same, whether or not you paint via a WM_PAINT message. For a push button, a better solution would be to use the ICustomButton and ICustomButtonDrawHandler classes. See Chapter 16, "Tool Bars, Fly-Over Help, and Custom Buttons," for details.

A paint handler also has the potential of painting outside the window it is attached to and onto the parent window. For example, the invalidated region of a window can include portions of the parent window if you use the Windows CS_PARENTDC class style or the OS/2 IWindow::parentClip style or CS_PARENTCLIP class style. You can avoid this problem by only painting into the rectangle formed by the intersection of the invalidated area and the boundary of the window. You can calculate this rectangle using code similar to the following in your paint handler:

```
IRectangle
  windowRectangle( event.dispatchingWindow()->rect() );
windowRectangle
  .moveTo( IPoint() );
IRectangle
  areaToPaint( event.rect() & windowRectangle );
```

Window Resize Handler

Chapter 2, "Object-Oriented User Interface Fundamentals," explains the importance of leaving the users in control. Part of designing an application so that users can perform tasks in the manner best suited for their needs is to allow them to freely size and position all frame windows. Enabling sizing support is the tricky part of the two. The canvas classes provide a great deal of function for sizable client windows (see Chapter 15, "Canvases," for more detail). Additionally, you can use the IResizeHandler class to create your own sizing code.

Virtual Functions

To use the IResizeHandler class, create a class derived from IResizeHandler and provide an implementation for its pure virtual function, windowResize. A window resize handler calls its windowResize function, passing it a reference to an IResizeEvent object, whenever a window that the handler is attached to changes in size. Because the operating system has already changed the size of the window by the time windowResize is called, the call serves as a notification. The IResizeEvent object passed to the function identifies both the previous and new window sizes. Call IResizeEvent::oldSize and IResizeEvent::newSize to obtain these values.

The Boolean value returned by your windowResize function determines whether Open Class Library allows any additional processing of the event. Generally, return false because many control classes have private resize handlers that would not otherwise be called (IMultiCellCanvas, for example).

Attaching a Window Resize Handler

You can attach a resize handler to any window, but attach it only to the window whose size you are monitoring. Unprocessed size events are not routed to any other windows for processing.

Chapter 18

Fonts and Views

- Describes Open Class Library classes that handle fonts and views
- Describes the IFont, IFontDialog and IFileDialog classes
- Read Chapters 4, 5, and 7 before reading this chapter.
- Chapters 15 and 23 cover related material.

This chapter describes Open Class Library classes that work with fonts, font selection, and file selection. Use these classes to change text-based controls that present text for users to edit or view.

What Is a Font?

A *font* is a set of visual characteristics that can be applied to character-based text. Fonts are an important part of user-interface design because they provide part of the visual "look," or design, of the interface. Use different fonts to highlight important information or to guide your user. Fonts can also improve readability. For example, a font with *serifs*, the horizontal strokes on the letters, improve readability for printed information such as this book because the serifs lead the eye to the next character. A *sans serif* (without serifs) font improves readability for characters displayed on a computer screen because they are easily distinguished against the light of the cathode ray tube. If you look at the fonts depicted in Figure 18-1, the Nimrod font is an example of a font with serifs, and the Arial font is an example of a sans serif font. Each font has a set of one or more visual attributes that makes it unique. These attributes are as follows:

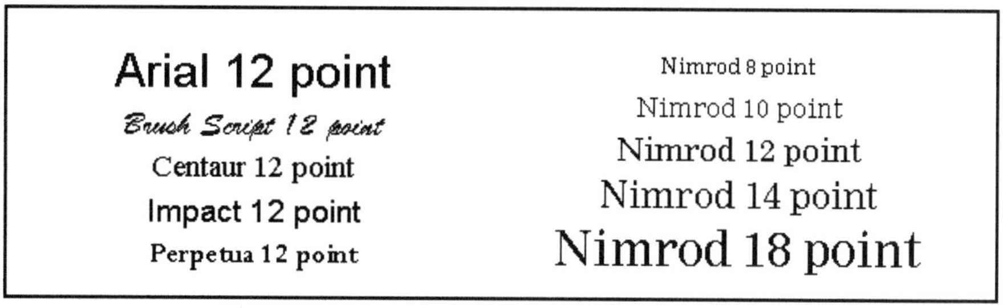

Figure 18-1. Examples of Font Typefaces and Sizes.

- **Typeface name**, a specific type family, is the main identifier for a font. Some common typeface names provided by the Windows or OS/2 operating systems are Arial, Courier, Helvetica and Times Roman. Each typeface name shares common characteristics within the family, such as the presence or lack of serifs, the spacing between characters or the shape of the vertices. Typeface names are typically trademarked.

- **Size**, a measurement of the height of a graphic character in a font. The standard unit of measurement of type is the point. A point is 1/72 of an inch (or 72 points to the inch). The width of the font is determined by the height defined and the aspect ratio of the font. This ratio is the width-to-height relationship of each character in a font.

- **Style**, additional information indicating the form and structure of the characters within a typeface name. Style information can specify whether a font is upright or slanted, or can indicate the weight of the characters. Weight is the degree of boldness of a typeface, caused by different thicknesses of the strokes that form a graphic character.

A font can be uniquely identified in terms of the above attributes, such as Arial Bold 12-point or Courier Italic 10-point. Figure 18-1 displays some examples of different typeface names and sizes.

What Is a View?

A *view* is a window that displays a set of information to interact with. Both the Windows and OS/2 operating systems supply a set of standard selection dialogs, which provide views of system information. For example, you can retrieve a list of all installed fonts on the system or all files on the system, and then choose from them. Figure 18-2 shows the classes in Open Class Library that you use to work with fonts and views. IFont provides a standard set of functions that you can use to create and manipulate fonts and to apply those fonts to windows within your application. IFontDialog and IFileDialog are classes that provide a wrapper for standard dialogs that the operating system provides. These view classes derive from the common base class IFrameWindow.

IFontDialogHandler, IFileDialogEvent, and IFileDialogHandler are classes that provide advanced functions for interacting with font and file dialogs. You typically use these classes to handle processing modeless dialogs or custom controls that you added to the dialog using a custom dialog template.

Constructing Font Objects

Create an IFont object using one of the four constructors described below. Because fonts are graphical and applied to windows, you typically use more than one type of constructor in an application. Each one has a specific use, depending on what information you have available to you at the time you need one.

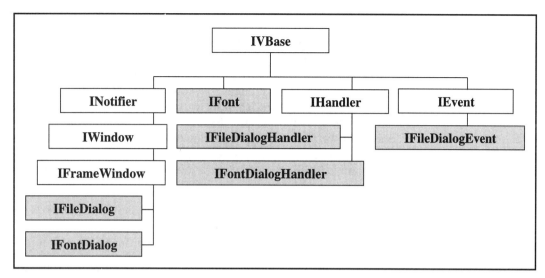

Figure 18-2. Font Classes and View Classes.

Creating a Default Font

Both the Windows and the OS/2 operating systems have a system default font. This font is used for all character-based displayed text unless you specify otherwise. In the Windows operating systems, this is the same as the stock font object SYSTEM_FONT. In the OS/2 operating system, this is the System Proportional font. Open Class Library provides a default constructor for IFont. The font object it creates represents the system default font.

Creating a Named Font

In addition to a default font, both the Windows and the OS/2 operating systems provide a standard set of fonts to use in your applications. Although your users can install additional fonts on their operating systems, you cannot rely on them doing so unless your application ships those fonts. Even the standard set of fonts that the operating systems provide could have been uninstalled, so there is no guarantee on them as well, although this is not a typical case. Most applications only need the standard set of fonts. However, because users of editors, browsers, and desktop publishing packages demand a variety of fonts, these applications typically provide additional fonts.

So that you can select a specific font, Open Class Library provides a constructor for creating a font object. You specify the name of the typeface, and any optional attributes such as size, type information and a graphic context. You specify the size in points.

The next two parameters are useFixedFont and useVectorFont. When you set useFixedFont to true, you get a fixed-space font; every character has the same width, making alignment and formatting calculations simple. The default is false, which means a font can be either proportionally spaced or fixed spaced.

The actual character information of a font is stored as either a *bitmap font* or a *vector font*, and both operating systems ship with examples of both of these. A bitmap font is so named because each character or symbol of the font is stored as a bitmap. This makes them fast to draw, but the characters do not *scale* well. Scaling refers to dynamically changing the size of the character. Instead of scaling, bitmap fonts store a different bitmap for each size, meaning only the specific sizes provided are available as choices. Vector fonts use line and curve commands, specifically stretching, shearing, and shaping to render the characters. (These functions are not available for bitmap fonts and are discussed a bit later in this chapter.) Vector fonts are slower to draw, but the fonts are device-independent so they scale up or down easily while maintaining their original shape. Because each character is described only once and scaled from that description, an infinite number of sizes are available to an application or a user.

Thus, you use the second parameter, useVectorFont, to indicate how the fonts are drawn, or rendered. Setting this parameter to true indicates that you want the font to use vectors to render it. The default, false, means that the font can be rendered as a bitmap or vector font.

Also, because typeface names vary between operating systems, avoid specifying an exact name within the code for portable applications. However, if your application needs to specify the fonts for displaying text, one approach is to define the typeface names at the top of the file. Then you can change them without searching through the code. Just remember that this still does not guarantee portability.

Creating a Font from a Window

In many cases, you don't want to specify a font by name, but you want to use the same font that another window uses. Open Class Library provides an IFont constructor for doing this. The window you specify on the constructor is queried for the characteristics of the font that is currently applied to that window. These characteristics are then used to create an IFont object with the same typeface name, size, and attributes of the original font.

Creating a Font from a Graphic Context

Another way to create an IFont object is to use an existing graphic context, represented by an IPresSpaceHandle object. The graphic context you specified is queried for the font that is currently selected into it. This information is then used to construct an IFont object with the same characteristics.

Modifying Font Objects

The IFont class provides a wide range of member functions to modify an existing IFont object. Change the typeface name using setName; set the point size to the desired size using setPointSize. Your application can query the current typeface name for a font by using name and the point size by using pointSize. Use setBold to add weight, setItalic to add a slant, setUnderscore to underline the text, and setStrikeout to draw a line through the text. Check any of these attributes using `isBold`, `isItalic`, `isUnderscore`, and `isStrikeout`. In the OS/2 operating system, use `setOutline` to draw only the character's outline and `isOutline` to check if this attribute is set.

You can also check other attributes of the current font. Use `isFixed` to determine if the font is a fixed-space font or a proportionally spaced font. Use `isBitmap` to determine whether the font is rendered using bitmap or vector font technology.

After creating the `IFont` object, apply the font to a window in one of two ways. You can use `IFont::setWindowFont`, passing the `IWindow` object to be modified, or you can use `IWindow::setFont`, passing the `IFont` object to be applied to the window.

The following example demonstrates using the `IFont` class to modify the font used to display the text of the sample application. First, an `IFont` object is created and applied to the main frame window, changing the font of the title text. That same `IFont` object is then modified by increasing the point size and is applied to the entry field. That `IFont` object is again modified by changing the name and shrinking the point size and is applied to the first check box. A new `IFont` object is created from the font in use by the first check box; its attributes are modified to slant the font and increase the weight; it is then applied to the second check box. Finally, a third `IFont` object is created, a default font, and applied to the last check box. Figure 18-3 displays the results.

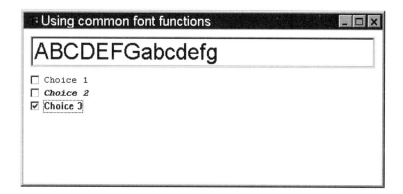

Figure 18-3. Using Common Font Functions.

Using IFont Objects - fonts\genfont\genfont.cpp

```cpp
#include <iapp.hpp>
#include <icheckbx.hpp>
#include <ientryfd.hpp>
#include <ifont.hpp>
#include <iframe.hpp>
#include <imcelcv.hpp>

// Specific font names vary between operating systems,
// complicating the issue of writing portable applications.
// Avoid embedding the names in the code and instead define
// them at the top of the code as we do here.
```

```
#ifdef IC_PM
#define OS_FONT_1    "Helvetica"
#define OS_FONT_2    "Courier"
#else   // Windows
#define OS_FONT_1    "Arial"
#define OS_FONT_2    "Courier New"
#endif

void main()
{
  // Create the frame, client canvas, and client controls.
  IFrameWindow aFrame( "Using Common Font Functions" );
  IMultiCellCanvas aClient( IC_FRAME_CLIENT_ID,
                            &aFrame, &aFrame );
  IEntryField myEntryField( 1001, &aClient, &aClient );
  ICheckBox myCB1( 1002, &aClient, &aClient );
  ICheckBox myCB2( 1003, &aClient, &aClient );
  ICheckBox myCB3( 1004, &aClient, &aClient );
  aFrame.setClient( &aClient );

  // Add the controls to the canvas.
  aClient
    .addToCell( &myEntryField, 2, 2 )
    .addToCell( &myCB1,        2, 4 )
    .addToCell( &myCB2,        2, 5 )
    .addToCell( &myCB3,        2, 6 );

  // Set the text of the entry field.
  myEntryField.setText( "ABCDEFGabcdefg" );

  // Set the text of the check boxes.
  myCB1.setText( "Choice 1" );
  myCB2.setText( "Choice 2" );
  myCB3.setText( "Choice 3" );

  // Create a font object, providing a typeface name
  // and point size and apply it to the frame.
  IFont font1( OS_FONT_1, 14 );
  aFrame.setFont( font1 );

  // Increase the point size; then, apply it to the entry field.
  font1.setPointSize( 24 );
  myEntryField.setFont( font1 );

  // Change the typeface name; decrease the point size,
  // and then apply it to check box 1.
  font1.setName( OS_FONT_2 ).setPointSize( 10 );
  myCB1.setFont( font1 );

  // Create a new font from check box 1.  Change the
  // font characteristics, and then apply it to check box 2.
  IFont font2( &myCB1 );
  font2.setBold().setItalic();
  myCB2.setFont( font2 );

  // Create a default font, and then apply it to check box 3.
  IFont font3;
  myCB3.setFont( font3 );

  // Show the frame and run the application.
  aFrame
    .setFocus()
    .show();
  IApplication::current().run();
}
```

Geometry Accessors

In addition to modifying an existing IFont object, your application often needs to query for information about the font in use, such as the height of an individual character or the width of a string of characters. This is important for formatting text or laying out text-based information. Open Class Library uses several of these geometry accessors to calculate the minimum size of windows that contain text in ICanvas and its derived classes. Note that all geometry accessors return values in numbers of pixels rather than points.

The two most common accessors are maxCharHeight and avgCharWidth. The first returns the maximum height of any character within the character set for the font, and the second returns the average character width for the font. Use charWidth to determine the individual width of a single character and textWidth to determine the width of an entire string of characters. The IFont class also provides the following geometry accessors:

- externalLeading, which queries the recommended spacing between lines of text for the font.

- internalLeading, which retrieves any space that the font designer includes in each character of the font.

- maxAscender, which finds the maximum ascent of any character. This is the distance between the baseline of the character and the maximum height that any character reaches. It is typically the height of the largest uppercase letter, where the baseline is the point at the bottom of an uppercase letter.

- maxDescender, which queries for the maximum descent. This is the distance between the baseline and the bottom of the letter that drops the lowest below the baseline, typically lowercase letters such as g, j, and y.

- maxSize, which determines the maximum size a character can be (the maximum width and height of the character).

Note that the maximum character height is equivalent to the maximum ascender, maximum descender, and the internal *leading* value added together. Leading is the space, in points, between the lines of type.

Advanced Font Topics

The previous topics describe what you need for most of your applications. However, IFont provides additional functions if you need additional control over a font. This control is especially important in graphic applications and in printing. These additional functions are supported only for vector fonts; you cannot use them with bitmap fonts. If you try, an exception is thrown.

Although you use the IFont function pointSize to change the size of each character, you may want to specify the exact width or height of the characters no matter how much it skews the character shape. Modify the width of the *character box* with setCharWidth, modify its height with setCharHeight, and change both at once using setCharSize. The character box is an imaginary box, which, if drawn, would surround each character. All values are expressed in pixels, which means that code written using these values is not device-independent. In addition to changing the size of the character box, you can change the shape of the character box or draw lines of characters at an angle. Use setFontShear for the former and setFontAngle for the latter.

IFont also provides two nested cursor classes: IFont::FaceNameCursor and IFont::PointSizeCursor. Use IFont::FaceNameCursor to navigate through a list of available typeface names on the operating system. When creating the cursor, you can specify that you want to look at all available fonts, all bitmap fonts, or all vector fonts. Use IFont::PointSizeCursor to provide a list of all available point sizes for a given typeface name. This is only necessary for bitmap fonts because you can scale vector fonts to any size.

The following example demonstrates using several of these functions in a graphical application. We use an IDrawingCanvas to paint a text string at a variety of angles and colors. Note that we call both setFontShear and setFontAngle for a Windows program but only setFontAngle for an OS/2 program. We do this because the OS/2 operating system implements automatic character rotation when you change the font angle, but in the Windows operating system you need to do this yourself to get the same result. Figure 18-4 displays the resulting window.

Advanced Font Techniques - fonts\advfont\advfont.cpp

```
#include <iapp.hpp>
#include <icolor.hpp>
#include <ifont.hpp>
#include <iframe.hpp>
#include <igrafctx.hpp>
#include <iglist.hpp>
#include <igstring.hpp>
#include <ipoint.hpp>
#include <istring.hpp>
#include "advfont.hpp"

// Specific font names vary between operating systems,
// complicating the issue of writing portable applications.
// Avoid hardcoding the names in the code as follows.
#ifdef IC_PM
#define OS_FONT_1    "Helvetica"
#else  // Windows
#define OS_FONT_1    "Arial"
#endif

IColor colArray[8]={IColor::blue, IColor::red, IColor::green,
                    IColor::black, IColor::cyan, IColor::yellow,
                    IColor::pink, IColor::darkGray };
IPoint ptArray[16]= { IPoint(0,4), IPoint(1,3), IPoint(2,2),
                      IPoint(3,1), IPoint(4,0), IPoint(3,-1),
                      IPoint(2,-2), IPoint(1,-3), IPoint(0,-4),
                      IPoint(-1,-3),IPoint(-2,-2),IPoint(-3,-1),
                      IPoint(-4,0), IPoint(-3,1), IPoint(-2,2),
                      IPoint(-1,3) };

void main()
{
  // Create the frame and a canvas client to draw on.
  IFrameWindow aFrame( "Using Advanced Font Functions" );
  FontDrawingArea aClient( IC_FRAME_CLIENT_ID,
                           &aFrame, &aFrame );
  aFrame.setClient( &aClient );
```

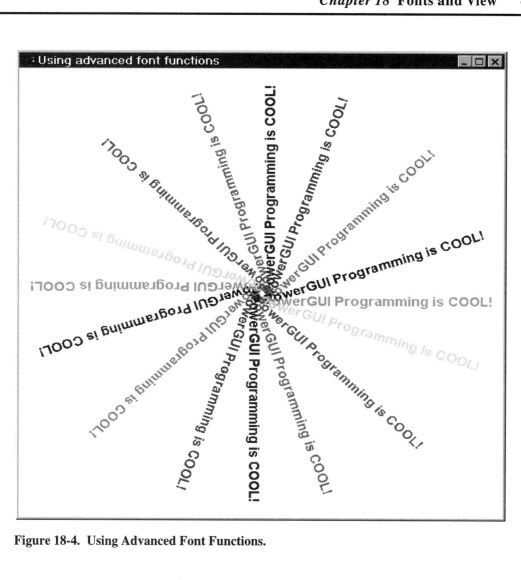

Figure 18-4. Using Advanced Font Functions.

```
  // Size and show the frame and run the application.
  aFrame
    .moveSizeToClient( aClient.rect() )
    .setFocus()
    .show();
  IApplication::current().run();
}

FontDrawingArea::FontDrawingArea( unsigned long windowId,
   IWindow* parent, IWindow* owner, const IRectangle& initial )
   : IDrawingCanvas( windowId, parent, owner, initial,
        IDrawingCanvas::defaultStyle() | IWindow::clipSiblings )
{
  // Initialize string with a catchy phrase.
  IString str( "PowerGUI Programming is COOL!" );
```

```
  // Get the graphic context of the canvas for drawing.
  IGraphicContext gc( this->handle() );

  // Create a graphic bundle for setting colors.
  IGraphicBundle gb(gc);

  // Create a graphic list for saving graphic strings.
  this->setGraphicList( new IGList() );

  // Create a font object, providing name and point size.
  IFont font( OS_FONT_1, 14, false, true );
  font.setBold();

  // Calculate the size of the displayed string in this font
  // and size the window accordingly, adding a buffer each way.
  unsigned long strSize = font.textWidth( str );
  IRectangle drawRect( IPoint( 20, 30 ),
                       ISize( 2*strSize+30, 2*strSize+30 ));
  this->moveSizeTo( drawRect );

  // Get the center point of the font drawing area.
  IPoint point( drawRect.centerXCenterY() );
  point -= IPoint( 20, 20 );

  // Iterate through the list of angles and colors, changing the
  // font and graphic attributes, and build a list of graphic
  // strings drawn at that angle with those colors.
  int i;
  for ( i=0; i<16; i++ )
  {
#ifdef IC_WIN
    font.setFontShear( ptArray[i] );
#endif
    font.setFontAngle( ptArray[i] );
    gb.setPenColor( colArray[i%8] );

    // Create a graphic string, starting at point
    // with text and font you want
    IGString* text = new IGString( str, point, font );
    text->setGraphicBundle( gb );
    text->drawOn(gc);

    // Add the graphic string (with attributes) to the list.
    this->graphicList()->addAsLast( *text );
  }
}

FontDrawingArea::~FontDrawingArea( )
{
  // Delete all the graphic objects in the drawing canvas.
  IGList::Cursor graphicsCursor( *graphicList() );
  for ( graphicsCursor.setToFirst();
        graphicsCursor.isValid();
        graphicsCursor.setToNext() )
  {
    IGraphic*
      graphic(&(graphicList()->graphicAt(graphicsCursor)));
    delete graphic;
  }
  delete graphicList();
}
```

Font Selection

At the beginning of the chapter we discussed the nonportability of many of the typeface names between operating systems. Another solution to this is to allow the application user to select the font to use. This is important for applications like editors, browsers, and desktop publishing packages. To meet this need, Open Class Library provides the IFontDialog class, which enables an application to create and display font dialogs in your application. A *font dialog* is a selection dialog that enables users to view a list of font typeface names, styles, and point sizes available on their systems and to select from them. In addition to a selection list, the selection dialog also contains a preview area that contains some sample text demonstrating what the currently selected typeface name, point size, and attributes looks like.

Creating a Font Dialog

Before you create an IFontDialog, you need to learn about another class first, the nested class IFontDialog::Settings. You use it to define the initial data, styles, and attributes of a font dialog. The IFontDialog::Settings object controls the appearance and use of the font dialog, and it also returns the font that the users choose.

To create an IFontDialog::Settings object, you typically pass an initial font on the constructor. If a font is not passed, the default font is used. Once the object is created, you customize the initial values using a variety of member functions. Use setFont to replace the initial font. Specify the new IFont value that you want to use to replace the current one. As mentioned earlier, the dialog contains a preview area that shows how the selected font will appear. Use setPreviewText to specify the string of text that will be used as the sample. Use setPosition to set the initial position of the dialog. Specify the position relative to the parent window of the dialog. Specify the text that will appear in the title of the dialog by using setTitle.

You may want some of your applications to use this dialog to select fonts for a specific display or printer device. In these cases, they can use setDisplayPS or setPrinterPS and specify the graphic context to query for the available fonts.

Your application can extend the font dialog functions by adding additional controls onto the dialog. An application uses setDialogTemplate and specifies the custom dialog template resource desired. Retrieving information from these controls is accomplished through the use of a handler.

Now that the settings object is initialized, you create the dialog from it. To create an IFontDialog object, provide the owning and parent window of the dialog and the settings object created above. Optionally, you can specify several dialog styles to control the appearance and functions of the dialog, as well as a handler to be attached to the dialog when it is created.

The font dialog by default is a *modal dialog*. This means that you cannot interact with the application until you dismiss the font dialog. Modify this behavior by specifying the IFontDialog::modeless style. See the "Displaying Application-Modal Frame Windows" topic in Chapter 5, "Frame Window Basics," for more information on modal windows.

The graphic engine of the Windows operating systems and the OS/2 operating system can synthesize a font. It does this when it cannot find an exact match for a requested set of parameters but through synthesis can come close. For example, suppose your application uses the font "MyFavoriteFont." In one part of that application, you want to use a bold version of this font. If "MyFavoriteFont Bold" does not exist, you cannot do this. However, using synthesis, the graphic engine could make the font appear bold by drawing each character twice, first in the original position and then again one pixel to the right. For most applications, it is important that certain attributes are reflected in the font as requested, which is why this feature is important. However, because font quality may degrade using this feature (for example, character outlines may not be as precise), you may want your applications to list only real fonts. To do this, an application sets the style `IFontDialog::noSynthesize`.

A number of additional buttons can be added to the font dialog. You can select from several styles to add these buttons. Use `IFontDialog::helpButton` to add a button to the dialog, which, when a user presses it, generates a request for help. See Chapter 23, "Using Help," for more information on using help. Use `IFontDialog::applyButton` to add a button that the user can use to apply the current selection without dismissing the dialog. Use this style with modeless dialogs. In the OS/2 operating system, use `IFontDialog::resetButton` to provide a button that resets the dialog to the initial values that were set when it was first displayed.

There are also several styles that you can use for filtering the types of fonts that will appear in the dialog list. If you want to list only those fonts rendered with bitmaps, specify `IFontDialog::bitmapOnly`. If you want to list only those fonts rendered with vectors, use `IFontDialog::vectorOnly`. For Windows operating systems, this includes both TrueType fonts and those vector fonts used in earlier versions of Windows. In the OS/2 operating system, this includes Adobe Type Manager fonts and vector fonts from early versions of the OS/2 operating system. Use `IFontDialog::fixedWidthOnly` to filter the list to display only fixed-space fonts. In the OS/2 operating system, use `IFontDialog::proportionalOnly` to list only proportionally spaced fonts.

Retrieving the Selection

After users dismiss a dialog, check whether they selected a font from the choices provided or whether they cancelled the dialog without making a selection. Check the users' actions with `IFontDialog::pressedOK`. If the users ended a dialog by pressing the **OK** push button, this member returns `true`. A value of `false` indicates that the users pressed **Cancel** or an error occurred.

If the users selected a font and pressed **OK**, then the font object that was used to initialize the settings object is modified to now represent the users' selections. This `IFont` object can then be applied to textual information in your application using `IFont::setWindowFont` or `IWindow::setFont`.

Adding a Handler

An important way to use the font dialog is to keep the dialog displayed while the results of any selections are applied. Do not dismiss the dialog until the users decide on their final choices. Open Class Library provides the IFontDialogHandler class to do this. Use this class, coupled with a font dialog created with the IFontDialog::modeless and IFontDialog::applyButton styles, to handle this trial-and-error method. The IFontDialogHandler class is also useful when you want your application to extend the functions of the font dialog by adding additional controls. User interaction with these new controls is handled by overriding dispatchHandlerEvent and adding the appropriate event-processing logic.

The following example shows a command handler that uses IFontDialog to enable users to select the font and attributes for displaying the graphic string in the previous example. It also demonstrates a class derived from IFontDialogHandler, MyDlgHandler, that you use to apply a selection without dismissing the dialog. Figure 18-5 displays the font dialog on the Windows operating system.

Selecting Fonts Using the Font Dialog - fonts\fontdlg\fontdlg.cpp

```
IBase::Boolean FontDialogExample::command(
                              ICommandEvent& cmdEvent )
{
  switch ( cmdEvent.commandId() )
  {
    case MI_FONTDLG:
    {
        // Create a font dialog handler, passing the frame
        // window for use during modeless processing.
        MyDlgHandler applyHandler( this );

        // Initialize a settings object with the current font.
        IFontDialog::Settings settings( &currentFont );

        // Set the preview text, title, and initial position.
        settings.setPreviewText( "PowerGUI is COOL!" );
        settings.setTitle( "Select a New Font" );
        settings.setPosition( IPoint( 450, 2 ) );

        // Create a modeless dialog containing an apply button,
        // and only list vector fonts.  Attach the font dialog
        // handler created above to handle the apply button.
        IFontDialog fntDlg( IWindow::desktopWindow(), this,
                       &applyHandler,
                       IFontDialog::modeless |
                       IFontDialog::applyButton |
                       IFontDialog::vectorOnly, settings );

        // Check if the user selected a font and if so, update
        // the drawing area using the new font.
        if (fntDlg.pressedOK())
          this->updateDemo( currentFont );

        return (true);
    }

    case MI_EXIT:
      this->close();
      return(true);
  }
}
```

```
IBase::Boolean MyDlgHandler::modelessApply(
            IFontDialog* modelessDialog, IFont* appliedFont )
{
   fhwnd->updateDemo( *appliedFont );
   return true;
}
```

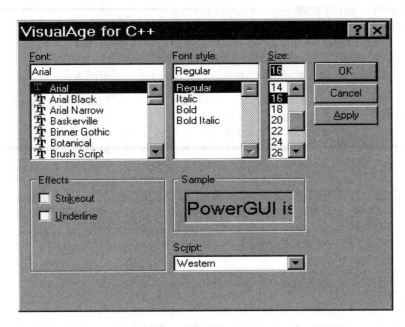

Figure 18-5. Font Dialog in the Windows Operating System.

File Selection

Although this chapter has focused on using and selecting fonts, many applications also work with information that is stored in files. Users of these applications need to be able to list existing files, select from them, and either load information or save new work. To meet this need, Open Class Library provides the IFileDialog class, which enables an application to create and display a file dialog in your application. A *file dialog* is a selection dialog that enables users to view the names of files available, both on their systems or across a network. Users can select from a list of drives, directories, and files, or they can enter a file name directly.

Creating a File Dialog

As in IFontDialog, you use the nested class IFileDialog::Settings to define the initial data, styles, and attributes of a file dialog. The IFileDialog::Settings object controls the appearance and use of the file dialog, and you can also use it to return the file name or names the users choose.

Use the default constructor to initially create an `IFileDialog::Settings` object. After the object is created, customize the dialog values using any of the following member functions. Most importantly, set the type of file dialog you want to create. Use `setOpenDialog` to indicate that the dialog will be an Open dialog. Use `setSaveAsDialog` to request a Save As dialog. The default type of dialog is an Open dialog.

Also as in `IFontDialog`, set the initial position of the dialog using `setPosition`. Specify the position relative to the parent window of the dialog. Specify the text that appears in the title of the dialog by using `setTitle`, and indicate that a custom dialog template is to be displayed with `setDialogTemplate`.

There are several member functions that affect the initial information displayed by the dialog. Specify the initial file name and directory to be displayed by using `setFileName`. Use `setInitialDrive` to select the initial drive that you want to list the contents from. In the OS/2 operating system, use `setInitialFileType` to indicate the initial extended attribute (EA) to filter the file name list with, and use `addFileType` to add additional EA descriptions to the filtering list.

Because a file dialog can be Open or Save As, your application can provide the users with an additional visual clue as to what actions will be performed when they choose a file. To do this, use `setOKButtonText` to change the text of the **OK** button to something more descriptive, such as "Open file" or "Save as."

After initializing the settings object, use it to create the dialog. To create an `IFileDialog` object, provide the owning and parent window of the dialog in addition to the settings object. You can modify the appearance and functions of the dialog by using several different styles, and you can specify a handler to be attached to the dialog.

You can also use `IFileDialog::helpButton` to add a help button to the dialog. When users press it, it generates a request for help.

Some applications such as editors and browsers work with multiple files at once. In this case, users may want to select more than one file at a time. Use `IFileDialog::multiSelection` to enable the dialog to support this. The default file dialog is a single-selection dialog, meaning that users can select only one file at a time.

Retrieving the Selection

After the users dismiss the dialog, check whether they selected a file name or names from the list, or whether they canceled the dialog without making a selection. Check the users' actions by using `IFileDialog::pressedOK`. If the users ended the dialog by pressing the **OK** push button, this member returns true. A value of false indicates that the users pressed **Cancel** or that an error occurred.

If the users selected a file name and pressed **OK**, then you can retrieve the file name or names. For a single selection style of dialog, use `IFileDialog::fileName` to get the selected file name. For a multiple selection style of dialog, first query for the count of the number of files selected using `IFileDialog::selectedFileCount`. Then, after you have retrieved the file count, iterate the list from 1 to the total number of files by using `IFileDialog::fileName` and by passing the index of the file to be retrieved.

Adding a Handler

As with `IFontDialog`, additional control over a file dialog is enabled through the use of a handler. Open Class Library provides both the `IFileDialogHandler` and `IFileDialogEvent` classes to facilitate adding this support to your application. Use the `IFileDialogHandler` class when you want your application to extend the functions of the file dialog by adding additional controls to the dialog. Or, use it to validate the users' file name selection before the dialog is dismissed. Handle the users' interactions with these new controls by overriding `dispatchHandlerEvent` and by adding the appropriate event-processing logic. Use `IFileDialogHandler` to validate a selected file name and override `validateName`. The first parameter of the event is an IString containing the file name that the user selected. If `validateName` returns `true`, the file dialog is dismissed and this file name is returned. If it returns `false`, your application does not accept the file name and the dialog is not dismissed.

The following example demonstrates using `IFileDialog` to create an Open dialog so users can select a file name that they will use to populate an edit window. It also shows how to create a Save As dialog that they can use to select a file name to save the contents of the edit window. Figure 18-6 displays the file dialog on the Windows operating system.

Selecting Files Using the File Dialog - fonts\filedlg\filedlg.cpp

```
#include <iapp.hpp>
#include <ifiledlg.hpp>
#include <imsgbox.hpp>
#include <istring.hpp>
#include "filedlg.hpp"
#include "filedlg.h"

void main()
{
  // Create a primary window that contains a read-only MLE.
  IFrameWindow primary( "Using the File Dialog", MAIN_WINDOW,
      IFrameWindow::defaultStyle() | IFrameWindow::menuBar );
  IMultiLineEdit
    mle( IC_FRAME_CLIENT_ID, &primary, &primary,
         IRectangle(),
         (IMultiLineEdit::classDefaultStyle
           | IMultiLineEdit::horizontalScroll
           | IMultiLineEdit::readOnly )
         & ~IMultiLineEdit::wordWrap );
  primary.setClient( &mle );

  // Create a command handler for the menu bar.
  MyCommandHandler cmdHandler( &primary, &mle );
  cmdHandler.handleEventsFor( &primary );

  // Set the input focus, and show the window.
  primary
    .setFocus()
    .show();

  // Start event processing.
  IApplication::current().run();
}
```

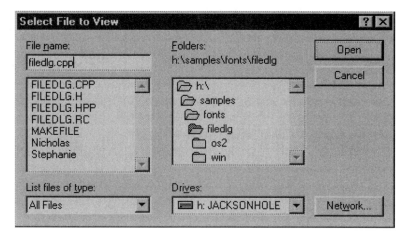

Figure 18-6. File Dialog in the Windows Operating System.

```
IBase::Boolean MyCommandHandler::command(
                                  ICommandEvent& cmdEvent )
{
  switch ( cmdEvent.commandId() )
  {
    case MI_OPENDLG:       // Open dialog processing.
    {
      // Initialize a dialog settings object.
      IFileDialog::Settings settings;

      // Set the initial file name, title and position.
      settings.setFileName( __FILE__ );
      settings.setOKButtonText( "Open" );
      settings.setTitle( "Select File to View" );
      settings.setPosition( IPoint( 50, 50 ) );

      // Create a file dialog using the default styles.
      IFileDialog fileDlg( IWindow::desktopWindow(),
                        frame, settings );

      // Check if a file name was selected.
      if (fileDlg.pressedOK())
      {
        // Empty any contents of the MLE.
        mle->removeAll();

        // Retrieve the file name selected.
        IString selectedFile = fileDlg.fileName();

        // Read the contents of the file into the MLE
        // and scroll to the top of the file.
        mle->importFromFile( selectedFile );
        mle->setCursorLinePosition( 0 );
      }
      return (true);
    }

    case MI_SAVEASDLG:     // Save As dialog processing.
    {
      // Initialize a dialog settings object.
      IFileDialog::Settings settings;
```

```
      // Set the initial file name, title, and position.
      settings.setFileName( "TEMPFILE" );
      settings.setTitle( "Select File Name to Save As" );
      settings.setPosition( IPoint( 50, 50 ) );

      // Make this dialog a Save As dialog.
      settings.setSaveAsDialog();

      // Create a file dialog using the default styles.
      IFileDialog fileDlg( IWindow::desktopWindow(),
                           frame, settings );

      // Check if a file name was selected.
      if (fileDlg.pressedOK())
      {
         // Retrieve the file name selected.
         IString selectedFile = fileDlg.fileName();

         // Double check with the user before overwriting file.
         IMessageBox msgBox( frame );
         IMessageBox::Response reply =
           msgBox.show( "Are you sure you want to overwrite
                        this file?", IMessageBox::okCancelButton |
                        IMessageBox::queryIcon );
         // If user concurs, overwrite the file.
         if (reply == IMessageBox::ok)
         {
            // Write the contents of the MLE to the file.
            mle->exportToFile( selectedFile );
         }
      }
      return (true);
   }

   case MI_EXIT:
      frame->close();
      return(true);
   }

   return(false);
}
```

Chapter 19

Advanced Frame Window Topics

- Describes topics dealing with frame windows not covered in Chapter 5
- Describes the IFrameWindow, IFrameExtension, and IFrameHandler classes
- Read Chapter 5 before reading this chapter.
- Chapters 20 and 25 cover related material.

Chapter 5, "Frame Window Basics," provides a description of the Open Class Library IFrameWindow class and the most-used features of frame window objects. This chapter describes some of those aspects in greater detail, covers less commonly used features, and provides a robust example of primary and secondary frame windows in an object-oriented application.

Frame Window Constructor Arguments

When you construct an IFrameWindow you must specify a certain set of frame attribute values. These attribute values are a subset of the complete set of frame attribute values. The subset contains those attribute values that roughly correspond to the set of attributes you would be required to provide for the creation of a frame window using the presentation system directly.

You do not need to explicitly specify all of these attribute values. In fact, most of the time you do not need to specify more than one or two. With IFrameWindow, you can control the default behavior of the objects so that construction of most frame windows is very simple. The examples in Chapter 5, "Frame Window Basics" illustrate this. Most of the time, you can construct your frame windows without having to handle the details and complexity covered in this chapter.

You can specify up to six different arguments on the IFrameWindow constructors: resource identifier, owner window, parent window, style, initial size and position, and window title. The next six topics describe each of these attribute values.

Specifying a Resource Identifier

The resource identifier constructor argument identifies the resources used to construct your frame window. You might need some or all of the resources described in Table 19-1 to construct a frame window. Even if your IFrameWindow does not need these resources, you still

Table 19-1. Frame Window Resource Types

Resource Type	How and When Used

dialog template	Some IFrameWindow constructors attempt to load the frame window definition from a dialog template resource with the specified resource identifier. These are the three constructors with signatures:
	
	`IFrameWindow ( unsigned long id = IC_DEFAULT_FRAME_ID,`
	`              FrameSource    source = tryDialogResource );`
	`IFrameWindow ( const IResourceId& resId,`
	`              IWindow*          owner = 0,`
	`              FrameSource       source = tryDialogResource );`
	`IFrameWindow ( const IResourceId& resId,`
	`              IWindow*          parent,`
	`              IWindow*          owner,`
	`              FrameSource       source = tryDialogResource );`
	
	Note: IFrameWindow does not attempt to load a dialog template resource if you use any of the other constructors or if you use IFrameWindow::noDialogResource as the value for the source argument.

icon	If you construct the frame window with the IFrameWindow::minimizedIcon style, it loads an icon resource with the specified resource identifier. This icon appears in the frame window's system menu button. The system also uses this icon to represent the frame window when a user minimizes it. If you require this resource, and the constructor cannot find it in the resource library, the IFrameWindow constructor throws an IAccessError exception.
menu	If you construct the frame window with the IFrameWindow::menuBar style, then a menu resource with the argument identifier is loaded. This menu defines the content of the frame window's menu bar. If you require this resource, and the constructor cannot find it in the resource library, the IFrameWindow constructor throws an IAccessError exception.
accelerator table	If you construct the frame window with the IFrameWindow::accelerator style, an accelerator table is loaded from the resource library and attached to the frame window. This table defines shortcut keys a user can press to select command choices. If the accelerator table cannot be found, the IFrameWindow constructor throws an IAccessError exception.
string	If you do not provide a title string as a constructor argument, then IFrameWindow attempts to load a string with the argument resource identifier. If the frame window can load the string, it uses it as the frame window's title text. If the frame window cannot find the string resource, then Open Class Library gives the frame window a default title. Normally, this is the name of the application's .EXE file.

must provide a resource identifier argument on the `IFrameWindow` constructor. There are two exceptions: you do not need one for the constructor you use to attach an `IFrameWindow` object to an existing frame window or for the default constructor.

The resource identifier argument has type `IResourceId`. Construct it from a numeric identifier if you want Open Class Library to load the resources from the default user-resource library. Alternatively, you can also just specify the numeric identifier so that Open Class Library constructs the `IResourceId` object automatically. Use the following expression to get the default resource library.

```
IApplication::current().userResourceLibrary()
```

To load the frame's resources from a different resource library, construct the resource identifier argument using both a numeric identifier and a resource library. Do this by explicitly specifying the library using an expression such as this:

```
IResourceId( RES_ID, "resource.dll" )
```

Chapter 24, "Using Resources" provides details on how to control the loading of resources.

The `IFrameWindow` object uses the numeric portion of the resource identifier as the frame's window identifier. If you need to obtain this identifier from the frame window, use the `IWindow::id` function to obtain its value instead of operating system provided functions.

Using an Owner Window

Frame windows can have an owner window. We group `IFrameWindows` into one of two categories based upon whether they have an owner. *Primary* windows are frames without an owner; *secondary* windows are frames with an owner.

The ownership of a frame window affects the behavior of the frame in important ways. When your application displays a modal dialog, the operating system enforces modality by disabling the owner window of the dialog. This prevents users from interacting with the owner until they dismiss the modal dialog. Ownership also affects the behavior of frame windows in the following ways:

- When a user minimizes, restores, or closes a primary window, the primary window minimizes, restores, or closes its associated secondary windows.

- Open Class Library performs some special processing when it detects the closing of the last primary window on a thread. When that happens, Open Class Library posts a `WM_QUIT` message to that thread. This causes a return from any pending calls to the `ICurrentApplication::run` or the `ICurrentThread::processMsgs` functions. By creating your application's windows as secondary windows owned by your application's main window, you cause event processing for your application to continue until its main, or primary, window is closed. See the "Closing Frame Windows" topic in Chapter 5 for greater detail.

- A frame window always brings secondary windows it owns to the foreground—to the top of the presentation system Z-order—when a user gives it the input focus.

This last feature has both positive and negative aspects. On one hand, this enables you to construct dialogs related to your primary window and to ensure that whenever a user activates the primary window, those related windows become visible, too. This is desirable for tool palettes and nonmodal utilities, such as an editor's search dialog. On the other hand, those secondary windows can get in the way, overlaying and obscuring the primary window with which a user really wants to interact. Because they are always displayed in the foreground, make secondary windows movable and sizable. In this way, a user can move them out of the way if they cover up something important on the primary window.

Use secondary windows to view actions and components of the objects being viewed in a primary window. Provide an owner argument only when constructing secondary frame windows. In other cases, you construct the frame window without an explicit owner, thus making it a primary window. You do this by passing a value of 0 for the owner window argument of the IFrameWindow constructor.

Using a Parent Window

Because they are just another type of presentation system window, frame windows have a parent window, too. For the most part, a frame's relationship to its parent is the same as that between any two presentation system windows. The child frame window is clipped to its parent. Because of this, child frame windows cannot readily be moved beyond the borders of their parent. The presentation system destroys the child frame window when it destroys the parent frame.

Typically, frame windows have the desktop window as parent. Thus, users can position their windows where they prefer. This means that you rarely provide a parent window constructor argument when creating an IFrameWindow. When you do not specify it explicitly, the frame's parent is the desktop window. To explicitly use the desktop window as the parent, specify either IWindow::desktopWindow() or 0 as the argument value.

Sometimes you need to construct frame windows that do not have the desktop as the parent. These frames are child windows. In almost all cases, make the parent and owner the same window. The following example shows how to load a child dialog as a page in an INotebook:

```
INotebook
  noteBook;
INotebook::PageSettings
  settings( myAttribute ); // Set page settings with
                           // appropriate attributes.
noteBook.addLastPage( settings,
                new IFrameWindow( dialogId,
                                    &noteBook, &noteBook ) );
```

A window arrangement containing child frame windows is characteristic of a *multiple document interface* (MDI). Many examples of MDI interfaces occur in Windows 3.x programs, including the Program Manager itself. The user interface styles in the Windows 95 desktop and the OS/2 Workplace Shell usually do not use MDI; they use secondary views or notebook dialogs instead. You can make a direct comparison of the two styles in the Windows 95 operating system by examining a similar function in the Explorer and File Manager programs. Explorer appears by default in the **Start->Programs** menu, and you can find the File Manager as fileman.exe in the Windows 95 directory. Explorer presents you with a list of the drives and directories on your system in a tree view in the left panel. When you select something, you see a detailed view on the right of what you have selected on the left. You can navigate the entire file system by expanding the tree in the left panel. File Manager uses an MDI-style interface. It presents you with a child frame window for each drive on your system. To move to a different drive, select the drive's icon or activate its window using the menu. If you minimize the view of a drive, the system draws its minimized icon at the bottom of the parent frame.

You can construct child frame windows easily enough; there are two constructors that accept parent window arguments. The standard `IFrameWindow` implementation provides basic child window behavior sufficient for using `IFrameWindow` objects as notebook pages, for example. However, Open Class Library does not provide any specific support for implementing the unique frame window behavior inherent in the MDI definition. You can only accomplish this by processing the appropriate events yourself and by managing the child windows, as necessary. Later in this chapter, you learn how to extend `IFrameWindow` to take advantage of special MDI support offered by the Windows operating system.

Specifying a Style

One of the most important attribute values of the frame window that you specify at construction time is its style. Some `IFrameWindow` styles control the appearance of the standard frame window components, such as the system menu, title bar, and border, that users use to interact with the frame window. The styles that control components roughly correspond to the underlying system styles that perform these functions. Open Class Library adds additional styles to give you control over the loading of menus, icons, and accelerators during `IFrameWindow` construction and in the initial positioning of the frame window.

Class `IFrameWindow` contains constant data members, which enumerate the set of valid frame window styles. These style members have type `IFrameWindow::Style`. This class is a derived bit flag class. See Chapter 26, "Data Types," for more information on the `IBitFlag` class.

The "IFrameWindow, Public Data" section of the *VisualAge for C++ Open Class Library Reference* lists the frame window styles. In this section, you find important information about how to use the styles when you construct frame windows. Consider the points in the following list for using frame window styles:

- `IFrameWindow` defines styles that correspond to each standard frame component. If you want your frame window to have a given standard component, such as the system menu or maximize button, turn on that style bit in the style argument that you pass to the `IFrameWindow` constructor. Conversely, turn off the style bit to remove the corresponding component. You can add or remove components from a frame dynamically. See Chapter 5 for information on how to do this.

- If you use the styles `minimizedIcon`, `menuBar`, or `accelerator`, then resources of type icon, menu, and accelerator table must be available to your application. These resources must have the identifier of and reside in the resource library, which is specified by the resource identifier argument provided to the frame window constructor. If you specify these styles, and the corresponding resource cannot be found, the `IFrameWindow` constructor throws an `IAccessError` exception.

Because the Open Class Library default style does not require you to define resources, the default that Open Class Library provides does not set these styles. You must explicitly add these styles when you construct the frame or use `IFrameWindow::setDefaultStyle` to set them for all subsequently constructed frame windows.

You can use function calls as an alternative to these styles. Use the `IFrameWindow::setIcon` function to set the icon, and use the `IMenuBar` and `IAccelerator` classes to set the menu and accelerators. You might need to use this approach when you construct the frame window from a dialog template because the constructors for dialog template frame windows do not accept the style argument.

- Specify the `titleBar` style if you want any of the standard frame components that appear on the title bar. This includes the system menu and minimize/maximize buttons. If you use these styles without specifying a title bar, Open Class Library implicitly turns on the `titleBar` style.

- With Open Class Library's `IFrameWindow` objects, you can create windows in the minimized or maximized state. If you specify either of the `minimized` or `maximized` styles on the `IFrameWindow` constructor, the window is automatically minimized or maximized. If you specify both of these styles, the window is created in the minimized state.

- The `deferCreation` flag is not really a style; it is a setting. This setting instructs `IFrameWindow` to defer the creation of the underlying presentation system frame window. As a result, any other styles specified with `deferCreation` on the constructor invocation are ignored. Typically, you use this setting when you need to create the presentation system frame window yourself. When you finally link the `IFrameWindow` object with an underlying presentation system window, specify all your `IFrameWindow` style flags at that point. Do that by calling the `create` or `initialize` member functions.

- Class `IFrameWindow` discards the `shellPosition` style if you construct your frame window with an explicit initial size and position rectangle because the default style includes `shellPosition`. If the style took precedence, you would have to override the default style whenever you wanted a specific initial size and position. By providing an explicit size and position, you indicate that you do not want `shellPosition`.

The style argument is optional. If you do not specify a style, `IFrameWindow` uses a default style. If the frame is constructed from a dialog template, it uses the styles and control flags specified in the dialog template. Otherwise, it uses the current default `IFrameWindow` style returned by the static member function `IFrameWindow::defaultStyle`. Unless you change it, the current default style is the same style as defined by `IFrameWindow::classDefaultStyle`. This default style includes each of the following style settings:

titleBar	minimizeButton	windowList
systemMenu	maximizeButton	appDBCSStatus
sizingBorder		

You can modify the default style in your application by calling
IFrameWindow::setDefaultStyle. When you do this, you turn certain styles on or off. Here is
an example of code that changes the default frame style to include the menuBar setting:

```
void main()
{
// All my frames will load menus from resource libraries.
IFrameWindow::setDefaultStyle( IFrameWindow::classDefaultStyle
                             | IFrameWindow::menuBar );
// ...
}
```

The **advframe\fstyle** program on the examples disk is another, more elaborate example that
accepts specification of the frame styles as command line arguments and creates a frame
window with the specified style. Use this program to test combinations of frame styles and to
show you how to manipulate style objects. You can use the program by entering a command
similar to this:

```
start fstyle default ~title
```

This command causes the program to create a frame with the default style but without a title
bar.

Specifying an Initial Size and Position

You can specify the frame window's initial size and position when you construct an
IFrameWindow.

If you construct the frame from a dialog template, the template specifies the frame's initial
size and position. For example, use the following template to construct an IFrameWindow.

```
DLGTEMPLATE IC_DEFAULT_FRAME_ID
  BEGIN
    DIALOG "Title", 1, 10, 10, 100, 40
      BEGIN
      /* Controls omitted for clarity ...  */
      END
  END
```

The result is a frame window positioned at IPoint(10,10) with ISize(100,40). When
constructing an IFrameWindow from a dialog template, you cannot specify an explicit initial
size and position for the frame window. It uses the initial size and position specified in the
dialog template resource.

If you are not constructing the frame window from a dialog template, use the
IFrameWindow::shellPosition style to give the frame a default initial size and position, the
shell position. This style results in a window sized and positioned by Open Class Library. You
get a large window in a different position from other recently created frame windows.

The shell position is better than hardcoding a position of the frame because variables such as
screen size are accounted for. However, following a user's lead is best. The ideal strategy is to
identify where each user last positioned the windows and to reopen them in the same size and
position.

However, the IFrameWindow constructor, which lets you specify an explicit initial size and
position, also requires parent and owner window arguments that you might not want to bother
with. You can establish the initial size and position of your frame windows as follows:

- Save the size and position of all of your application's windows. When a user reopens a view, position and size the frame window to the saved values. The easiest way to do this is to create the frame window with the shell position style, but hide it using `~IWindow::visible`. Then, position the frame to the stored values. Finally, show the frame.

- Use the shell position the first time you open a view.

- If you must force a view to a given size, for example, if your frame window's contents do not fill up the shell-positioned frame, preserve the default position.

Setting a Window Title

The frame window's title is much like the initial size and position attribute. Most of the time, Open Class Library obtains the title text for you. If `IFrameWindow` loads a dialog template, the dialog provides the title. Otherwise, the `IFrameWindow` constructor tries to load the title from a string resource with the same identifier as the frame window identifier. If the frame is a secondary window and there is no matching string resource, the frame title is the same as the owner window. If no other title is located, the `IFrameWindow` constructor sets the title to the name of the program executable file.

Only two constructors permit specifying an explicit title. You pass the title to these `IFrameWindow` constructors as a `const char *` pointer.

You can change the frame's title after construction by using an `ITitle` object. You might find this means of specifying an explicit title preferable to using the more awkward `IFrameWindow` constructors, which accept a title argument.

Frame Window Constructors

In the preceding section, we described the various `IFrameWindow` constructor arguments. In this section, we discuss all eight variations of `IFrameWindow` constructors.

Constructing from Existing Frame Windows

```
IFrameWindow( const IWindowHandle &hwnd );
```

Use this constructor to attach an `IFrameWindow` object to an existing presentation system frame window. The only argument is the window's window handle. Because the window already exists, all of the six frame constructor arguments discussed in the previous section are irrelevant when using this constructor.

With this constructor, you can continue to use existing code written without Open Class Library. For example, you might use this constructor to use the enhanced `IFrameWindow` capabilities to add frame extensions, such as an information area, to your existing application.

This support for other application code also extends to code that you implement using other C++ class libraries, including libraries from other C++ and library vendors. If you can obtain the window handle of the frame window, you can attach an IFrameWindow to it using this constructor.

This constructor warrants the following caveats.

- Pass the argument as an IWindowHandle, *not* an HWND. The system-defined type HWND is synonymous with unsigned long in the OS/2 operating system. If you use HWND as an argument in the OS/2 environment, you invoke the constructor that interprets the number as a resource identifier. If you have an HWND, you need to convert this to an IWindowHandle explicitly, as follows:

```
HWND
  hwnd = WinCreateWindow( ..., WC_FRAME, ... );
IFrameWindow
  frame( IWindowHandle( hwnd ) );
```

  A better solution is to store the window handle in an IWindowHandle to start with, as follows:

```
IWindowHandle
  hwnd = WinCreateWindow( ..., WC_FRAME, ... );
IFrameWindow
  frame( hwnd );
```

- Make certain that the window handle is not already attached to an IFrameWindow or IWindow object. If you attempt to attach another C++ window object to the same handle, the IFrameWindow constructor throws an IInvalidParameter exception. To avoid this error, test for the existence of an attached IWindow object by using IWindow::windowWithHandle as follows:

```
IWindowHandle
  hwnd;
//...hwnd set...
IFrameWindow
  *p = (IFrameWindow *)(IWindow::windowWithHandle( hwnd ) );
if ( !p )
    p = new IFrameWindow( hwnd );
```

Constructing Primary Frame Windows

```
IFrameWindow ( unsigned long id = IC_DEFAULT_FRAME_ID,
               FrameSource   source = tryDialogResource );
```

This is the default constructor for class IFrameWindow. Use it to construct primary windows from either dialog template resources or from standard frame window styles. The frame's parent is the desktop window, and it has no owner.

As explained in Chapter 5, "Frame Window Basics," you control the behavior of this constructor with respect to dialog template resources by using a value of the enumerated type FrameSource in the source argument. This constructor gets the rest of the frame window construction arguments, as follows:

- When you specify the value of source as IFrameWindow::noDialogResource, a standard frame window is constructed using the default style that is returned by IFrameWindow::defaultStyle. The constructor uses the id argument to create an IResourceId object associated with the default user resource library. The other resources required to construct the frame window, as determined by the default style, are obtained using this resource identifier. Its initial size and position is the next shell position—as returned by IFrameWindow::nextShellRect. The frame's title is either set from a string resource, with the argument resource identifier, or, if the frame cannot find the string, to the default title.

- When you specify IFrameWindow::dialogResource as the value of source, the constructor uses the id argument to construct an IResourceId object associated with the default user resource library. In this case, however, the constructor then attempts to create a frame window from a dialog template resource identified by the IResourceId object. The frame obtains its style, title, and initial size and position from the dialog template resource. If the dialog template resource cannot be loaded, the constructor throws an IAccessError exception.

- If you do not specify a value for source, or if you specify IFrameWindow::tryDialogResource, the constructor first attempts to construct the frame using a dialog template resource as if IFrameWindow::dialogResource is speci-fied. However, if the attempt to load the dialog template resource fails, the constructor does not throw an exception. Instead, it constructs a standard frame window as described for IFrameWindow::noDialogResource.

This constructor accepts, as an argument, a plain unsigned long. Because it has a default argument value, you can use this constructor to construct an IFrameWindow with no arguments. Any required frame resources are obtained using the resource identifier value IC_DEFAULT_FRAME_ID, which is defined in the header file ICCONST.H. Include this header in your resource script (.RC) file to define resources with the IC_DEFAULT_FRAME_ID identifier. See the beginning of Chapter 5, "Frame Window Basics," for examples of the use of this constructor.

Constructing Secondary Frame Windows

```
IFrameWindow ( const IResourceId& resId,
               IWindow*          owner = 0,
               FrameSource       source = tryDialogResource );
```

Use this constructor to create secondary frame windows. The additional IWindow* argument specifies the primary window, which is the owner of the newly constructed frame window.

Because it has a default argument value of 0, the owner argument is optional. When you do not provide an owner, this constructor builds a primary window just like the constructor we described in "Constructing Primary Frame Windows." The only difference is that you can use the resId argument to specify the resource library containing the frame resources.

The resulting frame window's attributes are determined in essentially the same manner as in the previous constructor. The only differences are that the resources come from the resource library referenced by the argument IResourceId object and that there may be an owner window. See examples of the use of this constructor in Chapter 5, "Frame Window Basics."

Constructing Child Frame Windows

```
IFrameWindow ( const IResourceId& resId,
               IWindow*          parent,
               IWindow*          owner,
               FrameSource       source = tryDialogResource );
```

Use this constructor to create child frame windows, optionally from a dialog template. Except to create page windows for a notebook, you rarely use child frame windows in applications that have the look and feel of the Windows 95 or OS/2 desktops. See Chapter 14, "Notebook Control," for more details on creating page windows for notebooks.

As with the preceding two constructors, this one accepts a resource identifier as its first argument and a source argument to control the search for dialog template resources. The frame obtains some construction attributes, such as style, initial size, position, and title, in the same way that the two preceding constructors do. This constructor permits you to specify a parent window other than the desktop window.

In most cases, make the same window both the parent and owner. This conforms to MDI conventions and works well for most applications.

However, if the secondary window is to be displayed in application modal fashion, do *not* make it a child frame window. The parent and owner windows of modal dialogs must meet the restrictions described in the topic "Displaying Application-Modal Frame Windows" in Chapter 5.

Here are typical examples of construction of a child frame window:

```
#define DIALOG_ID 101

IFrameWindow
 *parent;

// Get resources from the default user resource library.
IFrameWindow
  child( DIALOG_ID, parent, parent );

// Get resources from resource.dll.
IFrameWindow
  child( IResourceId( DIALOG_ID, "resource.dll" ),
         parent,
         parent );
```

Overloading, Ambiguity, and Default Argument Values

The three constructors that permit construction of frame windows from dialog templates provide a good example of how to exploit the C++ features of overloading and how to use default arguments to provide a simple and flexible interface for your objects.

While such a design might look complicated, it makes using the objects much easier. You can specify a resource identifier value, and the default resource library gets used. You can add an owner window argument to the code and not even realize that a different constructor is called. You can specify an explicit resource library without having to specify an owner.

Constructing Frame Windows with Nondefault Style

```
IFrameWindow( const IResourceId &resId,
              const Style &style );
IFrameWindow( const Style &style,
              const IResourceId &resId - IC_DEFAULT_FRAME_ID );
```

Use these two constructors to construct standard frame windows with other than the default style. Neither attempts to load the frame window definition from a dialog template resource. All frame windows constructed with these constructors are primary windows. The parent is the desktop window, and the frame has no owner. To construct a secondary or child window with other than the default style, use the miscellaneous frame window constructor that we describe in the next section of this chapter.

The two versions of this constructor conveniently permit you to pass the arguments in either order. The constructor accepts the style as the first argument and provides the default resource identifier. This permits you to construct a frame with just a style.

The remaining constructor arguments not explicitly specified, that is, title and initial size and position, default in the same manner as the previous constructors do.

When you use these constructors, you usually incorporate the default style into the style argument. If you want a specific style, use IFrameWindow's classDefaultStyle as follows:

```
// Construct a primary frame window with fixed style.
IFrameWindow
  myFrame( IFrameWindow::classDefaultStyle
           |
           IFrameWindow::menuBar );
```

Using classDefaultStyle ensures that your code is not changed if other code modifies the current frame window default style. If, however, you want your frame to reflect changes in the default style, use the IFrameWindow::defaultStyle function as follows:

```
// Construct a primary frame with with a style derived from the
// default.
IFrameWindow
  myFrame( IFrameWindow::defaultStyle()
           |
           IFrameWindow::menuBar );
```

Constructing Miscellaneous Frame Windows

```
IFrameWindow( const IResourceId &resId,
              IWindow *parent,
              IWindow *owner,
              const IRectangle &initRect,
              const Style &style = defaultStyle(),
              const char *title = 0 );
```

Use this constructor to specify all six of the possible IFrameWindow constructor arguments. Use it to construct IFrameWindows that do not lend themselves to construction via any of the simpler constructors. This constructor's signature is very much like the constructors provided for all of the window classes derived from IControl.

Because this constructor accepts title, style, and initial size and position arguments, dialog template resources are not loaded when you use it. If you use this constructor, you must specify the resource identifier, parent window, owner window, and initial size and position arguments. The constructor provides the standard defaults for style and title. If you want the default behavior for any of the first four arguments, specify those defaults as indicated in Table 19-2.

Why do you use this constructor? One reason is that this is the only constructor you can use to specify other than the default style for secondary windows. To do this, you use the constructor in much the same way that you use those described in the previous section. The only difference is that you specify one or more of the additional constructor arguments for the parent and owner windows. Here is a typical example, which creates a secondary frame window with the additional style of `minimizedIcon`:

```
IFrameWindow
  *primary;

IFrameWindow
  secondary( DIALOG_ID,
             IWindow::desktopWindow(),
             0,
             IFrameWindow::nextShellRect(),
             IFrameWindow::classDefaultStyle |
               IFrameWindow::minimizedIcon );
```

Choose between `classDefaultStyle` and `defaultStyle()` as a base for your style argument value using the same criteria that we described earlier for the simpler constructors.

This is the only constructor that accepts an explicit initial size and position. Use it when you want to specify a size and position that is different from the default to the constructor. However, as you saw in the "Initial Size and Position" section, there are other means of accomplishing the same end. Here is an example of how to construct a frame window with a fixed initial size and position:

```
IFrameWindow
  frame( IC_DEFAULT_FRAME_ID,
         IWindow::desktopWindow(),
         0,
         IRectangle( IPoint( 100, 100 ),
                     ISize( 200, 100 ) ) );
```

Table 19-2. Frame Window Constructor Arguments

Argument	What to Use to Obtain Default Attribute
resource identifier	IC_DEFAULT_FRAME_ID If you specify just a numeric value, the frame window loads the resources from the default user resource library.
parent	IWindow::desktopWindow() Most frame windows are not child frames, so make the desktop window the parent.
owner	0 If you are constructing a primary frame, specify 0 to indicate that your frame does not have an owner. Note that if you do not specify an owner, you might be able to use a simpler constructor instead.
initial size and position	IFrameWindow::nextShellRect() This static function of IFrameWindow obtains a shell position.

Constructing Frame Windows with Explicit Title

```
IFrameWindow( const char *title,
              const IResourceId &resId = IC_DEFAULT_FRAME_ID,
              const Style &style = defaultStyle() );
```

This IFrameWindow constructor provides a convenient way to construct a frame window with a title specified as a constructor argument. With this capability, you can write the simplest program, as follows:

```
#include <iframe.hpp>
void main() { IFrameWindow("Hello, World!").showModally(); }
```

Use this constructor for quick test applications, where the benefits of separating the title text from your code do not warrant the effort required to place the title in an .RC file and compile and bind the resource file to your application.

Windows created using this constructor are always primary windows. The parent window is the desktop window and there is no owner window. The frame calculates its initial size and position using IFrameWindow::nextShellRect. This constructor uses the conventional default values for the style and resource identifier arguments.

The frame style test application described earlier is a good example of the use of this constructor. That example shows that this constructor is also useful in cases where the title contents are dynamic.

Frame Extensions

You read about the basic concept of frame extensions in Chapter 5, "Frame Window Basics." Usually, you do not need to be concerned about how the frame window manages frame extensions. However, you can derive from the class IFrameExtension in order to customize frame extensions. You might want to do this to create extensions that draw fancier separators, or that dynamically change themselves in response to user interaction with the frame window. This section describes how to use a specialized frame extension class.

The public versions of addExtension use a private function to construct an IFrameExtension and add it to the collection of extensions managed by the frame window. If you derive a new class from IFrameWindow, you might have to add objects of that class to the collection. This is demonstrated in the function MyFrame::addMyExtension in the following example.

The example shows how you might design a frame-extension derived class that draws separator lines of user-selected width and color.

Derived IFrameExtension Interface - advframe\drawextn\myextns.hpp

```
#include <iframext.hpp>
#include <icolor.hpp>

class MyExtension : public IFrameExtension {
public:
  MyExtension( IWindow *control,
               IFrameWindow::Location loc);
  MyExtension( IWindow *control,
               IFrameWindow::Location loc,
               double size );
  MyExtension( IWindow *control,
               IFrameWindow::Location loc,
               int size );
virtual unsigned long
  separatorWidth ( ) const;

virtual void
  drawSeparator ( const IPresSpaceHandle &hps );

virtual MyExtension
 &setSeparatorWidth ( unsigned long width ),
 &setSeparatorColor ( const IColor& newColor );

private:
unsigned long
  width;
IColor
  color;
MyExtension ( const MyExtension&);
MyExtension
 &operator= ( const MyExtension&);
};
```

Derived IFrameExtension Implementation - advframe\drawextn\myextns.cpp

```
#include <icoordsy.hpp>
#include <igrafctx.hpp>
#include <igrect.hpp>
#include <irect.hpp>
#include "myextns.hpp"

MyExtension::MyExtension( IWindow *control,
                          IFrameWindow::Location loc )
    : IFrameExtension( control, loc, IFrameWindow::none ),
      width( 5 ),
      color( IColor::white )
    {
    }

MyExtension::MyExtension( IWindow *control,
              IFrameWindow::Location loc,
              double size )
    : IFrameExtension( control, loc, size, IFrameWindow::none ),
      width( 5 ),
      color( IColor::white )
    {
    }

MyExtension::MyExtension( IWindow *control,
              IFrameWindow::Location loc,
              int size )
    : IFrameExtension( control, loc, (unsigned long)size,
                       IFrameWindow::none ),
      width( 5 ),
      color( IColor::white )
    {
    }
```

```
unsigned long MyExtension:: separatorWidth ( ) const
    {
    return width;
    }
void MyExtension::drawSeparator ( const IPresSpaceHandle &hps )
    {
    IRectangle
      separator;
    Boolean isUpperLeft =
        (ICoordinateSystem::nativeOrientation() ==
         ICoordinateSystem::originUpperLeft );

    if ( location() == IFrameWindow::aboveClient)
        // Put separator beneath control.
        separator = control()->nativeRect()
          .moveBy( IPair( 0, isUpperLeft ?
                               control()->size().height() : -width) );
    else
      // Put separator above control.
      separator = control()->nativeRect()
        .moveBy( IPair( 0, isUpperLeft ?
                           -width : control()->size().height()) );

    separator.sizeTo( separator.size().setHeight( width-1 ) );

    // Draw the separator.   Don't draw it if width is 0.
    if (width != 0)
        {
        IGraphicContext gc(hps);
        gc.setFillColor(color);
        gc.setPenColor(color);
        gc.draw( IGRectangle( separator ) );
        }
    }

MyExtension& MyExtension::setSeparatorWidth ( unsigned long width )
    {
    this->width = width;
    return *this;
    }

MyExtension& MyExtension::setSeparatorColor (
                           const IColor& newColor )
{
    this->color = newColor;
    return *this;
}
```

Class `MyExtension` overrides the inherited virtual functions `separatorWidth` and `drawSeparator`. Other derived extension classes may override them to embellish the drawing of frame extensions.

You create a derived `IFrameWindow` class, which uses such an extension, using code like the **advframe\drawextn** program on the examples disk. This program lets a user select a color and a separator width, and then it updates the frame using those values. The frame extensions are objects of class `MyExtension`.

Implementation Details of IFrameWindow

We cover three aspects of the implementation:

- the IFrameHandler class, which handles frame window events,
- the process Open Class Library uses to construct frame windows,
- and details of the presentation system window used for frame window objects.

These aspects help you extend the features of IFrameWindow. In this section, you see how frame handlers work, learn why modifying a frame handler is difficult, and discover a simplified strategy for dealing with this problem.

Working with a Frame Handler

The IFrameHandler class provides for the handling of events that affect frame windows or that Open Class Library handles to implement the special features of IFrameWindow objects. IFrameWindow attaches one of these handlers to almost all frame windows when you call an IFrameWindow constructor. You can tailor your frame windows by deriving from this handler class and reimplementing the virtual functions that process particular frame events. Deriving from IFrameHandler and adding your own frame handlers to a frame window is much more complicated than it first appears.

Like most handlers, IFrameHandler objects convert the generic IEvents arriving at the dispatchHandlerEvent function to more specific IFrameEvents and pass those to a variety of virtual functions. You can override any of these functions to change the behavior of your frame window. However, we do not recommend overriding some of the virtual functions in IFrameHandler. The implementations of some of the functions in the base IFrameHandler class are dependent on one another for handling some complex tasks, such as the layout of the frame window's extensions. Fortunately, you generally do not need to override most of these functions. For example, there is little reason for you to add functionality to the format function.

The only functions you might want to override are closed and saved. However, you can better handle the former using a standalone ICommandHandler-derived class. See Chapter 5, "Frame Window Basics." The same approach works best for saved, too. The **advframe\framesav** program on the examples disk shows a SaveHandler class that provides an easier means for handling application save requests in the OS/2 operating system. In the Windows operating system, there is no separate event that the system sends to indicate that the application should save state data. (The IFrameHandler::saved function is not called in the Windows environment.) To get functionality similar to the following example, integrate its SaveHandler::saved function into your ICommandHandler-derived class for closed, and call it in response to the close event.

The default saved implementation saves the frame's window position using the OS/2 system function WinStoreWindowPos. When attached to a frame window, the handler restores the frame's position using its counterpart function, WinRestoreWindowPos.

Special Features of IFrameHandler

IFrameHandler is unlike most Open Class Library handler classes in two ways. The first way is that IFrameHandler provides certain concrete behaviors, such as frame-extension layout and special handling for events such as window activate and window close. Most Open Class Library handlers only provide behaviors when you derive from them. The second way is that Open Class Library attaches an IFrameHandler object to your frame window automatically when you construct an IFrameWindow object.

Consider what happens when you derive from IFrameHandler and attach your handler to a frame window. In your derived class, you override one or more of the virtual functions. Your handler, however, inherits the IFrameHandler implementation for the virtual functions that you do not override. When you add your handler to an IFrameWindow, you provide behaviors in your overridden functions and the IFrameHandler behaviors for the functions you do not override. Because there is already a default IFrameHandler object attached to the frame window, both your handler and the default IFrameHandler are processing events and applying behaviors to the frame window. Unless you carefully design your handler, some behaviors are applied twice, typically with undesirable results.

Customizing IFrameHandler Behavior

In certain circumstances, you might have to code classes that derive from IFrameHandler. You do this if you want your frame window to inherit some particular feature of frame windows, such as the ability to have extensions, but want to tailor the implementation of that feature, for example, to change the drawing of the frame extensions. How do you overcome the obstacles to doing this? The solution is to permit only one frame handler to be attached to your frame window.

The default frame handler gets attached to a frame window in the default implementation of the IFrameWindow::addDefaultHandler. This virtual function gets called from IFrameWindow::start, which in turn gets called from IFrameWindow::initialize. So why not override addDefaultHandler so that it adds a handler of a different type or disable the adding of a handler altogether?

You can do that, but it is difficult. This function gets called during the construction of the IFrameWindow. During construction, the object is still just an IFrameWindow, and your overridden virtual function is not in effect yet. The only way to make this work is to use the deferCreation style when you construct the IFrameWindow. When you use this style, create the presentation system frame window and connect it to the C++ frame window object. You can do both by calling IFrameWindow::initialize. Alternatively, you can create the presentation system window yourself and then call IFrameWindow::start to connect it to the C++ object.

It is easier to construct the base IFrameWindow in the normal fashion and then remove the default frame handler by calling IFrameWindow::removeDefaultHandler. You must then attach another frame handler. The following sample code lays out the basic structure for doing this:

```
class MyFrameHandler : public IFrameHandler {
// Override virtual functions here.  Make sure you properly
// call the inherited IFrameHandler function to ensure that
// you take necessary actions for key events.
};

class MyFrame : public IFrameWindow {
public:
// Provide your constructors here.  Note how you use the
// base class constructors in the normal fashion.
  MyFrame ( const IResourceId &resId )
    : IFrameWindow( resId )
    {
    // Remove default frame handler:
    removeDefaultHandler();
    // Add replacement frame handler:
    handler.handleEventsFor( this );
    }

private:
// Put the replacement handler here for convenience.
// You can place this object in a static member to
// share it among all MyFrame objects.
MyFrameHandler
  handler;
};
```

Managing Frame Window Construction

Another detail of frame windows is the order of the events that occur when you construct various ones. (You have already seen some of these events.) At the beginning of this chapter, you read about the constructor arguments and the various frame constructors. In the previous topic, you saw how Open Class Library attaches a default frame handler during construction. Now we look closer at the frame window construction process. Figure 19-1 shows the frame constructor logic.

When you use dialog templates, there are three concerns because of the way that frame window construction works. First, if you try to load a dialog from a template resource and the IFrameWindow cannot find the resource, it creates a standard frame window by default. If you consider this an error and the next two concerns do not bother you, use the IFrameWindow::dialogTemplate value for the source argument on the constructor. This causes an exception to be thrown in this case. Second, you cannot load a dialog and use a previously written dialog procedure. When IFrameWindow loads the dialog template, it always specifies a default dialog procedure. Third, you cannot process the dialog initialization event, which is WM_INITDIALOG in the Windows operating system and WM_INITDLG in the OS/2 operating system.

The example code at the end of this topic handles each of these concerns. The example implements these classes:

DialogWindow

This class derives from IFrameWindow. It differs from IFrameWindow in the following respects:

- It always loads the frame from a dialog template resource. If the resource library does not contain the resource, the dialog window object throws an `IAccessError` exception.

- It permits the use of your own dialog procedure. If you construct a `DialogWindow` and provide a dialog procedure, your procedure is used instead of the default dialog procedure.

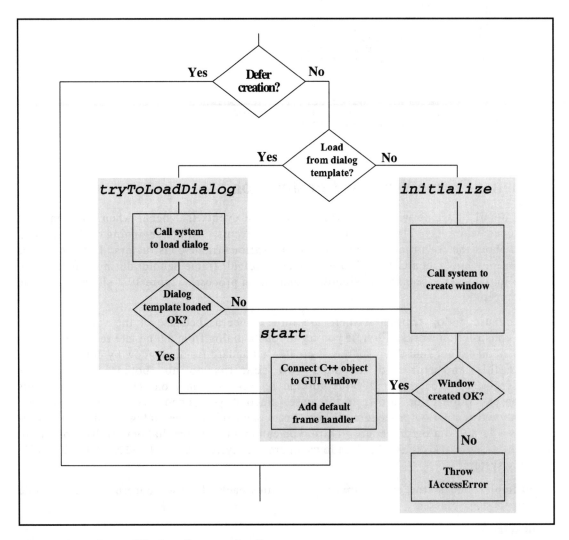

Figure 19-1. IFrameWindow Construction Process.

-   It permits a specialized handler to be used to handle dialog initialization. You cannot handle the dialog initialization message using an IHandler object. This is because the dialog is loaded and the dialog initialization message is sent during IFrameWindow construction and because you cannot register your handlers until after construction is completed.

The class DialogWindow avoids the unwanted IFrameWindow dialog-loading behavior by constructing its IFrameWindow base class using the deferCreation style. This style effectively disables IFrameWindow's attempt to create a presentation system window.

The actual dialog window construction occurs in the member function loadDialog. This function loads the dialog template from the resource library. If it cannot find the resource, IResourceLibrary::loadDialog throws an IAccessError exception. Because the function does not catch this exception, control is transferred back to your code at the point you attempted to construct the dialog window.

Notice that the DialogWindow member function loadDialog calls ICurrentThread::initializeGUI before trying to load the dialog template. Open Class Library does this within the IFrameWindow constructors, but only if it creates a presentation system window. Because the following code creates the window, it must initialize the windowing environment. See Chapter 20, "Applications and Threads" for more information on this topic.

If the dialog template loads successfully, the code passes the handle for the dialog window to the IFrameWindow::start function. This connects the C++ object to the presentation system window and attaches the default frame handler.

To enable your dialog handler to handle the dialog initialization message, the constructor that accepts a handler has to use a special dialog procedure when it loads the dialog template. This dialog procedure looks for the dialog initialization event and dispatches it to the dialog handler. To provide access to this handler, the constructor creates a modified creation parameter structure that holds a reference to the handler and the actual creation parameters passed to the constructor. The dialog procedure unwraps these creation parameters before calling the handler's initialize function.

The DialogWindow constructor accepts a dialog handler and attaches it to the dialog after constructing it. This means you can override dispatchHandlerEvent and handle other events in your handler.

DialogHandler

This class defines a specialized handler that has a virtual function initialize, which you can override to handle dialog initialization. Typically, you initialize your dialog's controls and set the focus to the appropriate control on your dialog by calling IWindow::setFocus.

DialogInitEvent

This class defines the dialog-initialization event. It provides the function `createParameters` that you can call to query the dialog creation parameters. It also provides the member function `setFocusChanged`. Call this function if you set focus on one of your dialog controls. The `setFocusChanged` function puts the proper notification in the event result field so that the system default dialog procedure handles your focus selection. If you do not set the focus, the system's default dialog procedure sets the focus to a default control. You can query the default control that gets the focus by calling the `DialogInitEvent::defaultFocusWindow` function.

DialogWindow Interface - advframe\tstdlg\dialog.hpp

```
#include <iframe.hpp>
#include <ireslib.hpp>

class DialogHandler;

class DialogWindow : public IFrameWindow {
public:
// Use this to construct a dialog using
// your own dialog procedure.
  DialogWindow( const IResourceId& resId,
                IWindow*          owner,
                IWinProc*         dlgProc = 0,
                void*             pCreateParms = 0 );

// Use this to construct a dialog using
// your own dialog handler.
  DialogWindow( const IResourceId& resId,
                IWindow*          owner,
                DialogHandler&    dlgHandler,
                void*             pCreateParms = 0 );
protected:
void
  loadDialog ( const IResourceId& resId,
               IWindow*           owner,
               IWinProc*          dlgProc,
               void*              pCreateParms );
private:
DialogWindow (const DialogWindow&);
DialogWindow& operator= (const DialogWindow&);
}; // class DialogWindow
```

DialogWindow Implementation - advframe\tstdlg\dialog.cpp

```
#include <ibase.hpp>
#ifdef IC_PM
  #define INCL_WIN
  #include <os2.h>
#else
  #include <windows.h>
#endif

#include "dialog.hpp"
#include "dlghndlr.hpp"

#include <ithread.hpp>
```

```
DialogWindow::DialogWindow( const IResourceId& resId,
                                 IWindow*         owner,
                                 IWinProc*        dlgProc,
                                 void*            pCreateParms )
   : IFrameWindow( deferCreation )
   {
   this->loadDialog( resId, owner, dlgProc, pCreateParms );
   }

struct DialogParms {
  DialogHandler
   &dlgHandler;
  void
   *pCreateParms;
};


#ifdef IC_PM

static void * _System dialogProc( unsigned long  hwnd,
                                   unsigned long  eventId,
                                   void           *parm1,
                                   void           *parm2 )
   {
   if ( eventId == WM_INITDLG )
      {
      DialogParms
       *p = (DialogParms*)parm2;
      DialogInitEvent
        initEvent( IEvent( hwnd,
                           eventId,
                           parm1,
                           p->pCreateParms ) );
      // Dispatch handler and check result.
      if ( p->dlgHandler.initialize( initEvent ) )
        // Do not pass the event on; the result is in the event.
        return initEvent.result();
      else
        // Pass the event to the default dialog procedure.
        return WinDefDlgProc( hwnd,
                              eventId,
                              parm1,
                              p->pCreateParms );
      }
   else
      return WinDefDlgProc( hwnd, eventId, parm1, parm2 );
   }

#else

static void* CALLBACK dialogProc( void*          hwnd,
                                  unsigned long  eventId,
                                  void*          parm1,
                                  void*          parm2 )
   {
   if ( eventId == WM_INITDIALOG )
      {
      DialogParms
       *p = (DialogParms*)parm2;
      DialogInitEvent
        initEvent( IEvent( hwnd,
                           eventId,
                           parm1,
                           p->pCreateParms ) );
```

```
      // Dispatch handler and check result.
      if ( p->dlgHandler.initialize( initEvent ) )
        // Do not pass event on; the result is in the event.
        return initEvent.result();
    }
  // Return 0 because the message is not processed.
  return 0;
  }

#endif


DialogWindow::DialogWindow( const IResourceId& resId,
                           IWindow*           owner,
                           DialogHandler&     dlgHandler,
                           void*              pCreateParms )
  : IFrameWindow( deferCreation )
  {
  DialogParms
    parms = { dlgHandler, pCreateParms };
  this->loadDialog( resId, owner, dialogProc, &parms );
  this->addHandler( &dlgHandler );
  }

void DialogWindow::loadDialog( const IResourceId& resId,
                               IWindow*           owner,
                               IWinProc*          dlgProc,
                               void*              pCreateParms )
  {
  IThread::current().initializeGUI();

  const IResourceLibrary
   &resLib = resId.resourceLibrary();
  IWindowHandle
    dlg = resLib.loadDialog( resId.id(),
                             0,
                             owner,
                             dlgProc,
                             pCreateParms );
  start( dlg );
  }
```

DialogHandler/DialogInitEvent Interface - advframe\tstdlg\dlghndlr.hpp

```
#include <ievent.hpp>
#include <ihandler.hpp>

class DialogInitEvent : public IEvent {
public:
  DialogInitEvent ( const IEvent& event );
IWindowHandle
  defaultFocusWindow ( ) const;
void
 *createParameters ( ) const;
DialogInitEvent
 &setFocusChanged ( );
};

class DialogHandler : public IHandler {
public:
virtual Boolean
  initialize ( DialogInitEvent& initEvent );
protected:
virtual Boolean
  dispatchHandlerEvent ( IEvent& event );
};
```

DialogHandler/DialogInitEvent Implementation - advframe\tstdlg\dlghndlr.cpp

```
#include "dlghndlr.hpp"

DialogInitEvent::DialogInitEvent ( const IEvent& event )
  : IEvent( event )
  {
  }

IWindowHandle DialogInitEvent::defaultFocusWindow ( ) const
  {
  return IWindowHandle( parameter1() );
  }

void *DialogInitEvent::createParameters ( ) const
  {
  return parameter2();
  }

DialogInitEvent& DialogInitEvent :: setFocusChanged( )
  {
  setResult( true );
  return *this;
  }

Boolean DialogHandler::initialize( DialogInitEvent& initEvent )
  {
  return false;
  }

Boolean DialogHandler::dispatchHandlerEvent( IEvent& event )
  {
  return false;
  }
```

DialogWindow Test Program - advframe\tstdlg\tstdlg.cpp

```
#include <ibase.hpp>
#ifdef IC_PM
  #define INCL_WIN
  #include <os2.h>
#else
  #include <windows.h>
#endif

#include <istattxt.hpp>
#include <ithread.hpp>

#include "dialog.hpp"
#include "dlghndlr.hpp"

class MyDialogHandler : public DialogHandler {
public:
virtual Boolean
  initialize( DialogInitEvent& initEvent )
    {
    IStaticText
      text( IWindow::handleWithParent(1, initEvent.handle() ) );
    text.setText( (char*)( initEvent.createParameters() ) );
    return false;
    }
};
```

```
#ifdef IC_PM
static void * _System myDlgProc( unsigned long   hwnd,
                                 unsigned long   eventId,
                                 void*           parm1,
                                 void*           parm2 )
  {
  if ( eventId == WM_INITDLG )
    {
    IStaticText
      text( IWindow::handleWithParent(1,  hwnd ) );
    text.setText( (char*)parm2 );
    }
  return WinDefDlgProc( hwnd, eventId, parm1, parm2 );
  }

#else
static void* CALLBACK  myDlgProc( void*           hwnd,
                                  unsigned long   eventId,
                                  void*           parm1,
                                  void*           parm2 )
  {
  if ( eventId == WM_INITDIALOG )
    {
    IStaticText
      text( IWindow::handleWithParent(1,  hwnd ) );
    text.setText( (char*)parm2 );
    }
  return 0;
  }

#endif

void main()
  {
  MyDialogHandler
    myHandler;
  DialogWindow
    dlg1( IC_DEFAULT_FRAME_ID,
          IWindow::desktopWindow(),
          myHandler,
          "myHandler" );
  DialogWindow
    dlg2( IC_DEFAULT_FRAME_ID,
          IWindow::desktopWindow(),
          myDlgProc,
          "myDlgProc" );
  dlg1.show();
  dlg2.show().setFocus();
  IApplication::current().run();
  }
```

Using the Presentation System Window

The Windows and OS/2 operating systems use different implementations for the underlying window objects that you use for frame and dialog windows. Most of the time, Open Class Library handles these differences so that you do not have to. However, sometimes you might need to deal with the differences in your application. In this topic, we discuss cases where these differences could affect how you write your application.

Working with Frame Components

Components include items such as the system menu, title bar, maximize, minimize and close buttons, and the border around the frame window. As you saw earlier in this chapter, many of these components are optional. Usually, you use the IFrameWindow style flags to control the appearance of the components and do not worry about them any more.

In some cases, it is useful to interact more directly with the frame components. For example, you use the ITitle class to manipulate the title bar decoration and the ISystemMenu class to control the appearance of the system menu. The interfaces for these classes look the same in the Windows and OS/2 versions of Open Class Library, but there are significant differences in the implementation. In the OS/2 operating system, the title bar, system menu, menu bar, and title bar buttons are all separate presentation system windows that are child windows of the frame window. They each have a full set of window attributes like window handle and window identifier. Likewise, scroll bars created with the IFrameWindow::horizontalScroll or IFrameWindow::verticalScroll styles are separate windows. In the Windows operating system, these components are actually part of the frame window itself. The system draws the components based on style settings of the frame window.

You need to be aware of this difference when you manipulate the components directly using system functions. For example, the handle function returns the same value for an ITitle object and its owner frame window in the Windows operating system. In the OS/2 system, the two objects have distinct values for handle. With the OS/2 version of VisualAge for C++, you can use the constructor:

```
IScrollBar ( unsigned long      id,
             IWindow*           parent );
```

to create a wrapper object for a frame window vertical scroll bar by using FID_VERTSCROLL for the id argument and the frame window for the parent argument. This will not work for the Windows version, because the scroll bar is actually part of the frame window.

Working with a Frame Window Control

The underlying presentation system control used for a standard frame window is also different between the operating systems. The Windows operating system does not define a standard frame window control. Typically, each application registers its own window class and provides the window procedure for it. Style flags control the appearance of components. Dialog templates use the pre-defined window class WC_DIALOG. The OS/2 system provides a pre-defined window class WC_FRAME for frame windows, including dialog templates. OS/2 applications typically use this window class for frame windows, and also control appearance with style flags.

The IFrameWindow constructors that create a presentation system window take care of the processing needed to create a frame window. However, you need to understand how Open Class Library does this if you use the constructor for existing frame windows:

```
IFrameWindow ( const IWindowHandle& hwnd );
```

because some features of IFrameWindow rely upon the underlying window class for processing. In addition, these differences make some techniques for manipulating frame window objects nonportable.

The Windows Open Class Library implementation uses the function `IFrameWindow::registerFrameClass` to create a presentation system window class for a standard frame window object. Because the window class of a window governs attributes that vary between frame window objects, such as the frame window's icon and background color, Open Class Library registers a new window class for each `IFrameWindow` object. The names of these classes begin with the string "ICL Frame". The ICL Frame window class also has an extra 32-bit window word. Open Class Library uses this word to store the window identifier of a top-level window. Use the `IWindow::id` function to access this identifier.

All of this means that the following restrictions apply to your Windows applications:

- Do not use `IWindow::windowWithParent` with the desktop window as parent to locate frame windows by identifier. The operating system does not store window identifiers for top-level windows. Instead, store a pointer to or the handle of the frame window that you need to find, and use it instead of the window's identifier.

- Unless the window class of the presentation system window is `WC_DIALOG` or begins with the string "ICL Frame", `IWindow::isFrameWindow` returns false and `IWindow::id` returns 0. For an illustration of how to create your own frame-window presentation system window class without this restriction, see the Multiple Document Interface Application example at the end of this chapter .

The OS/2 Open Class Library uses the `WC_FRAME` system-defined window class to create the presentation system window for standard frame windows. If you use a custom frame window control, follow these requirements for your OS/2 applications:

- Because the frame-extension layout support relies upon messages sent by the standard control, you must create custom controls that provide these messages. If you use the constructor for an existing frame window with your custom frame window control, create your custom control by subclassing `WC_FRAME` to preserve frame extension functionality.

- Because Open Class Library uses the standard window identifiers for the frame decoration controls, you must use them. These frame control identifiers are the FID_* values defined in the OS/2 developer's toolkit. Create your decoration controls using the standard identifiers in order to manipulate these objects with Open Class Library.

- Because the `IWindow::isFrameWindow` function returns false unless the window class of the control is `WC_FRAME`, subclass `WC_FRAME` when you create your custom control.

Frame Windows in Your Application

Up until now you have learned the various aspects of frame windows in isolation. You now see an extended example of how to use `IFrameWindow` objects in a realistic application. We then examine how to extend the `IFrameWindow` class to take advantage of operating system features that it does not support directly.

Using the Window Viewer Application

In this example, we design a graphical, object-oriented user interface for an application that provides a view of all the presentation system windows in your system. You see a potential use for such a utility for debugging in Chapter 28, "Problem Determination." Figure 19-2 shows the frame windows that comprise this sample application. It has three separate types of object views.

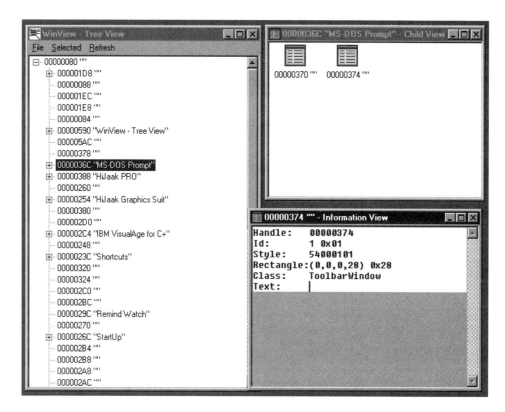

Figure 19-2. Window Viewer Application.

WinView - Tree View

This view shows the hierarchical arrangement of the windows active on your system. It uses a container-control tree icon view. Read about the details of using the container control in Chapter 13, "Container Control."

This frame window views the entire system and is, therefore, the primary window of this application. You can open secondary windows to display the child windows of a window or details about a window from this view.

WinView - Child View

This view shows the immediate child windows of a specific window. It uses a container-control icon view as its client window. This view is a secondary window; it is closed whenever the primary view closes. The application behaves this way because child windows are secondary components of their parent window; they cannot exist on their own apart from the window that contains them.

WinView - Information View

This view shows the details of a window, including its class, style, and location. It displays the details in a simple multiline edit control. For details about use of this control, see Chapter 9, "Edit Controls."

You can open the information view from either the tree view or the child view. Only one active information view for a window exists; if you open the view again, the application transfers focus to the existing information view.

Creating the Window Viewer Application

The logic of this application's `main` function creates and opens a `TreeView` of all of the windows in the system that are descendants of the desktop window. The code to do this is simple, requiring only three steps:

1. Construct a `TreeView` object.

2. Open it.

3. Call `IApplication::current().run()` to process window events. This function receives and processes window events until the primary view closes.

Window Viewer Usage - advframe\winview\winview.cpp

```cpp
#include <iwindow.hpp>

#include "treeview.hpp"
#include "hwindow.hpp"

int main (   )
{
  HWindow hwindow ( IWindow::desktopWindow()->handle() );
  TreeView
    view( hwindow );
  view.open();
  IApplication::current().run();
  return 0;
}
```

Defining the Primary View

The `TreeView` class provides a simple public interface: a constructor, member functions to open and close the view, and accessor functions for use by the handlers. Notice that the view class does not derive from `TFrameWindow`. Instead, the design uses composition and makes the frame a data member instead of a base class. Use this design approach whenever possible.

Because the trivial `TreeView` interface suffices, do not give it all of `IFrameWindow`'s functionality.

`TreeView` also has data members for the other components of the view: a reference to the window handle to display, a title, a container control to be used as the client window, and a container handler which is required to make the client window work properly. A menu and handlers process menu selections. In more complex views, you will likely find other components such as an information area object and additional handlers. All these are data members.

Use composition for all of the data members for these reasons:

- These components do not have to be derived from. You do not need to override any virtual functions that require derivation.

- It is easy to modify the view later. You can replace the client control with a different type, add or remove controls such as frame extensions, and add or replace handlers. All these actions are more difficult if the components are base classes.

The implementation of this view class is straightforward. It constructs the frame window as a primary window. Because the chosen view lays out the data across the screen vertically instead of horizontally, you have to adjust the frame's initial size and position by scaling the rectangle by half in the horizontal direction. The constructor uses the styles `IFrameWindow::menuBar` and `IFrameWindow::minimizedIcon` to load the menu and frame window icon automatically from the resource library. The frame has the default attributes `destroyOnClose(true)` and `autoDeleteObject(false)`, which is typical for primary windows. There is usually a single object of this type in automatic storage inside `main`, and it is destroyed when it goes out of scope. The frame must be destroyed when a user closes it. When the frame is closed, Open Class Library posts a `WM_QUIT` message that causes a return from the call to `IApplication::current()::run()`.

The following example illustrates these points:

Tree View Interface - advframe\winview\treeview.hpp

```
#include <iframe.hpp>
#include <ititle.hpp>
#include <icmdhdr.hpp>
#include <icnrctl.hpp>
#include <icnrhdr.hpp>
#include <imenubar.hpp>
#include "hwinobj.hpp"

class HWindow;
class TreeView;

class CommandHandler : public ICommandHandler {
public:
  CommandHandler( TreeView& view );
virtual Boolean
  command( ICommandEvent& event );
private:
  TreeView& fview;
CommandHandler( const CommandHandler& );
CommandHandler& operator= ( const CommandHandler& );
};
```

```
class TreeView : public IVBase {
public:
  TreeView ( HWindow &hwindow );
virtual TreeView
 &open      ( );
virtual TreeView
 &close     ( );
virtual TreeView
 &refreshView ( );
const IContainerControl
 &container( ) const;

protected:
virtual TreeView
 &populate ( );
virtual TreeView
 &populateChildren( HWindowObject* root );

private:
HWindow
 &hwindow;
IFrameWindow
  frame;
ITitle
  title;
IContainerControl
  client;
ICnrHandler
  handler;
IMenuBar
  fmenu;
CommandHandler
  fcommandHandler;
MenuHandler
  fmenuHandler;
TreeView ( const TreeView& );
TreeView& operator=( const TreeView& );
};
```

Tree View Implementation - advframe\winview\treeview.cpp

```
#include "treeview.hpp"
#include "hwindow.hpp"
#include "hwinobj.hpp"
#include "winview.h"

TreeView::TreeView ( HWindow& hwindow )
  : hwindow( hwindow ),
    frame( WND_MAIN, 0, 0,
           IFrameWindow::nextShellRect().scaleBy( 0.5, 1.0 ),
           IFrameWindow::defaultStyle() |
           IFrameWindow::menuBar | IFrameWindow::minimizedIcon   ),
    title( &frame ),
    client(IC_FRAME_CLIENT_ID, &frame, &frame, IRectangle(),
           IContainerControl::defaultStyle() |
           IContainerControl::noSharedObjects ),
    fmenu( &frame, IMenuBar::wrapper ),
    fcommandHandler( *this ),
    fmenuHandler( )

{
  title.setObjectText( "WinView" );
  title.setViewText( "Tree View" );

  client.setDeleteObjectsOnClose( true );
  client.showTreeTextView();
```

```
   frame.setClient( &client );
   handler.handleEventsFor( &client );
   fcommandHandler.handleEventsFor( &frame );
   fmenuHandler.handleEventsFor( &client );
}

TreeView &TreeView::open ( )
{
  frame.setFocus();
  frame.show();
  populate();
  return *this;
}

TreeView&  TreeView::close    ( )
{
   frame.close();
   return *this;
}

const IContainerControl& TreeView::container( ) const
{
   return client;
}

TreeView& TreeView::refreshView ( )
{
   client.setRefreshOff();
   client.deleteAllObjects();
   populate();
   client.setRefreshOn();
   client.refresh();
   return *this;
}

TreeView& TreeView::populate ( )
{
  HWindowObject* root =
     new HWindowObject( hwindow, APP_ICON_ID, &client );
  client.addObject( root );
  populateChildren( root );
  client.expand( root );
  return *this;
}

TreeView& TreeView::populateChildren( HWindowObject* root )
{
  HWindow::ChildCursor cursor( root->hWindow() );
  for ( cursor.setToFirst();
        cursor.isValid();
        cursor.setToNext()  )
    {
    HWindowObject* child =
       new HWindowObject( cursor.hWindow(), APP_ICON_ID, &client);
    client.addObject( child, root);
    populateChildren( child );
    }
  return *this;
}

CommandHandler::CommandHandler( TreeView& view ) :
  fview( view )
{ }
```

```
IBase::Boolean CommandHandler::command( ICommandEvent& event )
{
    Boolean handled = true;
    switch (event.commandId())
        {
        case MI_EXIT     :
            fview.close();
            break;
        case MI_OPENICON :
            {
            HWindowObject* object = (HWindowObject*)
                fview.container().cursoredObject();
            if (object)
                object->openIconView( );
            }
            break;
        case MI_OPENINFO :
            {
            HWindowObject* object = (HWindowObject*)
                fview.container().cursoredObject();
            if (object)
                object->openInfoView( );
            }
            break;
        case MI_REFRESH  :
            fview.refreshView( );
            break;
        default:
            handled = false;
        }
    return handled;
}
```

Defining Secondary Views

The class HWindowObjectView defines the common behavior of secondary views. The HWindowObjectView class is similar to the primary view class, TreeView. Its public interface has a destructor, a member function named open that opens the view, and an invalidateObject function that marks the object being viewed as invalid. The main difference is that HWindowObjectView derives from IFrameWindow to take advantage of the autoDeleteObject capability of IFrameWindow and to cause some cleanup to occur when a secondary view closes. To do that, put that code in the destructor of HWindowObjectView. If this class did not inherit from IFrameWindow, you would have to add a handler to look for the view closing and do the cleanup there. For the sake of simplicity, this sample uses derivation instead of another handler. It uses protected derivation to limit the chance that client code might exploit the fact that IFrameWindow is a base class.

HWindowObjectView constructs its IFrameWindow base object with the primary view as owner. It adjusts the size of the frame window like TreeView does. The constructor call specifies a nondefault frame style so that, in the OS/2 version, these secondary views do not move when the primary view moves.

The program creates these secondary views dynamically. As a user opens objects displayed in the primary view, the program creates these views using operator new. The HWindowObjectView constructor calls setAutoDeleteObject(true) to cause the deletion of the view when it closes. Because HWindowObjectView defines a protocol for showing an HWindowObject rather than an actual view, its constructor is protected. This forces a derived class to be created to define the actual view. Derived classes must pass their own client window pointer to the `HWindowObjectView` constructor because the client windows differ according to the actual type of view.

When a user double-clicks on a window object, the object's view opens (see `HWindowObject::handleOpen` in the example). `HWindowObjectView::open` first checks whether the view is minimized. If it is, then the view is restored. Thus, if a user opens a window and minimizes that view, the view is restored if the user opens the same object again. This is typical frame window management for your views.

Defining Window Viewer Objects

The class `HWindowObject` defines the common behavior of window viewer objects. `HWindowObject` derives from `IContainerObject` and defines how these objects work within the context of the application's container-control client windows. See Chapter 13, "Container Control" for a discussion of containers.

The responsibility for opening secondary views of an `HWindowObject` object lies within the object itself. This is because the object has the information about itself to identify which views are valid and which views, if any, are already open. The function `isIconViewAvailable` provides validity testing for a view. In this case, opening a child view of a window with no children results in an empty view. To avoid this behavior, the example program uses `isIconViewAvailable` to open an information view rather than a child view when a user double-clicks on an `HWindowObject` with no children.

The protected virtual functions `newIconView` and `newInfoView` create the view objects. If you want to change one of the views to show some additional information, for example, derive a new view class from `IconView` or `InfoView` to implement the new view. Also, create a derived class from `HWindowObject` to hold the additional information and override `newIconView` or `newInfoView` to create the new view object.

The window object also keeps track of which of its views are open. With this tracking, the window object can activate an existing view object using `HWindowObject::open`, and the view object can manage restoring itself as previously described. The window object also provides a means to notify a view when the data in it becomes invalid. In this example, view data can become invalid when a user selects the **Refresh** menu item, which uses a "brute force" technique to update the tree view. The `HWindowObject` destructor notifies any open views of the object by calling each view's `invalidateObject` member function.

The class `MenuHandler` derives from `ICnrMenuHandler` to handle pop-up menu requests on an `HWindowObject`. In the example, this handler is attached to the container in the tree view because only this view supports menu selections. However, you could also attach it to any other container control that contains an `HWindowObject`, such as the `IconView` client window.

Window Object/View Interface - advframe\winview\hwinobj.hpp

```cpp
#include <iframe.hpp>
#include <icnrctl.hpp>
#include <icnrmhdr.hpp>
#include <ititle.hpp>
#include "hwindow.hpp"

class IString;
class HWindowObjectView;

class HWindowObject : public IContainerObject {
public:
   HWindowObject ( const HWindow&      hwindow,
                   unsigned long       iconId,
                   IContainerControl*  cnr );
virtual
  ~HWindowObject();

virtual void
 handleOpen( IContainerControl* cnr );
virtual HWindowObject
 &openIconView( );
virtual Boolean
 isIconViewAvailable( ) const;
virtual HWindowObject
 &openInfoView( );
virtual HWindowObjectView
 &infoView ( );
virtual HWindowObjectView
 &iconView ( );
virtual HWindowObject
 &viewClosed ( HWindowObjectView* view );
virtual IContainerControl
 *container ( ) const;
const HWindow
 &hWindow( ) const;

protected:
virtual HWindowObjectView
 *newIconView ( );
virtual HWindowObjectView
 *newInfoView ( );

private:
IContainerControl
 *objCnr;
HWindowObjectView
 *ficonView;
HWindowObjectView
 *finfoView;
HWindow
 fhwindow;
};

class HWindowObjectView : protected IFrameWindow {
public:
   ~HWindowObjectView ( );
virtual HWindowObjectView
 &open ( );
virtual HWindowObjectView
 &invalidateObject ( );
protected:
   HWindowObjectView ( IWindow*       client,
                       HWindowObject& object,
                       const IString& viewName );
HWindowObject
 *object ( ) const;
```

```
private:
ITitle
  viewTitle;
HWindowObject
 *viewObj;
HWindowObjectView ( const HWindowObjectView& );
HWindowObjectView& operator=( const HWindowObjectView&);
};

class MenuHandler : public ICnrMenuHandler {
public:
  MenuHandler(  );
protected:
virtual Boolean
  makePopUpMenu( IMenuEvent& event );
};
```

Window Object/View Implementation - advframe\winview\hwinobj.cpp

```cpp
#include <ipopmenu.hpp>
#include "hwinobj.hpp"
#include "iconview.hpp"
#include "infoview.hpp"
#include "winview.h"

HWindowObject::HWindowObject( const HWindow&     hwindow,
                              unsigned long      iconId,
                              IContainerControl* cnr )
  : IContainerObject( IString(), iconId ),
    objCnr( cnr ),
    ficonView( 0 ),
    finfoView( 0 ),
    fhwindow( hwindow )
{
   IString wintext = hwindow.text();
   if ( wintext.length() > 20 )
      wintext.remove(21);
   wintext = hwindow.asHexString() + IString(" \"") + wintext +
             IString("\"");
   this->setIconText( wintext );
}

HWindowObject::~HWindowObject()
{
  if (ficonView)
     ficonView->invalidateObject();
  if (finfoView)
     finfoView->invalidateObject();
}

HWindowObject& HWindowObject::openIconView( )
{
   this->iconView().open();
   return *this;
}

HWindowObject& HWindowObject::openInfoView( )
{
   this->infoView().open();
   return *this;
}
```

```cpp
// This function is called by the container handler
// when the object is double-clicked.  Open the icon
// view if it is available; otherwise, open the
// information view.
void HWindowObject::handleOpen ( IContainerControl* )
{
   if (this->isIconViewAvailable() )
     this->iconView().open();
   else
     this->infoView().open();
}

HWindowObjectView& HWindowObject::iconView ( )
{
  if ( !ficonView )
    {
    ficonView = this -> newIconView();
    }
  return *ficonView;
}

HWindowObjectView& HWindowObject::infoView ( )
{
  if ( !finfoView )
    {
    finfoView = this -> newInfoView();
    }
  return *finfoView;
}

// Icon view is available as long as the object has children.
Boolean HWindowObject::isIconViewAvailable( ) const
{
   IContainerControl::ObjectCursor cursor( *(this->container()),
                                          this);
   return cursor.setToFirst() ;
}

// This function allocates a new icon view.
HWindowObjectView* HWindowObject::newIconView ( )
{
   HWindowObjectView* view = new IconView( *this );
   return view;
}

// This function allocates a new information view.
HWindowObjectView* HWindowObject::newInfoView ( )
{
  HWindowObjectView* view = new InfoView( *this );
  return view;
}

HWindowObject& HWindowObject::viewClosed( HWindowObjectView* view )
{
   if (view == this->finfoView)
      this->finfoView = 0;
   if (view == this->ficonView)
      this->ficonView = 0;
   return *this;
}

IContainerControl* HWindowObject::container ( ) const
{
  return objCnr;
}
```

```
const HWindow& HWindowObject::hWindow( ) const
{
  return fhwindow;
}

HWindowObjectView& HWindowObjectView::open ( )
{
  if ( isMinimized() )
    restore();
  setFocus();
  show();
  return *this;
}

HWindowObjectView::HWindowObjectView ( IWindow*       client,
                                       HWindowObject& object,
                                       const IString& viewName )
  : IFrameWindow( 0, 0, object.container()->parent(),
                  nextShellRect().scaleBy( 0.5, 0.5 ),
                  classDefaultStyle | noMoveWithOwner ),
    viewTitle( this ),
    viewObj( &object )
{
  viewTitle.setObjectText( object.iconText() );
  viewTitle.setViewText( viewName );
  setIcon( object.icon() );
  setClient( client );
  client->setOwner( this );
  setAutoDeleteObject( true );
}

HWindowObjectView::~HWindowObjectView ( )
{
  if ( viewObj )
    viewObj -> viewClosed( this );
}

HWindowObject* HWindowObjectView::object ( ) const
{
  return viewObj;
}

HWindowObjectView& HWindowObjectView::invalidateObject ( )
{
  viewTitle.setObjectText("<invalid>");
  viewObj = 0;
  return *this;
}

MenuHandler::MenuHandler( ) :
  ICnrMenuHandler( )
{ }

IBase::Boolean   MenuHandler::makePopUpMenu( IMenuEvent& event )
{
  Boolean result = false;
  IContainerControl* pcnr =
     (IContainerControl*)(event.dispatchingWindow());
  IContainerObject* pobj = popupMenuObject();
  if (pcnr && pobj)
    {
    pcnr->setCursor( pobj );
    IPopUpMenu* popup = new IPopUpMenu(POPUP_MENU, pcnr);
    popup->setAutoDeleteObject();
    popup->show(event.mousePosition());
    result = true;
    }
  return result;
}
```

The classes `IconView` and `InfoView` provide concrete implementations of secondary views for `HWindowObjects`. The icon view has a data member related to its client window—a handler for the container control client. The information view has a multiline edit control client and no data members. Each class also provides a `populate` member function, which initializes the contents of the client window. The code for these classes is in the **advframe\winview** directory on the examples disk.

Defining the Rest of Window Viewer

The remaining pieces of the window viewer application are the class `HWindow` and the application's resources. The class `HWindow` is derived from `IWindowHandle`, with some added member functions to return information about the system window in the format needed for the application. Look at the added member functions and notice that `IWindow` provides members to get most of the needed information. Using `IWindow` saves writing the system-dependent implementation code to get this information, so why not derive from `IWindow` instead of `IWindowHandle`? There are several reasons; all are rooted in the fact that this utility creates an `HWindow` object for every window in the system that is a direct or indirect descendant of the desktop window. These include Window Viewer's own windows, those created by the operating system itself, and those created by other unrelated applications.

First, using `IWindow` runs afoul of the Open Class Library restriction that there can only be one `IWindow` object for each system window. This applies to the Window Viewer application's windows because they are already `IWindow` objects. Open Class Library throws an exception when the application tries to create the second `IWindow` object to build the list of windows. This restriction is not that serious, because you could test for this situation by using `IWindow::windowWithHandle` and use the returned `IWindow` pointer if it is not 0.

Second, if you use `IWindow`, you can only create an `IWindow` object for an operating system window that the current process has created. If you used `IWindow` objects for gathering the window information, Window Viewer would only be able to show information on its own windows. The reasons for limiting `IWindow` objects to windows created by the current process are different, depending on the target operating system. In the OS/2 operating system, you cannot use the `WinSubclassWindow` function for a window handle created by another process. Because Open Class Library uses this function when it constructs an `IWindow` object, the constructor fails if you use it for an operating system window that was created in another process. In the Windows operating system, the reason for the restriction is that the `IWindow` implementation creates an `IThread` object for each thread that owns an `IWindow`. In order to create an `IThread` object, you must have access to the thread handle that the system assigns. Open Class Library has this handle for the threads in the current process but not for threads that the operating system or other applications own. For windows created outside of the current process, Open Class Library is unable to create the `IThread` object it needs; as a result you cannot use `IWindow` as a wrapper for such windows.

Because the `HWindow` class only needs simple information about windows, you can most easily implement it by using the presentation system APIs to get the information needed. The interface for `HWindow` is shown in the following example.

The application resources for the window viewer define the icons for both the application and the container objects, the application's main menu, and the pop-up menu that appears in the tree view.

The **advframe\winview** directory on the examples disk contains the complete window viewer program.

HWindow Interface - advframe\winview\hwindow.hpp

```
#include <istring.hpp>
#include <ihandle.hpp>

class HWindow : public IWindowHandle {
public:
  HWindow ( IHandle::Value handle=0 );

IString
  asHexString ( ) const;
IString
  id          ( ) const;
IString
  text        ( ) const;
IString
  rectangle   ( ) const;

IString
  windowClass ( ) const;
IString
  style       ( ) const;

Boolean
  isValid     ( ) const;

class ChildCursor : public IVBase {
public:
  ChildCursor ( const HWindow& parent );
virtual
 ~ChildCursor ( );

virtual Boolean
  setToFirst ( ),
  setToNext  ( ),
  isValid    ( ) const;

virtual void
  invalidate ( );

virtual HWindow
  hWindow    ( ) const;

private:
  ChildCursor ( const ChildCursor& cursor );
ChildCursor
 &operator = ( const ChildCursor& cursor );

IWindowHandle
  hwnd,
  hwndParent;
}; // HWindow::ChildCursor

};
```

The Multiple Document Interface Application

You have seen various ways to tailor the features of IFrameWindow to suit your requirements. For most applications, using one or more of the techniques described previously achieves the results you need. There are situations, however, where you need to do more to get the behavior you want. This section shows an example of tailoring IFrameWindow to take advantage of the Windows support for MDI applications.

The Windows operating system provides extensive support for MDI applications. This support includes automatically managing the appearance of the MDI windows and the menu items for navigating across the MDI application. To take advantage of these features, an application must adhere to a set of conventions described in the Windows SDK documentation. The MDIWindow class adapts IFrameWindow to these conventions. A simple application illustrates the results. Because the OS/2 operating system does not provide the added MDI support used by this example, it does not apply. With the OS/2 system, however, you can get basic MDI behavior by using IFrameWindow directly to create the MDI windows.

Defining the MDIWindow Class

The Windows operating system's conventions for MDI applications primarily affect how the windows in the application are created and how those windows process events sent to them. The main window of an MDI application, the *MDI frame*, is similar to a typical main window, except that it uses the special default window procedure DefFrameProc instead of the usual DefWindowProc. Each of the document windows contained within the MDI frame is an *MDI child*. These windows are also similar to typical IFrameWindows, except that they are created in a special way and use the window procedure DefMDIChildProc instead of DefWindowProc. The MDI frame window has a special child window, the *MDI client*, which manages the MDI child windows. When you create the MDI client, you can provide it with a reference to a menu item which a user can use to select the active window. Because the MDI client manages the MDI child windows, you typically perform an action such as minimize, restore, or close on an MDI child by sending a message to the MDI client window.

The MDIWindow class provides two constructors: one for creating MDI frame windows and one for creating MDI child windows. The MDI frame constructor is as follows:

```
MDIWindow( const IResourceId&       resId,
           IWindow*                 parent,
           IWindow*                 owner ,
           unsigned long            windowMenuId,
           unsigned long            childMenuId,
           const IRectangle&        initRect,
           const IFrameWindow::Style& style = defaultStyle(),
           const char*              title = 0 );
```

The MDI child constructor is as follows:

```
MDIWindow( const IResourceId&       resId,
           MDIWindow*               parent,
           const IRectangle&        initRect,
           const IFrameWindow::Style& style = defaultStyle(),
           const char*              title = 0 );
```

The details of these constructors as they relate to the components of an MDI application follow:

MDI Frame

To create an MDI frame window, you need the special default window procedure called for unprocessed events. You could do this in Open Class Library by writing a handler to call the procedure after all other handlers. However, this could result in a case where DefFrameProc is not called. If a handler calls IHandler::defaultProcedure, the default procedure for the window class is called, not DefFrameProc.

A more robust solution is to have DefFrameProc be the default procedure for the window class, thus ensuring it gets called for all unprocessed events. The example does not do it exactly like that, however, because the DefFrameProc needs an argument (the handle of the MDI client) that DefWindowProc does not need. The function MDIWindow::registerFrameClass sets up the MDI frame window class by registering the function MDIWindowProc as the window procedure. MDIWindowProc obtains the MDI client handle and passes all messages to DefFrameProc.

MDI Child

Creating an MDI child window is similar to creating the frame; a special window procedure has to be called for unprocessed messages. In this case, the signature of DefMDIChildProc is the same as DefWindowProc, so the example uses it as the window procedure for the window class. You do, however, have to create MDI child windows using the system function CreateMDIWindow instead of CreateWindowEx, which IFrameWindow::create uses. The function MDIWindow::initialize handles this case, and sets up some of the MDIWindow window styles and resources. Because IFrameWindow::create handles some details of menu and resource loading needed for an MDI frame, initialize calls it for MDI frame windows.

MDI Client

The main special feature of the MDI client window is that you create it using the system-provided window class MDICLIENT. Because this window is a necessary component of an MDI frame window, the constructor for MDI frames creates this window after creating the frame itself. Its window identifier is IC_FRAME_CLIENT_ID so that the IFrameWindow functions dealing with the client correctly identify it. Because the client window does not change for an MDI frame, the example overrides IFrameWindow::setClient to ensure that the MDI client window remains the client.

The MDI client needs to be able to access the menu bar to update it when MDI child windows are created and destroyed. The constructor for MDI frames accepts two arguments, which it uses to give the MDI client access to the correct menu items. The windowMenuId argument is the identifier of the menu item on the menu bar, which is to contain the menu items for activating MDI children. Typically, applications use the **Windows** menu item for this purpose. The childMenuId argument is the menu item identifier within the windowMenuId submenu, which contains the menu item for the first MDI child window. If there is more than one MDI child, the system numbers them sequentially starting with windowMenuId. Note that a side effect of this is that the IFrameWindow::menuBar style is required for an MDI frame window because the constructor needs to access the menu bar.

Both of the `MDIWindow` constructors accept the same `resid`, `initRect`, `style`, and `title` arguments that the `IFrameWindow` constructors do. The `parent` and `owner` arguments for the MDI frame constructor are also used like `IFrameWindow` uses them. The MDI child constructor accepts only an `MDIWindow` object as a parent because this is required for proper operation of the child. The implementations of both constructors use the `IFrameWindow::deferCreation` setting to construct the base `IFrameWindow` object because `MDIWindow::initialize` creates the window.

Because the Windows MDI support requires that special messages be sent to the MDI client to close, maximize, or restore an MDI child, `MDIWindow` overrides the `IFrameWindow` virtual functions `close`, `maximize`, and `restore`. The `MDIWindow` implementation of each of these functions checks whether the current object is an MDI child window and, if so, sends the appropriate messages to the MDI client. If the object is not an MDI child, the `IFrameWindow` implementation of the function is called.

`MDIWindow` also provides functions for managing the MDI arrangement. The class implements functions to determine the active MDI child window and to arrange the MDI child windows and minimized icons. The function `activateChild` is used when a user selects one of the menu items corresponding to an MDI child. Because the system assigns the identifier of the child windows as they are created, the example provides this function to encapsulate locating the MDI child that matches the menu item and activating it.

MDI Window Interface - advframe\mdi\mdiwin.hpp

```cpp
#include <iframe.hpp>

class MDIWindow : public IFrameWindow {
public:
 MDIWindow( const IResourceId&       resId,
            IWindow*                 parent,
            IWindow*                 owner ,
            unsigned long            windowMenuId,
            unsigned long            childMenuId,
            const IRectangle&        initRect,
            const IFrameWindow::Style& style = defaultStyle(),
            const char*              title = 0 );
 MDIWindow( const IResourceId&       resId,
            MDIWindow*               parent,
            const IRectangle&        initRect,
            const IFrameWindow::Style& style = defaultStyle(),
            const char*              title = 0 );

virtual MDIWindow
 &setClient    ( IWindow* newClient );

virtual MDIWindow
 &close         ( ),
 &maximize      ( ),
 &restore       ( );

virtual MDIWindow
 *activeChild( ) const;

virtual MDIWindow
 &activateChild( unsigned long childId ),
 &arrange       ( ),
 &cascade       ( ),
 &tile          ( Boolean horizontal=true );
```

```
protected:
MDIWindow
  &initialize        ( const IResourceId& resId,
                       const Style&        style,
                       IWindow*            parent   = 0,
                       IWindow*            owner    = 0,
                       const IRectangle&   initRect = IRectangle(),
                       const char*         title    = 0 );
unsigned long
  registerFrameClass ( const Style& style,
                       const IResourceId& resId ,
                       Boolean isChild );

private:
 IWindow
  *fclient;
 unsigned long
   fchildId;
 MDIWindow( const MDIWindow& );
 MDIWindow& operator=( const MDIWindow& );
};
```

In the implementation for `MDIFrame`, notice that we define a class `CmdHandler` derived from `ICommandHandler`. The purpose of this handler is to intercept `WM_SYSCOMMAND/SC_CLOSE` messages originating from an MDI child window. The handler handles these messages by calling the `close` function for the MDI child and then returns true. We need to do this because the processing of `SC_CLOSE` in the default `IFrameHandler` results in processing appropriate for standard frame windows but not for MDI child windows.

MDI Window Implementation - advframe\mdi\mdiwin.cpp

```
#include <windows.h>
#include <icmdhdr.hpp>
#include <icoordsy.hpp>
#include <iexcept.hpp>
#include <imenubar.hpp>
#include <isysmenu.hpp>
#include <ithread.hpp>
#include "mdiwin.hpp"

class CmdHandler : public ICommandHandler {
public:
  CmdHandler();
virtual Boolean
  systemCommand ( ICommandEvent& event );
static CmdHandler
  *defaultHandler();
private:
 static CmdHandler
   *defaultHdr;
};

CmdHandler* CmdHandler::defaultHdr = 0;

CmdHandler::CmdHandler()
  : ICommandHandler()
{ }
```

```cpp
IBase::Boolean CmdHandler::systemCommand( ICommandEvent& event )
{
  Boolean handled = false;
  if ((event.commandId() & 0xFFF0 ) == SC_CLOSE )
    {
    MDIWindow* mdichild = (MDIWindow*)event.window();
    if (mdichild)
      {
      mdichild->close();
      handled = true;
      }
    }
  return handled;
}

CmdHandler* CmdHandler::defaultHandler( )
{
  if (!CmdHandler::defaultHdr)
    CmdHandler::defaultHdr = new CmdHandler;
  return CmdHandler::defaultHdr;
}

MDIWindow::MDIWindow( const IResourceId&          resId,
                      IWindow*                    parent ,
                      IWindow*                    owner ,
                      unsigned long               windowMenuId,
                      unsigned long               childMenuId,
                      const IRectangle&           initRect,
                      const IFrameWindow::Style&  style,
                      const char*                 title ) :
  IFrameWindow ( IFrameWindow::deferCreation ),
  fclient      ( 0 ),
  fchildId     ( childMenuId )
{
    // Use MDIWindow::initialize instead of the one in IFrameWindow.
    this->initialize( resId, style, parent,
                      owner, initRect, title );

    // Create the MDI client window.
    IMenuBar menu( this, IMenuBar::wrapper );
    CLIENTCREATESTRUCT ccs;
    ccs.hWindowMenu = menu.menuItem( windowMenuId ).submenuHandle();
    ccs.idFirstChild = (unsigned int)fchildId;
    IWindowHandle hwnd =
      IWindow::create( IC_FRAME_CLIENT_ID,
                       0,
                       WS_CHILD | WS_CLIPCHILDREN | WS_VSCROLL |
                       WS_HSCROLL | WS_VISIBLE ,
                       "MDICLIENT",
                       this->handle(),
                       this->handle(),
                       IRectangle(0,0,0,0),
                       &ccs,
                       0,
                       defaultOrdering(),
                       0 );
    fclient = new IWindow( hwnd );
    fclient->setAutoDeleteObject( true );
}
```

```
MDIWindow::MDIWindow( const IResourceId&        resId,
                      MDIWindow*                parent,
                      const IRectangle&         initRect,
                      const IFrameWindow::Style& style,
                      const char*               title) :
  IFrameWindow ( IFrameWindow::deferCreation ),
  fclient ( 0 ),
  fchildId ( 0 )
{
    IASSERTPARM( (parent != 0) && (parent->client() != 0) );
    // Use MDIWindow::initialize instead of the one in IFrameWindow.
    this->initialize( resId, style, parent->client(),
                      parent->client(), initRect, title );
    CmdHandler::defaultHandler()->handleEventsFor( this );
}

MDIWindow& MDIWindow::setClient    ( IWindow* newClient )
{
  if (fclient == 0)
      IFrameWindow::setClient( newClient );
  return *this;
}

MDIWindow &MDIWindow::close ( )
  {
  IWindow* mdiClient = fclient ? 0 : this->parent();
  if (mdiClient)
      mdiClient->sendEvent( WM_MDIDESTROY,
                            IEventParameter1(this->handle()) );
  else
      IFrameWindow::close();
  return *this;
  }

MDIWindow &MDIWindow::maximize ( )
{
  IWindow* mdiClient = fclient ? 0 : this->parent();
  // Ignore the request if there is no maximize button.
  if ((this->style() & WS_MAXIMIZEBOX ) && (mdiClient) )
      mdiClient->sendEvent( WM_MDIMAXIMIZE,
                            IEventParameter1(this->handle()) );
  else
      IFrameWindow::maximize();
  return *this;
}

MDIWindow &MDIWindow::restore ( )
{
  IWindow* mdiClient = fclient ? 0 : this->parent();
  if (mdiClient)
      mdiClient->sendEvent( WM_MDIRESTORE,
                            IEventParameter1(this->handle()) );
  else
      IFrameWindow::restore();
  return *this;
}

// This function returns the active MDI child or 0 if there
// is none.
MDIWindow*  MDIWindow::activeChild( ) const
{
  MDIWindow* child = 0;
  if (fclient)
    child = (MDIWindow*) IWindow::windowWithHandle(
                (HANDLE)fclient->sendEvent( WM_MDIGETACTIVE ));
  return child;
}
```

```
MDIWindow&  MDIWindow::activateChild( unsigned long childId )
{
   if ((childId >= fchildId) && (fclient))
      {
      IWindow* child =
         IWindow::windowWithParent( childId, fclient );
      if (child)
         fclient->sendEvent( WM_MDIACTIVATE,
                             IEventParameter1(child->handle()) );
      }
   return *this;
}

MDIWindow&  MDIWindow::arrange          ( )
{
   IWindow* mdiClient = fclient ? fclient : this->parent();
   if (mdiClient)
      mdiClient->sendEvent( WM_MDIICONARRANGE );
   return *this;
}

MDIWindow&  MDIWindow::cascade          ( )
{
   IWindow* mdiClient = fclient ? fclient : this->parent();
   if (mdiClient)
      mdiClient->sendEvent( WM_MDICASCADE );
   return *this;
}

MDIWindow&  MDIWindow::tile             ( Boolean horizontal )
{
   IWindow* mdiClient = fclient ? fclient : this->parent();
   if (mdiClient)
      mdiClient->sendEvent( WM_MDITILE,
                           horizontal ? MDITILE_HORIZONTAL :
                                        MDITILE_VERTICAL);
   return *this;
}

MDIWindow& MDIWindow::initialize ( const IResourceId &resId,
                                   const Style       &style,
                                   IWindow           *parent,
                                   IWindow           *owner,
                                   const IRectangle  &initRect,
                                   const char        *title )
{
   // Save the extended style.
   setExtendedStyle(
      extendedStyle() | style.asExtendedUnsignedLong() );

   // Get styles and set up values for parent and owner windows.
   unsigned long
      frameStyle   = convertToGUIStyle( style ),
      exFrameStyle = convertToGUIStyle( style, true );
   IWindowHandle
      hParent = ( parent ) ? parent->handle() :
                             IWindow::desktopWindow()->handle(),
      hOwner  = ( owner )  ? owner->handle()  : IWindowHandle( 0 );
   Boolean
      isChild = ( hParent != IWindow::desktopWindow()->handle() );

   if ( isChild )
      frameStyle |= WS_CHILD;
   else
      frameStyle &= ~(unsigned long)WS_CHILD;
```

```
// Try to get the title from the resource library.  If it
// is not available, use whatever was provided.
HANDLE   fcdata = resId.resourceLibrary().handle();
if ( style & IFrameWindow::titleBar && !title )
   {
   IString titleString =
      resId.resourceLibrary().tryToLoadString( resId.id() );
   if ( titleString.length() )
      title = titleString;
   }
else if ( !(style & IFrameWindow::titleBar) )
   {
   // The WS_OVERLAPPED style implies title bar.  Make it a
   // pop-up window if the title bar area is not needed for
   // buttons or the system menu.
   if (!(frameStyle &
        (WS_CHILD|WS_MINIMIZEBOX|WS_MAXIMIZEBOX|WS_SYSMENU)))
      frameStyle |= WS_POPUP;
   }

IRectangle rect = ( style & IFrameWindow::shellPosition ) ?
                 IFrameWindow::nextShellRect() : initRect;

// Create our window class for the frame if necessary.
char* frameClass = (char*)
  registerFrameClass( style, resId, isChild );

// Create the window.  For Windows 95 and Windows NT 4.0,
// the WS_EX_MDICHILD extended style can be used with
// IFrameWindow::create to create an MDI child window.
// This style is not supported in Windows NT 3.51, so
// we have to use a more complex approach to support
// all operating systems.
if (isChild)
   {
   // Use CreateMDIWindow to create the MDI child.
   RECT parentRect;
   GetClientRect(hParent, &parentRect);
   ISize parentSize = ISize(parentRect.right - parentRect.left,
                            parentRect.bottom - parentRect.top);
   rect = ICoordinateSystem::convertToNative( rect, parentSize);
   IWindowHandle hwnd = CreateMDIWindow(
                           frameClass,
                           (LPSTR)title,
                           frameStyle,
                           (int)rect.minX(),
                           (int)rect.minY(),
                           (int)rect.width(),
                           (int)rect.height(),
                           hParent,
                           GetModuleHandle(0),
                           0);
   // Complete the functions IFrameWindow::create
   // would have completed.
   this->start( hwnd );
   this->setOwner( owner );
   // CreateMDIWindow forces WS_VISIBLE to on. Undo this for now.
   this->hide();
   }
```

```
      else
        {
        // Use IFrameWindow::create so we get the resource and
        // menu handling functions it provides.
        this -> create( resId.id(),
                        title,
                        frameStyle & (unsigned long)~WS_VISIBLE,
                        frameClass,
                        hParent,
                        hOwner,
                        rect,
                        fcdata,
                        0,
                        defaultOrdering(),
                        exFrameStyle );
        }


      // If one or both of the minimize/maximize buttons is missing
      // and there is still a system menu, disable the corresponding
      // item in the system menu.  Disabling rather than removing is
      // the action recommended in the SDK.
      if (frameStyle & WS_SYSMENU)
        {
        if ( (frameStyle & (WS_MINIMIZEBOX | WS_MAXIMIZEBOX)) !=
             (WS_MINIMIZEBOX | WS_MAXIMIZEBOX) )
          {
          ISystemMenu sysMenu( this );
          if ( !(frameStyle & WS_MINIMIZEBOX) )
            sysMenu.disableItem( ISystemMenu::idMinimize );
          if ( !(frameStyle & WS_MAXIMIZEBOX) )
            sysMenu.disableItem( ISystemMenu::idMaximize );
          // Restore is left enabled when the
          // WS_EX_DLGMODALFRAME style is used
          if ((exFrameStyle & WS_EX_DLGMODALFRAME) &&
             ((frameStyle & (WS_MINIMIZEBOX | WS_MAXIMIZEBOX))==0))
            sysMenu.disableItem( ISystemMenu::idRestore );
          }
        }

      // Handle requests to minimize or maximize the window.
      if ( style & IFrameWindow::minimized )
        this -> minimize();
      else if ( style & IFrameWindow::maximized )
        this -> maximize();

      // Handle request to show the window.
      if ( style & IWindow::visible )
        this -> show();

      return *this;
      }


  static LRESULT CALLBACK MDIWindowProc( void*          hwnd,
                                         unsigned int eventId,
                                         WPARAM       parm1,
                                         LPARAM       parm2 )
  {
    MDIWindow* frame = (MDIWindow*)IWindow::windowWithHandle( hwnd );
    if (frame)
      {
      return DefFrameProc( hwnd,
                           frame->clientHandle(),
                           eventId,
                           parm1,
                           parm2);
      }
```

```
    else
        {
        return CallWindowProc( (FARPROC)DefWindowProc,
                               hwnd,
                               eventId,
                               parm1,
                               parm2);
        }
}

unsigned long MDIWindow::registerFrameClass(
                        const Style& style,
                        const IResourceId& resId,
                        Boolean isChild )
{
    // Create a WNDCLASS structure for registering the new class.
    // We base this class on the WC_DIALOG class, but set up the
    // background brush, class style, and icon to match those
    // specified for the MDIWindow.  IFrameWindow uses the extra
    // window word.
    WNDCLASS
      wndclass;
    if (!GetClassInfo( 0, WC_DIALOG, &wndclass))
        ITHROWGUIERROR( "GetClassInfo" );
    if (style & IFrameWindow::dialogBackground )
      wndclass.hbrBackground = (HBRUSH)(COLOR_3DFACE + 1);
    else
      wndclass.hbrBackground = (HBRUSH)(COLOR_APPWORKSPACE + 1);
    wndclass.cbWndExtra = DLGWINDOWEXTRA + 4;
    wndclass.style =
      CS_DBLCLKS | CS_OWNDC | CS_VREDRAW | CS_HREDRAW ;
    if ( !( style & IFrameWindow::alignNoAdjust ) )
      wndclass.style |= CS_BYTEALIGNWINDOW;

    // If the minimizedIcon style is set, load the icon resource
    // and place it into the class structure. Otherwise, use the
    // default icon for dialogs.
    if ( style & IFrameWindow::minimizedIcon )
        {
        HINSTANCE
          hInstance = resId.resourceLibrary().handle();
        HICON
          hIcon;
        if ( !(hIcon = LoadIcon(
                       hInstance, MAKEINTRESOURCE( resId.id() ))))
            ITHROWGUIERROR( "LoadIcon" );
        else
            wndclass.hIcon = hIcon;
        }
    wndclass.lpszMenuName = 0;
    wndclass.hInstance = GetModuleHandle(0);

    // Here is the key difference between the MDIWindow window class
    // and the ones created by IFrameWindow.  We arrange for the
    // special MDI window procedures to be called.
    if (isChild)
      wndclass.lpfnWndProc = DefMDIChildProc;
    else
      wndclass.lpfnWndProc = (WNDPROC)MDIWindowProc;
```

```
    // Register a class whose name is ICL Frame_MDI + nnnn,
    // where nnnn is the ASCII string for the value of classID.
    // This results in each frame window having a unique class name
    // similar to ICL Frame_MDI1.
ATOM
    frameClass = 0;
static unsigned long
    classID = 0;
do
    {
    IString newFrameClass =  IString("ICL Frame_MDI") +
                             IString(classID);
    classID++;
    wndclass.lpszClassName = newFrameClass;
    frameClass = RegisterClass( &wndclass );
    if (!frameClass)
        {
        // If the class exists, try again with the next ID value.
        // Otherwise, throw an exception.
        if (GetLastError() != ERROR_CLASS_ALREADY_EXISTS)
            ITHROWGUIERROR( "RegisterClass" );
        }    // if not registered
    }
while (!frameClass);

    return MAKELONG( frameClass, 0 );
}
```

Creating the MDIWindow Application

The structure of an application using `MDIFrame` is similar to an application using `IFrameWindow`. In the **advframe\mdi** program on the examples disk, the class `MainWindow` contains an `MDIWindow` object for the MDI frame window, a menu bar, and a command handler. Because the MDI frame object is a private member, the class defines public functions for use by the command handler to access the MDI frame window. In the example, these functions are mostly trivial passthroughs to the `MDIWindow` object, but in a real application you might need them to allow `MainWindow` to keep track of the state of the MDI view. This can be important in an MDI application because you need to change the menu if an MDI child window containing a different type of data is created or activated.

The command handler `CommandHandler` is also typical, except for a few of the cases in the command function's `switch` statement. The `IC_ID_CLOSE`, `IC_ID_MINIMIZE`, and `IC_ID_RESTORE` command identifiers occur when a maximized MDI child is closed, minimized, or restored, respectively. It might seem odd that these events are sent as commands in this case, not system commands. However, remember that the buttons causing the events are located on the MDI frame window's menu bar rather than on the child window's title bar when the child is maximized. Thus, these events are like any other events originating from menu bar selections.

Instances of the `EditWindow` are MDI child windows. As in the Window Viewer example earlier in this chapter, the inheritance from `MDIWindow` is protected to control access to the object but still allow use of `IWindow::setAutoDeleteObject`.

Chapter 20

Applications and Threads

- Describes the application and thread classes in Open Class Library that you can use to add multiple thread support to your applications
- Describes the IApplication, ICurrentApplication, IThread, ICurrentThread, IStartedThread, IThreadFn, IThreadMemberFn<>, IResource, ISharedResource, IPrivateResource, IResourceLock, ICritSec, ITimer, ITimerFn, ITimerMemberFn, and ITimerMemberFn0 classes
- Chapters 24, 26, and 28 cover related material

This chapter describes the IThread class and related classes. These classes make it easy for you to exploit the power of multitasking in your applications.

We discuss threads: what they are, how they work, and what you use them for. Then we cover the support Open Class Library provides for this operating system feature, specifically the IThread class and the other classes you use in multithreaded applications.

Processes and Threads

The OS/2, Windows 95, and Windows NT operating systems are *pre-emptive multitasking* systems. This means that they can run multiple programs concurrently, and each of those programs has a chance to execute regardless of whether the other programs yield control. The tasking model of these systems has two layers:

- Process Level

  Processes are the heart of the systems' process model. A process corresponds to an executing application. Most operating system resources, such as memory and file handles, are owned at the process level. Open Class Library encapsulates process objects—to some extent—by the class IApplication. See the topic "Applications" later in this chapter for more on this subject.

- Thread level

  Threads are the smallest unit of execution. Conceptually, each operating system maintains the processor state—the current register values, flags, and instruction pointer —on a per-thread basis. A process can have multiple threads. Each thread has access to all of the operating system resources owned by its process.

These operating systems are multitasking in that they activate another thread and let it execute when either the current thread has used up its share of time (its *time slice*) or becomes suspended. They suspend a thread when the application code running on the thread requests some resource and that resource is not currently available. For example, a thread can request to read a file and the system suspends it until the file I/O is completed.

Most thread blocking occurs while threads wait until input and output are completed. If one process has requested to read a file, then the system suspends any other threads that require reading or writing to the same disk partition until the first disk operation has completed. Threads also must wait for input from a user. This is the most common reason threads of graphical user-interface applications are blocked; they are waiting for a user to move the mouse or press a key. This is one reason multiprocessing is so important. It lets the computer do work during the relatively long periods of time that the user spends entering information.

A more important reason to use multithreading, particularly for Presentation Manager applications, is that using multiple threads permits a user to do other work during the relatively long periods of time that your application is processing a user-input action. The following simple program illustrates this:

Multithreaded Demo Program - thread\simple\simple.cpp

```cpp
#include <iframe.hpp>
#include <istattxt.hpp>
#include <ipushbut.hpp>
#include <icmdhdr.hpp>
#include <ithread.hpp>
#include <istring.hpp>

enum { cmdThreaded, cmdNotThreaded, cmdDone };

static const char
  *prompt = "Press a button to perform action";

/*------------------------- Action --------------------------
| This simple class provides a single member function that  |
| sleeps for 15 one-second intervals, updating a static     |
| text window at each iteration.  At the end, a command      |
| event is posted to a frame window.                         |
-----------------------------------------------------------*/
class Action {
public:
  Action ( IFrameWindow &frame,
           IStaticText  &status )
    : frame( frame ),
      status( status )
    {
    }
virtual void
  performAction ( )
    {
    // Sleep for 15 seconds.
    for ( int i = 15; i; i-- )
      {
      status.setText( IString( i ) );
      IThread::current().sleep( 1000 );
      }
    status
      .setText( "" )
      .refresh();
    // Tell frame the action is "done."
    frame.postEvent( IWindow::command, cmdDone );
    }
```

```
private:
IFrameWindow
 &frame;
IStaticText
 &status;
Action ( const Action & );
operator = ( const Action & );
};


/*---------------------- CmdHandler ------------------------
| This class is a simple command handler that processes     |
| 3 separate commands:                                      |
|    cmdNotThreaded - Invokes Action::performAction on the  |
|                     current thread of execution           |
|    cmdThreaded    - Runs Action::performAction on a       |
|                     separate thread                       |
|    cmdDone        - Handles completion of an action by    |
|                     refreshing the frame window           |
-----------------------------------------------------------*/
class CmdHandler : public ICommandHandler {
public:
  // Handler attaches to frame + text.
  CmdHandler ( IFrameWindow &frame,
               IStaticText  &text,
               IStaticText  &status )
    : action( frame, status ),
      frame( frame ),
      text( text )
    {
    handleEventsFor( &frame );
    }
protected:
virtual Boolean
  command ( ICommandEvent &event )
    {
    switch ( event.commandId() )
      {
      case cmdThreaded:
        {
        frame.disable();
        text.setText( "Performing action on separate thread" );
        IThread
          thread;
        thread.start( new IThreadMemberFn<Action>
                      ( action, Action::performAction ) );
        break;
        }
      case cmdNotThreaded:
        frame.disable();
        text.setText( "Performing action on current thread" );
        action.performAction();
        break;
      case cmdDone:
        frame.enable();
        text.setText( prompt );
        break;
      }
    return true;
    }
private:
Action
  action;
IFrameWindow
 &frame;
IStaticText
 &text;
CmdHandler( const CmdHandler & );
operator = ( const CmdHandler & );
};
```

```
void main()
  {
// Create the main window.
IFrameWindow
   frame( "Multithreading Demo" );
// Use static text for client area and status window.
IStaticText
   client( IC_FRAME_CLIENT_ID, &frame, &frame ),
   status( 0, &frame, &frame );
// Create command handler to process button clicks.
CmdHandler
   handler( frame, status, client );
client.setAlignment( IStaticText::centerCenter );
status.setText( prompt );
// Create buttons to trigger actions.
IPushButton
   button1( cmdThreaded, &frame, &frame ),
   button2( cmdNotThreaded, &frame, &frame );
button1.setText( "On another thread" );
button2.setText( "On current thread" );
// Put status window above client; buttons below.
frame.addExtension( &status, IFrameWindow::aboveClient );
frame.addExtension( &button1, IFrameWindow::belowClient );
frame.addExtension( &button2, IFrameWindow::belowClient );
frame.setClient( &client );
// Make frame window a more reasonable size.
frame.moveSizeTo( frame.rect().scaleBy(.5) );
// Show the main window.
frame.setFocus();
frame.show();
// Process window events till user closes the main window.
IThread::current().processMsgs();
  }
```

This simple program illustrates the value of using multiple threads. If you press the button labeled **On current thread** while running this program under the OS/2 operating system, you lock out the user from the entire OS/2 system for fifteen seconds. If you press the button labeled **On another thread**, you can activate another application and work with it during those fifteen seconds. In the Windows operating systems, you can transfer control to another application, but this example program is disabled entirely during the fifteen seconds while the single thread is busy.

This example also illustrates how easy it is to use the Open Class Library thread support classes to make your applications multithreaded. You have to write only one line of code differently to do it right.

Applications

Open Class Library provides a minimal set of classes and functions to encapsulate operating system processes. Each application the user runs executes as a separate process.

IApplication Class

The IApplication class provides the general attributes and behavior of Open Class Library application objects. You might expect IApplication to provide functions for starting and manipulating secondary processes, much as IThread does for threads. However, because Open

Class Library has not yet implemented that level of function, this class provides only the support that its derivative ICurrentApplication class requires.

You can create objects of IApplication to represent applications that you start via some other means. To do that, provide the process identifier on the constructor of the IApplication object. You also use IApplication to set the priority of the threads in those applications. We discuss this capability later on in the topic, "Thread Priority."

ICurrentApplication Class

The class ICurrentApplication is a specialization of IApplication. Each application that you implement using Open Class Library includes a single object of this type to represent that application. You access the object that represents the currently executing process by calling the IApplication static member function current. This class adds function to make the current application object more useful than a generic IApplication object.

Program Arguments

One feature of the ICurrentApplication object is that it can hold the arguments to your program. Because the current application object is obtainable via a static member function, you can access these arguments anywhere in your application. Thus, you do not need to place the argc and argv arguments to main in static storage or to pass those values to the objects that require access to them. The functions that provide access to the program arguments are found in Table 20-1.

Typically, you call ICurrentApplication::setArgs from within main. However, you can call setArgs at any time. With this capability you can use the application arguments as general-purpose, process-scoped IString variables.

The User's Resource Library

Resources are application-specific entities that define various elements of your application, such as text strings, dialog templates, and icons. We describe resources at length in Chapter 24, "Using Resources."

You identify these resources via objects of class IResourceId. The identifiers consist of two elements: a reference to a specific resource library and a numeric "key" that uniquely identifies the resource within that library.

To simplify how you use these resource identifiers and replace resources, the resource library component of the resource identifier object defaults to the application's default *user's resource library*. The current application object maintains the identity of this object, which has type IResourceLibrary. With this feature you can use a generic IResourceId (constructed without an explicit IResourceLibrary) and switch to a different resource library. Then, you do not have to change all of the instances of those IResourceIds to refer to the new resource library.

Table 20-1. ICurrentApplication Program Argument Functions

Function	Description
setArgs	Stores the arguments in the current application object. You pass the same *argc* (number of arguments) and *argv* (array of char* argument pointers) that your main function receives.
argc	Returns the number of arguments.
argv	Returns a given command-line argument as an IString object. It accepts as argument the index of the requested argument. The argument indexes are always in the range 0 to argc-1.

ICurrentApplication provides two functions for maintaining the default user resource library. Call ICurrentApplication::userResourceLibrary to query the current default user resource library and ICurrentApplication::setUserResourceLibrary to assign a new default user resource library. By default, the former function returns a default IResourceLibrary object, which results in Open Class Library loading the resources from the program (.EXE) file rather than from a dynamic link library.

This design facilitates dynamic binding of your applications resources. For example, if you offer a menu choice for users to select their preferred language at run time, you could implement that using this code:

```
void setLanguage ( char code ) {
  IString
    libName = "MY_APP_" + code;
  IApplication::current().setUserResourceLibrary( libName );
}
```

Coupling this code with consistently using IResourceIds that use the default library results in the use of resources appropriate to the selected language.

Open Class Library's Resource Library

Open Class Library loads some resources for its own use. Examples of such resources are tool-bar button bitmaps, document framework dialogs, and multimedia control bitmaps. To enable the same degree of dynamic binding to such resources, ICurrentApplication maintains a separate *library resource library*.

Maintain this library by using the resourceLibrary and setResourceLibrary functions of ICurrentApplication. These functions work just as the ones do that maintain the user resource library.

If you are shipping the Open Class Library resource DLL with your application, add a call to ICurrentApplication::setResourceLibrary to your application's start-up code before any Open Class Library resources are loaded. You do this because you must rename that library to comply with the VisualAge for C++ license agreement. Call this function passing the new name of this library.

Controlling Program Execution

ICurrentApplication provides two functions that support a simple model for single threaded applications.

- ICurrentApplication::run, which is an alias for ICurrentThread::processMsgs. We discuss this function in detail in the topic "The Message Processing Loop" later in this chapter.

- ICurrentApplication::exit, which terminates the current application. It is equivalent to exiting the main thread of your application. In most cases, permit normal cleanup to occur by returning from main as usual. By calling the exit function, you bypass the destruction of active temporary and automatic objects.

IThread Class

Objects of class IThread provide C++ objects that correspond to threads of execution. However, the C++ objects are not the operating system threads. The two objects have the same relationship as do the windowing system's windows and the corresponding C++ IWindow objects. The diagram in Figure 20-1 shows the relationships among the various C++ objects and operating system threads, as follows:

- The IThread objects are pointers to objects of type IStartedThread. The latter class provides all of the implementation details of Open Class Library's thread support.

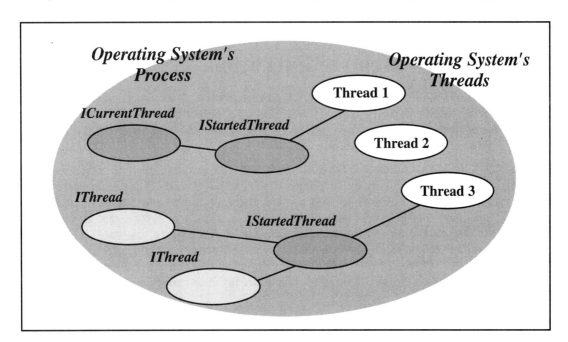

Figure 20-1. Operating System Threads and IThread Objects.

- The `IStartedThread` objects maintain a logical pointer to the associated operating system thread.

- Multiple `IThread` objects can refer to the same `IStartedThread` object and, in turn, to the same system thread. The `IThread` objects are effectively references to the associated `IStartedThread` object, which is, in turn, reference-counted. The `IStartedThread` objects disappear when all references are destroyed. The `IThread` object itself is effectively a reference to the `IStartedThread`. The `IStartedThread` object does not get destroyed until the thread of execution ends.

- Each Open Class Library application has a single object of type `ICurrentThread`. This derived `IThread` object maintains a reference to the `IStartedThread` object corresponding to the process' main thread. We discuss this current thread in greater detail in the next section.

- The process can have threads that do not correspond to `IThread` objects. Thread 2 is such a thread in the process depicted in Figure 20-1. The topic "Using IThread with Already Started Threads of Execution" covers this in detail.

Thread Termination versus IThread Object Destruction

Threads of execution never end when `IThread` objects are destructed! Because the `IThread` objects are not the threads themselves, and forcing the lifetimes of the separate entities to coincide is not possible, no attempt is made to try to turn the `IThread` destructor into a thread terminator.

The Current Thread of Execution

Open Class Library also provides the specialized thread class `ICurrentThread`. Open Class Library ensures that there is always one, and only one, object of class `ICurrentThread` by making the constructor for that class private. You access the single object by using the function `IThread::current`, as demonstrated in the following examples. This is a static member function of `IThread`. It creates the `ICurrentThread` object the first time you call it.

`ICurrentThread` is designed so its object adapts to the current thread. When code executing on thread1 uses it, it acts like thread 1. When code executing on thread 3 uses it, it acts like thread 3. You need this behavior when you require attributes of the current thread inside functions that can execute on any thread. For example, if you need to call an OS/2 API which requires the anchor block handle, you need to pass the anchor block handle for the current thread of execution. If the function is called on thread 1, you should pass thread 1's anchor block handle; if called on thread 3, you should pass thread 3's anchor block handle.

So, to implement a function that calls `WinGetCurrentTime`, you would simply code it as follows:

```
void millisecondsSinceSystemStartUp( ) {
  return WinGetCurrentTime( IThread::current().anchorBlock() );
}
```

`ICurrentThread` provides additional member functions for operations that you can apply only to the current thread of execution. For example, you cannot cause any thread but the current thread of execution to "sleep." Thus, `sleep` is a member function of class `ICurrentThread` instead of a member of its base class `IThread`.

Starting Threads

In this topic you learn how to use `IThread` to launch additional threads of execution.

You start additional threads via the `start` member function of `IThread`. You can also call this function indirectly by using certain `IThread` constructors; in effect, those constructors are simply a combined (plain) constructor and a call to `IThread::start`.

The most important argument that you need to provide when starting additional threads is the identity of the code you want to execute on that thread. With three overloaded versions of `IThread::start` and three corresponding constructors available, you can use any one of the three to specify a different flavor of code that you want executed. These versions are as follows:

- Functions compatible with the OS/2 operating system function `DosCreateThread`. For details on executing such functions on a separate thread, see "System-Compatible Thread Functions" later in this chapter. In that topic we also show you how to use `IThread` to replace your calls to the `CreateThread` API in the Windows operating system.

- Functions compatible with the VisualAge for C++ extended library function `_beginthread`. For details on starting threads to execute functions of this type, see "C Library Compatible Thread Functions."

- Any other code implemented by overriding a virtual function of class `IThreadFn`. You identify such code by passing a reference to an `IThreadFn` object which then executes that function. For details on using this technique to start new threads, see "IThreadFn Objects." Open Class Library also provides a template class derived from `IThreadFn`, which you can easily use to dispatch arbitrary member functions on a separate thread. For details on using this template class, `IThreadMemberFn`, see "Running C++ Member Functions on a Thread."

IThread Always Uses _beginthread

One reason C compilers provide some sort of "_beginthread" library function is because their run-time libraries require initialization on a per-thread basis. For this reason, it isn't always safe to use `DosCreateThread` or `CreateThread`, as any calls to the compiler's run-time library on that thread may fail.

However, `IThread` doesn't ever use plain `DosCreateThread` or `CreateThread` to start threads, even when starting threads to run functions compatible with `DosCreateThread`. `IThread` always starts threads using the C run time's _beginthread function. So, it is always safe to make calls to the compiler's run-time library on threads started using an `IThread` object.

System-Compatible Thread Functions

The OS/2 operating system starts all secondary threads using the DosCreateThread function. The first overloaded version of IThread::start is designed for compatibility with this system function.

```
void IThread::start( SystemFnPtr  pfn,
                     unsigned long arg,
                     Boolean       autoInitPM );
```

This function starts a new thread and then calls a user-provided function on that new thread of execution. Make your function of type IThread::SystemFnPtr, which, in turn, is an alias for type:

```
void ( _System * )( unsigned long )
```

This defines a pointer to a function with the following attributes:

- It must have _System linkage.
- It must accept a single argument of type unsigned long.
- It must return void.

This is the same type of function that you can use with the OS/2 operating system's DosCreateThread function. IThread supports functions of this type explicitly; so, you can replace using DosCreateThread with using IThread objects.

Open Class Library does not directly support starting functions compatible with the Windows operating system's CreateThread function because CreateThread executes a function with type:

```
unsigned long ( __stdcall * )( void * )
```

IThread does not directly support starting these functions. So, if you have existing code that you run on a separate thread using CreateThread, you cannot switch to using IThread objects unless you complete the following steps:

1. Write a wrapper function that has an IThread-compatible signature

2. Have that wrapper function call the CreateThread-compatible function.

In fact, this C++ template class "automatically" writes such wrapper functions for you as follows:

CreateThread-to-IThread Wrapper Functions - thread\starting\wrapper.hpp

```
/*-----------------------------------------------------------
| The template argument is the function you want to provide a |
| wrapper for.                                                |
-----------------------------------------------------------*/
template < unsigned long (__stdcall *WinFunction)( void * ) >
struct WrapperFor {
// This static member funtion is the actual wrapper.  It calls
// your function.
static void
  wrapper( void *p ) {
    WinFunction( p );
  }
// This operator permits objects of this template class to be
// converted to a function pointer that IThread accepts.
  operator IThread::OptlinkFnPtr () const {
    return (IThread::OptlinkFnPtr)wrapper;
  }
}; // WrapperFor<>
```

Create a wrapper function using an expression such as `WrapperFor<myFunction>()`, which creates a template class object. When you pass this object to `IThread`, it converts it to a function pointer using its operator `IThread::OptlinkFnPtr`. This operator returns a pointer to the static member function of the template class. Thus, when the thread starts, `IThread` calls that static member function. It, in turn, calls your function. You can see an example of how to use this class template in the example program **thread/starting/starting.cpp**.

C Library-Compatible Thread Functions

For the same reasons that Open Class Library provides a simplified means of starting threads, the VisualAge for C++ compiler provides an extended library function, `_beginthread`, which you can use instead of `DosCreateThread` or `CreateThread`. The second overloaded version of `IThread::start` is compatible with that compiler library function as follows:

```
void IThread::start( OptlinkFnPtr  pfn,
                     void          *arg,
                     Boolean        autoInitPM );
```

This function starts the thread and calls a user-provided function. The function you provide must be of type `IThread::OptlinkFnPtr`, which, in turn, is an alias for the following type:

```
void ( _Optlink * )( void * )
```

This defines a pointer to a function with the following attributes:

- It must have `_Optlink` linkage.
- It must accept a single argument of type `void*`.
- It must return `void`.

This is the same type of function that you can start on another thread using the compiler's `_beginthread` function. `IThread` supports functions of this type; so, you can replace using `_beginthread` with using `IThread`.

The following code comes from the example program that demonstrates how you can use `IThread` to replace your current use of the operating system's thread-creating functions or the compiler's `_beginthread` function. It includes each thread-creating scenario and demonstrates how to achieve the same result using an `IThread` object.

Starting Functions on a Thread - thread\starting\starting.cpp

```
/*---------------------- ThreadStarter ----------------------
| This class is a command handler that handles the starting of |
| threads using any of the six different methods.              |
---------------------------------------------------------------*/
class ThreadStarter : public ICommandHandler {
public:
virtual Boolean
  command ( ICommandEvent &event ) {
    switch ( event.commandId() ) {
      case createThread:
        #ifdef IC_PM
          TID
            tid;
          DosCreateThread( &tid,
                    compatibleWithOS,
                    (unsigned long)"Started via DosCreateThread",
                    0,
                    0x4000 );
        #else
          CreateThread( 0,
                      0x4000,
                      compatibleWithOS,
                      (void *)"Started via CreateThread",
                      0 );
        #endif
        break;
      case beginthread:
        _beginthread( compatibleWithCLibrary,
                    0,
                    0x4000,
                    (void *)"Started via _beginthread" );
        break;
      case createThreadUsingIThreadStart:
        {
        IThread
          newThread;
        #ifdef IC_PM
          newThread.start( compatibleWithOS,
                  (unsigned long)"Started via IThread::start" );
        #else
          newThread.start( WrapperFor< compatibleWithOS >(),
                      (void *)"Started via IThread::start" );
        #endif
        }
        break;
      case createThreadUsingIThreadCtor:
        {
        #ifdef IC_PM
          IThread
            newThread( compatibleWithOS,
                  (unsigned long)"Started via IThread ctor" );
        #else
          IThread
            newThread( WrapperFor< compatibleWithOS >(),
                      (void *)"Started via IThread ctor" );
        #endif
        }
        break;
      case beginThreadUsingIThreadStart:
        {
        IThread
          newThread;
        newThread.start( compatibleWithCLibrary,
                      (void*)"Started via IThread::start" );
        }
        break;
```

```
        case beginThreadUsingIThreadCtor:
          {
          IThread
            newThread( compatibleWithCLibrary,
                        (void*)"Started via IThread ctor" );
          }
          break;
      }
    return false;
    }
}; // ThreadStarter
```

IThreadFn Objects

Sometimes you want to dispatch another kind of function on a separate thread. To support that, the IThread class provides another overloaded version of IThread::start as follows:

```
void IThread::start( const IReference<IThreadFn> &fnObj,
                     Boolean autoInitPM );
```

The first argument is not a plain function pointer in this case; it is a smart pointer to a *thread function object*, an object of a class derived from IThreadFn. This class serves only to provide the following pure virtual function:

```
virtual void IThreadFn::run ( ) = 0;
```

When you start a thread using an IThreadFn function object, the IThread object eventually calls the function object's implementation of this run member function. You can implement this function any way you want to in the classes you derive from IThreadFn. The code that you put into your implementation gets executed on that thread.

This is how you execute, on a separate thread, code that does not fit into the DosCreateThread-compatible or _beginthread-compatible categories. Just package that code into a run function or write a run function that calls the code you want to execute on the new thread.

An Example of Executing a Function On a Separate Thread

You have a function that calculates *pi* to arbitrary precision and returns the result as an IString containing the ASCII representation of the value of *pi* as follows:

```
IString pi( unsigned digits );
```

Because this function might take a long time to run you want to run it in a separate thread and notify the user when the answer is ready.

This function is not compatible with DosCreateThread, CreateThread, or _beginthread. To start it on a separate thread, write a simple IThreadFn-derived class and implement the run function so that it calls pi. You also have that class take on the following additional responsibilities:

• To pass the number of digits that you specify on the constructor to the pi function when the thread starts.

• To update a window with the results when the calculation completes. You specify an IWindowHandle as a constructor argument to identify the window to be notified.

The following code illustrates how you write the code for this class:

Calculating Pi on Another Thread - thread\pithread\pithread.cpp

```
class PiOnAThread : public IThreadFn {
public:
  PiOnAThread ( unsigned digits,
                const IWindowHandle &window )
    : arg( digits ),
      win( window )
    {
    }
virtual void
  run ( )
    {
    IString
      result = pi( arg );
    UserEvent( 0, (char*)result ).sendTo( win );
    }
private:
unsigned
  arg;
IWindowHandle
  win;
};
```

This class is simple. You turn the pi function argument into a data member of the class and put a corresponding argument on the constructor for the class. You also include an argument that permits specifying which window is to be notified of the result. The class implements the run function by calling the desired function using the argument stored in the function object and then by sending the result to the window provided on the constructor.

You can then use this PiOnAThread class in another snippet from the same example program. The following code shows the implementation of a derived ICommandHandler class' command function that launches a thread to calculate *pi* when a user presses a push button:

```
virtual Boolean
  command ( ICommandEvent &event ) {
    Boolean
      result = false;
    if ( event.commandId() == button.id() ) {
      unsigned
        numDigits( input.text().asUnsigned() );
      output
        .addLineAsLast( "Calculating pi to "
                        +
                        IString(numDigits)
                        +
                        " digits..." );
      IThread
        calculatePi( new PiOnAThread( input.text().asInt(),
                                      output.handle() ) );
      result = true;
    }
    return result;
  }
```

Running C++ Member Functions on a Thread

So far, we have only discussed starting threads to execute simple nonmember functions. However, because you properly use C++, you likely want to execute member functions of your classes on separate threads.

Doing this is harder than you might think because C++ member functions cannot be called directly. You must apply them using an object or a pointer to an object. The `this` pointer is passed "under the covers" and the operating system's thread creation functions just cannot do that. Instead, you have to construct a nonmember function that can be started on a secondary thread. That function takes the object and the member function pointer you want applied and applies the function to the object.

Open Class Library provides a means that greatly simplifies doing all of that. You can use the `IThreadMemberFn` class template to generate `IThreadFn` objects which execute member functions of arbitrary classes on separate threads. The only restriction is that `IThreadMemberFn` limits support for member functions to those that accept no arguments and that return `void`.

An Example of Executing a C++ Member Function on a Separate Thread

Let us make a minor change to the last example. Instead of a simple nonmember `pi` function, we now have a `pi` member function of some class. This class also holds the desired number of digits and the handle for the window in which the results are to be displayed. We also have that class provide another member function called `update`. It calculates pi to some precision and updates the window with the result.

Running a C++ Member Function on a Thread - thread\picalc\picalc.cpp

```
class PiCalculator {
public:
// Construct the calculator with an MLE to be updated with the
// results.
  PiCalculator( IMultiLineEdit &mle )
    : digits( 0 ), results( mle ) {
    }
// This function calculates pi and updates the result window.
void
  calculate ( )
    {
    IString  result = pi( digits );
    UserEvent( 0, (char*)result ).sendTo( results.handle() );
    }
// Use this function to set the number of digits to calculate.
void
  setDigits ( unsigned int numDigits ) {
    digits = numDigits;
    }
private:
unsigned  digits;
IMultiLineEdit &results;
};
```

The calculate member function matches the criteria we established. Executing `PiCalculator::calculate` on a separate thread is simple when we use the `IThreadMemberFn` class template. The portion of that example program that starts the secondary thread follows:

Running a C++ Member Function on a Thread - thread\picalc\picalc.cpp

```
virtual Boolean
  command ( ICommandEvent &event ) {
    Boolean
      result = false;
    if ( event.commandId() == button.id() ) {
      unsigned
        numDigits( input.text().asUnsigned() );
      output
        .addLineAsLast( "Calculating pi to "
                        +
                        IString(numDigits)
                        +
                        " digits..." );
      calculator.setDigits( numDigits );
      IThread
        calculatePi(
            new IThreadMemberFn<PiCalculator>( calculator,
                                    PiCalculator::calculate ) );
      result = true;
    }
    return result;
  }
```

The IThread constructor argument is an object of the type generated by the class template. That template class' constructor requires two arguments. The first is the object to which the member functions is applied. The second argument is the address of a member function of the class of that object.

Using the IThreadMemberFn class template requires you to spell out your class name twice. A function template that provides a simpler means of generating IThreadMemberFn objects follows:

IThreadMemberFn Generator Function - thread\improved\improved.hpp

```
template < class T >
IThreadMemberFn<T> *memberFn( T &obj, void (T::*mem)(void) ) {
  return new IThreadMemberFn<T>( obj, mem );
}
```

Using this template function simplifies the specification of what member function you want to apply to what object. For example, the IThread construction in the example above is accomplished as follows:

```
IThread
  calculatePi( memberFn(calculator, PiCalculator::calculate) );
```

Setting the Attributes of New Threads

Three attributes of threads are pertinent at thread creation time. Each of these apply only if you are writing code to run on the OS/2 operating system. Open Class Library provides a set functions to manipulate these attributes; it also provides these functions on the Windows operating system for portability, but they don't do anything on that platform.

Automatic Presentation Manager Initialization

As we mentioned earlier, each means of starting additional threads—the three overloaded versions of IThread::start and the three corresponding constructors—accept an additional autoInitGUI argument. This argument specifies whether Open Class Library automatically initializes the windowing system (that is, Presentation Manager) as the thread starts. If the value of this attribute is true, then Open Class Library calls ICurrentThread::initializeGUI automatically when starting the new thread. We describe the effects of that function in detail in the topic, "Controlling Window Event Processing," later in this chapter.

This attribute applies only to threads on the OS/2 operating system. In the Windows operating system, there is no counterpart for the WinInitialize/WinCreateMsgQueue functions. All threads in Windows applications can create and manipulate windows.

Message Queue Size

Message queue size, too, is an OS/2 operating system-specific attribute. Open Class Library uses a default queue size of 30 messages, which is sufficient for most applications. In some cases you might need to set this to a larger value. For example, if you are posting events from one thread to a window on another thread, and that thread isn't processing those events as fast as you're generating them, you can fill up the queue.

You can specify the queue size when you call ICurrentThread::initializeGUI or when you set the default queue size via the static member function IThread::setDefaultQueueSize.

Stack Size

You can set the stack size specifically before starting the thread by using the default IThread constructor, setting the stack size via the setStackSize member function, and then starting the thread as the following example shows:

```
IThread
  thread;
thread.setStackSize( 65534 );
thread.start( someFunction, someArg );
```

In the OS/2 operating system, Open Class Library always starts threads without precommitting the stack pages. Because of this, you can specify a large stack size and not waste stack space if it isn't needed. In the cases where you need the extra stack space, then the OS/2 operating system commits the extra pages as the amount of data on the stack grows.

Although the Windows operating system supports specifying a stack size when you start a thread, it automatically extends the stack if the thread needs more stack space. It precommits the stack size that you specify at thread creation time. As a result, try to specify a smaller stack size and let the operating system allocate more stack space as needed.

The differences between the OS/2 and Windows operating systems in this respect make it difficult to come up with a portable stack-size strategy. Table 20-2 describes the stack size characteristics on the two systems. As you can see, the stack size that you specify at thread creation is used for fundamentally different purposes. Because of this, we recommend that

Table 20-2. Stack Allocation on Windows and OS/2 Operating Systems

	Windows	**OS/2**
Initial Stack Size	The number of bytes specified at thread creation via setStackSize.	One 4096-byte page plus a guard page. For thread 1, the entire stack is committed.
Maximum Stack Size	The application stack size specified at link time. The sum of the stack sizes of all the threads is subject to this limit.	The number of bytes specified at thread creation. For thread 1, the stack size is limited by the value specified at program link time.

your strategy is to specify stack sizes as accurately as possible and to use operating system-specific code to tailor your stack sizes as necessary.

Using IThread with Already Started Threads of Execution

There may be cases where you have additional threads of execution that you do not start by using Open Class Library's IThread class. The first, or primary, thread of your application is a good example. The operating system starts this thread automatically when your program is launched. Therefore, IThread cannot start it. You can have existing code that starts threads using DosCreateThread (on the OS/2 operating system), CreateThread (on the Windows operating system), or _beginthread and want to continue using that code without rewriting it to use IThread.

Fortunately, with Open Class Library, you can use the IThread member functions to manipulate these threads even though IThread does not start them. You do this by using the IThread constructor that accepts one argument which is an object of type IThreadId. You pass the thread identifier for the already started OS/2 or Windows thread. The IThread objects created in this fashion provide the full range of IThread function.

Controlling Thread Execution

In this topic, we cover the set of functions that provides various means of controlling the execution of threads.

Normal Termination

Figure 20-2 shows the call stack on entry to the PiCalculator::calculate member function from a previous example. There are three functions already in the call stack on entry to that function:

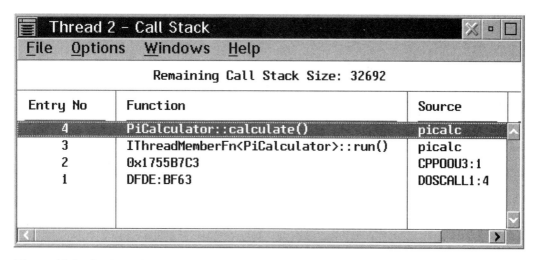

Figure 20-2. Chain of Command on Secondary Threads.

- `DOSCALL1:4` (on the OS/2 operating system; this would be a corresponding Windows function on the Windows operating system)

  This is the operating system function that first gains control when it starts a new thread.

- `CPPOOU3:1`

  This is the internal `IThread` function that is passed to `_beginthread`. It calls the `run` member function against the `IThreadFn` passed to it as an argument.

- `IThreadMemberFn<PiCalculator>::run`

  This is the overridden implementation of `run` from the template class object that we passed to the `IThread` constructor.

Your thread terminates when control returns back through this call stack and the operating system function at the top of the stack returns. Your code initiates the process by returning from the user-supplied function that you dispatched on the thread. In our example, this happens when `PiCalculator::calculate` returns.

As control returns back through this call stack, C++ objects on the stack are destructed, Open Class Library records the thread termination, and so on. All of the code that helped start your thread does what it needs to do to handle that thread's termination. This is the conventional means of thread termination: it simply returns from the code that you are running on the thread.

Abnormal Termination of Threads

There are other means of terminating a thread of execution. Both the OS/2 and Windows operating systems provide thread termination functions that you can call at any time to terminate a thread. The compiler's run-time library provides a function that does the same thing: _endthread. Open Class Library also provides a function for terminating a thread: ICurrentThread::exit.

Open Class Library also provides the function IThread::stop, which you can use to terminate another thread. This is the only means of thread termination that can terminate execution of one thread by executing code on another thread. While this might seem useful in some situations, try to avoid using this thread member function because this form of thread termination is tricky. The operating system puts the terminated thread into a suspended status where it stays until the system can terminate the thread properly. It is far more reliable to signal your secondary thread and have it terminate itself using a normal return.

Each of these techniques causes the flow of control in your thread to jump to the top of the call stack, bypassing any code that would normally get executed as control flowed back through the functions on the stack. As a result, destructors do not get called for any C++ objects on the stack, and cleanup code waiting to run will not be executed. In almost all cases, bypassing this code is a bad idea. For this reason, we call this *abnormal* thread termination. Thus, we recommend that you avoid terminating threads using these techniques.

Exiting the Thread's Message Processing Loop

Thread termination may seem more confusing when your thread is in the midst of processing its window message queue. For example, if your thread creates and displays windows, it likely has the following structure:

```
void _Optlink myThreadFunction( void * ) {
  // Create some windows.
  IFrameWindow
    frame("Main Window");
  // Show the frame.
  frame.show();
  // Process window events.
  IThread::current().processMsgs();
  // Terminate the thread.
  return;
}
```

A thread created to execute this function is not terminated until after it executes the return statement. But it can't do that until the call to ICurrentThread::processMsgs returns.

So, termination of some threads means termination of the message processing loop on that thread. You can find more information about exiting this loop in the topic "The Message Processing Loop" later in this chapter.

Suspend and Resume

You can suspend the execution of a given thread and resume it at any time using the functions IThread::suspend and IThread::resume. Be careful using IThread::suspend because it blocks thread execution unconditionally and you have to ensure that the thread is resumed at some point. Usually, it is better to use one of the more advanced thread synchronization techniques, such as semaphores, which we describe later in this chapter.

Sleeping

You can suspend the current thread for an arbitrary period of time by using the function `ICurrentThread::sleep`. The argument to this function specifies the number of milliseconds for which the thread will sleep.

This function is not designed to provide a means for threads to do *polling*, that is, spinning in a tight loop waiting for some event to occur. It is typically more efficient to let the system block your thread and wake it up when it is time to run than to do this on your own.

One application of `ICurrentApplication::sleep` is to force the current thread to give up the remainder of its time slice and yield control to other threads at the same or higher priority. Calling that function with an argument of 0 is expressly designed to accomplish that task.

Thread Priority

Both the Windows and OS/2 operating systems prioritize threads of execution. Each system has four categories of thread priority called *priority classes*. The OS/2 operating system prioritizes threads using a two-level scheme, also giving each thread a particular *priority level* within its priority class. The `IApplication` and `IThread` classes of Open Class Library provide a full set of functions to query and adjust the priority class and, on the OS/2 operating system, the priority level of each thread of execution.

The `IApplication` member functions change the priority of all of the application's threads. In addition, you can also use those functions to change the priority of child processes that you may have started using an operating system API call.

Priority Class

There are four priority classes. `IApplication::PriorityClass` is an enumeration that provides unique values for these four classes. The enumeration values are found in Table 20-3.

You can query a thread's priority class, via the function `IThread::priorityClass`. The `IApplication` class provides the `setPriority` function that you can use to change the priority of all a process's threads. To change the priority class of all the current process' threads to `timeCritical`, you would code a statement as follows:

```
IApplication::current().setPriority(IApplication::timeCritical);
```

You can set the priority class of a specific thread in the current application using the function `IThread::setPriority`. For example, to change the priority of a given thread to `timeCritical`, write the following statement:

```
aThread.setPriority( IApplication::timeCritical );
```

Priority Level

The OS/2 operating system supports 32 priority levels within each priority class. The default level within a class is 0, but you can adjust this level up or down within the range 0 to 31. By default, a thread's priority level is 0, which is the lowest priority level within the class. You can query a thread's priority level using the `IThread::priorityLevel` function. Note that

Table 20-3. Priority Classes

Priority Class	Description

IThread::idleTime
 	
OS/2:
    PRTYC_IDLETIME
 	
Windows:
    IDLE_PRIORITY_CLASS
	This is the lowest priority class. Use it for threads of background tasks that should not impact the execution of user-interface processes or more important tasks.
	
	Idle-time threads only run when the system has no other work at a higher priority to be done.

IThread::regular
 	
OS/2:
    PRTYC_REGULAR
 	
Windows:
    REGULAR_PRIORITY_CLASS
	This is the default priority class. Use it for most user-interface applications.

IThread::foregroundServer
 	
OS/2:
    PRTYC_FOREGROUNDSERVER
 	
Windows:
    HIGH_PRIORITY_CLASS
	This class is for threads that require being run at a higher priority than typical threads but don't have as stringent real-time requirements as "time critical" threads (see below).
	
	You must be careful when using this or the next priority class because threads with these priorities may prevent lower-priority threads from executing. This includes most user-interface threads, which run at normal priority. By preempting those threads, you prevent the users from interacting with the system, perhaps preventing them from taking action to block the foreground server thread.

IThread::timeCritical
 	
OS/2:
    PRTYC_TIMECRITICAL
 	
Windows:
    REALTIME_PRIORITY_CLASS
	This is the highest priority class. Use it only for threads that typically service real-time interrupts, such as communication processes.

Open Class Library supports the priority-level member functions even on the Windows operating system to provide portability for applications that use those capabilities on the OS/2 operating system. Those functions have no effect when called on the Windows operating system.

Both IApplication and IThread provide two ways to change a thread's priority level. IApplication::setPriority, which we introduced in the preceding topic, can accept an optional priority level argument in the range 0 to 31. Specifying a value sets all of the application's threads' priority levels to the argument value. IThread::setPriority, which we also introduced previously, also accepts an optional thread priority-level argument which has a similar effect to the IApplication function, but applies the change to a single thread.

There are also adjustPriority member functions of IApplication and IThread. These functions do not affect a process' or thread's priority class. They adjust the current priority level by some value in the range -31 to 31. The fundamental difference between the argument to adjustPriority versus the priority level argument to setPriority is that the former is a delta applied to the current priority level; the latter is an absolute priority level. Some examples follow:

```
// Change all threads in current process to highest level
// regular priority.
IApplication::current().setPriority( IApplication::regular, 31 );

// Change aThread's priority level to the highest (in same
// priority class).
aThread.setPriority( IApplication::noChange, 31 );

// Adjust priority level of all the current process' threads
// downward by 15.
IApplication::current().adjustPriority( -15 );

// Adjust current thread's priority level up by 15.
IThread::current().adjustPriority( +15 );
```

Be careful when manipulating thread priorities, particularly when your program runs on the OS/2 operating system. You can easily have a thread with increased priority take over the CPU and impact the responsiveness of your application. You can test the effects of tweaking thread priorities by running the example program implemented by **thread\threads\threads.cpp**.

Controlling Window Event Processing

Because the Windows and OS/2 operating systems maintain certain windowing system attributes on a per-thread basis, IThread objects have windowing system attributes. ICurrentThread also provides a number of functions that handle the windowing system and window event processing.

The Presentation System

The term *presentation system* refers to the per-thread attributes and associated windowing system's status information.

Presentation System Initialization

On the OS/2 operating system, initialize the presentation system for a thread by calling ICurrentThread::initializeGUI. This function is roughly equivalent to calling the Presentation Manager functions WinInitialize and WinCreateMsgQueue. There is one argument to this function, the size of the message queue. We already discussed the message queue size in "Setting the Attributes of New Threads."

You rarely need to call this function directly. Open Class Library calls it automatically when you start a secondary thread or when you create a primary window. You can write your programs to call this function regardless of which operating system they run on. It has no effect on the Windows operating system, where all threads in GUI applications automatically have their presentation system initialized.

Presentation System Termination

You can undo the effects of `initializeGUI` by calling the `ICurrentThread` function, `terminateGUI`. In the OS/2 operating system, this function invokes the Presentation Manager APIs `WinDestroyMsgQueue` and `WinTerminate`. In the Windows operating system, it has no effect.

Normally, you need to call this function only on the primary thread of your applications. Secondary threads, those started via use of `IThread`, automatically call this function as the thread terminates. You do not need to call this function because Presentation Manager automatically detects the thread termination and cleans up resources accordingly.

Anchor Block

To initialize the Presentation Manager environment, call `WinInitialize`. This establishes the *anchor block* handle for the current thread. The anchor block handle refers to the operating system object that Presentation Manager uses to record information about the thread and its windows. `ICurrentThread::initializeGUI` records this handle and stores it as an attribute of the `IThread` object. Obtain this handle by calling `ICurrentThread::anchorBlock`. You might need to do this if you want to directly call Presentation Manager APIs that require the `HAB` as a parameter. Because the Windows operating system has no anchor block handle, you do not need to call it on the Windows operating system; but if you do, the function always returns 1.

Message Queue

Presentation Manager initialization calls `WinCreateMsgQueue`. This API returns the handle of the Presentation Manager message queue for the thread. Open Class Library stores this handle as an attribute of the `IThread`. Obtain it by calling `IThread::messageQueue`.

The Windows operating system doesn't have a separate message queue handle. It identifies a thread's message queue using the thread identifier. So, Open Class Library returns this thread identifier when you call `IThread::messageQueue`. This ensures that your code works properly when you use functions that take the message queue handle as an argument, such as `IWindowHandle::postEvent` to post an event to a thread's message queue.

The Message Processing Loop

Both the Windows operating system and the OS/2 Presentation Manager are message-based windowing systems. They transmit input events from the user and system-generated events to the code that implements the windows. It places these messages on the thread's message queue as they occur. The application removes these messages from the queue and dispatches them to the window's window procedure.

The code that pulls these messages off of the message queue and dispatches them to the appropriate window procedure is the *message processing loop*. In a typical Windows application implemented in C this loop has the following form:

```
while ( GetMessage( &msg, 0, 0, 0 ) )
   DispatchMsg( &msg );
```

The Presentation Manager equivalent is almost identical, as follows:

```
while ( WinGetMsg( hab, &qmsg, 0, 0, 0 ) )
  WinDispatchMsg( hab, &qmsg );
```

The equivalent in Open Class Library is the statement:

```
IThread::current().processMsgs();
```

Starting the Message Loop

Calling IThread::current().processMsgs() performs the processing of the thread's message queue. It terminates when Open Class Library or you post a WM_QUIT message to the queue. You see how this message processing loop terminates in the next topic. An alias for this function invocation is IApplication::current().run().

The call to processMsgs, or IApplication::run, is unusual, especially if you are not familiar with the message-based application model. First, it does not return until an indeterminate point in the future. This means that you must ensure that other necessary actions occur prior to invoking this function. Most often the dispatching of the message processing loop occurs close to the end of your main function or at the end of the function you dispatch on the secondary thread.

An interesting feature of this function call is that it really doesn't yield control. Your code, specifically, your window handlers' functions, will execute with high frequency in the intervening period prior to this function call returning. You could interpret this call as a transfer of control from your main to your handlers.

IFrameWindow::showModally

There is yet another way to initiate a message processing loop. The underlying windowing systems perform that function as part of the processing of dialog windows. Because IFrameWindow::showModally is a wrapper for those system functions, you can use this Open Class Library function instead of the functions ICurrentThread::processMsgs and ICurrentApplication::run.

The advantage of the IFrameWindow function is that you most likely are already using IFrameWindow functions and can implement your entire program without including ITHREAD.HPP, or IAPP.HPP. This technique lets us reduce the smallest "Hello World" Open Class Library application to just two lines:

```
#include <iframe.hpp>
void main() { IFrameWindow( "Hello, World!" ).showModally(); }
```

Stopping the Message Loop

Remember that ICurrentThread::processMsgs does not return until you or Open Class Library posts a WM_QUIT event to the thread's message queue. The posting of a WM_QUIT event happens in one of three ways, as follows:

- Closing the last primary window on the thread. Open Class Library detects the closing of *primary windows*, those with the desktop window as parent and no owner, and posts a WM_QUIT message when the windowing system destroys the last primary window.

  An IObjectWindow is also considered a primary window. This ensures that secondary threads that service requests communicated via an object window run properly, too.

- A call to IThread::stopProcessingMsgs. This function provides a portable means of posting WM_QUIT, thereby forcing a return from processMsgs. You cannot post WM_QUIT portably because you need to include an operating-system-specific header file to obtain the value of the WM_QUIT message identifier.

- Explicit posting of a WM_QUIT. For example, the following statement causes return from processMsgs:

  ```
  aWindow.postEvent( WM_QUIT );
  ```

  Although nothing is wrong with using this technique to terminate the message processing loop, it has at least three disadvantages when compared to other techniques.

  - It is too procedural; it requires too much information on how things work. The fact that this causes return from processMsgs certainly isn't obvious.

  - It also bypasses the users. Usually, the application termination is triggered by closing the application's windows. When that happens, Open Class Library posts the WM_QUIT automatically, as we described in the previous bullet.

  - Finally, posting WM_QUIT is not easily portable. See the discussion of IThread::stopProcessingMsgs in the preceding bullet for the portable way to do it.

The Fourth Source of WM_QUIT

In the OS/2 operating system, WM_QUIT messages are also posted to your thread's message queue when a user selects **Close** on the Window List for one of the thread's windows. However, in this case "quit" really means "close the window." Thus, Open Class Library recognizes such WM_QUIT messages and treats them differently, as follows:

1. It posts a close message to the window to be closed.

2. The message processing loop continues.

Synchronizing Multiple Threads

After you add multiple threads to your application, you need to coordinate the sharing of process resources between those threads. This section describes two techniques that Open Class Library provides for synchronizing threads: resource locks and critical sections. We also provide an implementation of another technique that Open Class Library itself doesn't support: event semaphores.

Semaphores

The OS/2 and Windows operating systems provide objects called *mutual-exclusion semaphores* that enable separate threads and processes to synchronize access to shared resources. These objects ensure that two processes do not write to the same file at the same time and that two threads don't update static data simultaneously.

Open Class Library provides a set of C++ classes that encapsulates such semaphores and make it easy to synchronize your threads and processes.

Resources

The class IResource defines the abstract protocol for shared resources. This interface is simple; its two functions are shown in Table 20-4.

The default time-out argument is -1, which indicates that the thread is blocked indefinitely if the resource is not available. A time-out value of 0 causes the function to throw an IResourceExhausted exception immediately if the resource is already locked.

IResource is an abstract base class. You cannot create objects of this class. Use either of the derived classes ISharedResource or IPrivateResource, which we describe in the following topics.

We also discuss the use of resources in context of the **thread\picalc\picalc** example program. Part of that example program includes the following function, which is executed on each secondary thread:

Table 20-4. IResource Functions

Function	Description
lock	Call this function when a process, or thread, needs to gain exclusive access to the shared resource. The function returns after obtaining a lock (mutual exclusion semaphore) associated with the resource object. If a different process or thread has already locked the resource, the operating system blocks the requesting thread until the process or thread holding the resource unlocks it.
	This function accepts an optional argument that specifies the maximum amount of time it waits for an already locked resource. If this time-out period, which you specify in milliseconds, expires before the thread owning the resource unlocks it, IResource::lock throws an IResourceExhausted exception.
unlock	Call this function when the thread, which has previously locked a resource, is done with it. Only the thread that has locked the resource can unlock it. If you call this function from a different thread, an error results and the function throws an exception.

Where Thread Synchronization Is Needed - thread\picalc\picalc.cpp

```
// This function calculates pi and updates the result window.
void
  calculate ( )
    {
    IString  result = pi( digits );
    UserEvent( 0, (char*)result ).sendTo( results.handle() );
    }
```

This function requires thread synchronization because each secondary thread sends a user-defined event to the multiline edit control, potentially at the same time. This can cause output to the window to intermix the results of two or more calculations. That MLE control, within the context of this function, is a shared resource that you need to protect from being accessed by two threads at the same time.

To fix this, use `IResource` in one of the two following ways:

• As a base class for derived classes that represent shared resources. This technique is appropriate for objects that are always shared between processes or threads. Often, you derive from both `IResource` and some other base class that represents the nonshared nature of the objects. An example of this use of `IResource` is the following definition of a shared `IMultiLineEdit` class:

```
class SharedMLE : public IMultiLineEdit, public IPrivateResource {
};
```

The advantage of this technique is that it simplifies the locking and unlocking of these kinds of objects. You can lock and unlock the shared resources directly, because they are `IResource` objects, too. In our example, we would change the `PiCalculator` class to hold a `SharedMLE` results object and would rewrite the calculate function as follows:

```
void
  calculate ( )
    {
    IString  result = pi( digits );
    results.lock();    // Stop other threads.
    UserEvent( 0, (char*)result ).sendTo( results.handle() );
    results.unLock(); // Now we're done.
    }
```

• As a stand-alone object maintained in conjunction with the shared resource. Use this technique when sharing is an attribute of a single object instead of all objects of the class. Because we have just one `IMultiLineEdit` object to be shared in our example we might associate that object with an accompanying `IPrivateResource` object. Threads accessing the shared MLE would lock and unlock the corresponding resource, instead of the MLE itself, as follows:

```
// This function calculates pi and updates the result window.
void
  calculate ( )
    {
    IPrivateResource
      lock;
    IString  result = pi( digits );
    lock.lock();
    UserEvent( 0, (char*)result ).sendTo( results.handle() );
    lock.unLock();
    }
```

One risk in this technique is that only this function uses the locking mechanism. Because this MLE object is accessed from another location in this example (at the point where the thread is started), this technique doesn't work as well as the one shown previously.

Shared Resources

The class `ISharedResource` represents objects to be shared between processes. These objects correspond to named semaphores. Provide the name of the shared resource on the constructor for this class. You can access named shared resources via the resource name. Thus, you can construct two distinct `ISharedResource` objects with the same name and use them to protect a single shared resource. This is essential when sharing resources between processes. Just use the same resource name in each process.

Private Resources

You frequently represent resources that are shared by multiple threads of a single process as objects of class `IPrivateResource`. These objects use unnamed, nonshared mutual exclusion semaphores. You can share these semaphores only between threads within the same process.

One common usage for private resources is to serialize access to static data members of a class. Here is the code that we could add to another example program to prevent problems if the function is called on multiple threads simultaneously. The code in bold type shows what must be added to achieve the correct resource protection:

Protecting Static Data Members - thread\threads\thread.cpp

```
void Thread :: addColumnsTo ( IContainerControl &cnr ) {
  IPrivateResource
    staticGuard;

  staticGuard.lock();

  static Boolean
    doneAlready = false;

  if ( !doneAlready ) {
    iconColumn.showSeparators();
    nameColumn.showSeparators()
            .setHeadingText( "Name" );
    threadIdColumn.showSeparators()
                .setHeadingText( "Id" );
    statusColumn.showSeparators()
            .setHeadingText( "Status" );
    priorityClassColumn.showSeparators()
                    .setHeadingText("Class");
    priorityLevelColumn.showSeparators()
                    .setHeadingText( "Level" );
    doneAlready = true;
  }

  staticGuard.unLock();
```

```
cnr
  .addColumn( &iconColumn )
  .addColumn( &nameColumn )
  .addColumn( &threadIdColumn )
  .addColumn( &statusColumn )
  .addColumn( &priorityClassColumn )
  .addColumn( &priorityLevelColumn );
}
```

Resource Locks

Conventional usage of `IResource` objects has a familiar form. You can see it in each of the examples presented so far. For a given resource object, we follow these steps:

1. Call its `lock` member function.

2. Use the resource.

3. Call its `unLock` member function.

Notice how we bracket the access to the resource by the locking and unlocking of the resource. Experienced C++ programmers might recognize this as an opportunity to exploit C++ constructors and destructors to take care of the locking. A class whose constructor locked the resource and destructor unlocked it could then be used to manage the locking. You do this by defining an object of that class in the same scope as the code that operates on the resource.

Open Class Library provides a class that does exactly that, `IResourceLock`. Construct `IResourceLock` objects from a reference to the object you want to lock. The resource lock constructor locks the resource. The resource lock destructor unlocks the resource. This reduces the code that uses a `SharedMLE` object to the following code:

```
void
  calculate ( )
    {
    // Lock the results object for the duration of this block.
    IResourceLock
      lock( results );
    IString  result = pi( digits );
    UserEvent( 0, (char*)result ).sendTo( results.handle() );
    }
```

The main benefit of using `IResourceLock` versus locking and unlocking your resources manually is that doing so ensures you always unlock the resource. This holds true even if a C++ exception is thrown while you hold the lock. Conversely, do not use `IResourceLock` when you need the resource lock to span more than a single {}-delimited block. Instead of dynamically allocating an `IResourceLock` using `new`, just call `lock` and `unlock` directly on the `IResource` object.

Critical Sections

In a limited set of circumstances, you can use a simpler mechanism to limit access to process resources to a single thread: *critical sections*. The behavior of critical sections differs on the Windows and OS/2 operating systems. In the Windows operating system, entering a critical section only blocks other threads that attempt to enter critical sections themselves. In the

OS/2 operating system, entering a critical section automatically prevents all other threads in the process from being dispatched.

The main advantage of critical sections is that they can be more efficient than a mutual exclusion semaphore. However, the strict behavior of critical sections in the OS/2 operating system makes them less desirable than IPrivateResource objects, which use mutual exclusion semaphores.

Open Class Library provides the class ICritSec to facilitate using critical sections. ICritSec's constructor and destructor call the appropriate operating system functions to enter and exit the critical section. You embed code inside a critical section by preceding it with the declaration of an ICritSec object.

Warning: OS/2 Critical Section Ahead

Use critical sections with extreme caution. When you enter a critical section or construct an ICritSec object, the OS/2 operating system suspends all other threads in the application. They remain suspended until you exit the critical section or destroy the ICritSec object. This can lead to a *deadlock* if the thread within the critical section blocks. For example, consider the following solution to our shared MLE problem that we discussed previously:

```
void
  calculate ( )
    {
    // Lock other threads for the duration of this function.
    ICritSec
      lock;
    IString  result = pi( digits );
    UserEvent( 0, (char*)result ).sendTo( results.handle() );
    }
```

Although this code might look okay, it hangs the program when you run it in the OS/2 operating system because the MLE that receives the user-defined event is running on another thread. Sending the event to that window won't be completed till that window's thread processes the event. But because we've entered a critical section, that window's thread can't run. The application is deadlocked.

Thus, we recommend that you never enter a critical section in a block of code that might cause the OS/2 operating system to block the thread. Because you do not know what happens when you call other people's code, never enter a critical section in a block that executes code you didn't write yourself (or, at least that you don't know how it was written). This includes code in the compiler run-time library, including new and delete operators, or code in Open Class Library.

Event Semaphores

Both the OS/2 and Windows operating systems support another kind of semaphore: *event semaphores*. Event semaphores work like traffic lights. When such a semaphore is set, the "light" turns "green" and threads waiting for the semaphore proceed. When the semaphore is *reset*, the "light" turns "red" and threads that are running and that wait for the semaphore are blocked. Unlike mutual exclusion semaphores, which Open Class Library's IResource classes encapsulate, two threads that are waiting for the same event semaphore both start when a third thread sets the semaphore.

Although Open Class Library doesn't provide a class that encapsulates operating system event semaphores, you can easily provide your own implementation. You can find an implementation in the thread example code in the files signal.hpp and signal.cpp. These files implement a Signal class that provides a portable event semaphore wrapper that works on the OS/2 and Windows operating systems. The class supports both private and shared (that is, named) event semaphores. Signal objects provide three member functions as described in Table 20-5.

You typically use Signal objects to suspend one thread while waiting for another thread to complete some action. The various service thread techniques described in the following topic all rely on these objects to synchronize the startup of service threads.

Table 20-5. Signal Member Functions

Function	Description
signal	Turns the signal "green." Any waiting threads are unblocked and any threads that subsequently wait can proceed without stopping.
reset	Turns the signal "red." Any threads that subsequently wait for this signal are blocked until the signal() function is called.
wait	Suspends the current thread of execution if the signal is reset. The thread remains blocked until the object is signalled by calling its signal member function. This function accepts a time-out value that specifies the maximum number of milliseconds that the thread waits.

Service Threads

In all of the examples presented so far, we have dispatched a separate thread for each long-running task. Although this works well in many situations, it does incur additional costs that can be unacceptable in some cases. Specifically, this technique requires that a new thread be created, started, terminated, and destroyed every time there is some work to do. In our *pi* calculator examples, these thread start-up costs might exceed the time actually spent calculating the result.

A much better technique is to launch one or more *service threads* and keep them active, feeding them requests as such requests arise and suspending the service threads between requests. In this way, you amortize the thread start-up and shut-down costs over the life of your application and get faster response when lengthy processing needs to be done.

Designing a Service Thread

In this topic we describe how to design and implement service threads in a portable fashion using the building blocks of Open Class Library.

First, look at how we would want to use such service thread objects from a client application's perspective. Essentially, we want to replace the code that starts secondary threads with code that makes requests of the service thread. In the *pi* calculator example presented earlier, the threads started from within a command handler when a user pressed the **Calculate** push button. The nonservice-thread version of that command handler follows:

```
struct Controller : public ICommandHandler {
  Controller ( IFrameWindow    &frame,
               IPushButton      &button,
               IEntryField      &input,
               IMultiLineEdit &output )
    : frame( frame ),
      button( button ),
      input( input ),
      output( output ),
      resultHandler( output ),
      calculator( output ) {
    this->handleEventsFor( &frame );
  }
  ~Controller ( ) {
    stopHandlingEventsFor( &frame );
  }
virtual Boolean
  command ( ICommandEvent &event ) {
    Boolean
      result = false;
    if ( event.commandId() == button.id() ) {
      unsigned
        numDigits( input.text().asUnsigned() );
      output
        .addLineAsLast( "Calculating pi to "
                        +
                        IString(numDigits)
                        +
                        " digits..." );
      calculator.setDigits( numDigits );
      IThread
        calculatePi;
      calculatePi.start(
          new IThreadMemberFn<PiCalculator>(
                          calculator,
                          PiCalculator::calculate ) );
      result = true;
    }
    return result;
  }
private:
IFrameWindow
 &frame;
IPushButton
 &button;
IEntryField
 &input;
IMultiLineEdit
 &output;
ResultHandler
  resultHandler;
PiCalculator
  calculator;
  Controller( const Controller & );
  operator= ( const Controller & );
}; // Controller
```

The portion of this code that starts secondary threads is highlighted in boldface type. It is this code that we want to replace.

Rather than starting a new thread for each request, we want to notify some service thread object to perform another calculation. In addition, we want to send some notification back to our primary thread when the calculation is completed. These request and reply requirements are met perfectly by the PiCalculator::calculate function that this code already runs on the separate thread. So we'll leave the packaging of the request as-is. The only thing we need to change is the target to which we're sending that request. Instead of sending it to a new thread each time, we change the code so that it sends the request to a single ServiceThread object. But what ServiceThread object? We need to create one. The natural way to do it is to make the service thread object a data member of the Controller. This yields the following client code that uses our yet-to-be-designed ServiceThread object:

```
...
virtual Boolean
  command ( ICommandEvent &event ) {
    Boolean
      result = false;
    if ( event.commandId() == button.id() ) {
      unsigned
        numDigits( input.text().asUnsigned() );
      output
        .addLineAsLast( "Calculating pi to "
                        +
                        IString(numDigits)
                        +
                        " digits..." );
      calculator.setDigits( numDigits );
      serviceThread.postRequest(
          new IThreadMemberFn<PiCalculator>(
                          calculator,
                          PiCalculator::calculate ) );
      result = true;
    }
    return result;
  }
private:
ServiceThread
  serviceThread;
```

Implementing the Service Thread

Next, we decide how to implement this ServiceThread class. The implementation must meet the following requirements:

- The service thread must start a secondary thread at some point.

- The service thread object must be able to send requests from the client thread to the secondary thread.

- The service thread object must be able to queue incoming requests if they arrive faster than the secondary thread can process them.

- The secondary thread must block when there are no requests to process.

- The secondary thread must wake up as soon as a request comes along.

- The service thread implementation must be portable. Ideally, we would like to implement it using existing Open Class Library components.

Using an Object Window

Traditionally, multithreaded programs use an object window as the vehicle for communication with secondary threads. Using an IObjectWindow created on a secondary thread provides an almost ideal solution for our service thread implementation, as follows:

- We can post requests to the secondary thread by posting an event to the object window.

- The windowing system queues requests in the message queue of the secondary thread if they arrive faster than they can be processed.

- A standard message processing loop blocks the secondary thread when there are no pending requests to the object window.

- The secondary thread wakes up as soon as a request is posted to the object window.

- Open Class Library provides IObjectWindow objects and building blocks for constructing most of what we need.

The ServiceThread class has a simple interface, consisting of a constructor, destructor, and single member function, as follows:

Service Thread Interface - thread\piserve\service.hpp

```
class ServiceThread {
public:
/*---------------- Constructors/Destructor --------------------
| Note that the constructor automatically starts a secondary  |
| thread of execution and the destructor terminates that      |
| thread.                                                      |
-------------------------------------------------------------*/
  ServiceThread ( );
  ~ServiceThread ( );

/*-------------------- Request Handling ----------------------
| Use this function to post a request to the thread.          |
-------------------------------------------------------------*/
virtual void
  postRequest( const IReference<IThreadFn> &request );

private:
static void
  run ( void * );
ServiceThreadData
 *data;
}; // ServiceThread
```

Note that we only support requests packaged as IThreadFn objects. You could overload postRequest to accept function pointers, as IThread::start does. You would just have to provide a wrapper for those functions using an IThreadFn-derived class implemented here, as follows:

```
// Wrapper to convert non-member functions to IThreadFn objects.
class ServiceFn : public IThreadFn {
public:
  ServiceFn ( IThread::OptlinkFnPtr pfn, void *p )
    : type( optlink), oFunction( pfn ), arg( p ) {}
  ServiceFn ( IThread::SystemFnPtr  pfn, unsigned long p )
    : type( system ), sFunction( pfn ), arg( p ) {}
```

```
void
  run ( ) {
    // Call the stored function.
    switch ( type ) {
      case optlink: oFunction( arg ); break;
      case system:  sFunction( (unsigned long)arg ); break;
    }
  }
private:
enum { optlink, system }
  type;
union {
  IThread::OptlinkFnPtr
    oFunction;
  IThread::SystemFnPtr
    sFunction;
};
void
 *arg;
};

// Add these declarations/definitions to ServiceThread.
virtual void
  postRequest( IThread::OptlinkFnPtr pfn, void *arg ) {
    postRequest( new ServiceFn( pfn, arg ) );
  }
virtual void
  postRequest( IThread::SystemFnPtr pfn, unsigned long arg ) {
    postRequest( new ServiceFn( pfn, arg ) );
  }
```

Next, we look at the implementation of this ServiceThread class, as follows:

Service Thread Implementation- thread\piserve\service.cpp

```
struct ServiceThreadData {
IThread
  thread;
IObjectWindow
 *objWin;
Signal
  signal;
}; // ServiceThreadData

/*-------------- ServiceThread::ServiceThread ----------------
| The constructor allocates this object's implementation data. |
| It then starts the secondary thread and waits for that thread|
| to become ready.                                             |
---------------------------------------------------------------*/
ServiceThread :: ServiceThread ( )
  : data( new ServiceThreadData ) {
  data->thread
    .start( (IThread::OptlinkFnPtr)ServiceThread::run, data );
  data->signal.wait();
}

/*-------------- ServiceThread::~ServiceThread ----------------
| The destructor posts a WM_QUIT to the secondary thread using |
| IThread::stopProcessingMsgs.  It does *not* delete the       |
| object's data because the secondary thread is still using    |
| it.  The service thread deletes this object's data when it   |
| terminates.                                                  |
---------------------------------------------------------------*/
ServiceThread :: ~ServiceThread ( ) {
  data->thread.stopProcessingMsgs();
}
```

```
/*---------------- ServiceThread::postRequest -----------------
| A user-defined event is posted to the object window on the   |
| service thread.  We pass the address (effectively) of the    |
| IThreadFn object.                                            |
-------------------------------------------------------------*/
void
  ServiceThread :: postRequest
                ( const IReference<IThreadFn> &request ) {
  (*request).addRef();
  UserEvent( 0, (void*)(IThreadFn*)request )
    .postTo( data->objWin->handle() );
}


/*--------------------- ServiceHandler ----------------------
| This class handles user-defined events posted to the service |
| thread's object window.                                      |
|                                                              |
| It invokes the run() function against the IThreadFn          |
| referenced by mp1.                                           |
-------------------------------------------------------------*/
struct ServiceHandler : public UserHandler {
  ServiceHandler ( IObjectWindow *objWin ) {
    handleEventsFor( objWin );
  }

virtual Boolean
  handleUserEvent ( UserEvent &event ) {
    IThreadFn
     *request = (IThreadFn*)(void*)event.parameter1();

    request->run();
    request->removeRef();
    return true;
  }
}; // ServiceHandler


/*-------------------- ServiceThread::run --------------------
| This static member function executes on the service thread.  |
| It is passed the ServiceThreadData as input.  We create an   |
| object window, post the signal (to tell the thread that      |
| started this service thread that it's now ready), and        |
| process user-defined events that come into that object       |
| window.                                                      |
|                                                              |
| When the owner cancels this thread (by posting a WM_QUIT,    |
| most likely via IThread::stopProcessingMsgs), we delete the  |
| argument ServiceThreadData.                                  |
-------------------------------------------------------------*/
void ServiceThread :: run ( void *arg ) {
  ServiceThreadData
    data = (ServiceThreadData*)arg;

  data->objWin = new IObjectWindow;
  data->objWin->setAutoDeleteObject( true );

  data->signal.signal();

  ServiceHandler
    handler( data->objWin );

  IThread::current().processMsgs();
}
```

Using a Signal

You might notice that we use a `Signal` object to synchronize the code in the `ServiceThread` constructor, which executes on the client thread, and to synchronize the code that creates the object window, which runs on the secondary thread. Basically, we need to suspend the thread that creates the service thread until the service thread is ready to process requests. If we didn't, a call to the service thread's `postRequest` member function might fail, perhaps catastrophically, because the object window might not exist yet.

Event semaphores handle this situation. The `Signal` class meets our needs perfectly.

Using User-Defined Events

In the `ServiceThread` implementation, the use of the `UserEvent` and `UserHandler` classes is noteworthy. We used these objects in previous examples to handle the passing of results back to the primary thread. Our `ServiceThread` objects also need this capability to post requests to the secondary thread's object window.

Although Open Class Library provides the `IObjectWindow` class, it does not provide a portable means of sending such windows user-defined events or of handling such events. The `UserEvent` and `UserHandler` classes solve this problem. These classes eliminate the need to write nonportable code that obtains the proper system-dependent `WM_USER` values and also offer a higher-level interface for handling user-defined events.

User-Defined Event and Handler Classes - thread\userevt\userevt.hpp

```
class UserEvent : public IEvent {
public:
/*------------------- Constructor/Destructor ------------------
| Provide these attributes when creating a user event:        |
|   o An ID (which is ultimately added to WM_USER)            |
|   o Event parameter 1                                       |
|   o Event parameter 2                                       |
|                                                             |
| Within a handler, construct the UserEvent from the          |
| IEvent received in your dispatchHandlerEvent function.       |
| Most likely, you let the UserHandler objects take care of   |
| that for you.                                               |
-------------------------------------------------------------*/
  UserEvent ( unsigned int            id  = 0,
              const IEventParameter1 &mp1 = 0,
              const IEventParameter2 &mp2 = 0 );

  UserEvent ( const IEvent &genericEvent );

  ~UserEvent ( );

/*---------------------- Attributes -------------------------
| This function returns the user-defined event ID for this    |
| event object. Typically, you call this from within your     |
| UserHandler-derived classes' handleUserEvent override to     |
| determine the particular event that has occurred.           |
-------------------------------------------------------------*/
unsigned int
  userEventId ( ) const;
```

```
/*-------------------- Posting/Sending ----------------------
| Use these functions to post or send user-defined events    |
| to a window.                                                |
------------------------------------------------------------*/
void
  postTo ( const IWindowHandle &window ) const;

unsigned long
  sendTo ( const IWindowHandle &window ) const;

/*---------------------- Utilities -------------------------
| Use this function to obtain the base user event ID.         |
| This is required to implement UserHandler objects.          |
------------------------------------------------------------*/
static unsigned long
  baseId ( );

private:
  UserEvent ( const UserEvent & );
  operator= ( const UserEvent & );
}; // class UserEvent

class UserHandler : public IHandler {
protected:
/*----------------- Construtors/Destructor --------------------
| This is an abstract base class for your user-defined event  |
| handlers. Your derived class must provide the base class    |
| with the user-defined event identifier (or range of         |
| identifiers) that your handler is interested in.            |
------------------------------------------------------------*/
  UserHandler ( unsigned int id = 0 );
  UserHandler ( unsigned int low, unsigned int high );

  ~UserHandler ( );

/*--------------------- Event Handling ----------------------
| Override this to handle user-defined events of interest.    |
------------------------------------------------------------*/
virtual Boolean
  handleUserEvent( UserEvent &event ) = 0;

virtual Boolean
  dispatchHandlerEvent ( IEvent &event );

private:
unsigned int
  low,
  high;
}; // class UserHandler
```

Timers

The main idea of this chapter thus far has been to tell you how to use additional threads of execution to enable your applications to get work done while still providing timely response to user input events. In most of the example programs, the primary thread has called `ICurrentThread::processMsgs` and is consequently processing window events, that is, user input. Secondary threads are used to process something, such as to calculate *pi* to a specific number of digits, while the primary thread continues to handle user input.

The primary thread in such scenarios spends most of its time doing nothing except wait for the next user input. In some cases, you might want to take advantage of this otherwise wasted time and put the primary thread to use while waiting for a user to provide some input. You can use the same technique to do work that has to be done on the primary thread or can more conveniently be done on the primary thread, while still retaining timely response to input from a user.

To do this, use the support that the Windows and OS/2 operating systems provide for automatically generating periodic events. These events are posted and handled just like normal window events generated by user input. This topic is related to threads because you can use these *timer events* to enable your program's threads to do work while they would otherwise be idle waiting for user input.

Open Class Library encapsulates these timer events and the handling of them with the class ITimer. You work with ITimer objects in much the same way you work with IThread objects. You specify on the timer what code you want executed when the timer event occurs. You do this by using an ITimerFn object, which is similar to the IThreadFn objects that IThread uses. Instead of overriding the run member function, override the timerExpired member function of class ITimerFn.

You also have ITimerMemberFn and ITimerMemberFn0 class templates to assist in running C++ member functions when timer events occur. The former runs member functions that take one argument: the identifier of the timer that has gone off. The latter runs member functions that take no arguments.

The example program **thread\threads\thread.cpp** uses an ITimer object to increment the counter for that program's primary thread, as follows:

Example of use of ITimer - thread\threads\thread.cpp

```
/*---------------------- Thread::Thread ----------------------
| The constructor requires the container control that the    |
| thread is to be added to and a flag used to designate the  |
| primary thread.                                            |
------------------------------------------------------------*/
Thread :: Thread ( IContainerControl &cnr, Boolean primary )
  : IContainerObject ( ThreadData::name(),
                       primary ? THREAD1 : THREADS ) {
  // Create hidden data members.
  data = new ThreadData( cnr );
  // Start thread of execution (if necessary).
  if ( primary ) {
    data->flags |= isPrimary;
    data->thread = new IThread( IThread::current() );
    ITimer
      timer( new ITimerMemberFn0<Thread>(*this,
                                         Thread::timerTick) );
  } else {
    data->thread = new IThread( (IThread::OptlinkFnPtr)run,
                                this );
    // Secondary threads run at idle time (by default).
    data->thread->setPriority( IApplication::idleTime, 15 );
  }
  // Refresh container column data.
  this->threadId = data->thread->id().asString();
  this->refreshInfo();
  // Add container object to container and refresh it.
  cnr.addObject( this ).refresh();
}
```

```
/*-------------------- Thread::timerTick ----------------------
| This gets called on the primary thread.  Call performAction. |
--------------------------------------------------------------*/
void Thread :: timerTick ( ) {
  performAction();
}
```

Conclusion

In this chapter, we have described the basics of the Windows and OS/2 processes and threads, and have explained why your applications need to exploit them. To use threads effectively, you need to follow these steps:

1. Identify the portions of your application that can and should be executed on separate threads. These functions usually fall into one of the following two categories:

    -   Functions that perform input and output. Moving this code to another thread enables your application to perform other tasks while waiting for that input or output to be completed.

    -   Actions that would delay servicing of your application's message queue. Run this code on another thread so that your main thread can continue to service the message queue. This is essential in the OS/2 operating system so that the users can transfer control to another OS/2 application while your application is performing lengthy tasks.

2. Structure your application so that you can start the threadable portions identified in the previous step on a separate thread using IThread::start.

3. Use Open Class Library's thread synchronization support to maintain the integrity of your application's data in a multithreaded environment.

Chapter 21

Direct Manipulation

- Describes Open Class Library classes that you can use to add direct-manipulation support to your applications
- Describes the IDMHandler, IDMSourceHandler, IDMTargetHandler, IDMItem, IDMCnrItem, IDMMLEItem, IDMEFItem, IDMToolBarItem, IDMTBarButtonItem, IDMImage, IDMTargetEvent, IDMTargetDropEvent, IDMSourceDiscardEvent, IDMSourceEndEvent, IDMOperation, IDMSourceOperation, IDMTargetOperation, IDMItemProvider, IDMItemProviderFor<>, IDMRenderer, IDMSourceRenderer, and IDMTargetRenderer classes
- Read Chapter 4 before reading this chapter.
- Chapters 9 and 13 cover related material.

This chapter describes how you can use the direct-manipulation support classes of Open Class Library to provide your users with the ability to directly manipulate the objects they work with in your applications. Another commonly used term that describes direct manipulation is drag and drop. Both terms are used interchangeably throughout this chapter.

Do It Directly

Distinguishing features of the OS/2 operating system and Windows desktops are their respective object-oriented user interfaces. We described the benefits of the user-interface styles in Chapter 2, "Object-Oriented User Interface Fundamentals."

An important element of both desktops' interface is support for *direct manipulation,* which permits users to operate directly on the objects whose icons appear on the desktop.

Users will likely judge OS/2 and Windows applications based on the degree to which the interfaces support direct manipulation. If you want your application to stand out, your users to feel comfortable when using your application (along with the other OS/2 or Windows applications they will use), you need to provide direct manipulation in your applications.

Because Open Class Library provides C++ classes, you can easily add direct-manipulation support to your applications.

> ### Drag and Drop in a Nutshell
>
> The design of Open Class Library's direct-manipulation support provides as much default behavior as it can. As a result, it is extremely easy to include drag-and-drop support in your application without having to understand any of the underlying theory of the design.
>
> Here's all you need to provide default drag-and-drop support to your container controls:
>
> ```
> #include <idmhndlr.hpp>
> IDMHandler::enableDragDropFor(pCnr);
> ```
>
> pCnr is a pointer to your IContainerControl object.
>
> This gives users the ability to move and copy container objects within this control and between other containers in the same application.

Enabling Drag and Drop

For your application to support drag and drop, you need to attach handlers to your windows to process direct-manipulation requests. Open Class Library provides two handler classes and a common base class to accomplish this task.

Unlike most of the other handler classes that Open Class Library provides, the direct-manipulation handlers are more than just skeletons on which you build your handler logic. Instead, these handlers implement each of the handler virtual functions to compose a complete functional framework that you use as-is or extend via other means. In other words, you do not derive from these handler classes. Instead, you derive from the other classes in the direct-manipulation framework. This framework makes this task simpler than handling direct manipulation at the API level, which is what these handlers do.

Because the standard handler classes are sufficient for most applications, the direct-manipulation framework can create the appropriate handler objects and automatically attach them to your window when you need them. Thus, you can easily enable your windows for drag and drop.

Enabling Windows for Drag and Drop

Most of the time, especially in the case of containers, you want your windows that support drag and drop to be used as both the source and target of direct-manipulation operations. This requires that you attach a source and target handler to the window. You attach the *default source handler* and *default target handler* to a window by using the enableDragDropFor static member function of the class IDMHandler. We describe the default handlers later in the topic "The Default Source and Target Handlers."

For example, the following code enables a user to drag and drop container objects in the container control pointed to by pCnrCtl:

```
IContainerControl
  *pCnrCtl;

IDMHandler::enableDragDropFor( pCnrCtl );
```

There are five overloaded versions of `IDMHandler::enableDragDropFor` that accept the following argument types:

IContainerControl*

This version of Open Class Library's direct-manipulation framework can exploit the fact that the window is a container control. The default handlers relieve you of doing some of the additional work required to set up your window for drag and drop. The default behavior causes the container objects to be dragged. These generic container items provide basic drag-and-drop behavior. If this behavior is enough, you do not need to do more.

IMultiLineEdit*

This version of `enableDragDropFor` exploits the fact that the window is a multiline edit control and automatically takes the necessary steps to permit a user to directly manipulate the window's contents as text.

IEntryField*

This version sets up the argument entry field so that its contents can be dragged and dropped.

IToolBarButton*

This version provides the necessary support for the dragging and dropping of tool bar buttons within a tool bar or between tool bars in the same application.

IWindow*

This version of the function handles all other types of `IWindows`. When you use this version, take the additional steps required to enable the window for drag and drop. Specifically, you must attach an item-provider object to your window, as we describe in the topic "Providing Items to be Dragged and Dropped" later in this chapter.

Why Windows Aren't Handlers

It is worth noting that there is only one source and one target direct-manipulation handler, and you attach the same handler to all windows enabled for drag and drop.

The significance of this is that it demonstrates the value of separating the desktop event-handling behavior, from the window's behavior. Rather than deriving from each control to make a drag-and-drop control, Open Class Library can instead implement the handling of direct-manipulation events just once and then reuse this code over and over again.

Thus, you can see the value of the encapsulation that C++ libraries provide in general and the exploitation of those features by Open Class Library.

Enabling Source Windows

Sometimes, you might want to use a window solely as the source for direct-manipulation operations. In such cases, you need to attach to the default source handler to the window. Do this by calling one of the overloaded versions of the enableDragFrom static member function of class IDMHandler. We show an example of this in the following programmable menu buttons example. Here is the code that enables dragging from the menu bar's submenus. Note that this example only runs in the OS/2 operating system due to the differences in the menu support on the two platforms.

Enabling Menu Drag - dm\menudrag\menudrag.cpp

```
IDMHandler::enableDragFrom( &menuBar );
```

As with enableDragDropFor, enableDragFrom is also overloaded to distinguish between containers, multiline entry fields, entry fields, and other windows, such as a custom control. Note that if you are enabling other windows you also need to attach an item provider.

Enabling Target Windows

At other times you might want to use a window solely as the target for direct-manipulation operations. In this case, you need to attach only the default target handler to the window. An example of such usage might be a control that represents a device, such as a printer object.

You enable a window to be a target only by calling one of the overloaded versions of the enableDropOn static member function of class IDMHandler. We provide an example of this in the following drag information viewer example as well as in the programmable menu buttons example. The code that enables dropping on the information viewer follows:

Enabling Drop on Viewer - dm\dragview\dragview.cpp

```
// Replace default target renderer with the viewer target renderer.
DragViewTargetRender
  targetRenderer;
IDMRenderer::setDefaultTargetRenderer( targetRenderer );

// Enable the MLE as a target.
IDMHandler::enableDropOn( &mle );

// Construct and set the item provider for the drag viewer item.
IDMItemProviderFor< DragViewItem >
  itemProvider;

mle.setItemProvider( &itemProvider );
```

As with the other drag-and-drop enabling functions, enableDropOn is overloaded to distinguish between containers, multiline entry fields, entry fields, tool bars, and other windows. If you are enabling other windows, as in the example, you also need to attach an item provider.

Direct-Manipulation Items

Objects of Open Class Library class IDMItem represent the objects being dragged and dropped in your applications. IDMItem is the most important component of the direct-manipulation framework. Almost all of the code you write to support direct manipulation is related to implementing your application-specific and control-specific classes derived from IDMItem. As you learn in subsequent topics, there are other objects that participate in direct manipulation: handlers, events, and a variety of objects used to implement the underlying desktop behavior. Although these other objects play important roles in getting direct manipulation to work, they are just infrastructure that permit the important objects to be manipulated. Those objects are IDMItem objects.

The derivation of class IDMItem and its derived classes that Open Class Library provides are shown in Figure 21-1. IDMItem is the base class that defines the general behavior of all direct manipulation items. Although there are six IDMItem-derived classes, only five are portable. The sixth, IDMMenuItem, is an OS/2 operating system-only implementation. The five derived classes that are portable provide specializations of the base class, which represent the objects being dragged and dropped on five specific controls.

We examine some of these derived classes to show you how to develop your own item classes. In addition, we discuss the item classes used to implement a set of four direct-manipulation example programs.

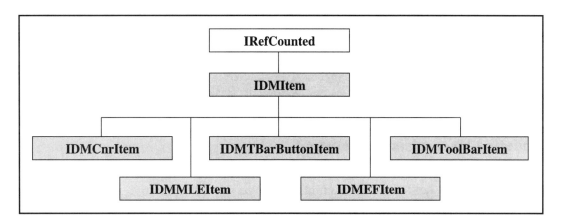

Figure 21-1. Direct Manipulation Item Classes.

Item Attributes

In this section, we discuss the behavior of direct-manipulation items and show you how to create derived item classes for your applications. However, before we do that, you need to know more about the various attributes whose values characterize these objects. We discuss those item attributes in this section.

Type

Direct-manipulation items require an explicit attribute that identifies the type of the item. Although your items are objects of C++ classes and those classes designate their type, you need another mechanism. The reason is that items are passed from window to window and application to application by generic desktop mechanisms that do not support the C++ type system.

Thus, direct-manipulation items have a type attribute. The value of this attribute is a sequence of character strings; each is the name of some type that the item is an element of. An item can be of many types. Usually, you order the types from most specific to least specific. For example, an item representing a file might have the types "C Source File," "Plain Text File," and "File." The first type in the list is the one that fully describes the nature of the item.

`IDMItem` provides a complete set of functions that you can use to maintain an item's types. However, you usually specify the item's type or types when you invoke the base `IDMItem` constructor. You also use these functions to query the item type of dragged or dropped items if your application supports the dropping of different kinds of items on your windows.

Open Class Library defines constants for a fixed set of type values. These have the type `IDM::Type` and are declared in `IDMCOMM.HPP`. Most of these types are general-purpose types and are compatible with the system-supported types.

At the desktop level, your item's type is represented by a character string consisting of all your supported types, separated by commas. Open Class Library masks this implementation detail to a considerable extent. You can instead treat your item's types as a collection of discrete type strings. The `IDMItem` functions handle decomposing and reconstructing the combined type string, which the desktop requires.

If your direct-manipulation items represent files, the convention is to match the item type to the file's content. If your items represent C++ objects, make the item's type value the same as its C++ class name.

Rendering Mechanisms and Formats

The terms *rendering mechanism* and *rendering format* refer to aspects of the protocol your application uses to transfer direct-manipulation items from the source to the target windows, and they refer to the operations you apply to the items in the process.

In terms of object attributes, the rendering mechanisms and formats identify the set of protocols your items and the associated renderer objects support. We discuss the details of those protocols at the end of this chapter. For the most part, the other direct-manipulation frameworks classes that Open Class Library provides handle implementing the protocols. All you need to do is specify whether your objects can be transmitted using them. We discuss the important rendering mechanisms and formats (RMFs) and show you how to choose the ones you need for your application.

You rarely work with rendering mechanism names independently of rendering format names and vice-versa. Most of the `IDMItem` functions that you use to maintain RMFs accept two arguments: a mechanism and a format. Most are overloaded so that you can pass a combined

RMF string. `IDMItem` also has static member functions that you can use to manipulate the actual RMF strings that the direct-manipulation support uses.

You do not need to remember the actual character strings that define the system's conventions for rendering mechanism and format names. Open Class Library provides constants for these as static members of the class `IDM`. For example, to add text file support to an item, you would add this code:

```
anItem.addRMF( IDM::rmFile, IDM::rfText );
```

We describe RMFs that the default Open Class Library's handlers and renderers support in the following list. We use the convention `<rm,rf>` to designate the combined RMF that uses rendering mechanism "rm" and rendering format "rf."

<rmLibrary, rfForThisProcess()>

This is an RMF that Open Class Library provides for doing efficient intraprocess dragging and dropping. The rendering format name includes the process identifier. The library-provided renderers exploit intraprocess mechanisms if they detect that the source and target windows are in the same process.

Note that the rendering format is not a constant. Instead, you construct the format string by calling the static member `IDMItem::rfForThisProcess`.

<rmLibrary, rfText>

Open Class Library provides this RMF to enable efficient dragging and dropping between separate processes in certain circumstances. The protocol used to transmit the item using this RMF works if the item contents are less than 256 bytes in length and do not contain embedded nulls. Use `IDMItem::generateSourceName` to determine whether your item can support this RMF. See the **dm\lboxdrag** program on the examples disk for an example.

<rmLibrary, rfSharedMem>

Open Class Library provides this RMF to enable general-purpose rendering of an item between processes. You need to use this RMF only if your item cannot support `<rmLibrary, rfText>`. Use this RMF to transfer arbitrary item contents between any two processes.

<rmFile, *>

Use the rendering mechanism `rmFile` if your items represent, or potentially represent, files. Usually, you need to add support for this RMF to your item to support dragging to or from the desktop.

Your item has additional responsibilities when it supports the file-rendering mechanism, such as setting the item's source file name, source container name, and attributes. Because `<rmLibrary, rfText>` also uses these attributes, this file-rendering mechanism is mutually exclusive with that RMF.

<rmDiscard, rfUnknown>

> This is the RMF your item must support for a user to drag it to the OS/2 desktop's shredder.

> This RMF is supported only in the OS/2 operating system.

<rmPrint, *>

> This is the RMF your item must support for a user to drag it to an OS/2 desktop printer object. To print, you need to know how to use the OS/2 Graphics Programing Interface (GPI) functions. Showing you how to do this is beyond the scope of this book. You can find out how to print your items using drag and drop by referring to the programming guides and references in the Developers Toolkit for the OS/2 operating system.

> This RMF is nonportable.

You work with your items' RMFs primarily when you construct the item. Usually, you call `IDMItem::addRMF` to add each of your items' supported RMFs. You can see how this is done for each of the example drag-and-drop programs that we present in this chapter by studying the item constructors in those programs. We show these constructors in a later topic.

To support a given RMF, you need to do more than call `addRMF` for it. For the `rmLibrary` RMFs, you must set the item's contents. The next section shows you how to do this. To support `rmDiscard`, or `rmPrint`, override the `IDMItem::sourceDiscard` and `IDMItem::sourcePrint` member functions in your derived class. To support `rmFile`, set your item's source file name, source container name, and attributes. We expand on this subject in the topic, "File Name and Path."

Contents

Open Class Library adds a pair of generic attributes to direct-manipulation items that make up the item's *contents*. One attribute is an `IString` that holds some representation of the item. You get and set this attribute by calling the functions `IDMItem::contents` and `IDMItem::setContents`, respectively. The other attribute is a `void*` value you get and set via the functions `IDMItem::object` and `IDMItem::setObject`.

Both attributes are transmitted from the source direct-manipulation item to the target item when you use any of the three `rmLibrary` rendering mechanisms and formats. Usually, you use the object attribute (pointer) when a user drags and drops your items within a single process. This is because the storage the object pointer points to is addressable only within the same process. Open Class Library renderer objects transfer the item content string via shared memory to the other process. Thus, you can use the string contents with the `rfText` and `rfSharedMem` rendering formats, too. Because the `IString` contents can hold arbitrary data, this mechanism provides you with a general-purpose interprocess communication technique to use for drag and drop.

The sample item constructors that we show in this chapter demonstrate how to set your item contents and then access the contents when a user drops the item.

File Name and Path

If you want to enable the target window to render the file, set the *source name* and *source container name* attributes at the source window. Set these attributes to null strings if you want to force the target to rely on the source side for rendering. In this case, the target sets the *target name* to notify the source where to render the file to.

Set these attributes whenever you add an RMF with the `rmFile` rendering mechanism. Usually, you do this in your item's constructor.

Supported Operations

Users can request any one of three distinct drag-and-drop operations: move, copy, or link. They indicate which operation they want by using augmentation keys, the Shift and Ctrl keys, before or during dragging of items. Set the supported operations attribute of your items to indicate which of these operations are valid for your item. If users request an unsupported operation or if they drag to a window that does not support the selected operation, the drag operation fails. The drag indicator then switches to the "not allowed" icon in that case.

Specify the operations that your item supports when you construct it. Open Class Library's direct-manipulation framework verifies the requested operation. You do not usually need to be concerned about the operation after you set the attribute at construction time. We discuss additional details of drag operations later in this chapter in the topic "Move, Copy, and Link."

Image Is Everything

The last item attribute we discuss is the *drag image*. This is the icon that appears when a user drags your item. You can assign an image to each of your items. The image can be any of the following ones:

- An icon or pointer that you identify as an icon resource or that you identify by an `IPointerHandle`.

- A bitmap that you identify as a bitmap resource or that you identify by an `IBitmapHandle`.

- An array of points that define a polygon that direct manipulation draws to represent the item as it is dragged. Note that only the OS/2 operating system supports this image format.

You work with direct-manipulation images using objects of class `IDMImage`. Items support the functions `IDMItem::image`, `IDMItem::hasImage`, and `IDMItem::setImage` that you can use to query, and set an item's drag image. By default, items do not have an image associated with them. Call `setImage` to give them one.

The direct-manipulation framework normally does not use images for individual items. Instead, it draws a generic *system image*. Call the function `IDMOperation::setImageStyle` to have the item images drawn. Apply the function to the source operation object, which we discuss in a later topic. This object is readily accessible when you construct your source direct-manipulation items. Whenever you use `IDMItem::setImage`, use code similar to the following:

```
anItem->setImage( anImage );              // Set item image.
srcOp->setImageStyle( IDM::stack3AndFade ); // Ensure it's used.
```

The programs we present in this chapter have examples of this.

Item Behavior

Open Class Library handlers translate the events that transpire during drag and drop into virtual function calls to your direct-manipulation items. In this topic, we discuss the most significant of these events and show you how to implement the corresponding functions.

You can readily identify the virtual functions of `IDMItem` that you need to override in your derived classes. All of the functions that the handlers and renderers call in response to significant source events have names that begin with "source": `sourceDiscard`, `sourceEnd`, `sourcePrepare`, `sourcePrint`, and `sourceRender`. The functions that the framework calls to signal events at the target end have names that begin with "target": `targetDrop` and `targetEnd`.

We discuss which of these functions you have to override most often in the following topics.

The Drop

Your item's override for the `targetDrop` function is called when a user drops your item on a window that can accept it. You almost always override the function because dropping would have no effect, otherwise. Remember that the object to which Open Class Library framework applies this function is the target item that resides in the target process. Your target window generally constructs this item from the source item that a user dragged over it. We discuss this construction process in detail in a later topic.

The argument to the `targetDrop` function is the target drop event, which is of type `IDMTargetDropEvent`. Normally, your item gets the target window from the event and adds itself to that window. Because you are using that window to show some object, you might instead add the item to the underlying object. Depending on the nature of your application, you might need to do both.

Your override returns `true` if you complete the drop processing for this item, or it returns `false` if the processing failed. The return value determines which renderer completion code, `IDM:targetSuccessful` or `IDM:targetFailed`, is returned to the source.

Here is the `targetDrop` implementation for the spin-button example program's `SpinButtonItem` class:

SpinButtonItem::targetDrop - dm\spindrag\spinitem.cpp

```
Boolean SpinButtonItem ::
  targetDrop ( IDMTargetDropEvent& event )
  {
  // Add dropped text to the spin button.
  ITextSpinButton
   *pSpin = (ITextSpinButton*)( event.window()->parent() );
  pSpin -> addAsLast( this->contents() );
  pSpin -> spinTo( this->contents() );
  return true;
  }
```

Next, we show the implementation of the `ListBoxItem`'s `targetDrop` function. It is more complicated because it handles removing the target emphasis that we are drawing in the list box. We discuss drawing target emphasis later. This example also shows you how you access the target operation to determine what operation is being performed and to determine if the source and target windows are the same. If so, we go to the source item, which we can do because it exists in the same process, and tweak it. Then, when the source version of the item detects completion of the move, it removes the correct item. You might need to look at the complete source for the list-box item class to fully understand the implementation of this function.

ListBoxItem::targetDrop - dm\lboxdrag\lboxitem.cpp

```
Boolean ListBoxItem :: targetDrop ( IDMTargetDropEvent& event )
  {
  IMODTRACE_DEVELOP("ListBoxItem::targetDrop");
  IListBox
   *tgtLB = (IListBox*)( event.window() );

  // Turn off target emphasis.
  ListBoxItemProvider
   *provider = (ListBoxItemProvider*)( tgtLB->itemProvider() );
  provider -> drawEmphasis( tgtLB, event, TgtLocation( after,
                                                       nil ) );

  // Calculate where the object is dropped.
  TgtLocation
    dropLoc = targetLocation( tgtLB, event.dropPosition() );
  // Add or replace the list item, based on drop location.
  switch ( dropLoc.type )
    {
    case before:
      tgtLB -> add( dropLoc.index, contents() );
      break;
    case on:
      tgtLB -> setItemText( dropLoc.index, contents() );
      break;
    case after:
      tgtLB -> add( dropLoc.index + 1, contents() );
      break;
    }
  // If source and target are the same, and the item is moved
  // forward, update source index.
  IDMTargetOperation::Handle
    tgtOp = IDMTargetOperation::targetOperation();
```

```
    if ( tgtOp->sourceWindow() == event.window()
        &&
        tgtOp->operation() == IDMOperation::move )
   {
   IDMItem::Handle
     srcItem = IDMItem::sourceItemFor( tgtOp->item( 1 ) );
   unsigned
     srcIndex = (unsigned)( srcItem->object() );
   if ( dropLoc.type != on
        &&
        dropLoc.index < srcIndex )
     srcItem->setObject( (void*)( srcIndex + 1 ) );
   }
   return true;
   }
```

Shredding

This capability is available in the OS/2 Operating System only. When a user drops your item on the OS/2 desktop shredder object, Open Class Library's direct-manipulation framework invokes your source item's sourceDiscard function. This occurs only when your item supports the rmDiscard rendering mechanism. Override sourceDiscard to remove the item from the source window and, if necessary, from the underlying object model.

The argument to this function is the IDMSourceDiscardEvent. Use this event in the same way that you use the events in the other item functions: to access the source window. The following example shows the implementation of the sourceDiscard function in the sample classes that support shredding.

ListBoxItem::sourceDiscard - dm\lboxdrag\lboxitem.cpp

```
Boolean ListBoxItem ::
  sourceDiscard ( IDMSourceDiscardEvent& event )
  {
  IListBox
   *srcLB = (IListBox*)( event.window() );

  // Get index of the dragged item.
  unsigned
    index = (unsigned)( this->object() );

  // Delete that item.
  srcLB->remove( index );

  // Mark deleted so sourceEnd doesn't delete it again.
  setObject( (void*)nil );

  return true;
  }
```

Wrapping Things Up

When the objects at the source and target ends of the direct manipulation operation have exchanged all of the window events that they need to, each window receives a final completion event. These events generate calls to virtual functions of your direct-manipulation items. Override these functions to take care of any cleanup you need to do when the drag and drop is completed.

Open Class Library's direct-manipulation framework invokes your source item's sourceEnd function. This occurs when the target item has completed its handling of the drop in its targetDrop function. You normally override sourceEnd to complete move operations or, perhaps, to complete link operations. The standard Open Class Library processing of the IDMSourceEndEvent event handles freeing most resources, such as the source operation and source items.

The argument source-end event provides an indicator to determine if the target succeeded in handling the drop. If not, you usually do not have to do anything. But, if you do, complete the operation at the source end of the direct-manipulation operation.

Here is the implementation of the sourceEnd function for the list-box example:

ListBoxItem::sourceEnd - dm\lboxdrag\lboxitem.cpp

```
Boolean ListBoxItem :: sourceEnd ( IDMSourceEndEvent& event )
{
IMODTRACE_DEVLOP("ListBoxItem::sourceEnd");
// If the move is completed and not sent to the shredder,
// delete the source item.
if ( event.wasTargetSuccessful()
     &&
     (unsigned long)( object() ) != nil
     &&
     event.dragItem()->sourceOperation()->operation() !=
                                        IDMOperation::copy )
  {
  unsigned
    index = (unsigned)( this->object() );
  ( (IListBox*)( event.window() ) ) -> remove( index );
  }
return true;
}
```

Your item's targetEnd function gets called when you use source rendering and the source has completed its processing in its sourceRender function. You do not use this style of rendering often, so we do not discuss the implementation of your targetEnd function in any more detail here.

The Source and Target Operations

Open Class Library maintains two objects to describe the active direct-manipulation operation. One object exists in the source process, the *source operation*. Another object exists in the target process, the *target operation*. Each of these objects has attributes that describe the active operation as a whole. Each operation object maintains a collection of the items that a user is dragging.

Your items need to access the operation objects to find information, such as the source and target window handles, the selected operation (move, copy, or link), and the mouse position of the drag or drop.

We cover IDMOperation and its derived classes in detail later in this chapter.

Providing Items to Be Dragged and Dropped

In the preceding section, we described the basic attributes of your direct-manipulation items. We also discussed how you tailor the behavior of your items to implement direct-manipulation support in your applications. Now, we begin the task of constructing your items and giving them the chance to apply that behavior. First, you learn to create direct-manipulation items.

Item Providers

Consider what happens when a user presses the mouse button and begins a drag operation. This action generates some conventional desktop mouse events that the system-provided windows translate to drag-and-drop events. The source direct-manipulation handler that Open Class Library provides and attaches to your window processes those events.

At this point, the direct-manipulation framework must do something specific to the application and window that a user is dragging from. Because the same source handler is being used for every window in your application, Open Class Library handlers cannot determine the details of the objects being shown in your windows: the source handler does not determine what type of direct-manipulation item to create.

In fact, the source handler goes to the source window to obtain the items. However, it does not do so directly. Instead, it uses an *item provider* object, which is attached to the window. This object is of a type that you derive from `IDMItemProvider`. You attach one of these objects to your window in much the same way that you attach handlers.

Item-Provider Functions

The class `IDMItemProvider` has functions that you inherit or override to provide all of the direct-manipulation support that is tailorable on a per-window basis. The more important of these functions are those that provide the direct-manipulation items at both the source and target sides of the drag-and-drop operation.

provideSourceItems

> Open Class Library's direct-manipulation source handler calls this function when a user begins a drag-and-drop operation. Implement this function so that you construct the appropriate direct-manipulation items and add them to the source operation passed as input to this function. We provide detailed guidelines on how to implement this function in the topic "Providing Source Items" later in this chapter.

provideTargetItemFor

> Open Class Library's direct-manipulation target handler calls this function when a user first drags an object or objects over the target window. It is called once for each item being dragged. Implement this function so that you construct the appropriate direct-manipulation item and return it. The target handler replaces the generic IDMItem stored in the target operation with the returned item. We provide detailed guidelines on how to implement this function in the topic "Providing Target Items" later in this chapter.

The item-provider class also has virtual functions that correspond to other behaviors that you might want to tailor for each of your windows. These IDMItemProvider functions are provideEnterSupport, provideLeaveSupport, and provideHelpFor. We discuss how you implement the first two of these in the topic, "To Drop or Not to Drop," later in this chapter.

Attaching Item Providers to Your Windows

Attach an *item provider* to windows that are enabled to be the source or target of a direct-manipulation operation by calling the function IWindow::setItemProvider. The argument is a pointer to an object of some type that you derive from the class IDMItemProvider. The source and target handlers subsequently access the item provider by using the function IWindow::itemProvider. It returns a pointer to the item provider previously set, or it returns 0 if no item provider is attached to the window.

The main job of the item provider is to furnish objects representing the objects being dragged or dropped. If you have reasonable defaults for the contents of certain controls, you can attach default item providers to windows of type IContainerControl, IMultiLineEdit, IEntryField, IToolBar, and IToolBarButton. In fact, Open Class Library's direct-manipulation framework assigns item-provider objects to do that if such windows are enabled for drag and drop and do not have a user-supplied item provider.

You can use your own item-provider object for windows of these types. Just call setItemProvider to attach an alternative one. You might do this for an entry field that a user uses to enter a date. The default for an entry field is to treat its contents as text. In this case, you might want to have a user drag and drop dates rather than text.

You must use your own item-provider object for windows that are not containers, multiline edit controls, or entry fields. There is no other way for Open Class Library's direct-manipulation framework to determine what items to drag and drop.

The IDMItemProviderFor Class Template

Open Class Library provides a class template, IDMItemProviderFor, that you can use to generate item-provider classes that correspond to your application-specific items. The template's argument is the name of your item class.

This class template overrides the key IDMItemProvider virtual functions and routes the requests to corresponding functions of your item class. IDMItemProviderFor<Item> processes those functions as follows:

provideSourceItems

The class template implements this function by invoking the static member function generateSourceItems of the template argument class.

provideTargetItemFor

The class template implements this function by constructing a new item object of the template argument class. The item is constructed from the generic IDMItem created by the target operation.

The intent of this class template is to automate (to some extent) the repetitive logic of most item-provider classes. In theory, by routing item-provider requests back to your item class, the template lets you isolate your code in a single class. In practice, however, you often need to override other IDMItemProviderFor virtual functions, especially provideEnterSupport.

You can still use this class template even if you need to extend the generated template class. To illustrate this, here is the declaration of the item-provider class that we use in the list-box direct-manipulation example program. In the case of the simpler programs, which use SpinButtonItems and DragViewItems, you can use the standard template classes, IDMItemProviderFor<SpinButtonItem> and IDMItemProviderFor<DragViewItem>.

ListBoxItemProvider Interface - dm\lboxdrag\lboxitem.hpp

```
class ListBoxItemProvider
  : public IDMItemProviderFor<ListBoxItem> {
typedef IDMItemProviderFor<ListBoxItem>
  Inherited;
public:
  ListBoxItemProvider ( IListBox* listBox = 0 );

virtual ListBoxItemProvider
 &provideItemsFor( IListBox* listBox );

virtual ListBoxItemProvider
 &drawEmphasis ( IListBox*                      listBox,
                 IDMTargetEvent&                event,
                 const ListBoxItem::TgtLocation& target );

virtual Boolean
  provideLeaveSupport( IDMTargetLeaveEvent& event ),
  provideEnterSupport( IDMTargetEnterEvent& event );

private:
// Make operator private to prevent attaching to wrong control.
ListBoxItemProvider
 *operator & ();
};
```

Providing Source Items

In this topic, you learn how to implement your direct-manipulation-item classes' generateSourceItem function. The IDMItemProviderFor class template's implementation of the function provideSourceItems calls that static member function. The instructions we provide are applicable regardless of which function you choose to implement.

Your implementation of whatever function you choose must complete the following three steps to enable your items to be dragged from your source window.

1. Create one or more objects of your direct-manipulation-item class.

2. Add the item or items to the source direct-manipulation operation that is passed as input to provideSourceItems/generateSourceItems.

3. Return true.

Constructing the Items

Create your direct-manipulation item on the heap by using operator new. This is because the item objects need to exist long after you return from the function that creates them. IDMItems are reference-counted objects. The object that usually maintains a reference to them is the source operation; it creates the reference to the item when you add it. This mechanism ensures that the items persist until the operation completes.

Usually, you create the item using a constructor that you provide especially for that purpose. All of the example programs we present here use this technique.

Adding the Items to the Operation

After you construct your item or items, add them to the source operation by calling IDMSourceOperation::addItem. Call this function from the item constructor or from the provideSourceItems or generateSourceItems function that constructs the items.

Setting the Return Code

generateSourceItems and provideSourceItems return a Boolean indicator to indicate whether a direct-manipulation operation can proceed. If you return false, then nothing happens when a user presses the direct-manipulation mouse button and moves the mouse. The effect is the same as if you had not enabled the source window for direct manipulation. You might return false if a user had not selected any objects in the source window or if a user did not begin the drag operation with the mouse positioned over a draggable object.

Examples of Providing Items

In this first example, we have a spin button as a frame extension on a simple editor application that uses a multiline edit control as the client window control. We want to drag text from the multiline edit control to the spin button and scroll through the spin-button elements looking for text to be dragged back into the editor window. The spin button operates like a multilevel clipboard; it is accessible using direct manipulation.

Here is how the spin-button component of this simple application provides source direct-manipulation items:

Providing SpinButtonItems - dm\spindrag\spinitem.cpp

```
Boolean SpinButtonItem ::
  generateSourceItems ( IDMSourceOperation* srcOp )
  {
  // Source item is object of this class.
  IDMItem::Handle
    item( new SpinButtonItem( srcOp ) );
  // Add it to the source operation.
  srcOp -> addItem( item );
  // Indicate an item is available to drag.
  return true;
  }

SpinButtonItem :: SpinButtonItem ( IDMSourceOperation* srcOp )
  : IDMItem( srcOp, IDM::text, IDMItem::copyable |
             IDMItem::moveable )
  {
  // Support intraprocess drag and drop only.
  this -> addRMF( rmfFrom( IDM::rmLibrary,
                           rfForThisProcess() ) );
  // Set item contents to selected spin button text.
  IEntryField
   *pEF = (IEntryField*)( srcOp->sourceWindow() );
  ITRACE_DEVELOP( pEF->selectedText() );
  this->setContents( pEF->selectedText() );
  }
```

In the next example, we provide source items when a user drags an item from a list-box control. You can see in this case how we return `false` if no item is dragged (which happens if the list box is empty or if a user drags from the end of the list). This example also shows how you can test whether the RMF <rmLibrary,rfText> can be used.

Providing ListBoxItems - dm\lboxdrag\lboxitem.cpp

```
Boolean ListBoxItem ::
  generateSourceItems( IDMSourceOperation* srcOp )
  {
  IMODTRACE_DEVELOP("ListBoxItem::generateSourceItems");
  Boolean
    result = false;
  IListBox
   *srcLB = (IListBox*)( srcOp->sourceWindow() );
  // Get index of dragged item.
  unsigned
    index = sourceIndex( srcLB, srcOp->position() );
  if ( index != nil )
    {
    //User not dragging from white space; add appropriate item.
    srcOp -> addItem( new ListBoxItem( srcOp, srcLB, index ) );
    srcOp -> setImageStyle( IDM::stack3AndFade );
    result = true;
    }
  return result;
  }

ListBoxItem :: ListBoxItem ( IDMSourceOperation* srcOp,
                             IListBox*           srcLB,
                             unsigned            index )
  : IDMItem( srcOp,
             IDM::text,
             IDMItem:: moveable | IDMItem::copyable,
             none )
  {
  IMODTRACE_DEVELOP("ListBoxItem::ListBoxItem");
```

```
    // Item contents is the list-box's item text.
    this -> setContents( srcLB->itemText( index ) );
    // Item object is the item index.
    ITRACE_DEVELOP("Selected text is " + srcLB->itemText(index));

    this -> setObject( (void*)index );
    // Try to use rfText.
    IString
      name = this -> generateSourceName(),
      rfs  = rfForThisProcess();
    if ( name.length() )
      { // Text fits; use rfText.
      this -> setSourceName( name );
      rfs += IString( "," ) + IDM::rfText;
      }
    else
      { // Text doesn't fit; use rfSharedMem instead.
      rfs += IString( "," ) + IDM::rfSharedMem;
      this -> setRequiresPreparation();
      }
    ITRACE_DEVELOP( "Rmfs is " + rfs );

    // Set up RMFs; we support dropping on shredder, too.
    this -> setRMFs( rmfsFrom( IDM::rmLibrary, rfs ) );

#ifdef IC_PM
    // We support dropping on the shredder in OS/2.
    this -> addRMF( IDM::rmDiscard, IDM::rfUnknown );
#endif

    // Use text icon when a user drags the item.
    ISystemPointerHandle
      icon( ISystemPointerHandle::text );
    IDMImage
      image( icon );
    this -> setImage( image );
    }
```

Reusing Inherited Item-Providing Logic

As more and more logic is added to functions that generate source items, you are more likely to want to reuse this logic. However, the structure of the direct-manipulation item-providing code makes it awkward to reuse these functions. The result of calling this code is that one or more direct-manipulation items of a specific class are added to the source operation. The problem is that the items are not of the right class; they are objects of your base class.

For example, you are using a list box to hold customer names. When a user drags an item from your list box, you might want to drag CustomerItems, not ListBoxItems. However, if you implement the CustomerItem member function, generateSourceItems, so that it calls ListBoxItem::generateSourceItems, you add ListBoxItems to the source operation. You can fix that because the source operation object provides a convenient set of functions that you can use to manipulate its items. You can replace those ListBoxItems with CustomerItems, as follows:

```
    class CustomerItem : public IDMItem {
    public:
      CustomerItem ( const IDMItem::Handle& item )
           : ListBoxItem( item )
        {
        //Extract customer name from contents
        //and build the customer item.
        }
```

```
static Boolean
  generateSourceItems ( IDMSourceOperation* srcOp )
    {
    Boolean
      result = ListBoxItem::generateSourceItems( srcOp );
    if ( result )
      for ( int i = 1;
            i <= srcOp->numberOfItems();
            i++ )
        srcOp->replaceItem(i,new CustomerItem(srcOp->item(i)));
    }
};
```

In addition to using replaceItem instead of addItem, CustomerItem has a constructor that accepts an object of the base item class rather than from the source operation.

This example shows how you can reuse an existing implementation of generateSourceItems. This technique is particularly useful in generating specialized container objects when you add direct-manipulation support to your detection of the dragging of a selected (versus nonselected) object by calling IDMCnrItem::generateSourceItems. After that, you iterate the items, replacing each with items specific to your container.

Providing Target Items

In this topic, you learn how to provide objects of your item class at your target windows.

The situation is much different at the target window than at the source window. First, the target items are created differently than they are created at the source. The items that a user drags already exist in the source process. Further, the basic item attributes are accessible at the target window because they are being passed by the desktop's drag-and-drop protocols. The data that is passed, however, is not in the form of generic IDMItem objects. Open Class Library's target handler and target operation solve this because they have the ability to interrogate the data and to construct a target operation and the proper number of generic IDMItem objects, respectively.

The generic IDMItem objects maintain the attributes of the dragged items. As IDMItem objects, they provide default processing when the target renderer calls virtual functions such as targetDrop. This is the reason you need to create objects of your item class on the target side. You use the same logic to provide your target items that you use to apply inherited generateSourceItems logic. Use the IDMOperation member function, replaceItem, to exchange objects of your item class for the more generic ones already added to the operation. Open Class Library automates the replacement of generic IDMItem objects with objects of your item class as we discuss in the next topic.

The Item-Provider's Role

The target operation calls the function provideTargetItemFor to get the replacement item for each of the generic items. It invokes this function on the item provider that you have attached to the target window. The generic item is provided as an argument to the function call.

Most of the time, you use the implementation of `provideTargetItemFor` that is generated by the class template `IDMItemProviderFor`. The implementation has the following basic structure:

```
...
return( (IDMItem::Handle)new Item( oldItem ) );
...
```

`Item` is the name of your item class, the template argument, and `oldItem` is the function argument of type `IDMItem::Handle`.

We accept this implementation as-is in all of the direct-manipulation example programs.

The Item's Target Constructor

Having accepted the template class' implementation of `provideTargetItemFor`, we now focus on the item constructor that function uses. Implement a matching constructor in your item class.

To do this, we show this constructor's implementation for the example `ListBoxItem` class as follows:

ListBoxItem Target Constructor - dm\lboxdrag\lboxitem.cpp

```
ListBoxItem :: ListBoxItem ( const IDMItem::Handle& dragItem )
  : IDMItem( dragItem )
  {
  IMODTRACE_DEVELOP("ListBoxItem::ListBoxItem(Handle)");
  // We only support copy and move.
  this -> enableLink( false );
  }
```

This constructor is simple to implement. Use the copy constructor of the base `IDMItem` class to copy the basic item attributes. The resulting item has the same attributes but with one important difference: the item is an object of your class so that your `targetDrop` function is called when a user drops an item on the target window. The only other steps you must take are as follows:

1. Limit the item's supported operations to those that your item truly supports. This prohibits a more functionally rich item from being dropped on your target window using an operation that the source window supports but the target window does not.

2. Limit the item's supported RMFs to those that your item supports. Again, this prevents the drop of an item that supports RMFs that you do not support.

You are not required to perform either of these steps. If you rely on other checks to avoid the problems, you can accept the operations and RMFs of the source items. However, you need to be aware of the potential problems.

To Drop or Not to Drop

To permit the direct-manipulation operation to take place requires more work. In this topic, you learn the process that the target objects use to determine whether a user can drop an item on the target window. The result of this process determines whether a user gets positive feedback while dragging the items over the target window, and it also determines what happens when a user drops the items.

Open Class Library's direct-manipulation framework makes the four checks you need for deciding whether a user can drop an item on your target window. You learn how the built-in checking is performed and how you can add your own checking if the default does not meet your requirements.

My Kind of Item

The first check you must make is whether the type of the dragged items is supported by the objects at the target window. Open Class Library supports all types of objects by default. As a result, you are responsible for checking the type if you need to do so. Perform that checking in your item provider's provideEnterSupport function.

Usually, you must check the type whenever you need to make assumptions about the format of the data that you extract from the source item. When you use Open Class Library's rendering mechanism, this checking applies when you rely on the item's contents or object values to contain particular values.

To verify the item's type, apply the hasType function to the target items, passing the required type. In your item provider's implementation of provideEnterSupport, insert code that resembles the following example:

```
...
IDMItem::Handle
  item = tgtOp->item[ 1 ];
// Check that dragged object is a bitmap or icon.
if ( item -> hasType( IDM::bitmap )
       ||
     item -> hasType( IDM::icon ) )
  {
  // ...code to process valid dragged items...
  }
...
```

Matching a Rendering Mechanism and Format

The second check is to determine if the source and target can match a rendering mechanism and format. The Open Class Library target handler iterates its set of renderer objects until it finds one that can render each of the dragged items. If it cannot find a renderer object for any of the items, the drop is not allowed.

You do not need to do your own checking for matching rendering mechanism and format. You can check the items' RMFs within your item-provider's provideEnterSupport function if you want to, but you do not need to do so. If there is a renderer that supports the item, the only reason that would prevent the user from dropping an item on your target is failure to satisfy one of these other checks.

Should We Operate?

The third check is to determine if the selected operation is acceptable to both the source and target windows. This means that the operation that a user selects is supported by both the source and target items. We discuss the details of the move, copy, and link operations in a later topic. All you need to know about the operation to determine if a drag-and-drop operation is permitted follows:

- If a user has not requested an explicit operation by pressing the Shift or Ctrl *augmentation keys*, Open Class Library's framework permits the drop if the source and target items have some commonly supported operation. The target item's supportedOperationsFor function determines the operations that the target supports. The argument to the function call is the selected RMF used to render the item.

  With this mechanism you can support different operations, depending on the rendering mechanism and format. For example, when a user is doing an interprocess drag and drop, you might not permit an object to be moved or linked. The following example implementation of supportedOperationsFor disables all but copy operations when you use the <rmLibrary, rfSharedMem> rendering mechanism and format.

  ```
  unsigned long SomeItem ::
    supportedOperationsFor ( const IString& rmf ) const
    {
    if ( rmf == IDMItem::rmfFrom( IDM::rmLibrary,
                                  IDM::rfSharedMem ) )
      // If you use <rmLibrary,rfSharedMem>, only copy is
      // supported.
      return IDMItem::copyable & this->supportedOperations();
    else
      // Use whatever the base class supports.
      return Inherited::supportedOperationsFor( rmf );
    }
  ```

- If a user requests a specific operation by pressing augmentation keys, the target and source must support the requested operation. If either item does not support the operation, the drop is not allowed. The set of operations supported by the target are those returned by the target item's supportedOperationsFor function.

Does It Make Sense?

The final and most important check that you must make before allowing an item to be dropped on a particular target window is to determine if it makes sense for a user to drop this item here.

This check is difficult because the situation is different in every scenario. Whereas Open Class Library's direct-manipulation framework can make the other checks with reasonable accuracy, you can only implement this check yourself, according to the semantics of your application and its objects.

Here is an example of an item provider's provideEnterSupport function, which does extensive semantic analysis to determine if the drop is permitted. If it determines not to permit the drop of the item, you must call the argument event's setDropIndicator function, setting the drop indicator to IDM::notOk (or IDM::neverOk).

ListBoxItemProvider::provideEnterSupport - dm\lboxdrag\lboxitem.cpp

```cpp
Boolean ListBoxItemProvider ::
  provideEnterSupport ( IDMTargetEnterEvent& event )
  {
  IMODTRACE_DEVELOP("ListBoxItemProvider::provideEnterSupport");
  // Get default dragover result.
  Inherited::provideEnterSupport( event );

  IDMTargetOperation::Handle
    tgtOp = IDMTargetOperation::targetOperation();

  IListBox
   *lb = (IListBox*)( event.window() );

#ifdef IC_WIN
  // Do not allow drops over the scroll bars.
  // The scroll bars in Windows are not controls;
  // thus, we calculate the scroll rectangles and
  // test for hits over the scroll areas.

  // Target position is in desktop coordinates.
  // We must map this to listbox window coordinates.
  IPoint
    lbPt = IWindow::mapPoint(event.position(),
                             IWindow::desktopWindow()->handle(),
                             lb->handle() );
  // fix for mapping problem on windows.
  lbPt += IPoint(1,1);

  unsigned
    hscrollHeight = ListBoxItem::horizontalScrollHeight( ),
    vscrollWidth = ListBoxItem::verticalScrollWidth( lb );

  IRectangle hscrollRect( lb->rect().left(),
                          lb->rect().top() - hscrollHeight,
                          lb->rect().right(),
                          lb->rect().top() ),
            vscrollRect( lb->rect().right() - vscrollWidth + 3,
                          lb->rect().bottom(),
                          lb->rect().right(),
                          lb->rect().top() - hscrollHeight );
  if ( hscrollRect.contains( lbPt ) ||
       vscrollRect.contains( lbPt ) )
    {
    event.setDropIndicator( IDM::notOk );
    // Undraw any existing target emphasis.
    drawEmphasis( lb,
                  event,
                  TgtLocation( ListBoxItem::after, nil ) );
    return true;
    }
#endif //IC_WIN

  ListBoxItem::TgtLocation
    tgtLocation
      = ListBoxItem::targetLocation( lb, event.position() );
```

```
if ( event.dropIndicator() == IDM::ok
     &&
     tgtOp->sourceWindow() == event.window() )
  { //If source equals target, prohibit dropping on same item.
  IDMItem::Handle
    srcItem = IDMItem::sourceItemFor( tgtOp->item( 1 ) );
  unsigned
    srcIndex = (unsigned)( srcItem->object() );

  // Disable conflicting drop on source window.
  unsigned long
    op = tgtOp->operation();
  if ( op == IDMOperation::drag )
    op = IDMOperation::move; // Default;
  if ( op == IDMOperation::copy )
    { // Can't copy to self.
    if ( (srcIndex == tgtLocation.index)
         &&
         tgtLocation.type == ListBoxItem::on )
      event.setDropIndicator( IDM::notOk );
    }
  else if ( op == IDMOperation::move )
    { // No sense moving to same place.
    if ( (srcIndex == tgtLocation.index)
         ||
         ( tgtLocation.type == ListBoxItem::before
           &&
           srcIndex == tgtLocation.index - 1 )
         ||
         ( tgtLocation.type == ListBoxItem::after
           &&
           srcIndex == tgtLocation.index + 1 ) )
      {
      event.setDropIndicator( IDM::notOk );
      }
    }
  }

// Draw target emphasis:
drawEmphasis( lb, event, tgtLocation );

return true;
}
```

Note that setting the drop indicator to `IDM::ok` is not sufficient to permit the drop to be made. Open Class Library's target handler still performs the checks for a matching RMF and a commonly supported operation.

Move, Copy, Link, or Get Out of The Way!

The desktop supports three distinct direct-manipulation operations, move, copy, and link. In the Windows operating system, link is commonly referred to as a shortcut. The protocol also supports adding application-specific drag-and-drop operations. The operation that your application performs depends on a number of factors. We discuss these factors from both the source and target windows' perspectives.

The Selected Operation

First, a user can request a specific operation by pressing some combination of augmentation keys. Usually, the Ctrl key forces a copy; the Shift key forces a move; and Ctrl+Shift forces a link (although users can define their augmentation keys to be different than these defaults if they choose). When a user presses these augmentation keys while dragging an item, only the selected operation can be performed. If the source or target do not support this selected operation, then a user cannot drop the item or items.

The drag image reflects the user-selected operation. This is a half tone image for a copy and, for the OS/2 operating system only, an image with a connecting line for a link. For the Windows operating system, the shortcut (link) is identified by a special symbol in the shape of a curved right arrow, which the system adds to the drag image.

Target Operation Selection

The more interesting case occurs when a user does not select a specific operation. This occurs when a user drags an item without pressing any augmentation keys. In this case, the target window determines which operation is to be performed. The system works this way so that different drop targets can implement different default operations, depending on the nature of the target. For example, a printer would default to copy while a shredder would default to move.

When target operation selection is required, the dragged items indicate whether the selected operation is `IDM::drag`, which is the default. Any target windows that accept such items when dragged over must specify its default operation. If the source does not support the target's default operation, a user cannot drop an item on the target.

Another feature of target operation selection is that the system changes the drag image to reflect the operation in effect at each target. As a result, the drag image becomes half tone, for example, when a user drags an item over a printer, and it reverts to the true (move) image when a user drags an item over a shredder.

Drawing Target Emphasis

The last functional aspect of direct manipulation that you learn is the drawing of target emphasis. Ideally, you display something in your target window to let users know what happens when they drop items. This is related to the visual cue that a user receives from the enhanced drawing of the drag image to indicate the operation that is to be performed. This cue tells users what happens when they drop items. The other cue a user needs is an indication of where the drop occurs. This kind of indication is called *target emphasis*.

You need to do some special drawing during drag and drop because the desktop is in a special state causing regular presentation drawing techniques not to work. Use the `IDMTargetEvent` member functions `presSpace` and `releasePresSpace` to obtain a special presentation space on which to draw. In addition, limit the kind of drawing you do so that you can efficiently update the display as a user drags an object across your window. Finally, you monitor the drag-and-drop operation and choose the correct times to draw and remove the target emphasis.

The list-box sample program that we use as an example in this chapter shows you how to draw target emphasis. The Windows specific code that we identify with the directive, IC_WIN, is necessary because the list box's scroll bars are not controls in the Windows operating system. Therefore, we include the additional logic to prevent the drawing of target emphasis on the scroll bars.

First, we show you the functions that actually do the drawing as follows:

ListBoxItem Target Emphasis Drawing - dm\lboxdrag\lboxitem.cpp

```
typedef ListBoxItem::TgtLocation TgtLocation;

static TgtLocation
  lastTarget( ListBoxItem::after, nil );

static void draw ( IGraphicContext&   gc,
                   IListBox*          lb,
                   const TgtLocation& target )
  {
  if ( target.index != nil )
    {
    // First, get offset from top of list box:
    unsigned
      offset = target.index - lb->top() + 1,
      height = ListBoxItem::itemHeight( lb );

    // Next, adjust it if before this item:
    if ( target.type == ListBoxItem::before )
      offset--;

    // Calculate that item's rectangle's bottom, taking into
    // account the platform's coordinate system:
    unsigned
      bottom;
    if ( ICoordinateSystem::applicationOrientation()
         == ICoordinateSystem::originUpperLeft )
      {
      bottom = height * offset;
      }
    else
      {
      bottom = lb->rect().height() - height * offset;
      // Lower bottom by 2 pels to align the emphasis.
      bottom -= 2;
      }

    // Get the width of the vertical scroll bar.
    unsigned
      vscrollWidth =
        ListBoxItem::verticalScrollWidth( lb );
#ifdef IC_WIN
    // Get the height of the horizontal scroll bar.
    unsigned
      hscrollHeight =
        ListBoxItem::horizontalScrollHeight( );
#endif
```

```
// Draw line or box.
   IPoint
     origin( 0, bottom );
   if ( target.type == ListBoxItem::on )
      {
      IPoint
        topRight;
      if ( ICoordinateSystem::applicationOrientation()
           == ICoordinateSystem::originUpperLeft )
         {
         topRight = IPoint( lb->rect().width(),
                            bottom - height + 2 );
         }
      else
         {
         topRight = IPoint( lb->rect().width(),
                            bottom + height );
         }

      // Adjust the origin so the left side of the box is
      // visible.
      origin += IPoint( 1, 0 );

      // Adjust the end point if the vertical scroll bar is
      // visible.
      topRight -= IPoint( vscrollWidth, 1 )

#ifdef IC_WIN
      // Do not draw emphasis over the horizontal scroll bar.
      IPoint
        bottomLeft( origin.x(),
                    lb->rect().top() - hscrollHeight - 1 );
      if ( origin.y() >= bottomLeft.y() )
         {
         IGPolyline myLine( IPointArray(4) );
         myLine.setPoint( 0, bottomLeft );
         myLine.setPoint( 1, IPoint( origin.x(),
                                     topRight.y() ) );
         myLine.setPoint( 2, topRight );
         myLine.setPoint( 3, IPoint( topRight.x(),
                                     bottomLeft.y() ) );
         myLine.drawOn( gc );
         return;
         }
#endif //IC_WIN

      IRectangle theBox( origin, topRight );
      IGRectangle myBox( theBox );
      myBox.drawOn( gc );
      }
   else
      {
#ifdef IC_WIN
      // Do not draw emphasis over the horizontal scroll bar.
      if ( bottom >= (lb->rect().top() - hscrollHeight - 1) )
         return;
#endif //IC_WIN

      // Adjust the end point if the vertical scroll bar is
      // visible.
      IPoint
        end( lb->rect().width() - vscrollWidth + 1, bottom );
      IGPolyline myLine( IPointArray(2) );
      myLine.setPoint( 0, origin );
      myLine.setPoint( 1, end );
      myLine.drawOn( gc );
      }
   }
}
```

```
ListBoxItemProvider
  &ListBoxItemProvider::drawEmphasis( IListBox*         listBox,
                                      IDMTargetEvent&   event,
                                      const TgtLocation& target )
  {
  // If same target, it's already drawn.
  if ( target == lastTarget )
    return *this;

  // Get the graphic context and set the drawing attributes.
  IGraphicContext
    gc( event.presSpace() );

  gc.setMixMode( IGraphicBundle::xor );
  gc.setDrawOperation( IGraphicBundle::frame );
  gc.setPenColor( IColor::white );
  gc.setPenWidth( 1 );

  // "Undraw" current target emphasis.
  draw( gc, listBox, lastTarget );

  // Set new target and draw it.
  lastTarget = target;
  draw( gc, listBox, lastTarget );

  event.releasePresSpace();
  return *this;
  }
```

The drawing is done using the mixed mode IGraphicBundle::xor. You do most target emphasis drawing this way because it makes removing the emphasis simple; you just redraw it to undo it.

The only remaining detail is to make sure that you draw target emphasis at the appropriate times and that you remove target emphasis when a user drags an item from your target window or drops an item on it. In this example, we make certain that we erase the previously drawn target emphasis by recording the location where we last drew it (with a special value to indicate that there was no target emphasis drawn). Drawing at a new location consists of drawing at the previous location (thereby erasing it) and recording the new location and drawing at it.

Normal drawing occurs in the item provider's provideEnterSupport function. Clean up on two other occasions, also:

- A user drags an item from the target window in the item provider's member function, provideLeaveSupport.

- A user drops an item on the target window in the item's targetDrop function.

We have already shown you all of this code except for the implementation of ListBoxItemProvider::provideLeaveSupport, which follows:

ListBoxItemProvider::provideLeaveSupport - dm\lboxdrag\lboxitem.cpp

```
Boolean ListBoxItemProvider ::
  provideLeaveSupport ( IDMTargetLeaveEvent& event )
  {
  IListBox
   *listBox = (IListBox*)( event.window() );
  this -> drawEmphasis( listBox,
                        event,
                        TgtLocation(ListBoxItem::after, nil) );
  return false;
  }
```

"Under the Covers"

In the rest of this chapter, we examine the implementation of Open Class Library's direct-manipulation support. You do not have to understand the implementation beyond the responsibilities you have as an implementor of direct-manipulation item and item provider classes. However, if you have previous experience with the direct-manipulation structures and the API of the OS/2 operating system, or you have experience with OLE objects and API in the Windows operating system, this additional insight into the implementation might be helpful.

A Peek at Platform Specifics

Given the power of direct manipulation as a user-interface technique, implementing support for it using a native API can be a fairly daunting task. To help you use the simplified set of C++ objects in Open Class Library, we describe the nature of the OS/2 and Windows operating systems objects that they represent.

OS/2 Operating System Objects

There are a large number of structures that OS/2 direct-manipulation support utilizes. The structures that define the representation of the objects being manipulated are as follows:

DRAGINFO

> Represents ongoing direct-manipulation operations.

DRAGITEM

> Represents the objects being manipulated by a user.

DRAGIMAGE

> Defines the representation of the objects being manipulated.

There are additional structures that contain higher-level objects, such as bit masks and string handles, and they are manipulated using various APIs. Discussion of these structures is beyond the scope of this book, so we do not cover them.

Windows Objects

The Windows direct-manipulation support utilizes OLE objects. The OLE objects that define the representation of the objects being manipulated are as follows:

IDragObject

Manages the transfer of data from the source to the target.

IDropSource

Processes the callback functions that dispatch source-related direct-manipulation events.

IDropTarget

Processes the callback functions that dispatch target-related direct-manipulation events.

There are additional objects and image-related structures. Discussion of these objects and structures are beyond the scope of this book, so we do not cover them.

An Overview of the Direct-Manipulation Framework Classes

This section provides a short explanation of Open Class Library's model for direct manipulation. We introduce the various classes that implement direct-manipulation support and describe briefly the responsibilities of each class. More important, we indicate what interest you will likely have in those classes.

The object diagram, shown in Figure 21-2, provides an overview of the objects involved in direct manipulation and the relationships between these objects. The "Drag Information" and "Drag Item" entries have different meanings for the OS/2 and Windows operating systems. In the OS/2 operating system, they represent the DRAGINFO and DRAGITEM structures, respectively. In the Windows operating system, they represent objects of the private classes, IDragInfo and IDragItem, respectively. The objects—actually, classes—of interest are as follows:

Handlers and Events

Windows that permit the user to directly manipulate their contents must have direct-manipulation handlers attached to them. As with other Open Class Library handlers, the direct-manipulation handlers operate on a set of event objects, in this case, those that encapsulate the desktop's drag-and-drop messages.

Your interest in these handlers is to attach them to your windows. Even that task is greatly simplified. For details, see "Enabling Drag and Drop" at the beginning of this chapter.

Operations

These objects—different kinds on the source and target sides of the operation—represent the pending direct-manipulation operation. The direct-manipulation handlers take care of the creation and deletion of these objects. You access these objects to get and set various attributes of the ongoing drag-and-drop operations. For more details, see "Direct Manipulation Operations," later in this chapter.

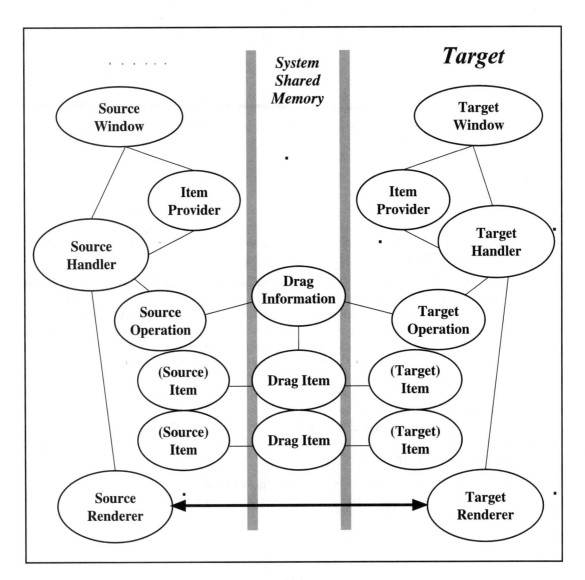

Figure 21-2. Direct-Manipulation Framework Objects.

Items

These objects represent the application objects being manipulated. Most of your efforts to support direct manipulation in your application involve deriving classes from the Open Class Library base item class. Much of the tailoring involves setting the attributes of these item objects. For details on how to define your direct-manipulation item classes, see "Direct-Manipulation Items," at the beginning of this chapter.

ItemProviders

These objects are extensions to the standard windows of your application. They make it possible for your windows to provide the direct-manipulation objects specific to your application.

Open Class Library supplies specialized provider classes for containers, entry fields, multiline edit controls, tool bars, and tool bar buttons. It also provides a class template that you can use to generate a provider class specific to your items. See "Providing Items to Be Dragged and Dropped," earlier in this chapter for details.

Renderers

These objects handle the transfer of items from the source to the target window. The base renderers that Open Class Library provides handle this transfer for the standard rendering techniques. These meet your needs in most cases.

For more details on how these objects work see "Rendering" at the end of this chapter.

Handlers and Events

Direct manipulation is accomplished by users pressing a mouse button and moving the mouse while they press the button. In the OS/2 operating system the, desktop handles the lower-level button-down and mouse-move events and translates them to direct-manipulation messages. In the Windows operating system, the message translation is achieved jointly via Open Class Library's direct-manipulation support and the desktop. These are the messages your window must handle to support direct manipulation.

In the context of Open Class Library design, these responsibilities are handled by objects of some IHandler-derived class. With a class that handles the direct-manipulation messages, attaching such handlers to your windows enables direct manipulation of the window's contents.

Open Class Library provides a set of classes, as pictured in Figure 21-3, to handle the direct-manipulation events.

IDMHandler

This is an abstract base class. It provides common implementation for each of the derived direct-manipulation handler classes. This class also provides some static member functions that provide support for attaching handlers to your windows, thereby enabling them for drag and drop. This default support is almost always all that you need in your applications.

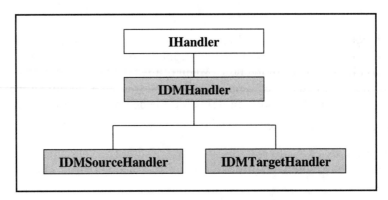

Figure 21-3. Direct-Manipulation Handler's Class Hierarchy.

IDMSourceHandler

This class provides support for the handling of direct-manipulation events for the source window.

IDMTargetHandler

This class provides support for the handling of direct-manipulation events for the target window.

The Default Source and Target Handlers

The enabling static functions of class IDMHandler, which we describe at the beginning of this chapter, attach the default handlers. These handlers are objects of the classes IDMSourceHandler and IDMTargetHandler or of classes derived from those classes. The default handler objects are maintained via static functions of class IDMHandler: defaultSourceHandler, setDefaultSourceHandler, defaultTargetHandler, and setDefaultTargetHandler.

You can access these default handlers and modify them by invoking handler functions that set the various handler attributes. For example, if your application uses some new rendering mechanism that you have implemented using derived IDMRenderer classes, you could add this rendering mechanism to all windows using code like the following example:

```
MySrcRenderer
  *pSrcRenderer = new MySourceRenderer;

MyTgtRenderer
  *pTgtRenderer = new MyTargetRenderer;

IDMHandler::defaultSourceHandler().addRenderer( pSrcRenderer );
IDMHandler::defaultTargetHandler().addRenderer( pTgtRenderer );
```

Make certain that the lifetime of such renderer objects spans the time that the default handlers will be using them and remove the renderers prior to deleting them. You can find out more about renderer objects in "Rendering" later in this chapter.

Replacing the Default Handlers

You can replace the default source and target handlers entirely. Usually, you only want to do this to override one of the virtual functions of one of the handler classes and to permit this modified handler to be attached to windows using the enable functions of `IDMHandler`. You specify the new default handlers via the `IDMHandler` functions `setDefaultSourceHandler` and `setDefaultTargetHandler`. Call these functions before enabling any windows for drag and drop.

Direct-Manipulation Operations

The information managed by the handlers is anchored by an *operation* object that represents the ongoing direct-manipulation operation. These objects are instances of the classes shown in Figure 21-4.

IDMOperation

This is an abstract base class that provides common behavior and implementation for the two concrete-derived classes.

IDMSourceOperation

This class represents a direct-manipulation operation from the source window's perspective. It basically encapsulates the attributes of the operation and permits manipulation of the attributes that are under the source window's control.

IDMTargetOperation

This class represents a direct-manipulation operation from the target window's perspective. It only permits changing the attributes that are under the target window's control.

The handler objects handle allocating and freeing these operation objects at the appropriate time. Most of the time, you interact with these operation objects when they are passed as arguments to some of the virtual functions of the item-provider class that you have written. Usually, you use the operation in one of two ways:

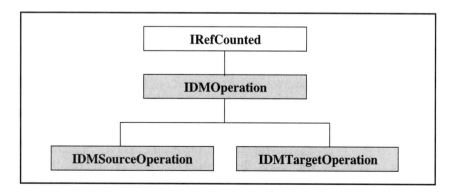

Figure 21-4. Direct-Manipulation Operation's Class Hierarchy.

- In its role as the collector of the items being manipulated. From this perspective, IDMOperation objects look like sequences of items.

- As the holder of the set of attributes that apply to the direct-manipulation operations as a whole. Examples of such attributes are the style used to display the objects being dragged and the type of operation being performed (move, copy, or link).

The Lifetime of Direct-Manipulation Operation Objects

IDMOperation is derived from class IRefCounted. The reasons for this are twofold as follows:

- The objects are allocated and freed by part of the direct-manipulation framework (not by you). However, you might want to keep a reference to the object beyond the period of time that the rest of the framework needs it.

- The objects might be needed long after the events that caused their creation have occurred. For example, rendering that takes a long time often must be done in a separate thread. As the other thread runs asynchronously, you need a more elaborate scheme to ensure that these objects "live" until any such secondary threads are completed.

You can ignore this complication by making sure you always access such reference-counted objects using the appropriate *reference* objects. In the case of IDMSourceOperation, and IDMTargetOperation, do the referencing using the corresponding nested Handle class.

For more information, see "Reference Counting" in Chapter 26, "Data Types."

Using Your Own Operation Classes

The operation classes encapsulate some of the low-level drag-and-drop APIs of the desktop. To give you control over the use of those APIs while still permitting you to take advantage of the robust function built into the direct-manipulation framework of Open Class Library, there is a way for you to replace the standard operation objects with objects of classes derived from the base IDMSourceOperation and IDMTargetOperation classes.

To modify this aspect of the behavior of the direct-manipulation framework, complete the following steps:

1. Derive from IDMSourceOperation or IDMTargetOperation or both, and override the virtual functions for which you want to modify the behavior.

2. Derive from the corresponding source or target handler classes or both.

3. Override the allocateOperation function of the handler class. Implement this function by allocating an object of your derived-operation class and returning a handle for it.

4. Make your derived handler or handlers the default as described in "Replacing the Default Handlers."

A C++ Design Note

The mechanism for replacing the operation classes that the direct-manipulation framework of Open Class Library uses demonstrates an important aspect of C++ class library and framework design. The problem is reconciling the power of a framework with the fact that by doing lots of work on your behalf, it becomes more difficult to tailor the framework's behavior. In this case, we find that the framework manages the complex task of creating and freeing these operation objects. However, if we were limited to using objects of the base class only, then we would fail to fully exploit the virtues of C++ inheritance.

A good way to measure the capabilities of a C++ class library or framework is to ask this question:

Can you readily override each of the key virtual
functions of each of the key objects in the framework?

In this instance, at least, with Open Class Library you can answer "Yes."

Rendering

The last set of objects that participate in direct manipulation are the *renderers*. These are objects of Open Class Library's rendering classes `IDMSourceRenderer` and `IDMTargetRenderer`. Figure 21-5 shows the renderer class hierarchy.

Renderer objects transmit the direct-manipulation items between the source and target windows after a user drops them. The transfer occurs using some protocol mutually agreed to by the source and target applications. With the Open Class Library framework, the agreement as to what protocol to use is negotiated between the source and target handlers. Each handler maintains a collection of renderers. The handler searches this collection to find a renderer to use for each item. Renderers are chosen depending on the type, supported operations, and supported rendering-mechanism and format attributes of the item.

The default source and target handlers have a single renderer object attached to them. The source handler attaches an object of type `IDMSourceRenderer`. The target handler attaches an object of type `IDMTargetRenderer`. These default renderers can usually handle all of your direct-manipulation operations. They support each of the protocols we described in the

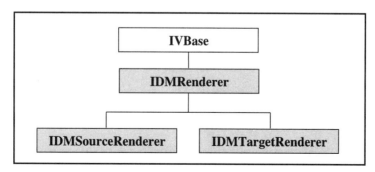

Figure 21-5. Renderer Class Hierarchy.

section "Item Attributes—Rendering Mechanisms and Format." These renderers are sufficient because they fully support the efficient transfer of arbitrary item contents. So, if you want to transfer unusual data, you do not need a new renderer. Instead, you set your item contents to the data you want the renderer to transfer.

Adding Your Own Rendering Formats

If you need to support additional rendering mechanisms and formats, derive new classes from IDMSourceRenderer and IDMTargetRenderer. Create objects of each renderer class and add them to the default source and target renderers using the addRenderer member function.

Rendering requires handling of an additional set of direct-manipulation window events. The source and target handlers dispatch those events to the renderers in much the same way that some events are eventually dispatched to the items. To add a new rendering mechanism, process the events by overriding the functions sourceRender, targetRender, and so on. Alternatively, you can accept the bulk of the default processing of these events and override the lower-level functions that do the renderer-specific work. These are the functions doRender, renderAtSource, and so on

The following drag information viewer example shows an interesting twist: it replaces the default target renderer with one that allows all drag objects to be dropped on the viewer. Subsequently, the viewer displays the information contained within the underlying drag objects and structures. Override the IDMTargetRenderer member functions, canRender and targetRender, in the new class, DragViewTargetRenderer. Relevant sections of code are shown in the following example:

Drag Information Viewer - dm\dragview\dragview.cpp

```
DragViewTargetRender
  targetRenderer;
IDMRenderer::setDefaultTargetRenderer( targetRenderer );
.
.
.
IDM::DropIndicator DragViewTargetRenderer::
                  canRender( const IDMItem::Handle& )
  {
  return( IDM:: ok );
  }

DragViewTargetRenderer& DragViewTargetRenderer::
            targetRender( IDMTargetDropEvent&    event,
                          const IDMItem::Handle& dragItem )
  {
  IMODTRACE_DEVELOP( "DragViewTargetRenderer::targetRender" );

  // Call targetDrop override for the drag viewer item.
  Boolean
    bRc = dragItem->targetDrop( event );

  // Indicate to the source that rendering of the item has
  // completed.
  informSourceOfCompletion( dragItem,
                            ((bRc) ? IDM::targetSuccessful
                                   : IDM::targetFailed) );

  return( *this );
  }
```

Detailed instructions for overriding the rest of these functions are beyond the scope of this book. Refer to the Open Class Library reference documentation and rely on your understanding of the underlying desktop's operations. Open Class Library supports the common rendering mechanisms and formats and provides the means of rendering your items that should satisfy most of your requirements.

Conclusion

In this chapter, we described Open Class Library components that you can use to add drag-and-drop support to your applications. Adding that support is easy. It involves the following tasks:

- Adding drag-and-drop handlers to your windows

- Deriving direct-manipulation item classes to hold the data that you want a user to drag and drop.

- Overriding the important functions in your item class to get application-specific behavior when a user drops items on your windows.

- Constructing an item-provider object to attach to your window that ensures your items get used.

We described each of these tasks in this chapter and we provided detail on all of the issues related to adding drag-and-drop support to your application. Four separate full-function examples were presented to show you how to do that. Finally, we discussed the details of the design and implementation of Open Class Library's direct-manipulation support to help you to better understand how it works.

Chapter 22

Dynamic Data Exchange Framework

- Describes Open Class Library classes that you can use to add Dynamic Data Exchange support to your applications
- Describes the IDDETopicServer, IDDEClientConversation, IDDEEvent, IDDEAcknowledgeEvent, IDDEClientAcknowledgeEvent, IDDEAcknowledgePokeEvent, IDDEDataEvent, IDDEAcknowledgeExecuteEvent, IDDEServerAcknowledgeEvent, IDDEExecuteEvent, IDDESetAcknowledgeEvent, IDDEClientHotLinkEvent, IDDERequestDataEvent, IDDEServerHotLinkEvent, IDDEPokeEvent, IDDEBeginEvent, IDDEEndEvent, IDDEClientEndEvent, IDDEClientHotLinkSet, IDDEActiveServer, and IDDEActiveServerSet classes
- Read Chapter 4 before reading this chapter.
- Chapter 20 covers related material.

Dynamic Data Exchange (DDE) is a client-server protocol for communicating between two applications running in the same machine. In a client-server model, the client application sends requests to a server application. The server application handles these requests from client applications and returns information or data to the client, if appropriate. In this chapter when we use "data," we are referring to a raw buffer of data; when we use "information," we are referring to the data as well as information about the data. DDE is a common protocol that is implemented by all of the Windows operating system platforms as well as the OS/2 operating system.

This chapter describes the Open Class Library classes that comprise the DDE framework. First, we provide an overview of DDE to define the native operating system function that is abstracted in Open Class Library's DDE framework. Next, we briefly discuss Open Class Library's DDE design. Then, we provide a topic on how to add DDE client support to an application. This includes a detailed discussion of the important DDE client functions and DDE events that you use to pass information to an application. Finally, we provide a topic on how to add server support to an application including, again, a detailed discussion of the DDE events that you use to pass information to the application program.

DDE Overview

In the following topics, we describe DDE in terms of the functionality provided by the underlying operating system's implementation. Because DDE is based on the client-server application model, a DDE client application must request a conversation with a DDE server application. Once the server accepts a conversation, the client can send a variety of predefined requests to the server. A server application sends information or data plus positive and negative acknowledgements to client applications. A server application cannot send requests to a client application. The only unsolicited communication that a DDE server application can have with a client application is to notify it that it is ending a conversation.

DDE can be difficult to use for a number of reasons. Some of the larger issues are as follows:

- The DDE protocol lacks a clear definition, thus requiring study to implement it correctly.

- Exchanging data between applications requires memory. You must correctly coordinate the allocation, accessing, and freeing of memory between the client and server applications.

- You must register all private DDE data formats in the operating system's atom table.

- You must create a window message queue for each conversation because all communication occurs through operating system messages.

The primary reason to use Open Class Library's DDE framework is that these issues are taken care of and hidden from you by the framework. As a result, you can concentrate your programming efforts with DDE at a much higher level of abstraction. Using Open Class Library's DDE framework, you can focus on requesting or providing data without focusing on the ugly operating-system-level details of DDE.

DDE Is Transaction-Based

All communications between DDE client and server applications occur within the context of a DDE *conversation*. Once a DDE client application has successfully initiated a conversation with a DDE server application, all subsequent communications are in the form of asynchronous transactions. These transactions are asynchronous because they are implemented using operating system messages that are posted, not sent, to the other application. This can lead to complications because the DDE messages and control blocks that the operating system messages pass contain a minimal amount of information to tie a response to a particular request.

As a result of the possible confusion inherent in any asynchronous communications, the DDE protocol requires server applications to respond to requests from any one client in the exact order that they are received in. The Open Class Library's DDE framework fulfills this requirement. On the server side, it enforces this synchronization; on the client side, it tracks all outstanding transactions, making sure they are responded to in the correct order. It also provides you with information about your original request along with the response data.

Applications, Topics, and Items

For the purpose of initiating a DDE conversation, the conversation is uniquely identified by the application name of the DDE server and the name of the *topic*. A topic is a logical data context. For example, for a word processing or spreadsheet DDE server application, the topic is usually the file name of a document or spreadsheet. For a DDE news server, the topic could be an area of interest. Once a conversation is initiated, it is uniquely identified by a pair of window handles, one provided by the client application and one by the server application.

An *item* is a named data object that can be passed as part of a transaction within a DDE conversation. An item can be as small as a simple data type, such as an integer or character string, or as large as a bitmap or data file.

Data Formats

Whenever a DDE application requests or provides data, it must specify the format of the data. This is the way DDE applications determine how to package and unpackage, or interpret, the data that they pass back and forth. Before a DDE application can use a data format, the application must ensure that the data format is uniquely identified by registering its name in the operating system's atom table. The operating system defines a number of constant names for industry-standard data formats and adds them to its atom table.

Open Class Library's DDE framework ensures that any format that your application specifies is defined in the atom table. You can forget about atoms being used. An Open Class DDE client application simply requests data in a format the DDE server application it is conversing with supports. An Open Class DDE server application provides data in formats that DDE client applications can process.

`IDDE::Format` in `IDDECOMM.HPP` contains synonyms for the DDE formats that are predefined in and common to both the OS/2 and Windows operating systems. The standard format for exchanging text data is `IDDE::textFormat`. It is the default format for all functions that require a format. Table 22-1 provides a brief description of the formats contained in the `IDDE` class.

Table 22-1 (Part 1 of 2). DDE Data Formats

IDDE::Format	Description
bitmapFormat	Specifies that the data is a BITMAPINFO2 structure.
codePageTextFormat	Specifies that the data is contained in a CPTEXT structure. The text portion of the structure must be in IDDE::textFormat format. Use this format to send text in a code page other than the default.
dibFormat	Specifies that the data is a Device-Independant Bitmap File Format (DIB) structure.
difFormat	Specifies that the data is in Data Interchange Format (DIF). Software Arts developed this format for exchanging data with Visicalc spreadsheet programs.
displayBitmapFormat	Specifies that the data is a bitmap in a private data format.
displayMetafileFormat	Specifies that the data is a metafile in a private data format.

Table 22-1 (Part 2 of 2). DDE Data Formats

IDDE::Format	Description
displayMetafilePictureFormat	Specifies that the data is a metafile picture in a private data format.
displayTextFormat	Specifies that the data is text in a private data format.
linkFormat	Specifies that the data is in link-file format which contains the information necessary to establish a DDE hot link. You typically use it in paste-link clipboard operations. The layout is: applicationName(0x00)topicName(0x00)itemName(0x00)(0x00).
metafileFormat	Specifies that the data is a metafile.
metafilePictureFormat	Specifies that the data is a Metafile Picture Format (MFP) structure.
oemTextFormat	Specifies that the data is in the same format as IDDE::textFormat.
paletteFormat	Specifies that the data is a PALETTEINFO structure.
sylkFormat	Specifies that the data is in Microsoft Symbolic Link format. Use it to exchange spreadsheet information in an ASCII-text format.
textFormat	Specifies that the data is a null-(0x00) terminated character string. The data can include a carriage return (0x0D), a line feed (0x0A), or both to mark the end of a line. This is the standard format for exchanging text.
tiffFormat	Specifies that the data is in Tag Image File Format (TIFF). Aldus, Microsoft, and Hewlett-Packard developed this to describe bitmapped data.

Note: In the Windows platforms, specify any private format as a string not as an atom. Simply pass the atom inside of double quotes, and the DDE framework converts it to an atom.

The DDE Framework Design

On the DDE server side, IDDETopicServer is the primary class. It represents a DDE server for a single topic. An IDDETopicServer object can have as many concurrent conversations as you want, and these conversations can be with the same or different applications. The only restriction is that they must all be on the same topic.

On the DDE client side, IDDEClientConversation is the primary class. An IDDEClientConversation object represents a single conversation with a single DDE server application. You can reuse an IDDEClientConversation object. For example, when you end a conversation with a DDE server application, you can use the IDDEClientConversation object to begin a conversation with any DDE server application on any topic.

IDDEClientConversation and IDDETopicServer contain virtual callback functions that provide you with DDE conversation information. These functions typically pass an IDDEEvent object, or one of its derived classes that contains a DDE request or response. Most of these functions have a default behavior that typically does nothing. Override each callback function that you need and provide an appropriate behavior.

For an `IDDETopicServer` object, the callback functions pass requests for data or requests for the server to carry out an action. The default implementation for most of these functions returns `false` to indicate that the DDE server does not support this particular DDE transaction type. To support a particular transaction type, override the function and provide an appropriate implementation. This typically involves setting information or data into the passed DDE event.

`IDDETopicServer::requestData` is pure virtual, so you must derive from `IDDETopicServer` to provide an implementation for it. We made this function pure virtual so that you cannot create an `IDDETopicServer` object. We designed it this way because, essentially, it does nothing by default. Thus, you need to provide implementations for its callback functions for it to have value. The rest of the callback functions have a default implementation so that you can quickly and easily derive a class from `IDDETopicServer`, adding your own implementations for the remaining functions. This enables you to build a DDE server application incrementally, supporting only the DDE transaction types that make sense for your application.

For an `IDDEClientConversation` object, the callback functions pass you the responses that the DDE server application has sent to your requests. The default implementation for these functions is to do nothing. However, because you made the request to the DDE server application, you want the response the server has sent to you. Override these callback functions to process the responses, and the data and information that is part of each response.

`IDDEClientConversation::data` is pure virtual, also. Thus, you must derive from `IDDEClientConversation` to provide an implementation for it. We made the `data` function pure virtual for the same reasons we made the `requestData` function of `IDDETopicServer` pure virtual: You cannot create an `IDDEClientConversation` object because the class cannot do anything reasonable with the responses sent by a server application. Provide implementations for the callback functions to turn this into a useful class for your applications. As in the `IDDETopicServer` class, the remainder of the callback functions have default implementations so that you can quickly and easily derive a class with minimal capability from `IDDEClientConversation`. This enables you to add function to your DDE client application incrementally by providing implementations for the other functions based on the needs of your application.

Start the Message Queue!

Because DDE uses object windows to communicate, an application that uses it needs to process window messages. Even if your application has no interface components, the `IThread` member function `processMsgs` must be executed. Although there are several ways to accomplish this, you normally call `IApplication::current().run()`.

The Generic DDE Event Classes

Because IDDETopicServer and IDDEClientConversation objects pass data and information in the form of event objects, we describe the DDE events that DDE clients and servers use in this topic. We discuss the events that are specific to a client or server application later in this chapter. Figure 22-1 shows the hierarchy of DDE classes.

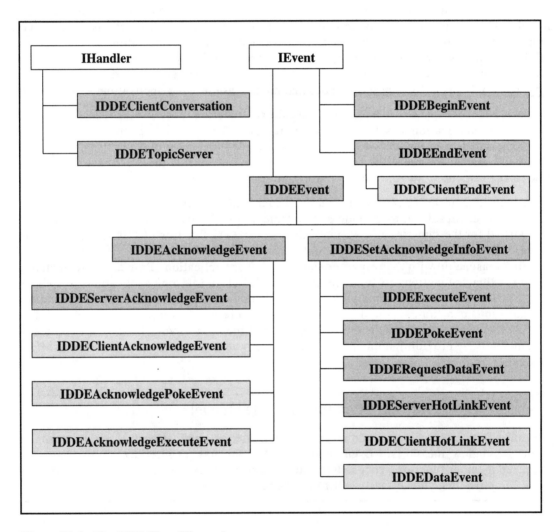

Figure 22-1. The DDE Class Hierarchy.

The IDDEEvent Class

IDDEEvent is the main DDE Event class from which most other DDE event classes derive. The only exceptions to this are the event classes associated with beginning and ending a conversation: IDDEBeginEvent, IDDEEndEvent, and IDDEClientEndEvent. This class provides two important functions: the item and format functions. The item function returns the name of the data item for which the event is sent. The format function returns the name of the format that the data item is either rendered in or requested to be rendered in. Because an object of an IDDEvent derived class is usually passed, you can usually obtain the names of the item and data format.

The IDDEAcknowledgeEvent Class

IDDEAcknowledgeEvent is the parent of all DDE event classes used to pass acknowledgement information. For many DDE transactions, one of the valid responses—and in some cases, the only allowed response—is an acknowledgement. These acknowledgements can be positive or negative. Negative acknowledgements indicate that the transaction was not processed and contain information about why the acknowledgement is negative. The IDDEAcknowledgeEvent class contains the member functions common to all acknowledgement event classes that Open Class Library's DDE framework provides. The following list describes each IDDEAcknowledgeEvent function:

- Call isAckPositive first for any event derived from IDDEAcknowledgeEvent. If the function returns true, the acknowledgement is positive, and there is no reason to call any of the class's other functions. If it returns false, use the other IDDEAcknowledgeEvent member functions to determine why the acknowledgement is negative.

- The isApplicationBusy function returns true if the application you are conversing with is too busy to process your request.

- The isMessageUnderstood function returns false if the application you are conversing with cannot recognize your request. The function might return false if you request a DDE server application to execute an unsupported command.

- The DDE protocol provides for one byte of application-specific data that can be set on any acknowledgement. Normally, this field is used only for negative acknowledgements, but the protocol does not prevent it from being set on a positive acknowledgement. The applicationSpecificData function returns this byte of data. The format of the data in this field must be defined and recognized by any pair of applications using it.

The IDDEClientAcknowledgeEvent Class

IDDEClientAcknowledgeEvent, which is derived from IDDEAcknowledgeEvent, provides three functions for determining what type of transaction the acknowledgement is for. These functions are required because the acknowledged function and the

`IDDEClientAcknowledgeEvent` event are used to pass acknowledgements for the `requestData`, `beginHotLink`, and `endHotLink` transactions.   Use the functions `isAckToRequestData`, `isAckToBeginHotLink`, and `isAckToEndHotLink` to determine the initiating transaction.

The IDDESetAcknowledgeInfoEvent Class

`IDDESetAcknowledgeInfoEvent` is the parent of all DDE event classes for which you can set acknowledgement information.   Many of the transactions (defined by the DDE protocol) accept an acknowledgement as a valid response from the server application.   Some of the transactions, such as the request for a hot link, require an acknowledgement for the response. In some cases, a DDE server application can request an acknowledgement from a DDE client application.   In all cases where you might need to send an acknowledgement to the application you are conversing with, you are passed an object of a class derived from `IDDESetAcknowledgeInfoEvent`. Use this class's functions to provide details about a negative acknowledgement.   You can also use the application-specific data field on positive acknowledgements.   The following list describes each `IDDESetAcknowledgeInfoEvent` function:

- Call `setApplicationBusy` to set the application busy flag if you cannot process a request or the information returned in response to a request because your application is busy.

- Call `setMessageNotUnderstood` to set the flag indicating that you could not recognize a request or a response to a request that was sent by the application with which you are conversing.

- The DDE protocol provides for one byte of application-specific data that can be set on any acknowledgement.   Use `setApplicationSpecificData` to set the contents of this field.   Normally, this field is used only for negative acknowledgements, but the protocol does not prevent it from being set on a positive acknowledgement.   The format of the data contained in this field must be defined and recognized by any pair of applications using it.

The IDDEEndEvent Class

`IDDEEndEvent` is the parent of the `IDDEClientEndEvent` class.   It provides a function common to all events used to notify you that a conversation is ending: the `sourceOfEnd` function.   Use it to determine why the conversation is ending.   The possible values and meanings of the `Source` enumeration returned by this function follow:

- `client` indicates that the DDE client application that this `IDDETopicServer` object is conversing with is ending the conversation.

- `server` indicates that the DDE server application that this `IDDEClientConversation` object is conversing with is ending the conversation.

- `error` indicates that this `IDDEClientConversation` or `IDDETopicServer` object is ending the conversation due to an error encountered trying to communicate with the other application in the client-server pair.   This value is used particularly when the object receives a bad return code when trying to post information to the conversing application.

This typically occurs if the conversing application terminates without ending the DDE conversation. In our original design, the object threw an exception when one of these errors occurred. We later decided that throwing an exception, which would likely terminate the application, was not warranted just because the conversing application terminated. Instead, the application receiving the error cleans up and ends the conversation, and then notifies you by passing you an IDDEEndEvent object or IDDEClientEndEvent object using conversationEnded.

DDE Clients

IDDEClientConversation is the key DDE client abstraction in Open Class Library. The other classes for implementing a DDE client are the DDE event classes. The hierarchy of client DDE event classes is shown in Figure 22-1. We cover each event class in detail in the topic covering the DDE request where it is actually used. For example, we cover the IDDEAcknowledgeExecuteEvent class in the topic "Executing Remote Commands."

To provide DDE client support in your application, follow these steps. For multiple concurrent conversations, follow these same steps for each concurrent conversation. (Also remember that although an IDDEClientConversation object represents a single conversation with a single server, you can reuse the object for a subsequent conversation once you end the current conversation.)

1. Derive a class from IDDEClientConversation to provide implementations for the virtual callback functions that you need. Provide an implementation for the data pure virtual function.

2. Create an object of the class that you derived from IDDEClientConversation.

3. Initiate a conversation with a DDE server application on a specific topic.

4. Request services from the DDE server. These requests for services (transactions) are usually requests for data, requests to accept data from you, or requests to execute commands on your behalf.

5. Handle the request responses that the DDE server sends you in your virtual callback function overrides.

6. End the conversation with this DDE server application when you do not need any more services from this particular DDE server.

7. Destroy the object of the class derived from IDDEClientConversation or reuse the object by starting over at Step 3.

These are all the steps you need for adding DDE client function to your application.

Constructing a DDE Client

Open Class Library provides two constructors for creating IDDEClientConversation objects. The default constructor's signature is as follows:

```
IDDEClientConversation( Boolean useEventThread = true );
```

Notice that the only argument to the default constructor is a Boolean, which defaults to true. This argument specifies whether the IDDEClientConversation object can create a separate thread to process incoming messages from the DDE server application. We recommended that you let the argument default to true because you gain benefits from allowing a secondary thread to process incoming messages.

Note: This argument has no effect in the Windows operating system due to a restriction in its native DDE implementation. Therefore, the following information regarding the benefits of using threads does not apply in Windows platforms.

When you specify true for the useEventThread argument, the constructor creates an OS/2 operating system queue using the DosCreateQueue API. Next, the constructor creates a secondary thread, passing it a function that remains in a while (true) loop, reading and processing the IEvent objects in the queue using the DosReadQueue API. Every time the DDE client application receives an inbound message from the DDE server application, the IDDEClientConversation object writes an IEvent object to this queue using the DosWriteQueue API. You gain two benefits by letting the IDDEClientConversation object use a separate thread:

- The IDDEClientConversation object can guarantee that you process all messages in the exact order that they are received from the server application.

  All messages from the DDE server application are added to the end of an OS/2 operating system queue in the form of an IEvent object. They are only removed from this queue in the order they are received, and are, therefore, processed in the correct order.

  If you do not allow the IDDEClientConversation object to use a secondary thread, the incoming DDE messages are processed as they are received. It might seem that this would guarantee that they are processed in the correct order, but it doesn't. The IDDEClientConversation object passes information from the server message to the application using a callback function. If the callback function creates a modal dialog, the dialog creates its own message queue and dispatches messages from it. This could cause your application to process messages from the DDE server application out of order, depending on how quickly the user dismisses the dialog. Although your application does not finish processing the current message until the dialog is dismissed, the dialog could dispatch subsequent messages from the DDE server application during this time.

- The IDDEClientConversation object can help you avoid violating the operating system's 1/10-second rule described in Chapter 20, "Applications and Threads." You cannot accidentally violate this rule because the secondary queue is created without a message queue.

If you choose to specify false for the useEventThread argument, and in all cases for the Windows platforms, avoid using dialogs inside any of the callback functions and always return promptly from the callbacks for the previous reasons. If you let the useEventThread argument default to true, the IDDEClientConversation object throws an IOutOfSystemResource exception if the thread creation fails.

The second `IDDEClientConversation` constructor has the following signature:

```
IDDEClientConversation( const char* applicationName,
                        const char* topicName,
                        Boolean useEventThread = true );
```

The application and topic names are used to begin a conversation with a DDE server application with the specified name on the specified topic after the `IDDEClientConversation` object has been successfully initialized. This constructor works as a short cut to eliminate the need for calling `begin`. If you use this constructor, you don't know if the conversation has been successfully initiated because constructors do not return anything. So, you must use `inConversation` to find out if the implicit call to `begin` was successful.

Both constructors create an `IObjectWindow` object to communicate with DDE server applications. Because the `IDDEClientConversation` class derives from the `IHandler` class, you have a complex handler that you work with a bit differently than you do with other handlers in Open Class Library. One major difference is that the `IDDEClientConversation` object adds itself as a handler to the `IObjectWindow` object; you do not add it.

Each `IDDEClientConversation` object also creates several collections to keep state information. The collections of interest to you are: an `IQueue` collection of transactions for which the responses are outstanding and an `ISet` collection of active hot links.

The `IDDEClientConversation` copy constructor is private, so you cannot make a copy of an `IDDEClientConversation` object. Because these objects communicate with other processes using only window handles to identify themselves, it would not make sense to construct one `IDDEClientConversation` from another. (What would this new object communicate with?) It does make sense to create a new `IDDEClientConversation` object using one of the two regular constructors. For the same reason, `IDDEClientConversation::operator=` is also private.

Requesting a DDE Conversation

In the previous topic, we described a way to begin a DDE conversation as part of constructing an `IDDEClientConversation`. The second way you can request a conversation is to call `begin` on the `IDDEClientConversation` object. For this function, specify the name of the application you want to have a conversation with and the name of the topic you want to have a conversation about. For example:

```
Boolean bStarted =
  aConversation.begin( "Financial Server","NYSE Stock Quotes")
```

The `begin` function returns `true` if the `IDDEClientConversation` object initiates a conversation with the requested application on the requested topic. If the `IDDEClientConversation` object is already conversing on any topic, it throws an `IInvalidRequest` exception. Again, you can reuse the `IDDEClientConversation` object for a subsequent conversation once you end the current conversation.

The `IDDEClientConversation` class provides a second version of `begin` that requires an `IWindowHandle` reference as its only argument. With this version of `begin`, you can use objects of this class without the standard conversation initialization as defined by the DDE protocol. However, you must use this version if you have already agreed with another application to have a DDE conversation and have an alternate method of exchanging the required window handles. For this version of begin pass the window handle that the DDE server application provides.

You can obtain the window handle that the IDDEClientConversation object uses for conversing with server applications by calling clientHandle. One example for bypassing normal conversation initialization is to use DDE for direct manipulation. Because you are already communicating with the other process and have an alternate means of exchanging your window handles, you might choose to use this version of begin.

Requesting Data

Use requestData to request data from a server application, specifying the name of the data item and, optionally, the format of the data. The format defaults to IDDE::textFormat. For example:

```
aConversation.requestData( "XYZ Corp." );
```

The IDDEClientConversation object throws an IInvalidRequest exception if it is not currently conversing with a server application.

A server application can respond to a request for data in one of two ways. It can either send the data item in the requested format to the client application or send a negative acknowledgement indicating that it cannot provide the data item in the requested format.

DDE Data

The DDE Framework gets data from applications in the form of a void* pointer to a data buffer and a length. DDE gives you data in the form of an IString object. Thus, the IString object may contain a trailing null character. This occurs if the application that provides the data counts the null-terminating character as part of the buffer.

Strip any trailing nulls from the IString object before performing any C++ string operations on the contents, such as using strcat for concatenation. IString::stripTrailing strips all trailing nulls in an IString buffer.

If the server application sends the requested data item, the IDDEClientConversation object creates an IDDEDataEvent object and passes a reference to this event by calling data. Because this is a pure virtual function you must provide an implementation for it. You can call the following functions of the IDDEDataEvent object to get detailed information about the event:

- data

  Returns an IString object containing the data you requested from the server application.

- isAckRequested

Returns `true` if the server application requests an acknowledgement when the client application receives the data. If the server requests an acknowledgement, the `IDDEClientConversation` object automatically sends it. The `IDDEClientConversation` object uses the value returned from the `data` function to determine whether to send a positive or negative acknowledgement to the server application. If it returns `true`, it sends a positive acknowledgement. If it returns `false`, it sends a negative acknowledgement. If the server application does not request an acknowledgement, the return value of the `data` function is not used. The client application cannot send an unsolicited acknowledgement.

- `isDataFromHotLink`

  You need the `isDataFromHotlink` function because `IDDEClientConversation` uses the `data` function and `IDDEDataEvent` event to pass data for both data requests and hot links. Returns `false` if the server application sends the data item in response to a `requestData`. It returns `true` if the server application sends the data item because of a data item change for an active hot link. (Hot links are described in the next topic.)

If the server application sends a negative acknowledgement to the data request, the `IDDEClientConversation` object creates an `IDDEClientAcknowledgeEvent` object and passes a reference to this event by calling `acknowledged`.

Requesting a Data Hot Link

The DDE protocol supports *hot links*, ongoing links to data items. Once you establish a hot link with a DDE server application for a particular data item, the server informs you whenever the value of the data changes. To request a hot link to a data item with a server application, use `beginHotLink`. Its prototype follows:

```
IDDEClientConversation
   &beginHotLink( const char*   item,
                  IDDE::Format  format = IDDE::textFormat,
                  Boolean       sendData = true,
                  Boolean       pacing = false );
```

Just as for `requestData`, the only required argument is the name of the data item. The first optional argument is the format you want the data to be rendered in. The format defaults to `IDDE::textFormat`. Use the two additional optional arguments to customize the type of hot link you are requesting.

The first of these arguments specifies the type of hot link you are requesting. If you specify `true` for the `sendData` argument (the default), you are requesting a *data hot link*. If a data hot link is accepted, the DDE server application sends you a copy of the data item every time its value changes. If you specify `false` for the `sendData` argument, you are requesting a *notification hot link*. If this type of hot link is accepted, the server notifies you every time the data changes, but the new value is not sent.

The second optional argument specifies whether you want the DDE server application to pace the rate at which updates for this data item are sent to you. The default for this argument is `false`. If you specify `true` for the pacing argument, every time the DDE server application sends either data or a notification for this data item, it waits until it receives an acknowl-

---

Tuning Your Hot Links

A hot link can seriously impact the performance of your application in two situations. The first occurs when you have a highly active hot link that is flooding your application with hot-link updates. The second occurs when you have a hot link that involves transferring large amounts of data with each hot-link update.

You can prevent these situations from degrading your application's performance:

- When you begin the hot link, specify `false` for the `sendData` argument of `requestHotLink`. When it is critical to update your local copy of the data item, call `requestData` to obtain the current value of the data item from the server. This is an especially appropriate technique when you have a hot link to a data item that changes values frequently. You can also use this technique for large data items.

- When you begin the hot link, specify `true` for the pacing argument of `requestHotLink`. This prevents subsequent hot-link updates from being sent to your application until it has finished processing the current update. This is an appropriate technique when you have a hot link to large data items or need a long time to process data items. This technique is not as helpful for data items whose values change frequently.

---

edgement from you indicating that you are ready for any additional updates. The `IDDEClientConversation` object sends this acknowledgement automatically when you return from the `data` or `hotLinkInform` callback functions; it uses the returned value to determine whether to send a positive or negative acknowledgement.

The `IDDEClientConversation` object throws an `IInvalidRequest` exception if it is not currently conversing or if it already has an active hot link for this data item in the requested format. Note that you can request as many hot links as you want for an item, as long as they are all for different formats. The server can respond to this request with either a positive or negative acknowledgement. Request the data item using `requestData` if you want an initial value for the data item because the server application can only send an acknowledgement in response to a request for a hot link according to the DDE protocol.

The `IDDEClientConversation` object creates an `IDDEClientAcknowledgeEvent` object and passes a reference to it by calling the `acknowledged` callback function.

Handling Hot Link Data

Once you have established a data hot link, the server sends you the new value of the data item every time the value of the data item changes in the DDE server application. When the `IDDEClientConversation` object receives the updated data item, it creates an `IDDEDataEvent` object and passes a reference to this event when calling the `data` function. Again, this is a pure virtual function so you must override the function to provide an implementation for it.

We described the three functions that the `IDDEDataEvent` objects provide, `data`, `isAckRequested`, and `isDataFromHotLink`, in the "Requesting Data" topic earlier in this chapter. See that topic for the description of the `IDDEDataEvent` class and its member functions.

The `isAckRequested` function returns `true` if the DDE server application requested an acknowledgement, which it does if pacing is active for the hot link. The `IDDEClientConversation` object automatically sends the acknowledgement to the server if it has been requested. The `IDDEClientConversation` object uses the return value from the `data` function to determine whether to send a positive or negative acknowledgement to the server application.

Handling Hot Link Notifications

Once you have established a notification hot link, the server sends a notification that the value of the data item has changed every time the value of the data item changes in the DDE server application. When the `IDDEClientConversation` object receives the notification, it creates an `IDDEClientHotLinkEvent` object and passes a reference to this event by calling `hotLinkInform`. Explicitly request the updated data item from the DDE server application using `requestData` to get the new value.

The `IDDEClientHotLinkEvent` class has two member functions, `isAckRequested` and `isDataRequested`. Do not call `isDataRequested` in this context because it would not make sense to do so. You already know that `hotLinkInform` is called only for notification hot links (where data is never sent). Open Class Library provides `isDataRequested` only because each `IDDEClientConversation` object also keeps `IDDEClientHotLinkEvent` objects in an `ISet` object. This is how `IDDEClientConversation` keeps track of all of its active hot links. In this context, you need the function to determine what type of hot link the object represents.

The `isAckRequested` function returns `true` if the DDE server application requested an acknowledgement, which it does if pacing is active for the hot link. The `IDDEClientConversation` object automatically sends the acknowledgement to the server if it is requested. The `IDDEClientConversation` object uses the return value from the `hotLinkInform` function to determine whether to send a positive or negative acknowledgement to the server application.

Obtaining Information about Active Hot Links

Use the `hotLinks` function to obtain the current set of active hot links. The `hotLinkCount` function returns the number of currently active hot links for this `IDDEClientConversation` object. Each `IDDEClientConversation` object uses an `ISet` object to keep track of all of the active hot links. The prototype of `hotLinks` is as follows:

```
IDDEClientConversation
   &hotLinks( IDDEClientHotLinkSet& hotLinkSet );
```

`IDDEClientHotLinkSet` derives from `ISet` and is defined in `IDDECSET.HPP`. Include this header file to use the `hotLinks` function. This separate header file contains the collection classes that the `IDDEClientConversation` class uses. This technique reduces overhead due to static functions created by the collection template classes if you don't use any of the functions that take or return a collection class.

To get the set of all hot links, create an IDDEClientHotLinkSet object and call hotLinks. The IDDEClientConversation object creates a copy of each IDDEClientHotLinkEvent object in its internal hot link set and adds it to the set. If you remove any of these event objects from the set, you must delete them when you are through using them. Open Class Library provides an IDDEClientHotLinkSet destructor that deletes each of the IDDEClientHotLinkEvent objects in the set.

Use IDDEClientHotLinkEvent::isAckRequested to determine if a hot link supports pacing and IDDEClientHotLinkEvent::isDataRequested to determine if a hot link is a data or notification hot link. Use the IDDEEvent item and format functions to obtain the remaining information about each hot link.

The primary reason for obtaining this set of hot links from an IDDEClientConversation object is to make the set of active hot links in your client application persistent. You can save the information contained in this set when your application ends, and then use it to request the same set of hot links the next time your application runs.

Ending Hot Links

The IDDEClientConversation class provides two functions for ending hot links, endHotLink and endHotLinks. To end a single hot link, call endHotLink, specifying the name of the data item and, optionally, the format of the data. The format defaults to IDDE::textFormat. For example, if you have multiple active hot links, all in different formats, with a DDE server application on the "XYZ Corp" data item, end just one of the hot links as follows:

```
aConversation.endHotLink("XYZ Corp", IDDE::textFormat);
```

Use endHotLinks to end multiple hot links with one function call. The endHotLinks function has one optional argument, the name of the data item, which defaults to 0. To end all hot links for all data formats of a particular data item, specify the name of the data item. For example, the following code ends all hot links to the "XYZ Corp" data item for all data formats:

```
aConversation.endHotLinks("XYZ Corp");
```

To end all hot links for all data items for an IDDEClientConversation object, call endHotLinks with no parameters. The IDDEClientConversation object throws an IInvalidRequest exception if it is not currently conversing, or if no active hot links match the arguments specified.

The server application can respond to an endHotLink or endHotLinks request with either a positive or negative acknowledgement. For either one, the IDDEClientConversation object creates an IDDEClientAcknowledgeEvent object and passes a reference to this event by calling acknowledged.

Poking Data

The DDE protocol supports the concept of *poking data* from a DDE client application to a DDE server application. Poking data is a request to a DDE server application to set a specified data item to a value passed by the client application. The IDDEClientConversation pokeData function sends a poke data request to the conversing DDE server application.

The pokeData function has three required arguments and one optional argument. The first required argument is the name of the data item that the DDE server is to update to a new value. The second and third required arguments are a void*, a pointer to a buffer containing the new data item value, and an unsigned long, its length. By using a void* and length instead of just a char* to point to the new data item value, you can poke both character strings and buffers of data. The optional argument is the format that the data is sent in; it defaults to IDDE::textFormat.

The following example requests a DDE server application to set the value of the "XYZ Corp" data item to 82. It specifies a private data format, "private_IString." The example creates an IString object from the unsigned long. The DDE server application must recognize the format of the data so that it can receive the data as an IString object, and convert it back to an unsigned long using IString::asUnsigned.

```
unsigned long ulValue = 82;
  IString strValue(ulValue);
  aConversation.pokeData( "XYZ Corp",
                          strValue,
                          strValue.length(),
                          "private_IString" );
```

The IDDEClientConversation object throws an IInvalidRequest exception if it is not currently conversing.

The server application responds to this request with a positive or negative acknowledgement. In either case, the IDDEClientConversation object creates an IDDEAcknowledgePokeEvent object and passes a reference to this event by calling pokeAcknowledged.

The only function that the IDDEAcknowledgePokeEvent class provides is pokedData, which returns an IString object containing the data item value that you requested the DDE server application to poke. This IString object is constructed from the void* pointer and length you passed as arguments in the pokeData call to which this IDDEAcknowledgePokeEvent is a response. (The IDDEClientConversation object keeps the details of all outstanding transactions in an IQueue object.)

Executing Remote Commands

The DDE protocol provides a way for DDE client applications to send commands and command strings to DDE server applications to execute them remotely. Typically, you would send macros and commands to word processing or spreadsheet applications that support a command language and support this aspect of the DDE protocol.

Use `IDDEClientConversation::executeCommands` to send commands to DDE server applications. The `executeCommands` function has two required arguments, a `void*`, which points to the command string buffer, and an `unsigned long`, which is the length of the command string buffer. The DDE server application defines the format of the contents of a command string buffer, unlike all other DDE transactions where the format of the data buffer is defined by the specified DDE data format. Refer to the documentation of the DDE server application you are sending commands to in order to determine the required format of the command buffer. The `IDDEClientConversation` object throws an `IInvalidRequest` exception if it is not currently conversing.

The server application responds to this request with a positive or negative acknowledgement. In either case, the `IDDEClientConversation` object creates an `IDDEAcknowledgeExecuteEvent` object and passes a reference to this event by calling `executeAcknowledged`.

The only function that the `IDDEAcknowledgeExecuteEvent` class provides is `commands`, which returns an `IString` object containing the command string that you requested the DDE server application to execute. This `IString` object is constructed from the `void*` pointer and length passed in the `executeCommands` call to which this `IDDEAcknowledgeExecuteEvent` is a response. (The `IDDEClientConversation` object keeps the details of all outstanding transactions in an `IQueue` object.)

Ending a Conversation

To end the current conversation, call `IDDEClientConversation::end`. The `IDDEClientConversation` object first cleans up and then resets all of its instance data to the original values from which the object was first constructed. Then, it posts a message to the DDE server application that instructs it to end the conversation. The `IDDEClientConversation` object throws an `IInvalidRequest` exception if it is not currently engaged in a conversation.

The DDE server application responds by posting an identical termination message to the DDE client application acknowledging the end of the conversation. Then, the `IDDEClientConversation` object creates an `IDDEClientEndEvent` object and passes a reference to this event by calling `conversationEnded`.

You can call the `application` and `topic` functions of `IDDEClientEndEvent` to get details about the conversation that just ended. The `application` function returns an `IString` object containing the name of the DDE server application with which you were conversing. The `topic` function returns an `IString` object containing the name of the topic you were conversing about with the DDE server application.

You can also call `sourceOfEnd`, which the parent class of `IDDEClientEndEvent`, `IDDEEndEvent`, provides to determine who initiated the end of the conversation. This information is important because an error can cause the conversation to end and because the one transaction that the DDE protocol allows a DDE server application to initiate is an end conversation transaction. In both cases, `conversationEnded` is called to inform you that the conversation is ending. See "The Generic DDE Event Classes" earlier in this chapter for a detailed description of the `IDDEEndEvent` class.

Miscellaneous Client Functions

The IDDEClientConversation class provides additional functions for obtaining information on the status of an IDDEClientConversation object and the current conversation, if it is engaged in one. Following is a brief description of two of these member functions:

- The isCaseSensitive function returns true if the DDE server application that this IDDEClientConversation is conversing with indicates it enforces case sensitivity. The server provides this information when the conversation is initiated.

- The outstandingTransactionCount function returns the number of outstanding transactions for this IDDEClientConversation object as an unsigned long. Outstanding transactions are those that the IDDEClientConversation object has not received a response to from the DDE server application.

Finding Active DDE Servers

There are several ways to obtain information about active DDE server applications and the topics they support. One of these methods is defined by the *System* topic, which is a topic all DDE server applications are encouraged to support. You can find detailed information about the System topic in the online *Presentation Manager Guide and Reference*.

The DDE protocol also provides an older mechanism for obtaining information about active servers. Because most DDE server applications support this alternate mechanism, Open Class Library provides explicit support for it with the supportedTopics and supportingApplications functions. You can use these functions even when the IDDEClientConversation object is conversing.

For both functions, you construct an empty IDDEActiveServerSet object and pass a reference to it as an argument to the function. IDDEActiveServerSet derives from ISet, and it contains IDDEActiveServer objects. Both classes are defined in IDDECSET.HPP. You need to include this header file to use supportedTopics and supportingApplications.

Open Class Library provides a destructor for the IDDEActiveServerSet class that deletes each IDDEActiveServer object it contains. If you remove any of the IDDEActiveServer objects from the set, you must delete them. The IDDEActiveServer class provides the following three functions:

- The application function returns an IString object containing the name of the DDE server application.

- The topic function returns an IString object containing the name of a topic supported by this DDE server application.

- The isCaseSensitive function returns true if the DDE server application indicates that it enforces case sensitivity for conversations on this topic.

Finding All Supported Topics

Use `supportedTopics` to find information about all topics that currently active DDE server applications support. This function's prototype is as follows:

```
IDDEClientConversation
    &supportedTopics( IDDEActiveServerSet& activeServerSet,
                      const char* applicationName = 0 );
```

To find all topics supported by all applications, let the `applicationName` argument default to 0. Then, an `IDDEActiveServer` object is added to the set for each unique application and topic pair supported on your system. If you specify an application name, only the topics supported by that application are represented by an `IDDEActiveServer` object in the set.

Finding All Applications Supporting a Topic

Use `supportingApplications` to find all currently active applications that support a particular topic. This function's prototype is as follows:

```
IDDEClientConversation
    &supportingApplications( IDDEActiveServerSet& activeServerSet,
                             const char* topicName );
```

Then, an `IDDEActiveServer` object is added to the set for each application that supports the specified topic.

Dynamic Data Exchange Servers

`IDDETopicServer` is the key DDE server abstraction in Open Class Library. The other classes you use to implement a DDE server are the DDE event classes. The hierarchy of DDE event classes is shown in Figure 22-1. Each of these classes is covered in detail in the topic that covers the DDE transaction where they are actually used. For example, the `IDDEExecuteEvent` class is described in a later topic, "Supporting Command Execution."

An `IDDETopicServer` object can participate in an unlimited number of concurrent conversations. Multiple `IDDETopicServer` objects can also support the same topic in your application. If you choose to do this, determine how you want to split the conversation load among the multiple servers that you create for the same topic. An `IDDETopicServer` object must always support the topic it is constructed for; you cannot change the topic.

Take the following steps to provide DDE server support in your application. Follow them once for each DDE topic you want to support in your application because an `IDDETopicServer` object can only support conversations for a single topic.

1. Derive a class from `IDDETopicServer` to provide implementations for the virtual callback functions associated with DDE transactions that you want your DDE topic server to support. Provide an implementation for the `requestData` pure virtual function.

2. Create an object of the class that you derived from `IDDETopicServer`.

3. Wait for DDE client applications to initiate conversations with you. Accept as many of the conversations as you want.

4. Wait for transaction requests from the DDE client applications with which you are in conversation. Process the requests within a conversation in the order that they arrive in. These requests consist of requests for data, requests for hot links, requests to execute commands, and requests to accept data from client applications.

5. At any time, you can end one or more of the conversations.

6. Destroy the object of the class derived from IDDETopicServer. The IDDETopicServer destructor automatically ends all conversations in which the IDDETopicServer-derived class is currently engaged.

At a high level, these are all the steps for adding DDE server function to your application.

Constructing a DDE Server

There is only one constructor for creating IDDETopicServer objects. Following is the prototype of this constructor:

```
IDDETopicServer( const char*    applicationName,
                 const char*    supportedTopic,
                 IFrameWindow*  owner = 0,
                 Boolean        useEventThread = true );
```

The first two arguments are required and the last two are optional. The first required argument is the name of your application, and the second one is the name of the topic that this IDDETopicServer object supports. DDE client applications must specify an application name and a topic name when they request a conversation.

The first optional argument is an IFrameWindow*, which defaults to 0. If your application has a main window, we recommend that you pass a pointer to it in your first IDDETopicServer constructor. The IDDETopicServer constructor creates a static IFrameWindow object and can use the IFrameWindow* as the objcct's owner. (There is one IFrameWindow object shared by all IDDETopicServer objects. This IFrameWindow object is reference-counted to ensure that it is not destroyed until there are no more IDDETopicServer objects.)

Specifying an IFrameWindow* prevents a problem that you can have when your application is ending. The operating system window associated with each IFrameWindow object must be destroyed before the message loop exits. This requirement is described in Chapter 20, "Applications and Threads." Therefore, you must ensure that all IDDETopicServer objects are destructed in order for the static IFrameWindow object to be destructed so that your application can end. These destructions may not occur if you create any IDDETopicServer objects on the stack inside of main, unless you specify this IFrameWindow* argument.

The second optional argument to the IDDETopicServer constructor is a Boolean, which defaults to true. This argument specifies whether the IDDETopicServer object can create a separate thread to process incoming messages from DDE client applications. We highly recommend that you let this default to true because of the benefits you gain from allowing the use of a secondary thread for processing incoming messages. See the "Constructing a DDE Client" topic earlier in the chapter for a detailed description of these benefits as well as potential problems if you do not use secondary threads.

Note: This argument has no effect in the Windows operating system due to a restriction in the native DDE implementation.

The `IDDETopicServer` constructor creates an `IObjectWindow` object to communicate with DDE client applications. Because the `IDDETopicServer` class derives from `IHandler`, you have a complex handler that you work with a bit differently than you do with other handlers in Open Class Library. One major difference is that the `IDDETopicServer` object adds itself as a handler to the `IObjectWindow` object.

The `IDDETopicServer` object also creates several collections to keep state information. The collections of interest to you are an `ISet` collection to keep track of all conversations, and an `ISet` collection of hot link items, where each element in the set points to an `ISet` collection of active hot links for that item.

The `IDDETopicServer` copy constructor is private, so you cannot make a copy of an `IDDETopicServer` object. Because `IDDETopicServer` objects communicate with other processes using only window handles to identify themselves, it would not make sense to construct one `IDDETopicServer` from another. (What would this new object communicate with?) It does make sense to create a new `IDDETopicServer` object using the regular constructor. For the same reason, the `IDDETopicServer` operator= is also private.

Accepting DDE Conversations

When an `IDDETopicServer` object receives a request to begin a conversation from a DDE client application, it verifies that the request is valid. The `IDDETopicServer` object checks the application and topic names supplied in the request with the names contained in its instance data, ignoring mismatches due to differences in case. (The strings are all folded to uppercase, so the matching is case-insensitive.)

If either the application or topic names do not match, the request to begin a conversation is discarded. The exception to this is a 0-length `char*` for either the application or topic name. The DDE protocol allows DDE client applications to use 0-length character strings as wildcards for application and topic names. In this way, DDE clients can find all topics supported by a particular application, all applications that support a particular topic, or all active application-topic pairs. See the "Finding Active DDE Servers" topic earlier in this chapter for more information on using wildcards.

If the names match, the `IDDETopicServer` object creates an `IDDEBeginEvent` object and passes you a reference to this event by calling `acceptConversation`. You are passed an `unsigned long` representing a unique conversation ID in addition to the `IDDEBeginEvent` object. If you accept this request for a conversation, this ID is passed on all subsequent transaction requests from this DDE client. You can also use this ID to end this conversation at a later time. Remember that conversation requests are sent, not posted, by the DDE client application, so you must return as quickly as possible from `acceptConversation`.

Call `IDDEBeginEvent::application` to get the name of the application with which the DDE client wants to converse. `IDDEBeginEvent::topic` returns the name of the topic that the DDE client wants to have a conversation about. The `acceptConversation` function is not called unless the application and topic names match the topic server's, so the only reason to call these two functions is if you want to know if any wildcards are being used. (For example, you may not want to accept conversations initiated using wildcards.)

If you return `false` from `acceptConversation`, the `IDDETopicServer` object does not respond to the DDE client, and the conversation is not accepted. If you return `true`, you indicate that you want to accept the conversation, and the `IDDETopicServer` object responds to the DDE client application to reflect this. The default behavior of `acceptConversation` is to return `true`, effectively accepting all conversation requests. If you want to have a case-sensitive conversation, call `IDDEBeginEvent::setCaseSensitive` and it is communicated to the DDE client application.

Supporting Data Requests

When an `IDDETopicServer` object receives a request for data from a DDE client application, first it ensures that it has an active conversation with the client application. If it does, the `IDDETopicServer` object creates an `IDDERequestDataEvent` object and passes a reference to this event by calling `requestData`. Because `requestData` is a pure virtual function you must provide an implementation for it. The conversation ID for the DDE client is also passed by `requestData`.

Because the `IDDERequestDataEvent` class derives indirectly from `IDDEEvent`, you can call the `IDDEEvent` `item` and `format` functions to determine what data item is requested and in what format. If you want to provide the requested data, use one of the two overloaded versions of `IDDERequestDataEvent::setData`. The first version of `setData` accepts a `const char*` to support character strings. The second version supports buffers of data. It accepts a `const void*` argument to point to the data buffer and a `unsigned long` argument for the length of the buffer.

By calling `IDDERequestDataEvent::requestAck`, you can also request that the client application send an acknowledgement when it receives the data. To indicate to the `IDDETopicServer` object that you have provided the requested data, you must return `true` from `requestData`. If you cannot provide the requested data, return `false` from `requestData`. This causes the `IDDETopicServer` object to send the client application a negative acknowledgement.

If you request an `acknowledgement` from the DDE client application, the client returns an acknowledgement to your `IDDETopicServer` object after it processes the data it receives. When this acknowledgement is received, the `IDDETopicServer` object creates an `IDDEServerAcknowledgeEvent` object and passes a reference to it by calling `acknowledged`. Do not call the `IDDETopicServer` `hotLinkUpdate` or `endConversation` functions from within `acknowledged`. If you do, the instance data of `IDDETopicServer` may be corrupted or a deadlock may occur.

The `IDDEServerAcknowledgeEvent` provides two functions, `data` and `isAckToHotLinkUpdate`. Use the `data` function to obtain an `IString` object containing the data value you provided to the client application. This `IString` object is constructed from the `void*` pointer and length passed as arguments in the `IDDERequestDataEvent` function, `setData`. (The `IDDETopicServer` object keeps the details of all outstanding acknowledgements in an `IQueue` object.)

Use `isAckToHotLinkUpdate` to determine if this acknowledgement is for data that you sent in response to a request for data or for data that you sent as the result of an updated hot-link data item. In this case, the function returns `false` because the acknowledgement applies to data that you sent to satisfy a request for data from the client application.

Supporting Hot Links

Because the DDE protocol supports ongoing hot links to data items, you must send the updated data item's value or a notification (depending on the type of hot link) whenever the value of the data item changes. When an `IDDETopicServer` object receives a request for a hot link, it first ensures that it has an active conversation with the client. If it does, the `IDDETopicServer` object creates an `IDDEServerHotLinkEvent` object and passes a reference to this event by calling `beginHotLink`. The conversation ID for the DDE client is also passed by `beginHotLink`.

Because the `IDDEServerHotLinkEvent` class is indirectly derived from `IDDEEvent`, you can call the `IDDEEvent` `item` and `format` functions to determine what data item a hot link is being requested for and in what format. Use `isDataRequested` to determine what type of hot link the DDE client application is requesting. If this function returns `true`, a data hot link is being requested; if the function returns `false`, a notification hot link is being requested. You do not have to send updated data item values for a notification hot link: just send a notification that the data item value has changed.

Use `IDDEServerHotLinkEvent::isPacingRequested` to determine if the DDE client application is requesting pacing for the hot link. Pacing means you must request an acknowledgement from the client application every time you send it a data item value update or notification. You must then wait until the client application sends you an acknowledgement before sending any subsequent updates or notifications. A DDE client application can use this to avoid being overrun with updates from a highly active hot link.

If you want to accept the hot link, return `true` from `beginHotLink`. This causes the `IDDETopicServer` object to send the client application a positive acknowledgement. If you do not want to accept the hot link, return `false` from `beginHotLink`. This causes the `IDDETopicServer` object to send the client application a negative acknowledgement. The default behavior of `beginHotLink` is to return `false`.

When an `IDDETopicServer` object receives a request to end one or more hot links from a DDE client application, it first ensures that it has an active conversation with the client. If it does have one, and if it has a matching hot link to the client application, the `IDDETopicServer` object creates an `IDDEEvent` object and passes a reference to this event by calling `hotLinkEnded`. The conversation ID for the DDE client is also passed by `hotLinkEnded`.

Note that you do not have a choice about accepting a request to end a hot link. If the DDE client application specifies a 0-length string for the format, all hot links for the specified item are ended. If the client application specifies a 0-length string for the data item name, all hot links with this client are ended. Call the `item` and `format` member functions of `IDDEEvent` to obtain the name of the data item and data format for which a hot link is being ended.

Providing Hot Link Data

Keep track of all of the data items for which you have accepted a hot link. When the value of one of these data items changes, call IDDETopicServer::hotLinkUpdate to pass the name of the changed data item. If you pass a 0 or a 0-length string for the name of the data item, the IDDETopicServer object throws an IInvalidParameter exception. If there is not an active hot link for the specified data item, the IDDETopicServer object throws an IInvalidRequest exception. The hotLinkUpdate function returns an usigned long containing the number of hot links for which it sent a notification, or an updated data item value.

The hotLinkUpdate function creates an IDDERequestDataEvent object and passes a reference to this event by calling requestHotLinkData once for each format that this data item has a data hot link for. The hotLinkUpdate function then sends the updated data item's value to each DDE client that has a hot link for that item and format. Thus, you do not have to keep track of all of the formats you have accepted hot links for on each data item. The IDDETopicServer object keeps track of everything for you. Do not call the IDDETopicServer hotLinkUpdate or endConversation member functions from within this function. If you do, IDDETopicServer instance data may be corrupted or a deadlock may occur.

Because IDDERequestDataEvent is indirectly derived from IDDEEvent, you can call the IDDEEvent item and format member functions to determine what data item is being requested and in what format. You must provide the data because you agreed to accept this hot link and called hotLinkUpdate to indicate that you have an updated value for the data item. Use one of the two overloaded versions of IDDERequestDataEvent::setData to provide the data. The first version of setData accepts a const char* to support character strings. The second version supports buffers of data. It accepts a const void* argument to point to the data buffer and a unsigned long argument for the length of the buffer.

By calling the requestAck function of IDDERequestDataEvent, you can also request the client application to send an acknowledgement when it receives the data. If pacing is active for any of the hot links, the IDDETopicServer object automatically requests an acknowledgement. The IDDETopicServer object enforces pacing if it is active for a hot link. If an acknowledgement is outstanding for a hot link with pacing, no update is sent to the client application. When the client application sends the outstanding acknowledgement, the IDDETopicServer object sends the client the latest update or notification if the data item has changed while the acknowledgement was outstanding. If data is required, the IDDETopicServer object calls requestHotLinkData as described above.

If you request an acknowledgement from the DDE client application, the client returns an acknowledgement to your IDDETopicServer object after it has processed the data that you provided. When this acknowledgement is received, the IDDETopicServer object creates an IDDEServerAcknowledgeEvent object and passes a reference to this event by calling acknowledged. Do not call the IDDETopicServer hotLinkUpdate or endConversation member functions from within acknowledged. If you do, IDDETopicServer instance data may be corrupted, or a deadlock may occur.

The IDDEServerAcknowledgeEvent object provides two functions, data and isAckToHotLinkUpdate. Call data to obtain an IString object containing the data value that you provided to the client application. This IString object is constructed from the void* pointer and length that you passed as arguments in the `IDDERequestDataEvent::setData` call. (The `IDDETopicServer` object keeps the details of all outstanding acknowledgements in an `IQueue` object.)

Use `isAckToHotLinkUpdate` to determine if this acknowledgement is for data that you sent as the result of a request for data or for data that you sent as the result of an updated hot-link data item. In this case, the function returns `true` because the acknowledgement applies to data that you sent for a hot-link update.

Supporting Requests to Poke Data

When an `IDDETopicServer` object receives a request to poke a new value for a data item, it first ensures that it has an active conversation with the client application. If it does, the `IDDETopicServer` object creates an `IDDEPokeEvent` object and passes a reference to this event by calling `pokeData`. The conversation ID for the DDE client is also passed on `pokeData`.

To indicate to the `IDDETopicServer` object that you have accepted the poke data request, return `true` from `pokeData`. This causes the `IDDETopicServer` object to send the client application a positive acknowledgement. If you cannot process the poke data request, return `false` from `pokeData`. This causes the `IDDETopicServer` object to send the client application a negative acknowledgement. The default behavior of `pokeData` is to return `false`, indicating that you cannot process the poke data request.

Supporting Command Execution

When an `IDDETopicServer` object receives a request to execute a command string, it first ensures that it has an active conversation with the client application. If it does, the `IDDETopicServer` object creates an `IDDEExecuteEvent` object and passes a reference to this event by calling `executeCommands`. The conversation ID for the DDE client is also passed on `executeCommands`.

Use `IDDEExecuteEvent::commands` to obtain an `IString` object containing the command string that the client wants you to execute.

To indicate to the `IDDETopicServer` object that you have successfully executed the command string, return `true` from `executeCommands`. This causes the `IDDETopicServer` object to send the client application a positive acknowledgement. If you cannot execute the command string, return `false` from `executeCommands`. This causes the `IDDETopicServer` object to send the client application a negative acknowledgement. The default behavior of `executeCommands` is to return `false`, indicating that you cannot execute the command string.

Handling Conversation Terminations

When an `IDDETopicServer` object receives a request to end a conversation, it first ensures that it has an active conversation with the client application. If it does, the `IDDETopicServer` object creates an `IDDEEndEvent` object and passes a reference to this event by calling conversationEnded.   The conversation ID for the DDE client is also passed on conversationEnded.

You can call `IDDEEndEvent::sourceOfEnd` to determine what initiated the end of the conversation. This is important because an error can cause the conversation to end, as well as a request to end the conversation from the DDE client application. In both cases, conversationEnded is called to inform you that the conversation is ending. See "The Generic DDE Event Classes" topic earlier in this chapter for a detailed description of the `IDDEEndEvent` class.

The IDDETopicServer object responds by posting an identical termination message back to the DDE client application to acknowledge the end of the conversation.

Miscellaneous Server Functions

The `IDDETopicServer` class provides miscellaneous functions for obtaining information about the status of an `IDDETopicServer` object and the conversations in which it is currently engaged. Following is a brief description of two of these member functions:

- The DDE protocol does not allow a server application to initiate a conversation with a client application. It does allow a client and server application to engage in a conversation without going through the standard conversation initialization. The `beginConversation` function takes the window handle of a DDE client as its only argument. Use it if you have already agreed with a client application to have a DDE conversation, and if you have an alternate method for exchanging the required window handles. Use `IDDETopicServer::serverHandle` to obtain the topic server's window handle to pass to the client application. The IDDETopicServer object throws an IInvalidParameter exception if the specified window handle is not valid. The IDDETopicServer object also throws an IInvalidRequest exception if it is already engaged in a conversation with a DDE client application using the specified window handle.

- The endConversation function ends a conversation with a DDE client application. This is the only transaction that a DDE server application can initiate. The only argument to this function is an unsigned long, which is the conversation ID that uniquely identifies the conversation. If there is not a current conversation with the client application identified by the conversation ID, the IDDETopicServer object throws an IInvalidRequest exception. When the DDE client application acknowledges the end of the conversation, the IDDETopicServer object creates an IDDEEndEvent object and passes a reference to this event by calling conversationEnded. The conversation ID for the DDE client is also passed on conversationEnded.

Chapter 23

Using Help

- Describes how to provide help in your application
- Describes the IHelpWindow and IHelpHandler classes
- Describes the ICnrHandler, IContainerColumn, IContainerObject, IPageHandler, IMessageBox, IFileDialog, IFontDialog, and IDMItemProviderFor classes in regards to how they support help
- Chapters 5, 6, 13, 14, 16, 18, 21, 24, and 27 cover related material.

An important part of creating an application is providing it with online help. Online help can welcome a user to a new user interface and describe the visual cues it uses and the real-world analogies it draws upon. It can encourage exploration, demonstrate features, and provide guidance for solving problems. Online help offers the advantage of being less disruptive than printed documentation because it does not require a user to leave the keyboard.

Open Class Library provides help support through the IHelpWindow and IHelpHandler classes, as well as several associated event classes. Figure 23-1 shows their class hierarchy. Additionally, Open Class Library provides help support for containers, notebooks, menus, tool bars, and message boxes, and for drag and drop, which is scattered in a number of other classes.

This chapter describes the help support in Open Class Library. In the cases where some information appears in other chapters, this chapter provides references to where you can find it. For example, this chapter does not describe information areas and fly-over help. Both of these features display short help text that a user does not request via the F1 key. See Chapter 5, "Frame Window Basics," for information on the IInfoArea class, which you primarily use to show descriptions for menu items. See Chapter 16, "Tool Bars, Fly-Over Help, and Custom Buttons," for information on the IFlyOverHelpHandler and IFlyText classes. Their primary use is to show descriptions for the tool bar button that the mouse pointer is over.

Help Fundamentals

Online help information has many forms. Most applications provide *contextual* (also known as *context-sensitive*) and *general* (also known as *extended* or *task-oriented*) help for elements in their user interface. Contextual help presents a user with usage information for the item with the input focus, such as an entry field, button, menu choice, or object in a container. General help provides information that applies to an application window as a whole. This help

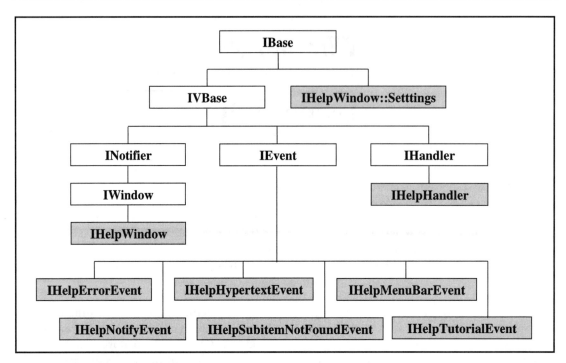

Figure 23-1. Help Class Hierarchy.

typically describes the purpose of the window, the tasks that a user can perform, and how elements of the window interact with each other.

Other types of online help include a *table of contents* and *help index*, which list the topics you are providing help for, *using help* which describes how to use the help system, a *keys help panel* that lists keys that have a special purpose in your application, and a *tutorial* that teaches how to use your application.

To add help to your application, follow these steps:

1. Add elements to the user interface that enable a user to request help.

2. Create the help information, which can include help panels and a help index.

3. Provide the code to enable help support and to associate specific help panels with specific windows in your application.

Enabling a User to Request Help

An application typically gives a user three ways to request help: by pressing the F1 key, by selecting a **Help** push button, and by selecting a help-related menu choice. Build these mechanisms into your user interface to enable a user to access help information.

F1 Key

The operating system converts an F1 key press into a help request. In response to such a help request, an application generally displays contextual help for the control or menu item with the input focus. If no contextual help exists, it displays general help for the frame window.

Help Push Button

A user can also request help information by selecting a **Help** push button. This essentially produces the same result as pressing the F1 key.

Chapter 10, "Button Controls," describes how you can create a help push button by using the style `IPushButton::help` or calling `IPushButton::enableHelp`. To prevent the input focus from changing to the push button when a user selects it with the mouse, use the `IButton::noPointerFocus` style or `IPushButton::disableMouseClickFocus` function. Clicking a help push button with the mouse then generates a contextual help request for the current control instead of the help push button.

The Windows operating system supports a "What's This?" title bar button in dialog boxes as an alternative to a **Help** push button; Open Class Library does not currently support this feature. The styles `DS_CONTEXTHELP` and `WS_EX_CONTEXTHELP` control the appearance of the "What's This" button.

Help Menu Choices

Menu bars typically contain choices for accessing help information. Figure 23-2 shows an example of a **Help** pull-down menu for a Windows and OS/2 application.

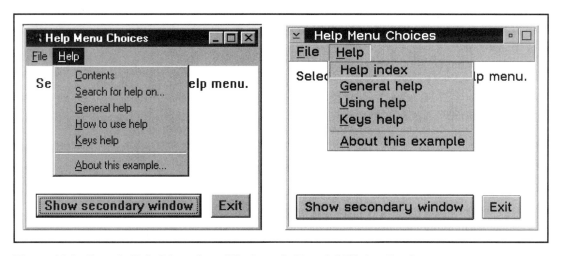

Figure 23-2. Sample Help Menu for a Windows (left) and OS/2 Application.

You can add help-related menu choices to both a menu bar and pop-up menu. The menu resource that defines the **Help** menu shown in Figure 23-2 follows. The operating system does not automatically add these choices for you.

Help Menu Resources - help\helpmenu\helpmenu.rc

```
#include "helpmenu.h"

#ifdef IC_PM /* OS/2 resources */

#include <os2.h>

MENU ID_MENUBAR
{
  SUBMENU "~File",                   ID_FILE
  {
    MENUITEM "Close\tF3",            ID_CLOSE,          MIS_SYSCOMMAND
  }
  SUBMENU "~Help",                   ID_HELP
  {
    MENUITEM "Help ~index",          SC_HELPINDEX,      MIS_SYSCOMMAND
    MENUITEM "~General help",         SC_HELPEXTENDED,   MIS_SYSCOMMAND
    MENUITEM "~Using help",           ID_USINGHELP
    MENUITEM "~Keys help",            SC_HELPKEYS,       MIS_SYSCOMMAND
    MENUITEM SEPARATOR
    MENUITEM "~About this example",   ID_PRODUCTINFO
  }
}
...
#else /* Windows resources */

#include <windows.h>

ID_MENUBAR MENUEX
{
  POPUP "&File"                      ID_FILE
  {
    MENUITEM "Close\tF3",            ID_CLOSE
  }
  POPUP "&Help",                     ID_HELP
  {
    MENUITEM "&Contents",            ID_HELPCONTENTS
#ifdef IPF_COMPATIBLE
    MENUITEM "Help &index",          SC_HELPINDEX
#else
    MENUITEM "&Search for help on...",  SC_HELPINDEX
#endif
    MENUITEM "&General help",        SC_HELPEXTENDED
    MENUITEM "&How to use help",     ID_USINGHELP
    MENUITEM "&Keys help",           SC_HELPKEYS
    MENUITEM SEPARATOR
    MENUITEM "&About this example...",  ID_PRODUCTINFO
  }
}
...
#endif
```

Creating Help Information

Applications provide most of their help information as help panels. You define help panels in a help source file and then compile that file into a help file. Open Class Library supports two formats for help files. For an OS/2 application, your help files must be in the format defined by the *Information Presentation Facility* (IPF), the help component of the OS/2 operating system. For a Windows application, you can use IPF help files or help files formatted for the help component of the Windows operating system, *Windows Help*.

VisualAge for C++ does not provide any tools for converting help files from one format to the other, so the choice of which to use is mostly one of portability versus native look and feel. For portability, use IPF help files in both the Windows and OS/2 operating systems (this also gives you native look and feel in the OS/2 operating system). If you are developing an application only for the Windows operating system, or if native look and feel in the Windows operating system is important to you, use the Windows Help format. (Note, however, that if you can locate a third-party tool that converts between Window Help and IPF help files, you no longer have to sacrifice native look and feel for portability.) You identify the format of the help files you are using when you construct an `IHelpWindow` object. See the topic "Creating a Help Window Object" for more details

As you build your help information, keep in mind the relative strengths and weaknesses of online information as compared to printed material. Strengths include the ability to search entire documents for specific text, provide hypertext or hypergraphic links between related parts of a document, display information specific to the context of a help request, and incorporate multimedia or a tutorial into the help information.

IPF Help Files

Both OS/2 and Windows applications can use IPF help files. When a frame window receives a help request in the OS/2 operating system, by default it calls IPF to service that request. VisualAge for C++ for Windows includes a version of IPF. When you use IPF help panels in the Windows operating system, Open Class Library calls this version of IPF to display the help panels.

Use any text editor to create the source files for IPF help files. You use the IPF tag language to code the help information. The language provides tags for defining help panels, formatting text into paragraphs and lists, and defining related help information such as a table of contents, index, and hypertext links between information. The following example uses the `:h3.`, `:p.`, and `:hp2.` tags to define a simple contextual help panel for a menu choice:

Help Panel Definition - help\helptbl\helptbl.ipf

```
...
:h3 res=PANEL_CLOSE.Close Help
:p.This is contextual help for the :hp2.Close:ehp2. menu choice.
:p.Select this choice to close the window.
...
```

After creating a help source file, compile it with the IPF compiler packaged with VisualAge for C++, `IPFC.EXE`. You can use the IPF compiler to generate either a help file (with a `.HLP` file extension) that your application uses to display help panels or an online manual (with an `.INF` file extension). View an online manual using `VIEW.EXE` in the OS/2 operating system and `IVIEW.EXE` in the Windows operating system.

For more details on the IPF tag language, compiler, and help files, refer to the *Information Presentation Facility Programmer's Guide and Reference* included with VisualAge for C++.

Although the IPF compiler does not support the use of C/C++ #define macros in its help source files, you can emulate this support. Doing so allows the use of symbolic constants for help panel identifiers, such as we used for the value of the :h3. tag's res attribute in the previous example. This enables you to avoid synchronization problems by defining the value of a macro in a single location while using it in several locations, such as a help source file, a help table in a resource file, and source code. To use C/C++ macros in a help source file, follow these steps:

1. Include the file that defines the macros into the help source file.

2. Use the preprocessor of the C++ compiler to substitute the values of the macros. Run the C++ compiler against the help source file using the compiler options **/Pc- /Pe+ /Tp**. This creates an .I file.

3. Use the IPF compiler to compile the .I file that the preprocessor produces. This creates a .HLP or an .INF file.

Note that this technique requires you to replace apostrophes with the IPF symbol &apos. to avoid error messages from the C++ preprocessor. You may have to use similar symbol substitutions in other cases as well.

Windows Help Files

Only Windows applications can use help files created for Windows Help. These files are not portable to the OS/2 operating system. Open Class Library calls the Windows API WinHelp to display help information from these files.

Create help source files for Windows Help as rich-text format (RTF) files. You can create these files best using an RTF editor enabled for this kind of work, such as Microsoft Word 6.0. Such editors enable you to easily define help panels and format text into paragraphs and lists. A text editor requires you to use control-character tokens to mark up the help information, whereas an RTF editor generates the tokens for you. The definition of a help panel follows:

Help Panel Definition - help\helptbl\helptbl.rtf

```
...
${\footnote Close Help}
#{\footnote PANEL_CLOSE}\par \pard \cf1 \f2 \fs28 \tx0
  \b Close Help\b0 \par \pard \fs20 \par \pard \li0 \fi0
  \tx0 This is contextual help for the \b Close \b0 choice.
\par \pard \par \pard \li0 \fi0
  \tx0 Select this choice to close the window.
...
```

You must also create a help project file to name and define characteristics of the help source file. You can also code advanced configuration information into the help project file. After creating these files, use the help compiler for Windows Help packaged with VisualAge for C++, HCW.EXE, to compile the project file and the help source file into a help file (with a .HLP file extension) that your application uses to display help panels.

For more information on RTF tokens, the Windows Help help compiler, and the Windows Help help files, view the *Help Author's Guide* included with VisualAge for C++ for Windows. You can view this help information by typing **winhlp32 hcw.hlp** on the command line or through the Microsoft Help Workshop, which you start by running HCW.EXE without any command line arguments.

Basic Contextual and General Help

Once you add help support to your user interface and create the help information, you must supply the code for your application to display contextual and general help. This code enables Open Class Library to work with IPF or Windows Help to service help requests by displaying the appropriate help panel based on the context of a user's request.

Creating a Help Window Object

The main step for enabling help support in your application is to create an object of the IHelpWindow class. This class is your interface with the help system: IPF or Windows Help. Without an IHelpWindow object, you cannot display help panels by calling IHelpWindow::show, and Open Class Library and the help system cannot automatically display help panels for you in response to user requests.

In addition to enabling basic help support, you can also use an IHelpWindow object to specify configuration information. This information includes the title bar text for the help panel window, the name of the help file containing your help panels, the location of help table resources, and the help panel to display when a user selects the **How to use help** or **Using help** menu item.

A help window object is specific to the thread on which you create it. Therefore, use it to service help requests only for windows you create on the same thread. To provide help for windows you create on another thread, create an IHelpWindow object on that thread for those windows to use.

The following example creates a help window object that is associated with a primary window. See the next topic for a discussion of associated windows.

Creating a Help Window - help\helpmenu\helpmenu.cpp

```
// Create a primary window with a help menu.
HelpMenuWindow
  primary( ID_PRIMARY, 0 );

// Create the help window and associate it with the primary window.
IHelpWindow::Settings
  settings;
settings
 .setTitle( "Help Menu Choices - Help" )
 .setLibraries( "HELPMENU.HLP" )
 .setHelpTable( ID_HELPTABLE );
```

```
#ifdef IPF_COMPATIBLE
  IHelpWindow
    help( settings, &primary,
          IHelpWindow::classDefaultStyle
          | IHelpWindow::ipfCompatible );
#else
  IHelpWindow
    help( settings, &primary );
#endif

  // Attach static help-specific handlers to the associated window.
  helpCommandHdr
    .handleEventsFor( &primary );
  keysHelpHdr
    .handleEventsFor( &primary );
```

Associating a Help Window Object with Your Application

To provide help support for the windows in your application, you must associate your frame windows with an IHelpWindow object. These frame windows are *associated windows*. To service a help request, the help system (for this discussion, we treat Open Class Library as part of the help system) must locate an associated window. The help system uses the IHelpWindow object of the associated window to identify a help file and an optional help table to find the help panel to display.

During a help request, the associated window is also important for the following reasons:

- The help system sends help-related notifications to the associated window. Use an IHelpHandler object to process these notifications. For example, you can process errors that occur during the display of a help panel by overriding IHelpHandler::handleError (its default implementation is to display a message box).

- IPF closes a help panel window when the application or a user closes the associated window. IPF also returns input focus back to the associated window when a user closes a help panel window. (When using Windows Help help files, the associated window is not used during window closing because multiple applications can share the same help panel window.)

- IPF uses the associated window as the default relative window (more on relative windows, shortly).

Passing an IFrameWindow* to an IHelpWindow constructor, as we did in the previous example, associates that frame window with the IHelpWindow object. Calling the setAssociatedWindow function of IHelpWindow also makes an IFrameWindow object an associated window. You can associate a frame window to only one IHelpWindow object, although many frame windows can be associated with the same help window object. You must create the frame window and help window on the same thread. See the next topic for more information on associating these frame windows.

To find an associated window, the help system first checks the active frame window. If it is not an associated window, the help system searches up the parent and owner chains of the active window. If it finds no associated window, the help request goes unserviced, and the user sees no help panel.

Associate all of your primary windows with an IHelpWindow object. If you create multiple primary windows in your application, you can associate all of them to the same IHelpWindow object (as long as you create all on the same thread). To process the help notifications that these frame windows receive as a result, attach help handlers to them. If a primary window is not an associated window, the help system has no way to find one because there are no windows in its parent or owner window chain to search.

If you use IPF help files, also associate your secondary windows. Although these windows support help without your calling IHelpWindow::setAssociatedWindow (if their owning primary windows are associated windows), making them associated windows gives them the activation behavior described earlier in this topic. This also makes each secondary window a relative window, so that IPF positions the help panel window to avoid covering it. Attach the same help handlers to your secondary windows that you attach to your primary windows.

The following code makes a secondary window an associated window:

Associating a Secondary Window - help\helptbl\helptbl.cpp

```
SecondaryWindow
  *frame = new SecondaryWindow( ID_SECONDARY_MODELESS,
                                event.dispatchingWindow() );
frame->setAutoDeleteObject();
IHelpWindow
  *help = IHelpWindow::helpWindow( frame );
help->setAssociatedWindow( frame );
frame->show();
```

Setting Active and Relative Windows

Related to the concept of associated windows are *active windows* and *relative windows*. When servicing a request using help tables (more on them shortly), the help system treats the active window as the window that a user requested help from. IPF uses the relative window to position the help panel window (IPF attempts to avoid covering the relative window). When using Windows Help help files, the relative window has no effect.

Calling IHelpWindow::setActiveWindow sets both the active and relative window. Unlike associated windows, you can specify only one active and one relative window for an IHelpWindow object; setting a new active window or relative window replaces the previous one. If you do not set the active window or reset it to 0, the active window defaults to the frame window that the operating system identifies as having activation. If you do not set the relative window or reset it to 0, it defaults to the associated window.

Generally, you only need to call IHelpWindow::setActiveWindow in the OS/2 operating system for frame windows used as page windows of a notebook. See the topic "Dialog Page Windows of a Notebook" for more information.

Identifying Contextual and General Help Panels

In most cases, Open Class Library and the help system work together to service a help request by displaying the contextual or general help panel for the current window. As a result, you typically do not need to process help requests by calling `IHelpWindow::show` to display a help panel; you only need to identify the contextual or general help panel that each window uses.

Open Class Library gives you two methods to identify contextual and general help panels. The method you choose is independent of whether you define your help information as an IPF or Windows Help help file. You can use both methods in the same application—and even for different controls or menu choices in the same frame window. Both methods require that you define help panels with numeric identifiers rather than names.

The first method is to call `IWindow::setHelpId` and `IMenu::setItemHelpId`. Currently, these functions are available only in VisualAge for C++ for Windows. The second method is to use help table resources. This is the mechanism that the OS/2 help system, IPF, uses to determine the contextual or general help panel to display when servicing a help request. Open Class Library emulates this use of help tables in the Windows operating system.

Help assigned via `IWindow::setHelpId` or `IMenu::setItemHelpId` takes precedence over help assigned via help tables. If a user requests help for a window and that window has a help panel assigned with `IWindow::setHelpId`, Open Class Library displays that help panel. Otherwise, if the window is a frame window, Open Class Library or the help system processes the request using help tables. If it is not a frame window, it passes the help request up its parent window chain until it is processed via `IWindow::setHelpId` or help tables. If a user requests help for a menu item and it has a help panel assigned via `IMenu::setItemHelpId`, Open Class Library displays that help panel. Otherwise, Open Class Library or the help system processes the request using help tables.

The IWindow::setHelpId and IMenu::setItemHelpId Functions

Use `IWindow::setHelpId` to assign a help panel to a window. For a frame window, calling this function is equivalent to defining a general help panel in a help table. If you assign a help panel to a canvas, it also acts as general help for the child windows of the canvas. For other windows, calling this function is equivalent to defining contextual help through a help table.

Use `IMenu::setItemHelpId` to assign contextual help for a menu item in a menu bar, the system menu, or pop-up menu.

Using these functions, you can dynamically change the help panels you assign to windows and menus. You can remove a help panel you previously assigned with either function by calling it again with a value of 0. Additionally, help support through these functions does not require that you use unique window and menu item identifiers to display unique help panels, as is the case with help tables. However, these functions require that the `IWindow` or `IMenu` object for the window or menu exists for as long as you need help support for the object.

The following code shows the use of these functions:

Identifying Help Panels at Run Time - help\helpid\helpid.cpp

```
// Assign contextual and general help.
list
  .setHelpId( PANEL_LISTBOX );
primary
  .setHelpId( PANEL_PRIMARY );
menubar
  .setItemHelpId( ID_FILE,    PANEL_FILE )
  .setItemHelpId( ID_CHOICE1, PANEL_CHOICE1 )
  .setItemHelpId( ID_CHOICE2, PANEL_CHOICE2 )
  .setItemHelpId( ID_CLOSE,   PANEL_CLOSE );
```

Help Tables

You can use help table resources to statically identify the contextual and general help panels for elements in your user interface. When you identify help panels for windows and menus in a help table, you do not need IWindow or IMenu objects for them. You specify these elements in a help table simply by their window or menu item identifiers.

If a help request reaches a frame window that has no help assigned via IWindow::setHelpId, Open Class Library or the help system uses help tables to service the request. In the OS/2 operating system, the frame window calls IPF via a system help hook. IPF uses the help tables and its subtables to do a lookup to determine the proper contextual or general help panel to display, based on the identifier of the window with the input focus. In the Windows operating system, Open Class Library does this lookup.

To do the lookup, Open Class Library (or IPF) uses the frame window that a user requested help from (the active window) to find an IHelpWindow object and an entry in its help table. This entry provides both a general help panel and a help subtable. Open Class Library (or IPF) uses the identifier of the control or menu item from which a user requested help to locate an entry in the help subtable. This entry provides a contextual help panel. If Open Class Library (or IPF) does not find an entry that matches the control or menu item, it displays the general help panel for the frame window.

You define help tables in a resource file using the keyword HELPTABLE, and help subtables using the keyword HELPSUBTABLE. A help table contains many HELPITEM statements; each identifies a frame window and its general help panel and help subtable. A help subtable contains many HELPSUBITEM statements; each identifies a control or menu item and its contextual help panel. For controls, only create HELPSUBITEM entries for those that accept the input focus, such as buttons and entry fields. Include menu items from menus that the frame window or its controls own, such as the menu bar, system menu, or pop-up menus. An application typically uses one help table and many subtables for each thread. You compile the resource file using the resource compiler to produce a resource library. See Chapter 24, "Using Resources," for information on building resource libraries.

A frame window that requires a unique general help panel must have a window identifier unique from all other frame windows. This allows you to create an entry in a help table just for the frame window. Controls that need unique contextual help panels must have window identifiers that are unique in the subtable to which they belong. IPF reserves the use of the window identifier 0xFFFF, so do not assign this value to any frame window or child window that can accept the input focus. Also, do not define a help panel with an identifier of 0xFFFF.

Figure 23-3 illustrates the relationship between a help table, a help subtable, an application window, and a contextual help panel.

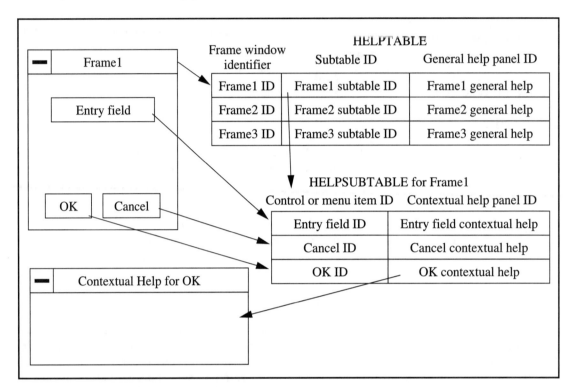

Figure 23-3. Relationship of Help Tables to an Application Window.

A help table resource for an OS/2 and Windows application follows:

Help Table Resources - help\helptbl\helptbl.rc

```
#include "helptbl.h"

#ifdef IC_PM /* OS/2 resources */

#include <os2.h>

...

HELPTABLE ID_HELPTABLE
{
  HELPITEM ID_PRIMARY,
              SUBTABLE_PRIMARY,        PANEL_PRIMARY
  HELPITEM ID_PRIMARY2,
              SUBTABLE_PRIMARY2,       PANEL_PRIMARY2
  HELPITEM ID_SECONDARY_MODELESS,
              SUBTABLE_SEC_MODELESS,   PANEL_SEC_MODELESS
  HELPITEM ID_SECONDARY_MODAL
              SUBTABLE_SEC_MODAL,      PANEL_SEC_MODAL
}
```

```
HELPSUBTABLE SUBTABLE_PRIMARY
{
  HELPSUBITEM ID_LISTBOX,        PANEL_LISTBOX
  HELPSUBITEM ID_FILE,           PANEL_FILE
  HELPSUBITEM ID_CHOICE1,        PANEL_CHOICE1
  HELPSUBITEM ID_CHOICE2,        PANEL_CHOICE2
  HELPSUBITEM ID_CLOSE,          PANEL_CLOSE
}

HELPSUBTABLE SUBTABLE_PRIMARY2
{
  HELPSUBITEM ID_ENTRY1,         PANEL_ENTRY1_PRIMARY2
  HELPSUBITEM ID_HELP_BUTTON,    PANEL_HELP_BUTTON_PRIMARY2
}

HELPSUBTABLE SUBTABLE_SEC_MODELESS
{
  HELPSUBITEM ID_ENTRY1,         PANEL_ENTRY1_SEC_MODELESS
  HELPSUBITEM ID_HELP_BUTTON,    PANEL_HELP_BUTTON_SEC_MODELESS
}

HELPSUBTABLE SUBTABLE_SEC_MODAL
{
  HELPSUBITEM ID_ENTRY1,         PANEL_ENTRY1_SEC_MODAL
  HELPSUBITEM ID_HELP_BUTTON,    PANEL_HELP_BUTTON_SEC_MODAL
}

#else /* Windows resources */

#include <windows.h>

...

ID_HELPTABLE HELPTABLE
{
  ID_PRIMARY,             SUBTABLE_PRIMARY,       PANEL_PRIMARY
  ID_PRIMARY2,            SUBTABLE_PRIMARY2,      PANEL_PRIMARY2
  ID_SECONDARY_MODELESS,  SUBTABLE_SEC_MODELESS,  PANEL_SEC_MODELESS
  ID_SECONDARY_MODAL,     SUBTABLE_SEC_MODAL,     PANEL_SEC_MODAL
}

SUBTABLE_PRIMARY HELPSUBTABLE
{
  ID_LISTBOX,        PANEL_LISTBOX
  ID_FILE,           PANEL_FILE
  ID_CHOICE1,        PANEL_CHOICE1
  ID_CHOICE2,        PANEL_CHOICE2
  ID_CLOSE,          PANEL_CLOSE
}

SUBTABLE_PRIMARY2 HELPSUBTABLE
{
  ID_ENTRY1,         PANEL_ENTRY1_PRIMARY2
  ID_HELP_BUTTON,    PANEL_HELP_BUTTON_PRIMARY2
}

SUBTABLE_SEC_MODELESS HELPSUBTABLE
{
  ID_ENTRY1,         PANEL_ENTRY1_SEC_MODELESS
  ID_HELP_BUTTON,    PANEL_HELP_BUTTON_SEC_MODELESS
}

SUBTABLE_SEC_MODAL HELPSUBTABLE
{
  ID_ENTRY1,         PANEL_ENTRY1_SEC_MODAL
  ID_HELP_BUTTON,    PANEL_HELP_BUTTON_SEC_MODAL
}

#endif
```

Other Kinds of Help

Most applications provide more than just contextual and general help. Figure 23-2 shows **Help** pull-down menus that show other standard forms of help. Near the figure is the resource that defines the menu.

Open Class Library does not service these help requests through help tables and help subtables. Open Class Library and the help system have built-in support for some of these forms of help, such as a **General help** menu choice that runs the SC_HELPEXTENDED system command. However, others you must process with the IHelpHandler class.

Keys Help Panel

Define a Keys Help panel to list and describe the special-purpose keys that your application uses. To create a **Keys help** choice in the menu bar, define a menu item that runs the SC_HELPKEYS system command. The default processing for this system command is to generate a help notification that you process in a help handler (the operating system does not provide a default Keys Help panel).

Specify the Keys Help panel by overriding the IHelpHandler::keysHelpId function in a help handler attached to your associated windows. Your keysHelpId function specifies the help panel to use by storing the panel identifier as the event result. Return a value of true from keysHelpId to indicate that no other handler needs to process the event. A help handler that identifies a Keys Help panel (one with a help panel identifier of PANEL_KEYS_HELP) follows:

Displaying a Keys Help Panel - help\helpmenu\hkeyshdr.hpp

```
#include <ihelphdr.hpp>
#include "helpwin.h"    // For PANEL_KEYS_HELP.

class KeysHelpHandler : public IHelpHandler {
protected:
virtual Boolean
  keysHelpId ( IEvent& event )
  {
    event.setResult( PANEL_KEYS_HELP );
    return true;
  }
}; // KeysHelpHandler
```

A **Keys help** choice also appears by default in the menu bar of an IPF help panel window. Your help handler is also called when a user selects that menu choice.

Using Help Panel

The Using Help panel describes the features of the help system and explains how to view the help information you have provided. This type of help is also known as *help for help*. The operating system provides a default Using Help panel. You can replace the default by calling the IHelpWindow::setUsingHelp function and passing it the help panel identifier of your own Using Help panel.

To display the Using Help panel from a menu, create a command handler that calls
`IHelpWindow::show` with the `IHelpWindow::using` enumeration. Code from a command
handler that displays the Using Help panel follows:

Command Handler for Displaying "Using Help" - help\helpmenu\hcmdhdr.hpp

```
...
  case ID_USINGHELP:
  {       // A user has selected the "Using help"
          //(or "How to use help") choice.
    IHelpWindow
     *help = IHelpWindow::helpWindow( event.window() );
    help->show( IHelpWindow::using );
    dontPassOn = true;
    break;
  }
...
```

Help Contents Panel

The table of contents panel shows a hierarchy of topics that you have provided in the help file.
For an IPF help file, the help compiler builds this list from the way you have tagged your help
file. The `:h1.` through `:h3.` tags you use (or the heading tags you list on the `:docprof.` tag)
define the topics in the contents. For a Windows Help help file, you create this panel yourself
and identify it in the help project file.

To display the help contents from a menu, create a command handler that calls
`IHelpWindow::show`, passing it the `IHelpWindow::contents` enumeration.

Help Index Panel

The help index panel shows a list of topics you have provided in the help file. For both an IPF
and Windows Help help file, the help compiler builds this list from the way you tag your help
file. For IPF, the `:i1.` and `:i2.` tags you use define the topics in the index. For Windows Help,
you create an index entry using a K-footnote.

To display the help index from a menu, create a menu item that runs the `SC_HELPINDEX` system
command.

Product Information Window

Use a product information window to display information about your application. This
information could include a logo, copyright, trademarks, or a user's registration number. To
create a product information window, process a user's request to display it in a command
handler by creating an `IMessageBox` or `IFrameWindow` object. Code for a command handler
that processes the **About this example...** choice in the menu resource for Figure 23-2 follows.

Command Handler for Product Information - help\helpmenu\hcmdhdr.hpp

```
. . .
  case ID_PRODUCTINFO:
  {        // A user has selected the "Product information" choice.
    IMessageBox
      msg( event.dispatchingWindow() );
    msg
      .setTitle( "About This Example" )
      .show( "This is the help menu example program from "
               "\"Power GUI Programming with VisualAge for C++.\"",
             IMessageBox::noIcon | IMessageBox::moveable,
             PANEL_PRODUCT_INFO_MSG );
    dontPassOn = true;
    break;
  }
. . .
```

Special-Case Contextual and General Help

The topic "Basic Contextual and General Help" describes the use of the `IWindow::setHelpId` and `IMenu::setItemHelpId` functions and help tables for supporting contextual and general help. For most windows, following these steps is all you need to do to enable help support. However, some windows require special considerations for displaying contextual or general help. These windows include containers, notebooks, and message boxes.

Containers

When a user presses the F1 key when a container or an object in the container has the input focus, the container performs special processing of the `WM_HELP` message. As a result, it does not route the `WM_HELP` message to its parent window, so you cannot plan on the request being processed through help tables and subtables.

Instead, the container generates a notification event that you can process with the `help` virtual function of the `ICnrHandler` class. `ICnrHandler` passes this function an `ICnrHelpEvent` object that identifies the container object with the input focus. If a user is editing the container object, the event also identifies a column in details view. To make things easier, `ICnrHandler::help` has a default implementation for displaying a help panel if you identify the panel in one of following ways:

- Override the `IContainerObject::helpId` virtual function
- Call the `IContainerColumn::setHelpId` function
- Call `IWindow::setHelpId`.

See Chapter 13, "Container Control," for additional details.

The following code shows how a container object overrides `IContainerObject::helpId` to supply the `PANEL_CONTAINER` contextual help panel:

Help for a Container Object - help\helpothr\helpothr.hpp

```
class CnrObject : public IContainerObject {
public:
virtual void
  handleOpen ( IContainerControl* container );
virtual unsigned long
  helpId      ( ) const;
virtual IContainerObject
 *objectCopy ( );
};
```

Help for a Container Object - help\helpothr\helpothr.cpp

```
unsigned long CnrObject::helpId ( ) const
{
  // Return the help panel identifier for a container object.
  return PANEL_CONTAINER;
}
```

Unfortunately, this strategy for handling contextual help does not apply to the use of a **Help** push button. The container does not detect such a help request because the button routes the request to its owner window, which is not typically the container. If you require a user interface that combines a container and a **Help** push button on the same frame window, display the general help panel for the frame window in this case.

Dialog Page Windows of a Notebook

When you use a frame window as the page window of a notebook, you are using it as a child frame window. For contextual and general help requests to be serviced through help tables and subtables, create a help subtable for the dialog. Alternatively, you can assign contextual and general help for dialog page windows using the IWindow::setHelpId function.

The remainder of this topic deals with considerations for the OS/2 operating system. To use help tables with a dialog page window, identify the child frame window as the active frame window. Without adding this special code, IPF instead recognizes the notebook's frame window as the active window and uses it to search help tables and subtables.

The following code shows a handler class that calls IHelpWindow::setActiveWindow whenever the operating system activates the window. This call makes the child frame window both the active window and the relative window. We attach this handler to all dialog page windows.

Making a Child Frame Window the Active Window - help\helpothr\childhlp.hpp

```
class ChildHelpHandler : public IHandler {
public:
virtual ChildHelpHandler
 &handleEventsFor       ( IFrameWindow* child ),
 &stopHandlingEventsFor ( IFrameWindow* child );
protected:
virtual Boolean
  dispatchHandlerEvent  ( IEvent& event );
ChildHelpHandler
 &setActiveWindow       ( IEvent& event,
                          Boolean active = true );
```

```
private:
virtual IHandler
  &handleEventsFor        ( IWindow* window  ),
  &stopHandlingEventsFor  ( IWindow* window  );
}; // ChildHelpHandler
```

Making a Child Frame Window the Active Window - help\helpothr\childhlp.cpp

```
IBase::Boolean
  ChildHelpHandler::dispatchHandlerEvent ( IEvent& event )
{
  unsigned long
    activeWindow = true;
  switch ( event.eventId() )
  {
    case WM_ACTIVATE:
      // The frame window is gaining or losing activation.
      activeWindow = event.parameter1().number1();
      // Fall into the WM_HELP case.
    case WM_HELP:
      // Add this in case help is initialized or this handler
      // is attached after the frame window is activated.
      this->setActiveWindow( event, activeWindow );
      break;
    default:
      break;
  }
  return false;
}

ChildHelpHandler&
  ChildHelpHandler::setActiveWindow ( IEvent& event,
                                      Boolean active )
{
  IHelpWindow
    *help = IHelpWindow::helpWindow( event.window() );
  if ( help )
  {
    IFrameWindow
      *frame = 0;
    if ( active )
    {
      frame = (IFrameWindow*)event.window();
    }
    help->setActiveWindow( frame, frame );
  }
  return *this;
}
```

Using `IWindow::setHelpId` enables you to avoid the entire problem of trying to correct for an incorrect active window. Because no significant problems result from having an incorrect active window, you do not need to use the `ChildHelpHandler` class. Also, do not attempt to make a dialog page window an associated window.

Other Page Windows of a Notebook

The page windows of a notebook can be any type of window. If they are not frame windows, they are typically containers or canvases. The container requires its own help processing. The use of the `ICnrHandler` class, described in the previous topic "Containers" also applies to containers when used as page windows of a notebook.

Windows other than a container or a frame window forward WM_HELP messages to their parent window. As a result, standard help processing can occur via IWindow::setHelpId and help tables. In the case of help tables, the help subtable of the frame window containing the notebook is used to service the help request.

However, having several page windows share the same help subtable can cause problems. If you want different controls to use different contextual help panels, give those controls unique window identifiers. Often, it is not practical to limit the window identifiers that you use in this way. You also cannot assign different general help panels to each page window if the page windows are not frame windows. The general help panel of the notebook's frame window effectively becomes the general help panel for each of the page windows. You can provide unique general help for each of these page windows, however, by dynamically providing the general help panel rather than relying on help tables and subtables for this feature. This technique is described in the section "Dynamic Contextual or General Help."

You can also use the IWindow::setHelpId function to assign the contextual help appropriate for the controls on different page windows and to assign general help to each of the canvas page windows. The help panels you assign to the canvas page windows act as general help in the sense that the help system displays them for child controls without contextual help. However, a **General help** menu item displays the general help for the frame window containing the notebook rather than the general help panel for the current canvas page window. The technique to dynamically change the general help of the notebook's frame window can solve this problem.

Notebook Tabs

You cannot use help tables and subtables to process contextual help for a notebook tab. As is the case with container, notebooks generate their own notification events when a user presses the F1 key while a major or minor tab has the input focus. To process this notification, provide a page handler and override the IPageHandler::help function. The IPageHelpEvent that is passed to this function identifies the notebook page with the tab. Attach this handler to the notebook or its owner window.

Example code for such a handler follows. This handler requires the notebook to store the identifier of the help panel for each tab as the user data for the page.

Help for a Notebook Tab - help\helpothr\helpothr.hpp

```
class NotebookTabHelpHdr : public IPageHandler {
protected:
virtual Boolean
  help ( IPageHelpEvent& event );
}; // NotebookTabHelpHdr
```

Help for a Notebook Tab - help\helpothr\helpothr.cpp

```
IBase::Boolean NotebookTabHelpHdr::help ( IPageHelpEvent& event )
{
  // Display help for a notebook tab.  Get a previously stored help
  // panel identifier from the user data of the page window.
  Boolean
    stopProcessingEvent = false;
  IPageHandle
    page = event.pageHandle();
  INotebook::PageSettings
    settings = event.notebook()->pageSettings( page );
  unsigned long
    panel = settings.userData();
  if ( panel )
  {
    event.helpWindow()->show( IResourceId( panel ) );
    stopProcessingEvent = true;
  }
  return stopProcessingEvent;
}
```

Message Boxes

To define the general help panel for a message box, pass the help panel identifier when you call `IMessageBox::show`. You cannot define contextual help for the push buttons of a message box. Help table and subtable entries that you create for a message box are not used, as well as any calls to `IWindow::setHelpId`. When constructing the `IMessageBox` object, you must also specify an owner window that is or leads to an associated window.

Avoid using the identifier of the help panel for a message box as a window identifier for a frame window. The current implementation of `IMessageBox` in the OS/2 operating system may otherwise display the help panel of the message box for one of your frame windows.

Following is an example of a message box with general help. The identifier for the general help panel is `PANEL_PRODUCT_INFO_MSG`. See Chapter 27, "Error Handling and Reporting," for more information on the `IMessageBox` class.

Message Box with General Help - help\helpmenu\hcmdhdr.hpp

```
IMessageBox
  msg( event.dispatchingWindow() );
msg
  .setTitle( "About This Example" )
  .show( "This is the help menu example program from "
         "\"Power GUI Programming with VisualAge for C++.\"",
         IMessageBox::noIcon | IMessageBox::moveable,
         PANEL_PRODUCT_INFO_MSG );
```

File and Font Dialogs

These windows do not process help requests in the same way that other frame windows do. As a result, you cannot use the `IWindow::setHelpId` function with these dialogs or their child controls. However, you can service their help requests using help tables. To do this, create a help subtable for the file or font dialog and adding an entry for it to the help table of its owning frame window. Note that you can only use help tables for these dialogs if you display them as secondary windows. See the **help\helpothr** program for an example.

Drag and Drop

A user can request help while dragging an object by pressing the F1 key during the drag operation. To process this help request, create an item-provider class derived from the template class IDMItemProviderFor and provide an implementation for the provideHelpFor virtual function. Open Class Library calls this function so that the object being dragged can supply help when a user presses F1. Requesting help cancels the drag operation.

The following example code illustrates this technique:

Help while Dragging a Container Object - help\helpothr\helpothr.hpp

```
class CnrDragHelpProvider : public IDMItemProviderFor< IDMCnrItem > {
public:
virtual Boolean
  provideHelpFor ( IDMTargetHelpEvent& event );
}; // CnrDragHelpProvider
```

Help while Dragging a Container Object - help\helpothr\helpothr.cpp

```
IBase::Boolean
  CnrDragHelpProvider::provideHelpFor ( IDMTargetHelpEvent& event )
{
  IHelpWindow
   *help = IHelpWindow::helpWindow( event.dispatchingWindow() );
  help->show( IResourceId( PANEL_DROP ));
  return true;
}
```

Managing Contextual or General Help Dynamically

The IWindow::setHelpId and IMenu::setItemHelpId functions provide you with an easy way to dynamically change the contextual or general help of a window or menu item.

Even if you do not use these functions and instead provide help through a help table and subtables, you can still dynamically control contextual help panels. On the OS/2 operating system, you can also dynamically control the help panel displayed for general help.

To allow a help handler to manage contextual help for a special control, omit an entry for the control from its frame window's help subtable. You must then create a handler derived from IHelpHandler, providing an implementation for its helpSubitemNotFound virtual function. IHelpHandler calls helpSubitemNotFound when the user requests contextual help for any control without a help subtable entry.

To manage general help in the OS/2 operating system, provide a value for the frame window's general help panel that does not correspond to an actual help panel. You must then create a handler derived from IHelpHandler, overriding the handleError virtual function. IHelpHandler calls handleError when a user requests general help and the general help panel cannot be found (in the Windows operating system, this case simply results in the display of an error message). Based on run-time information (for example, whether a push button is enabled or disabled), you can display the appropriate help panel using the IHelpWindow::show function.

The `DynamicPageHdr` class in the **help\helpothr** example program shows how you can override the `helpSubitemNotFound` and `handleError` virtual functions to dynamically control the contextual and general help for a notebook page window. The `helpSubitemNotFound` function follows:

Dynamically Displaying Help - help\helpothr\helpothr.hpp

```
class DynamicPageHelpHdr : public IHelpHandler {
protected:
virtual Boolean
  handleError      ( IHelpErrorEvent& event ),
  subitemNotFound  ( IHelpSubitemNotFoundEvent& event );
};
```

Dynamically Displaying Contextual Help - help\helpothr\helpothr.cpp

```
IBase::Boolean DynamicPageHelpHdr::subitemNotFound
                         ( IHelpSubitemNotFoundEvent& event )
{
  Boolean
    stopProcessingEvent = false;
  if ( event.isWindow() )
  {
     // The help system cannot find an entry in a help subtable for
     // the control with the input focus.  By omitting the entry,
     // we can hook this error case to dynamically display the
     // contextual help panel for the current control.  In our case,
     // we can display different help panels for two controls with
     // the same window identifier.
     unsigned long
       topicId = event.topicId(),
       subtopicId = event.subtopicId(),
       helpPanel = 0;
     if ( topicId == ID_PAGE1  &&  subtopicId == ID_ENTRY3 )
     {
        helpPanel = PANEL_ENTRY3;
     }
#ifdef IC_PM
     // For Windows, we can also use the IWindow::setHelpId function
     // for dynamically controlling the contextual help panel of a
     // control.  We call IWindow::setHelpId in place of using the
     // below code, which would have worked just as well, for the
     // ID_ENTRYC entry field.
     else if ( topicId == ID_PAGE2  &&  subtopicId == ID_ENTRYC )
     {
        helpPanel = PANEL_ENTRYC;
     }
#endif
     if ( helpPanel )
     {
        IFrameWindow
         *frame = (IFrameWindow*)event.dispatchingWindow();
        IHelpWindow
         *help = IHelpWindow::helpWindow( frame );
        help->show( IResourceId( helpPanel ) );
        event.setResult( true );
        stopProcessingEvent = true;
     }
  }
  return stopProcessingEvent;
}
```

Chapter 24

Using Resources

- Describes Open Class Library classes you can use to load and manage operating system resources from a resource library
- Describes the IResourceLibrary, IResourceId, IDynamicLinkLibrary, IBitmapHandle, ISystemBitmapHandle, IPointerHandle, ISystemPointerHandle, IProcedureAddress, and IDLLModule classes
- Chapters 5, 6, 8, 15, 20, 23, and 29 cover related material.

Resources are user-interface elements such as text strings, bitmaps, icons, dialog boxes, menus, and accelerator tables. These resources are read-only data that you store in your application's executable file. Perhaps the largest benefit from using resources is that you can build and maintain them separately from the code of your application. This enables you to build applications for different natural language environments and to make changes to the text of the application without modifying code. It also enables you to use graphical designers to build screen layouts and images without requiring them to understand the logic you use to display these items.

This chapter describes some basic concepts involved in using resources, including how to package and load your resources, and it describes how Open Class Library makes using operating system resources easier. Figure 24-1 displays the classes in Open Class Library that you use to load and interact with resources. Detailed information on creating specific types of resources are covered in the following chapters:

- Dialog boxes are discussed in Chapter 5, "Frame Window Basics."
- Menus and accelerators are covered in Chapter 6, "Menus and Keyboard Accelerators."
- Bitmap and icon resources are discussed in Chapter 8, "Static Controls."
- Help table resources are covered in Chapter 23, "Using Help."

Resource File Fundamentals

A *resource script file* is a text file containing statements that describe the typical components of a user-interface application. You can describe dialog boxes, menus, the location of bitmaps and icons, accelerator tables, string tables, and help tables using the resource tag language. If you intend to build resources using a resource script file, refer to *VisualAge for C++ Tools Reference* for a description of how to code the necessary resource statements.

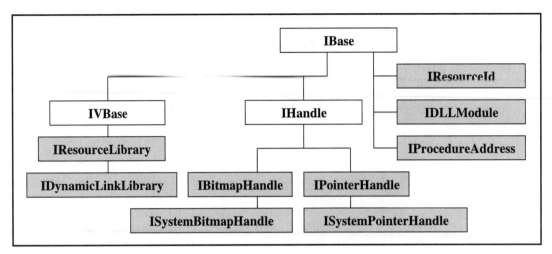

Figure 24-1. Resources Class Hierarchy.

Typically, you use resource editors, such as the ones provided with VisualAge for C++, to create your resource script file. In particular, the resource workshop or dialog box editor can help you define dialog boxes containing any of the operating system-supported windows, such as entry fields, list boxes, combination boxes, buttons, and static text controls. These editors generate a resource script file. You can use this file as a starting point for adding additional resources to your application. Use the resource compiler to convert the resource script file into a binary image so that it can be added to your application.

Once you have the binary image for your resources, add it to either the application's main executable file or a separate dynamic link library (DLL). In the Windows operating system, use the linker to add this binary image. In the OS/2 operating system, use the resource compiler to attach this binary image. The primary use of a DLL is to build code that the operating system loader links to your application's executable file (EXE) when the application executes. Although we touch on this use of a DLL later in the chapter, we start by describing the use of a DLL as a storage place for resources.

Chapter 5, "Frame Window Basics," describes how you use Open Class Library to load dialog boxes from a resource file. Many of the Open Class Library sample applications that VisualAge for C++ provides use resources; use them as a reference to help you add resources to your application. Chapter 15, "Canvases," describes an alternative, more flexible approach to using dialog boxes in your application.

Building a Resource DLL

Using a DLL is a good choice for delivering the resources associated with your application. If you store your resources separately from the application's main executable file, you can write a single application to support many different natural languages, such as English, German, and French. You can build your application to support more than one natural language and can switch between languages while your application is running. In the topic "Application

Framework Support of Resources," we describe how Open Class Library provides explicit support to help you switch from resources in one DLL to resources in another. The Hello 6 sample program that VisualAge for C++ provides is a good example of how to build such an application.

When writing portable applications, you need to be aware of the differences in resource formats between the OS/2 and Windows operating systems. VisualAge for C++ for Windows has several tools to assist your applications in translating resources from one operating system to the other. Use IBMPCNV.EXE and IBMPCNI.EXE to convert bitmaps and icons from one operating system's format to the other's format. IRCCNV.EXE is a utility that converts resource script files from one format to the other. The only caveat is that it does not support conversion of dialog resources. Hello 6 is also a good example of using these tools to build a portable application.

Storing resources in a separate DLL also speeds the building of your application. When you do not store your resources in your application's EXE, you do not need to reattach the resources every time you link the executable file.

The steps involved in storing resources in a DLL are straightforward. The following example demonstrates these steps by showing how to build a DLL with a single piece of text in a resource file:

1. Create a separate header file to provide the numeric identifiers that the resource script file and your application program use to identify the resources as follow:

    Numeric Resource Identifiers - reslib\dlltext\mytext.h

    ```
    #define MY_TEXT    100
    ```

2. Create the resource script file with the text string stored in a STRINGTABLE resource as shown in the following code. See the chapters referenced previously for examples of more complex resource script files.

    Resource Script File - reslib\dlltext\myeng.rc

    ```
    #include "mytext.h"
    #ifdef IC_PM  /* OS/2 resources      */
    #include <os2.h>
    #else         /* Windows resources */
    #include <windows.h>
    #endif
    STRINGTABLE PRELOAD
    BEGIN
      MY_TEXT,      "Using resources is easy"
    END
    ```

3. Build a dummy source file to put into the DLL as shown in the following code. This step is necessary because a DLL must be linked with at least one object module.

    Dummy DLL Function - reslib\dlltext\dummy.cpp

    ```
    void ADummyFunction()
    {
    }
    ```

4. For the OS/2 operating system only, create a module definition file to describe the contents of your DLL as shown in the following code. Note that the library name must match the name of the DLL.

    Module Definition File - reslib\dlltext\myeng.def

    ```
    LIBRARY MYENG
    DESCRIPTION 'English Resource DLL'
    DATA     NONE
    ```

5. Compile the dummy file into an object file and the resource script file into a resource file as follows:

    ```
    icc -c -Ge- -Gm+ dummy.cpp
    #ifdef IC_PM
    rc -r myeng.rc myeng.res
    #else
    irc -r myeng.rc -Fomyeng.res
    #endif
    ```

6. Link the object file and resource file into a DLL as shown in the following code. In the Windows operating system, you can pass the resource file to the linker directly; in the OS/2 operating system, attach the resource file as a separate step.

    ```
    #ifdef IC_PM
    icc -Ge- -Gm+ /Femyeng.dll dummy.cpp myeng.def
    rc myeng.rc myeng.dll
    #else
    icc -Ge- -Gm+ /Femyeng.dll dummy.obj myeng.res
    #endif
    ```

Open Class Library Support for Resources

You need three pieces of information to load an operating system resource: the type of the resource, its unique numeric identifier, and the identity of the executable file where you placed the resources. Classes in Open Class Library represent each of these pieces of information. This chapter also discusses the design and use of these classes, and it shows you how they handle the mechanics of loading resources. Open Class Library's application framework does most of the work for you.

Accessing Resources

The base class, IResourceLibrary, defines the protocol necessary to load specific kinds of resources. It represents the storage location for resources in an application's EXE. The previous example showed how to put a string resource into a DLL. If instead of using a DLL we put the resource directly into an EXE, you could load and print the string with the following code:

EXE Resource Example - reslib\exetext\exetext.cpp

```
#include <iostream.h>
#include <istring.hpp>
#include <ireslib.hpp>
#include "mytext.h"

void main(int argc, char *argv[], char *envp[])
{
  IResourceLibrary resLib;
  IString str = resLib.loadString(MY_TEXT);

  cout << "The resource text is [" << str << "]" << endl;
}
```

`IDynamicLinkLibrary` is derived from `IResourceLibrary` and represents resources stored in a DLL. Any resource that you can load from an EXE using an `IResourceLibrary` object, you can load from a DLL using an `IDynamicLinkLibrary` object. In addition, as we describe later in the topic "Dynamic Binding and IProcedureAddress," `IDynamicLinkLibrary` has support for dynamically linking to functions contained in the DLL. With only a slight change to our previous program, we can load the resources from `MYENG.DLL` as follows:

DLL Resource Example - reslib\dlltext\dlltext.cpp

```
#include <iostream.h>
#include <istring.hpp>
#include <ireslib.hpp>
#include "mytext.h"

void main(int argc, char *argv[], char *envp[])
{
  IDynamicLinkLibrary dllLib("myeng");
  IString str = dllLib.loadString(MY_TEXT);

  cout << "The resource text is [" << str << "]" << endl;
}
```

You rarely need to use an `IResourceLibrary` or `IDynamicLinkLibrary` object to load resources, however. Many classes in Open Class Library let you pass the numeric resource identifier and they handle the task of loading the resource. Table 24-1 shows how the `IResourceLibrary` functions relate to the classes in Open Class Library that use them. It also shows the relationship between these functions and the Software Developer's Toolkit resource keywords that you use to create these resources in a resource script file.

Using the Application Framework's Support for Resources

To make it easier for you to use resources, Open Class Library enables you to store an `IResourceLibrary` or `IDynamicLinkLibrary` object in the application framework. By default, Open Class Library uses the resource library stored in the framework whenever it loads a resource that you do not specifically provide a resource library for.

If you do not provide a resource library, the framework loads resources using the resource library obtained by calling `ICurrentApplication::userResourceLibrary`. By default, this resource library is in your application's EXE. To use a DLL instead, call `ICurrentApplication::setUserResourceLibrary` with the name of a DLL. To switch to a

Table 24-1. Relationship of Resource Constants to IResourceLibrary Functions

Resource Keyword	IResourceLibrary Function	Related Classes	Reference
ACCELTABLE (OS/2) ACCELERATORS (Windows)	loadAccelTable	IAccelTableHandle IAccelerator IAcceleratorTable	Chapter 26 Chapter 6
BITMAP	loadBitmap	IBitmapControl IBitmapHandle ISystemBitmapHandle	Chapter 8 Chapter 26 Chapter 26
DLGTEMPLATE (OS/2) DIALOG (Windows)	loadDialog	IFrameWindow	Chapter 5
HELPTABLE	loadHelpTable	IHelpWindow	Chapter 23
ICON POINTER (OS/2) CURSOR (Windows)	loadIcon loadPointer	IIconControl IPointerHandle ISystemPointerHandle	Chapter 8 Chapter 26 Chapter 26
MENU (OS/2) MENUEX (Windows)	loadMenu	IMenu, IMenuBar IPopUpMenu	Chapter 6
MESSAGETABLE	loadMessage	IString IMessageBox	Chapter 26 Chapter 27
STRINGTABLE	loadString	IString	Chapter 26

different DLL later, call the function again with the name of the new DLL. To revert to using the application's EXE for resources, call the function and pass a 0 pointer for the DLL name.

ICurrentApplication::setUserResourceLibrary constructs and stores either an IDynamicLinkLibrary if you pass the name of a DLL or an IResourceLibrary if you pass 0. ICurrentApplication::userResourceLibrary returns a reference to this resource library. Any time Open Class Library needs a resource library and you don't explicitly provide one, it calls this function. This behavior enables you to build an application that can easily switch from one set of resources to another.

Specifying DLL Names

When you provide the name for a DLL, you usually do so by specifying just the file name without the path or file extension (.DLL). When you specify it this way, the OS/2 operating system searches the directories specified in the LIBPATH environment variable to find the first DLL with a matching name; the Windows operating system searches the directories listed in the PATH environment variable.

If you do not want the operating system to search the environment-specified path first for a DLL, add the path and file extension to fully qualify the file name.

Using setResourceLibrary or setUserResourceLibrary

A common mistake is to confuse the two `ICurrentApplication` functions `setResourceLibrary` and `setUserResourceLibrary`. These functions control two different sets of resources. `ICurrentApplication::setResourceLibrary` indicates the source of the resources which Open Class Library uses. These are resources such as the bitmaps for the standard tool bar buttons or the pushpin on the tool bar. See Chapter 29, "Packaging and Performance Tuning," for more information on using this function. `ICurrentApplication::setUserResourceLibrary` controls the source of user-defined resources and is one of the main subjects of this chapter.

The following example creates a simple frame window containing a piece of text from our resource DLL. This example demonstrates two things. First, it shows you how to store the resource library in the application framework. Second, it demonstrates how classes in Open Class Library use this framework for loading resources. When the sample puts text into the `IStaticText` field, it only provides the resource identifier. `IStaticText::setText` is responsible for loading the text from the application's resource file stored in the framework.

Dynamically Changing Resources - reslib\stattxt\stattxt.cpp

```
#include <iframe.hpp>
#include <iapp.hpp>
#include <istattxt.hpp>
#include "mytext.h"

void main(int argc, char *argv[], char *envp[])
{
    // Store the location of our resources from MYENG.DLL
    // in the application framework.
    IApplication::current()
      .setUserResourceLibrary("myeng");

    // Create a frame and a text field for the client area.
    IFrameWindow frame("Text from a Resource File");
    IStaticText text(100, &frame, &frame);

    // Align the text field and add the text from a resource.
    text
      .setAlignment(IStaticText::centerCenter)
      .setText(MY_TEXT);

    // Put the text field in the client and show the window.
    frame
      .setClient(&text)
      .setFocus()
      .show();

    // Run the application.
    IApplication::current().run();
}
```

Using Numeric Resource Identifiers

As you have already seen, you reference all resources in a resource file using the numeric identifier provided on the resource definition. The numeric identifier for these resources is limited to a value less than 64K. The last example demonstrated how functions in Open Class Library use this identifier to load resources from your application's resource library. What if you want to load most of your resources from the application's resource library, but you want to load a small number of specialized resources from a different resource library?

You can switch the application's resource library by calling setUserResourceLibrary multiple times, but this solution only works in a single-threaded application. Under this scenario, you can ensure that no other function loads a resource from the application's resource file during the time you have it changed. However, this is not acceptable in a multi-threaded application unless you limit all uses of resources to a single thread.

The class IResourceId is designed to solve this problem. In addition to storing the numeric resource identifier, an IResourceId object also stores a reference to a resource library. If you do not provide a resource library when you construct an IResourceId, the IResourceId constructor stores a reference to the application's default resource library by calling ICurrentApplication::userResourceLibrary.

Usually, you do not specify the resource library when constructing an IResourceId. You have seen that by not doing this, you have the ability to switch resource libraries while the application is running. However, if you have some resources in a location different from the application's main resources, you can use them at any time by providing a different resource library on the IResourceId constructor. To modify the last example so that it loads the text for the static text field from the application's EXE instead of using the application's resource library stored in MYENG.DLL, you code the following:

```
// Put text from the EXE resource file into the text field.
text.setText(IResourceId(MY_TEXT,IResourceLibrary()));
```

Figure 24-2 displays the relationship between Open Class Library resource classes and the resources in the EXE or DLL.

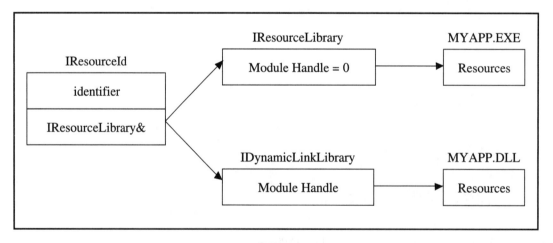

Figure 24-2. Resource Component Relationships.

The control classes in Open Class Library that accept `IResourceId` objects in their interface use the resource library stored in the `IResourceId` to load whatever resources are necessary. For example, `IStaticText::setText` contains code that is similar to the following for loading its text:

```
IStaticText::setText(const IResourceId& resid)
{
   IString newText = resid.resourceLibrary().loadString(resid);
   // The rest of the routine would be here.
}
```

IBitmapHandle and IPointerHandle

`IBitmapHandle` and `IPointerHandle` are classes that encapsulate the operating system handle for bitmaps (`HBITMAP`) and icons (`HPOINTER` in the OS/2 operating system, `HCURSOR` and `HICON` in the Windows operating systems). The implementation of these two classes uses a reference-counting mechanism that enables bitmaps and icons to be loaded once and used multiple times. Only use these bitmaps and icons through their respective handle classes to take advantage of this performance benefit.

Assume you are building a class that requires a bitmap. You need to keep this bitmap to periodically update the display. You can accomplish this by storing an `IBitmapHandle` object in the private data of the class to bind a reference to the bitmap. You then add functions to enable the bitmap to be identified to the object. It might look something like the following example:

```
class MyBitmapControl : public IControl
{
 public:
// Normal constructors
MyBitmapControl
 &setBitmap      (const IBitmapHandle& bitmap),
 &setBitmap      (const IResourceId& bitmapId),
 &setBitmap      (unsigned long bitmapId);
private:
IBitmapHandle
  aBitmap;
};
```

Note that we provided three separate versions of the `setBitmap` function. The first one takes an `IBitmapHandle` and enables the bitmap to be loaded outside our class and passed in so that an already loaded bitmap can be reused. The second version enables us to load the bitmap from the information in the `IResourceId`. The last version resolves the ambiguity that results by calling this function with a number because both an `IResourceId` and an `IBitmapHandle` can be implicitly constructed from a number. This last function results in the number being used as a bitmap identifier, not an `IBitmapHandle`. This function loads the bitmap from the default application resource library. Implement these three functions similar to the following code:

```
MyBitmapControl&  MyBitmapControl::setBitmap(
                              const IBitmapHandle& bitmap)
{
  this->aBitmap = bitmap;
  refresh();
  return *this;
}
```

```
MyBitmapControl& MyBitmapControl::setBitmap(
                                    const IResourceId& bitmapId)
{
  setBitmap(bitmapId.resourceLibrary().loadBitmap(bitmapId));
  return *this;
}

MyBitmapControl& MyBitmapControl::setBitmap(
                                    unsigned long bitmapId)
{
  setBitmap(IResourceId(bitmapId));
  return *this;
}
```

ISystemBitmapHandle and ISystemPointerHandle

Both the OS/2 and Windows operating systems deliver several built-in bitmaps and icons. It is unnecessary to put these icons and bitmaps into a resource file, so using them is particularly easy. ISystemBitmapHandle and ISystemPointerHandle both provide a set of enumerations for specifying the particular bitmap or icon to use. For example, if you need the bitmap for a folder in your application, you use the following code:

```
ISystemBitmapHandle folder(ISystemBitmapHandle::folder);
```

Dynamic Binding and IProcedureAddress

There are two ways to bind to and execute functions contained in a DLL. The most common method occurs when you statically link to the function by using an import library containing the function. When you do this, the operating system opens the DLL whenever users start your application. Although this method is the most common, it may cause one or more DLLs to be loaded for your application even though your application never calls any functions in those DLLs. Further, if you use a large number of DLLs in your application, your application may take a long time to load and display its initial window.

For this reason, operating systems support a feature called *dynamic binding*. Dynamic binding means that an application can reference a set of functions in a DLL, the references get resolved at run time, and the DLL is only loaded when requested. Dynamic binding enables you to control when your DLL gets loaded because you explicitly load it yourself. To use functions in a DLL that you have dynamically loaded, the operating systems provide a mechanism to query the address of functions by using either the name of the function or the ordinal assigned to the function. Using dynamic binding in combination with querying a function's address ensures that you don't load a DLL unless you intend to execute a function in the DLL.

The class IDynamicLinkLibrary enables you to dynamically load a DLL. The class IProcedureAddress enables you to determine the address of functions in the DLL. If you are dynamically linking to functions in the DLL, ensure that the DLL stays open for the length of time that the function needs it. You do this by keeping an IDynamicLinkLibrary object around while you need it. The class IProcedureAddress works with IDynamicLinkLibrary to manage this for you. It does this by establishing a link to the DLL on its constructor and by releasing it in its destructor.

Assume we need to bind to a C function in a DLL called isValid that takes an integer argument and returns an integer result. To keep it simple, we add the function to the DLL that we created for our English resources, MYENG.DLL. To our DUMMY.CPP in the DLL, we add the following code and rebuild the DLL:

Loading a Function Address - reslib\procaddr\dummy.cpp

```
extern "C"
{
  #pragma export(isValid, "isValid", 1)

  //Return true if "number" is less than 10.
  int isValid( int number)
  {
    if (number<10)
      return 1;
    else
      return 0;
  }
}
```

To use the function isValid in the MYENG.DLL requires the following code:

Loading a Function Address - reslib\procaddr\procaddr.cpp

```
#include <iprocadr.hpp>

// Define the type of our function.
typedef int (*IntReturningInt)( int );

void main( )
{
  // Use IProcedureAddress to bind to our function in the DLL.
  IProcedureAddress<IntReturningInt>isValid("isValid","MYENG");

  int checkIt=0;
  int valid=0;

  while ( checkIt != 99 )
  {
    cout << "Enter a number (99 to quit)" << "\n";
    cin >> checkIt;
    valid = isValid(checkIt);
    cout << "isValid() returned " << valid << "\n";
  }
}
```

In summary, you dynamically bind functions in a DLL to reduce the time it takes to load and execute an application. Thus, you avoid loading the DLL until you need it. With the current implementation of IProcedureAddress, you can achieve this by "scoping" an IProcedureAddress to the function that calls it, as we did in the preceding sample. The problem with this strategy is that the DLL is unloaded when the IProcedureAddress goes out of scope and is destructed if no other reference binds it. Note that we are dynamically binding to a C function. Dynamically loading and calling a C++ member function is complex, so we do not recommend it. Before you dynamically load a DLL that uses thread local storage in Windows 95, read the warnings about thread local storage in the VisualAge for C++ for Windows documentation. Also, see "Using Static Objects" in Chapter 29, "Packaging and Performance Tuning," for an idea of how to accomplish this using static objects.

DLL Reference Counting

IDynamicLinkLibrary also adds support to reference-count the use of the DLL. The IDynamicLinkLibrary constructor opens the DLL if it is not already open, and the IDynamicLinkLibrary destructor closes the DLL if no other IDynamicLinkLibrary objects reference it. The implementation of IDynamicLinkLibrary uses another object called IDLLModule to manage the use of the DLL. Creating and destroying IDynamicLinkLibrary objects increments and decrements the use count of an IDLLModule object. On the first request to open the DLL, IDLLModule opens it. On additional requests to open the DLL, IDLLModule increments the use count. If you want to keep a DLL open, keep an IDynamicLinkLibrary object around to bind a reference to the DLL.

Chapter 25

Storing Data in a Profile

- Describes Open Class Library classes you can use to store and retrieve profile information from initialization files
- Describes the IProfile and IProfile::Cursor classes
- Chapter 26 covers related material.

This chapter describes how you can use the Open Class Library IProfile class to store and retrieve data in text, binary, or integer format from system and user profiles or initialization files. Open Class Library provides the IProfile class to support both system and application profiles.

Overview

The operating system provides a set of functions that you can use to organize, read, and write pieces of data into special files. The system itself uses these functions to store system configuration information, such as information about the classes and instances of objects on the desktop.

Many applications have a similar need to store information that must be preserved between invocations of the application. For example, the VisualAge for C++ debugger stores information about the options you have set and the breakpoint settings to be used when you debug a given application in its profile. Think of profiles, and the data you store in them, as a means of storing variables that preserve their values between runs of your program. The IProfile class provides a way to use these special files and store data using Open Class Library, which is easily accessed by your applications.

Using the Profile—A Simple Example

The IProfile class provides functions to query and set persistent application data based on application-defined key and value pairs. The profile data set stores information using the following two keys:

- Application name, which is stored as a string
- Key name, which is stored as either a string or an integer

In the following example, we use the IProfile class to store information about a fictitious software product in the Windows registry or an OS/2 initialization (.ini) file, and then we retrieve that same information:

Basic Profile Example - profile\basicpro\basicpro.cpp

```cpp
#include <iprofile.hpp>
#include <iostream.h>

int main()
{

// We construct an IProfile object and provide the name of our
// key or .ini file.
#ifdef IC_PM
    IProfile  profile ( "Jennware.ini" );
#else
    IProfile  profile ( "Jenn's Software" );
#endif

// We add two elements under that key.
    profile.addOrReplaceElementWithKey ("Bitmap",
                                        "horse.bmp",
                                        "Visual Jenn" );

    profile.addOrReplaceElementWithKey ("User count",
                                        61368,
                                        "Visual Jenn" );

// Print to screen.
    cout << "The key value pairs are:  " << endl;

// We cursor through our profile.
    IProfile::Cursor cursor (profile, "Visual Jenn");
    for (cursor.setToFirst();
         cursor.isValid();
         cursor.setToNext())

// We retrieve the stored key value pairs and display them on
// the screen.
    {
        IString keyName = profile.applicationOrKeyAt (cursor);
        cout << keyName << ":   ";
        if (keyName == "User count")
           cout << profile.integerWithKey (keyName,"Visual Jenn")
                << endl;
        else
           cout << profile.elementWithKey (keyName,"Visual Jenn")
                << endl;
    }
}
```

Behind the Scenes

The Windows operating system stores its configuration information in a special file called the *registry*. The purpose of the registry is to provide one source for configuration and user-preference information, to track and configure devices and applications, and to provide security. The data in the registry is critical to the correct operation of the operating system and it varies according to the Windows platform used. The registry preserves case information but ignores the case in all operations; so, application and key names are not case-sensitive. Users can access the registry by using the registry editor that the operating system provides.

The registry is a hierarchical database made up of keys that are linked together to form tree structures. The registry has six *root keys* that serve as entry points to the database for any application. Each key can contain subkeys and data entries. Links provide a mechanism to traverse the database from a root key to other keys. Each key in the registry has a name and a default value.

An OS/2 profile resembles a simplistic relational database and you can use it as such. It is comprised of a number of "tables"—applications. Each table consists of a number of "rows"—key and data pairs. Profiles do not provide database features such as data integrity and data security. They only provide a convenient means of organizing and storing nonessential application data.

The OS/2 operating system uses the following two special profiles:

- *System profile*, which primarily holds operating-system configuration information. This file (usually \os2\os2sys.ini on your OS/2 boot drive) holds information about system colors, print spooler settings, and similar basic information. You cannot store information here, but sometimes you might need to read from it.

- *User profile*, which holds information that conceptually is an attribute of a user of the system. This includes per-user information that your application maintains. You can store data in this profile, however, we recommend you store as little as possible. (You learn more about this later in this chapter.) This profile is usually named \os2\os2.ini, and it is found on your OS/2 boot drive.

The structure of these profiles is the same as the profiles you create and maintain within your own applications using the IProfile class. Each file is comprised of individual pieces of data. Each piece of data is identified by a *key*.

Collections of data are combined into groups identified by an *application* name. The application names and keys are null-terminated character arrays. The application names must be unique within a profile. The keys must all be unique within a given application. You can use the same key in more than one application. Figure 25-1 shows the structure of a profile.

Open Class Library uses the same concepts on the Windows platform, but it stores both profiles in the Windows registry. If you want to use a system profile, Open Class Library stores it under the HKEY_LOCAL_MACHINE\\Software key in the registry. When you specify a user profile, IProfile uses the HKEY_CURRENT_USER\\Software key.

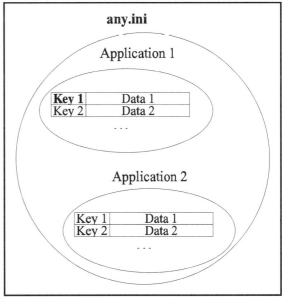

Figure 25-1. Profile Structure.

Open Class Library stores application-defined profiles under the key `HKEY_LOCAL_MACHINE\\Software\\profileName`, where `profileName` is a name that the application supplies.

Figure 25-2 demonstrates the structure of the registry using the Windows registry editor. Notice that the keys created by the preceding example are contained in the registry once you run the program. The system profile name we specify is reflected and the value of the key is shown as two items: the data itself and the data type.

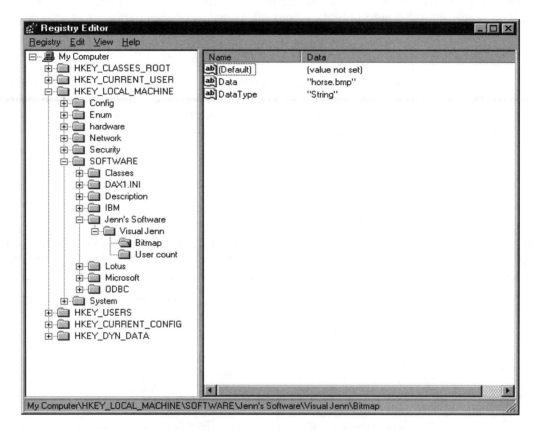

Figure 25-2. Windows Registry Structure.

Constructing Profile Objects

As you saw in the previous example, you need to create `IProfile` objects first, which cause the profile to open automatically. After you have constructed an `IProfile` object, you can immediately begin reading and writing to that object.

The general purpose IProfile constructor accepts as an argument the name of the profile file. If this isn't a fully-qualified file name, then the operating system searches for the profile using the current drive or the current directory.

If the operating system cannot find the profile, then it creates and opens a new Windows registry key or OS/2 .ini file for the new profile. In the OS/2 operating system, it is difficult to detect whether or not you have the correct file name. You have to resort to using plain file input/output functions to detect this situation. The sample code provided at the end of this chapter shows how you can implement an enhanced profile that lets you detect when a profile does not exist.

IProfile provides two static functions, systemProfile and userProfile, that return IProfile objects corresponding to the system and user profiles, respectively. If you need to perform only one operation on that profile, then you can apply the appropriate function to the result of one of the functions, as follows:

```
if ( IProfile::systemProfile().includesApplication("MYAPP" ) )
   // The application is already present.
else
   // The application is not present.
```

If you are going to use the system or user profiles for more involved processing, then invoke the static function once to construct a local IProfile object. Then, use that local object to access the profile.

```
// Access user profile through local object for efficiency.
IProfile
   userProf( IProfile::userProfile() );
```

Storing Your Profile Name in the User Profile

Before putting configuration and initialization data into the Windows registry or OS/2 .ini files, ensure that your application divides the data between system data and user data.

Storing vast amounts of data in the user profile complicates the process of backing up and restoring your application profile data and the system profile data. Instead, store your application data in a profile specific to your application. Use the user profile only to store the location of this application profile.

This strategy works well because the operating system tracks the user profile location. The system takes care of accessing it, regardless of how you have installed your system or in what directory you have placed the file. Storing your application's profile name in this way ensures that you can always locate that name and, subsequently, your application profile.

In the Windows operating system, similar rules apply. Store data that exceeds one or two kilobytes (K) in a data file and refer to it by using a key in the registry. Do this because the Windows registry is user-configurable, but is limited by system resources.

The same IProfile code that creates a different .ini file in the OS/2 operating system creates a new registry key in the Windows operating system.

Another useful convention when using OS/2 .ini files is to give users the ability to specify where they want your application to place its profile data. The first time your application runs, it detects that you have not already stored a profile path and prompts the user for one. We show this technique in the following example:

```
IString
  profPath;

try
  {
  // Get previously stored path if there is one.
  profPath = IProfile::userProfile().elementWithKey( "profPath",
                                                      "MYAPP" );
  }
catch ( const IAccessError &exception )
  {
  // Prompt user for directory to place profile in.
  ProfPathDialog
    dialog();
  dialog.showModally();
  profPath = dialog.text();

  // Save path in user profile for next time.
  IProfile::userProfile()
    .addOrReplaceElementWithKey( profPath, "profPath", "MYAPP" );
  }

IProfile
  myProfile( profPath + "\MYAPP.INI" );
```

Working with Application Names

As described previously, you group the various data objects in a profile into separate applications. The IProfile class provides you functions that work with these profile applications in various ways.

The Default Application Name

Many IProfile member functions accept an application name as an argument. However, often you find yourself specifying the same application name on many function calls because your application only interacts with a particular subset of the profile data. An IProfile object maintains a *default application name*, which makes profiles more usable. You set the default application name via IProfile::setDefaultApplicationName. If you do not specify the application name for a function that accepts an application name as an argument, IProfile uses the value you specified for the defaultApplicationName. The default application name is the value that IProfile uses if you do not specify an argument; it is not the default argument itself, which is 0.

This default name provides the default argument value for almost all the member functions that accept an application name argument.

Removing All of the Keys in a Profile Application

You can delete all the key and data pairs within a given application using the IProfile member function deleteElementWithApplication. This function requires the name of the application you want to remove as an argument. The default argument is the default application for the profile, so specify the correct application name or specify that you do intend to delete the default application name.

Enumerating All of the Applications in a Profile

In most cases, you know what applications and keys are in your profiles because your application is the only one writing to it. Sometimes, particularly when writing profile maintenance utility programs, you want to figure out what applications a given profile contains. The IProfile class provides facilities for doing that.

You can use the nested class IProfile::Cursor to enumerate all of the applications in a profile as well as all of the keys within an application (we describe this in a later topic). To enumerate applications, construct the IProfile::Cursor by providing a reference to the IProfile you want to examine. The cursor class provides the standard set of cursor functions: setToFirst, setToNext, setToPrevious, invalidate, and isValid. You obtain the application name where the cursor is using the IProfile member functions applictionOrKeyAt. This function returns an IString with the application name. The following example shows the enumeration of all of a profile's applications:

```
IProfile::Cursor
  cursor( aProfile );

for ( cursor.setToFirst();cursor.isValid();cursor.setToNext() )
  {
  IString
    nextApp = aProfile.applicationOrKeyAt( cursor );
  // Do something with nextApp.
  }
```

Reading and Writing Data

You find a collection of key and data pairs within a profile application. The keys must be unique within the application but not within the profile as a whole. The application name plus the key form a concatenated key.

IProfile supports two kinds of data, IString (for text and arbitrary structures), and long (for any numeric values).

Reading and Writing String Data

Most of the time you are reading and writing textual data to your profile. IProfile supports this by using IString objects to specify the data to be written and by returning IString objects from the member functions that read data.

You write data using the `IProfile` member function `addOrReplaceElementWithKey`. The following example shows how simple it is to use this function:

```
IString
  app,
  key,
  data;

aProfile
  .addOrReplaceElementWithKey( key, data, app );
```

Note that the key always comes first. The third argument, the application name, is optional. If you want the key and data pair written to the default application for the profile as shown, leave this argument off of the call.

Because an `IString` can hold embedded nulls, `IProfile` supports the writing of data with embedded nulls using this same technique. For example, the following code writes a "shallow" copy of an object of any arbitrary class to the profile. It does not copy the entire object if the object stores pointers or references.

```
MyClass
  myObject;

aProfile
  .addOrReplaceElementWithKey( key,
                     IString( &myObject,
                              sizeof myObject ) );
```

Read `IString` data from the profile using the `IProfile` member function `elementWithKey` as shown in the following example:

```
IString
  data = aProfile.elementWithKey( key );

MyClass
  myObject( *(MyObject*)(char*)aProfile );
```

This example shows how to extract `MyObject`, which is embedded in the `IString` that is read from the profile. As in all cases where you use such code, ensure that the objects actually hold the kind of data that you specify and that you always match the code that saves and restores objects. Using the `IProfile` class, you can only retrieve information from the Windows registry that was placed there using an Open Class application and the `IProfile` class.

Reading and Writing Numeric Data

`IProfile` also supports storing integral numeric data directly, without having to convert it to or from an `IString`. The `addOrReplaceElementWithKey` function is overloaded to accept a value of type `long`. By casting to type `long`, you can write other integral numeric data using this function. Usually, you do not need an explicit cast; the value you provide as an argument is converted while still preserving the bit value. The following code writes an unsigned short value to the profile:

```
unsigned short
  data;

aProfile.addOrReplaceElementWithKey( key, data );
```

Read numeric data using the `integerWithKey` member function of `IProfile`. For example, to restore the value written in the previous example, use the following code:

```
unsigned short
  data = aProfile.integerWithKey( key );
```

The compiler performs the conversions in this example, which ensures that the value restored is the same as the original. Always restore a value to the same type of variable from which you saved it. Unfortunately, neither profiles nor the `IProfile` class stores any indicator of the type of data they hold. For example, you cannot tell if you wrote a particular data object as a `long` or an `unsigned char`. In fact, you cannot even tell if you wrote it as an `IString` or a `long`. Data written in one format can always be read in the other format.

`IProfile` writes out all numeric data as four bytes of binary data. These four bytes are simply the bits of the `long` argument to `addOrReplaceElementWithKey`. As a result, you can identify objects that may be numeric by checking the length. If you read the object as an `IString` and its length is not exactly four bytes, then it was not written as a numeric value. If the length is four, then you can reread the value as an integer.

Compatibility with Operating System Profile Functions

You can read from and write to profiles directly using the Windows `Reg` or the OS/2 `Prf` functions. In this section, we explain how you can write data using one technique and read it using another.

The Windows operating system provides some extended registry functions for use with 32-bit systems. On 16-bit systems, you use the corresponding standard function. For example, use `RegSetValue` or `RegSetValueEx` to write data and `RegQueryValue`, `RegQueryValueEx`, or `ReqQueryMultipleValues` to obtain the value of that data.

The OS/2 functions support data in slightly different formats.

Data written with `RegSetValueEx` or `PrfWriteProfileData` is read using the `IProfile` member function `elementWithKey`. The resulting `IString` contents matches the data buffer that was written. In the event that the data written was the contents of a variable of type `long`, the value can be obtained using `IProfile::integerWithKey`. If the data written consists solely of decimal digits and an optional leading minus sign, obtain the numeric value returned by `RegQueryValueEx` or `PrfQueryProfileInt` by using `IProfile::elementWithKey`. Then, convert the contents using `IString::asInteger`.

Data written with `IProfile::addOrReplaceElementWithKey` and an argument of type `long` is read using `RegQueryValueEx` or `PrfQueryProfileData`. This function reads the four bytes of data, which can then be converted to a long value by various means, such as using a union or casting the buffer address to type `long*`.

Data written with `RegSetValue` or `PrfWriteProfileString` is read using the `IProfile` member function `elementWithKey`. Because the string data written includes a terminating null and `IProfile` cannot determine how it was written, the resulting string's contents includes a terminating null. (In the OS/2 operating system, it may have been written using

PrfWriteProfileData and might already have a null character at the end.) This null would be in addition to the null that IString places at the end of the string's contents. Most of the time, using the resulting IString as a null-terminated character array is not affected by this.

Data written with IProfile::addOrReplaceElementWithKey and an argument of type IString can be read using RegQueryValueEx or PrfQueryProfileData. IProfile does not normally write the trailing null in text data objects. This means if you read data written by IProfile using standard OS/2 functions, you must use PrfQueryProfileData and append the null byte yourself. You do not do this if the data is simply a buffer instead of a text string. If the data written is an ASCII representation of a number in the range -32768 to 32767, use PrfQueryProfileInt to read this data directly into a variable of type long.

Enumerating the Data Elements

You can query the set of keys you store within a given profile application by using an IProfile::Cursor. To do this, you use a technique similar to enumerating the profile application names as described previously. To enumerate the keys, construct the cursor by providing both the name of the application and the IProfile to be examined. Call IProfile::applicationOrKeyAt to obtain the key name at the cursor argument's current position.

The following is an example of the basic code you use to enumerate all of the keys in a given profile application:

```
IString
  appName;

IProfile::Cursor
  cursor( aProfile, appName );

for ( cursor.setToFirst();cursor.isValid();cursor.setToNext() )
  {
  IString
    nextKey = aProfile.applicationOrKeyAt( cursor );
  // Do something with nextKey.
  }
```

Deleting Data

You can remove data from a profile using the IProfile member function, deleteElementWithKey. This function removes a single key and data pair. Use deleteElementWithApplication to remove all of the key and data pairs within a single application name.

The new function, deleteProfile, removes the specified profile from the system. Uninstall utilities use this function to erase the .ini file or remove the appropriate key and subkeys in the registry.

Sample Programs

We have included two sample programs that display the contents of an arbitrary profile. They provide the complete set of IProfile read functions, but they do not write any data. One program is a command-line program; the other uses the same classes to give a graphical representation of the profile contents.

In addition to demonstrating the use of IProfile objects, the programs have the following features:

- A class ViewProfileArgs that manages the program's arguments. The constructor for this class parses the user input, validates it, and stores the resulting program options for subsequent querying.

- An enhanced derivative of IProfile, named EnhancedProfile, which adds additional support for detecting missing profile files at construction time and adds a function to dump the profile contents to an output stream.

- Additional classes, ProfileApplication and ProfileKey, which simplify working with application profiles and key and data pairs.

The complete definition of the classes that implement the profile readers are contained on the example program disk. Table 25-1 indicates the location of the profile reader components after you install these programs.

To run either program, type: profile /?

This gives you the command-line arguments you need to display the profile. For example, to view the system profile, type: profile /s.

Table 25-1. Profile Reader Components

Component	Example Location
Profile Viewer Example Program	profile\viewprof\viewprof.cpp
EnhancedProfile, ProfileApplication, and ProfileKey Interfaces	profile\viewprof\enhprof.hpp profile\advpro\enhprof.hpp
EnhancedProfile, ProfileApplication, and ProfileKey Implementation	profile\viewprof\enhprof.cpp profile\advpro\enhprof.cpp
ViewProfileArgs Interface	profile\viewprof\vprofarg.hpp profile\advpro\vprofarg.hpp
ViewProfileArgs Implementation	profile\viewprof\vprofarg.cpp profile\advpro\vprofarg.cpp
GUI Profile Viewer Example Program	profile\advpro\profile.cpp
ProfileAppObject and Application View Interface	profile\advpro\appview.hpp
ProfileAppObject and Application View Implementation	profile\advpro\appview.cpp
ProfileKeyObject and KeyView Interface	profile\advpro\keyview.hpp
ProfileKeyObject and KeyView Implementation	profile\advpro\keyview.cpp
ProfileObject and ProfileObjectView Interface	profile\advpro\profobj.hpp
ProfileObject and ProfileObjectView Implementation	profile\advpro\profobj.cpp
ProfileView Interface	profile\advpro\profview.hpp
ProfileView Implementation	profile\advpro\profview.cpp

Chapter 26

Data Types

- Describes the basic data type classes that Open Class Library provides
- Describes the following classes: IPair, IPoint, ISize, IRange, IRectangle, IString,
  I0String, IBuffer, IStringTest, IStringTestMemberFn<>, IStringParser,
  IDBCSBuffer, IAccelTblHandle, IAnchorBlockHandle, IBitmapHandle,
  IEnumHandle, IHandle, IMessageQueueHandle, IModuleHandle, IPointerHandle,
  IPresSpaceHandle, IProcessId, IProfileHandle, ISemaphoreHandle, IStringHandle,
  ISystemBitmapHandle, ISystemPointerHandle, IThreadId , IWindowHandle, IDate,
  ITime, IBitFlag, IColor, IDeviceColor, IGUIColor, IRefCounted, IReference<>

Open Class Library provides data-type classes to define and implement the behavior of the more complex user-interface and application components of the library. These classes are also useful outside the context of Open Class Library, and they provide examples of how to exploit the power of C++ to declare and implement new data types.

The Open Class Library data types provide textbook examples of using C++ as a data abstraction tool. They generally do not make use of the additional C++ features that enable object-oriented programming. One characteristic distinguishes these data types from the more functionally rich, larger-scale objects of Open Class Library: they encapsulate data rather than provide behavior, thus making data easier for you to use.

Using Data Type Objects

This section provides general advice on using the Open Class Library data types. You use objects of these data types to describe data members of other classes or to hold concrete information during execution of member functions. Such usage matches the key design points for the data types: they are relatively small and have straightforward, efficient constructors and destructors.

Use these data types exactly as you would use the built-in types of C++. In general, this means you do not need to be concerned with the creation or implementation of the objects. The classes exploit the features of C++ so that object construction, assignment, copying, and so on all work the way you expect, just as they do for the built-in types.

Further, these data types define operators in ways that make sense. If an addition operation makes sense for the type, then the class defines operator+. If a function is the best match for the concept of an addition operation for that type, then the class implements that function as operator+. When you use these types, you simply write your code in a way that seems natural and intuitive. The classes do what you expect.

You can use Open Class Library data types as data members of other classes, as arguments or return values of member functions, and as automatic variables in member functions.

Data Members

You often use data type objects as data members of other classes. For example, a Customer class might have an IString data member that holds the customer name. You allocate and create these data members when you allocate and create the enclosing object.

Open Class Library data types are designed as follows:

- They are space-efficient. The enclosing objects do not pay a size penalty for having data members of these data types, even if the data members are not initialized or are undefined. This means it is just as efficient to have a null IString data member as a null IString pointer.

- Their constructors and destructors are efficient. This is important because inefficiencies in this area accumulate in the enclosing objects.

To take advantage of these efficiencies, define data members as actual objects of the data types rather than as pointers or references, thus saving time and space costs. The extra complexity of managing pointers also defeats the inherent simplicity of the data types. The code to manage the pointers costs more space than it usually saves.

Most of the Open Class Library data types have default constructors that result in reasonable values. The constructors of classes that use these types for data members do not even have to explicitly create those data members.

Arguments or Return Values

Using data types as arguments or return values requires member functions to get or set the data. The data types are designed so that you can easily and efficiently pass data type objects as arguments to, or return them as results from, member functions.

Open Class Library classes almost always return data types by value. Fortunately, these objects are efficiently copied. Functions that return by value relieve you from being concerned with managing storage for their results.

In addition, Open Class Library classes almost always accept arguments of data types as references to constant objects. For example, member functions that accept a size argument declare that argument to be of type const ISize&. Passing such arguments by value is less efficient. The compiler passes a reference in a single register's contents. But more important, the copy constructor call necessary to pass the argument by value is unnecessary because the called function does not need its own copy.

Although data type arguments could be passed using a pointer, Open Class Library uses references because they better convey the semantics of such interfaces. In most cases, such arguments are required by the function. A pointer, which could be 0, does not accurately describe the interface. Also, the use of a reference indicates that indirection occurs only for performance reasons. You write the code for both the caller and called function as if the argument is passed by value.

Automatic Variables

You can also use data type objects to hold local data in member functions. For example, you can use automatic instances to hold function results or to calculate new data member values. In this case, dynamic allocation is inappropriate. To allocate temporary data using operator new is unnecessary and prone to error because you might forget to free the temporary object. Note that in all of the examples in this chapter, none of the data type objects is allocated dynamically on the heap with operator new.

Ordered Pairs

A basic data type that Open Class Library provides is a general purpose, two-dimensional vector, or *ordered pair*, of signed long values. The base class for this type is IPair. The library provides three derived classes that represent specific applications of such ordered pairs. They are IPoint, ISize, and IRange.

IPair Base Class

The IPair base class provides most of the implementation for all of the types of ordered pairs. It consists of a pair of coordinates of type IPair::Coord, which is an alias for long. Although you can use objects of type IPair, you almost always use the derived classes described in Table 26-1 to ascribe a specific semantic interpretation to the ordered pair.

IPair provides almost all of the functionality of each of these specific types of ordered pairs. We do not describe these functions completely here because many of them are intuitive. You can manipulate IPair objects much like you do a built-in type. For example, IPair objects define all of the mathematical operators and they work as you would expect them to (+ adds, - subtracts). This section mentions each functional category of IPair, and we discuss any interesting or nonobvious details of the functions in the category.

Table 26-1. Derived Ordered-Pair Classes

Class	Description
IPoint	Presents the ordered pair as a point in two-dimensional space.
ISize	Presents the ordered pair as a width and height.
IRange	Presents the ordered pair as the boundaries of a range of numbers.

Almost the entire implementation is inlined. Most functions consist of one or two assignments of simple expressions. In most cases the compiler generates efficient code for these functions.

IPair Constructors

You can create an IPair object from 0, one, or two coordinate values. If you do not provide any coordinate values, IPair assigns both the value 0. You can also create an ordered pair from an existing IPair object using the generated copy constructor. The derived classes provide their own constructors. If you derive your own ordered-pair classes, your constructors will probably use the IPair constructor that accepts values for both coordinates.

Accessing the Coordinate Values

Access the two coordinate values that the IPair object maintains by using the functions coord1 and coord2. Set them to new values by using the functions setCoord1 and setCoord2. Usually, you use objects of some derived class, and those derived classes assign the coordinates more meaningful names. For example, the class IPoint uses the functions x, y, setX, and setY.

Comparison Functions

You can compare any two IPair objects for equality or inequality. Compare them using any of the other logical comparisons operators >, <, >=, or <=. One ordered pair is less than another ordered pair if both coordinates are less than the corresponding coordinates in the other ordered pair. If you plot the two ordered pairs being compared on conventional x-y axes, the lesser pair is below and to the left of the greater pair.

Assignment Functions

You assign one IPair object to another using operator=. IPair provides other assignment operators that perform some mathematical operation on the ordered pairs and assign the result to the left-hand argument.

Mathematical Operators

The standard mathematical operators for ordered pairs are addition, subtraction, multiplication, and division. IPair also supports the remainder operator (%). Each operator performs the specified operation on the corresponding coordinates of the two operands. For example,

```
IPair( 1,2 ) * IPair( 2, 3 ) == IPair( 2, 6 )
```

Because an IPair is created from an integral expression, you can add IPair objects, for example, to an int. The expression:

```
IPair( 1048, 762 ) / 2
```

evaluates to

```
IPair( 524, 381 )
```

Open Class Library declares the operators as friend functions rather than as member functions of IPair so you can use numbers on either side of the operator. You can write 5 * aPair or aPair * 5.

The multiplication and division functions are also overloaded to accept an argument of type double. This permits greater precision when they operate on points using a floating-point factor or divisor.

Miscellaneous Functions

IPair provides other ordered-pair functions. Table 26-2 describes these functions.

Table 26-2. Miscellaneous Ordered-Pair Functions

Function	Description
transpose	Swaps the coordinates of the ordered pair. There are two versions. One is a member function that transposes the ordered pair to which the function is applied. The other is a nonmember function that accepts an IPair and returns a new transposed IPair. Use the nonmember function to preserve the original IPair.
dotProduct	Calculates the dot product of the IPair object that the function is invoked against and an argument IPair. The dot product for the IPairs (x1,y1) and (x2,y2) is defined to be x1*x2 + y1*y2. Written in terms of IPairs, an example is: 　　IPair(3,4).dotProduct(IPair(-8,-6)) == 0 Lines from the origin to these two points are perpendicular.
scaleBy	Multiplies the two coordinates of the ordered pair by different floating point values. This is in contrast to operator *, which always multiplies the coordinates by the same floating point value or by integral expressions. The result replaces the ordered pair to which this function is applied.
scaledBy	Similar to the preceding function, scaledBy differs in that it does not modify the ordered pair to which you apply the function. Instead, it returns the result as a new ordered pair. Use this function to preserve the original ordered pair.
maximum	Returns the larger of the ordered pair to which the function is applied and an argument ordered pair. The two comparands are compared using operator >.
minimum	Returns the smaller of two ordered pairs.
asString	Returns an IString object that contains a representation of the ordered pair. The result is in the form "(coord1,coord2)" with the coordinate values as decimal digits.
ostream extractor	This extractor puts the result returned by asString to the stream.

IPoint Class

The most commonly used of the ordered-pair derived classes is IPoint. Open Class Library window and control classes use IPoint and IRectangle, which is built on IPoint, to handle window geometry.

IPoint provides an abstraction to general ordered pairs. Specifically, the two coordinates are treated by the point as the x and y coordinates in two-dimensional space. IPoint provides the functions x, y, setX, and setY so that you can access the coordinates from that perspective.

IPoint provides essentially the same constructors as IPair does. You can use an additional constructor to create an IPoint object from an object of type POINTL (defined in both the Windows and OS/2 developer's toolkits). IPoint also provides a conversion function asPOINTL.

IPoint inherits all its other functions from class IPair.

IPoint and POINTL

An IPoint object is bitwise-compatible with both the Windows and OS/2 POINTL structures. You can choose to exploit this by passing IPoint* as PPOINTL, but IPoint provides support for converting from and to type POINTL, so it is unnecessary to take that risk. However, the risk is small. If you are concerned that the compiler or Open Class Library might change so that these types are no longer compatible, add the following code to your programs to detect such a change:

```
IASSERT( (sizeof POINTL == sizeof IPoint) &&
         (offsetof(POINTL,y) == offsetof(IPoint,y)) );
```

This comment also applies to ISize and SIZEL.

ISize Class

Another specialized ordered pair that Open Class Library commonly uses is ISize. It interprets the ordered pair as width and height values. Thus, this class has functions width, height, setWidth, and setHeight that you can use to manipulate these values.

ISize provides the common constructor types that you find in IPair and IPoint. In addition, two other constructors create an ISize object from Windows and OS/2 RECTL and SIZEL structures. The resulting ISize values represent the size of that rectangle. ISize also provides asRECTL and asSIZEL functions that return a suitable structure based on an ISize object.

IRange Class

The other ordered-pair derived class that Open Class Library provides is IRange. Objects of this class represent number ranges. The coordinates are the lower and upper bounds of that range. The coordinate accessing functions are lowerBound, upperBound, setLowerBound, and setUpperBound.

The lower and upper bounds or any `IPair` object creates `IRange` objects. `IRange` also furnishes a default constructor that constructs the range [0,0] and a generated copy constructor.

`IRange` provides a range-specific function called `includes`. This function accepts a number as an argument and returns a `Boolean` to indicate if the argument falls within the number range. Use this function as shorthand for the logical expression:

```
( aRange.lowerBound() <= x ) && ( aRange.upperBound() >= x )
```

IRectangle Class

The class `IRectangle` does for rectangles what `IPoint` and `IPair` do for points. The same way that `IPoint` objects simplify the manipulation of `POINTL`-type data and leave you with simpler and more readable code, `IRectangle` simplifies your code that manipulates window size, position rectangles, and other windowing geometry.

Mathematically speaking, an `IRectangle` object represents a locus of points in two-dimensional space. The rectangle defines the set of points by the two points that lie at the (minimum x, minimum y) and (maximum x, maximum y) corners of the rectangle. The coordinate system orientation of the application determines the relative locations of these two points. In an application with lower-left orientation, the (minimum x, minimum y) point is the lower-left corner, and the (maximum x, maximum y) point is the upper-right corner. In an application with upper-left orientation, the two points are the upper-left and lower-right corners, respectively. The rectangle includes all points both greater than or equal to the first point and less than the second point. `IPoint` objects represent these points. Figure 26-1 shows an `IRectangle` object in upper-left orientation and labels its important attributes.

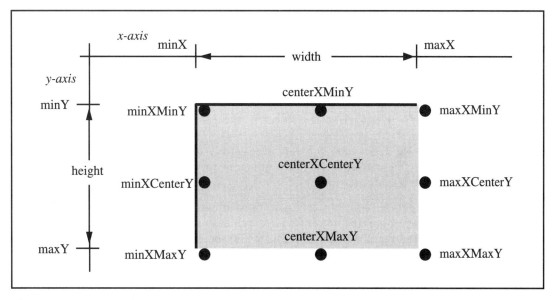

Figure 26-1. Schematic of an IRectangle Object in an Upper-Left Orientation.

Notice that the rectangle is skewed towards the upper-left corner of the page. The rectangle does not include its maximum x and maximum y edges. This ensures the integrity of the mathematical property that the area of the rectangle (the number of discrete points within it) is always equal to the width of the rectangle multiplied by its height.

Rectangle Attributes

The `IRectangle` class provides functions that return separate attributes of the rectangle, functions that return various points on the perimeter of the rectangle, and a function that returns the point nearest the center of the rectangle. Figure 26-1 shows these points and labels them with the name of the `IRectangle` function that returns them. The function names are orientation-independent. `IRectangle` also provides a set of synonym functions that imply orientation. For example, the `bottomLeft` function is a synonym for `minXMinY`, and `topRight` is a synonym for `maxXMaxY`. In the synonym function names, bottom and top indicate minimum and maximum y, and left and right indicate minimum and maximum x. They thus have a correct denotation in applications with lower-left orientation.

Four functions return the coordinates of the boundaries of the rectangle. The boundaries and labels, which again match the function names, appear on the x and y axes in Figure 26-1. Other functions return the width and height of the rectangle. `IRectangle::size` returns an `ISize` object with the width and height of the rectangle, and `IRectangle::area` returns the product of the width and height of the rectangle.

Rectangle Constructors

Use any of the sets of arguments in Table 26-3 to create an `IRectangle` object.

Rectangle Operators

The `IRectangle` class provides the operators in Table 26-4. (There is no intuitive meaning for the addition and multiplication operators.)

Rectangle Transformations

You can stretch and move `IRectangle` objects in a variety of ways. Although there are eight basic transformations, you can specify the arguments to each of them in different ways. Table 26-5 describes the transformations.

Notice there are two separate functions for each transformation. The ones whose names are in present tense modify the rectangle and return a reference to it. The functions whose names are in past tense describe the result of the function, which is a new rectangle. Thus, the former modify the rectangle and the latter do not.

Table 26-3. IRectangle Constructors

Arguments	Description
None	The default null constructor returns a rectangle located at (0,0) with size (0,0).
two points	This constructor interprets the argument points as the opposite corners of the rectangle you are constructing. These points are either the lower-left and upper-right corners or the upper-left and lower-right corners, depending on the relationship of the points you provide and the orientation of the application.
a point and a size	The resulting rectangle has its (minimum x, minimum y) corner at the specified point and has the specified size. This is similar to the way you specify Windows and OS/2 operating system window rectangles (x, y, cx, and cy values).
four coordinate values	The four values become the coordinates of the rectangle's minimum y, minimum x, maximum y, and maximum x edges, respectively. Although this looks like the way you specify window rectangles in the Windows and OS/2 operating systems, it does not produce the desired result if you use it this way. For example, specifying an initial window rectangle as IRectangle(100,100,100,100) produces a window with no height or width because its minimum and maximum points are the same, not a window with size (100,100).
a RECTL object	This object permits conversion from a standard presentation system rectangle structure to an IRectangle object. You can convert the reverse way using the member function asRECTL.
a RECT object (Windows operating system only)	Converts from a Windows RECT structure to an IRectangle object. There is no reverse conversion function.
a width and a height	The (minimum x, minimum y) corner is at (0,0).
any ordered pair	The ordered pair specifies the width and height of the rectangle, and the rectangle position is at (0,0). The argument pair can be an ISize or IPoint object. The result is the same.

Table 26-4. IRectangle Operators

Operators	Description
== and !=	These comparison operators check whether the two operands are identical.
& and &=	These operators provide for rectangle intersection. The result is a rectangle comprised of the points in both argument rectangles. If the rectangles do not overlap, the result is a null rectangle. See Figure 26-2 .
| and |=	These operators provide for rectangle union. The result is the smallest rectangle that contains both of the argument rectangles. See Figure 26-2.

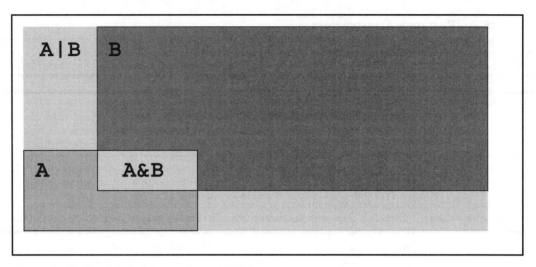

Figure 26-2. Rectangle Intersection and Union.

Table 26-5. IRectangle Transformation Functions (Part 1 of 2)

Functions	Arguments	Description
Centering at a given location		
centerAt centeredAt	const IPoint &	Moves the rectangle so that its center ends up at the argument point.
Expanding from the center		
expandBy expandedBy	const IPair &	Expands the rectangle by increasing the width and height by different amounts, which the coordinates of the argument pair specify. Each corner is adjusted by this amount away from the center.
	Coord	Expands by the same factor in both directions.
Moving relative to current position		
moveBy movedBy	const IPair &	Moves the rectangle from its current position by the vector specified in the argument ordered pair. Use combinations of positive and negative coordinates to move the rectangle in any direction.
Moving to an absolute position		
moveTo movedTo	const IPoint &	Moves the rectangle so that its (minimum x, minimum y) corner is at the argument position.

Table 26-5. IRectangle Transformation Functions (Part 2 of 2)

Functions	Arguments	Description
Scaling		
scaleBy scaledBy	const IPair &	Multiplies each point in the rectangle by the argument ordered pair. This function moves the (minimum x, minimum y) corner of the rectangle using sizeBy to resize the rectangle at its current position. Scaling by (-1,-1) rotates the rectangle 180 degrees from the coordinate system's origin.
	Coord	Multiplies the points of the rectangle by the argument coordinate value. This function scales the rectangle by the same amount in each direction.
	double	Multiplies the point of the rectangle by the floating-point value.
	double, double	Scales the rectangle by different factors in the x and y directions.
Shrinking towards the center		
shrinkBy shrunkBy	const IPair &	Adjusts the position of each corner of the rectangle by the specified amounts in either direction (towards the center for positive coordinate values).
	Coord	Moves the corners of the rectangle the same amount horizontally and vertically.
Sizing to an absolute size		
sizeTo sizedTo	const IPair &	Sets the size of the rectangle to the value specified by the argument. The position of the rectangle remains the same.
Sizing to a relative size		
sizeBy sizedBy	const IPair &	Multiplies the size of the rectangle by the argument ordered pair and resizes the rectangle to that size. The position of the rectangle remains the same.
	Coord	Scales the width and height by the same factor.
	double	Scales the width and height by the same floating-point value.
	double, double	Scales the width and height by different floating-point value.

Testing Functions

Table 26-6 describes the `IRectangle` functions that test the characteristics of the rectangle.

Table 26-6. IRectangle Testing Functions

Function	Description
contains	Accepts an IPoint object as an argument. It determines whether the rectangle contains this point and returns true or false accordingly.
intersects	Accepts another rectangle as an argument. It returns an indicator of whether the two rectangles have any points in common.

Character Strings

The Open Class Library classes `IString` and `IOString` provide a comprehensive and efficient C++ encapsulation of character strings.

Standard C and C++ character arrays and the built-in techniques for handling them are prone to numerous problems, as follows:

- If you allocate the storage for the array dynamically, you must explicitly free this storage, something you might forget to do.

- You must allocate enough space for the terminating null character. Otherwise, whatever occupies the following byte of memory is overwritten when you do something like `strcpy` into that string.

- You must place the null character in the last element of the array. Otherwise, the bytes that follow in memory are interpreted as part of the string, and you are likely to overwrite them or they can cause you to overwrite data elsewhere.

- If you have functions that return character arrays, you must determine what allocates the space for them and what deletes them. This not only complicates the interface, but often results in storage not being released.

Replacing char* with an IString Object

In the `IString` implementation objects are bitwise identical to an equivalent `char*` pointer. Thus, you can redefine a plain C structure with `IString` in place of `char*` and still be compatible with both C++ and C, even though the latter does not detect that the field holds a C++ object. Open Class Library exploits this feature of `IString`. For example, `IContainerObject` redefines portions of the OS/2 container `MINIRECORDCORE` structure so that the `char*` elements can be replaced with `IString` objects.

Where Do You Start: 0 or 1?

The string objects defined by the class IString are indexed starting at 1. The string objects defined by the class I0String are indexed starting at 0. In all other respects, these two classes are identical. You can use either version of IString.

Open Class Library interfaces are defined in terms of IString, but because an I0String object is essentially an IString object, you can use the former everywhere in your code. Then, the string objects are converted as needed. If you prefer the conventional 0-based indexing that you use for C arrays, use I0String. By placing typedef I0String String; in ISYNONYM.HPP, you can use String as a shorthand for I0String.

In the version of I0String shipped with Open Class Library in VisualAge for C++ for Windows, version 3.5, however, a virtual destructor was inadvertently added to the I0String class but not to the IString class. The two classes are now temporarily bitwise incompatible. If you use I0String in place of IString, your code might not compile (for example, with the IStringParser class). And, if you use I0String in a class derived from IContainerObject to provide information for the container, the details view does not work. For more information on this problem, see the Frequently Asked Questions document shipped with the product.

All these problems are solved if you use IString objects rather than traditional C character arrays. In addition, objects of this type provide a comprehensive set of functions that operate on the string contents. The IString class turns character strings into a first-class data type of C++ with the following characteristics:

- IString objects free the dynamically allocated character arrays that they manage.

- The class terminates all strings with a null character.

- The class provides conversions from and to traditional char* pointers so that an IString object's contents are efficiently passed to code that receives data in this format.

Operator char* versus Operator const char*

There is some danger in permitting the IString contents to be implicitly accessed using operator char*. By rights, the function should be operator const char*. The only reason it works the way it does is that prior to the updated toolkit that shipped with IBM's C Set ++ 2.0, the declarations for all of the OS/2 and Presentation Manager functions used non-const character pointers. If IString permitted conversion to const char* only, users would have to do inordinate numbers of casts to type PSZ. So, the operator was declared non-const out of necessity. By the time IBM updated the OS/2 toolkit, programmers had written code that was dependent on being able to convert to a non-const pointer.

Thus, ensure that you do not inadvertently pass an IString object to a function that modifies the pointed-to storage unless you know what the effects on the IString object will be. Passing such a pointer to strcat, for example, might prove to be a mistake.

Implementation of the IString Class

You can use `IString` objects effectively without understanding the implementation of the class. However, if you understand the implementation, you can use the class better and avoid pitfalls.

First, look at a simple `IString` object. The following code declares and defines an `IString` object with contents consisting of the character string "Hello, World!":

```
IString s( "Hello, World!" );
```

This `IString` object results in the arrangement of `IString` and `IBuffer` objects shown in Figure 26-3.

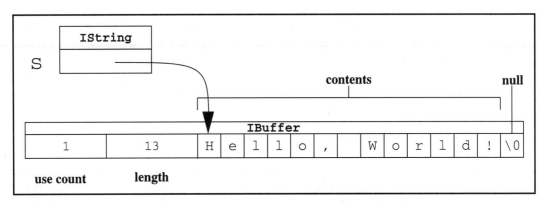

Figure 26-3. Simple IString Object Configuration.

In this configuration, note the following points:

- The `IString` variable s occupies only four bytes and the contents of those bytes is a `char*` pointer to the contents.

- The character array to which the `IString` object points includes a trailing null character. The contents include only the bytes preceding this null. The extra byte is solely for the purpose of making the string contents compatible with code that handles null-terminated C character arrays.

- The character array to which the `IString` points is a portion of an enclosing `IBuffer` object. The `IBuffer` object implements the language-sensitive behavior of `IString` objects. The `IString` object delegates functions that are language-sensitive to this `IBuffer` object.

- Because `IString` objects are essentially smart pointers to `IBuffer` objects, you rarely, if ever, need to allocate `IString` objects dynamically on the heap. You gain nothing by adding an additional layer of pointers and dynamic storage allocation calls. The following code results in two dynamic storage allocations: one to allocate space for the `IString` object, and another to allocate space for the `IString` object's contents:

```
IString
  *p=new IString( "Dynamic" );
```

The following alternative version requires only a single dynamic storage allocation request for the IString object's contents:

```
IString s( "Dynamic" );
```

- The IBuffer object caches the length of the IString object for performance reasons. The strlen function or equivalent is not called every time the length of the contents is required. The length does not include space for the terminating null character. In this example, the length is 13, which is just enough space for "Hello, World!".

- The IBuffer object also contains a use count. This value and its usage are discussed next.

Consider what happens when the IString object's contents include a null character. In the example, if you execute the following code, the blank within "Hello, World!" is changed to a null character:

```
s[7] = '\0';
```

This results in the object's configuration shown in Figure 26-4. The only difference is that the seventh byte of the contents is now a null character rather than a blank. Notice that the length of the contents has not changed.

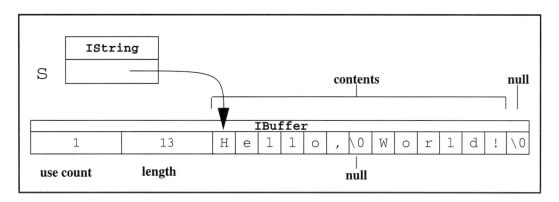

Figure 26-4. An IString Object with an Embedded Null.

The next example shows you how the IString class shares the string contents that the IBuffer object defines. First, add a statement to the example as follows:

```
IString s2( s );
```

This line creates another IString object named s2 and gives it the same value as s. This produces the objects pictured in Figure 26-5.

The figure shows that if you create two IString objects and assign one to the other, you get a single IBuffer object that is shared by the two IString objects. The use count on the IBuffer object is incremented each time the buffer is shared, and it is decremented when a reference to the buffer is removed. When the use count goes to 0, the IBuffer object is deleted.

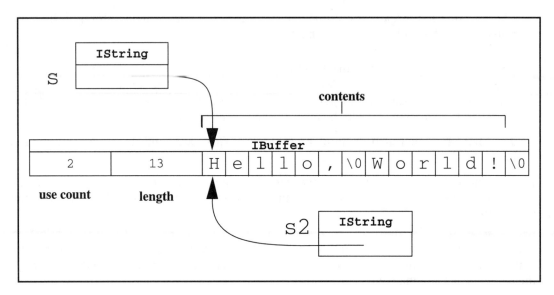

Figure 26-5. An IString Object with a Shared IBuffer Object.

An IString object shares its contents whenever possible. Most often, this happens when you assign one IString object to another. Assignments happen implicitly, too. For example, returning an IString object from a function effectively assigns the returned IString object to the variable reserved in the calling code. This sharing does not extend to the assignment of char* strings, including literal strings. An IString object must make a copy of these strings.

The final example shows what happens when you manipulate one of the two IString objects that share the same buffer contents. Consider the following expression:

```
s = "Good-bye";
```

This statement must change s so that its contents are now the string "Good-bye". The contents of s2 must remain unchanged. The question is: how does the IString class handle a modification to one of the IStrings objects that shares its contents? The example results in IString and IBuffer objects' configurations as shown in Figure 26-6.

As this figure shows, when s changes, it allocates a new IBuffer object to hold its new contents. The string decrements the use count for the old IBuffer object when s is changed to point to the new IBuffer object. Had the use count gone to zero, the original IBuffer would have been deleted. In this example, however, the original IBuffer object remains with s2 still pointing to it.

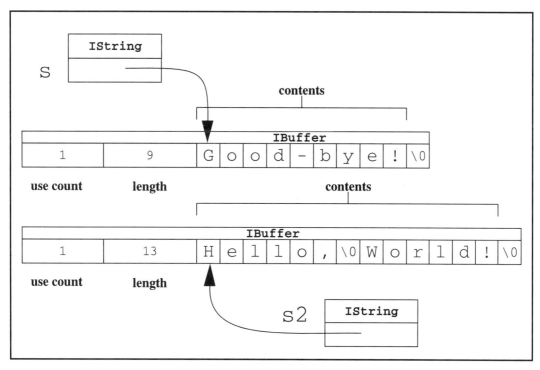

Figure 26-6. IStrings After Copy-on-Write.

Copy-on-Write

The technique of detaching from the old shared contents and allocating new contents when one of the references changed is called *copy-on-write*.

There is some overhead involved in implementing this technique. The class must manage the reference counts and add additional logic to deal with sharing the representation. However, such a scheme is usually beneficial, especially for a general-purpose string class. Such strings are frequently passed between objects on function calls as either arguments or return values. By using a copy-on-write implementation, neither the caller nor the called function need to track what the other party is doing with the strings.

If the caller takes the IString results and just reads the value, then no copy is made. Only when the caller subsequently modifies the result is a copy made. Since such modifications are relatively unlikely, delaying the copy until it is necessary will probably provide a savings.

Reference versus Value Semantics

Your code could implement a C++ string class that has s2's value change as s changes, and vice-versa. Objects that change in this way exhibit *reference-semantics*; that is, they behave as if the objects are pointers.

However, concrete data types should always exhibit *value-semantics*; that is, they behave as if the objects are distinct values rather than pointers. The latter behavior follows from the definition of concrete data types: they represent concrete objects, and two instances, therefore, represent two separate objects. As a consequence, operations performed on one should not affect the other. For this reason, all of the Open Class Library concrete data type classes provide value semantics.

String Constructors

The IString class has 18 public constructors. This may seem like an inordinate number, but each one provides some specific feature that the others do not. Further, the constructors fall into a small set of categories that make it easy for you to choose the appropriate constructor for a given task.

Most of the time you use a constructor that allows you to specify the initial contents of the IString object. You can create an IString object from almost any primitive C++ type. The resulting object contains the most reasonable ASCII representation of the argument value.

A list of the most important, interesting, and useful hints and tips about creating IString objects follows:

- The default constructor builds a string with empty contents. It has length zero. If you convert this string to a char*, the result points to a null character. Therefore, a null IString object is more convenient to use than a null char* pointer that you must check before accessing its contents.

- The copy constructor is important because it provides the only means for two IString objects to share the same string contents.

- The constructors that take char* pointers (plain, signed, or unsigned) all make a copy of the argument character array, up to and including the terminating null character.

- For efficiency, always create a new IString object from an existing one rather than from the existing string's contents (as a char*). Conversely, if you want to copy an existing string, cast the source IString to type char*, as follows:

    ```
    IString source( "source string" );
    // Force a copy of the buffer.
    IString copy( (char*)source );
    ```

- If you create an IString object from a char* pointer with value 0, the it initializes itself to be null.

- You can create an IString object from the contents of up to three separate buffers of arbitrary data. One advantage of these constructors is that they are much more efficient than using concatenation to build up the string's contents. Here are some additional details to note about these types of IString constructors:

  - The argument buffer pointers are of type void*, denoting that these buffers are not null-terminated. You must also pass the buffer length because the buffers can contain embedded null characters.

  - The buffer pointer values can be 0. If they are, the corresponding portion of the string contents are filled with the pad character. The pad character is an optional argument on these constructors. The default pad character is a blank.

  - The pad character is only in effect for 0-valued buffer pointers. If you try to create an IString object with the following code, you do not get "helloxxxxx":

    ```
    IString padded( "hello", 10, 'x' );
    ```

    Instead, the IString constructor uses the ten bytes residing at the location specified by the "hello" literal string.

  - Use these constructors to allocate IString objects that you plan to use as buffers. For example, IString(0,1024) creates an IString object with an empty 1024-byte buffer.

- If you create an IString object from a numeric type (a type other than char), the resulting string's contents are an ASCII representation of that number. For example,

  ```
  IString( 1234 ) == "1234"
  IString( 3.14159 ) == "3.14159"
  ```

Null IString Objects

The IString class shares a single null IBuffer contents object among each and every null IString object in your application. This is important because it means defining a null-valued IString object is extremely efficient because allocation of dynamic storage does not occur. This is part of the reason why allocating IString objects dynamically using operator new is rarely necessary.

Overloaded String Operators

The IString and IOString classes provide a complete set of unary and binary operators. We do not discuss these operators in detail because most of them work the way you would expect. However, to provide some insight into the power and usefulness of some of the more obscure IString operators, we describe the operators that you can use to twiddle the bits of the IString contents. Table 26-7 describes these operators.

The second operand of the bitwise binary operators is replicated (or truncated) by the operators. In effect, the second operand becomes the same size as the first operand.

Table 26-7. IString Bitwise Operators

Operator	Description	Examples
operator&	Bitwise AND. Result bits are set only if the bits of both operands are set.	IString s("5"); s & "\x0F" == "\x05" s & "\xFF" == s IString("a") & "\xDF" == "A"
operator|	Bitwise OR. Result bits are set if the corresponding bit is set in either or both operands.	IString s("Hello"); s | " " == "hello" IString s2("\x0\x1\x2"); s2 | "0" == "012"
operator^	Bitwise exclusive OR. Result bits are set only if the corresponding bits in the operands are different.	IString s("BiCapitalized"); s ^ " " == "bIcAPITALIZED" s ^ "????" ^ "???" == s
operator~	Unary bitwise negation. Result bits are the inverse of the operand bits.	~IString(" ") == "\xDF"

If you use IStrings objects to manipulate textual data only, you may not find a use for these operators. However, if you are using IStrings to hold binary data, these operators greatly simplify that operation. If you are writing a computer hardware simulator, an IString object can hold the emulator's "memory" and might be able to emulate the machine's exclusive OR instruction by using IString::operator^. Or, you might use an IString object to hold bitmap bits and then want to manipulate those bits using the higher-level IString operators.

The exclusive OR operator is interesting. Applying it twice with the same operand creates an identity operation; that is, the result is the original operand. Thus, you can use this operator to implement a simple (but not totally secure) encryption scheme.

The following code reads data from stdin, performs an exclusive OR with an arbitrary key, and writes the result to stdout:

Using IStrings with Binary Data - data\cipher\cipher.cpp

```
#include <istring.hpp>
#include <iostream.h>
#include <stdio.h>

int main ( int argc, char *argv[] )
  {
  int
    result = 0;

  // Get a key.
  IString
    key( argv[1] );
```

```
     // Ensure a key was specified.
     if ( key.length() )
        {
        // Put input and output files in binary mode.
        if ( !freopen( "", "rb", stdin )
              ||
             !freopen( "", "wb", stdout ) )
           {
           cerr << "Error opening input/output files.\a" << endl;
           result = 2;
           }
        else
           {
           // Read from stdin, XOR the bytes with the key,
           // and write to stdout.
           IString
             buffer( 0, 4096 ); // Allocate 4K buffer.
           while ( true )
              {
              size_t
                n = fread( (char*)buffer, 1, buffer.length(), stdin );
              buffer ^= key;
              fwrite( (char*)buffer, 1, n, stdout );
              if ( n < buffer.length() )
                 break;
              }
           }
        }
     else
        {
        cerr << "You must specify a key!\a" << endl;
        result = 1;
        }
     return result;
     }
```

From this code example, you see how to use an IString object to manage a buffer rather than to simply hold some text. You gain the benefit of the storage management support inherent in IString and obtain all of the string manipulation functions that IString provides.

Use this cipher program from a command prompt as follows:

```
C>cipher "some secret key" <input.txt >output.txt
C>cipher "some secret key" <output.txt
```

This sequence of commands writes the original file to stdout. The intermediate output.txt file holds the contents of input.txt, thus rendering the contents unusable without the user having the secret key.

String Searches

The IString class provides a comprehensive set of string search functions. Table 26-8 lists a set of *canonical* search functions. Canonical functions search the string from left to right starting the search at the position you specify. If you do not specify an explicit starting position, the search starts at the beginning of the string. You can also search a string from right to left. The functions to do that have similar names, but have the prefix *last*: lastIndexOf, lastIndexOfAnyOf, and lastIndexOfAnyBut. These functions accept a starting position and search from that point back to the beginning of the string. By default, they start searching from the end of the string.

Table 26-8. IString Search Functions

Search Function	Description
indexOf	Searches for the next occurrence of the argument string and returns the position at which the next occurrence was found. It returns 0 if the argument string is not found.
indexOfAnyOf	Interprets the argument as a set of characters. Use this function to search a string for characters in this set. The returned value is the position in the string of the first character that is a member of the argument set. If the string holds none of the argument characters, the function returns 0. Use this function to search for the next occurrence of any of a set of delimiters, to find the next numeric digit, and so on.
indexOfAnyBut	Searches for characters not in the argument set. This is similar to indexOfAnyOf, but does not search for characters in the argument set. Thus, use it to find the next nonnumeric digit, the next non-whitespace character, and so on.

Table 26-9 lists a set of search function arguments which you can use to specify a search argument.

Table 26-9. IString Search Function Arguments

Argument Type	Description
IString&	An IString object. You can also pass an IString argument as a char* in almost all cases (except when the IString contains embedded nulls). Using an IString argument does provide some performance advantages, too. For indexOf, the IString argument is the string for which you are searching. For indexOfAnyOf or indexOfAnyBut, the characters in the string are the set of characters that are accepted or rejected.
char*	A char* pointer to an array of characters. Use it when you pass a literal string as the search argument. The search functions treat the char* argument the same as they treat an IString argument.
char	A single character. It is passed to the search functions directly without having to build an IString object or character array around it. In this case, indexOf and indexOfAnyOf are identical.
IStringTest&	An arbitrary "string-test" object. For complex search criteria that the basic IString search functions do not cover, you can usually implement the criteria using a class derived from IStringTest. The indexOf function passes the string test object one character at a time until a character tests true. indexOfAnyOf works the same way. If you pass indexOfAnyBut an IStringTest object, the function passes the object characters until one tests false.

Even with 24 search functions, choosing the right function is not difficult if you understand the underlying model. To determine the right function to use, decide whether you want to search for a given string, one of a set of characters, or a character not in a given set. Then decide whether you want to search from the beginning of the string or the end. Do not be concerned about the search argument because the C++ overloaded functions ensure that the proper function gets called.

In addition to the basic set of search functions, IString also provides the advanced search functions described in Table 26-10.

Table 26-10. Advanced IString Search Functions

Search Function	Description
isAbbreviationFor	Tests whether the IString object is an acceptable abbreviation for the argument string. The string passes this test if it matches the argument string and has sufficient length (which you specify as an additional, optional argument).
isLike	Performs a fuzzy comparison of two character strings.

The following code uses the isAbbreviationFor function to evaluate a "PRINT" string abbreviation.

```
IString keyword( "PRINT" );
IString input1( "PR" );
IString input2( "P" );

// These expressions evaluate to true.
input1.isAbbreviationFor( keyword );
input2.isAbbreviationFor( keyword );

// This expression evaluates to false.
input2.isAbbreviationFor( keyword, 2 );
```

Use the isAbbreviationFor function to test input for command keywords, validate input data, and so on. Also use it as shorthand for testing whether the beginning of one string matches another. The expression aString.isAbbreviationFor(anotherString) is identical to the expression aString == anotherString.subString(1, aString.length()). The first expression, in addition to being much easier for you to type and your program to read, is also far more efficient than the latter. The subString call in the second version requires your program to create a copy of the portion of the string being compared.

Although the isLike function is not quite a full, regular-expression parser, it is built in and it is efficient. Use it to implement sophisticated searches with minimal effort. For example, the following program searches, or greps, a file for lines that match an arbitrary pattern.

Grep for Matching Pattern - data\igrep\igrep.cpp

```
#include <istring.hpp>
#include <fstream.h>

int main ( int argc, char *argv[] )
  {
  int
    result = 0;
```

```
// Validate the input arguments.
if ( argc != 3 )
   {
   cerr << "Usage:  igrep  <file>  <pattern>\a" << endl;
   return 0;
   }

IString
   file( argv[1] ),
   pattern( argv[2] );

// Pad the pattern at both ends with wildcards (so the pattern
// is found anywhere in an input line)
pattern = IString( 0, 1,
                   (char*)pattern, pattern.length(),
                   0, 1,
                   '*' );

// Open the input file.
ifstream
   input( file );

if ( !input )
   {
   cerr << "Error opening file.\a" << endl;
   return 0;
   }

// Read lines, looking for a pattern.
unsigned
   lineNo = 0;
while ( input )
   {
   IString
      line = IString::lineFrom( input );
   lineNo++;
   if ( line.isLike( pattern ) )
      {
      result++;
      cout << IString( lineNo ).rightJustify( 4 ) << " "
           << line << endl;
      }
   }
return result;
}
```

You can include special characters in the isLike function argument string to further qualify the search. The special character * matches an arbitrary string of 0 or more characters. For example, aString.isLike("*") returns true for all strings, and aString.isLike("*{*}*") returns true for all strings that contain a matched set of braces. The character ? matches exactly one arbitrary character. For example, aString.isLike("x ?=*") returns true for any string containing code that applies any operator-plus-assignment operator to the variable x, and aString.isLike("?*") returns true for any string containing at least one character.

IStringTest Class

In Table 26-9, you saw that all of the basic IString search functions are overloaded to accept an IStringTest object. Use the version of those functions that takes an IStringTest argument to implement your own special-purpose search functions.

The `IStringTest` class helps you to easily and efficiently search a string's contents for the next punctuation character. Without the version of `indexOfAnyOf` that accepts an `IStringTest` object, you would have to resort to code like this: `aString.indexOfAnyOf( ";':\"\",.?" )`. The problem with this code is that the argument does not include the whole set of punctuation characters. ANSI C specifies that the `ispunct` function of the Standard C library returns `true` for any characters considered to be punctuation. And even if you write a test program to determine the exact set of punctuation characters, that is not an ideal solution because the set can vary based on the C locale in effect.

Instead, you need to somehow pass the `ispunct` function to the `IString` object and get it to call that function instead of searching against the argument set that contains the characters. `IStringTest` enables you to do that. To exploit this capability, derive from the `IStringTest` class and override the virtual member function `test` to implement your character-testing logic. `IString` calls the `IStringTest` object's `test` function, which tests individual characters during execution of the various search functions.

The base `IStringTest` class has a constructor that accepts a pointer to a C function of the same type as the standard C library character test functions `ispunct`, `isspace`, `isdigit`, and so on. To apply this function to `IString` objects, find the position of the next punctuation character using: `aString.indexOfAnyOf( ispunct )`.

If you want to use your own string-testing logic, you have two choices. One choice is to write a C function that applies the test, and then wrap this function with a generic `IStringTest` object. For example, to search for the next occurrence of either white space or punctuation, write the following code:

```
extern "C" int myTest( int c )
{
  return isspace( c ) || ispunct( c );
}
```

Then use this function as follows:

```
aString.indexOf( myTest )
```

The alternative is to derive a new class from `IStringTest` and override the `test` member function, as follows:

Deriving from IStringTest - data\strngtst\strngtst.cpp

```
class MyTest : public IStringTest {
public:
  MyTest ( )
    : IStringTest( user, 0 )
      {
      }
  virtual int test ( int c ) const
      {
        return isspace( c ) || ispunct( c );
      }
};
```

Then use this class as follows:

```
aString.indexOf( MyTest() )
```

There are some things to watch for when deriving from the `IStringTest` class. First, `IStringTest` has no default constructor. You have to implement a constructor in any derived class and explicitly create the `IStringTest` base class in the constructor's member initializer list. IStringTest provides a protected constructor expressly for use by such derived classes. This constructor accepts two arguments:

- An enumerator that specifies the type of the value the IStringTest object is holding. When deriving from IStringTest, specify user.

- A void* pointer. This is a pointer or integral value of your choosing. It gives you a way to reuse the space that the base IStringTest class uses to hold its C function pointer. You most often specify 0 for this value.

Second, the virtual function test is a const member function. Make sure your overridden function's signature matches. Cast away the const when your derived IStringTest objects must maintain state information during the search. In the following example, a derived IStringTest object returns true until it encounters a character that is not greater than or equal to the preceding one.

```
class Ascending : public IStringTest {
public:
  Ascending ( )
    : IStringTest( user, 0 ),
      previous( 0 )
    {
    }
  virtual int
    test ( int c ) const
    {
      if ( (unsigned char)c >= previous )
        {
          ((Ascending*)this)->previous = c;
            return true;;
        }
      else
        {
          return false;
        }
private:
  unsigned char  previous;
};
```

Note how you must "cast away const" in the body of the test member function to update the test object's data member.

Open Class Library provides one IStringTest-derived class template called IStringTestMemberFn. This class template makes it easy for you to use a member function of any of your classes to search IStrings.

The template argument for IStringTestMemberFn is the name of the class containing the member function that is to supply the string search logic. Objects of a template class created using IStringTestMemberFn require two arguments to be created:

- An object of the class whose member function you are using.

- A pointer to the member function to be used to test the string's characters. The member function must meet the protocol required by IString and IStringTest, that is, it must accept a single argument of type int and return a Boolean.

The class template accepts any valid combination of const or non-const objects and const or non-const member functions. The following example shows how to use this class template. First, you need a class with a member function that qualifies.

```
class Tester {
public:
virtual int
  isAscending ( int c )
    {
    if ( (unsigned char)c >= previous )
      {
      previous = c;
      return true;;
      }
    else
      return false;
    }
private:
unsigned char
  previous;
};
```

The isAscending function of this class implements the same ascending check as you saw in the previous example. Normally, your class is one you are using elsewhere in your program, and it possesses some data or logic that lends itself to searching your IString objects.

To use Tester::isAscending to search a string, you write code as follows:

```
Tester
  tester;

IStringTestMemberFn<Tester>
  testObj( tester, Tester::isAscending );

result = input.indexOfAnyBut( testObj );
```

The class template generated by IStringTestMemberFn holds a reference to the object you pass on the constructor. Thus, you must take care that this object's lifetime extends beyond that of the template class object. Usually, you just create the class template objects at the point of the IString search function invocation and let it be deleted immediately after performing the search.

Testing

IString also provides a set of functions that test the contents of a string. The testing functions are similar to the searching functions in the previous topic, "String Searches." The former returns a Boolean answer to questions of the form "does the string contents meet some criterion?" The latter returns a more precise answer to questions of the form of "at what position is the first character that meets or fails some criterion?"

The testing functions are effectively a subset of the searching functions. The most substantive difference is that the testing functions have names more suited to that purpose. For example, rather than indexOf, the testing function is named includes. Rather than !indexOfAnyBut(isalpha), the equivalent testing function is isAlphabetic.

Editing

Your character string data does not consist solely of constants. IString provides a comprehensive set of functions that lets you manipulate the contents of an IString. Each edit operation applies some change to the string and returns a reference to the edited object.

What's in a Name?

Should IString provide two functions that do the same thing? The answer is yes because the source code you write is not just read by the compiler; you, and possibly others, also read it.

The naming convention for the member functions of Open Class Library are based on making your source code readable. You can read a book and understand it, even though the ideas are new to you, because the words in the book follow certain syntactic and semantic rules built into the language in which it is written. You can use what you know about the language to form an educated assessment of the meaning of what you read.

Source code is no different. Our use of natural language extends to the way we think. If you think "if the string has any blanks in it, then I need to...," it is much easier to write, and later read, code of the form:

```
if ( aString.includes( isspace ) )
  ...
```

The code in this case follows the conventions we expect from natural language. Member functions in Open Class Library can be categorized into parts of speech. Some are nouns; these nouns describe the returned object. Some are verb phrases; these make sense in context of if and while statements. Some are imperatives; these make sense when directed at objects to instruct them to do something.

We not discuss the editing functions in detail here. We do, however, discuss some of the more advanced editing functions and provide general information that guides you in using the others.

Having just read about searching and testing of IStrings, you are now familiar with the idea of using IStringTest objects to do specialized searching and testing. There is one category of IString editing functions that use IStringTest objects. They are the strip functions shown in Table 26-11.

Table 26-11. Strip Functions

Function	Description
strip	Removes both leading and trailing characters that meet the argument condition.
stripLeading	Removes characters from the beginning of the string. The characters are removed starting at the beginning of the string and continuing until a character is encountered that fails to pass some test specified by the function argument.
stripTrailing	Removes characters starting from the end of the string and working backward that meet the argument test condition.

Each of these functions has overloaded versions that accept an IStringTest object as an argument. For example, you write such code as follows to strip all leading and trailing punctuation from an IString. And, as with the search functions, you use the class template

IStringMemberFn or extend IStringTest further by deriving from it and adding logic to strip off arbitrary characters.

```
aString.strip( ispunct );
```

Another of the IString editing functions is overlayWith. Use this function to overlay a portion of the string with the contents of another string. This function provides a more efficient way to build up compound strings from pieces than the commonly used concatenation operator.

In the following example, IString objects hold a drive letter, a path name, a file name, and a file extension. You want to create from these parts a fully qualified file name. You might be tempted to write the following code statement:

```
IString
    filename = drive + ":" + path + "\\" + file + "." + ext;
```

Because of the way IString manages storage, this code does about seven times as much work as is necessary. Each invocation of IString::operator+ allocates space for new IString contents and copies both operands into it. To counter this, use overlayWith as follows:

```
int length = drive.length() +
             path.length() +
             file.length() +
             ext.length() +
             3;
IString
    filename( 0, length );
filename
    .overlayWith( drive )
    .overlayWith( ":", length = drive.length() )
    .overlayWith( path, length += 1 )
    .overlayWith( "\\", length += path.length() )
    .overlayWith( file, length += 1 )
    .overlayWith( ".", length += file.length() )
    .overlayWith( ext, length += 1 );
```

Although this version is more difficult to read, it results in a single allocation of an IString buffer. It also copies the contents of each of the various components only once. Therefore, if code efficiency is critical, you may have to sacrifice code readability.

Word Functions

IString also provides functions that handle the string contents as a set of white-space-delimited words. These functions provide logical access to this set of words, and let you search for a given sequence of words. In this section we discuss some of these functions described in Table 26-12.

The logical sequence of words these functions handle always use 1-based indexing. This applies to the 0-based IOString functions as well. These functions search a string for a given phrase (that is, a sequence of words as contained in an argument string) and return either the position in the string at which the phrase begins or the index of the word at which the phrase begins. The difference is rather subtle, so remember that all IString functions with the prefix index return character positions within the string.

The wordIndexOfPhrase function is invaluable when translating user input to an index of an array of possible values. For example, consider a program that accepts as input any one of the subset of IString editing function names {center, leftJustify, rightJustify}, an argument

Table 26-12. Word Functions

Function	Description
indexOfPhrase	Returns the character position in the string at which the argument phrase begins. It returns 0 if it does not find the argument phrase. For example, IString("a b c").indexOfPhrase("b c") returns 3.
wordIndexOfPhrase	Searches for the argument phrase and returns the index of the first word of that phrase within the string. IString("a b c").wordIndexOfPhrase("b c") returns 2.

string, a number, and a pad character. The program's output is the contents of the input string modified as indicated by the requested function and its arguments. One solution is to use an array of IString member function pointers and to translate the function name argument into an index into this array, as follows:

```
typedef
unsigned (IString::*editFn)( unsigned, char );

editFn table[] = { IString::center,
                   IString::leftJustify,
                   IString::rightJustify );

IString fns = { center leftJustify rightJustify );

unsigned i = fns.wordIndexOfPhrase( argv[1] );
cout << (input.*table[i-1])( n, pad ) << endl;
```

Because word indexing is 1-based, wordIndexOfPhrase returns 0 if the input string is invalid. This behavior is used by placing the address of a default function in the first element of the editFns array. This function then gets used if you provide invalid input or do not provide any input.

String Parsing

You can also use IString to split up a text string into its component parts, or *tokens*. This technique is called *parsing*. The IStringParser class provides this function for Open Class Library. The following code uses IStringParser to separate name into tokens:

```
#include <istring.hpp>
#include <istparse.hpp>
#include <iostream.h>

int main ()
  {
  IString firstName, lastName, rank, starship;
  IString name ( "Jean-Luc Picard,Captain,USS Enterprise" );
  name >> firstName >> lastName >> "," >> rank >> "," >> starship;
  cout << "firstName is "<< firstName << endl <<
          "lastName is " << lastName  << endl <<
          "rank is "     << rank      << endl <<
          "starship is " << starship  << endl;
  return 0;
  }
```

The output from this program is as follows:

```
firstName is Jean-Luc
lastName is Picard
rank is Captain
starship is USS Enterprise
```

Notice that we do not refer to the IStringParser class directly, and you might have to look twice to determine where we use an object of that class. Further, all constructors for the IStringParser class are protected, so you cannot create an object of this class directly. Instead, you create IStringParser objects by invoking a friend function: one of nine overloaded versions of operator>>. Do this as follows:

- Provide an IString object as the left-hand argument of the operator. This string specifies the text you want parsed by the subsequent parsing expressions.

- Provide as the right-hand argument any of the various types of *tokens* or *patterns* accepted by the operator>> functions. We describe these in Table 26-13.

Table 26-13. Right-hand Arguments for IStringParser Friend operator>>

Argument Type	Description
IString& token	The next token in the left-hand argument of the expression is copied into the IString object. The delimiter between tokens is a space. If only one operator>> is used in an expression, the resulting token is the entirety of the original string.
const IString& pattern const char* pattern char pattern	The parser position moves to the first occurrence of the pattern in the source string. Subsequent calls to operator>> in the same expression begin parsing from the new position. If the pattern is not found, the parser moves off the end of the source string.
unsigned long delta int delta	The parser position moves to the right by the delta. The movement is relative to the current parser position, not to the beginning of the string. Subsequent calls to operator>> in the same expression begin parsing from the new position.
const IStringTest& test	The IStringTest object is applied to each character in the source string beginning at the current parser position and continues until a character tests true. If no character tests true, the parser moves off the end of the source string.
IStringParser::Command command	The parser position moves using one of the IStringParser::Command enumerations {reset, skipWord, skip}. IStringParser::reset returns the parser to the beginning of the string. IStringParser::skipWord and IStringParser::skip cause the parser to skip over the next word (space-delimited token).
const IStringParser::SkipWords& skipObject	The parser skips the number of words indicated when the IStringParser::SkipWords object is constructed.

The return value of the expression is an `IStringParser` object. When returned, this object has already completed its first parsing operation depending on the type of the right-hand argument. You can use the resulting `IStringParser` object to do additional parsing by applying the same right-shift operators (>>) to the parser object.

This example shows the step-by-step explanation of how the parsing in the previous example occurs:

```
name >> firstName // Calls operator>>(const IString&,IString&).
                  // This creates an IStringParser object, uses it
                  // to parse the first token (set the contents of
                  // the variable firstName), and returns
                  // the parser.
         >> lastName  // Calls IStringParser::operator>>(IString&).
                  // The parser returned by the first operation is
                  // used to parse the next token and set the
                  // contents of lastName.  The tokens are space
                  // delimited.
         >> ","   // Calls IStringParser::operator>>(const char*).
                  // This advances the parser to the next
                  // occurrence of the pattern ",".
  >> rank >> "," >> starship;  // Makes similar calls to those
                  // described above.  The token placed in the
                  // rank variable is delimited by commas.
                  // The remainder of the text is
                  // parsed into the variable starship.
```

You can also create an `IStringParser` object by applying the left-shift operator (`operator<<`) to an `IString` object. The right-hand operand in this case is an `unsigned long` that indicates an absolute column position. When this operator is used, the parser position in the source string moves to the column specified. Column positions are 1-based. Further parsing operations continue from this new position in the source string. We discuss absolute column positioning in more detail later.

All `IStringParser` objects are temporary. Because the constructors are protected, you use the shift operators to create an `IStringParser` object. If you need to, make the parser object live long enough to access it later. You could add the following code, but we do not advise doing so:

```
IStringParser &parser = (IStringParser &)( aString >> aToken );
```

Instead, to do subsequent parsing, capture the remainder of the text in an `IString` token and resume parsing with that as the starting point.

Extracting Tokens

The most useful parsing operation is to extract some portion of the *parse text* (the portion of the original text yet to be parsed) into an `IString` variable. The previous example demonstrates how to do this: apply the right-shift operator to an `IStringParser` or `IString` object when you are beginning a parsing statement, and specify the `IString` variable that is to receive the next token as the right-hand argument.

The result is that the next token from the text being parsed is assigned to the `IString` variable. To identify the next token requires some explanation. The string parser assigns to the `IString` variable the portion of the text being parsed between its current position (that is, where it left off in parsing the preceding text) and the position indicated by the following parsing operations:

- If there is no subsequent parsing operation, the string parser assigns the remainder of the parse text to the string.

- If the next parsing operation is to extract another token, the string parser assigns to the string the next word from the parse text.

- If the next parsing operation is to match some pattern, the string parser assigns to the string the portion of the parse text lying between the current position and the position at which the pattern is located.

- If the next parsing operation involves column positioning, the parser assigns to the string the portion of the parse text that lies between the current position and the position specified by that column position.

This basic description of extracting tokens coupled with the semantics of C++ leads to the following observation: the value of an IString variable that is assigned a token during parsing will likely change as the parsing proceeds. The following example shows this:

```
IString
  text( "one two" ),
  a, b, c;
text >> a;          // a == "one two"
text >> b >> c; // b == "one", c == "two"
```

Both parsing statements begin by calling the function operator>>(IString&,IString&). This function constructs an IStringParser object from the first argument and then calls operator>>(IString&). That function has to extract the next token and assign it to its argument. But what does it assign? Because it is called exactly the same way in both cases, it has to do the same thing, which is to assign the parse text in its entirety. Only when the second call to that function occurs (which happens only in the second case) does the string parser complete the parsing of the first token. Thus, the value of the variable b changes from "one two" to its final value of "one". This works this way because the IStringParser object keeps a parsing history. As the text is parsed, a history of what has been done is saved. When the next operator is applied, the object can correct its action.

Matching Patterns

After basic extracting of tokens, you will likely find the ability to control the building of tokens based on the contents of the parse text to be the most useful feature of the string-parsing component of Open Class Library. With pattern matching, you can adjust the position in the parse text to skip over uninteresting portions and to locate more important tokens. For example, the following program invokes the system dir command and parses the output to find the oldest and newest files:

String parsing with pattern matching - data\stparse\stparse.cpp

```cpp
#include <idate.hpp>
#include <itime.hpp>
#include <istring.hpp>
#include <istparse.hpp>
#include <iostream.h>
#include <stdlib.h>
#include <fstream.h>
int main ()
{
    // List a directory and redirect it to a file.
#ifdef IC_PM
    int rc = system ("dir /N > dir.out");
#endif
#ifdef IC_WIN
    int rc = system ("dir > dir.out");
#endif
    if (!rc)
    {
        // Create an input stream.
        ifstream input( "dir.out" );
        if ( !input )
        {
            cerr << "Error opening file.\a" << endl;
            return 0;
        }
        // Create variables to hold parsing tokens.
        IString line,
                pattern1 = IString( 0, 1,
                                    "bytes",
                                    IString("bytes").length(),
                                    0, 1,
                                    '*' ),
                pattern2 = IString( 0, 1,
                                    "<DIR>",
                                    IString("<DIR>").length(),
                                    0, 1,
                                    '*' ),
                month, day, year,
                hour, minutes, AMPM,
                date,
                time,
                size,
                sizeEAs,
                filename,
                oldestFilename,
                newestFilename;
        IDate oldestDate, newestDate(1,1), theDate;
        ITime oldestTime, newestTime(0,0), theTime;

        // Skip the first five lines of the output that contain nonpertinent
        // information.
        for (int i=0; i<5; i++)
            IString::lineFrom (input);
```

```
              // Read lines and look for the oldest and newest files.
              while ( input )
              {
                 // Get a line.
                 line = IString::lineFrom( input );
                 // If the line is the summary information at the bottom,
                 // quit the loop.
                 if (line.isLike (pattern1))
                    break;
                 // Only process the line if it contains information for a file,
                 // not a directory.
                 if (!line.isLike (pattern2))
                 {
                    // Parse the line into its tokens.
                    // OS/2 has an EA size field; Windows does not.
#ifdef IC_PM
                    line >> date >> time >> size >> sizeEAs >> filename;
#endif
#ifdef IC_WIN
                    line >> date >> time >> size >> filename;
#endif
                    // Strip leading or trailing white space from the file name.
                    filename.strip();
                    // Our output file will always be the newest, so exclude it.
                    if (filename != "DIR.OUT")
                    {
                       // Parse the date and create an IDate object.  Hardcode the
                       // default separators.  A more robust solution would query
                       // them from the system.
#ifdef IC_PM
                       date >> month >> '-' >> day >> '-' >> year;
#endif
#ifdef IC_WIN
                       date >> month >> '/' >> day >> '/' >> year;
#endif
                       IDate theDate (IDate::Month(month.asInt()),
                                      day.asInt(),
                                      year.asInt()+1900);
                       // Parse the time and create an ITime object.
                       time >> hour >> ":" >> 1 >> minutes >> 2 >> AMPM;
                       ITime theTime (((AMPM == "a") ||
                                       (AMPM == "A")) ?
                                          hour.asInt() : hour.asInt() + 12,
                                          minutes.asInt());
                       // Check to see if the date of the current file is older
                       // than the oldest or newer than the newest.  If so, reset
                       // the variables.
                       if ((theDate < oldestDate) ||
                           ((theDate == oldestDate) && (theTime <
                                                        oldestTime)))
                       {
                          oldestDate = theDate;
                          oldestFilename = filename;
                          oldestTime = theTime;
                       }
                       if ((theDate > newestDate) ||
                           ((theDate == newestDate) && (theTime >
                                                        newestTime)))
                       {
                          newestDate = theDate;
                          newestFilename = filename;
                          newestTime = theTime;
                       }
                    }
                 }
              }
```

```
            // Report our findings.
            cout << "Oldest file is " << oldestFilename <<
                    " with date " << oldestDate.asString() <<
                    " and time " << oldestTime.asString() <<
                    endl;
            cout << "Newest file is " << newestFilename <<
                    " with date " << newestDate.asString() <<
                    " and time " << newestTime.asString() <<
                    endl;
        }
        else
            cout << "Dir command could not be completed." << endl;
        return 0;
    }
```

Sample output from this program follows:

```
    Oldest file is CDFS.IFS with date 12-12-94 and time 18:25:00
    Newest file is CONFIG.SYS with date 08-26-96 and time 19:34:00
```

The following example uses the `char*`, `IString&`, `char`, and `int` versions of `operator>>`. Parsing the whole line invokes `IStringParser::operator>>(IString&)` repeatedly. Because the tokens are separated by spaces, there is no need to search for any specific delimiter.

```
            // Parse the line into its tokens.
    #ifdef IC_PM
            line >> date >> time >> size >> sizeEAs >> filename;
    #endif
```

However, when the date is parsed, the day, month, and year are delimited by special characters, so `IStringParser::operator>>(char)` is used.

```
            // Parse the date and create an IDate object.
    #ifdef IC_PM
            date >> month >> '-' >> day >> '-' >> year;
    #endif
```

Positioning by Relative Column Offsets

Sometimes the data you want to extract is dictated by the format of the data rather than by its content. For those situations, use parsing operations that specify positioning within the parse text at columns relative to the position at which the last pattern was matched. This invokes `IStringParser::operator>>(int)`.

The **data\stparse** example shown previously uses this technique. To parse the time into its component, use `IStringParser::operator>>(char*)` and `IStringParser::operator>>(int)` as follows:

```
    // Parse the time and create an ITime object.
    time >> hour >> ":" >> 1 >> minutes >> 2 >> AMPM;
```

The hour >> ":" portion of the code places the part of the source string prior to the ":" into the hour variable. (Notice that the use of ":" is identical to ':' because the `char*` string is only one character long.) After the hour is parsed, the parser position is on the ":" in the source string. Next, a call to `IStringParser::operator>>(int)` is made and the parser position is moved forward one position to skip the ":". The parser then places the rest of the source string into the minutes variable. `IStringParser::operator>>(int)` is called again, the parser position moves forward 2 places, and the source string contents between the prior position and the current position are placed in the minutes variable. The last call to `operator>>` places the remainder of the source string in the AMPM variable. So, for example, if time is "3:22A", after parsing occurs hour contains "3", minutes contains "22", and AMPM contains "A".

Positioning by Absolute Column

You can use the left-shift operator to position the parser to an absolute column position. This is most useful when the format of the string data you are parsing is well-defined and consistent. Unlike using `IStringParser::operator>>(unsigned long)`, which moves the parser position relative to the current position, `IStringParser::operator<<(unsigned long)` moves the parser to an absolute 1-based column position in the text being parsed. You can modify the **data\stparse** example to parse the `time` variable using this technique. The code is as follows:

```
// Parse the time and create an ITime object.
IString temp;
time >> hour << 2 >> temp << 3 >> minutes << 5 >> AMPM;
```

The parsing begins as it did before. However, when the parser encounters the first `IStringParser::operator<<(unsigned long)`, it moves the parser position to the column specified, which is 2, and copies all the text between the previous position (the beginning of the string) and the current position to the `hour` variable. Subsequent calls to `IStringParser::operator<<(unsigned long)` work in exactly the same way. The data between columns 2 and 3 is copied to `temp`, between 3 and 5 is copied to `minutes`, and the remainder of the string is copied to the last variable. You can "see" this behavior by looking at the code. Each variable is delimited by the column numbers that define its content, where the first column is inclusive and the last is not. Thus, because the `temp` variable is between 2 and 3 in the parse statement, its data is defined as starting in column 2 and extending to column 3.

We also defined `IString temp;`, a temporary variable, to hold a column that we wanted to "throw away" or skip when using absolute column positioning. To avoid doing this every time we wanted to skip one or more columns, `IStringParser` provides two ways to skip columns.

Skipping

Sometimes you need to skip over items when parsing data. Instead of defining temporary variables each time to hold the superfluous data, you can use `IStringParser::skip` to indicate to the parser object that you want to skip the next token. The token is defined by its context. The following code uses this technique in the **data\stparse** example to parse the `time` variable:

```
// Parse the time and create an ITime object.
time >> hour << 2 >> IStringParser::skip << 3 >> minutes << 5 >> AMPM;
```

By its context, the token that is skipped is defined as "the token that starts in column 2 and extends to column 3," just like the `temp` variable was. You could also use `IStringParser::skip` in parsing the line variable. When the line is parsed, portions are parsed into variables called `size` and `sizeEAs`, but these items are never used; they are thrown away. You could use `IStringParser::skip` instead, as follows:

```
// Parse the line into its tokens.
#ifdef IC_PM
    line >> date >> time >> IStringParser::skip >>
        IStringParser::skip >> filename;
#endif
```

Again, the context of the parsing statement defines the skipped tokens. Because we do not specify any special characters or positions as delimiters, two space-delimited tokens are skipped.

`IStringParser::skip` is part of the `IStringParser::Command` enumeration that contains the reset, skip, and `skipWord` literals.   `IStringParser::reset` sets the parser position back to the beginning of the parse text. `IStringParser::skip` and `IStringParser::skipWord` are equivalent.

If you want to skip more than two or three items in a parse statement, the repeated use of `IStringParser::skip` can become cumbersome. With the `IStringParser::SkipWords` class, you can skip as many tokens as you want with one call to `IStringParser::operator>>`. To do that, you construct the `IStringParser::SkipWords` object with an `unsigned long` that indicates how many tokens you want to skip, and then use the object in your parsing. The default number of words to skip is one. When we use `IStringParser::SkipWords`, the code to parse the input line in the **data\stparse** example becomes:

```
    IStringParser::SkipWords wordsToSkip(2);
    // Parse the line into its tokens.
#ifdef IC_PM
    line >> date >> time >> wordsToSkip >> filename;
#endif
```

REXX

If you have used the REXX programming language, you probably noticed that the `IString` searching and editing functions resemble those that REXX provides. The same is true with the `IString` parsing function that `IStringParser` provides. If you are familiar with REXX, you can quickly adapt to string parsing in C++ using the function that the `IStringParser` class provides.   For example, the following REXX code displays the directories that compose the `PATH` environment variable:

```
    path = VALUE( "PATH", , "OS2ENVIRONMENT" )
    while path <> ""
      do
        parse var path dir ";" path
        say dir
      end
```

Using `IStringParser`, you implement the same function as follows:

```
    IString
      path( getenv( "PATH" ) );
    while ( path.length() > 0 )
      {
      IString
        dir;
      path >> dir >> ";" >> path;
      cout << dir << endl;
      }
```

Follow these steps to convert REXX to C++:

1. Drop the `parse var` (or `parse value` and `with`) portions of the REXX statement.

2. Insert a right-shift operator (`operator>>`) between each element in the REXX parse statement.

IStringTest in Parsing

If you have a specialized set of tokens that you want to skip or to accept in your parsing text, you can use an `IStringTest` object as an argument to `IStringParser::operator>>`. The `IStringTest` object is called for each character until it returns `true`. For example, if you want to skip all of the parse text until you find any type of punctuation, use the following code:

```
#include <istring.hpp>
#include <istparse.hpp>
#include <iostream.h>
#include <ctype.h>

extern "C" int myTest( int c )
{
  return ispunct( c );
}

int main ()
{
  IString input ("Some text delimited by%The rest of the text."),
          beginningOfString,
          restOfString;
  input >> beginningOfString >> myTest >> 1 >> restOfString;

    // Report our findings.
  cout << "Beginning is " << beginningOfString << " and
     restOfString is " << restOfString << endl;
  return 0;
}
```

The output from this program is as follows:

```
Beginning is Some text delimited by and restOfString is The rest of the
text.
```

See the previous section on `IStringTest` for more details on how to use that class.

Conversions

You can convert the contents of an `IString` object to a variety of other formats. The Open Class Library string classes provide functions that convert an `IString` object's contents to other data types. These conversions fall into two main categories: those that return an object of some built-in C++ type (described in Table 26-14) with a value derived from the contents, and those that return another `IString` object (described in Table 26-15) whose contents are a reinterpretation of the characters of the original string.

`IString` provides a full set of functions that interpret the `IString` contents as a numeric value using one of the four conventions described in Table 26-15. It then converts that numeric value to an `IString` object, which reinterprets the value according to one of the other four

---

Watch Out for Overflow!

An `IString` object can hold any sequence of digits. But the built-in C++ types can hold only a finite range of values. As a result, converting to a numeric type using `asInt`, `asUnsigned`, or `asDouble` may fail if the string's contents express a value that cannot be contained in the requested built-in type. Ensure that the strings you convert using these functions contain reasonable values.

Table 26-14. Conversion Functions Returning a Built-in C++ Type

Conversion Function	Description
operator char*	The string is converted to a char* pointer to the contents. This happens implicitly. The compiler accomplishes this with a user-defined conversion operator. Because many plain C functions take as an argument char* pointers, you probably do not want to invoke an explicit asCStringPtr function each time. (After all, IString is intended to serve as an improved char* pointer.) There are actually three separate char* types that an IString object can be converted to: char*, signed char*, and unsigned char*. The compiler selects the proper one based on what you are doing with the generated pointer.
asInt	The string is converted to type long int. This makes sense only if the IString object is a representation of an integer value. This function is a little forgiving of non-integer data in that it converts the leading digits of the string and skips any extra characters that are not valid for an integer's representation. Note that asInt uses the sprintf function to convert the string so it handles scientific notation, too. If you only need an int or a short int, convert to type long int using asInt. The compiler then applies normal integral conversions to convert the type to the one you need.
asUnsigned	The string is converted to type unsigned int. This returns an unsigned integral value representing the IString contents. The primary difference between this function and asInt is that it can return larger values in cases where the string represents a number larger than what fits in a signed long int.
asDouble	The string is converted to a floating-point value. Use this function if the IString contains a decimal point.

Table 26-15. Conversion Functions Returning Another IString Object

Contents	Description
characters	All IString contents can be considered plain characters.
decimal digits	An IString comprised solely of decimal digits can also be considered to represent the numeric value of that string of digits. For example, the string "123" can be interpreted as a representation of the number 123. An IString object can be considered this way if it passes the test applied by the IString function isDigits.
binary digits	An IString comprised solely of binary digits can also be considered to represent the numeric value of that string of digits. For example, the string "01010001" can be interpreted as a representation of the number 0x51. An IString object can be considered this way if it passes the test applied by the IString function isBinaryDigits.
hexadecimal digits	An IString comprised solely of hexadecimal digits can also be considered to represent the numeric value of that string of digits. For example, the string "af511" can be interpreted as a representation of the number 0x0AF511. An IString object can be considered this way if it passes the test applied by the IString function isHexDigits. **Note:** The hexadecimal digits "a-f" can be either uppercase or lowercase, or even mixed uppercase and lowercase within the same string.

conventions. The functions that do the conversion all have names like <input>2<output>, where <input>, and <output>, indicates binary (b), character (c), decimal (d), or hexadecimal (x). For example, IString("cat").c2x() converts the string "cat" to "636174." Use the following program to see how these conversion functions work.

IString Conversion Test Program - data\convert\convert.cpp

```cpp
#include <istring.hpp>
#include <istream.hpp>

typedef IString String;

typedef String& (String::*pStringConversionMember)();
typedef String (*pStringConversionFunction)(const String &);

// Array of IString conversion functions that operate on the
// calling string.
static pStringConversionMember
  members[] = { String::b2c, String::b2d, String::b2x,
                String::c2b, String::c2d, String::c2x,
                String::d2b, String::d2c, String::d2x,
                String::x2b, String::x2c, String::x2d };

// Array of IString static conversion functions that return a new string.
static pStringConversionFunction
  functions[] = { IString::b2c, IString::b2d, IString::b2x,
                  IString::c2b, IString::c2d, IString::c2x,
                  IString::d2b, IString::d2c, IString::d2x,
                  IString::x2b, IString::x2c, IString::x2d };

// Array of command-line options.
static String
  options( "b2c b2d b2x "
           "c2b c2d c2x "
           "d2b d2c d2x "
           "x2b x2c x2d " );

int main( int argc, char *argv[] )
  {
  if ( argc == 3 )
    {
    // Get conversion function name.
    String opt( argv[1] );

    // Get string to be converted.
    String arg( argv[2] );

    // Get the index of the conversion function in the options array.
    // Note that indexing begins at one and 0 is returned if no
    // conversion function is matched.
    unsigned int i = options.wordIndexOfPhrase( opt );

    // Perform the conversions and print the results.
    if ( i )
      {
      String opt = options.word(i--); // Note the index must be
                                      // decremented for
                                      // the function call.

      String input  = arg;
      String result = functions[i](arg); // Call the static function
                                         // to return a new string.

      // Print the results.
      cout << opt << "(\"" << input << "\")   \t=\t" << result << "\n";
      cout << "(\"" << input << "\")." << opt << "()\t=\t";
```

```
        // Call the nonstatic function to operate on the string itself and
        // print the results.
        (input.*members[i])();
        cout << input << "\n";

        // Reverse the given option (for example, from b2x to x2b).
        opt.reverse();
        i = options.wordIndexOfPhrase( opt ) - 1;
        result = functions[i](input);
        cout << opt << "(\"" << input << "\")    \t=\t" << result << "\n";
        cout << "(\"" << input << "\")." << opt << "()\t=\t";
        (input.*members[i])();
        cout << input << "\n";

        if ( result != arg || result != input )
            cout << "Something is wrong with this!\a\n";
        else
            cout << "This seemed to work OK!\n";
        }
    else
        cout << "Invalid conversion function\nChoose one of:\n\t"
            << options << '\n';
    }
    else
        cout << "Invalid input\nSyntax is:   convert opt input\n";

    return 0;
    }
```

This program produces the following output when invoked with "c2x cat":

```
C>convert c2x cat
c2x("cat")        =        636174
("cat").c2x()     =        636174
x2c("636174")         =        cat
("636174").x2c()      =        cat
This seemed to work OK!
```

Debug Information Function

The function `asDebugInfo` also renders the contents of an `IString` object. This function displays information about the internal representation of the string. Using the function in an expression such as:

```
IString( "Hello, World!" ).asDebugInfo()
```

yields the following output:

```
IString(@232396,pBuffer->IBuffer(@590672,refs=1,len=13,
     data=[Hello, World!]))
```

This output reveals information about the `IBuffer` object holding the contents of the string. Comparing the output from a number of different `IString` objects provides insight into how the string contents are shared.

IBuffer Class

As mentioned before, `IString` is really nothing more than a smart pointer to an object of class `IBuffer`. Whereas `IString` itself is simply a data type, `IBuffer` is not. Almost all of the functions of `IBuffer` are virtual because `IBuffer` provides the portion of `IString` that needs to be overridden by derived classes. We discuss the reason for permitting this overriding of `IBuffer` behavior in the next section, which is about `IDBCSBuffer`. In this section we discuss the `IBuffer` class in general and the relationship between the `IString` and `IBuffer` objects.

As you saw previously, the char* data member of IString objects is a pointer to a portion of an IBuffer object. IString delegates to the IBuffer object by doing some simple arithmetic on that pointer. One important function delegated this way is the allocation of a new IBuffer when the string's contents change. Rather than allocate an IBuffer object explicitly, the IString object invokes the newBuffer function against the IBuffer object to which it is currently pointing.

IBuffer::newBuffer is a virtual function that can be implemented differently in classes derived from IBuffer. Its design is based on the fact that each derived IBuffer class actually re-implements that virtual function. It allocates an object of the derived class rather than a generic IBuffer. This is a subtle but crucial point of the IString and IBuffer design. It enables the IBuffer class to be replaced without requiring any change in the IString class. This is another example of the application of the design for extensibility that recurs throughout Open Class Library.

The effect of this design is that once an IString object connects to an object of some specialized IBuffer class, that specialized IBuffer class is used despite changes to the contents of the IString. This means you can create an IString object using some specialized IBuffer and pass that IString to another function, which may know nothing of the IBuffer-derived class. Even if that function makes changes to the string, it is still connected to your derived IBuffer object.

For example, to share an IString object between two different processes, place the IString in shared memory. Because the IString object points to an IBuffer object, it is in memory that is accessible to both processes. IBuffer does not, by default, appear in shared memory. Thus, you need an extensible design such as the one Open Class Library's IString and IBuffer implementation provides.

To get IString to use your IBuffer-derived class, call the IBuffer::setDefaultBuffer function and pass a null buffer object of your class. IString generates all new string contents from that null buffer through the use of its newBuffer function. Your IBuffer-derived class must override the virtual function IBuffer::allocate so that it returns a properly sized object of your class. Due to the assumptions that Open Class Library makes about the IBuffer contents for performance reasons, you cannot add data members to your IBuffer-derived class.

The following program illustrates how to install your own class derived from IBuffer as a replacement for the base IBuffer that Open Class Library provides.

Replacing IString's IBuffer - data\mybuffer\mybuffer.cpp

```
#include <iostream.h>
#include <istring.hpp>
#include <ibuffer.hpp>

class MyBuffer : public IBuffer {
public:
  MyBuffer( unsigned len )
    : IBuffer( len )
    {
    }
```

```
virtual IBuffer
 *allocate ( unsigned len ) const
     {
     return new (len) MyBuffer( len );
     }
virtual const char
 *className ( ) const
     {
     return (const char*)"MyBuffer";
     }
};

void main()
   {
   IString
     withDefault( "withDefault" );
   cout << withDefault.asDebugInfo() << endl;

  // Allocate null buffer.
  MyBuffer
    root(0);
  IBuffer::setDefaultBuffer( &root );
  IString
    withMyBuffer("withMyBuffer");
  cout << withMyBuffer.asDebugInfo() << endl;
  }
```

Sample output from this program follows:

```
IString(@360408,pBuffer->IBuffer(@1522128,refs=1,len=11,
        data=[withDefault]))
IString(@360384,pBuffer->MyBuffer(@1522176,refs=1,len=12,
        data=[withMyBuffer]))
```

IDBCSBuffer

Open Class Library provides a single class derived from IBuffer named IDBCSBuffer. It implements a polymorphic subset of IString to provide support for *multibyte character set*s (MBCS). When your programs execute on systems that support MBCS, IString uses objects of type IDBCSBuffer to hold the string contents. All MBCS-sensitive IString functions are overridden in IDBCSBuffer to ensure that it properly handles MBCS data.

The MBCS handling in IString manages two separate issues. First, the string editing functions protect against splitting the bytes that make up a multibyte character. For example, consider the following code:

```
// "Dx" means a MBCS character with first byte 'D',
// and second byte 'x'.
IString mbcs( "abDxDycd" );

mbcs = mbcs.subString( 4 );
```

What should the value of mbcs be after this code executes? If IString had no MBCS support, the result would be xDycd. This is wrong, however, because there is no single-byte character x in the original string.

IDBCSBuffer ensures that the two bytes of an MBCS character are never split. The result of the code shown above is " Dycd". The orphaned second byte of the MBCS character 'Dx' is converted to a blank. IDBCSBuffer provides such protection in all of the string editing functions that need it.

The second MBCS issue relates to searching the string for single-byte characters that match the second byte of an MBCS character. For example, what should the expression IString("abDxDycd").indexOf("x") return? In MBCS environments, the result is 0 because there is no string x in the string being searched. The byte with value x is the second byte of an MBCS character, which is distinct from the single-byte character at that code point.

IDBCSBuffer also overrides the various IBuffer search functions to ensure the search results accurately reflect the meaning of multibyte data.

Handles

Both the Windows and OS/2 operating systems developer's toolkits make programming less complicated by adding a few abstractions. For example, you use handles for objects rather than pointers to structures. Such handles give you one of the benefits of C++ object-oriented programming.

The Windows Software Development Kit (SDK) defines its handle types as synonyms for the HANDLE type, which is a synonym for void*. The Developer's Toolkit for OS/2 defines its handle types as synonyms for a common LHANDLE type, which itself is a synonym for unsigned long. This is all that can be done in C because it has no facility for defining new types.

Because all of the handle typedefs are just synonyms for the same type, you can inadvertently use one kind of handle where you need to use another. For example, you can pass an HBITMAP to a function that requires an HICON, but the compiler does not warn you about the error. Further, you cannot overload functions based on different handle types.

Open Class Library provides a set of handle classes that use C++ to solve these nagging problems. The handle classes provide three main benefits:

- An abstract interface between presentation system objects and Open Class Library's model of them as C++ objects. The C++ objects, such as IWindows, have handle attributes. Those handles, in turn, are convertible to the handle of the associated presentation system objects. You can then use the handle to make presentation system function calls.

- Additional type safety. Because each handle type is a unique C++ class, Open Class Library specifies a specific type of handle, and you get an error if you pass a different type of handle to a function.

- Overloaded functions based on handle type. Classes such as IGraphicPushButton and IDMImage accept bitmap or icon handles and can detect the difference. You do not have to pass a handle type; consequently, you cannot specify the wrong type.

IHandle Base Class

The IHandle base class defines the basic handle type. It is roughly equivalent to the HANDLE type in the Windows SDK and the LHANDLE type in the Developer's Toolkit for OS/2. It provides support for holding the handle value and has a conversion operator with which any IHandle can be converted to type IHandle::Value. IHandle::Value is a synonym for the presentation system toolkit definition. IHandle uses this alias to provide portability between platforms. You use the conversion operator, the constructor for IHandle, and all its derived classes to bridge these objects to presentation system code as follows.

First, you replace any occurrences of a presentation system handle type with an object of the equivalent Open Class Library handle class. For example, in the Windows operating system, you might have the following existing code.

```
HWND hwnd;
hwnd = CreateWindowEx( ... );
```

Convert this code to use objects of class IWindowHandle by replacing HWND with that class name.

```
IWindowHandle hwnd;
hwnd = CreateWindowEx( ... );
```

Conversely, you can extract the handle from an Open Class Library object and use this handle as a presentation system handle. Do this to invoke a function that Open Class Library does not support. The following is from the OS/2 operating system:

```
WinShutdownSystem( IThread::current().anchorBlock(),
                   IThread::current().messageQueue() );
```

This example uses two different Open Class Library handles: the anchor block handle returned by ICurrentThread::anchorBlock and the message queue handle returned by ICurrentThread::messageQueue.

When you write code that must use both Open Class Library functions and presentation system functions, always declare your handle objects using Open Class Library handle classes. Your objects will be C++ objects in your code, and they are converted to plain handles when you call presentation system functions. Doing the opposite—storing presentation system handles and converting those to Open Class Library handle objects—is possible, but you lose all the benefits of additional type-safety and overloading.

IHandle-Derived Classes

You do not need to write code that works with IHandle objects. Open Class Library provides classes derived from IHandle that represent specific presentation system handle types, and you use these abstract types. Table 26-16 identifies each of the handle classes.

Table 26-16. IHandle-Derived Classes, their Presentation System Types, and their Uses

Handle Class	Windows Type	OS/2 Type	Where Used
IAccelTblHandle	HACCEL	HACCEL	IAccelerator, IAcceleratorTable
IAnchorBlockHandle	N/A	HAB	IThread
IBitmapHandle	HBITMAP	HBITMAP	IBitmapControl IGraphicPushButton IDMImage IResourceLibrary
IEnumHandle	N/A	HENUM	IWindow
IMenuHandle	HMENU	N/A	IMenu IMenuItem IResourceLibrary ISubmenu
IMessageQueueHandle	N/A	HMQ	IThread
IModuleHandle	HMODULE	HMOD	IDynamicLinkLibrary
IPointerHandle	HBITMAP• HCURSOR• HICON	HPOINTER	IIconControl IGraphicPushButton IFrameWindow IDMImage IResourceLibrary
IPresSpaceHandle	HDC	HPS	IPaintEvent IFont IWindow
IProcessId	N/A	PID	IApplication
IProfileHandle	HKEY	HINI	IProfile
IRegionHandle	HRGN	N/A	IGraphicContext IGRegion
ISemaphoreHandle	HANDLE	HMTX	IResource
IStringHandle	N/A	HSTR	IDMItem
ISystemBitmapHandle	HBITMAP	HBITMAP	See IBitmapHandle
ISystemPointerHandle	HCURSOR	HPOINTER	See IPointerHandle
IThreadId/IThreadHandle	HANDLE	TID	IThread
IWindowHandle	HWND	HWND	IWindow

Date and Time

Open Class Library provides the classes IDate and ITime that represent dates and times. IDate objects represent any date between January 1, 4713 BC and October 17, 5874777. ITime objects represent any point in time, to the nearest second, in the range 00:00:00 (midnight) to 23:59:59. Both IDate and ITime provide a full suite of member functions that enable you to manipulate their data in a variety of useful ways.

IDate objects maintain their value using a Julian day number. These values start at 1, which represents the date January 2, 4713 BC. The next day's Julian day number is 2, the next 3, and so on. Julian day numbers for the present are quite large. For example, June 20, 1961 is Julian day number 2437471. The upper limit for IDate is determined by the Julian day number at which its arithmetic overflows.

You can treat IDate objects as if they are comprised of separate attributes for month, day, and year. IDate provides member functions to retrieve each of these components.

To provide type safety and reduce the need for argument checking, IDate defines an enumeration for the month values. Months are handled as IDate::Month objects. The enumeration values are the full month names January through December. IDate::January has the value 1. This is important if you are creating dates from numeric input.

Some IDate functions handle days of the week as arguments or return values. The enumeration type IDate::DayOfWeek defines the type of these objects. The enumeration values are the full day names Monday through Sunday. IDate::Monday has the value 0, IDate::Sunday has the value 6.

ITime objects maintain their value internally as the number of seconds past midnight. You can view ITime objects as if they consist of separate hour, minute, and second values. The class provides member functions to return each of those elements.

Because dates and times are both small concrete values for which the default copy constructor and assignment operators are sufficient, almost all IDate and ITime functions return new dates and times by value. The only functions you use to change a date or a time are the operator-assignment functions, such as operator+=.

IDate and ITime Constructors

You create a date or time object from just about any combination of values sufficient to uniquely identify the particular date or time you want to represent. To create a date object, you need a month, day, and year. Alternatively, you can specify a year and a day in that year. One constructor accepts an unsigned long Julian day number. The IDate class uses this constructor internally.

To create a time object, specify the hour, minute, and second. If you do not need full precision, omit the number of seconds and they default to zero. Alternatively, you can specify just the number of seconds. This constructor is also designed mostly for internal use by the ITime class.

The default constructors create date and time objects that represent the current date and current time. Use the special static member functions IDate::today and ITime::now to obtain the current date and time. We recommend these functions if you explicitly want the current date and time because using the default constructors might mean you are going to assign a specific value later.

Note the following aspects of date and time constructors:

- There are IDate constructors that accept month/day/year and day/month/year. The former is the convention in the United States while the latter is the convention in Europe. Use either one. Because the month argument is of type IDate::Month, the compiler calls the appropriate constructor.

- The constructor that accepts year/day works differently. Because both year and date are ints, if you create an IDate using IDate(328, 1984), the compiler processes it as January 1, 4713 BC rather than November 23, 1984, as you intended.

- The ITime constructor that accepts a long argument treats a negative value as the corresponding time, counting backwards from midnight. It works that way so that time arithmetic works right. For example, ITime(0, 20) - 60 yields ITime(-40), which is 23:20:00 on the preceding day.

Accessing Attributes

IDate provides a full set of functions to access the month, day, and year components of a date. It provides functions to obtain the month name and the name of the day of the week as a string. Other functions return such results as the number of days in a given month in a given year.

With so many functions that return so many similar results, which function do you need to call? Table 26-17 lists each function. The left column shows the range of the results, and the right column shows the function or functions you call to obtain those results. If you want to get the number of days in a given year, scan the table for "365 or 366" because this is the kind of value you need. ITime does not have as many similar functions. It just has member functions hours, minutes, and seconds that return the expected attribute.

Date Static Functions

Selecting the correct IDate function to obtain the data you need is complicated by static member functions that overlap the nonstatic member functions (in some cases). For example, you use the expression aDate.dayName() to get the name of the day of the week represented by aDate. The expression, IDate::dayName(IDate::Saturday) obtains the string corresponding to the IDate::DayOfWeek enumeration value passed as an argument. The function names are the same, but the functions do fundamentally different things.

The IDate static functions that might cause confusion all require arguments, as they do not have an object on which to operate. So, the general rules are: do not pass an argument to the nonstatic member functions and do not pass an IDate object to a static member.

Table 26-17. Sample Return Values from IDate Functions

Desired Result	Function
"Monday"	dayName
0-31	dayOfMonth
28-31	daysInMonth
IDate::Monday	dayOfWeek
1-366	dayOfYear
365 or 366	daysInYear
"November"	monthName
IDate::October	monthOfYear

To determine the number of days in the month in which a given date occurs, use this code. (There is no daysInMonth nonstatic member.)

```
IDate::daysInMonth( aDate.monthOfYear() )
```

Formatting

IDate and ITime provide powerful formatting capabilities. You can convert a date or time object to a string result using the overloaded function asString. The result is a string that contains arbitrary text mixed with arbitrary attributes of the date or time object converted to text.

The asString function accepts as an argument a *format string*. This is a string of text in which you place special conversion specifiers at the point where you want attributes of the date or time object to appear. IDate and ITime use the strftime function of the C run-time library to implement the asString function; therefore, they support all of the conversion specifiers that strftime supports.

An example of how you use IDate::asString to produce formatted dates follows.

```
IDate aDate = IDate( IDate::November, 24, 1990 );
cout << aDate.asString( "Allison was born on a %A" );
```

This code produces the following output:

```
Allison was born on a Friday
```

Here is an example of using ITime::asString to get the time in 24-hour military time format:

```
ITime aTime = ITime( 14, 30 );

cout << aTime;                          // produces 02:30:00
cout << aTime.asString( "%H:%M:%S" );   // produces 14:30:00
```

There are default versions of asString for both IDate and ITime. The default format for IDate is "mm-dd-yy" or "mm/dd/yy" based on the operating system setup. You can provide an argument to asString to request the year as four digits instead of two. The default format for ITime is "hh:mm:ss."

Both classes support output to streams. By default you get the default asString result. If you want another format, call asString yourself. The previous example, showing how to get an ITime object formatted in the 24-hour format, illustrates this.

There are two restrictions for using asString:

- Do not use the time-related conversion specifiers when formatting a date, and do not use the date-related conversion specifiers when formatting a time. If you do, all those specifiers are converted to undefined values. If you need to build a string with a combined date and time, you must do it in two steps.

- This function does not support the full range of dates supported by IDate. Because IDate::asString uses strftime, it only works with dates that the latter function handles, which are dates beginning January 1, 1 AD. To format a date earlier than that, you have to do it yourself using the individual IDate functions.

The formatting of dates and times reflects your application's current locale setting. For the French locale, the day names are in French.

Dates and Times from Strings

Although IDate and ITime have functions for formatting dates and times as strings, interpreting a string as a date or time is more difficult. There is no C library function that does the inverse of strftime. To convert string input to a date or time, you must write code to analyze the string and figure out what date or time it represents.

The **data\str2date** program on the examples disk contains a dateFrom function that performs the inverse of IDate::asString. You pass in both the format specifier and the formatted date, and it figures out the IDate that produces that formatted string.

Arithmetic

You can perform the following arithmetic on date and time objects:

- Add or subtract an integral value N to or from an IDate to get a new IDate. The result represents the date N days prior to or later than the original IDate. For example, to find out the date 25 days after a billing date, use this code:
  ```
  IDate billingDate;
  IDate dueDate = billingDate + 25;
  ```
  This calculates the proper dueDate regardless of the number of days in the month or whether it is a leap year.

- Subtract two IDate objects to yield the number of days between them. Because you don't add two dates together, IDate does not provide operator+.

- Add or subtract two ITime objects to produce the sum or difference of the times. Because you can create an ITime from a number, an expression such as aTime + 180 yields a time 3 minutes later than aTime.

Because you can compare two dates or two times, `IDate` and `ITime` provide a full set of comparison operators.

Where Were You on September 3, 1752?

Because the world has many different calendar systems, it is difficult to describe a date so that everyone understands it. For this discussion a calendar system is "the system by which we give names to dates." For example, some calendar systems count years starting at a different point than the conventional one to which readers in the United States are accustomed. When somebody using such a calendar says, "July 4, 1776," they may not be talking about the date you think they are.

The `IDate` class calendar system is the standard calendar system that has been in use in the United States. The Julian day-number scheme used to implement `IDate` is straightforward. The day after day number N is day number N+1. However, be aware of two oddities in the Julian calendar:

- There is no year 0. The year 1 BC was followed by the year 1. Equivalently, `IDate( -1, 365 ) + 1 == IDate( 1, 1 )`. If you create an `IDate` using year 0, you get an invalid date. All invalid dates are displayed as January 1, 4713 BC. You can test if a date is valid using any of the `IDate::isValid` functions.

- There are no dates for September 3, 1752 through September 13, 1752. The day after September 2 was September 14.

  The missing 11 days made up for the errors in the calendar system in use prior to that date. Because our planet Earth does not take exactly 365 days to orbit the sun, and one leap-year every four years did not completely solve that problem, the calendar fell behind.

  At the time this flaw was detected in 1599, Pope Gregory IX revised the calendar to eliminate leap years in years divisible by 100 but not divisible by 400. To correct for the extra leap-year days, 11 days were skipped. That system is in use today and keeps the calendar and the Earth's orbit in sync.

  However, because the Pope revised the calendar, the English Anglicans did not revise their calendars for another 153 years, in September 1752. Thus, the expression `IDate( IDate::September, 3, 1752 ).isValid()` returns `false`.

Bit Masks

Almost all of the window and control classes of Open Class Library have a nested `Style` class, which represents combinations of style attributes valid for windows of those classes. Most of the attributes are represented by on or off settings. The combination of style attributes comprise a *bit mask*, an unsigned numeric value with some of its bits representing the settings of particular attributes.

Representing these combinations of attributes with a class required solutions to the following C++ problems:

- You must specify only valid combinations of attribute settings. This precludes using plain integral expressions because that would permit users to specify any value.

- You must be able to combine separate attributes values to compose valid combinations.

- You must be able to extend the set of attributes for one window class by defining an extended set in a derived window class. This permits the combination of the two kinds of attributes in the derived class.

Open Class Library solves these problems by providing the `IBitFlag` class and a set of macros to generate the declarations of derived classes. This section describes how to use the `Style` classes built using `IBitFlag` and these macros and how to use these facilities to define your own bit-mask classes.

Defining Base Bit-Mask Classes

`IBitFlag` is an abstract base class that holds two `unsigned long` data members that are used to store the bits defined by derived classes.

Basic concrete bit-mask classes are derived from `IBitFlag` using the following macro:

```
INESTEDBITFLAGCLASSDEF0( className, enclosingClass );
```

The `className` argument specifies the name to be given to the `IBitFlag` derived class that this macro generates. The `enclosingClass` argument specifies the name of the class in which the generated class is nested. Examples of the use of this macro in Open Class Library are as follows:

- `INESTEDBITFLACCLASSDEF0( Style, IWindow );`

  This invocation occurs within the declaration of the class `IWindow`. It generates the declaration of the class `IWindow::Style`. Objects of that class define a set of general window style attributes.

- `INESTEDBITFLAGCLASSDEF0( Style, IDMImage );`

  This invocation occurs within the declaration of class `IDMImage`. It generates the declaration of the class `IDMImage::Style`, which is used to create objects that specify combinations of direct manipulation image attributes.

Use the `INESTEDBITFLAGCLASSDEF0` macro to create *base* bit mask classes, which are distinguished by the fact that objects of these classes cannot be created from more primitive bit-mask objects.

The following example shows how to use this macro and the `IBitFlag` class in general. It also shows how this component of Open Class Library provides a more robust solution to this kind of problem.

The standard C++ `ios` class declares the following nested enumeration type:

```
enum open_mode  { in=1, out=2, ate=4, app=010, trunc=020,
                  nocreate=040, noreplace=0100, bin=0200,
                  binary=bin   /* OS2 specific */
                } ;
```

These enumeration values, designed to be OR-ed, result in numeric values that are passed to various `ios` functions, such as the `ifstream` constructor. The enumeration values define a typical set of bit-mask values, each of them specifying a unique bit. They are OR-ed to produce a single numeric value representing arbitrary combinations of these bits. For example, (`ios::in` | `ios::nocreate` | `ios::binary`) specifies that the open mode for an input file is to be read in binary mode and is not to be created if it does not already exist.

There are, however, subtle problems with this approach. The `ifstream` constructor has a `mode` argument of type `int`, which means it is possible to pass in any integer value, including enumeration values from another attribute set as follows:

```
ifstream infile( "myfile", 392 | ios::hardfail );
```

Although such usage does not make sense, it is difficult to prevent.

To solve these problems, use Open Class Library's `IBitFlag` class and its support macros. Follow these steps:

1. Declare a class representing these mode settings, using the `INESTEDBITFLAGCLASSDEF0` macro:

   ```
   class ios {
     // ...
     INESTEDBITFLAGCLASSDEF0( Mode, ios );
     // ...
   };
   ```

   This generates the declaration of the class `ios::Mode`.

2. Change the declaration of the argument on the `ifstream` constructor and wherever `ios::Mode` arguments are appropriate.

3. Change the declaration of the enumeration values to declarations of objects of type `ios::Mode`.

Creating Bit-Flag Objects

In the preceding section, we described how to use the `INESTEDBITFLAGCLASSDEF0` macros to generate the declaration of a nested `IBitFlag`-derived class. The constructor for the class that this macro generates is protected. Thus you can only create objects from already existing objects, using either assignment or the copy constructor.

Where do these source objects come from? Clearly, you do not want to create such objects from arbitrary numeric values, which would permit creating bit masks with invalid combinations. A key characteristic of `IBitFlag` and its generated derived classes is that the base set of bit-mask objects are carefully regulated. Specifically, the macro-generated classes make the enclosing class a friend of the bit-mask class. This enables members of the enclosing class to use the protected constructor that accepts an arbitrary numeric argument. Thus, only the enclosing class determines the valid bit combinations because these bit masks are attributes of an aspect of that class.

Typically, the enclosing class defines the valid bit combinations, the base set of `enclosingClass::className` objects, as a set of static data members. For example, in the case of `IDMImage::Style`, you find these static data members:

```
class IDMImage : public IVBase {
//...
INESTEDBITFLAGCLASSDEF0(Style, IDMImage);
static const Style
  ptr,
  bmp,
  polygon,
  stretch,
  transparent,
  closed;
//...
};
```

This code declares six distinct `IDMImage::Style` values named `IDMImage::ptr`, `IDMImage::stretch`, and so on. These style values are all static data members of class `IDMImage`. They are also `const` data members, which ensures that they cannot be altered. With these declarations, you create your own variables of type `IDMImage::Style` as follows:

```
IDMImage::Style myStyle = IDMImage::polygon;
```

To continue the previous example of fixing the `mode` enumerations of class `ios`, you convert its declarations of enumeration values to the following static data members:

```
...
static const Mode
  in,
  out,
  ate,
  app,
  trunc,
  nocreate,
  noreplace,
  binary,
  bin;
...
```

Define these static data members in the implementation file for the enclosing class. For example, in `IWINDOW2.CPP`, you would find these definitions:

```
const IWindow::Style
  IWindow::visible = WS_VISIBLE,
  IWindow::synchPaint = WS_SYNCPAINT;
```

For `ios::Mode`, you would place the following definitions in the implementation file for class ios:

```
const ios::Mode
  ios::in = 1,
  ios::out = 2,
  ios::ate = 4,
  ios::app = 010,
  ios::trunc = 020,
  ios::nocreate = 040,
  ios::noreplace = 0100,
  ios::binary = 0200,
  ios::bin = 0200;
```

If you get unresolved external errors during linking, check to see if you defined these static bit-mask values.

Extract the `unsigned long` representation of an `IBitFlag` or `IBitFlag`-derived object using the member function `asUnsignedLong`. Typically, you do this only when implementing the enclosing class's member functions that accept arguments of the bit-mask type. If these bit masks match the ones that the presentation system uses (which is often the case in Open Class Library), then aStyle.asUnsignedLong() can be passed directly to the presentation system functions that require such style attribute values. If they do not match, many Open Class Library classes provide a convertToGUIStyle function that you can call to obtain a style that can be passed to system functions.

Extended Styles

Classes that have many styles may reach the limit with only one unsigned long value. So, IBitFlag provides a second unsigned long that you can use to double the available bits. This second value is called an *extended style*. To define an extended style, you pass a second argument to the IBitFlag constructor. In the previous examples, this value was not passed and thus defaulted to zero. Many Open Class Library classes use extended styles. For example, the IFrameWindow implementation file IFRAME.CPP contains the following extended styles:

```
const IFrameWindow::Style
...
   IFrameWindow::titleBar        ( 0, FCF_TITLEBAR ),
   IFrameWindow::systemMenu       ( 0, FCF_SYSMENU ),
   IFrameWindow::menuBar          ( 0, FCF_MENU ),
   IFrameWindow::hideButton       ( 0, IFS_HIDEBUTTON ),
   IFrameWindow::minimizeButton   ( 0, FCF_MINBUTTON ),
   IFrameWindow::maximizeButton   ( 0, FCF_MAXBUTTON ),
   IFrameWindow::verticalScroll   ( 0, FCF_VERTSCROLL ),
   IFrameWindow::horizontalScroll( 0, FCF_HORZSCROLL ),
   IFrameWindow::deferCreation    ( 0, IFS_DEFERCREATE ),
...
```

Access the actual unsigned long value for styles created this way by using the asExtendedUnsignedLong member function. When extended style values need to be passed to presentation system functions, call convertToGUIStyle and set the second argument to true to indicate extended styles only.

In addition to increasing the available styles, you can use extended styles to keep two styles from interfering with each other. For example, you may want to provide a wrapper for a set of styles that has overlapping values, as in the ios::Mode example. To make the bin and binary members unique, even though they represent the same value, you change the definitions as follows:

```
const ios::Mode
   ios::in = 1,
   ios::out = 2,
   ios::ate = 4,
   ios::app = 010,
   ios::trunc = 020,
   ios::nocreate = 040,
   ios::noreplace = 0100,
   ios::binary = 0200,
   ios::bin( 0, 0200 );
```

These changes result in ios::binary and ios::bin being set independently of each other.

Extended styles and regular styles behave and operate identically. All of the operators defined for IBitFlag and discussed in the following sections apply to extended styles. You can use them between regular and extended styles seamlessly.

Combining Values

After declaring bit-mask classes, defining the set of valid bit combinations, and declaring variables equal to one of the valid bit settings, you now combine multiple bits into a composite bit-mask value. When working with integer bit values, use the standard C++ bitwise | operator so that the `IBitFlag` class and its derivatives use the same operator. Then, the bit-mask classes generated from the `IBitFlag` macros define an `operator|` which you use to `OR` bit-mask objects to create valid composite values.

For example, the following expression calls `IDMImage::Style::operator|`, yielding an object of type `IDMImage::Style`:

```
IDMImage::bmp | IDMImage::stretch
```

The resulting bit mask is then used like any of the base values defined as static members of class `IDMImage`.

Turning Off Bits

You may also want to turn off bits in an existing `IBitFlag` bit mask. For example, the following code uses the current default `IWindow` style to turn off the visible bit:

```
IWindow::setDefaultStyle( IWindow::defaultStyle() &
                          ~IWindow::visible );
```

Using a style to turn off bits is like the way you manipulate integer bit-mask values in C++. As it does with combining bits, Open Class Library defines the appropriate set of operators for the bit-mask classes that it generates to make such usage result in the desired operations.

Negating bits is complicated by the fact that you designate the bit to be turned off by an expression of the form ~bitValue. Because `bitValue` is an object of some `IBitFlag` class and not a number, you cannot apply the unary negation operator without that operator explicitly being defined for that type. If you do, the compiler returns an error.

Therefore, the `IBitFlag` macros generate class declarations that include the following elements:

- A declaration for a nested class with name `Negated` concatenated with your style class name. Using the Open Class Library convention, this is `NegatedStyle`. You can then write the following code:

    ```
    IWindow::Style::NegatedStyle invisible = ~IWindow::visible;
    ```

- An `operator~` that takes a bit-mask object and returns a corresponding negated bit-mask object.

- An `operator&` that you use to combine negated bit-mask values with other bit masks to turn off the desired bits.

The utility of the `IBitFlag` class comes from these operators. This component of Open Class Library shows how you can use C++ to implement powerful data types. Basically, if you can state the requirements for the data type using the basic notation of C++ operators and more primitive types, you can implement that type.

Bit-Mask Testing

Another common task is to test that a given bit is set by using this code:

```
if ( aStyle & IWindow::visible )
   ...
```

The design goal is to match the way you write this code using plain C++ built-in types. The IBitFlag class and its derivatives meet this goal by defining another overloaded operator&. We previously discussed one operator& that you can use to turn off bits; it accepts as an argument a negated bit-mask value. Another operator& accepts as an argument a particular bit-mask value. This operator returns an unsigned long. You can then test the result using an if or while statement.

Composite Bit-Mask Classes

The most complicated aspect of the IBitFlag class and the bit-mask types it helps define is declaring bit-mask classes that are a superset of another set of valid bit masks. For example, how do you declare an IControl::Style class whose valid bit settings include those bits defined by IWindow::Style plus some additional bits appropriate to class IControl?

This problem resembles inheritance in some respects. An IWindow::Style is an IControl::Style. But inheritance works in the opposite direction from that of the enclosing classes. So, you cannot use normal C++ inheritance. Instead, the derived style must explicitly permit creating objects as objects of the base bit-mask type. For example, for the following code:

```
IControl::Style myStyle = IWindow::visible;
IControl::setDefaultStyle( IControl::defaultStyle() &
                           ~IWindow::synchPaint );
```

the IControl::Style class must support the following functionality:

- Creating an IControl::Style object (the derived bit-mask class) from an object of type IWindow::Style (the base bit-mask class)

- Operators that can combine IControl::Style objects with IWindow::Style objects in the same way as other IControl::Style objects.

Open Class Library provides additional macros to implement such derived bit-mask classes.

Additional Bit-Flag Macros

Open Class Library provides four macros in addition to the INESTEDBITFLAGCLASSDEF0 macro that we previously described. These macros, INESTEDBITFLAGCLASSDEF1 through INESTEBITFLAGCLASSDEF4, work in much the same way but accept specifying from one to four additional base bit-mask classes.

Specify the base classes using the name of the enclosing class. For example, the following code generates the declaration of IControl::Style:

```
INESTEDBITFLAGCLASSDEF1( Style, IControl, IWindow );
```

This declares IControl::Style so that IWindow::Style objects can be freely promoted to the former type, as is required. These macros require that the base style class has the same name as the nested class being generated. You cannot use these macros to generate a class Derived::Style compatible with Base::Attribute. If you need to do that, generate your own class declarations using the provided macros as a base.

In addition to the standard IBitFlag-derived class generated by INESTEDBITFLAGCLASSDEF0, these macros generate additional public constructors that accept as an argument an object of the base type. This conversion capability enables the various operators to accept objects of the base bit-mask type on the right-hand side.

Bit-Flag Operator Function Macro

The INESTEDBITFLAGCLASSDEFn macros generate code to enable you to AND and OR base bit-mask values to compose derived bit-mask classes. However, such use is restricted to the appearance of the base values on the right-hand side of bitwise operations.

To make operations commutative, additional operator functions are declared that are global rather than simple member functions. Open Class Library provides one more macro to generate these additional operators:

```
INESTEDBITFLAGCLASSFUNCS( className, enclosingClass );
```

For example, at the bottom of the ICONTROL.HPP file, you find the following code:

```
INESTEDBITFLAGCLASSFUNCS( Style, IControl );
```

This generates nonmember operator functions. Because they are not member functions, the left-hand argument of operations, if it is a base bit-mask type, is converted automatically so that the operator can be invoked.

Colors

Open Class Library window classes provide support for querying and setting the color of various areas of the windows. As a result, there is a need to define C++ classes to represent these colors. The IColor class and its derivatives, IDeviceColor and IGUIColor, are the classes of objects you use when querying and setting the colors of IWindow objects.

IColor defines the basic attributes of all color objects. A *color* is basically a mix of red, green, and blue values. You can create an IColor object from any combination of red, green, and blue values, and you can extract the red, green, or blue values for any color.

IColor also provides an enumeration of a set of standard color mixes. These define specific red, green, and blue mixes. You can create an IColor object from one of these enumeration values. In many cases, this form of constructor is preferred because you do not have to determine the red, green, and blue values that comprise a standard color.

You can also construct an IColor object from a SystemColor enumeration that defines presentation system colors that your users can set. SystemColor defines values for all of the system color categories, such as the notebook page background color, the default button color, and the active frame border color. These enumeration values correspond to the COLOR_* constants defined in the Windows SDK, and the SYSCLR_* constants defined in the Developer's Toolkit for OS/2. An IColor object constructed from a SystemColor value is linked to the presentation system's settings so that the object changes if the user changes the settings. However, if you use one of the setRed, setGreen, or setBlue functions on one of these objects, the link is broken.

A common use of these classes and the values extracted from them is to provide arguments to Open Class Library's 2-D Graphics classes. For example, you can pass an IColor object to IGraphicBundle::setPenColor to set the color used when lines are drawn that have a pen width greater than one. The **genhdrs\painthdr** program on the examples disk shows how to do this.

IColor provides functions to access various forms of the color. See Table 26-18.

Table 26-18. IColor Functions

Function	Description
asRGBLong	This function returns a single unsigned long value that indicates all three of the red, green, and blue components of the color.
value	This function returns the IColor::Color standard color nearest to the color with this object's red, green, and blue components.
index	This function returns the logical color table index closest to this color.

Derived Classes

The derived class IGUIColor constructs color objects corresponding to the system colors that the user defines, similar to IColor(SystemColor). The difference is that IGUIColor provides a setColor accessor whereby you can set the system color. Instead of just a one-way link from the system color to the object, IGUIColor provides a two-way link that propagates changes in both directions. Setting a system color using an IGUIColor affects all windows in the system.

The IDeviceColor class provides support for device-independent colors. It enables you to create three special color objects that represent device-independent color indexes for the device background, the device's neutral color, and the device's default color. These colors take on the actual color index appropriate to the device with which you are working (for example, a printer device or a screen device).

Reference-Counting

When you use data types, you usually work directly with objects rather than indirectly using pointers. You allocate most of these objects in automatic storage, that is, they are allocated on the stack when entering a function or block. Also, you might allocate them as data members of an enclosing object. Usually, you do not allocate objects of these types on the heap using `operator new`.

An advantage to using such objects is that you can manage the allocation and deallocation of them easily. The automatic objects are created when they enter the block and deleted when they exit. The data members are created when their enclosing object is created and are deleted when the enclosing object is deleted.

Sometimes objects must be allocated dynamically. This is the case when the lifetime of such objects must span the scope of a block, when the type of an object is not known until run time, or when the size or number of objects is not known ahead of time. In such cases, problems inevitably arise when deciding how to manage the lifetime of the dynamically created objects.

Using *reference-counting* is a means of managing this problem. Reference-counting is based on the idea that you can define a C++ class that serves as a *smart pointer*. By using a class object instead of a pointer, you can cause a destructor to be called when the pointer goes out of scope or when the object of which the pointer is a data member is deleted. You can call `operator delete` in this destructor, thereby causing the pointed-to object to be deleted.

Here is a class template for a smart pointer that can point to any type of object:

```
template < class T >
class SmartPointer {
public:
  SmartPointer ( T *p = 0 )
    : ptr( p )
    {
    }
  ~SmartPointer ( )
    {
    delete ptr;
    }
  SmartPointer<T> &operator = ( T *p )
    {
    T *temp = ptr;
    ptr = 0;
    delete temp;
    ptr = p;
    }
  operator T* ( ) const
    {
    return ptr;
    }
  T *operator -> ( ) const
    {
    return ptr;
    }
private:
T *ptr;
};
```

You use objects of the template class `SmartPointer<T>` instead of plain `T*` pointers. Here is an example:

```
struct SomeClass { void foo(); };

void someFunction( unsigned long size ) {
  SmartPointer<SomeClass>
    array( new SomeClass[ size ] );
  for ( int i = 1; i <= size; i++ )
    array[ size - i ].foo();
};
```

In this example, the array is allocated dynamically because the dimension is passed as an argument to the function. If you used SomeClass*, you would need to add a delete at the end of the function. The SmartPointer object does that in this example.

Next, consider the complications that arise when you try to use such smart pointers across object interfaces. What happens if one smart pointer is assigned to another? The result is that the pointed-to object is deleted twice. This leads us to reference-counting. You need to store a count of the number of smart pointers that point to the object. Assigning or copying a smart pointer increments the count. The smart-pointer destructor now only decrements this count. When the count becomes 0, the pointed-to object is deleted.

Open Class Library's IRefCounted class implements the smart-pointer behavior. It has a data member that maintains a use count and member functions that adds or removes references. When the reference count becomes 0, the IRefCounted object deletes itself.

Open Class Library also provides the IReference class template. Use this template to generate classes whose objects can be used as smart pointers to objects of some IRefCounted-derived class.

Open Class Library itself uses the reference-counting classes. For example, IThreadMemberFn derives from IRefCounted, and objects hidden inside the implementation of IThread serve as IReference<IThreadMemberFn> objects. The direct-manipulation classes IDMOperation and IDMItem are also IRefCounted objects.

Note the following points when you use IRefCounted and IReference:

- Remember that code of the form class X : public IRefCounted { ... }; means that objects of class X are allocated dynamically, accessed with smart pointers, and are deleted when there are no more smart pointers pointing to them.

- Almost always allocate IRefCounted objects on the heap using operator new. Be careful allocating such objects on the stack. If you do and accidentally bind such an object to an IReference object, then you have a problem when the IReference object deletes the IRefCounted object.

- Do not use IRefCounted objects as data members for much the same reason. Instead, use an IReference object that refers to the actual data object.

- Avoid using true pointers or C++ references to IRefCounted objects. Using plain pointers or references does not properly increment the use count of the IRefCounted object, and the object may be deleted.

- Take care when initializing IReference objects. The IReference class template is designed to support the following usage:
  ```
  class X : public IRefCounted {
    //...
  };

  IReference<X>
    x = new X();
  ```

The `IRefCounted` constructor initializes its use count to 1, and the `IReference` constructor does not increment it. As a consequence, the following code creates an error:

```
void someFunction ( X *pX )
    {
    IReference<X>
      x = pX;
    // ...
    }
```

The reason is that the creation of the `IReference` does not properly increment the `IRefCounted` object's reference count. Instead create the `IReference` object and initialize it in separate steps, as follows:

```
void someFunction ( X *pX )
    {
    IReference<X>
      x;
    x = pX;
    // ...
    }
```

The `IReference` assignment operator increments the use count. You avoid this problem if you do not use plain pointers to `IRefCounted` objects as suggested previously.

Chapter 27

Error Handling and Reporting

- Describes the C++ exception-handling model and the exception classes that Open Class Library provides
- Describes the IException, IAccessError, IAssertionFailure, IDeviceError, IInvalidParameter, IInvalidRequest, IResourceExhausted, IOutOfMemory, IOutOfSystemResource, IOutOfWindowResource, IException::TraceFn, IExceptionLocation, IBaseErrorInfo, IGUIErrorInfo, ISystemErrorInfo, IWindow::ExceptionFn, and IMessageText classes
- Chapters 4, 23, and 28 cover related material.

This chapter describes how Open Class Library handles error conditions and the implications this has for your application code. The chapter starts with a brief discussion of signals and operating system exceptions and then discusses the error-handling mechanism as defined by C++.

When you use exception handling, the structure of your application programs changes because the model for reporting errors is changed. It is important for you to understand how exception handling works and how Open Class Library uses exceptions so that you can write applications that take advantage of this style of reporting and handling errors.

This chapter also describes several classes closely related to error handling. These include classes for loading error messages from the operating system and displaying error information to the user in a message box. Finally, the chapter describes how to obtain the exception information that Open Class Library logs and how to provide your own trace function for managing the output of this information.

Operating System Exception Handling & C Signals

Operating system exceptions and C signals are similar in several ways. Both are mechanisms for reporting abnormal conditions that occur during the execution of a program. Windows and OS/2 exceptions are generated by the operating system, whereas C signals are generated by the C++ run time. Both exceptions and C signals usually terminate the application by default, but they allow the application to register handlers to process the errors and possibly avoid termination. Some of the causes of exceptions and C signals are synchronous, such as dividing by 0 and other math errors. Other causes of exceptions and C signals are asynchronous, such as when the user presses Ctrl+Break.

C signals are described in the *VisualAge for C++ Tools Programming Guide*. VisualAge for C++ provides an exception handler that maps most of the operating system exceptions to C signals. This enables you to handle most of the errors that these two mechanisms report using only C signals.

C++ exception handling is not intended or designed to handle the exceptions defined by operating system exceptions and C signals. Operating system exceptions and C signals transfer control directly to the handler registered for the particular exception or signal. This means that catch blocks, which are the C++ exception handlers, cannot *catch* these exceptions or signals. Therefore C++ exception handling complements, but does not replace, Windows or OS/2 exceptions and C signals. Open Class Library does not use Windows or OS/2 exceptions or C signals, so we do not describe them further. However, you can use these facilities in your applications to handle error conditions that Open Class Library does not report to you using C++ exceptions.

Exception Handling in C++

Exception handling in C++ provides a way for a function to notify its caller when it encounters an error condition from which it cannot recover. C++ provides three keywords to support exception handling: try, catch, and throw. The notification process is called *throwing the exception*. An exception is an expression and, therefore, can be an object of any type. A caller of a function has the option of catching any exception that the function throws using try and catch blocks. You can enclose any section of code for which you want to catch exceptions in a try block. A try block must be followed by one or more catch blocks, also referred to as *exception-handlers*. The following code shows typical try and catch block usage:

```
try {
    myObject.someFunction();
}
catch ( IAccessError& exc ) {
    // Recovery is possible because we have detailed information
    // about the error.
    app.recover( exc );
}
catch ( IException& exc ) {
    // If the exception is recoverable, let the user decide whether
    // to continue.  Set the default response to cancel.
    IMessageBox::Response response = IMessageBox::cancel;
    if ( exc.isRecoverable() ) {
        IMessageBox msgBox( &mainWindow.frame() );
        response = msgBox.show( exc );
    }
    if ( response == IMessageBox::cancel ) {
        // Perform some cleanup and rethrow the exception.
        app.cleanup();
        throw;
    }
    else                    // The user has chosen retry.
        app.recover( exc );
}
catch ( ... ) {
    // We don't have enough information to continue;
    // cleanup and rethrow the exception.
    app.cleanup();
    throw;
}
```

```
// If we catch the exception and don't rethrow it
// using throw, the program resumes here.
```

Notice that the catch blocks in the example are ordered with the most specific exception-handler listed first. IAccessError is derived from IException, so we placed the catch block for IAccessError first. When a matching catch block is found, control is given to the first statement in the block. The exception is then considered to have been handled, and the C++ run time does not look for any additional catch blocks. Therefore, always specify catch blocks that provide you with the most detailed information first. If an IAccessError exception was thrown and the order of the first two catch blocks was changed, the IException& catch block would catch the exception because an IAccessError is derived from an IException .

Specifying catch (...), indicates that you want to catch all exceptions, regardless of type. Because it is the most generic catch block possible and you have no way of getting any information about the exception, list it last in a series of catch blocks.

When an exception is thrown, the C++ run time transfers control to the matching catch block associated with the nearest active try block. A try block is active if one of the functions it contains, or any function called directly or indirectly by the functions it contains, is currently in control. A matching catch block is one whose specified exception type matches that of the thrown object. When you catch an exception, you have the choice of continuing the program at the point immediately following the last catch block in the group, or rethrowing the exception if you cannot recover from the error condition. If the exception is rethrown, the C++ run time again searches for the nearest matching catch block. If a catch block cannot be found, the C++ run-time terminate function is called. By default, it calls the C++ run-time abort function, which ends the application. See the "Replacing the Terminate Function" topic later in this chapter for information on how to provide your own terminate function.

The exception mechanism just described is known as the *termination model* of error handling. In this model of exception handling, control is never returned to the point where the exception was thrown. The *resumption model* of error handling, which allows an exception handler to handle an error and then resume at the point where the exception was thrown, is not supported by C++.

When an exception is thrown and the C++ run time is looking for the closest active try block, the call stack is said to be *unwound*. This means that functions on the call stack are terminated as the C++ run time backs up looking for a try block. Destructors for all automatic objects (those created on the stack) in those terminated functions are called as the stack is unwound.

Benefits of Using C++ Exceptions

C++ exception handling is intended to replace the use of return codes. Open Class Library uses exceptions because of the many benefits they provide. One of the most important benefits of using exceptions is that your error-handling code can be completely separated from your application logic. The error-prone method of passing and checking return codes after each function call is no longer necessary. This separation of normal processing from error handling leads to cleaner code, which is easier to understand and maintain. This separation also enables you to place exception handlers at strategic locations, places where it makes sense to try and recover instead of at every function call.

Another important benefit of using exceptions is the fact that the stack is unwound when an exception is thrown, and destructors of all local objects are called as the objects are removed from the stack. This means that you can guarantee resources are cleaned up and freed, even when an exception occurs, as long as you provide destructors that release all resources. If an exception is thrown from a constructor, a destructor is called for any subobjects that are already constructed.

You can use exception handling in conjunction with constructors and destructors to implement an elegant technique for managing resources that Bjarne Stroustrup refers to as "... resource acquisition is initialization."[1] This is a technique in which resources are acquired during the construction of objects and are subsequently cleaned up and released in destructors. One example of this in Open Class Library is `IPrivateResourceClass`, where the resource acquired is a *mutex semaphore*. If your code uses this class, you do not have to wrap code that uses a mutex semaphore in a `try` block to ensure that the semaphore is closed and released if an exception is thrown while it owns the semaphore. The destructor takes care of this cleanup for you.

Another important benefit of using exceptions is that they are implemented in such a way that an application cannot ignore them. If you ignore an exception, your application terminates. This forces you to acknowledge the error and make a conscious decision to continue the program. Under the return-code paradigm, a program could continue incorrectly because it failed to check the return code from a function call.

Several other benefits are also worth mentioning. Because the `throw` statement throws an expression, as opposed to an integer, it is possible to throw any of the built-in types as well as any user-defined types. This allows detailed error information to be returned to any interested exception handler, which increases the chances that the exception handler can recover from the error.

Returning errors from constructors is also a problem in C++ if you do not use exception handling. Constructors cannot return anything, so they cannot notify clients of an error condition with return codes. At best, they can place an object in an invalid state and hope the client notices and recovers. Exceptions safely solve this problem because destructors for subobjects are called when an exception is thrown from a constructor.

Open Class Library's Error-Handling Strategy

Open Class Library's strategy of using exception handling for processing all errors, including the design of the exception classes, was strongly influenced by the ideas of Bjarne Stroustrup. We adopted his idea that exception handling is error handling. Throwing exceptions has

---

[1]Bjarne Stroustrup. *The C++ Programming Language*. Reading, Massachusetts: Addison-Wesley Publishing Company, 1991.

completely replaced the use of return codes in Open Class Library. Open Class Library also only *throws* exceptions in true error situations.

All of the classes in the Open Class Library exception-handling component are self-contained. This means that the exception classes do not depend on any classes in Open Class Library outside of the exception component. This ensures that no exceptions are thrown while an exception is already being processed. For example, the exception classes use character arrays instead of an IString object so that the IString implementation is free to use exceptions where needed. The exception classes also temporarily replace the *new-handler* when they allocate dynamic storage so that they get control if an error occurs. This ensures that exceptions are not recursively thrown.

Open Class Library defines a small hierarchy of classes derived from IException that represents all exceptions that Open Class Library can throw. Figure 27-1 shows the User Interface Library exception class hierarchy. Figure 27-2 shows the Collection Class Library exception class hierarchy. Notice that both hierarchies are derived from a common base class, IException. IException defines the interface and attributes of all exceptions that Open Class Library throws. Therefore, a minimum level of information is always available for an exception that Open Class Library throws. See the topic "The Root of All Exceptions" later in this chapter for detailed information about IException.

Defining the exceptions as a hierarchy with a single root class guarantees that a program can catch any exception thrown within an enclosing try block by Open Class Library using catch (IException& exc). If all exceptions did not derive from one base class, client code would have to code a catch block for each exception type or use the catch (...) syntax to catch all exceptions thrown by the libraries.

The exceptions that Open Class Library defines are based on the logical type of the error condition, not on the class that throws the exception. In other words, there is not an IDDEInvalidRequest or IContainerResourceExhausted exception type. This helps to minimize the number of exception types needed to describe errors that Open Class Library encounters. This, combined with the fact that all exception classes are derived from a common base class, allows users to catch logical groups of exceptions at various places in the hierarchy.

The Root of All Exceptions

IException is the base class for all of the other exception types that Open Class Library defines and throws. IException defines the common interface for all exceptions and provides the majority of the implementation for them. In general, throw an object of a class derived from IException rather than IException so that the type of the exception conveys meaningful information about the error.

Open Class Library functions create objects of classes derived from IException for all error conditions the functions encounter. Each exception object contains the following:

- A stack of exception message text strings (descriptions)
- An error ID

- A severity code

- An error code group

- Information about where the exception was thrown

See the "Exception Information Logging" topic later in this chapter for detailed information about logging out the information contained in an IException object. The classes derived from IException all override name in order to return their own name instead of their parent's.

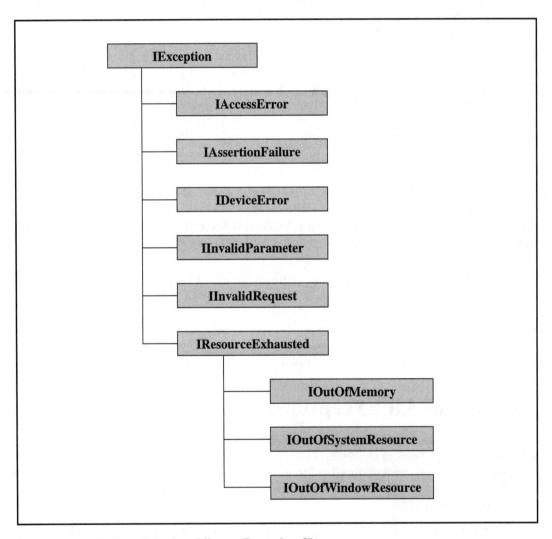

Figure 27-1. The User Interface Library Exception Classes.

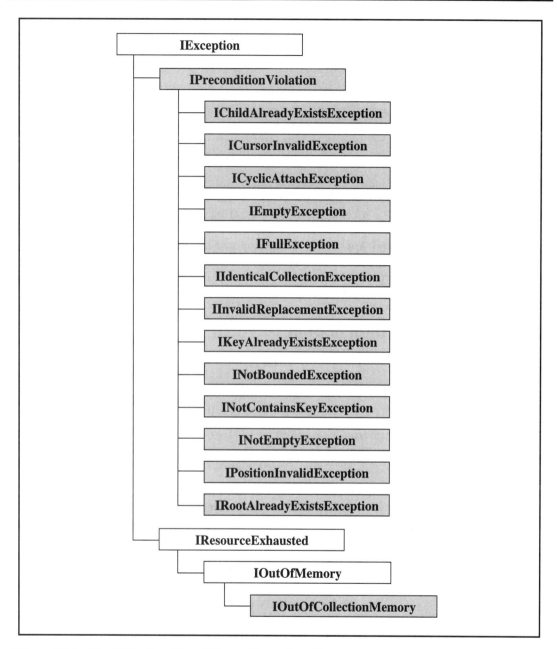

Figure 27-2. The Collection Class Library Exception Classes.

Constructing an Open Class Library Exception

The only required argument for constructing an IException object is an error text string. Optionally, you can provide an error ID, which defaults to 0, and the severity of the exception, which must be one of the values of the IException::Severity enumeration. The choices are recoverable and unrecoverable (the default). You can modify all of these attributes after the exception has been constructed. When you catch an exception, you use this information along with the type of an exception to determine if you can recover from an error.

The ErrorCodeGroup enumeration categorizes an exception by the class library that throws it. You cannot specify the value on the constructor, and it always defaults to baseLibrary. Use setErrorGroup to change this value and errorCodeGroup to retrieve the current value. This enumeration is provided so that you can uniquely identify an error in cases where more than one library, toolkit, or operating system uses the same error code for different errors.

You can use the setSeverity, and isRecoverable functions to set and determine the severity of the error. To set and get the error ID of the error, use the setErrorId and errorId functions. Open Class Library obtains the error ID from the operating system when operating system and windowing errors are encountered. The name function is provided solely for logging the type of the exception. Thus, do not use the name function to determine the type of the exception. Instead, use multiple catch blocks if the type of the exception is pertinent to your program logic. See the discussion about catching groups of exceptions and the ordering of catch blocks in the "Open Class Library's Error Handling Strategy" topic earlier in this chapter.

Exception Location Information

Perhaps the most important exception information, from a debugging perspective, is the array of location information that every IException object keeps. Each IExceptionLocation object contains a function name, the file name this function is contained in, and the line number in this file where an IException object has been created or rethrown.

The IEXCEPTION_LOCATION macro is provided so that you can easily obtain this location information. The macro creates an IExcepionLocation object using the VisualAge for C++ __FUNCTION__, __FILE__, and __LINE__ predefined macros.

Every time the addLocation function is called, it adds an IExceptionLocation object to the end of an array. Only five IExceptionLocation objects are kept in the array. The addLocation function always replaces the last object when the array is full. This ensures that the original location of the error is preserved. Use the locationCount function to retrieve the number of locations in the array. Use the locationAtIndex function if you want to retrieve an IExceptionLocation object at a 0-based index to obtain location information.

Create Exceptions on the Stack

Always create exceptions on the stack to avoid the problem of determining how to delete the exception object. When an exception is thrown, the compiler makes a copy of the exception so that it can unwind the call stack. This is the object that the compiler passes to any matching exception handler, not the object you created and threw.

The other reason for creating exceptions on the stack is that it avoids the problems that would occur if operator new failed due to an out-of-memory condition.

Exception Text

`IException` keeps a stack of exception text strings that you can use to obtain or provide information about the error condition. This stack has no size limit, and it has a 0-based index. `IException` provides two functions for adding error text strings to the exception object. The `setText` function adds an exception text string to the top of the stack. The `appendText` function appends the exception text string to the exception string on the top of the stack. The `textCount` function returns the number of exception strings in the stack. The `text` function returns the text at the specified index, which by default is 0, meaning the top of the stack.

This stack is provided so that a range of information about an error can be stored in an exception object. The exception strings at the bottom of the stack contain the most specific information about the error. This is the information that is of most use when debugging or diagnosing a problem. The exception strings at the top of the stack are more general because they are usually added "farther" from the point of the error. This more general exception text is likely to be the kind of information you want to present to a user in a message box.

The Open Class Library Exception Classes

The following is a brief description of each of the classes derived from `IException`. The examples are provided to show a typical error condition for which a particular exception type is used. These examples use the macros that are typically used to throw exceptions in the Open Class Library. These macros use the helper exception classes `ISystemErrorInfo` and `IGUIErrorInfo` in some cases to obtain error information from the Windows and OS/2 operating systems.

IAccessError

Open Class Library throws an exception of this type for operating system errors when none of the other exception classes are appropriate. In general, this is most of the Windows and OS/2 errors (other than resource exhaustion problems, for which Open Class Library provides several other exception classes). The majority of exceptions that Open Class Library throws are of this type.

Use this exception type for any error returned by Windows and OS/2 functions, when none of the other exception classes are a better fit. The following code is an example of typical usage of this exception type:

```
unsigned long rc = DosKillThread( threadId );
if ( rc != 0 )
  ITHROWSYSTEMERROR( rc,
                     "DosKillThread",
                     IBaseErrorInfo::accessError,
                     IException::recoverable );
```

IAssertionFailure

Open Class Library throws an exception of this type when a condition asserted to be true evaluates to false. Open Class Library typically uses this exception type when checking the input parameters to a function, and it uses the IASSERT macro to throw this exception. IASSERT checks the assertion and throws an exception only if the macro IC_DEVELOP is defined. Open Class Library developers typically define IC_DEVELOP only during development and testing. Note that the macro sets the errorCodeGroup to other.

The following is an example of typical usage of IASSERT to throw this exception type:

```
IString IDDEInfo__stringFromAtom ( unsigned long atom )
{
    IASSERT(atom != 0);
...
}
```

IDeviceError

Open Class Library does not currently throw any exceptions of this type. When a member function makes a hardware-related request of the operating system or the presentation system that the system cannot satisfy because of a hardware failure, the member function creates and throws an object of the IDeviceError class. An example of a failing hardware-related request is attempting to print to a disconnected printer.

IInvalidParameter

Open Class Library throws an exception of this type when an input parameter to a function in production-level code is in error. Use this exception type whenever you need to guarantee the correctness of an input parameter in your production-level code. The following is an example of typical usage of this exception type in Open Class Library:

```
IDDETopicServer& IDDETopicServer :: beginConversation
                 ( const IWindowHandle& clientHandle )
{
    IASSERTPARM(clientHandle.isValid());
...
}
```

The reason the example uses an IInvalidParameter exception instead of IAssertionFailure is that a window handle can only be validated at run time, so this is an error that even rigorous testing of an application cannot eliminate. Open Class Library provides the IASSERTPARM macro for throwing this exception type because it throws it extensively. IASSERTPARM always throws an exception if the assertion fails. Note that the macro sets the errorCodeGroup to other.

IInvalidRequest

Open Class Library throws an exception of this type when the current state of an object is not valid for the called function. Use this exception type when you need to verify that the state of an object is valid for a function call. The following is an example of typical usage of this exception type in Open Class Library:

```
IDDEClientConversation& IDDEClientConversation :: requestData
          ( const char* item,
            const char* format )
{
   IASSERTSTATE(inConversation());
...
}
```

Open Class Library provides the IASSERTSTATE macro for throwing this exception type because it throws it extensively. Note that the macro sets the errorCodeGroup to other.

IOutOfMemory

Open Class Library throws an exception of this type when a request for memory fails. Open Class Library's new-handler throws an exception of this type when dynamic storage is exhausted. We describe the new-handler later in this chapter in the "Open Class Library's New-Handler" topic.

Note: A stack-exhausted situation results in an operating system exception, which is completely different than a C++ exception. See the "Operating System Exception Handling & C Signals" topic.

Use this exception type when memory is exhausted if you override operator new. This makes your new-handler consistent with the method Open Class Library uses to report dynamic memory allocation failures.

IOutOfSystemResource

Open Class Library throws an exception of this type when an operating system resource is exhausted. Use this exception type when a call to an operating system function returns a code indicating that a resource is exhausted. The following is an example of typical usage of this exception type in Open Class Library:

```
unsigned long ulRc = DosCreateQueue(&ulClQHandle,
                                    (unsigned long)0,
                                    (PSZ)strQueueName);
if (ulRc)
   ITHROWSYSTEMERROR(ulRc,"DosCreateQueue",
                     IBaseErrorInfo::outOfSystemResource,
                     IException::recoverable);
```

IOutOfWindowResource

Open Class Library does not currently throw any exceptions of this type. Use this exception type when a call to a presentation or window system function returns a code indicating a resource is exhausted.

IResourceExhausted

Open Class Library does not currently throw any exceptions of this type. This exception type is the base resource exhaustion class. Use one of the classes derived from IResourceExhausted for resource exhaustion errors to provide specific information about the resource that is exhausted.

Catching Exceptions

Use `try` blocks judiciously in an application, because there is a small performance penalty associated with trying to catch exceptions. Regardless of this, you generally do not need to catch an exception unless you can partially recover from the error, can perform some cleanup, or want to present the error information to the user.

One reason for catching an exception, even when none of the reasons listed in the previous paragraph are valid, is to trace the flow of control leading up to the exception. You can do this by using the Open Class Library `IRETHROW` macro to rethrow the exception. This macro records the current function, source file, and line number. Because the C++ run time unwinds the call stack when an exception is thrown, you can get a good idea of the program flow prior to the exception using this technique.

Depending on the severity of the error, it may be better for the program to end rather than continue with incorrect results. A good place to use `try` blocks is at component or subsystem boundaries where the damage can be localized. In the topics that follow, we describe several strategic places to catch exceptions.

Catching Exceptions Thrown from Handlers

Open Class Library contains a `try` block in the `IWindow::dispatch` function because a majority of exceptions can be caught here in a typical application. The support that Open Class Library provides for catching exceptions thrown from handlers and the functions they call is described in the "Exception Support" topic of Chapter 4, "Windows, Handlers, and Events."

See the sample at the end of this chapter for information about how to register an exception handler with `IWindow`. The name of the class derived from `IWindow::ExceptionFn`, in the sample is `ExceptionViewer`. Its `handleException` function displays a message box to the user.

Note: Both of the static functions `IWindow::setExceptionFunction` and `IWindow::exceptionFunction` return a pointer to the previously registered `IWindow::ExceptionFn` class, if any. This makes it possible for you to temporarily replace the exception-handling function and later restore it.

Catch Exceptions as References

Always catch exceptions as references so that a copy of the exception is not made. This is important if you catch an exception with a handler for one of its base classes, such as `IException`.

For example, here is what would happen if you caught an `IInvalidParameter` object using `catch (IException exc)`. In this case, the compiler uses the copy constructor for `IException` to copy the caught exception. This results in lost or sliced information as the original `IInvalidParameter` object has been replaced by an `IException` object.

Catching Exceptions in main

Wrap the contents of the main routine in a try block if you want to catch as many of the exceptions thrown in your program as possible. It is not possible to catch exceptions thrown from constructors of static objects because they are constructed before main is entered. Wrapping the contents of your main routine in a try block gives you one last opportunity to release any resources and do any cleanup before your application ends. Usually, your application does not try to recover at this point.

The following code is taken from the sample program at the end of the chapter and demonstrates catching exceptions using a try block inside of main. The example assumes that no errors occur in the construction of the IFrameWindow, mainWindow, which precedes the try block. This allows the IFrameWindow object to be used in the construction of an IMessageBox object.

```
int main(int argc, char *argv[], char *envp[])
{
    ExceptionViewer mainWindow;
    try {
        IApplication::current().run();
    }
    catch ( IException& exc) {
        IMessageBox msgBox(&mainWindow.frame());
        msgBox.setTitle("Exception caught in main routine");
        msgBox.show(exc.text(),
                    IMessageBox::okButton    |
                    IMessageBox::errorIcon   |
                    IMessageBox::moveable );
    }
}
```

Why Can't I Catch That Exception?

If you think that your code is causing an exception to be thrown, and you are unable to catch the exception, read on. The **/Gx+** compiler option disables the generation of C++ exception-handling code. If the exception is thrown using one of the Open Class Library macros that does error logging, you still get the error output. This can fool you into thinking that the exception is being thrown, but that is not the case if the application was compiled with the **/Gx+** option. The error logging is done before the C++ run time processes the throw statement and terminates the application. Not even a terminate function registered by your application is called.

Replacing the C++ terminate Function

You can replace the C++ run-time terminate function by registering your own *termination* function using the C++ set_terminate function. As previously mentioned, the terminate function is called if no exception handler (matching catch block) is found. It is also called for two other reasons as well:

- The stack is found to be corrupted while an exception is being processed.

- A destructor called during stack unwinding, caused by an exception being *thrown*, tries to throw an exception.

An error occurs when a user-supplied terminate function tries to return to its caller instead of terminating and no arguments are passed to the registered function so that no error information is available. As a result of these limitations, only register your own termination function in addition to having a strategy for catching exceptions. Use your termination function only as a final safety net and terminate it by calling abort. The following example shows a user-written termination function and how to register it:

```
void customTerminate()
{
   cerr << "My terminate function was called\n";
}

set_terminate(&customTerminate);
```

Errors Allocating Dynamic Memory

Use operator new to allocate dynamic storage. If operator new cannot allocate the requested storage, it returns 0. In order for Open Class Library and your code to detect errors allocating dynamic memory, the return code from all calls to operator new needs to be checked. Open Class Library avoids this by using exceptions for handling errors. Checking return codes tends to clutter up the code, making it harder to read and maintain. To avoid this problem, Open Class Library provides a *new-handler* function, which integrates errors allocating dynamic memory with exception handling.

The Open Class Library's New-Handler Function

C++ has provided the set_new_handler function to register a *new-handler* function, which is invoked when a dynamic storage allocation failure occurs. Open Class Library uses this capability to eliminate the need to check return codes on every call to operator new. A static structure in IBASE.CPP registers a new-handler function. This new-handler function throws an IOutOfMemory exception whenever it is called. This allows your code to handle dynamic memory allocation failures using the same strategy you use for any other exception.

Open Class Library's exception-handling implementation avoids causing any exceptions while processing an exception. Recursive exceptions would cause terminate to be called. The Open Class Library exception-handling component sets the new-handler function to 0 any time it needs to call operator new so that it gets back a 0 return code if operator new fails. The previously registered new-handler function is reregistered after the return code is checked.

Registering Your Own New-Handler Function

You can temporarily or permanently replace the new-handler function that Open Class Library provides with your own new-handler function. The following code is an example that replaces the current new-handler function with customNewHandler.

```
void customNewHandler( ) {
    // Handle new failures your way here.
    cerr << "Dynamic memory allocation failure.\n";
}

fooBar() {
    void(*pOldNewHandler)() = set_new_handler(customNewHandler);
    pBuffer = new char[100];
    set_new_handler(pOldNewHandler);
}
```

The set_new_handler function returns the address of the current new-handler function, which the sample saves in pOldNewHandler. At the end of the fooBar function, it restores the previous new-handler function.

Throwing Exceptions

This section explains how to use the classes and macros that Open Class Library provides to throw exceptions when you detect errors in your code. Open Class Library provides a number of macros and exception helper classes to simplify the throwing of exceptions.

Using Macros to Throw Exceptions

The IBaseErrorInfo class is an abstract base class that defines the interface for its derived classes: ICLibErrorInfo, IGUIErrorInfo, IMMErrorInfo, and ISystemErrorInfo. These classes retrieve error information and text that you can subsequently use to create an exception object.

In prior releases of Open Class Library, the base class was named IErrorInfo, but the Windows operating system also uses the IErrorInfo class name. If you are not ready to migrate your code to the new class name, add **/DIUSE_IERRORINFO** to your compiler options. This adds a typedef to your code so that IErrorInfo is defined as a synonym for IBaseErrorInfo. Note that you cannot use this solution when your code also includes the Windows IErrorInfo class.

IEXCEPT.HPP contains macros that create an exception object, log the error information contained in the exception object, and throw the exception. Some of the macros create objects of the ISystemErrorInfo or IGUIErrorInfo helper classes. Logging the error information is described in detail in the "Exception Information Logging" section later in this chapter. We cover ISystemErrorInfo and IGUIErrorInfo in the "Obtaining Operating System Error Information" and "Obtaining Presentation System Error Information" topics later in this chapter.

Open Class Library provides other macros for throwing exceptions, but they are less flexible or less efficient than the macros we describe. These macros are more efficient because they call static functions to create the exception object, call functions to add location information and log the error information out, create the helper objects when necessary, and throw the exception. This topic also describes the macros Open Class Library primarily uses to throw exceptions.

For a complete list of the macros that Open Class Library uses to throw exceptions, refer to the *Open Class Library Reference Guide*.

ASSERT

This macro provides assertion support in Open Class Library, which is almost identical to assertion support provided in the C library ASSERT.H. The big improvement over C assertions is that this macro integrates assertion support with exception handling. When the IC_DEVELOP macro constant is defined, the expression passed to IASSERT is evaluated. If the expression evaluates to 0, the macro calls the IException static function, assertParameter, which throws an IAssertionFailure exception. If IC_DEVELOP is not defined, the test is compiled out. In other words, the macro does not generate any code in this case.

Use this macro for any expressions you want to assert in your application. Also, define IC_DEVELOP only during the development and testing of your code. When your code is ready to be delivered, do not define the IC_DEVELOP macro constant so that the assertions are compiled out. IASSERT is defined in IEXCBASE.HPP.

The following code is an example of typical usage of the IASSERT macro in Open Class Library. This example generates this exception text: "The following expression must be true, but evaluated to false: atom != 0".

```
IString IDDEInfo__stringFromAtom ( unsigned long atom )
{
   IASSERT(atom != 0);
   // remainder of function.
}
```

IASSERTPARM

This macro is identical to the IASSERT macro except it does not depend on the IC_DEVELOP macro constant and, therefore, always evaluates the input expression. (It cannot be compiled out.) If the expression evaluates to 0, the macro calls the IExcept__assertParameter static function, which throws an IInvalidParameter exception. The error group other is added to the object. Open Class Library typically uses this macro to check for null pointers, but you can use this macro to check the validity of any parameter. For example, use this macro to check the validity of input parameters to functions in your classes and applications. The following code is an example of typical usage of the IASSERTPARM macro in Open Class Library. This example generates the following exception text: "UIL0001: The following expression must be true, but evaluated to false: clientHandle.isValid()".

```
IDDETopicServer& IDDETopicServer :: beginConversation
                ( const IWindowHandle& clientHandle )
{
   IASSERTPARM(clientHandle.isValid());
   // remainder of function.
}
```

IASSERTSTATE

This macro is similar to the IASSERT and IASSERTPARM macros in that it also asserts an expression, typically a member function call. The difference is that the expression is not usually related to any of the input parameters. If the expression evaluates to 0, the macro calls the IExcept__assertState static function, which throws an IInvalidRequest exception. The error group other is added to the object. Open Class Library uses this macro to ensure that the state of an object is valid for the called function.

Use this macro to verify that the state of an object is valid for a function call in any of your classes. IASSERTSTATE is defined in IEXCEPT.HPP.

The following code is an example of typical usage of the IASSERTSTATE macro in Open Class Library. This example automatically generates this exception text: "UIL0001: The following expression must be true, but evaluated to false: inConversation()".

```
IDDEClientConversation& IDDEClientConversation :: requestData
            ( const char* item,
              const char* format )
{
    IASSERTSTATE(inConversation());
    // remainder of function.
}
```

ITHROWERROR

Open Class Library uses this macro to throw exceptions containing error text loaded from a message file. See the "Custom Error Messages" topic later in this chapter for information on creating message files and loading message text from a message file.

The macro takes three arguments: the ID of the message to be loaded from the current message file, one of the values of the IBaseErrorInfo::ExceptionType enumeration, and one of the values of the IException::Severity enumeration. The exception type is used to determine what type of exception object to create, and the severity is used to determine if the exception is recoverable.

The valid values for the IBaseErrorInfo::ExceptionType, and IException::Severity, enumerations are listed in the description of the ITHROWGUIERROR2 macro. The macro calls the IExcept__throwLibraryError static function.

You can use this macro to load custom error text from a message file. ITHROWERROR is defined in IEXCEPT.HPP. See an example of the ITHROWERROR macro in the "Custom Error Messages" section later in this chapter.

The ITHROWERROR1 macro is identical to the ITHROWERROR macro except it has a fourth argument, which is text to be substituted into the retrieved message. See the "Custom Error Messages" topic for detailed information on the mechanism that message files provide for handling substitution text.

This macro replaces ITHROWLIBRARYERROR and no longer requires you to use the Open Class message file. You can specify the message file of your choice for your own custom messages.

ITHROWERROR1

This macro can throw any of the Open Class Library-defined exceptions. It is identical to the `ITHROWERROR` macro except it has another parameter for the substitution text for the retrieved message.

ITHROWGUIERROR2

Open Class Library uses this macro when a call to an operating system function fails and the documentation indicates that information about the error is available via `WinGetLastError`. This macro takes three arguments: the name of the operating system function that returned the error code, one of the values of the `IBaseErrorInfo::ExceptionType` enumeration, and one of the values of the `IException::Severity` enumeration. The failing operating system function name is prepended to the exception text. The exception type is used to determine what exception object type should be created, and the severity is used to determine if the exception is recoverable.

The valid values of the `IBaseErrorInfo::ExceptionType` enumeration are: `accessError`, `deviceError`, `invalidParameter`, `invalidRequest`, `outOfSystemResource`, `outOfWindowResource`, `outOfMemory`, and `resourceExhausted`. The valid values of the `IException::Severity` enumeration are `recoverable` and `unrecoverable`.

The macro uses the `IGUIErrorInfo` class to retrieve detailed information about the error. This information is used to set the error code and error text of the exception object. See detailed information about the `IGUIErrorInfo` class in the "Obtaining Operating System Error Information" topic later in this chapter. The macro calls the `IGUIErrorInfo::throwGUIError` static function.

Use this macro whenever a call to the operating system fails and the documentation indicates additional information about the error can be obtained by calling `WinGetLastError`. The following code is an example of typical usage of the `ITHROWGUIERROR2` macro:

```
unsigned long ulAtom;
ulAtom = WinAddAtom(WinQuerySystemAtomTable(),
                    (PSZ)atom);
if (!ulAtom)
   ITHROWGUIERROR2("WinAddAtom",IBaseErrorInfo::invalidParameter,
                   IException::recoverable);
```

ITHROWSYSTEMERROR

Open Class Library uses this macro when a call to an operating system API results in an error. The macro takes four arguments: the return code from the operating system function, the name of the function, one of the values of the `IBaseErrorInfo::ExceptionType` enumeration, and one of the values of the `IException::Severity` enumeration. The name of the failing function is prepended to the exception text. The exception type is used to determine what type of exception object to create, and the severity is used to determine if the exception is recoverable.

The valid values for both the `IBaseErrorInfo::ExceptionType` and `IException::Severity` enumerations are listed in the previous description of the `ITHROWGUIERROR2` macro.

The `ITHROWSYSTEMERROR` macro uses the return code in conjunction with the `ISystemErrorInfo` class to retrieve detailed information about the error from the OS/2 operating system. This information is used to set the error text of the exception object. See detailed information about the `ISystemErrorInfo` class in the "Obtaining Operating System Error Information" topic later in this chapter. The macro calls the `ISystemErrorInfo::throwSystemError` static function. Note that the `ITHROWSYSTEMERROR` macro sets the `ErrorCodeGroup` to `operatingSystem`.

Use this macro whenever a call to an OS/2 function fails. The following code is an example of typical usage of the `ITHROWSYSTEMERROR` macro in Open Class Library:

```
unsigned long rc = DosKillThread( threadId );
if ( rc != 0 )
  ITHROWSYSTEMERROR( rc,
                     "DosKillThread",
                     IBaseErrorInfo::accessError,
                     IException::recoverable );
```

IRETHROW

Use this macro to rethrow an exception that you have caught but cannot recover from. The macro has no arguments, and it does not work unless you are inside a `catch` block. This is because `IRETHROW` does not specify anything on the `throw` statement, which is the correct way to rethrow an exception. Outside the context of a `catch` block, a `throw` statement by itself is meaningless.

The main benefit of using the `IRETHROW` macro is that it logs out all of the exception information, including the current location information, before rethrowing the exception. Using `IRETHROW` provides some detailed information on the program flow leading up to the exception. See the discussion about using `IRETHROW` to trace program flow in the earlier section "Catching Exceptions."

Throwing Exceptions without Using Macros

In this topic, we briefly discuss throwing an object of one of the exception classes without using the previously described macros, and some of the helper classes you can use to obtain information about errors. You might want to use the native Open Class Library exception classes directly if you do not want to log out the error information before throwing or rethrowing an exception. Also, if you throw an exception type not defined by Open Class Library, do not use the macros.

If you want to have location information added to an `IException` object that you create and have the error information in that `IException` object logged, use the `ITHROW` macro to throw the exception, as follows:

```
IInvalidRequest invReq("setup() must be called first.");
ITHROW(invReq);
```

If you throw the exception using the `throw` statement, you can still add location information or log the error information as illustrated in the following example:

```
IInvalidRequest invReq("setup() must be called first.");
invReq.addLocation(IEXCEPTION_LOCATION());
invReq.logExceptionData();
throw invReq;
```

Obtaining Presentation System Error Information

Use the `IGUIErrorInfo` class to retrieve error information from the presentation system or window system. Use this class if you get a bad return code from a call to the presentation system for which the documentation indicates further error information is available. Normally, you use the `ITHROWGUIERROR2` macro for this situation. You can use this class directly if you unsure if the presentation system has error information available.

If you provide the optional `GUIFunctionName` argument when constructing an `IGUIErrorInfo` object, it is used as a prefix to the error text that the presentation system provides. The `isAvailable` function returns `true` if the error information was successfully retrieved. Use `throwError` to create and throw an exception using the information contained in an `IGUIErrorInfo` object. The following code is an example of how you would throw an `IAccessError` exception:

```
IGUIErrorInfo errInfo;
if (errInfo.isAvailable())
   errInfo.throwError(IEXCEPTION_LOCATION());
```

Obtaining Operating System Error Information

Use the `ISystemErrorInfo` class to retrieve information from the operating system. Use this class anytime you get a bad return code from the Windows or OS/2 operating system. The one required argument is the return code.   As it does for the `IGUIErrorInfo` class, `ISystemErrorInfo` prefixes the error text with the name of the failing function if you provide the optional second argument. Normally, you use the `ITHROWSYSTEMERROR` macro to throw an exception for an operating system error. One reason you might want to use this class directly is if you need to do some special processing with the error information before you throw an exception.

The `isAvailable` function returns `true` if the error information was successfully retrieved from the operating system. Use `throwError` to create and throw an exception using the information contained in an `ISystemErrorInfo` object. The following code is an example of how you would throw an `IAccessError` exception:

```
ISystemErrorInfo errInfo;
if (errInfo.isAvailable())
   errInfo.throwError(errInfo.errorId(), IEXCEPTION_LOCATION());
```

Deriving a New Exception Class

You can easily to derive a new class from `IException` or any of its derived classes. The following example shows everything you need to provide for a complete `IException`-derived class:

CustomException Interface - exceptns\newexcp\custexcp.hpp

```
#include <iexcbase.hpp>

class CustomException : public IException
{
public:

  CustomException ( const char*    errorText,
                    unsigned long errorId = 0,
                    Severity      sev = unrecoverable );

virtual
 ~CustomException ( );

  CustomException ( const CustomException& excp);

virtual const char
 *name ( ) const;

private:
operator = ( const CustomException& );
};
```

CustomException Implementation - exceptns\newexcp\newexcp.cpp

```
#include "newexcp.hpp"

CustomException::CustomException ( const char*    errorText,
                                   unsigned long errorId,
                                   Severity      sev )
        : IException(errorText, errorId, sev)
{ }

CustomException::~CustomException ( )
{ }

CustomException::CustomException ( const CustomException& excp)
        : IException(excp)
{
   // Copy your instance data here.
}

const char* CustomException::name ( ) const
{
   return "CustomException";
}
```

In this example, we do not attempt to inline the constructor or any of the virtual functions because the compiler currently does not inline them. See Chapter 29, "Packaging and Performance Tuning," for the reasons. If you try to inline any of these functions, a static version is generated in each compilation unit that needs them. The copy constructor is required so that the compiler can make a copy of the exception object when it is thrown. You must also supply a name function, as shown in the example, if you want the logExceptionData function to log the type of the exception correctly.

There is an easier way for you to provide a new derived exception class if you do not add any new functions or instance data. Use the IEXCLASSDECLARE macro to declare your new class and use the IEXCLASSIMPLEMENT macro to provide the implementation for it. These macros are provided in IEXCBASE.HPP. The following code is equivalent to the previous example for deriving a new class:

```
IEXCLASSDECLARE(CustomException, IException);
IEXCLASSIMPLEMENT(CustomException, IException);
```

Custom Error Messages

Open Class Library uses message files for loading custom error messages. These messages are used in error situations when the presentation system or operating system provides no appropriate error message or when Open Class Library provides more detailed error information. Message files are useful because they allow your application to load messages in different languages without recompilation.

Creating a Message File

You can create a message file to allow your application to provide custom error messages. For the OS/2 operating system, use the MKMSGF utility, which is part of the Developer's Toolkit for OS/2, to create these message files. This utility is described in detail in the online *Developer's Toolkit for OS/2 Tools Reference*. Each message in a message file has a unique ID and the associated message text.

For the Windows operating system, the mechanics of building and delivering message files are different; they are handled as resources.

Use the message compiler, MC.EXE, to convert message text files into binary resource files which can then be input to the resource compiler, IRC.EXE. The output from irc is a resource (.res) file, which you can bind to your application or DLL using the linker.

Use IMessageText to retrieve the messages on both the OS/2 and Windows operating systems.

Loading the Messages

We provide the IMessageText class for loading message text from an OS/2 or Windows message file. IMessageText is defined in IMSGTEXT.HPP. The IMessageText constructor requires two arguments: the message ID and the name of the message file from which to retrieve the message. Include the file extension, typically MSG, in the message file's name parameter. The following example loads the text for Message 3 from SAMPLE.MSG:

```
IMessageText sampleMessage(3,"SAMPLE.MSG");
```

You can also pass up to nine optional text strings on the IMessageText constructor. These are substitution strings used to replace occurrences of %1, %2 ... in the specified message. If the number of substitution strings does not match the number of %n occurrences in the message, no substitution occurs. This substitution capability allows you to reuse your error messages when they are similar.

The OS/2 operating system first tries to load the message from any message segment bound to your application. (Refer to the description of the MSGBIND utility in the online *Developer's Toolkit for OS/2 Tools Reference* for information on how to bind your message file to your executable.) If the message is not found, the OS/2 operating system searches for the specified message file. The search for this file proceeds as follows:

1. In the system root directory

2. In the current working directory

3. Using the DPATH environment variable

4. Using the APPEND environment variable

You can retrieve the name of the current message file using the IBase::messageFile static function. Open Class Library finds this file name using the following algorithm:

1. If the IBase::setMessageFile static function is called, the name of the message file that it specified is returned.

2. The value of the ICLUI_MSGFILE environment variable is returned if you have set it.

3. The default Open Class Library message file is returned.

The easiest way to load your own custom messages is by using the ITHROWERROR and ITHROWERROR1 macros, which also throw the exception for you. See the "Using Macros to Throw Exceptions" topic earlier in the chapter for detailed information on these macros.

Using a Message Box to Display an Exception

If you want to present exception information to the user, you can use a message box. See the sample program at the end of the chapter for several examples of using IMessageBox to display exception information.

Constructing a Message Box

The only constructor for IMessageBox accepts an IWindow* parameter. This value identifies the window that you want to be the owner window of the message box. If you decide to provide help for the message box, Open Class Library uses its owner window to find the associated help window for displaying the help panel. See Chapter 23, "Using Help," for more information.

Use the IMessageBox::setTitle function to set the title bar text of the message box. If you do not set the title text, the text from the title bar of the owner IWindow is used.

Showing a Message Box

Open Class Library provides six overloaded versions of the show function. All of the versions have a required argument for providing the message text and an optional help ID argument for providing help. The style of the IMessageBox is determined by an IMessageBox::Style or IMessageBox::Severity, depending on which version of show you use to display the message box. Refer to *Open Class Library Reference* for a description of which styles Open Class Library sets for each severity.

The IMessageBox class provides many styles for customizing the message box, such as the following customizations:

- The type of icon and buttons to be displayed

- The modality of the message box

- Whether the message box is movable

These styles are also well documented in the *Open Class Library Reference*.

Figure 27-3 shows a message box.

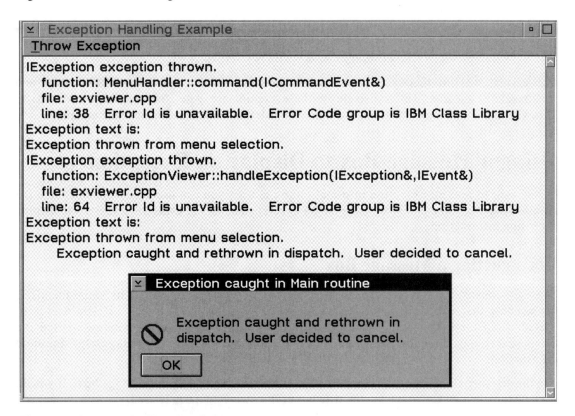

Figure 27-3. Exception Logging Output.

Checking the User's Response

All of the IMessageBox::show functions return an IMessageBox::Response, which is an enumeration of all of the types of buttons allowed on message boxes. The valid values of this enumeration are enter, ok, cancel, abort, retry, ignore, yes, no, and unknown. Check this return value to determine what push button the user selected. The following code is from the example at the end of the chapter, which demonstrates how to check the user's response.

```
IMessageBox::Response response =
    msgBox.show(exc.text(),
                IMessageBox::retryCancelButton |
                IMessageBox::errorIcon        |
                IMessageBox::moveable );
if (response == IMessageBox::retry)
    // Do something.
```

Using Exception Classes with Message Boxes

One of the versions of IMessageBox::show requires only an IException& argument. The function retrieves the message text from the IException object. This version of show displays the *error* icon, which is a circle with a diagonal line through it. If IException::isRecoverable returns true, the message box displays the **Retry** and **Cancel** push buttons. Otherwise, the message box contains only the **OK** push button. (This version of IMessageBox::show is not used in the example at the end of the chapter because we needed to be able to move the message box to capture the screen image for Figure 27-3.)

Open Class Library provides another version of show that requires an IBaseErrorInfo& argument. Thus, you can use objects of its derived classes, IGUIErrorInfo and ISystemErrorInfo, to display a message box. The show function retrieves the message text from the IBaseErrorInfo object. The message box contains an error icon and the **OK** push button.

As you can see, these two versions of show are easy to use. If you need to customize your message box using styles that these versions of show do not support, just retrieve the exception text and use one of the other versions of show.

Providing Help with Message Boxes

You can provide help for any IMessageBox object by providing the help ID of the help window as the last argument to the show function. See Chapter 23, "Using Help," for more information on the help component of Open Class Library. You must create an IHelpWindow object and use the IHelpWindow::associateWindow function to associate the help object with the owner window of the IMessageBox object. This is the owner window that you provide on the IMessageBox constructor. The message box includes a **Help** push button when you pass a help panel identifier to the show function.

Exception Information Logging

The logExceptionData function of IException logs all available information about an exception. It is called by all of the exception-throwing macros described earlier in this chapter in the "Using Macros to Throw Exceptions" section. The exception information is extremely useful for debugging because it contains information that identifies the exact location of the throw or rethrow. Figure 27-3 shows the exception information that the example program logs at the end of the chapter. Notice that the error has been logged twice, once when it was thrown and once when it was caught and rethrown.

Applications That Just End

If you have an application that suddenly ends with no warning, there is a good chance that an exception is being thrown. The easiest way to see if this is what has happened is to look at your exception output.

Open Class Library uses `ITrace` to log exception output by default. See Chapter 28, "Problem Determination," for more information on this subject.

Location of Logged Output

The `IException::logExceptionData` function calls `operator new` to allocate a buffer for storing the exception information. If `operator new` fails, the function writes the exception information to the standard error device, `stderr`. Otherwise, it passes the buffer of exception information to the registered exception trace function.

`IBASE.CPP` registers a default trace function, which writes the buffer using `ITrace`.

You can use the `setTraceFunction` to register your own trace function that overrides the default. Open Class Library uses this function in `IBASE.CPP` to register an exception trace function that writes the buffer of data to wherever `ITrace` output is being written. See Chapter 28, "Problem Determination," for a description on how to set the environment variables, `ICLUI_TRACE`, `ICLUI_TRACETO`, and `ICLUI_TRACEFILE`. These variables control trace activation and the location of `ITrace` output.

Registering an Exception Trace Function

Objects of the class `IException` and its derived classes use `IException::TraceFn` to log exception object data.

`IBASE.CPP` registers a default `TraceFn`-derived object. It uses `ITrace` to write the buffers of data so that the buffers are written to wherever the `ICLUI TRACETO` environment variable directs the output from `ITrace`.

If you want to modify some aspect of tracing, derive your own class from `IException::TraceFn` and register it with `IException` using `IException::setTraceFunction`. `IException::logExceptionData` calls `IException::TraceFn::logData`, passing it the exception object. By default, `logData` calls `IException::TraceFn::write`, passing it a buffer of data.

You can completely take over exception logging by overriding the `logData` function. The `IException` object is passed so that you can completely customize the logging of exception data. If you only want to change how the buffers of exception data are logged, override the `write` function.

We provide the `exceptionLogged` function so that you can determine when the default `logData` function has passed the last buffer of exception data to the `write` function. Thus, you can gather all of the exception data by overriding the `write` and `exceptionLogged` functions for situations where you must write all of the exception data with one call.

Follow these steps to register a function for logging exception information:

1. Derive a class from `IException::TraceFn`.

2. In the derived class, override the `write` pure virtual function or the `logData` function.

3. Create an object of the class you derived from `IException::TraceFn`.

4. Register this object with the Open Class Library exception-handling routines using the `IException::setTraceFunction` static function.

The sample program in the next topic shows how to register an exception-trace function. The name of the class derived from `IException::TraceFn` in the example is `ExceptionViewer`. Its `trace` function writes the buffer of information to an `IMultiLineEdit` object.

Exception-Handling Sample

The following exception-handling sample demonstrates many of the techniques and subjects we covered in this chapter as follows:

-   Throwing and catching exceptions

-   Using a `try` block in `main`

-   Registering an exception function with `IWindow`

-   Using `IMessageBox`

-   Registering an exception-tracing function

ExceptionViewer Interface - exceptns\exviewer\exviewer.hpp

```
#include <iframe.hpp>
#include <imle.hpp>
#include <icmdhdr.hpp>

class ExceptionViewer;

class MenuHandler : public ICommandHandler
{
public:
 MenuHandler ( ExceptionViewer &excViewer )
                : viewer(excViewer) {}

protected:
virtual Boolean
  command     ( ICommandEvent& event );

private:
ExceptionViewer
 &viewer;
};
```

```
class ExceptionViewer : public IException::TraceFn,
                        public IWindow::ExceptionFn
{
public:
 ExceptionViewer  ( );

IFrameWindow
  &frame           ( )    { return frameWindow; }
IMultiLineEdit
  &mle             ( )    { return mleWindow; }

// Callback functions from IException and IWindow::ExceptionFn.
virtual void
   write ( const char* buffer );
virtual Boolean
   handleException (IException& exception, IEvent& event);

private:
IFrameWindow
   frameWindow;
IMultiLineEdit
   mleWindow;
MenuHandler
   menuHandler;
};
```

ExceptionViewer Implementation - exceptns\exviewer\exviewer.cpp

```
#include <iapp.hpp>
#include <imsgbox.hpp>
#include "exceptns.hpp"
#include "exceptns.h"

ExceptionViewer::ExceptionViewer ( )
        : frameWindow(IFrameWindow::defaultStyle() |
                      IFrameWindow::menuBar,
                      WND_MAIN),
          mleWindow(0x5002, &frameWindow, &frameWindow),
          menuHandler(*this)
{
   IException::setTraceFunction(*this);
   IWindow::setExceptionFunction(this);
   mle().disableDataUpdate();
   frame().setClient(&mle());
   menuHandler.handleEventsFor(&frame());
   frame().show();
};

Boolean MenuHandler::command(ICommandEvent& event)
{
   switch (event.commandId()) {
      case THROW_EXCEPTION:
         IException exc("\nException thrown from menu selection.
                       \n",
                       0, IException::recoverable);
         ITHROW(exc);
         return true;
   };
   return false;
}

void ExceptionViewer::write ( const char* buffer )
{
   mle().addAsLast((char*)buffer);
}
```

```
Boolean ExceptionViewer::handleException (IException& exc, IEvent& event)
{
    IMessageBox msgBox(&frame());
    msgBox.setTitle("Exception caught in dispatch routine");
    IMessageBox::Response response =
        msgBox.show(exc.text(),
                    IMessageBox::retryCancelButton |
                    IMessageBox::errorIcon        |
                    IMessageBox::moveable );
    if (response == IMessageBox::retry) {
        mle().addAsLast("Exception caught in dispatch.
                        User decided to retry.\n",
                        0, IMultiLineEdit::noTran );
        return true;
    }
    else {
        exc.setText("Exception caught and rethrown in dispatch.
                    User decided to cancel.");
        IRETHROW(exc);
    }
}

int main(int argc, char *argv[], char *envp[])
{
    ExceptionViewer mainWindow;
    try {
        IApplication::current().run();
    }
    catch ( IException& exc) {
        IMessageBox msgBox(&mainWindow.frame());
        msgBox.setTitle("Exception caught in Main routine");
        msgBox.show(exc.text(),
                    IMessageBox::okButton   |
                    IMessageBox::errorIcon  |
                    IMessageBox::moveable );
    }
}
```

Chapter 28

Problem Determination

- Describes techniques for preventing programming errors, and tips for isolating and fixing them when they occur
- Describes the ITrace class
- Chapters 27 and 29 cover related material.

Because we are all human beings, making and correcting programming errors are normal parts of the iterative cycle of application development. An important goal is to move the identification of these errors as early in the development cycle as possible.

The best case is that you are typing the code in error and the code parser running as a background task points out the mistake and corrects it. The worst case is that you have completed testing your application, sent it to your customers, and then they find a subtle behavior in a limited circumstance that causes your application to fail.

Between these two bounds, you identify problems using exhaustive unit and system testing, Beta testing, functional trace analysis, memory diagnostics, and code inspections. Because these techniques are expensive in terms of people's time, this chapter starts by addressing some ways to avoid common programming errors. Then, we move on to tools, tips, and techniques for finding and fixing errors once they occur.

An Ounce of Prevention . . .

Before we discuss how to find errors once they occur, we would like to spend a little time discussing some techniques to keep these errors from occurring in the first place.

Use Type Safety

One of the primary mechanisms C++ provides for identifying errors early in the development cycle is its ability to provide a type-safe functional interface. With type safety, you can design a function and limit the conditions under which that function gets called. It also provides the earliest possible warning when an error occurs using an interface. As you design the error-reporting strategy for a class and its functions, ask the question, "Can I describe the limitations of this class directly in the interface?" Doing so can save your users countless hours of debugging.

Use References Instead of Pointers

If you have done much C programming, more than likely you have spent a good deal of time using pointers. In C, you use pointers not only as a way to allocate storage on the heap, but also as a way to reduce the amount of data passed between functions. The primary problem with the latter usage is that it requires the called function to handle the pointer having a 0 value. If the function cannot operate successfully with a 0 value, it must report an error to the caller.

A better way of requiring a function to be called with only valid objects is to use *references* instead of pointers. References document the requirement instead of waiting until run time to notify the caller with an exception.

Carefully Manage the Lifetime of Objects

Failure to manage the lifetime of objects allocated on the heap can cause several problems. The system may abort the application when you attempt to use a deleted object, or you might hang the entire system from a storage leak because you allocate objects but never delete them. Limiting the use of heap-allocated objects can reduce these kinds of problems. Where possible, allocate objects on the stack or as part of the instance data of another object.

If you must use the heap to allocate an object, be clear about how it is deleted. If possible, allocate objects in a constructor and free them in a destructor. If this is not possible, consider using a reference-counting scheme so you delete an object when its last reference is removed. You can also describe what frees the storage through a naming convention on functions.

Don't forget to provide copy constructors and assignment operators when storing pointers in instance data. Try to avoid using multiple methods for deleting an object because the object is easily misplaced. It is best if what creates an object deletes it. In the "Memory Allocation Tracing" topic later in this chapter, you find diagnostic tools that you can use to track down memory allocation errors when they occur.

The Cost of Instance Data

We have just recommend limiting the use of heap-allocated objects in favor of storing the object as an instance of another object. However, there are at least two problems with this recommendation. First, this can increase compilation time because the compiler must have the size of all objects in the instance data. A pointer can be identified to the compiler using a forward class reference, which does not require the complete class declaration. The other problem is that the amount of debugging information will increase because the compiler has access to the class definition of the instance data class and includes the necessary information to describe it.

Limit the Use of Multiple Inheritance

Adding multiple inheritance to your application increases its complexity in ways that might not be evident from the start. As with anything that increases the complexity of an application, use multiple inheritance only when you really need it. Typically, construction from components using a HAS-A relationship provides the necessary level of function without the added problems of multiple inheritance.

If you do use multiple inheritance, do not cast the "this" pointer. Depending on the actual class hierarchy, and the compiler implementation, the "this" pointer might not point to the actual memory for any of the base objects in your multiple-inheritance instance.

VisualAge for C++ Diagnostics Aids

Besides the diagnostic messages of the compiler and linker, VisualAge for C++ provides several useful facilities for finding programming errors.

The Program Debugger

The VisualAge for C++ debugger (the Windows version is called **idebug**, the OS/2 version **icsdebug**) offers an extensive set of features that can help you isolate problems in your program. Using the debugger is beyond the scope of this book, but later on in this chapter you learn how to use a few of the features as they relate to solving some common problems. If you haven't already done so, take the time to work your way through the *VisualAge for C++ User's Guide* and *How Do I...* sections for this tool. You are sure to find useful features.

The Performance Analyzer

The VisualAge for C++ Performance Analyzer tool (the Windows version is **iperf**, the OS/2 version **icsperf**) is useful for understanding the run-time characteristics of your application. The Performance Analyzer records trace information about your application while the application is running. You can then use its set of analysis tools to study the behavior of your program. The Performance Analyzer can show you timing information in several different formats as well as display the order of execution of the functions. The output can be in the form of a table or a graph. You can also define your own trace events and view them with the normal Performance Analyzer trace events. There are several ways to control the amount of trace data recorded, including by level of nesting, by function, and by statements you insert into your program. It is worth your time experimenting with these output-limiting tools because a large program can create a tremendous amount of trace data. Figure 28-1 shows the call nesting diagram, and in Chapter 29, "Packaging and Performance Tuning," you see an example of how to use the Performance Analyzer tool.

You can also get performance data about your application's usage of some of the system APIs that it is calling. To do this, link your application with special versions of the system libraries provided with VisualAge for C++ for this purpose. Refer to the *VisualAge for C++ Users Guide* for details on how to use the special system libraries.

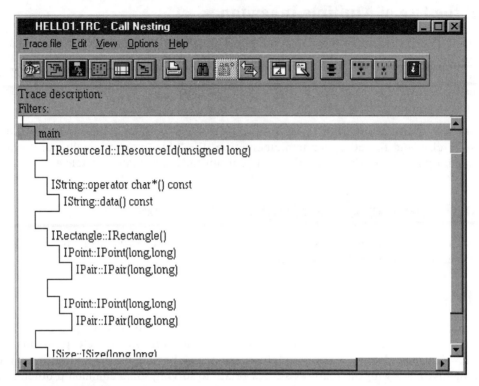

Figure 28-1. Performance Analyzer Call Nesting Diagram.

Run-Time Tracing

VisualAge for C++ can track various aspects of your program while it is running. You can cause trace information for functions and data to be written to the standard error stream, the standard output stream, a file, or a system queue. The product can also monitor memory allocation and deallocation for storage overlays and leaks.

Function and Data Tracing Using ITrace

The class ITrace provides a simple means of writing trace statements during the execution of your program. Macros exist for writing trace statements. You can remove them from the final product by changing the definition of a macro constant at compile time. Table 28-1 summarizes the use of these macro constants and their effect on the trace macros.

ITrace supports writing buffered data to the standard output stream and nonbuffered data to the standard error stream or a system queue. VisualAge for C++ for Windows also supports tracing to a named file, which, unlike the other output streams, you can use when tracing a Windows 3.1 application. You control tracing by calling static functions in the class ITrace, or by setting environment variables prior to starting the program. By default, ITrace does not

Table 28-1. Trace Macro Usage

Macro constant defined	Macro definitions enabled
none	IFUNCTRACE_RUNTIME IMODTRACE_RUNTIME ITRACE_RUNTIME
IC_TRACE_DEVELOP	IFUNCTRACE_RUNTIME IMODTRACE_RUNTIME ITRACE_RUNTIME IFUNCTRACE_DEVELOP IMODTRACE_DEVELOP ITRACE_DEVELOP
IC_TRACE_ALL	IFUNCTRACE_RUNTIME IMODTRACE_RUNTIME ITRACE_RUNTIME IFUNCTRACE_DEVELOP IMODTRACE_DEVELOP ITRACE_DEVELOP IFUNCTRACE_ALL IMODTRACE_ALL ITRACE_ALL

write trace statements. You can start tracing in an application built to write trace data by using any of the following commands prior to starting the application:

```
SET ICLUI_TRACE=ON
SET ICLUI_TRACETO=QUEUE
SET ICLUI_TRACETO=STDERR
SET ICLUI_TRACETO=ERR
SET ICLUI_TRACETO=STDOUT
SET ICLUI_TRACETO=OUT
SET ICLUI_TRACETO=FILE
```

The first of these commands causes ITrace to write trace data to the current output location. The default output location is a system queue. In the 32-bit Windows operating systems this queue is a mailslot, \\.\mailslot\PRINTF32. In the OS/2 environment it is \QUEUES\PRINTF32. The second statement explicitly directs the output to the queue. The next two statements cause ITrace to write trace data to the standard error stream; the fourth and fifth statements direct the trace data to the standard output stream. The last statement directs the trace data to a file. When you direct output to a file, you identify the file name using this command:

```
SET ICLUI_TRACEFILE=c:\trace.out
```

It causes the trace data to be written to the file c:\trace.out. You can disable tracing once it is enabled by undefining the appropriate environment variable with one of the following commands:

```
SET ICLUI_TRACE=
SET ICLUI_TRACETO=
```

By default, ITrace attaches a prefix string containing the output line number and the identifier of the process and thread to each line of trace data. You can disable the writing of prefix information by using the following command prior to starting the application. This command turns tracing on as a side effect:

```
SET ICLUI_TRACE=NOPREFIX
```

In the OS/2 environment, any time an application writes data to the trace, ITrace approximates the remaining bytes of stack space and adds this information to the trace prefix. To write the stack information, use the following command prior to starting the application:

```
SET ICLUI_CHECKSTACK=TRUE
```

Open Class Library also recognizes the environment variables described previously with a space substituted for the underscore in the variable names.

The function-tracing macros IFUNCTRACE_RUNTIME, IFUNCTRACE_DEVELOP, and IFUNCTRACE_ALL create an ITrace object on the stack, with the name and line number of the current function. When the ITrace constructor receives a name as input, it processes the call by tracing the entry and exit of a function. Therefore, it stores a reference to the name and writes this name and the line number in the trace data. When the function is completed and the ITrace object goes out of scope, the ITrace destructor is called. The destructor again writes the name of the function in the trace data.

To use this technique effectively, code the function trace macro as the first line of code in the function. This way, all code in the function occurs between the entry and exit tracing. In the following example, the function foo traces its name on entry, writes the value of its input parameter in hex, and traces its name on exit.

Storing References

An ITrace object stores a reference to the function name so that it can write the function name from its destructor. Callers of ITrace must ensure that the function name string exists for the life of the ITrace object. For general class design this is not a good solution, because the string passed in at construction might be the result of a temporary object of a class such as IString. For performance reasons, ITrace does not support temporary objects. But, it also does not reject them. Avoid code such as the following, which causes problems when using ITrace:

```
foo ()
{
    IMODTRACE_DEVELOP(IString("foo"));
}
```

Simple Trace Example - debug\trace\trace.cpp

```
#include <itrace.hpp>
#include <istring.hpp>

int foo(unsigned long count);

void main()
{
    IMODTRACE_DEVELOP("main");
    foo(10);
}

int foo(unsigned long count)
{
    IFUNCTRACE_DEVELOP();
    ITRACE_DEVELOP(IString("The count is ")+IString(count).d2x());
    return 0;
}
```

When you compile this file with the macro IC_DEVELOP defined, the following results appear in the trace data:

```
00000000 000058:01 +main(14)
00000001 000058:01    +foo(unsigned long)(20)
00000002 000058:01       >The count is 0A
00000003 000058:01    -foo(unsigned long)
00000004 000058:01 -main
```

Notice that the process identifier is 58, the thread ID is 1, and the function foo was called on line 14 of the source module with a value of 0x0A. The indenting of the trace text indicates the nesting of trace objects on the stack. The + indicates where an ITrace object was created and the - indicates where an ITrace object was deleted. This example shows a common usage of the IFUNCTRACE_ and IMODTRACE_ macro sets. Placing one of these macros at the beginning of a scoping block causes traces to be written that correspond to entry and exit from the block, respectively.

The Trace Browser Application

The following code is a simple example of reading information from the system queue used by ITrace. The application contains two main parts: a primary thread and a secondary thread. A browser application in the primary thread includes a basic frame window with a container for the trace data in the client area. A separate thread reads the queue, creates an IContainerObject with each line of data, and posts it to the main thread for addition to the container. Figure 28-2 displays sample output in the Trace Browser window.

You will find a more sophisticated version of this example in the **debug\tracebox** program on the examples disk. This debugging utility adds filtering the trace input and display, suspending the trace recording, and copying the trace data to the clipboard.

If you actually build and run prtque, make sure you run prtque in an environment with tracing turned off (SET ICLUI_TRACE=OFF) or you risk setting up an infinite loop. Run your application to be traced with tracing to the system queue enabled (SET ICLUI_TRACETO=queue).

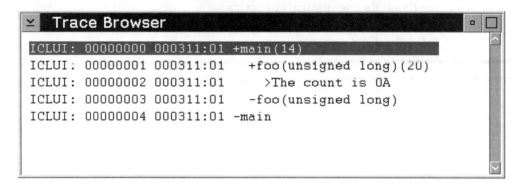

Figure 28-2. The Trace Browser Window.

TraceBrowser Interface - debug\prtque\trbrowse.hpp

```
#include <iframe.hpp>
#include <icnrctl.hpp>
#include <ithread.hpp>
#include <ihandler.hpp>
#include "querdr.hpp"

class TraceBrowser;

// Handler processes Queue requests.
class TraceBrowserHandler : public IHandler{
public:
  TraceBrowserHandler ( TraceBrowser& browser)
       : browserWindow(browser) {}
protected:
virtual Boolean
  dispatchHandlerEvent ( IEvent &event );
private:
TraceBrowser
 &browserWindow;
TraceBrowserHandler (const TraceBrowserHandler&);
TraceBrowserHandler operator= (const TraceBrowserHandler&);
};

// Main window
class TraceBrowser : public IFrameWindow {
public:

 TraceBrowser   ( const IString& queueName  );

IContainerControl
 &container     ( )   { return cnrWin;}
QueueReader
 &queueReader   ( )   { return reader;}
IThread
 &readerThread  ( )   { return thread;}
```

```
private:
TraceBrowserHandler
  queueHandler;
IContainerControl
  cnrWin;
QueueReader
  reader;
IThread
  thread;
TraceBrowser (const TraceBrowser& );
TraceBrowser& operator= (const TraceBrowser& );
};
```

TraceBrowser Usage - debug\prtque\prtque.cpp

```
#include <istring.hpp>
#include <ithread.hpp>
#include "trbrowse.hpp"

const unsigned PMQUEUE_SIZE = 2000;
IString        QUEUE_NAME("PRINTF32");    // base name of queue


int main( )
{
    // Note that we increase the size of the PM
    // message queue to try to avoid filling
    // it up.
    IThread::current().initializeGUI(PMQUEUE_SIZE);

    // Create the trace browser window.
    TraceBrowser traceWindow(QUEUE_NAME);

    // Give the window the focus and show it.
    traceWindow
      .setFocus()
      .show();

    IThread::current().processMsgs();
    IThread::current().terminateGUI();
    return 0;
}
```

TraceBrowser Implementation - debug\prtque\trbrowse.cpp

```
#include <ifont.hpp>
#include "trbrowse.hpp"
#include "trbrowse.h"

TraceBrowser::TraceBrowser ( const IString& queueName )
        : IFrameWindow("Trace Browser"),
          queueHandler(*this),
          cnrWin        (IC_FRAME_CLIENT_ID, this, this, IRectangle(),
                         IContainerControl::defaultStyle() |
                         IContainerControl::noSharedObjects ),
          reader      (queueName, this->handle()),
          thread      ( )
{
  // Attach handler to our frame.
  queueHandler.handleEventsFor(this);
```

```
      // Change the font & show text view with extended selection.
      IFont font("Courier", 8);
      container()
        .showTextView()
        .setExtendedSelection()
        .setFont(font);

      // Make the container the client and start the queue.
      (*this)
        .setClient(&container())
        .postEvent(START_QUEUE);
}

IBase::Boolean  TraceBrowserHandler::dispatchHandlerEvent ( IEvent& event
)
{
  switch (event.eventId())
  {
    case ADD_OBJECT:
    {
      browserWindow.container()
        .addObject((IContainerObject*)(void*)event.parameter1());
      return true;
    }
    case START_QUEUE:
    {
      // Start Reader in a separate Thread.
      browserWindow.readerThread()
        .start(new IThreadMemberFn<QueueReader>
                  (browserWindow.queueReader(),
                  QueueReader::run));
      return true;
    }
    default:
      break;
  } // endswitch
  return false;
}
```

QueueReader Interface - debug\prtque\querdr.hpp

```
#include <ihandle.hpp>
#include <istring.hpp>

// Retrieves messages from queue, creates objects from them,
// and sends them to main window.
class QueueReader {
public:
QueueReader  ( const char*           queueName,
               const IWindowHandle& receiver);
~QueueReader ( );

void
  run            ( );
unsigned long
  queueHandle    ( ) const { return qHandle;}
IWindowHandle
  targetHandle   ( ) const { return target;}
```

```
private:
IWindowHandle
  target;
unsigned long
  qHandle;
char
  *queueData;
IString
  fqueueName;

QueueReader      (const QueueReader&);
QueueReader
  &operator=      (const QueueReader&);
};
```

QueueReader Implementation - debug\prtque\querdr.cpp

```
#include <ibase.hpp>
#ifdef IC_PM
  #define INCL_DOSQUEUES
  #define INCL_DOSPROCESS
  #include <os2.h>
#else
  #include <windows.h>
#endif

#include <iexcept.hpp>
#include <icnrobj.hpp>
#include <ihandle.hpp>
#include <ithread.hpp>
#include "querdr.hpp"
#include "trbrowse.h"

#if (IC_MAJOR_VERSION < 320)
  #define IBaseErrorInfo IErrorInfo
#endif

#define    BUFFERSIZE    999

#ifdef IC_PM
const char    QUEUE_PATH[] = "\\QUEUES\\";
#else
const char    QUEUE_PATH[]   = "\\\\.\\mailslot\\";
#endif

// Set up the queue for reading.
QueueReader::QueueReader ( const char*          queueName,
                           const IWindowHandle&  targetWindow)
              : target    (targetWindow),
                qHandle   ( 0 ),
                queueData( 0 )
{
  fqueueName = IString(QUEUE_PATH) + IString(queueName);
#ifdef IC_PM
  unsigned long rc = DosCreateQueue(
                        &qHandle,
                        QUE_FIFO | QUE_CONVERT_ADDRESS,
                        fqueueName);
  if (rc!=0)
    ITHROWSYSTEMERROR(rc, "DosCreateQueue",
                      IBaseErrorInfo::accessError,
                      IException::recoverable );
```

```
#else
  qHandle = (unsigned long)
    CreateMailslot(
      fqueueName,
      BUFFERSIZE,
      MAILSLOT_WAIT_FOREVER,
      (LPSECURITY_ATTRIBUTES) NULL);
  if ( qHandle == (unsigned long)INVALID_HANDLE_VALUE )
    ITHROWGUIERROR2("CreateMailSlot",
                    IBaseErrorInfo::accessError,
                    IException::recoverable );

  queueData = (char *)GlobalAlloc( GPTR, BUFFERSIZE+1 );
#endif
}

// Delete the queue.
QueueReader::~QueueReader ( )
{
#ifdef IC_PM
  DosCloseQueue(queueHandle());
  if (queueData)
    DosFreeMem(queueData);
#else
  CloseHandle( (HANDLE)queueHandle() );
  if (queueData)
    GlobalFree((HGLOBAL)queueData );
#endif
}

// Our Thread function reads the queue.
void QueueReader::run ( )
{
  IContainerObject* pobj;
  unsigned long    dataLength;

#ifdef IC_PM
  unsigned long    rc;
  REQUESTDATA      request;
  BYTE             priority = 0;

  request.pid = IThread::current().id();
#endif

  while(1)
    {
    dataLength = 0;
#ifdef IC_PM
    rc = DosReadQueue (queueHandle(),
                       &request,
                       &dataLength,
                       (void**)&queueData,
                       0,
                       0,
                       &priority,
                       0);
    if(rc!=0)
      ITHROWSYSTEMERROR(rc, "DosReadQueue",
                        IBaseErrorInfo::accessError,
                        IException::recoverable );
#else
    ReadFile( (HANDLE)queueHandle(),
              queueData,
              BUFFERSIZE,
              &dataLength,
              (LPOVERLAPPED)NULL );
    queueData[dataLength] = '\0';
#endif
```

```
    // Create an object and post a request to the main
    // thread to add it to the container.
    pobj = new IContainerObject(queueData);

#ifdef IC_PM
    DosFreeMem(queueData);
    queueData = 0;
#endif
    Boolean loop = true;
    while(loop)
        {
        try
            {
            loop = false;
            targetHandle().postEvent(ADD_OBJECT, pobj);
            }
        catch (IException& )
            {
            // If we can't post (message queue full?),
            // wait and try again.
            loop = true;
#ifdef IC_PM
        DosSleep(100);
#endif
            }
        }  // while posting
    } // while
}
```

TraceBrowser Constants - debug\prtque\trbrowse.h

```
// Note: 0x1000 is in WM_USER range
#define ADD_OBJECT      0x1000 + 100
#define START_QUEUE     0x1000 + 101
```

Open Class Library Debug DLLs

You can increase the coverage of the tracing to include Open Class Library code by using the debug versions of the DLLs provided on the VisualAge for C++ for Windows CD-ROM. (The trial version of the product on the CD-ROM accompanying this book does not include these DLLs, however.) These DLLs produce extensive trace data using ITrace, which is interleaved with any trace information produced by your application. If you are using VisualAge for C++ for OS/2, you can build the debug DLLs using the IBM VisualAge C++ for OS/2 Open Class Library Source product (a separate option).

The debug DLLs are in the iocsrc\dll subdirectory on the VisualAge for C++ for Windows CD-ROM. They have the same names as the retail versions but are considerably larger. Many of the VisualAge for C++ tools, including the debugger and editor, use Open Class Library. When you use the debug DLLs with your application, rename the debug DLLs and your application's references to them. You do this by using the **dllrname** tool. Chapter 29, "Packaging and Performance Tuning," describes in detail how to do this.

Once you have setup the debug DLLs, run your application in the usual way to capture the combined trace. You can examine the trace by using the previous trace browsing tools or a text editor if you have directed it to a file. To keep the trace volume to a manageable level, Open Class Library's debug DLLs do not generate traces for all function calls. They do, however, trace many significant operations. The debug DLLs are built with the IC_TRACE_DEVELOP macro set, so any IMODTRACE_ALL or ITRACE_ALL macros you see in the source are not expanded.

You can also use the debugger to trace into the Open Class Library code when you are using the debug DLLs. If you do this, add the directories `iocsrc\cppwob3`, `iocsrc\cppwod3`, `iocsrc\cppwof3`, `iocsrc\cppwom3`, and `iocsrc\cppwou3` on the CD-ROM to your `CAT_PATH` environment variable before starting **idebug**. The debugger can then locate Open Class Library source files.

If you want to use the debug DLLs for VisualAge for C++ for OS/2, build the DLLs using the Open Class Library Source product. In the `iocsrc` subdirectory that the source product install creates, there is a command file `debugbld.cmd` to build the DLLs. Running this program results in the debug DLLs being created in the `iocsrc\dll` subdirectory. You can use these DLLs in much the same way as described for the Windows version. If you want to use the debugger to trace into the VisualAge for C++ for OS/2 debug DLLs, add the directories `iocsrc\cppoob3`, `iocsrc\cppood3`, `iocsrc\cppoom3`, `iocsrc\cppoou3` and `iocsrc\include` to your `PMD_PATH` environment variable before starting the debugger. Prefix each of the directories listed with the name of the base directory in which you installed the Open Class Library Source product.

Memory Allocation Tracing

VisualAge for C++ provides a useful debug memory management component that checks for attempts to access previously released storage and storage overlays. It also writes the contents of all allocated storage. Enable memory debugging by adding **/Tm+** to the compiler options you use to compile your source files. Memory debugging adds additional arguments to all `operator new` and `operator delete` functions.

To use these diagnostic tools, you must change your code if you have added class members for `operator new` and `operator delete`, or if you have replaced the global `operator new` or `operator delete` functions. You must add optional versions of these calls that include parameters for the file name and line number of the call. You declare these functions similarly to the following example:

```
class MyObject
{
public:

#ifdef __DEBUG_ALLOC__
void
 *operator new     ( size_t        size,
                     const char*    fileName,
                     size_t         lineNumber),
  operator delete ( void*,
                     const char*    fileName,
                     size_t         lineNumber );
#else
void
 *operator new     ( size_t size),
  operator delete ( void* );
#endif
};
```

Open Class Library uses this technique in several places. Examine the declarations of operator new and operator delete in ICNROBJ.HPP and IBUFFER.HPP and the corresponding definition of these functions in ICNROBJN.INL, ICNROBJD.CPP, IBUFFERN.INL, and IBUFFERD.CPP.

After you have rebuilt your application with the memory debug component, determine if your application leaks memory by failing to free storage allocated with operator new. In the past, you could add code to the end of your main routine to call a "heap-walk" type function that listed storage left allocated. The VisualAge for C++ function _dump_allocated examines the storage you've allocated via the C++ run time. It then writes diagnostic messages to the standard error stream for any storage that remains. However, the best place to put the call to _dump_allocated is not in your main routine, because storage allocated by static objects will not have been freed yet. Put the call to _dump_allocated into the destructor of the highest priority static object, so that it is called after static objects are freed. You can do this, or create a source file with the following code in it. Use #pragma priority in this source file to ensure that the memory dump static object gets destructed last. If you do not use static objects, put the following code into the .CPP file that contains main:

```
// Dump Memory statistics.
#ifdef __DEBUG_ALLOC__
class MemoryDump
{
public:
  ~MemoryDump()
    {
      _dump_allocated(20);
    }
};


// Create a MemoryDump object.
static MemoryDump dumpAllStorage;

#endif
```

Some Common Problems

We do not spend much time discussing the errors reported using the compiler and linker. The messages displayed by the VisualAge for C++ compiler describe errors and identify their location in the source code. We spend most of our time discussing the problems that occur once your application is up and running.

Why Are References Unresolved When Linking?

Missing Virtual Function Table

The compiler generates the virtual function table, which it uses to resolve addresses to virtual functions in your classes. VisualAge for C++ puts the table in the compilation unit containing the first non-inlined virtual function. Eventually, when linking your application, the linker reports something similar to the following message:

```
no_vft.obj(no_vft.cpp) :   error LNK2029:
     'NoVFT::virtual-fn-table-ptr' : unresolved external
```

The error occurred during the compiling and linking of the following code:

```
class NoVFT
{
   public:
virtual aMissingVirtualFunction();
};

main(int argc, char *argv[], char *envp[])
{
   NoVFT noVFT;
}
```

The error occurs because we did not provide the implementation of the virtual function that VisualAge for C++ uses to pick a compilation unit for the virtual function table. As a result, the compiler did not generate the virtual function table. To resolve this problem, add the option **/Wvft+** to your compiler options to find out which function the compiler has targeted for the virtual function table. Adding this option when compiling our short sample yields the following message:

```
no_vft.cpp(1:7) : informational EDC3281:
     The virtual function table for "NoVFT" will be defined
     where "NoVFT::aMissingVirtualFunction()" is defined.
```

Now, add an implementation for aMissingVirtualFunction. This error often results from declaring but not implementing a virtual destructor.

Missing Libraries

Open Class Library header files contain pragma library statements. These statements cause the compiler to automatically generate references to the link libraries needed for the implementation of the classes. Thus, in general you do not have to specify Open Class Library or compiler run-time libraries to the linker. However, you disable this automatic process if you use the linker switch **/NOD**. So, do not use this switch unless you absolutely have to.

If you are using system calls in your program, you may have to explicitly list the appropriate libraries on the linker command line. VisualAge for C++ libraries automatically link the system libraries they need, but if you use a function from a different library, you have to explicitly specify the library.

Why Did My Application Suddenly Quit Running?

You start your program, the disk light flashes, perhaps you see your frame window on the display, and then suddenly your program ends. You don't see a trap panel, an error message, or anything else to suggest what problem occurred. More than likely, an object in the program threw a C++ exception. The C++ run time then ended the application because it could not find a catch block to handle the exception. To verify this, turn tracing on in Open Class Library and examine the trace output.

It is simple to add code to your application to display these exceptions in a message box. Unfortunately, you cannot use this approach to display all exceptions, because a message box requires the presentation system to be successfully initialized. The following code displays most exceptions. The code encloses the entire contents of the `main` routine in a `try` block and then displays the exception text in a message box when the code throws an exception.

Displaying Exceptions - debug\excdisp\excdisp.cpp

```
#include <iframe.hpp>
#include <istattxt.hpp>
#include <istring.hpp>
#include <iexcbase.hpp>
#include <imsgbox.hpp>

void main( )
{
try {
    IFrameWindow frame(100);
    IStaticText txt(101, 0, 0); // Causes an assertion exception.
    frame.setFocus().show();
    IApplication::current().run();
  }
  catch(IException& exc) {
    IMessageBox abortIt(IWindow::desktopWindow());
    abortIt.setTitle("Exception Caught");
    abortIt.show(exc.text(), IMessageBox::okButton);
  }
}
```

Figure 28-3 shows the output of the program. To correct the error that caused the exception, change the parent and owner passed to the `IStaticText` constructor to the address of the `IFrameWindow` object.

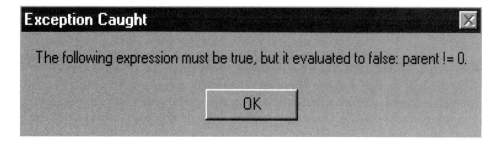

Figure 28-3. Displaying an Exception in a Message Box.

How Do I Find an Application Error?

In different operating systems they call this type of error an application error, system error, or illegal operation; they mean the same thing. A program has accessed an invalid memory location or one for which it does not have access permission. Figure 28-4 shows the message you can get when an illegal operation occurs. The VisualAge for C++ debugger makes finding the cause of these application errors easy. This error occurred because we used a pointer with a value of 0 to call a function on an object, as shown in this example:

Application Error - debug\zeroptr\zeroptr.cpp

```
#include <iframe.hpp>

void main( )
{
  IFrameWindow* pframe = 0;
  pframe->show();
}
```

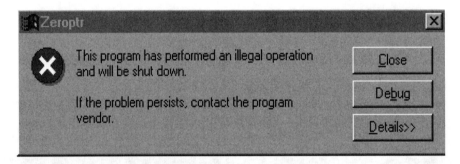

Figure 28-4. Application Error Panel.

To find the cause of this error, start the debugger with the name of the program and press the run icon on the tool bar. The debugger executes the program to the error and then displays its application error panel. Press **Examine/Retry** on this panel to display the source window with the line of code where the error occurred highlighted. If that does not identify the problem, you can use other tools in the debugger to analyze the problem further. For example, you might try the following three tools:

• Open a Local Variables window at the point of the error in your program to examine your data. In Figure 28-5, you can see that the pframe variable of our example has a value of 0, indicating that we did not initialize our pointer field.

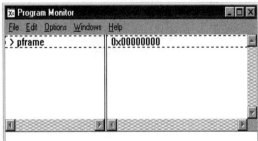

Figure 28-5. Program Monitor.

- Open a Mixed-source view containing the C++ source code, the assembler instructions, and a Registers view to examine the exact cause of the error. Figure 28-6 displays these views. In the Mixed-source view, the current line of the program uses the EAX register to load a storage address. The Register view displays the value of the EAX register. As you can see, the value of the EAX register is 0. Therefore, we tried to access storage based on an address of 0.

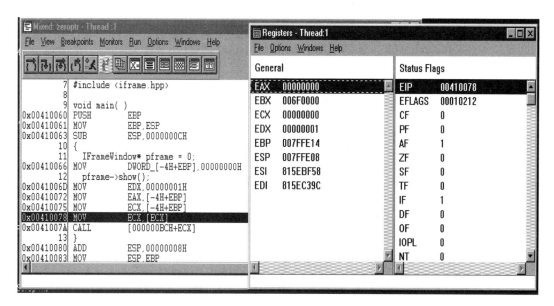

Figure 28-6. Debugger Mixed-Source and Registers View.

- Open a Call Stack view to see the callers of the function in error, and then open Source views on each caller to examine the request causing the error. This is particularly helpful when the application error occurred, where you don't have the source code. Use the call stack to back up to the point in your program that you do have the source. Often, you can see what is wrong.

Another problem, which can show similar symptoms, is incorrectly ordering window member data in a class declaration. This can cause the constructor for a child control to be called before its parent has been created. Avoid this problem by remembering that the order of member construction is determined by the order of the members in the class declaration rather than the order of calls specified in the constructor initializer list.

How Do I Use Debug on Demand?

In the Windows NT environment, there is an alternative to starting the program under **idebug** to examine an application error. The Windows NT system offers a feature called *debug on demand*, which allows a failing program to be loaded into a debugger at the point of failure, even if it was not started under the debugger. To have debug on demand load **idebug** as the debugger, enter this command:

```
dod e:\ibmcppw\bin
```

e:\ibmcppw\bin is the directory where **idebug** is installed. After you install VisualAge for C++, you only have to enter this command once. If you want to remove **idebug** (as the debug on demand debugger), use this command:

```
dod /u
```

To activate debug on demand at the point of a failure, select **Cancel** from the application error message box. The debugger is loaded and the error panel is displayed just as if you had started the program with **idebug**. You can then examine the error.

Why Is My Application Trapping before main()?

With static objects, you can now write an application that completely executes prior to the C/C++ run time calling your main() routine. By default, the debugger does not stop at a break point prior to this code being executed. To debug static objects, request the debugger to debug initialization code by adding the parameter **/i** to the invocation of the debugger.

```
IDEBUG /i myapp myParms
```

You also can start the debugger from its VisualAge for C++ desktop icon or at a command prompt (with no parameters) and then click the box "Debug program initialization" in the **Program Startup** window.

Why Is My Handler Callback Never Called?

As you have already seen, the event-handling framework uses a series of callback functions in IHandler objects. To receive a particular notification, you derive a class from a handler and provide your own implementation for a callback virtual function. If you do not define your virtual function exactly as it exists in the base class, the handler dispatcher does not call the function at run time. In particular, it is easy to overlook the const on the function or parameter declaration, or the reference symbol (&) on a parameter. After checking that you have correctly defined the function, verify that you have created the handler correctly and activated it by calling handleEventsFor on the correct window. Also, make sure that your handler object has not been deleted either explicitly or because it has gone out of scope.

If your function is still not being called, it is possible that another handler is processing the event. If a handler returns true from its dispatchHandlerEvent function, Open Class Library does not call any more handlers for that event. It dispatches events to a window's handlers in the reverse order that the handlers called handleEventsFor. For example, if you attach a keyboard handler to a window and then attach a mouse handler to the window, the mouse handler is called before the keyboard handler. If there is a problem in the mouse handler that causes it to return true for keyboard events, none of the keyboard handler's callback functions are called for the window.

You can create a trace of all of the events that come to a handler by overriding the dispatchHandlerEvent function. In your derived class, the dispatchHandlerEvent function logs the incoming event and then calls the dispatchHandlerEvent in the base class. For the keyboard-handler class MyKeyboardHandler, the code would look like the following example:

```
IBase::Boolean  MyKeyboardHandler::dispatchHandlerEvent(IEvent& event)
{
    ITRACE_ALL(IString("HWND=") +
               IString(event.handle().asUnsigned()).d2x()+
               IString(", Msg=") +
               IString(event.eventId()).d2x()+
               IString(", P1=") +
               IString((unsigned long)event.parameter1()).d2x()+
               IString(", P2=") +
               IString((unsigned long)event.parameter2()).d2x());
    return IKeyboardHandler::dispatchHandlerEvent(event);
}
```

When compiled with the IC_TRACE_ALL macro defined, this code writes all of the messages that the handler detects to the trace.

To see which messages are coming to the window, use a tool that can monitor these messages. There are a number of such tools available, including **spy** in the Microsoft Win32 SDK and the Message Queue Monitor in the OS/2 version of the VisualAge for C++ debugger.

To use the VisualAge for C++ for OS/2 debugger to monitor messages, start **icsdebug** and open the Message Queue Monitor. Figure 28-7 displays an example of this monitor. We open this view to learn why the keyboard handler attached to our frame window did not call our override of the characterKeyPress virtual function. We initialized the monitor to capture WM_CREATE messages so that we could verify the handle of our frame window and WM_CHAR messages to see if the OS/2 operating system dispatched them to our frame window. Figure 28-7 shows that our window does receive the WM_CHAR messages. Therefore, the problem must be somewhere else.

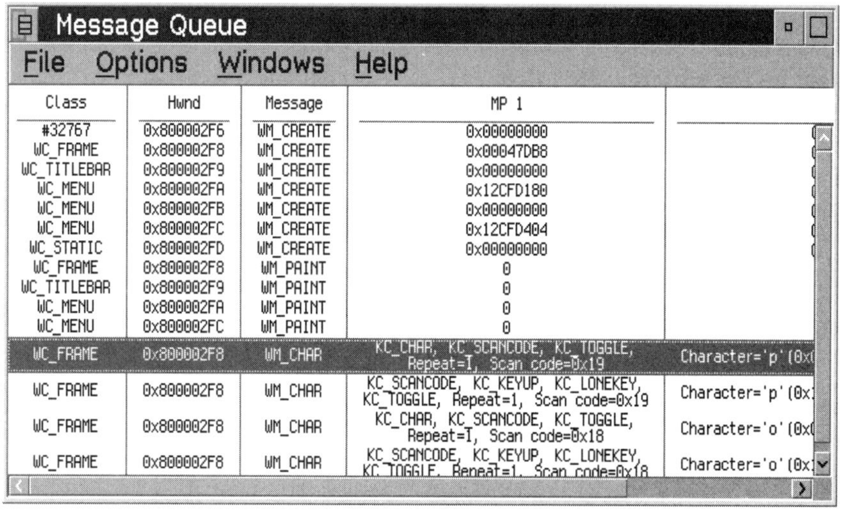

Figure 28-7. VisualAge C++ Debugger Message Queue Monitor.

Why Can't I See My Window?

The following sample creates a static text field on a frame window:

Invisible Window - debug\invisibl\invisibl.cpp

```
#include <iframe.hpp>
#include <iapp.hpp>
#include <istattxt.hpp>

void main( )
{
  IFrameWindow frame(100);
  IStaticText text(101, &frame, &frame,
                   IRectangle(50,50,50,50));

  text
    .setText("Initial Text");
  frame
   .setFocus()
   .show();

  IApplication::current().run();
}
```

Although this seems simple enough, when you run the application, the static text is not seen. You double check the constructor for the static text field just to make sure you've done it right. Did you give it a size? Yes, you've coded it as a 50-by-50 pixel rectangle. Does the style of the static text field contain IWindow::visible? You read the documentation for IStaticText::defaultStyle, and it lists IWindow::visible as a default style. What next?

You need a tool to inspect the actual window characteristics as the system shows the window. Using spy utilities, including the VisualAge for C++ for OS/2 debugger, you can view the basic properties of a window as it is being displayed. In addition, if you review the advframe\winview sample in Chapter 19, "Advanced Frame Window Topics," you will find another tool that provides information about the window that you need to determine what is happening with the current example's static text field.

Use the VisualAge for C++ for OS/2 debugger's Window Analysis feature to track down why you cannot see the text field. Start **icsdebug** with the program, set a break point on the line containing IApplication::current().run(), and run the application to the break point. Select **Monitors->Window analysis** from the menu of the Source view to open the Window Characteristics view. Click the mouse on the right arrow in the bottom corner of the notebook to turn to page two of the notebook. Select **Monitors->Window characteristics** from the Window Analysis view menu to open the Window Characteristics view.

Your window characteristics look similar to Figure 28-8. Select **Options->Display style...** to add columns to the display if needed. Close examination reveals that we have created the static text field identified by the OS/2 window class WC_STATIC with no width or height. The IRectangle constructor that accepts four values uses those values to represent two opposite corners of a rectangle. In our sample, we are creating a static text field with one corner at 50, 50 and the other corner in the same place. Therefore, our rectangle has no size.

Other problems can occur that result in an invisible window. One of the more common of these is that the window is hidden by another one. This can occur if two windows share the same parent and their rectangles overlap. Only one of the windows shows up in the overlapping area. Inspecting window characteristics as we did with the 0 size window can help you identify this situation.

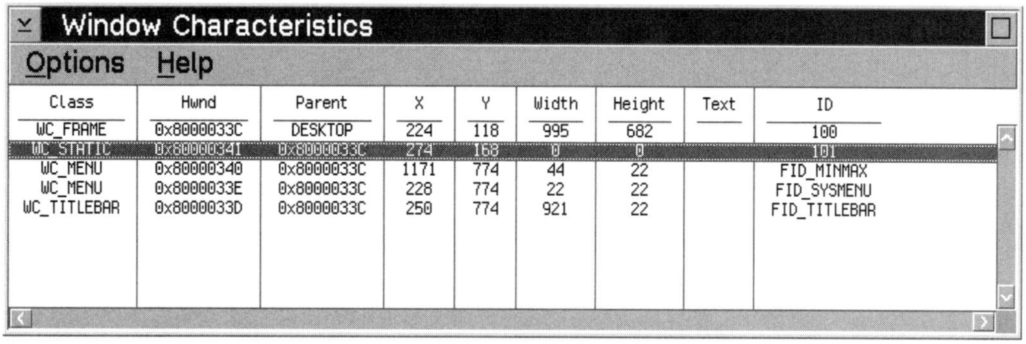

Class	Hwnd	Parent	X	Y	Width	Height	Text	ID
WC_FRAME	0x8000033C	DESKTOP	224	118	995	682		100
WC_STATIC	0x80000341	0x8000033C	274	168	0	0		101
WC_MENU	0x80000340	0x8000033C	1171	774	44	22		FID_MINMAX
WC_MENU	0x8000033E	0x8000033C	228	774	22	22		FID_SYSMENU
WC_TITLEBAR	0x8000033D	0x8000033C	250	774	921	22		FID_TITLEBAR

Figure 28-8. VisualAge C++ Debugger Window Characteristics.

How Do I Find a Storage Overlay?

The memory debug diagnostics described earlier in this chapter identify the exact block of corrupted storage, but they might not do so until sometime after the corruption occurs. To request that the memory debug diagnostics check memory more often, add calls to the function _heap_check throughout your code. This function writes a diagnostic message and terminates your application when it detects a corruption of storage.

Another means of finding a storage corruption is to use the debug memory management functions in combination with the debugger. Use the debug functions to identify where the program allocated the corrupted storage. When the compiler detects the overwrite, it will abort the application. Although you cannot set a break point to catch the abort, you can easily write a signal handler to catch it. In the following example, we register a signal handler, which causes a trap on a SIGABRT, to give the debugger control during the abort. When the debugger displays the application error panel, open the Call Stack monitor and find your last function.

Termination Signal Handler - debug\sigterm\sigterm.cpp

```cpp
#include <signal.h>
#include <string.h>
#include <stdio.h>
#include <new.h>

void TrapOnTerm(int signal)
{
  // Cause a trap
  char* psz=0;
  strcpy(psz, "junk");
}

void main( )
  {
    signal(SIGABRT, (_SigFunc)TrapOnTerm);

    // Now cause a memory overlay for a termination.
    char* pszBuffer = new char[10];
    strcpy(pszBuffer, "Memory overlay Memory overlay");

#ifdef __DEBUG_ALLOC__
    // And run the heap check to detect it with /Tm+.
    _heap_check();
#endif
  }
```

Chapter 29

Packaging and Performance Tuning

- Describes how to optimize and package your final application for delivery
- Chapters 24 and 28 cover related material.

Congratulations! Because you have completed the code for another winning product, it is now time to wrap things up and deliver your product to the manufacturer. Depending on your application and customers, this might involve little additional work, or it might require detailed performance analysis and tuning. This chapter helps you understand what you need to do to distribute your product. We discuss the packaging of the Open Class Library components and the steps you might take to repackage these components with your application. We also describe a detailed tuning process you can use to ensure that the final product is small and that it loads and executes as quickly as possible.

Building the Final Application

You have undoubtedly used the dynamic-link libraries in VisualAge for C++ during the development phase because it shortens the time to link an application. Now, you must decide whether to deliver your application using the dynamic-link libraries or to link your application statically with the VisualAge for C++ run-time code. Both choices have advantages and disadvantages—there is no right answer. Your final choice depends on your particular application and customers.

Statically linking your application with the VisualAge for C++ run-time code means your final executable file (the EXE) will contain all of the code necessary to run your application. Dynamically linking your application means that the VisualAge for C++ run-time code will be provided in separate dynamic-link libraries (DLLs) that you will deliver as part of your application. Only your code will be directly linked into the executable file. You also might choose to separate some of your code into individual DLLs.

DLLs provide a means for several applications to share the same code both on the hard disk and in memory. If your application contains several executable files that have the VisualAge for C++ DLLs as a common code base, seriously consider using dynamic linking, and then deliver the VisualAge for C++ DLLs with your product. Because there are license restrictions involved, the next topic, "Dynamic Linking and Using DLLRNAME," describes how to do this.

DLLs allow you to share code on the hard disk because of a system setting that makes a single copy of the code and the data in a DLL available to all applications. The Windows operating system uses the PATH environment variable to locate DLLs, and the OS/2 operating system uses the LIBPATH setting to identify the path to search for DLLs. If you use DLLs, you must make sure that the names of the DLLs shipped with your product do not conflict with any existing or future DLLs in your user's system. If there is a conflict, your users will usually be unable to run either your application or another application on their systems. Consequently, if you build your application as a single executable file, consider statically linking your application to keep this problem from occurring.

Tables 29-1 and 29-2 describe the libraries you use for both static linking and dynamic linking of an Open Class Library application. The VisualAge for C++ linker automatically searches the link libraries for C/C++ run-time code and Open Class Library functions that your application uses. You can select dynamic linking by compiling your entire application with the **/Gd+** compiler switch, or you can select static linking with the **/Gd-** switch. When you link your application, ensure that the **/Gd** setting is the same for all of your object modules so that you do not get a mixture of static and dynamic linking. If you mix statically linked and dynamically linked components, your application, at best, will be larger than necessary due to duplicate copies of the VisualAge for C++ components, and, at worst, you will encounter linker or run-time errors due to the duplicate copies of the VisualAge for C++ run-time data.

Table 29-1. Libraries Used in Building an Open Class Library Application for the Windows Operating System

Import Libraries	Dynamic Libraries	Static Libraries	Purpose
CPPWOB3I.LIB	CPPWOB3I.DLL	CPPWOC3.LIB	Base and data classes, collections
CPPWOU3I.LIB	CPPWOU3I.DLL	CPPWOC3.LIB	UI application, controls, drag drop
CPPWOD3I.LIB	CPPWOD3I.DLL	CPPWOC3.LIB	DDE
CPPWOM3I.LIB	CPPWOM3I.DLL	CPPWOC3.LIB	Multimedia
CPPWOF3I.LIB	CPPWOF3I.DLL	CPPWOC3.LIB	Compound Document Framework
CPPWM35I.LIB	CPPWM35I.DLL	CPPWM35.LIB	C/C++ run time

Table 29-2. Libraries Used in Building an Open Class Library Application for the OS/2 Operating System

Import Libraries	Dynamic Libraries	Static Libraries	Purpose
CPPOOC3I.LIB	CPPOOB3.DLL	CPPOOC3.LIB	Base and data classes, collections
CPPOOC3I.LIB	CPPOOU3.DLL	CPPOOC3.LIB	UI application, controls, drag drop
CPPOOC3I.LIB	CPPOOD3.DLL	CPPOOC3.LIB	DDE
CPPOOC3I.LIB	CPPOOM3.DLL	CPPOOC3.LIB	Multimedia
CPPOM30I.LIB	CPPOM30.DLL	CPPOM30.LIB	C/C++ run time

Dynamic Linking and Using DLLRNAME

Dynamic linking with the VisualAge for C++ run-time libraries means you will be delivering VisualAge for C++ DLLs as part of your application. The license agreement for VisualAge for C++ requires you to rename any VisualAge for C++ dynamic-link libraries you ship with your product. This reduces the chances of DLL name space collisions, which can occur if two VisualAge for C++ applications reside on the same system with different levels of VisualAge for C++ code.

VisualAge for C++ provides the **dllrname** utility to help you rename DLLs. Be aware that you cannot use the system **rename** command to rename DLLs because the linker records the name of the DLL inside the DLL. The loader requires that the name inside the DLL must match the external name of the DLL. The **dllrname** utility changes both the external and internal names of the DLL, the references to that name inside other DLLs, and the executable files that use the DLL. However, **dllrname** does not change the use of dynamically loaded DLLs. DLLs could be dynamically loaded using either the class `IDynamicLinkLibrary` in the Open Class Library or the system `LoadLibrary` or `DosLoadModule` functions. See the *VisualAge for C++ User's Guide* for more information on the use of **dllrname**.

In the VisualAge for C++ for Windows, Version 3.5 product, there are two DLLs shipped with the product that are loaded dynamically and may be required by your application. These DLLs are dynamically loaded even if you statically link your application. One of the DLLs is `CPPWOT3.DLL`, which is needed when you use a control with the `pmCompatible` style, when you use `IContainerControl`, or when you use any of the three `IFrameWindow` constructors that attempt to load a dialog template. See Chapter 5, "Frame Window Basics," for a detailed discussion of these constructors. The other dynamically loaded DLL is `LIBIPF32.DLL`, which is required if you use the `ipfCompatible` style on one or more `IHelpWindow` objects. As noted in the product `README.TXT` file for this version, you cannot use **dllrname** on these DLLs. If your application requires them, you must reship them using the original names.

The following example shows you how to use **dllrname** to rename the VisualAge for C++ DLLs used in the Open Class Library sample application Hello6. You can find the Hello6 sample in the `ibmcppw\samples\ioc\hello6` directory on the product CD-ROM. If you installed the samples, it is installed in the same subdirectory on your hard drive. You can use the **dllrname** utility to discover which DLLs the program is linked to. To do this with Hello6, change to the directory containing hello6.exe and enter:

```
dllrname hello6.exe
```

You get output similar to the following:

```
Licensed Materials - Property of IBM
IBM C/C++ Tools Version 2.0 - DLL Rename Utility
(C) Copyright IBM Corp., 1993, 1995. All Rights Reserved
US Government Users Restricted Rights - Use, duplication or disclosure
restricted by GSA ADP Schedule Contract with IBM Corp.

Processing file hello6.exe.
 File hello6.exe has not been changed.
 4 names found in file hello6.exe.
 Imported DLL name CPPWOB3I has been left unchanged.
 Imported DLL name CPPWOU3I has been left unchanged.
 Imported DLL name KERNEL32 has been left unchanged.
 Imported DLL name cppwm35i has been left unchanged.

Complete.  0 error(s) detected.
```

Because CPPWOU3I.DLL, CPPWOU3I.DLL, and CPPWM35I.DLL are being used, we must rename these three DLLs. Many of the VisualAge for C++ DLLs reference other DLLs, so repeat this process for each of the DLLs found for the executable. In this case, however, we have already found all of the DLLs that need to be renamed. You can verify this in the **dllrname** output after you actually rename them.

To start the renaming process, create a new directory and copy your executable files and the DLLs they use into it. For example, the following code shows this step:

```
MD \RENAME
CD \RENAME
COPY \IBMCPPW\BIN\CPPWOU3I.DLL
COPY \IBMCPPW\BIN\CPPWOB3I.DLL
COPY \IBMCPPW\BIN\CPPWM35I.DLL
COPY \IBMCPPW\SAMPLES\IOC\HELLO6\HELLO6.EXE
```

Now, use the **dllrname** command to rename all of these DLLs and the references to them in HELLO6.EXE. The **dllrname** utility requires that the old and new names of the DLLs must be the same length. In this example, we chose to replace the CPP prefix of the standard DLL names with the characters PGP.

```
DLLRNAME HELLO6.EXE CPPWOU3I.DLL CPPWOB3I.DLL CPPWM35I.DLL
    CPPWOU3I=PGPWOU3I CPPWOB3I=PGPWOB3I CPPWM35I=PGPWM35I
```

The output from **dllrname** follows:

```
IBM C/C++ Tools Version 2.0 - DLL Rename Utility
(C) Copyright IBM Corp., 1993, 1995. All Rights Reserved
US Government Users Restricted Rights - Use, duplication or disclosure
restricted by GSA ADP Schedule Contract with IBM Corp.

Processing file hello6.exe.
 1 external names in file hello6.exe have been left unchanged.
 4 names found in file hello6.exe.
 Imported DLL name CPPWOB3I has been changed to PGPWOB3I.
 Imported DLL name CPPWOU3I has been changed to PGPWOU3I.
 Imported DLL name KERNEL32 has been left unchanged.
 Imported DLL name cppwm35i has been changed to PGPWM35I.
```

```
Processing file cppwou3i.dll.
   8 external names in file cppwou3i.dll have been left unchanged.
   11 names found in file cppwou3i.dll.
   Executable name CPPWOU3I has been changed to PGPWOU3I.
   Imported DLL name ADVAPI32 has been left unchanged.
   Imported DLL name COMCTL32 has been left unchanged.
   Imported DLL name CPPWOB3I has been changed to PGPWOB3I.
   Imported DLL name GDI32 has been left unchanged.
   Imported DLL name KERNEL32 has been left unchanged.
   Imported DLL name SHELL32 has been left unchanged.
   Imported DLL name USER32 has been left unchanged.
   Imported DLL name comdlg32 has been left unchanged.
   Imported DLL name cppwm35i has been changed to PGPWM35I.
   Imported DLL name ole32 has been left unchanged.
   File cppwou3i.dll has been renamed to PGPWOU3I.DLL to match internal DLL
   name.

Processing file cppwob3i.dll.
   2 external names in file cppwob3i.dll have been left unchanged.
   4 names found in file cppwob3i.dll.
   Executable name CPPWOB3I has been changed to PGPWOB3I.
   Imported DLL name KERNEL32 has been left unchanged.
   Imported DLL name USER32 has been left unchanged.
   Imported DLL name cppwm35i has been changed to PGPWM35I.
   File cppwob3i.dll has been renamed to PGPWOB3I.DLL to match internal DLL
   name.

Processing file cppwm35i.dll.
   1 external names in file cppwm35i.dll have been left unchanged.
   2 names found in file cppwm35i.dll.
   Executable name cppwm35i has been changed to PGPWM35I.
   Imported DLL name KERNEL32 has been left unchanged.
   File cppwm35i.dll has been renamed to PGPWM35I.DLL to match internal DLL
   name.

Complete.  0 error(s) detected.
```

Finally, move your executable file and the renamed DLLs to another system, and make sure everything works as before. In our example, we encounter a problem when we do this. The application terminates when you select **Settings->Open** in the main menu. The reason is that we need CPPWOT3.DLL because the ANotebookWindow constructor in ANOTEBW6.CPP is using the constructor:

```
IFrameWindow ( const IResourceId& resId,
               IWindow*          owner = 0,
               FrameSource       source = tryDialogResource );
```

which is attempting to load the DLL. To solve this problem, we copy CPPWOT3.DLL to our distribution directory. Because Hello6 uses Windows Help help files by default, we do not need LIBIPF32.DLL.

You may also find that your application requires the Open Class Library resource DLL. Some of the features, such as the tool bar, direct manipulation, and the document framework, load resources from the resource DLL at run time. If the resources are not available, an exception is thrown when the resource load fails. The U.S. English language version of the resource DLL is named CPPWOR3U.DLL in the Windows version and CPPOOR3U.DLL in the OS/2 version, and the license agreement allows you to reship these with your application. For more information on handling Open Class Library resources in your application, see Chapter 24, "Using Resources."

Tuning Your Application

Tuning an application refers to reducing the code size both on disk and in memory and to reducing the time needed to load and run the application. Because the size of the code directly affects both the load time and run-time characteristics of your application, it is best to do size tuning before performance tuning.

Reducing the Code Size of the Executable

Reducing the code to its smallest possible size decreases the cost of shipping your application and enhances the load and run-time performance of your application. By following these guidelines, you can reduce the size of your application on disk. Some of these guidelines may become outdated as the features of the compiler change in future releases.

- Compile the application with full optimization using the compiler switch **/O+**. Optimization dramatically affects the size of the resulting code.

- Eliminate all compiler-generated functions.

  The C++ language defines situations in which a compiler must generate functions where they are needed. The compiler can generate constructors, assignment operators, and destructors where it needs them. Although this feature of the language can speed up the development cycle, it usually results in the code being larger then it needs to be. This occurs because the compiler generates these functions in every compilation unit that needs them. Although these functions are small, if there are many compilation units, the amount of duplication can become quite high. You can solve this by providing these functions in a single compilation unit, even if the function implementation is empty.

- Minimize the use of inline functions.

  Inline functions, another useful feature of the C++ language, can also cause problems. If you instruct the compiler to inline a function that cannot be inlined, the result is a static version of the function in every compilation unit that uses it. Adding exception handling to the language has reduced the number of functions that can be inlined because of the need to clean up objects constructed on the stack when an exception occurs. The simplest guideline is to restrict inline code to the setting and querying of the fundamental data types. If you decide to inline functions that do more than that, follow these guidelines:

  - If a class inherits from another class that has a destructor, the compiler will no longer inline any of the class's constructors or its destructor. To be safe, provide outline versions of all constructors and destructors, even if they are empty.

  - Do not inline virtual functions.

  - Do not inline functions with automatic instances or compiler temporary instances that require destruction.

  - Do not inline functions that call `operator new` in a class with a user-provided constructor.

- Do not inline functions that you reference by address. The compiler will generate a static version to obtain an address.

- Use the **/Winl** compiler switch so the compiler warns you about cases where it cannot inline what you instructed it to inline. This causes the EDC3542 message to be issued for each offending function.

• If you are using the collection classes, compile the final version of your code with the macro INO_CHECKS defined. Without INO_CHECKS, the collection classes add inline calls to verify that a cursor is valid prior to using it. This checking should be unnecessary once you have completed testing your application.

• Link without debugging information.

If you follow the preceding guidelines, you can get your linked application close to its smallest size.

To find the compiler-generated static functions, compile the module, and request an assembler listing using the **/Fa+** compiler option. Then, examine the listing for nonpublic functions. Later in this chapter, we describe a utility that helps you do this without poring over several thousand lines of assembler code.

Reducing Application Load Time

At least initially, your users will typically gauge the performance of your application by the length of time they have to wait before they can interact with a window on the display (the load time). This, of course, has little to do with the actual performance of your application. If your application loads slowly, your users may mutter comments like *"What a pig that product is, it takes thirty seconds just to load."* Although the load time is somewhat dependent on the application code and your code can increase that time, it is not the primary factor. The primary factor in increasing load time is usually more closely related to the amount of code and data that the operating system must load, not the amount of code it must execute. (This conclusion is based on the assumption that another application has not already loaded the code and data.)

The 32-bit Windows operating systems and the OS/2 operating system all load code and data into storage in 4K chunks called pages. When you call a function that is not in memory, a page fault is generated that causes the system to load the needed page into memory. Although a function may only be a hundred bytes, the system loads the full 4K page containing the function. In addition, it loads any data pages needed by the function. The worst-case scenario for loading an application is that the start-up functions are spread evenly throughout the pages in the executable file. When this happens, the operating system can load almost the entire executable file before the application can complete its initialization.

An object-oriented style usually results in more functions with less code per function and with functions arranged into compilation units by classes. Further, the typical application initially constructs many objects and makes only a few function calls on each object. Unfortunately, this style of programming approaches the worst-case scenario for loading pages because many unused functions are sprinkled throughout the functions used during application start up.

Due to this problem, the Open Class Library developers took specific steps to reorganize the code and data in the DLLs to minimize the actual number of pages that get loaded. The size of your application may require you take some of these same steps. If so, the following sections describe changes you can make to enhance the load-time performance of your application.

To tune your application's load-time, first run trace scenarios to learn the order in which functions execute during initialization. Then, add `alloc_text` pragmas on code and `data_seg` pragmas on data in the source code to group the functions and data in the DLL. This ensures that the operating system loads the smallest number of pages into storage prior to showing the application to users.

If your OS/2 application contains DLLs, you can also reduce load time of the DLLs by exporting the functions by ordinal values rather than by name. Refer to the *VisualAge for C++ User's Guide* for details on using the **cppfilt** utility to generate the ordinal values for your module definition file.

Generating Trace Data

You can use the Performance Analyzer tool to identify those functions that get called when the application starts up. To use the Performance Analyzer, build a special version of your code that uses the compiler options **/Gh+** to generate hook code and **/Ti+** to include debugging information. Also, compile with optimization turned on (**/O+**) so that inlining occurs wherever possible. Then, link the application with the **/Ti+** or **/B" /DE"** linker options and with the Performance Analyzer object file (CPPWPA3.OBJ for the Windows operating system, CPPOPA3.OBJ for the OS/2 operating system). The Performance Analyzer can execute an application built in this manner and display a variety of views of the trace data to help you determine which functions were called.

Figure 29-1 displays a portion of a Statistics diagram containing some of the functions used in the Hello1 sample program. We have modified the Hello1 sample by adding a call to the function `PerfStop`. This function causes the Performance Analyzer to stop tracing after executing most of the functions needed to display a window. Therefore, the Performance Analyzer displays those functions that Hello1 calls during initialization.

Hello1 Changes for Start-Up Tuning - shipapp\hello1\hello1.cpp

```
#include <istattxt.hpp>
#include <iframe.hpp>
#include <icoordsy.hpp>
#include <istring.hpp>

#ifdef IC_PM
#include <icsperf.h>      // Include prototype for PerfStop()
#else
#include <iperf.h>        // Include prototype for PerfStop()
#endif

// Define a static object.
IString appName("Hello World - Version 1");
```

```
int main()
{
  ICoordinateSystem::setApplicationOrientation(
          ICoordinateSystem::originLowerLeft );
  IFrameWindow mainWindow (appName);
  IStaticText hello(IC_FRAME_CLIENT_ID, &mainWindow, &mainWindow);
  hello.setText("Hello World");
  hello.setAlignment(IStaticText::centerCenter);
  mainWindow.setClient(&hello);

  mainWindow.sizeTo(ISize(400,300));
  mainWindow.setFocus();
  mainWindow.show();

  // We shut down tracing now.
  PerfStop();

  IApplication::current().run();
  return 0;
} /* end main() */
```

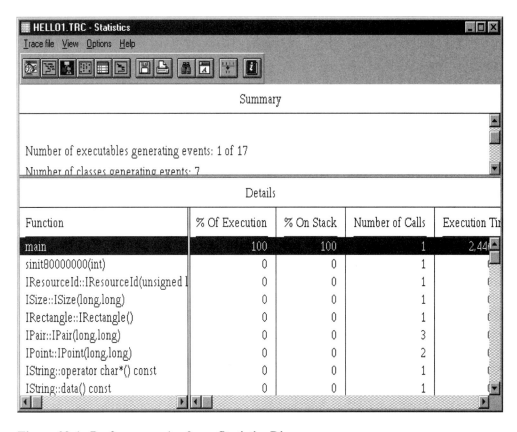

Figure 29-1. Performance Analyzer Statistics Diagram

Ordering the Code into Segments

Use the information in the Statistics diagram to construct `alloc_text` pragmas for those functions shown in the diagram. For example, you could put the Open Class Library `IWindow::show` function into the segment `ICLTop` with the following pragma:

```
#pragma alloc_text( ICLTop, IWindow::show())
```

You can use the `alloc_text` pragmas in this manner to achieve a fine degree of control over the grouping of functions in the DLL. It is sometimes sufficient to place all functions executed during the start-up phase into the same named segment and then place this segment at the top of the DLL. If the application is large, you may wish to further refine the ordering by using more than one named segment and to place code into the segments based on frequency of use across several test scenarios. You can order the functions within segments and the data in data segments by ordering the modules in the linker response file. In the VisualAge for C++ for Windows CD-ROM, you will find an example of pragmas used for page-tuning the start-up functions in the file `IOCSRC\CPPWOB3\IPAGETUN.H`. Later in this chapter, you will see an example of using the `alloc_text` pragma.

Using Static Objects

At first glance, static objects may seem like a useful feature of the C++ language. The C++ run-time library constructs them when it starts your application, so you can write code with the assurance that these objects are available when needed. Unfortunately, because there are several problems with using static objects, the Open Class Library designers worked to minimize their use. We recommend that you do the same. Static objects are a concern because they affect the loading of your application. The compiler generates code to construct all static objects when your application loads, whether the application needs them or not. For a DLL, all static objects in the DLL are constructed whenever the DLL is loaded. Another problem with static objects is that the language definition leaves the order of initialization and destruction up to the compiler implementation. This can become a problem if you have a static object that depends on another static object in a different compilation unit.

Using static functions that return a reference to an object is a better approach to ensure that you have created objects when you need them. These functions construct the object when called if it is not already constructed. Therefore, the object is not constructed until it is used. If you do not create containers, for example, then the application does not create the container static objects.

You still must delete these objects when you no longer need them or when the application closes. You can delete them when the application ends by adding the static object pointers to a class with only a destructor to delete the objects. You then declare a static object of this class so that the C++ run-time library calls the destructor when the application closes.

The following example demonstrates the use of this technique and creates an object of the class `IDynamicLinkLibrary` for a user DLL, named `MYENG.DLL`. `APPSTAT.HPP` defines the interface to a class called `AppStatics`. This class contains a static accessor function `AppStatics::englishDLL` for a static `IDynamicLinkLibrary` object and a static pointer to this object. `APPSTAT.CPP` declares the static object, initializes the pointer to the

IDynamicLinkLibrary object, and implements the destructor to delete the
IDynamicLinkLibrary object when the C++ run-time library deletes the static AppStatics
object. After that, a short example demonstrates the use of the static function to load a text
string from resources contained in the DLL.

AppStatics Interface - shipapp\appstat\appstat.hpp

```
#include <ireslib.hpp>

class AppStatics
{
public:
// Destructor for cleanup.
  ~AppStatics ();

// DLL Accessor function.
static IDynamicLinkLibrary
 &englishDLL();

private:
static IDynamicLinkLibrary
 *engDLL;
};
```

AppStatics Implementation - shipapp\appstat\appstat.cpp

```
#include <ireslib.hpp>
#include "appstat.hpp"

// Define static instance of AppStatics.
AppStatics appStatics;

// Initialize AppStatics object pointer
IDynamicLinkLibrary* AppStatics::engDLL = 0;

// Destructor to close the DLL.
AppStatics::~AppStatics ( )
{
  if(engDLL != 0)
    delete engDLL;
}

// Static accessor for the DLL.
IDynamicLinkLibrary& AppStatics :: englishDLL( )
{
    if(!engDLL)
      engDLL = new IDynamicLinkLibrary("myeng");
    return *engDLL;
}
```

AppStatics Usage - shipapp\appstat\main.cpp

```
#include <iostream.h>
#include <istring.hpp>
#include "appstat.hpp"
#include "mytext.h"

void main ( )
{
  IString str = AppStatics::englishDLL().loadString(MY_TEXT);

  cout << "The resource text is [" << str << "]" << endl;
}
```

The preceding example only partially addresses the problem of controlling the order of static object construction and destruction. We ensured that the AppStatics object is initialized when needed, so any references to it by another static object constructor will work correctly. We did not, however, ensure that the object is destructed after all other users of it are destructed. The VisualAge for C++ compiler provides pragma `priority` for controlling static-object construction order. This is an implementation-specific feature, so the method for ordering static object construction and destruction may be different for other compilers.

Finding Static-Object Initialization Functions

To construct static objects, the compiler generates static functions that it calls during program initialization to call the constructors on the objects. The compiler creates these functions in the compilation unit where you define the static objects. This can result in page faults in many different parts of the DLL (or EXE) at load time. If you compile a module containing static objects and request the assembler output, you will find these functions. You may have noticed that the preceding Hello1 sample has a static IString object, appName, for the application name. This static object causes the compiler to generate initialization code similar to the following:

Static Initialization Function

```
__sinit80000000__Fv     proc
        call    _ProfileHook32
        push    ebp
        mov     ebp,esp
        push    offset FLAT: _Exception_CPP
        push    fs:[0h]
        mov     fs:[0h],esp
        push    0ffffffe0h
        sub     esp,014h
        push    ebx
        push    edi
        push    esi
        jmp     @BLBL5
        align   04h
@BLBL6:

; 15 IString appName("Hello World - Version 1");
        mov     edx,offset FLAT:@CBE2
        mov     eax,offset FLAT:appName
        sub     esp,08h
        call    __ct__7IStringFPCc
        add     esp,08h
        mov     dword ptr [ebp-020h],01h;          __es
        pop     esi
        pop     edi
        pop     ebx
        add     esp,018h
        pop     fs:[0h]
        leave
        ret
@BLBL5:
        mov     dword ptr [ebp-020h],0h;           __es
        mov     dword ptr [ebp-018h],offset FLAT:@a2a__fsm_tab; __es
        jmp     @BLBL6
        align   04h
__sinit80000000__Fv     endp
```

The names of static initialization functions begin with "__sinit," followed by a number based on the initialization priority of the data. You can adjust the initialization priority of static data by using the pragma `priority`.

The compiler generates similar functions to call the destructors of static objects when the application closes. These termination functions begin with "__sterm."

To reduce the number of pages executed during initialization, you can use `alloc_text` pragmas to logically place these static initialization functions at the top of the DLL and the static termination functions at the bottom of the DLL. It is not obvious how to do this because the compiler makes up the function names as it compiles. Fortunately, it is not too difficult to write a simple program that compiles a series of files and determines the names of these functions. You see an example of this program shortly.

Finding Static Exception Handling Functions

The current VisualAge for C++ implementation of exception handling generates static functions to call destructors during the processing of an exception. A design goal of Open Class Library was to limit the use of exceptions to error conditions that should not occur once you debug your application. Consequently, moving these functions to a segment that does not get loaded until an actual error occurs reduces the amount of memory required for a normally running application. The compiler helps in this regard because it automatically places the generated exception code in a segment called EH_CODE, and it places the data structures associated with exception handling in a segment called EH_DATA. You can see the generated functions and data by compiling a module that uses exception handling and requesting the assembler output. Search for the string "__dftdt" in the assembler file. You will see something similar to the following example from our modified Hello1:

```
__dftdt__7IStringFv    proc
        call    _ProfileHook32
        push    ebp
        mov     ebp,esp
        sub     esp,08h
        mov     [ebp+08h],eax;  this
        mov     edx,02h
        mov     eax,[ebp+08h];  this
        call    __dt__7IStringFv
        add     esp,08h
        leave
        ret
__dftdt__7IStringFv    endp
```

You will also find references to these generated functions in a series of tables with labels containing the string "__fsm_tab." The compiler uses these tables to ensure that destructors are called when an exception occurs within a block.

Generating the Pragmas for Static Functions

In the previous topics, we identified several functions that the compiler might create as static functions due to static-object construction, static-object destruction, or attempts to inline functions that it cannot inline. The following VisualAge for C++ editor macro demonstrates the generation of alloc_text pragmas for the static functions in a group of modules. The macro takes a file specification as input and writes pragmas to the initprag.h file as follows:

- Static initialization functions are placed in the segment InitSegment.
- Static termination functions are placed in the segment TermSegment.
- Static functions for exception handling are left alone because they are already in a separate segment.
- All remaining static functions are placed in the segment StaticSegment.

Generate Pragmas for Static Functions - shipapp\genprags\genprags.lx

```
/*-----------------------------------------------------------------
    genprags.lx  - The primary purpose of this macro is to
        generate the alloc_text pragmas for initialization,
        termination, and static functions.  If you have a command line
        REXX interpreter available, you can copy this file to genprags.cmd
        and run it from the command line.  If this option is available it
        is recommended since this program can take a while and will lock
        up the edit session while it is running as a macro.

    The macro functions by generating and parsing the
        assembler code (-Fa) for all specified files. Static
        functions are identified because they have a PROC
        statement with no coooresponding PUBLIC statement.
        The static functions identified in this manner are
        searched for various tokens to determine the segment
        they should be placed in and the appropriate
        alloc_text pragmas generated.

    Requires as inout:
     wildCardFileName   - files to process of the form '*.cpp'

    Generates as output:
     initprag.h

    ---------------------------------------------------------------*/

call RxFuncAdd 'SysLoadFuncs', 'RexxUtil', 'SysLoadFuncs'
call SysLoadFuncs

/* set up to run as either a macro or a command file */
parse upper source osname . me
me = strip(me)
lastDot = lastPos('.', me)
if substr(me, lastDot) = ".LX" then do
    isMacro = 1
end
else do
    isMacro = 0
end
if isMacro = 1 then do
  /* insure that message and messageline are on */
  'extract messageLine into messageLineSetting'
  'extract messages   into messagesSetting'
  'set messages      on'
  'set messageLine on'
end

/*
  Read and parse arguments
*/
PARSE UPPER ARG wildCardFileName  '(' optionsUpper
```

```
kDebug = 0        /* set to 1 for debug info */
if pos("DEBUG", optionsUpper) > 0 then kDebug = 1

wildCardFileName = strip(wildCardFileName)
if wildCardFileName = "" then
  wildCardFileName = "*.CPP"

/*
  Initialize constants
*/
publicString = "public"
procString   = "proc"
extrnString  = "extrn"
kStaticWord  = "static"


rootDirectory       = directory()
assemblerFile       = rootDirectory"\genprag$.asm"
objectFile          = rootDirectory"\genprag$.obj"
OutFile             = rootDirectory"\genprag$.out"
pragmaFile          = rootDirectory"\genprag$.h"
filteredPragmaFile  = rootDirectory"\initprag.h"

InitSegment     = "InitSegment"
TermSegment     = "TermSegment"
StaticSegment   = "StaticSegment"

/*
 check for file already in ring
*/
if isMacro = 1 then do
  'EXTRACT DOCLIST'
  if doclist \= '' then
    'EXTRACT DOCNUM INTO SAVEDOCNUM'
  else
    savedocnum = 0
  do while doclist \= ''
    parse var doclist docnum doclist
    'GODOC DOCNUM 'docnum
    if rc <= 1 then do
      'EXTRACT NAME into currentDocName'
      if translate(currentDocName) = translate(filteredPragmaFile) then
        'qquit'
    end
  end
  if savedocnum \= 0 then
    'GODOC DOCNUM 'savedocnum
end

if stream(pragmaFile,'C','QUERY EXIST')<>'' then
    call osCmd '@DEL 'pragmaFile


/*
  Write a prolog to the output file
*/
rc = lineOut(pragmaFile, "// Generated by "me )
rc = lineOut(pragmaFile, "// Arguments were "wildCardFileName  )
rc = lineOut(pragmaFile, " " )


/*
  Collect a list of the files to process
*/
cppFiles. = 0
if kDebug = 1 then
  call sayErr 'wildCardFileName='wildCardFileName
rc=SysFileTree(wildCardFileName,'cppFiles','FO','*****')
```

```
/*
 Process each CPP file
*/
do fileNumber=1 TO cppFiles.0
  call refreshDisplay
  call sayErr "Processing file "fileNumber" of "cppFiles.0"
("cppFiles.fileNumber")"
  /* Erase the assembler file and create the next one */
  if stream(assemblerFile,'C','QUERY EXIST')<>'' then
      call osCmd '@DEL 'assemblerFile
  iccOptions = "-c -Ft- -O+ -W2 -Q+ -Gm+ -Gd+"
  if 0 \= osCmd( '@ICC' iccOptions '-Fa'assemblerFile '-Fo'objectFile
cppFiles.fileNumber' > 'outFile ) then do
      call sayErr "ICC failed"
      if isMacro = 1 then
          'lx 'outFile
      else
          call osCmd 'type 'outFile
      exit 1
  end

    /*
      Build a table of public symbols from the assembler file.
    */
    filePublics. = 0
    call SysFileSearch publicString, assemblerFile, 'filePublics', 'C'
    if kDebug = 1 then do
        call sayErr "FilePublics.0 = "filePublics.0
        call refreshDisplay
    end
    publicList. = 0
    do j=1 to filePublics.0
        filePublics.j = translate(filePublics.j, ' ', '09'x)   /* remove
tabs */
        parse var  filePublics.j publicKeyword function
        if kDebug = 1 then
          call sayErr "PUBLIC: " publicKeyword function
        /* We want the statements of the form                      */
        /* public __functionName                                   */
        /* but not segment declarations and such.                  */
        if strip(publicKeyword) = publicString  then do
          publicList.0 = publicList.0 + 1
          currentPublic = publicList.0
          publicList.currentPublic = strip(function)
        end  /* if */
    end  /* do */


    /*
      Build a table of procedures ("proc", both public & static).
    */
    fileProcs. = 0
    call SysFileSearch procString, assemblerFile, 'fileProcs', 'C'
    procList.  = 0
    do j=1 to fileProcs.0
        fileProcs.j = translate(fileProcs.j, ' ', '09'x)
        parse value fileProcs.j with fileProcs.j ";" comment
        /* The following logic attempts to eliminate lines that get
           included that are not "proc" statements (e.g. lines with
           words like "process").
        */
        if words(fileProcs.j) = 2 & word(fileProcs.j,2) = procString then do
          procList.0 = procList.0 + 1
          currentProc = procList.0
          procList.currentProc = strip(word(fileProcs.j,1))
          if kDebug = 1 then
            call sayErr "PROC: "fileProcs.j
        end  /* if */
    end /* do */
```

```
    /*
        Flag the functions in the procList as being PUBLIC or
        STATIC (STATICS are in the procList but not the publicList).
    */
    staticsFound = 0
    do j=1 to procList.0
        found = 0
        do k=1 to publicList.0 while found = 0
            if procList.j = publicList.k then do
                found = 1
                procList.j.scope = publicString
            end
        end   /* do */
        /* Not found in public list so must be a static */
        if found = 0 then do
          procList.j.scope = kStaticWord
          staticsFound = 1
        end /* if */
    end /* do */

    /*
        Determine the alloc_text pragmas for functions meeting
        one of the criteria.
    */
    if staticsFound = 1 then do
      /* Determine the File Name and write an #ifdef for it */
      cppOffset = pos('.', cppFiles.fileNumber)
      lastSlash = lastPos('\', cppFiles.fileNumber)
      cppNameLength = cppOffset - lastSlash -1
      cppFileName = substr(cppFiles.fileNumber, lastSlash+1, cppNameLength)
      rc = lineOut(pragmaFile, "#ifdef _"||translate(cppFileName)||"_CPP_")

      /* Now dump out the segment definitions for Statics  */
      do procNumber=1 to procList.0
        if procList.procNumber.scope = kStaticWord then do
            writePragma = 1
            outBuffer = "#pragma alloc_text("
            /* Do not write out Exception Functions because  */
            /* they are in EH_CODE already.                  */
            if pos("__dftdt", procList.procNumber) > 0   |  ,
               pos("__dftbdt", procList.procNumber) > 0   then
              writePragma = 0
            if pos("__dftct", procList.procNumber) > 0 then
              outBuffer = outbuffer||StaticSegment
            /* Write out Initialization functions */
            else if pos("__sinit", procList.procNumber) > 0  then
              outBuffer = outbuffer||InitSegment
            /* Write out termination functions */
            else if pos("__sterm", procList.procNumber) > 0 then
              outBuffer = outbuffer||TermSegment
            else
              outBuffer = outbuffer||StaticSegment

            outBuffer = outBuffer||"," procList.procNumber||")"
            if writePragma = 1 then
                rc = lineOut(pragmaFile, outBuffer)
        end
      end /* do procNumber */

    rc = lineOut(pragmaFile, "#endif")
    rc = lineOut(pragmaFile, "")
  end /* do staticsExist */
end /* do fileNumber */
rc = stream(pragmaFile, 'C', 'close')
```

```
/*
  Use CPPFILT on the pragma file
*/
call oscmd '@CPPFILT /q' pragmaFile ' > ' filteredPragmaFile

/* cleanup temporary files */
if kDebug - 0 then do
   if stream(assemblerFile,'C','QUERY EXIST')<>'' then
      call osCmd '@DEL 'assemblerFile
   if stream(objectFile,'C','QUERY EXIST')<>'' then
      call osCmd '@DEL 'objectFile
   if stream(outFile,'C','QUERY EXIST')<>'' then
      call osCmd '@DEL 'OutFile
   if stream(pragmaFile,'C','QUERY EXIST')<>'' then
      call osCmd '@DEL 'pragmaFile
end

/* restore previous settings and view the results if a macro */
if isMacro = 1 then do
   'set messageLine 'messageLineSetting
   'set messages   'messagesSetting
   'lx 'filteredPragmaFile
end

exit 0

/* Utility function to call a system function */
oscmd:
  parse arg theCmd

  if pos('@', theCmd) \= 1 | kDebug \= 0 then
    call sayErr theCmd
  if pos('@', theCmd) = 1 then
    Address 'CMD' substr(theCmd, 2)
  else
    Address 'CMD' theCmd
  return rc

/* Utility function to write error message    */
sayErr:
procedure expose isMacro
parse arg theString
if isMacro = 1 then
   'msg 'theString
else
   say theString
call refreshDisplay
return

/* Utility function to update the display    */
refreshDisplay:
procedure expose isMacro
if isMacro = 1 then
   'sshow'
return
```

The macro works by compiling each of the files specified on input to generate an assembler listing. It examines the assembler code to find the compiler-generated static functions. If it finds any generated static functions other than exception-handling functions, it outputs pragmas to place each function in the desired segment. It then uses the VisualAge for C++ tool **cppfilt** to unmangle the function names and produce the final output file initprag.h.

For example, to generate an include file with alloc_text pragmas for the Hello6 sample program, execute the following command:

```
GENPRAGS ibmcppw\samples\ioc\hello6\*.cpp
```

Then, include the file `initprag.h` in the Hello6 implementation files. For example, add to the top of `ADIALOG6.CPP` the lines:

```
#define _ADIALOG6_CPP_
#include "initprag.h"
```

The actual output of this program run against the implementation files in Hello6 follows:

```
// Generated by D:\USR\MACROS\GENPRAGS.LX
// Arguments were *.CPP

#ifdef _ADIALOG6_CPP_
#pragma alloc_text(StaticSegment,
ADialogCommandHandler::~ADialogCommandHandler())
#endif
#ifdef _AEARTHW6_CPP_
#pragma alloc_text(StaticSegment,
ATwinkleTimeHandler::~ATwinkleTimeHandler())
#pragma alloc_text(StaticSegment,
ATwinkleTimeHandler::ATwinkleTimeHandler(AEarthWindow*))
#pragma alloc_text(StaticSegment, IGraphicBundle::__dftct())
#pragma alloc_text(StaticSegment, IPoint::__dftct())
#pragma alloc_text(StaticSegment, IRectangle::__dftct())
#endif
#ifdef _AHELLOW6_CPP_
#pragma alloc_text(StaticSegment, TimeUpdate::~TimeUpdate())
#pragma alloc_text(StaticSegment, ACommandHandler::~ACommandHandler())
#pragma alloc_text(StaticSegment, ASelectHandler::~ASelectHandler())
#pragma alloc_text(StaticSegment, AHelpHandler::~AHelpHandler())
#pragma alloc_text(StaticSegment, APopUpHandler::~APopUpHandler())
#pragma alloc_text(StaticSegment, TimeUpdate::TimeUpdate(AHelloWindow*))
#pragma alloc_text(StaticSegment, APopUpHandler::APopUpHandler())
#pragma alloc_text(StaticSegment, AHelpHandler::AHelpHandler())
#pragma alloc_text(StaticSegment, IResourceId::IResourceId(unsigned
long))
#endif

#ifdef _ANOTEBW6_CPP_
#pragma alloc_text(StaticSegment,
ANotebookCommandHandler::~ANotebookCommandHandler())
#endif
```

An examination of this output reveals several interesting things. First, because there are no functions of the form "__sinit" or "__sterm," Hello6 must not use any static objects. This is a good start. However, if you examine the entries for StaticSegment segment, you see several constructors and destructors with pragmas defined. Instead of leaving these functions with pragmas (which place them in the static segment), create outlined versions of these functions in a compilation unit.

Ordering the Segments

The order in which the linker encounters segment names when it scans the input files is generally the order in which the linker places them in the executable (subject to operating-system-dependent requirements). To ensure that your tuning work is most effective, force a specific segment-ordering with respect to the segments you define. You can do this with directives to the linker that cause it to encounter your segments in the order that you want them placed in the output file. The specific syntax of the directives varies by environment.

The Windows version of **ilink** accepts a **/SECTION** directive on the command line. It allows you to name and set certain attributes of each segment. For example, we would set up the segment ordering in our Hello6 example by adding the following directives to the link commands in the makefile:

```
/B" /SECTION:InitSegment,ER /SECTION:CODE32,ER /SECTION:StaticSegment,ER
     /SECTION:TermSegment,ER "
```

This places `InitSegment` before the default `CODE32` segment, and then it places the rest of our segments at the end. The `ER` attributes mean **E**xecute **R**ead-only, and they are the defaults for code.

With the OS/2 version of **ilink**, you can do the same thing using directives within a module definition file. We would create a module definition file for Hello6 that looks like the following example and add the name of the file to the link command line in the makefile:

```
        NAME HELLO6
        DESCRIPTION  'Hello6'
SEGMENTS
   InitSegment
   CODE32                      ; Remaining CODE32
   StaticSegment
   TermSegment
```

Windows Linker Segment Ordering

You have seen how to get your segments ordered by listing them in **/SECTION** directives on the linker command line in the order you want them in. This is how it is supposed to work. However, the Version 3.5 linker does not work this way. Windows system conventions call for segments whose names contain "$" characters to be sorted in the load module by the part of the name after the $. Unfortunately, the linker sorts all of the segments by name. Until the linker is changed, you need to select the names of your segments so that they collate in the order you want them to. In our Hello6 example, we would change `InitSegment` to `AInit` so that it appears before `CODE32`.

Finishing Up the Tuning

The final steps in the tuning process are to remove functions from `StaticSegment` and `TermSegment` that appear in the Performance Analyzer trace runs and to order the object files in the linker response file for the linker. The primary result of both of these final steps is to reduce the storage requirements for your application after it is started up and is running.

The `StaticSegment` and `TermSegment` segments are for seldom-used functions or for functions used at termination time. But, functions that appear in the trace don't meet these criteria. Therefore, you need to move the referenced functions out of `StaticSegment` and `TermSegment` so that these segments are not loaded because of them.

Similarly, the order that the object files are presented to the linker determines the placement of functions and data within segments. Because we do not group all of the functions in the DLL, present heavily used object files to the linker first so that they appear first in the default segments. Also, try to keep objects used together near each other to maximize localization.

Index

CUSTOMER NOTE: IF THIS BOOK IS ACCOMPANIED BY SOFTWARE, PLEASE READ THE FOLLOWING BEFORE OPENING THE PACKAGE.

This software contains files to help you utilize the models described in the accompanying book. By opening the package, you are agreeing to be bound by the following agreement:

This software product is protected by copyright and all rights are reserved by the author, John Wiley & Sons, Inc., or their licensors. You are licensed to use this software on a single computer. Copying the software to another medium or format for use on a single computer does not violate the U.S. Copyright Law. Copying the software for any other purpose is a violation of the U.S. Copyright Law.

This software product is sold as is without warranty of any kind, either express or implied, including but not limited to the implied warranty of merchantability and fitness for a particular purpose. Neither Wiley nor its dealers or distributors assumes any liability for any alleged or actual damages arising from the use of or the inability to use this software. (Some states do not allow the exclusion of implied warranties, so the exclusion may not apply to you.)